© Charles Knight murals in the Hayden Planetarium of the American Museum of Natural History.

The HOME UNIVERSITY ENCYCLOPEDIA

—An Illustrated Treasury of Knowledge—

Prepared under the Editorship of

C. RALPH TAYLOR

Advisory Editor

CARL VAN DOREN

WITH SPECIAL ARTICLES AND DEPARTMENTAL SUPERVISION BY 462 LEADING EDITORS, EDUCATORS AND SPECIALISTS IN THE UNITED STATES AND EUROPE

(Revised Edition)

1953

COMPLETE IN TWELVE VOLUMES

VOLUME I

PERIODICAL PUBLISHERS' SERVICE BUREAU, INC.

New York   Sandusky, Ohio   San Francisco

NELSON NEW LOOSE-LEAF ENCYCLOPEDIA
FIRST PUBLISHED AND COPYRIGHTED, 1905
REVISED AND COPYRIGHTED, 1934,
BY THOMAS NELSON & SONS, NEW YORK
REVISED, ABRIDGED AND COPYRIGHTED,
1935, 1936, 1937, 1938, 1940, 1941, 1942, 1943, 1944, 1945, 1946, 1948, 1951, 1952, 1953
BY BOOKS INC., NEW YORK

All rights reserved, including the right to reproduce this
book, or portions thereof, in any form

PRINTED AND BOUND IN THE UNITED STATES OF AMERICA

LIST OF CONTRACTIONS USED IN THIS WORK

ac., acres.
agric., agricultural.
Ala., Alabama.
alt., altitude.
Alta., Alberta.
Amer., America or American.
anc., ancient.
ann., annual.
Ar., Arabic.
Aram., Aramaic.
Ariz., Arizona.
Ark., Arkansas.
arr., arrondissement.
A. S., Anglo-Saxon.
A. V., Authorized Version.
aver., average.
b. p., boiling point.
bor., borough.
Brit., Britain or British.
B. C., British Columbia.
bur., burgh.
c. (circa), about.
C., centigrade.
Cal., California.
cap., capital.
cf., compare.
co., county.
Colo., Colorado.
Com., Commission.
comm., commune.
Conn., Connecticut.
cub. ft., cubic feet.
Dan., Danish.
D. C., District of Columbia.
Del., Delaware.
dep., department.
dist., district.
div., division.
Du., Dutch.
e., east.
eccles., ecclesiastical.
ed., edition; edited.
e.g., for example.
Eng., England or English.
episc., episcopal.
et. seq., and the following.
F., Fahrenheit.
Fla., Florida.
fort. tn., fortified town.
Fr., French.
ft., feet.
Ga., Georgia.
Ger., German.
gov., government.
Gr., Greek.
Heb., Hebrew.

I., isl., island.
Ia., Iowa.
ibid., the same.
i.e., that is.
Ill., Illinois.
in., inches.
Ind. T., Indian Territory.
Ind., Indiana.
Ire., Ireland or Irish.
Ital., Italian.
Kan., Kansas.
Ky., Kentucky.
l., lake.
La., Louisiana.
Lat., Latin.
lat., latitude.
l. bk., left bank.
lit., literally.
long., longitude.
m., miles.
Man., Manitoba.
Mass., Massachusetts.
Md., Maryland.
Me., Maine.
M. E., Methodist Episcopal.
Meth., Methodist.
Mich., Michigan.
Minn., Minnesota.
Miss., Mississippi.
Mo., Missouri.
Mont., Montana.
m. p., melting point.
mrkt. tn., market-town.
Mt., mts., mount, mountain, -s.
munic., municipal.
n., north.
Neb., Nebraska.
N. B., New Brunswick.
N. C., North Carolina.
N. Dak., North Dakota.
Nev., Nevada.
N. H., New Hampshire.
N. J., New Jersey.
N. Mex., New Mexico.
N. S., Nova Scotia.
N. T., New Testament.
N. W. T., Northwest Territories.
N. Y., New York.
O., Ohio.
Okla., Oklahoma.
Ont., Ontario.
Ore., Oregon.
O. T., Old Testament.
par., parish.

parl., parliamentary.
Pa., Pennsylvania.
P. E., Protestant Episcopal.
P. E. I., Prince Edward Island.
Per., Persian.
P. I., Philippine Islands.
p., population.
Port., Portuguese.
P. R., Puerto Rico.
Presb., Presbyterian.
prom., promontory.
prov., province.
pueb., pueblo.
Que., Quebec.
q.v., which see.
R., riv., river.
r. bk., right bank.
R. C., Roman Catholic.
R. R., or ry., railroad or railway.
R. I., Rhode Island.
R. V., Revised Version.
R. R. jn., railroad junction.
s., south.
Sans., Sanskrit.
Sask., Saskatchewan.
S. C., South Carolina.
Scot., Scotland or Scottish.
S. Dak., South Dakota.
seapt., seaport.
Sp., Spanish.
sp. gr., specific gravity.
sq. m., square miles.
stn., station.
s. v., under the word.
Syr., Syriac.
temp., temperature.
Tenn., Tennessee.
terr., territory.
Tex., Texas.
tn., town.
trans., translated.
trib., tributary.
U. S., United States of America.
Va., Virginia.
vil., village.
vol., volume.
Vt., Vermont.
w., west.
Wash., Washington.
wat.-pl., watering-place.
W. Va., West Virginia.
Wis., Wisconsin.
Wyo., Wyoming.
yds., yards.

© *U. S. Army*

Underwater atomic explosion at Bikini.

© *U. S. Navy*

Atomic bomb damage to Hiroshima. October 26, 1945.

VOLUME I

A

A. The original sound in English of the letter *A* was that which it had in the Greek and Latin tongues. In most European languages (French, German, Welsh, etc.) it has retained this value, and occasionally also in English words ('psalm'). It is phonetically described as the mid-back 'wide' vowel. *A* is the standard Greek form transmitted to the Latin alphabet. The Hebrew name *aleph* (Greek *alpha*), means an ox. Some think the original sign represented a head and horns. *A* is in musical notation the sixth note of the natural diatonic scale of C, and the first note of the relative minor scale; called *la* in Italy, France, and Spain. In modern international pitch, *A* has 435 vibrations per second, or 435 multiplied or divided by any power of 2. In concert pitch, *A* has about 900 vibrations a second. Continental tuning forks are set to this note. Most stringed instruments have a string tuned to it, which in the violin is the second string, in the viola and violoncello the first, and in the contrabasso generally the third. It is the note given for tuning the orchestra. The key of *A* major has three sharps. *A*, as a symbol of order or eminence, denotes the first of a series, or the chief of a class. *A*, in the calendar, is the first of the seven dominical letters. In old books of which only the alternate pages are numbered it denotes left-hand pages. *A* as a symbol in logic is the universal affirmative. In medical formulæ *A* or *aa* (Gr. *ana*) signifies that equal parts of each ingredient are to be taken. See ALPHABET; ABBREVIATIONS.

A.A.A., Agricultural Adjustment Administration. See **United States, New Deal.**

Aachen. See **Aix la Chapelle.**

Aalborg, ancient city and port in northeast Jutland, Denmark. It is an important railroad and commercial centre, and has an evangelical bishopric; p. 42,819.

Aalen, industrial and commercial city, seat of province of the same name, Württemberg, Germany. Aalen is built on the site of an old Roman settlement; p. 12,171.

Aali Pasha (1815-71), Turkish statesman, born in Constantinople. He was five times grand vizier and an ardent advocate of reform.

Aar, or **Aare,** chief Swiss tributary to the Rhine. Its length is 175 m.

Aard-Vark (Dutch 'earth-pig'). See **Cape Ant-Eater.**

Aard-wolf (*Proteles cristatus*), a burrowing, nocturnal animal, closely related to the hyæna. It is confined to South Africa.

Aarestrup, Carl Ludwig Emil (1800-56), Danish lyric poet. His *Efterladte Digte* created a sensation by their erotic tone.

Aarhus, or **Aarhuus,** port on e. coast and largest city of Jutland, Denmark, with a good harbor. It has tobacco and cotton manufactures and iron and oil industries; p. 76,-226.

Aaron, the elder brother, colleague and interpreter of Moses. According to the Pentateuch, he was consecrated to the high-priesthood, and was consequently regarded as the ancestor of all lawful priests in Israel. Though always second to Moses, he was joined with him in the performance of miracles; his budding rod was deposited in the Ark. His great sin was the making of the golden calf; for a subsequent fault he was denied entrance into Canaan, and died, aged 123, on Mount Hor, in Edom.

Aaron's Beard, the name of two different plants—*Hypercium calycinum* ('rose of Sharon'); and *Saxifraga sarmentosa* ('mother of thousands').

Aaron's Rod, a name applied to various plants with tall flowering stems, especially to the great mullein or hag taper (*verbascum thapsus*), but also to the golden-rod.

Aaron's Tomb (*Kabr Harun*), east peak (4,360 ft.) of Mt. Hor, is, according to ancient tradition, the place where Aaron was buried. See HOR.

Aasen, Ivar Andreas (1813-96), Norwegian philologer and author. Aasen reconstructed an eclectic 'national' language (*Landsmaal*) out of the existing Norwegian dialects.

Aasvär Islands, near the Arctic Circle,

w. of Norway about 10 mi. They have important herring fisheries.

Ab, in Jewish calendar, 5th month of the ecclesiastical and 11th of the civil year; part of our July and August. The 9th of Ab was set aside to commemorate the destruction of the Temple (586 B.C. and 70 A.D.).

Ababdeh, pastoral Arab Mohammedan tribe living in the hilly district about the frontiers of Upper Egypt and Nubia, between the Red Sea and the Nile.

Abaca, or **Abaka.** See **Manila Hemp.**

Abaco, Great, or **Lucaya,** one of the Bahama Islands; p. 3,993.

Abaco, Little, n.w. of Great Abaco.

Abacus, an instrument to facilitate calculation, used by the ancient Greeks, Romans, Egyptians, Hindus, and Mexicans. It consists of a board in which parallel grooves are cut to contain pebbles, or a rectangular frame of wires on which beads are strung.

Abacus, in architecture, a flat stone, square, octagonal, or circular, and either plain or variously ornamented, placed above the capital of a column.

Abaddon, Hebrew word for 'ruin' or 'destruction.'

Abalone, a flatly coiled mollusk (*haliotis*) of the sea-coast; numerous in Southern California. The shell is used as mother-of-pearl, and the flesh is dried and eaten.

Abancourt, Charles Xavier Joseph d' (1758-92), a supporter of Louis XVI in the French Revolution, was made Minister of War (June, 1792), and was killed at Versailles by the populace.

Abandonment. The leaving of a person or persons to whom one is legally bound, or the relinquishment of property or rights, with the intention of not returning to such person or persons, or of not reclaiming such property or rights. Abandonment of wife and family has in many of the United States been made a penal offence, and is in most States a ground for divorce. See DESERTION.

Abano (**Bagni** or **Terme**), watering place, province Padua, Italy, foot of Euganean Hills. Its hot sulphur springs (98 to 181° F.) were known to the Romans.

Abarim ('those on the other side'), a range of highlands e. of the Dead Sea, containing Pisgah, where Moses viewed the Promised Land, and 2 m. to the e., Mount Nebo, 'the lonely mountain,' where Moses died and was buried.

Abatement, in law, is the interruption or suspension of a legal claim. *Abatement of nuisance* is the forcible removal by the injured party of an inconvenience constituting an infringement of his property rights. Such removal is legally permissible if accomplished without unnecessary damage or disturbance.

Abatis, a fortification made by felling trees, stripping them of their smaller branches, and securing them with the sharpened trunks in the earth and the branches pointing upward and outward toward the enemy.

Abattoir (Fr. *abattre,* 'to slaughter'), a slaughter-house for cattle and other animals used for food. A public health officer and a veterinary surgeon always supervise the operation of a good abattoir, and in the U. S., government officials inspect meat for interstate or foreign trade. See MEAT; PACKING INDUSTRY. Consult Schwartz' *Abattoirs and Cattle Markets* (1903); Cash's *Our Slaughter-House System* (1907); Ayling's *Public Abattoirs* (1908.)

Abba (Aramaic, 'father'), a devotional expression for the Divine Father, and apparently the chief appellation of God used by Jesus in prayer.

Abbadie, Antoine Thomson d' (1810-97), French savant and explorer, was born at Dublin; educated in France, whither his parents removed in 1818; sent by the Académie des Sciences on a mission to Brazil (1835); occupied with the exploration of Abyssinia (1837-48).

Abbas (c. 566-652), uncle of Mohammed, was taken prisoner at the battle of Bedr, and afterward became the leading supporter of the faith; was the founder of the dynasty of the Abbasides, who were califs of Bagdad from 750 until the Mongol conquest in 1258. See CALIF.

Abbas I, 'The Great' (1557-1628), Persian monarch, ascended the throne in 1586. His dominion extended from the Tigris to the Indus. He established the capital at Ispahan, and was the author of many important reforms.

Abbas Hilmi (1874-1923), Khedive of Egypt, son of Mohammed Tewfik, succeeded to the throne in 1892, but was deposed by the British in 1914 when he threw in his lot with the Turks.

Abbas Mirza (1783-1833), Prince of Persia, son of Shah Feth-Ali, was commander in the Russian campaigns of 1811-13 and 1826-8, in which Persia lost her Caucasian territories; was recognized as Shah by the treaty of 1828.

Abbas Pasha (1813-54) succeeded his

uncle, Ibrahim Pasha, as viceroy of Egypt (1848). His reign was profligate and reactionary.

Abbate, Niccolo dell' (1512-71), Italian painter, was born in Modena. His best works are the altar piece of San Pietro (Modena), and *Execution of the Apostles Peter and Paul* (Dresden).

Abbazia, health resort, Italy, formerly Austria, at the head of the Gulf of Fiume. There is an old abbey church, from which Abbazia takes its name. It is known as the Nice of the Adriatic and the Italian Riviera; p. 2,479.

Abbe, Cleveland (1838-1916), American astronomer and meteorologist, born in New York City, in 1868 was appointed director of the Cincinnati Observatory. His works on meteorology are of high authority.

Abbe, Robert (1851-1928), American surgeon, brother of Cleveland Abbe. He was eminent for his radium research.

Abbe, Truman (1873-), American surgeon, son of Cleveland Abbe. In 1904 he published notes on the physiological and therapeutic action of radium and three years later he was awarded a silver medal at the Jamestown exposition for his researches in this field.

Abbess, female superior of a nunnery, chosen by the secret votes of the nuns. She must be over forty years old, and have kept the vows of the order for at least eight years. She is installed by episcopal benediction, and exercises the temporal and spiritual duties of an abbot, except confession and preaching.

Abbeville (*Abbatis Villa*), town, department Somme, France, on an island and both banks of the Somme River, 15 m. from its mouth in the English Channel. Exports grain, fodder, flour, cloth, and rope; imports tar, coal, salt, wool, wine, and cattle. It is noted for its Church of St. Wolfram. Abbeville was founded in the ninth century. It was fortified by Charlemagne and Hugh Capet, and later became the residence and capital of the courts of Ponthieu. It became a city in 1130; p. 20,320.

Abbeville, city, South Carolina, co. seat of Abbeville co., 97 m. w. by n. of Columbia. Cotton and other agricultural products are raised in the neighborhood; and in the town are cotton gins, manufactories of cottonseed oil and fertilizers, and cotton mills; p. 4,930.

Abbey, the abode of a community of monks or nuns. As a Christian institution it originated among the early Christian hermits of the Egyptian desert as a cluster of separate huts built round that of an anchorite of distinguished piety; anticipated as a form of community by the Buddhists, Essenes, and Therapeutae; it is a natural corollary of the ascetic principle. As the monastic system became organized, there arose a form of architecture suited to its needs. The principle adopted by the Benedictines, that an abbey should be entirely self-contained, led to great complexity in the many thousand buildings erected by that order throughout Western Europe. Among British abbeys are Westminster, Canterbury, York, Tewkesbury (Benedictine), Durham, Fountains (Cistercian), Bolton, Bristol, Holyrood (Augustin-

Westminster Abbey.

ian). The first English abbey was founded at Bangor in 560. Henry VIII. suppressed many of the smaller foundations in 1525 and following years, and abolished all institutions of this kind in 1539 and 1540. See PRIORY; MONASTERY; MONASTICISM. Consult Wishart, *Short History of Monks and Monasticism* (1900); Cram, *Ruined Abbeys of Great Britain* (1905); Champney, *Romance of the French Abbeys* (1905); Dixon, *Abbeys of Great Britain* (1908); Gasquet, *Greater Abbeys of England* (1908); Hibbert, *Dissolution of the Monasteries* (1910); James, *Abbeys in England* (1926).

Abbey, Edwin Austin (1852-1911), American illustrator and figure painter, was born in Philadelphia. Abbey is best known to Americans for the frescoes—fifteen panels telling the story of the Holy Grail—in the Boston Public Library (1901), and for the eight immense paintings in the dome of the Pennsylvania capitol at Harrisburg (1908); and to the English for the picture of King Edward's coronation (1904), now in Windsor Castle.

Abbot, the head of a monastery. The name was first given as a title of honor to any monk, then to aged or distinguished monks, finally to the superior alone. In the East the corresponding title is archimandrite or hegumenos. In the West, in orders founded after the eleventh century, superiors are known, not as abbots, but as priors, guardians, rectors, provosts, etc. An abbot may be chosen for life or for three years; must be at least twenty-five years old, and a priest; the choice is made by the professed monks who are in holy orders, and confirmed by the bishop, or, in case of exempt monasteries, by the superior abbot or by the Pope; as a rule, receives solemn benediction for his office at the hands of a bishop; he may empower priests to absolve his subjects, etc.; in important cases he must obtain the consent of the community. He may preside over one house, or over many; he may be exempt from episcopal jurisdiction, and be subject directly to the Pope; he may possess quasi-episcopal jurisdiction over a whole district.

Commendatory abbots are persons who enjoy the revenues of an abbey without necessarily being monks.

Abbot, Charles Greeley (1872-   ), American astrophysicist, was born at Wilton, N. H. He was educated at Mass. Inst. of Technology, and was director, Smithsonian Astrophysical Observatory (1907-44); also secretary, Smithsonian Institution (1928-44).

Abbot, Ezra (1819-84), American Biblical scholar, was born at Jackson, Me., and educated at Bowdoin College. He was a member of the New Testament committee for revision of the English Bible.

Abbot, George (1562-1633), English prelate, was born at Guildford, Surrey. He was Archbishop of Canterbury (1611-33), and one of the translators of the King James New Testament. Consult Hook's *Lives of the Archbishops of Canterbury.*

Abbot, Henry Larcom (1831-1927), American engineer officer, was born in Beverly, Mass. He received his military education at West Point. Under General Humphreys he took part in the hydrographic survey of the Mississippi delta, of which he wrote (with Humphreys) an elaborate report, *Physics and Hydraulics of the Mississippi River.* During the Civil War he saw service in the Manassas campaign; was wounded at Bull Run, and took part in constructing the defences of Washington. He also served in the Virginia Peninsula Campaign (1862), and in the operations before Richmond in 1864-5. In 1865 he was chief of artillery in the operations before Fort Fisher, and in the Department of Virginia. He attained the rank of brigadier-general. After the war he was engaged in the military and scientific duties of the Corps of Engineers, until his retirement from active service in 1895. He received the degree of LL.D. from Harvard in 1886. He was a member of the Board of Consulting Engineers which formed, in 1896, the adopted plan of the Panama Canal.

Abbot of Unreason, also **Lord of Misrule,** the master of the revels at the season of Christmas, the former being his title in Scotland, the latter in England. His 'reign' lasted from All-Hallows Eve to Candlemas Day.

Abbotsford, the home of Sir Walter Scott from 1812 to 1832, is an estate on the right bank of the Tweed, 3 m. from Melrose. The house stands on a terrace between the river and the road from Melrose to Selkirk, and is a picturesque, irregular building in the Scottish baronial style. See SCOTT, SIR WALTER. Consult Smith and Crockett's *Abbotsford* (1905).

Abbott, Austin (1831-96), American lawyer, son of Jacob Abbott, was born in Boston, and was graduated from New York University (1851). He was counsel for Theodore Tilton in his celebrated suit against Henry Ward Beecher.

Abbott, Benjamin Vaughan (1830-90), American lawyer, son of Jacob Abbott (q.v.), was born in Boston, Mass., and was graduated from New York University (1850). He draughted the present penal code of New York State; and was one of the three commissioners that revised the U. S. statutes in 1870-73.

Abbott, Charles Conrad (1843-1919), American archæologist and naturalist, was born in Trenton, N. J. He was graduated in medicine from the University of Pennsylvania (1865). While assistant curator of the

Peabody Museum, Cambridge, Mass., he gathered a fine collection of 20,000 archæological specimens, which he presented to that museum. His published writings includes: *Cyclopædia of Natural History* (1886).

Common People of Ancient Rome (1911); *Roman Politics* (1923).

Abbott, Grace (1878-1939), social worker, born at Grand Island, Nebraska. After a few years spent in teaching, she went as

Abbotsford House.

Abbott, Frank Frost (1860-1924), American educator, born in Redding, Conn., and graduated from Yale (1882; PH.D. 1891; Hon. A.M. 1912). From 1891 to 1908 he was associate professor and professor of **Latin**

resident worker to Hull House, Chicago. Was director of the child labor division of the Children's Bureau, Washington, D. C., 1917-1919, and later chief of U. S. Children's Bureau, retiring in 1934. She became prof.

Sir Walter Scott's Library.

in the University of Chicago; and in 1908 became professor of Latin at Princeton. He wrote: *A History of Rome* (1906); *Society and Politics in Ancient Rome* (1909); *The*

of public welfare, U. of Chicago. Later was U. S. member of advisory com. on traffic in women and children, League of Nations.

Abbott, Jacob (1803-79), American clergyman and writer, was born in Hallowell, Me., and was graduated from Bowdoin College (1820). He was ordained in the Congregational ministry; and after 1840 devoted himself to writing, spending his life in New York City and in foreign travel. He was a prolific and popular writer of stories for the young, and published over 200 volumes, including *Harper's Story Books* (36 vols.), the *Rollo Books* (36 vols.), the *Franconia Stories* (10 vols.), the *American Histories for Youth* (8 vols.), and *Histories for the Young* (19 vols).

Abbott, John Stevens Cabot (1805-77), American writer, brother of Jacob Abbott (q.v.), was born in Brunswick, Me. After 1844 he devoted himself to literature, and wrote many historical works, including: *American Pioneers* (12 vols.); *The French Revolution; History of the Civil War; History of Frederick the Great*.

Abbott, Lyman (1835-1922), American minister and editor, son of Jacob Abbott (q.v.). He practiced law, studied theology, was ordained in the Congregational ministry. In 1888 he succeeded Beecher as pastor of Plymouth Church, Brooklyn. In 1899 he resigned his pastorate to devote himself to the editorship of *The Outlook* and to literary work. Dr. Abbott's numerous published works include: *Christianity and Social Problems* (1897); *Henry Ward Beecher* (1903); *The Spirit of Democracy* (1910); *Letters to Unknown Friends* (1913).

Abbreviations are portions of a word, generally the first letter or syllable, used in place of the word to save time and space. In ancient Greek and Roman inscriptions, in the rabbinical writings, and in the manuscripts of the Middle Ages, abbreviations were especially abundant; but with the invention of printing these became largely unnecessary.

Abbreviators, the former draughtsmen of papal bulls, etc.

Abd (Arabic, 'slave,' 'servant,' 'worshipper'), in Mohammedan countries, forms, in composition with Allah (God) and with other names or attributes of deity, many of the common Arabic personal names—*e.g.*, Abdullah, Abd-el-Kader.

Abd-el-Aziz, Mulai (1878-1943), sultan of Morocco, succeeded in 1894 to the throne and attempted to introduce European customs and methods of government. In 1907 Mulai Hafid, elder brother of Abd-el-Aziz, was proclaimed sultan; and in 1908, after futile opposition, Abd-el-Aziz surrendered the throne.

Abd-el-Kader, or **Abdul-Kadir, Emir** (1807-83), Algerian patriot, was the son of a marabout of Mascara. Preaching a *jihad* (holy war) against the French, he opened the campaign at Oran in 1833. Concluding a treaty with the French, he was recognized as emir in 1834; but war was soon resumed, and Abd-el-Kader fled to Morocco in 1843. In 1847 he gave himself up and was sent to Toulon. Released in 1852, he received a pension of $20,000 (1863), and finally resided at Damascus. He wrote a work on the Consolations of Philosophy (translated into French under the title *Rappel à l'Intelligent: Avis à l'Indifférent*). Consult lives by Churchill and Pichon.

Abdera, town, which stood in ancient Thracia. Although the birthplace of such distinguished men as the philosophers Democritus, Protagoras, Anaxarchus, and the historian Hecatæus, Abdera was the Gotham of antiquity, and 'Abderite' was a proverbial name for a simpleton.

Abderhalden, Emil (1877-), German biochemist, was born in Switzerland. He is notable for his work on proteins.

Abdication, the resignation of office by a ruler or sovereign, may result from various causes. It was from being wearied with dominion that Diocletian (395 A.D.) and, in more modern times, Christina of Sweden (1654) resigned their sovereignty. The World War and the troubles that followed in its wake resulted in a number of abdications. Modern times have seen Abdul-Hamid II. of Turkey (1907), Ali Mirza of Persia (1909), Manuel II. of Portugal (1910), Hsuan-Tung of China (1912) and Nicholas, Czar of Russia, (1917) retire before the storm of revolution; have seen, too, the abdication of King Constantine of Greece (1917), of Emperor William II. of Germany (1918), of Ferdinand of Bulgaria (1918), of Charles V. of Austria (1918), of the Sultan of Turkey (1922), of King George of Greece (1924), of King Alfonso of Spain (1931) and of King Prajadhipok of Siam (1935); Emperor Napoleon I, of France twice, (1814 and 1815). See EDWARD VIII, ABDICATION.

Abdomen, in vertebrates, is the cavity supported by the pelvis, separated from the thorax by the diaphragm, and surrounded by muscular body walls. It contains the stomach, intestines, liver, bladder, and internal genital organs. A delicate serous membrane, the *Peritoneum,* lines the abdomen and covers its viscera, permitting a smooth, gliding movement of the organs (see PERITONEUM). For abdominal surgery, see SURGERY. See also INTESTINES; LIVER; STOMACH.

In Systematic Zoology the term Abdomen is used to describe the posterior region of the body in insects, crustaceans, arachnids, and other arthropods which have the body divided into regions. The abdomen in arthropods is typically segmented, or divided into rings; but the segments tend to disappear in parasitic or much-modified forms.

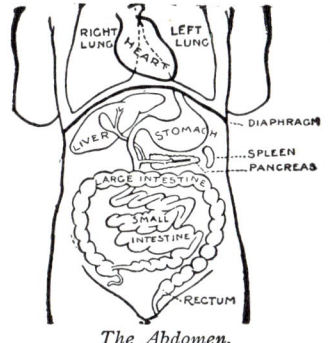

The Abdomen.

Abduction, a term meaning the unlawful taking away of a free person, or of a slave belonging to another. In the United States, abduction is the taking and carrying away of a child, a ward, a wife, or other relative, by fraud, persuasion, or open violence. Any one who takes away any female under the age of eighteen years from her father, mother, guardian, or other person having the legal charge of her person, without her consent for the purpose of prostitution, is guilty of a felony. The gist of the offence is the enticing and carrying away. A b d u c t i o n throughout the United States is a felony, and in some States may be punished by fine, not exceeding $10,000, or by separate or solitary confinement at labor for a period not exceeding twenty-five years. See KIDNAPPING.

Abdul-Aziz Ibn Saud (c1880-), King of Saudi Arabia, which includes the sultanate of Nejd, and kingdom of Hejaz and its dependencies. His father was driven out, 1891. Abdul began war against usurper, 1901. King since 1926.

Abdul-Hamid I., or **Ahmed IV.** (1725-89), sultan of Turkey, who succeeded to the throne in 1774. In the first year of his reign Turkey, disunited by revolts in Egypt and Syria, and defeated by Russia, was compelled to sign the Treaty of Kuchuk-Kainardji (1774), by which the questions of the Near East definitely enter into European diplomacy. War broke out again in 1786, and Turkey again sustained reverses, which brought about the death of the sultan.

Abdul-Hamid II. (1842-1918), succeeded his brother, Amurath v., as sultan of Turkey in 1876. His long reign was marked by reactionary measures, misgovernment, and foreign interference. Compelled to grant a constitution and an amnesty to exiles in 1908, he opened the first Turkish Parliament in the same year, but next year was forced to abdicate in favor of his brother, Reshid Effendi, known as Mohammed v. (q.v.).

Abdul-Kadir. See **Abd-el-Kader.**

Abdul-Medjid II. (1823-61), sultan of Turkey, succeeded his father, Mahmud II. (1839), and in 1841 concluded peace with Mehemet Ali of Egypt. In 1853 he resisted those claims of Russia to a protectorate over his orthodox subjects, which led to the Crimean War.

Abdur-Rahman Khan (?1830-1901), ameer of Afghanistan (1880-1901). He showed masterly skill and energy in consolidating his power, and in promoting European arts and manufactures and was considered a wise and intelligent ruler.

Abdur-Rahman I. (731-788), founder (756) of the Ommiad dynasty of Cordoba, Spain, was born in Damascus.

Abdur-Rahman II. (788-852), fourth Ommiad ruler of Cordoba, and son and successor of Al-Hakim I. (822). He wrote *Annals of Spain* in Arabic.

Abdul-Rahman III., or **Abderame** (891-961), eighth and greatest ruler of the Ommiad dynasty in Spain, ascended the throne in 912. He did much to promote Mohammedan unity in Spain.

Abe, Nobuyuki (1875-), Japanese army officer and pub. official; acting war minister 1928; appt. premier, 1939; succeeded in 1940 by Prince Fuminaro Konoye.

Abecedarians, a small sect among the Anabaptists in Germany in the sixteenth century, noted for their dislike to learning. They thought it best not even to learn to read, as a knowledge of the Scriptures was all that was necessary, and this was communicated by the Holy Spirit direct to the believer without the medium of the written word.

A Becket, Thomas. See **Becket.**

A Beckett, Gilbert Abbott (1811-56), English barrister, magistrate, and man of letters, was born in London. He founded *Figaro* in London, the forerunner of *Punch* and also wrote the *Comic Blackstone* and the *Comic Histories of England* and *Rome*.

Abel, the second (perhaps twin) son of Adam; a shepherd, who, having offered to God a more acceptable sacrifice than his brother Cain, was slain by the latter out of jealousy. In the New Testament 'righteous Abel' is regarded as the first martyr, and as a hero of faith. Around his name many Jewish and Mohammedan legends have gathered.

The Gateway, Marischal College, Aberdeen, Scotland.

Abel, Sir Frederick Augustus (1827-1902), English chemist, was born in London. He was an authority on explosives, and with James Dewar was inventor of cordite.

Abel, John Jacob (1857-1938), American pharmacologist, was born in Cleveland, O., and educated at the Univ. of Mich. and in Europe. He was professor of pharmacology at Johns Hopkins University (1893-1932), and editor of the *Journal of Pharmacology and Experimental Therapeutics* (1909-32). He was the first to obtain epinephrin and insulin in crystalline form.

Abel, Niels Henrik (1802-29), Norwegian mathematician, was born in Findö. He distinguished himself by his able development of the theory of elliptical functions and algebraic equations.

Abélard, or **Abailard, Pierre** (1079-1142), French theologian and scholastic philosopher, was born at Le Pallet, near Nantes, whence he received the epithet 'Doctor Palatinus.' He lived when the controversy of scholastic philosophy between Nominalism and Realism was at its height; studied under Roscellin, and then under William of Champeaux, the champions, respectively, of the opposing principles. He became, at thirty-six years of age, the most famous teacher in Europe, and his school at Notre Dame was crowded by students from every land. He rose above the abstract controversy of the schools, and taught a critical as opposed to the prevalent dogmatic method.

Abélard is best remembered for the story of the love of Héloise. Within the precincts of Notre Dame lived Héloise, the niece of the canon Fulbert, then seventeen years of age, and already remarkable for her beauty and accomplishments. They fled together to Brittany, where with the consent of her uncle Héloise was privately married to Abélard and bore him a son. Not long after, Héloise, with singular devotion, denied the marriage, that her love might be no hindrance to Abélard's advancement in the church. Abélard became a monk and Héloise took the veil.

Having suffered imprisonment for heresy, by judgment of the synod of Soissons in 1121, Abélard retired to a hermitage—the 'Paraclete'—where eager students surrounded him; and later he was called to preside over the abbey of St. Gildas-de-Rhuys in Brittany, while Héloise directed a sisterhood at Paraclete. Leaving the abbey after ten years, Abélard again became a teacher of great influence; but his enemies accused him of heresy, and Abélard set out for Rome, to die in the priory of St. Marcellus, near Châlon-sur-Saône. His body was taken to Paraclete, where Héloise was laid beside him in 1163. In 1817 their remains were placed in one tomb within the churchyard of Père-la-Chaise in Paris.

The best collective edition of Abélard's work is that of Victor Cousin. Consult also works by Wilkens, Carrière, Deutsch, and Gingold (1906); Gabriel Compayré's *Abélard and the Origin and Early History of Universities* ('Great Educators' Series); Pope's *Epistle of Eloisa to Abélard*; *Life* by Joseph McCabe; Wright's *Lives and Letters of Abélard and Héloise*; Richardson's *Abélard and Héloise*; George Moore's *Héloise and Abélard*.

Abelites, a Christian sect of the fourth

and fifth centuries, living in North Africa, whose principal distinction was their refusal to propagate children, holding it to be the original sin, although they accepted matrimony, and adopted children.

Abenaki. See **Abnaki**.

Abenakis Springs, Quebec, Canada, summer resort, with mineral springs, on the St. Francis River.

Abencerrages, an ancient and powerful Moorish family of Granada. Their story is found in Gines Perez de Hita's *Guerras Civiles de Granada,* on which Chateaubriand's *Aventures du dernier des Abencérages* and Cherubini's opera are based.

Aben-Ezra. See **Ibn-Ezra**.

Abercrombie, John (1780-1844), Scottish physician, was born in Aberdeen. He published *The Intellectual Powers* (1830) and *The Moral Feelings* (1833).

Abercrombie, John Joseph (1802-77), American soldier, was born in Tennessee, and was graduated from West Point (1822). In 1865 he retired from active service with the rank of brigadier-general.

Abercromby, James (1706-81), British soldier, was born in Glassbaugh, Scotland. He was sent to America in 1756, and two years later became commander-in-chief of the British and Colonial forces. On July 8, 1758, he led an army of 15,000 men against Ticonderoga (q.v.), but was repulsed with the loss of 2,000; and in September, 1758, he was superseded.

Aberdeen, the chief city and seaport of North Scotland, on the North Sea; 130 mi. n.e. of Edinburgh by rail (Tay and Forth bridges). Aberdeen is a handsome town, built mainly of granite, and so called 'the Granite City.' The chief industries are quarrying and working in granite, salmon and herring fisheries, fish curing, engineering, chemical tanning, brewing, paper making, and shipbuilding; p. 158,969. It was often bombed by Ger. in World War II.

Aberdeen, city, South Dakota, county seat of Brown co. Its artesian wells furnish valuable water power, and there are manufactures of flour, chemicals, brick, clothing, and artesian well supplies, also grain elevators and creameries; p. 17,015.

Aberdeen, city, Chehalis county, Washington, at the head of Gray's Harbor. It has extensive lumber industries, including mills, cooperages, and shipyards, and fish and clam packing houses; p. 18,846.

Aberdeen, George Hamilton Gordon, Fourth Earl of (1784-1860), British statesman, was born in Edinburgh, and was educated at Cambridge. He was Colonial Secretary in 1834-5. In 1841 he again became Foreign Secretary in Peel's administration, his chief services as such being the conclusion of the Chinese War, the Ashburton Treaty (1842), and the Oregon Treaty (1846). Consult *Life,* by his son, Sir A. Gordon.

Aberdeen and Temair, John Campbell Gordon, First Marquis of (1847-1934), British administrator, grandson of the fourth earl, succeeded to the title in 1870. He served as lord-lieutenant of Ireland (1886), Governor-General of Canada (1893-8), and again as lord-lieutenant of Ireland (1905-15).

Aberdeenshire, maritime county in the n.e. of Scotland, bounded on the n. and e. by the North Sea. Toward the sea the land is fertile and comparatively level, but a great portion lies in the mountainous region of the Grampians, which form in the s.w. the group of the Cairngorms. About 37 per cent of the area is cultivated, the chief crops being oats, barley, and turnips, while nearly 8 per cent. is under wood. Aberdeenshire is famous for its cattle, the principal breed being the hornless variety known as Polled Angus. The coast fisheries are very productive. The county town is Aberdeen. Area, 1,980 sq. mi.; p. 301,016.

Aberdeen, University of, comprises the two separate foundations of King's College and Marischal College, which were united in 1860.

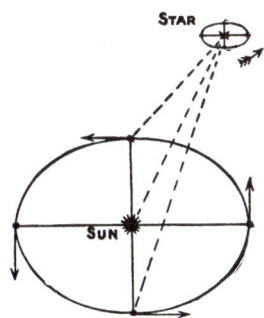

Apparent Annual Path of a Star Due to Aberration of Light.

Aberration of Light, an apparent displacement of the heavenly bodies, due to the combined effects of the earth's orbital motion and of the finite velocity of light. Each star, consequently, describes about its true position, a small ellipse, the semi-major axis of which represents the arc traversed by the earth during the interval of light transmission from the sun, and is known as the 'constant of aberration.' Its accepted value is 20.47 in. And since it stands for the ratio of luminous to terrestrial speed, the distance of the sun can thence be deduced when the velocity of light has been independently determined. The aberrations of light was discovered by the English astronomer Bradley in 1727, while seeking to determine the parallax of certain fixed stars. See PARALLAX.

Aberration, Spherical and Chromatic, in optical instruments, means the deviation of part of a pencil of rays from the point through which every component ray of the pencil should pass, if the theoretical conditions for distinct vision are to be rigorously fulfilled.

Aberystwyth, port and watering place, Cardiganshire, Wales, on the River Ystwith; 245 m. n.w. of London by rail. The seat of the University College of Wales and of the Welsh National Library. Exports, lead and blende ore; p. 11,220.

Abettor. See **Accessory.**

Abgar, the titular name of twenty-eight kings of Osroene (in Mesopotamia, of which Edessa was the capital), one of whom was said to have sent a letter to Jesus, asking Him to share his kingdom and cure his disease, and to have received a reply from Christ.

Abhorrers, in English history, a name given (1679-80) to the Court or Prerogative Party, who signed addresses to Charles II. 'abhorring' the petitions of the 'Petitioners.' The Abhorrers later received the nickname of 'Tories,' and the Petitioners that of 'Whigs.'

Abiathar ('Father of Plenty'), son of Ahimelech or Ahijah the high priest, but later joined Adonijah in his revolt, and was therefore deposed from the priesthood by Solomon.

Abib, in the Jewish calendar, the first month of the ecclesiastical year, on the 14th of which the feast of the Passover is celebrated; later named Nisan, and corresponding nearly to April.

Abies. See **Fir.**

Abigail ('Father has rejoiced'), wife of Nabal the Carmelite. After Nabal's death, she became the wife of David. In speaking to David she called herself 'thine handmaid,' and her name has thus come to be colloquially used for a waiting maid or servant.

Abijah, the name of several individuals —in Bible: 1, king of Judah (c920-917), (Abijam), son and successor of Rehoboam; 2, son of Jeroboam I, died in infancy; 3, descendant of Eleazar, son of Aaron, chief of eight of the twenty-four courses of David's priests; 4, second son of Samuel, whose corrupt administration gave the elders of Israel a plea for their demand for a king.

Abilene, a district of the ancient kingdom of Iturea, formed into one of four tetrarchies by the Romans (36 B.C.-23 B.C.).

Abilene, Texas, co.-seat Taylor co.; Simmons University and Abilene Christian College.

Abimelech ('My father is king' or 'is Molech'). (1.) A king of Gerar, who, owing to Abraham's misrepresentation, took Sarah into his harem; but being warned in a dream, restored her to her husband. (2.) Son of Gideon and a Shechemite woman, who persuaded the Shechemites to make him their king, and by assassination got rid of his seventy half-brothers except Jotham.

Abingdon, town, Virginia, county seat of Washington co. Industries are brick works, canning and wagon factories, and flour and lumber mills; p. 3,158.

Abington, town, Massachusetts, county seat of Plymouth co., 20 m. s.e. of Boston. Boots and shoes are manufactured, and there are machine shops; p. 5,872.

Abington, Mrs. Fanny (1737-1815), English actress. During her career on the stage (1755-99) she created thirty original characters, her most famous being Lady Teazle.

Abiogenesis. See **Biogenesis.**

Abipones, South American aborigines who formerly inhabited the Gran Chaco, Argentina, between the Bermejo and Rio Grande. Consult Church's *Aborigines of South America* (1912).

Abishai, nephew of King David, and one of his most daring and faithful followers. He became one of the captains of the kingdom.

Abjad is the first of eight mnemonic words which give the numerical order of the Arabic alphabet from 1 to 1,000.

Abjuration. The *Oath of Abjuration* was imposed in 1701 upon members of the British Parliament and all holders of public offices, including clergymen, teachers, barristers, etc. It was a declaration in favor of King William and the Revolution Settlement, and against the 'late King James,' and concluded with the words, 'upon the true faith

Ablative of a Christian.' It has by subsequent enactments been merged in a general oath of allegiance to the person of the reigning sovereign.

Ablative Case, a grammatical inflection of nouns and pronouns used to denote the place, person, or thing from which something is taken away. It is found in Indo-European languages, particularly Latin, in which it also expresses other relations; Sanskrit, Oscan, and Umbrian. In Greek its functions have been diverted to the genitive case; and in other languages, as English, it is usually replaced by the prepositions *in, with, by, from,* etc.

Ablaut. The use of the term ablaut in philology is due to Jacob Grimm (*Deutsche Grammatik*); the word *gradation* is frequently employed as its equivalent in English. It finds special application in the comparative grammar of the Indo-Germanic languages, especially in the Germanic so-called 'strong verbs,' where, as in Anglo-Saxon, for example, there are six distinct classes, differentiated by varying but regular ablaut rows (compare English *sing, sang, sung; write, wrote, written*). Consult Skeat's *English Etymology*.

Ablegate, a special papal envoy, sent to confer the symbols of office upon a newly appointed cardinal or other dignitary.

Ablution, a right symbolizing the purification of the soul by the cleansing of the body. In the Roman Catholic Church the word indicates the washing of the chalice and the priest's fingers with water and wine after mass.

Abnaki, Abenaki, or **Abnakis,** an Indian tribe of the Algonquin Confederacy, formerly inhabiting the State of Maine. They now number less than 2,000 persons, located in New Brunswick, Quebec, and Maine.

Abner ('Father is Ner'), a Hebrew warrior, cousin of Saul, and captain of the army. He proclaimed Ish-bosheth king, abandoned him for David, and was killed by Joab.

Abo (Finnish, **Turku**), port of Finland, and capital of Finland until 1812; site of cathedral and university; p. 73,700.

Abo-Björneborg (Finnish, **Turku-Pori**), department of Finland; area, 8,500 sq. m.; p. 536,079; capitals, Turku and Pori.

Abolitionists, a term applied, broadly, in the United States to those who, before the Civil War, advocated the abolition of slavery; but especially applied to those who urged immediate abolition, without compensation to the slave owners, and who, disavowing the Federal Constitution as a proslavery document, endeavored to attain their object by moral agitation rather than by political action.

What is distinctively known in American history as the Abolition Movement began in 1831 with the establishment by William Lloyd Garrison of an intensely anti-slavery journal, *The Liberator,* devoted to agitation for the immediate and unconditional emancipation of all slaves in the United States. This movement found expression through effective anti-slavery organizations such as the New England Anti-Slavery Society (formed 1832) and the American Anti-Slavery Society (formed 1833). Among other prominent Abolitionists may be mentioned Wendell Phillips, Theodore Parker, Samuel May, Lucretia Mott, and Gerrit Smith. See SLAVERY.

Consult Garrison's *William Lloyd Garrison;* William Birney's *Life and Times of James G. Birney;* Hume's *The Abolitionists* (1905); Herbert's *The Abolition Crusade and Its Consequences* (1912).

Aborigines. This word was first used of the original inhabitants of Italy; it was afterward extended to the inhabitants of other countries when first known; now it generally means the natives found in a country by European colonists—as, for example, the North American Indians. The word is also used of plants and animals, to denote the flora and fauna indigenous to a place.

Abortion, in medicine, denotes the expulsion of the product of conception (the impregnated ovum) from the womb before the sixth month of pregnancy. If the expulsion takes place after that date, and before the proper time, it is termed a *premature labor* (q.v.) or *miscarriage.* In law, however, no such distinction is made.

CAUSES.—The causes of abortion may depend upon the health of the fœtus, or on that of the mother. Illness of the mother during pregnancy, either by lowering the general health or by a more direct action, may induce abortion or miscarriage. Among predisposing causes are a diseased condition of either parent, especially a syphilitic taint, and most fevers. Among the direct causes of abortion may be placed blows on the abdomen, falls, any violent muscular efforts, and severe mental shock. Moreover, the death of the fœtus from any cause is sure to occasion abortion.

Criminal Abortion.—In law, procuring, or attempting to procure abortion, whether by the woman herself or by another, is a felony in most of the States of the United States, unless the act be necessary to preserve the mother's life.

It cannot be too generally known that all attempts at procuring criminal abortion, either by the administration of powerful drugs or the application of instruments, are accompanied with extreme danger to the pregnant woman. See INFANTICIDE.

Aboukir, or **Abukir,** (ancient *Kanobos*), village, Abourkir Bay, Egypt; 13 m. n.e. of Alexandria. Abourkir Bay, 16 m. wide, was the scene of the Battle of the Nile (Aug. 1, 1798) in which Nelson defeated the French. In the vicinity are many ancient remains.

About, Edmond François Valentin (1828-85), French novelist and dramatist, was born in Dieuze, Lorraine. His fame rests principally upon his novels—all of which have been translated into English.

Abra, river and province, Luzon, Philippine Islands. Area, 1,484 sq. mi.; p. 55,000.

Abracadabra, a cabalistic word or formula constructed from the letters of the alphabet, used by Basilidian Gnostics of the 2d century, and later as a spell to secure the assistance of good spirits against evil; supposed, when written in the form of a triangle and worn round the neck for nine days, to act as a charm against fevers, etc.

Abraham. A native of Ur of the Chaldees (in Mesopotamia, or, less likely, Uru, now Mugheir, in Babylonia), married to his half-sister Sarai, he migrates to Haran in Upper Mesopotamia; thence, in obedience to a divine command, to Canaan, which land is thereupon promised to his seed. Thenceforward he lives the life of a nomad chief, wandering mainly in the districts around Shechem, Beth-el, and Hebron. While sojourning in Egypt, he imperils Sarai's honor by misrepresenting her as only his sister; but he shows true self-denial in giving the choice of pasture land to his nephew Lot, and true courage in his successful attack upon the victorious Chedorlaomer; while the tenderness of his nature is evinced in his unwillingness to expel Hagar and Ishmael from his tent at Sarai's instigation, and in his pathetic intercession on behalf of Sodom.

The promises grow ever in splendor; Jehovah makes a covenant with him, ordaining the rite of circumcision, and changing his name from Abram to Abraham (and Sarai's to Sarah), as the credentials thereof; heavenly messengers are commissioned to visit him, and his prayers have power on high. At length Isaac is born, and the crowning expression of Abraham's faith is given in his willingness to obey God even to the extent of offering up the son of promise as a sacrifice. After Sarah's death Abraham marries Keturah, and has six sons by her; and at last, at the age of 175, he is laid to rest beside Sarah in the cave at Machpelah.

The patriarch plays a great rôle in later Judaism, as also in the New Testament; many remarkable legends have gathered round his name; and to the Arabs he is, as Ibrahim, the first and greatest Moslem.

On the more debatable or extra-Biblical points, the commentaries (Dillmann, Delitzsch, Driver) and the recent Bible dictionaries (Hastings' and Cheyne's) may be consulted. For Assyrian relations, consult Tomkins' *Studies on the Times of Abraham,* and Sayce's *Patriarchal Palestine;* for Abraham's place in Biblical history and theology, Schultz's *Old Testament Theology* (Eng. trans.), and Kittel's *History of the Hebrews* (Eng. trans.). There is a late apocryphal book, *The Testament of Abraham,* published in *Texts and Studies* (1892).

Abraham-a-Santa-Clara—family name, **Ulrich Megerle**—(1644-1709), a great pulpit orator of the Roman Catholic Church; born near Messkirch in Baden. The sermon, *Up, up, ye Christians!* (1683), against the Turkish menace, was used by Schiller in *Wallenstein's Lager.* His most typical book is *Judas der Ertz-Schelm* (1686-95).

Abraham, Heights of, or **Plains of Abraham,** s.w. of Quebec, along the St. Lawrence River, the scene of the battle between Wolfe (q.v.) and Montcalm (Sept. 13, 1759), which added Canada to the British empire. In 1908 the Plains were made a Canadian National Park.

Abrahamites, a Syrian sect in the ninth century who denied the divinity of Christ. Also applied to a deistic sect in Bohemia in the 18th century, who professed to be followers of Huss; they were expelled from Bohemia in 1783.

Abraham's Bosom, a term applied by the Jews to the abode of the righteous after death. Consult Salmond's *Christian Doctrine of Immortality.*

Abrasives, substances producing wear by friction, used for grinding, polishing, and scouring in the arts and in manufacture. The principal natural abrasives are *corundum* (q.v.), a crystalline aluminum oxide of about

90 per cent. purity, and *emery* (q.v.), of about 65 per cent. purity. More reliable in quality are the artificial abrasives: carbide of silicon, known as *carborundum* (q.v.) or by other trade name; *alundum* (q.v.), an aluminum hydrate, manufactured from bauxite, much used in the grinding of steel; and crushed steel. Consult U. S. Geological Survey's annual report, *Mineral Resources of the United States.*

Abravanel, or **Abarbanel, Isaac Ben Jehuda** (1437-1508), minister of state to King Alfonso v. of Portugal, and from 1483 to 1492 chancellor to Ferdinand the Catholic, king of Castile. He was distinguished for his high intellectual and moral qualities; author of a number of philosophical and exegetical treatises.

Abridgment, a shortened or condensed form of a book. At law a fairly made abridgment is deemed a new work, and is not an infringement of copyright. If the text of the work is reproduced in part, the production is legally not an abridgment, but a compilation, and is held to be an infringement of copyright. See COPYRIGHT.

Abrogation is a term derived from the Canon Law, where it meant the total as opposed to the partial repeal of a pre-existing law. In modern times it denotes, strictly speaking, the tacit nullification of a rule of law, which is generally brought about through the adoption by the courts, or enactment by the legislature, of a new rule inconsistent therewith.

Abruzzi, Prince Luigi Amadeo, Duke of the (1873-1933), Italian Arctic explorer and geographer, third son of Amadeo, Duke of Aosta, and cousin of the king of Italy, was born in Madrid. On Sept. 30, 1911, he commanded the squadron which attacked Preveza, the first action of the Italian-Turkish War. He was commander-in-chief of the Italian Navy (1915-1917) during the World War. Consult Filippi's *Ascent of Mount St. Elias* (Eng. trans.); *On the 'Polar Star' in the Arctic Sea* (Eng. trans.); *Ruwenzori* (1908).

Abruzzi and Molise, a territorial division (compartimento) of Central Italy. It is traversed by the two main ranges of the Central Apennines. In the higher parts the climate is severe. Forestry and pasturage are the chief occupations; cereals and wine are produced in the fertile lower valleys. Area, 6,565 sq. mi.; p. 1,519,000.

Absalom, King David's third son, born at Hebron. Because of his personal charms, Absalom became a universal favorite, and his ambition made him a danger to the realm. Though forgiven by his father for the murder of his half-brother Amnon, he stirred up sedition, and raised a formidable insurgent force. His army was routed by the royal troops in the wood of Ephraim, and Absalom, fleeing upon a mule, was caught by his hair in a tree, and killed by Joab, to the great sorrow of the king.

Absalon, or **Axel,** archbishop of Lund (1128-1201), was born in Sjælland, Denmark. Absalon was of the best type of the mediæval warrior priests, one of the greatest of Danish statesmen, yet pious and conscientious. A scholar himself, he supplied his clerk, Saxo Grammaticus (q.v.), with the materials for his great history.

Abscess (*Apostema*), a circumscribed collection of pus formed within some tissue or organ of the body, through the presence of specific organisms, such as streptococci. The vessels supplying the area dilate so that there is an increased flow of blood into the part; the organisms multiply, and throw out certain poisons or toxins which, attacking the tissue cells and white blood corpuscles, destroy them, and thereby produce the pus corpuscles. Once formed, this pus may either become dried up to form a caseous or cheesy mass, or it may escape by bursting through the skin or into a canal such as the rectum, urethra, etc.

Absciss Layer, a layer of cork formed in autumn between the base of the leaf and the stem in many deciduous trees. It divides across the middle, and causes the fall of the leaf, half of the cork remaining to cover the leaf scar. See CORK.

Absconding is fleeing or remaining away from one's usual residence, or the place where one is generally found, in order to avoid legal proceedings.

Absentee, a term applied, by way of reproach, to landlords who derive their rent from one country, and spend it in another.

Absinthe, absinth; *Fr.* absant, a green liquor made by distillation, containing alcohol and a number of essential oils, the chief among the latter being the oil of wormwood or absinthum (*Artemisia absinthum*), to which the deleterious properties of the liquid are in great measure due.

Absolute, that which is freed from relation, limitation or dependence. As an adjective it is therefore applied (1) to the essence of a thing apart from its relations or appearances, and (2) to the complete or perfect state of being. Hence comes its substantival meaning of 'The Absolute' as the self-existent, self-sufficient Being, that which is free from all limitation, the all-inclusive Reality. The absolute in one form or another is a central feature of the philosophical systems of Spinoza, Schelling, and Hegel. For absolute monarchy, see ABSOLUTISM. For absolute alcohol, see ALCOHOL. For absolute zero of temperature, see TEMPERATURE.

Absolution, originally a legal term, was adopted by the prelatical churches to express the remission of sin, or of certain consequences of sin, in virtue of power committed by Christ to His Church. The Council of Trent defines absolution from sin as a judicial act on the part of the priest, who, as judge, passes sentence on the penitent, and who acts in the name of God.

The word absolution is also used of certain prayers said over a corpse before it is taken from the church to the cemetery.

Absolutism is the term applied to that form of government in which no constitutional checks are imposed on the power of the monarch. Louis XIV. of France was the great champion of absolutism on the continent of Europe. His famous dictum was *L'état, c'est moi* ('I am the state'). See GOVERNMENT; SOVEREIGN.

Absolutists, a name given to a Spanish political party which in 1819 wished to abrogate the constitution of 1812, and to restore the absolute power of the throne.

Absorbents. In medicine, the term absorbents is applied to such substances as magnesia, chalk, etc., which absorb or neutralize acid fluids in the stomach; in chemistry, to anything that takes up into itself a gas or a liquid (to such a drying agent as caustic soda, which withdraws moisture from the air); and in physiology (animal and vegetable), to the vessels by which the processes of absorption are carried on, such as the lymphatics in animals and the extremities of the roots in plants. See LYMPHATICS.

Absorption in Plants can only take place when the substance to be absorbed has been changed into the liquid form of solution; for all food has to pass through the actual cell walls by a process of osmosis. See PLANTS, *Nutrition*.

Absorption of Gases by liquids depends on the pressure, the temperature, and the nature of the particular gas and liquid. If the temperature remains constant, and the pressure is altered, the amount of gas absorbed is directly proportional to the pressure (Henry's Law): thus one volume of water at $15.5°$ C., and under ordinary atmospheric pressure, takes up one volume of carbon dioxide; while under a pressure of two atmospheres it absorbs an equal volume at that pressure, but, in accordance with Boyle's Law, twice as great a mass of the gas. See OCCLUSION; GASES, LAWS OF.

Absorption of Light occurs whenever light falls upon a material surface and suffers refraction and reflection. Neither of these phenomena could be produced unless the light penetrated some distance into the substance.

Most substances exert a general absorption, so that all kinds of radiation suffer diminution in passing through them; but they also exert a selective absorption, certain rays being more freely absorbed than others. It is this selective absorption which gives rise to the varied tints and colors of bodies, the color of any body being determined by the excess of the corresponding kind of light in the radiations sent back from it or transmitted through it. See COLOR; DISPERSION.

Absorption Lines and Bands. When sunlight falls upon a prism the emergent rays are split up into a band of color called the Solar Spectrum. Closely examined, this color band is found to be crossed by a large number of dark lines. If the source of light be changed the spectrum changes with it. See SPECTRUM.

Abstemii, a name formerly given to those who refused to partake of the cup of the eucharist because of their aversion to wine.

Abstinence. See **Temperance; Fasting.**

Abstract and **Abstraction.** An abstract term or idea, in the logical sense, is one which expresses a quality or essence regarded apart from the individuals or particular objects of which it may be predicated—color, man, wisdom. (See NOMINALISM.) *Abstraction* is the selective process by which such ideas are formed; for example, in forming the abstract idea of Man, the particular differences which distinguish one man from another are disregarded, and only the qualities common to all men, or those that belong to man as such, are retained. Abstraction in this sense is one aspect of generalization.

Abstract, in Law, means a concise summary of the contents of a document, and corresponds to a *précis* in diplomacy.

In Arithmetic the term is applied to numbers considered by themselves, without reference to any objects enumerated. Thus, 9,

12, are abstract numbers, 9 dogs, 12 dollars are concrete numbers.

Abstract of Title is a concise statement of the instruments and events under and by means of which a person derives his title to property. The abstract is usually compiled from the public records, though the original instruments should, if possible, be compared.

Abt, Franz (1819-85), German composer, was born in Eilenburg, Prussia. He was *Kapellmeister* at Zürich (from 1841) and at the Hof Theatre, Brunswick (from 1852).

Abu, is much used in Arabic in the formation of personal and topographical names. The common view is that 'paternity' is the primary meaning; but W. Robertson Smith assigns 'possession' as the primary and 'paternity' as the secondary meaning.

Abu-Bekr, ('father of the maiden') (573-634), received this name in allusion to his daughter Ayesha, the only maiden among the wives whom Mohammed married. A man of wealth and position among the Koreish, as well as a native of Mecca, he was one of the first to believe in the Prophet, and was his sole companion in the Hejira; and on the death of Mohammed (June 8, 632) was elected head of the Moslems, with the title of Calif (*khalifa, 'successor'*). He reigned two years. He was buried at Medina, near the grave of Mohammed. See CALIF.

Abulfaraj (Latin, *Abulfaragius*) best known as **Bar-Hebraeus** (1226-86), Syrian scholar, was born at Malatia, Armenia. Son of a Jewish physician who became a Christian, he became bishop of Aleppo (1252) and archbishop of the Eastern Jacobites (1264). The last classical author in Syriac literature, he wrote the *Chronicum Syriacum* or Universal History. He also wrote commentaries in Syriac and Arabic on Aristotle, and treatises on theology, philosophy and science.

Abulfeda (1273-1331), Arabic geographer and historian, born at Damascus, early achieved distinction in the field (against Crusaders and Mongols) and by his pen. Of his many works the most celebrated are a *Universal History* down to his own day, and a *Geography*.

Abu, Mount, in Southwest Rajputana, India. It is a celebrated place of pilgrimage, especially for the Jains, who have a magnificent group of five temples at Delwara.

Abutilon, or **Flowering Maple,** a genus of shrubs belonging to the order Malvaceæ, with maple-like leaves and bell-shaped flowers, usually drooping. They are desirable garden and window plants, although tender.

Abutment, in architecture and engineering, that portion of a pier, bridge, or wall constructed to receive the thrust of an arch or vault.

Abydos, ancient city Upper Egypt, near the modern Araba el Madfuna, on the left bank of the Nile. During the 19th dynasty it was a place of great commercial importance; later it declined, and in early Christian times was in ruins.

Here are the ruins of the temple built by Seti I., during the 19th dynasty, and fragments of another temple, built by Rameses II.

The neighborhood is filled with private tombs, which in the early part of 1909 yielded many objects of ornament; vases, the oldest in existence, and small engraved tablets of ivory and ebony inscribed with history of events of the time from 4700 B.C. onward.

Consult Amélineau's *Les Nouvelles Fouilles d' Abydos* (3. vols., 1899-1904); Caulfield's *Temple of the Kings at Abydos* (1902); Petrie's *Abydos* (1902-4); Murray's *Osireion at Abydos* (1904).

Abydos, ancient town near Canakkale, Turkey, Asia Minor, on the Hellespont, here less than one mile wide, opposite to ancient Sestos. Here Xerxes crossed (480 B.C.) by a bridge of boats. It is associated with the tradition of Hero and Leander.

Abyssal Animals. Scientific exploration with delicate and trustworthy instruments, recording the conditions they encounter at any designated depths, have proved that the great abysses of the ocean support a varied population. All the large groups of marine animals are represented there.

A striking characteristic of virtually all abyssal animals is the uniformity of the body color. Though the colors are most diverse when a collection from one locality is studied, they are quite uniform if the individuals themselves be considered.

The last volume of the *Challenger* monographs, entitled *Summary of Results,* gives a historical account of deep-sea dredging. For American work in this field, consult the publications of the U. S. Bureau of Fisheries; Agassiz' *Three Cruises of the Blake;* Goode and Bean's *Oceanic Ichthyology.*

Abyssinia, officially known now as **Ethiopia** (Ethiopian and Amhar, *Ityopya;* Latin, Æthiopia), a Semitic country in Northeast Africa, lying, roughly between 6° and 15° N. lat., and 35° and 43° E.

Ethiopia: Emperor Haile Selassie, Wearing Crown.

long. It is composed of the former kingdoms of Tigré, with Lasta, in the n. and n.e.; Amhara, with Gojjam, in the center and w., and Shoa in the s.; also portions of Somaliland and Galla in the s.e. and s. It is wholly an inland country. The area of the country is estimated at about 305,731 sq. m., and the population was estimated in 1939 as 9,450,000. The largest cities are the capital Addis Ababa (c. 150,000), Diredawa (c. 30,-000), and Harar (c. 25,000).

Ethiopia consists chiefly of an elevated, irregular table-land, with a general elevation of 6,500 ft., rising in parts to 8,000 and 10,000 ft., and in summits to 15,000 ft. There are many forest tracts of magnificent trees, with a dense undergrowth of ferns and parasitic creepers. The determining physical agency has been volcanic, with subsequent erosion. Earthquakes are common in the northern section, and there are hot springs.

The climate is determined by altitude, according to which a native division recognizes three zones. There are two seasons—the rainy, which lasts from June to September, and the dry.

The lowlands are unhealthful, hot, and humid. Their vegetable life is tropical, com-. prising sugar-cane, cotton, coffee, **indigo**, aloe, baobab, tamarind, banana, sycamore, fig, tamarisk, and acacia: the total loss of foliage during the dry season **is characteristic**. The climate of the middle zone is quite pleasant; the uppermost region is subject to bitter n. winds. Among the products of the middle zone are the vine, bamboo, oil palm, banana, wheat, teff, dagusa, tobacco, pomegranate, orange lemon, olive, and peach. In the highlands, which are chiefly pastoral, **wheat, barley, and oats are grown up to 12,000 feet, above which the vegetation is** alpine. In general the soil is extremely fertile. In the northern country the slopes of **the valleys are laid out in terraces and ir**rigated, and three crops annually may be harvested from the same ground.

In the lowlands are found the elephant, two-horned rhinoceros, hippopotamus, zebra, giraffe, gazelle, and many birds, reptiles, and insects; in the highlands, the buffalo, antelope, wolf, jackal, lynx, hyæna, lion, leopard, and ibex. Monkeys and baboons are found up to elevations of 10,000 feet above the sea. The minerals comprise iron, gold, coal, saltpetre, sulphur, copper and silver, platinum, potash, and there are numerous mineral springs. Precious stones are plentiful, especially emeralds and agates. Some diamonds have been found.

The dominant race is Semitic. The Hamitic is the aboriginal race. The Negritic people are known as Shankela or Shangalle. Pigmies are met with s. of Kaffa and the Oromo, as in the Doko. The court or official language is Amharic, but Geez or Ethiopic is that of the church and literature; Tigrai is the language of the Tigré.

The native industries are the weaving of cotton and mohair fabrics, and the working of metals and leather. The chief exports are gold, civet, ivory, rubber, hides, goat skins, coffee, wax, and native butter. The annual value of the imports and exports is about $12,000,000.

Up to the time of its conquest by Italy in 1935 and 1936, the government was a despotic monarchy.

The national religion is Monophysite Christianity, but Judaism is found among the Agau or Falasha; Islam is the faith of the Afar, Somali, and most of the Galla. Education is restricted to the teaching of the secular and regular clergy. A cabinet formed on European lines was introduced in 1919 but was somewhat vague in function.

History.—By the evidence of speech, the Abyssinians—*i. e.,* the dominant Semitic race —are immigrants from Southern Arabia, where to this day a cognate dialect quite distinct from Arabic is spoken. The Abyssinian empire dates from the 1st century B.C. or the 1st century A.D., when these colonists founded the kingdom of Aksum, or Axum, on the downfall of the empire of the Ptolemies.

In 1923 Abyssinia was admitted to the League of Nations. The Empress Zauditu died in April, 1930; she was succeeded by Ras Tafari, who was crowned at Addis Ababa on Nov. 2, 1930, amid scenes of barbaric splendor. He took the name of Haile Selassie.

In December, 1925, Great Britain and Italy agreed that they would support each other to secure the right for the British to build a dam at Lake Tana, the source of the Blue Nile, for the irrigation of the Soudan, and for the Italians to build a railroad between Eritrea and Italian Somaliland. A protest was made in 1926 to the League of Nations by Abyssinia, who had not been consulted. The matter was dropped by Great Britain and Italy, and in a joint statement issued in Rome on September 29, 1934, Italy and Abyssinia recorded their mutual attitude of friendship and non-aggression.

Abyssinia was conquered by Italy in a war which had its inception in a clash in December, 1934, on the Somaliland border between tribesmen and Italian colonial troops. The war was waged until May 5, 1936, when Addis Ababa was taken by the Italians. On May 9 Premier Mussolini proclaimed the annexation of Abyssinia to Italy. The Emperor fled to Great Britain and his title was later claimed by Emmanuel III, King of Italy. (See *Italy*.)

In May 1941 following the defeat of the Italian army by the British, Haile Selassie was restored to his throne. In 1952 Ethiopia united with Eritrea in an E. Afr. Federation.

Consult Rey's *In the Country of the Blue Nile* (1927); Abzug's *Spearhead* (1946).

Acacia, a genus of usually thorny trees and shrubs, belonging to the bean family (order Leguminosæ, sub-order Minosaceæ), of which over 400 species are found in tropical and subtropical regions throughout the world, but more extensively in Australia and Africa. They are evergreen, and have small flowers.

A. vera yields the true gum arabic. *A. catechu* yields a resinous extract, catechu, used in medicine as a powerful astringent.

Académie Française. See **Academy.**

Academy, an institution for the cultivation of learning, of letters, or of art. The name has been applied to many and various organizations, such as schools, universities, colleges for instruction in particular arts and sciences, and societies of scholars, literary men, and artists.

The ACCADEMIA DELLA CRUSCA, founded in Florence in 1582, had as its object the purification of the Italian language. It publishes *Transactions.*

INSTITUT DE FRANCE. In 1795 the Institut de France was founded with three sections, reorganized with four in 1803 and 1816, and enlarged in 1832 by the admission of the *Académie des Sciences Morales et Politiques.*

The ACADEMIE FRANCAISE, originated (1630) as the informal weekly meetings of a few literary friends. Though assemblies of any kind were illegal at that time, Richelieu offered his patronage and the society was incorporated in 1637 as the Académie Française. Its famous Dictionary has furnished an authoritative national standard of orthography and accuracy of language.

It was completed Sept. 5, 1935, after 40 years of labor. This same year the "Forty Immortals" celebrated the three-hundredth anniversary of the Academie.

Memoirs and reports of sessions are published. Among its works are *Histoire Littéraire de la France; Recueil des Historiens de France; Corpus Inscriptionum Semiticarum.*

The ACADEMIE DES SCIENCES, founded by Colbert in 1666, formed the basis of the Institute as constituted in 1795. It publishes *Memoirs* and *Reports.*

The ACADEMIE DES BEAUX-ARTS (1655) was united with the Academy of Architecture as the fourth section of the Institute. Five volumes and two parts (one-half) of the 6th volume of the *Dictionnaire de l'Académie des Beaux-arts* have been published (1912).

ROYAL BRITISH ACADEMY.—It was not until June 28, 1901, that the British Academy was founded, having for its object the promotion of the study of moral and political science, including history, philosophy, law, politics and economics, archæology and philology. A royal charter was granted by the King in Aug., 1902.

The AKADEMIE DER WISSENSCHAFTEN (Academy of Sciences) is the oldest academy in Germany—founded in Berlin in 1700 by Frederick I., after the plan of Leibniz.

In Holland there are the Royal Academy of Sciences at Leyden, the oldest in the country; another at Haarlem, founded in 1752; and another at Amsterdam (1855). Each of these publishes *Verhandelingen* (*Transactions*).

The Royal Academy of Sciences at Vienna, founded in 1847, is divided into two sections —philosophical and scientific.

Belgium has the *Académie Royale des Sciences* at Brussels and *Académie Royale d' Archéologie* at Antwerp.

In Portugal there is the *Academia Real das Sciencias* at Lisbon, founded in 1779, reorganized in 1851.

The Royal Academy of Sciences in Stockholm (1741) is divided into seven classes, and numbers 90 members. A committee of the Academy awards the Nobel Prizes (q.v.) for Physics and for Chemistry.

UNITED STATES.—In the United States the tendency has been to form learned societies of unlimited membership, rather than academies in the restricted sense in which that term is generally used on the Continent. Of the latter type of academies, however, the United States has the American Academy of Arts and Letters (1780), the National Academy of Sciences (1863), and the National Institute of Arts and Letters (1898), with the Academy of Arts and Letters (1904).

The American Philosophical Society, founded by Franklin in Philadelphia (1743), is the oldest scientific society in the United States. It has 500 resident and 70 foreign members, and a library containing the world's largest collection of Frankliniana. Its publications include *Transactions, Proceedings, Memoirs,* and a *Year Book.* A list of American learned societies is included in the article SOCIETIES (*q.v.*).

Consult *Handbook of Learned Societies and Institutions of America* (Carnegie Institution of Washington, Publication No. 39; 1908); Matthew Arnold's 'Literary Influence of Academies,' in *Essays in Criticism* (First Series); Harnack's *Geschichte der Preussichen Akademie der Wissenschaften* (4 vols., 1901); Rosengarten's *American Philosophical Society* (1909); Robertson's *History of the French Academy* (1910); *Minerva,* an admirable annual guide, in German, to all universities, museums, libraries, and societies; *Official Year Book of the Scientific and Learned Societies of Great Britain and Ireland.*

Academy of Arts and Letters, American, was founded in 1904 by the National Institute of Arts and Letters (See INSTITUTE OF ARTS AND LETTERS) as an inner circle of the latter society, its aim being 'to represent and further the interests of the fine arts and literature.' It was incorporated in 1916. Membership is limited to 50.

Academy of Arts and Sciences, American, an institution founded in Boston in 1780. There are 792 Fellows and 43 Fellows Emeriti; also 124 foreign honorary members.

Academy of Medicine, American. See **Medicine, American Academy of.**

Academy of Natural Sciences, an institution founded in Philadelphia in 1812, the oldest natural science society in the United States.

Academy of Political and Social Science, American. See **Political and Social Science, American Academy of.**

Academy of Sciences, National. See **National Academy of Sciences.**

Academy (the Royal) of Arts, London, was founded in 1768, with Sir Joshua Reynolds as its first president. An annual exhibition of painting and sculpture is held in Burlington House, Piccadilly, lasting from May till August.

Academy, U. S. Military. See **Military Academy.**

Academy, U. S. Naval. See **Naval Academy.**

Acadia, or **Acadie,** a name supposed to be derived from a Micmac expression meaning 'abounding in.' It is first found in a petition of De Monts to the king of France asking for permission to colonize a part of the New World. The territory which was granted to De Monts was of uncertain limits, and so extensive as to include within its borders the present cities of Montreal and Philadelphia. Later, its bounds were defined and limited to the province of New Brunswick, the peninsula of Nova Scotia, and part of Maine. The first settlement and most important town was Port Royal, founded in 1604, now known as Annapolis Royal, and situated on Annapolis Basin, an arm of the Bay of Fundy. In 1621 Acadia, enlarged by the addition of the island of Cape Breton and the Gaspé peninsula, was granted to Sir William Alexander, who named it Nova Scotia. Then followed a long struggle between England and France for the possession of the coveted territory, which was eventually brought under English control by the Treaty of Paris in 1763. See NOVA SCOTIA.

Acadia University, a coeducational institution situated in Wolfville, Nova Scotia.

Acanthite, a mineral form of silver sulphide (Ag_2S), nearly related to argentite. It occurs in slender, iron-black, prismatic crystals of the normal orthorhombic type. Acanthite is found with other ores of silver in Freiberg, Saxony, and in other German localities.

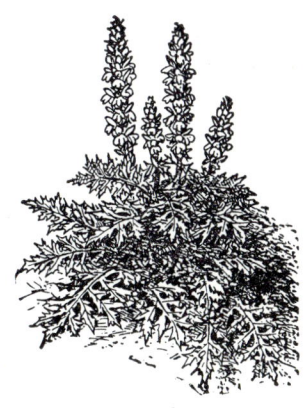

Acanthus

Acanthus, or **Bear's-Breech,** a genus of about 20 tall, herbaceous plants in tropical and subtropical Europe, Asia, Africa and Australia. The varieties native to the country about the Mediterranean have large, thorny-toothed leaves, which are supposed to have suggested the acanthus (q.v.) of ancient architecture. The varieties familiar in the United States are chiefly tender garden or hothouse plants, such as Justicia, or Thunbergia.

Composite Capital, with Acanthus Ornament

Acanthus, in architecture, a conventionalized leaf decoration believed to have been designed after the leaf of the *acanthus spinosus*. It is seen in characteristic form in the Corinthian capital of ancient Grecian architecture. In modified forms the acanthus also served for the decoration of furniture, laces, vases, and personal ornaments. See ARCHITECTURE.

A Cappella, or **Alla Cappella,** a musical term implying that a composition is to be sung as ecclesiastical music. Frequently it means that the voices are unaccompanied, or accompanied only by an instrument (usually the organ) played in unison with the voices.

Acarnania, district, Northwest Greece; with Ætolia it forms the province of Arcanania and Ætolia, stretching north from the Gulf of Patras, and including part of the Gulf of Arta; area, 3,034 square miles; p. 175,000.

Acarus (Demodex) Folliculorum, the pimple mite, a minute parasitic mite which infests the hair follicles and sebacious glands in man. It is very common in comedones ('black heads') and seems to have no deleterious influence.

Acatalectic Measures, metres which do not allow of the excision of an unaccented syllable at the beginning or the end of the line. See CATALECTIC.

Accault, Michel, a Frenchman who, with an explorer named Du Gay, accompanied Father Hennepin, at the instance of La Salle, in Hennepin's discoveries in the upper waters of the Mississippi. In 1680 all three were made prisoners by a wandering band of Sioux.

Accelerando, (Italian), a musical term indicating that the *tempo* is to be gradually increased.

Acceleration, the rate at which the velocity of a moving body changes. It is positive when the velocity is increasing, negative (with the minus sign) when it is decreasing. The acceleration of a falling body, due to gravity, amounts to 32.2 ft. per second. If the body influenced by gravity is moving upward, as a ball thrown into the air, its acceleration by gravity is negative, and is represented by —32.2 ft. per second. See KINEMATICS; KINETICS.

Accent, the stress laid in pronunciation upon one syllable of a word—corresponding to *emphasis,* the stress laid in elocution upon a word or words in a phrase. For accent in its metrical aspect, see VERSE.

Accent, a grammatical sign used to distinguish the varying sounds of the same vowel. They are three in number—*viz.,* grave (`), acute (´), and circumflex (^), as exhibited in the French words *père, été, tête.*

Accent, in music the regular recurrence of stress or emphasis upon certain notes—always (unless syncopated) upon the first note of a bar; while a slighter accent falls on the third note of a bar in common time, or the fourth in a bar in 6/8 time.

Acceptance. See **Bill; Bill of Exchange.**

Access, Right of, a legal right in the nature of an easement, which a riparian owner possesses, of uninterrupted access to the sea or navigable river. This is a right of property, and cannot be cut off through the grant by the state of the shore to a railroad company or other private owner. See RIPARIAN RIGHTS.

Accessories, the paraphernalia, other than the shield, of a heraldic achievement—*viz.,* the helm, wreath, crest, cap, crown, mantling, badge, scroll, etc. See HERALDRY.

Accessory, a term used by lawyers to distinguish certain classes of accomplices from the chief actors in the commission of felonies. An accessory *before the fact* is one who deliberately instigates others to commit a felony, but who does not himself take a part in its commission. An accessory *after the fact* is one who, knowing that a felony has been committed, takes active steps to shelter the felon from justice, or to enable him to escape. See CRIME.

Accidence, that part of grammar which deals with inflections, or changes in the form of words produced by the declension of nouns and adjectives or the conjugation of verbs. See GRAMMAR; INFLECTION.

Accident, in the narrower and stricter sense an occurrence which is due neither to design nor to negligence; in its wider sense, any casualty whether caused by fault or not. (See ACCIDENTS, INDUSTRIAL; AIRCRAFT DISASTERS; FIRE DISASTERS; MARINE DISASTERS; MINING; RAILROADS, *Accidents.*)
See INSURANCE, ACCIDENT.

Accident, in logic, a predicate which neither is contained in nor can be inferred from the definition of its subject—the predicate *black* as applied to the subject *crow*. If all crows without exception were black, blackness would be an 'inseparable accident' of the subject *crow*; otherwise it is a 'separable accident.' See PREDICABLES.

Accidental Colors, the imaginary complementary colors which are seen when, after looking fixedly at a bright-colored object, the eye is turned to a white or light-colored surface. If the object was red, the accidental color is green. Blue corresponds in like manner to yellow. See COLOR.

Accidentals, in music, are signs of chromatic alterations of the notes, differing from the signature in applying only to particular notes, and not extending their effect beyond the bar in which they occur, or according to others, the first note of the next bar. They indicate a temporary change of key.

Accident Indemnity. See **Employers' Liability.**

Accident Insurance. See **Insurance, Accident.**

Accidents, Industrial. The term 'industrial accident,' as ordinarily used, connotes a personal injury sustained by an employee in the course of his employment, and includes both fatal and non-fatal injuries.

Accipitrés, a term applied by Linnæus to birds of prey, such as the hawk (Accipiter). See BIRDS OF PREY.

Acclimatization, the process whereby animals or plants become adapted to, and so thrive in, a climate different from that in which they are indigenous. Biologically considered, acclimatization is part of the general process of modification of organism by environment.

In America some interesting experiments in naturalization have been made. Many European birds have been set at liberty by local societies, and a few species promise to become Americanized. The camel breeds well in a half-wild state in Nevada and Arizona; while alpacas, though repeatedly tried, have nowhere thriven. Ostrich farming (q.v.) has been successful in the Western United States, as well as in the Argentine Republic. Australasian trees, notably the eucalyptus, thrive in California, and successful experiments have been made with them in the cotton-growing States; the tea plant also grows well in various parts of the United States. Consult Darwin's *Animals and Plants under Domestication;* Wallace's *The Geographical Distribution of Animals;* Ireland's *Tropical Colonization;* Peschel's *The Races of Man and Their Distribution;* Semple's *Influences of Geographical Environment* (1911).

Accolade, (1) The ceremony by which knighthood is conferred: formerly an embrace round the neck, now the touch of a sword on the shoulder. (2) In musical score, the brace connecting the staves. (3) In architecture an ornamental moulding over a window or doorway, characterized by reverse curves tangent to the curves of the arch, rising to a finial or other ornament above.

Accommodation, in commerce, is either a loan of money directly, or the service rendered when one becomes security for a sum advanced to another by a third party, as by a banker.

Accommodation Bill. See **Bill of Exchange.**

Accommodation of Vision. In the camera, when the object distance changes, a distinct image on the sensitive plate may always be obtained by moving the lens. In the eye a distinct image cannot be obtained in this way, since the distance from lens to retina is constant. The edge of the crystalline lens, therefore, is surrounded by a powerful muscle which can alter the convexity of the lens sufficiently to cause the eye to focus correctly. This adjustment of the focus is called accommodation. The theory of the accommodation of vision was advanced by Thomas Young, but to Helmholtz belongs the credit of the proof. See EYE; VISION. Consult Helmholtz' *Physiological Optics* (Eng. trans. 1924).

Accompaniment, in music, the instrumental or subservient vocal parts assisting a solo part. It is either *ad libitum,* when it may be omitted at pleasure, or *obligato,* when it forms an integral part of the composition.

In the scores of earlier masters, frequently very faint indications are given of the parts of the accompaniment beyond a 'figured bass—the bass part with certain recognized figures written above it—indicating the harmony to be played to each note.

Accomplice, any person who in any way is associated with another in the commission or attempted commission of a criminal offence. An accomplice is punishable with his associates either as principal in the first or second degree or as accessory (q.v.).

Accord and Satisfaction, a term signifying a discharge of an obligation arising out of contract or tort by a new agreement based upon a good and sufficient consideration. The claimant must undertake to accept and the debtor undertake to pay or do something to satisfy the cause of action—this is the accord; and actual payment or fulfilment of the newly constituted debt or obligation must follow—this is the satisfaction. A cardinal part of the doctrine is that the satisfaction must constitute a good and sufficient consideration for the 'accord.' See CONTRACT.

Accordion, a portable musical instrument, with keyboard and mechanical contrivance for wind, invented by Damian at Vienna in 1829. Each key gives two notes, one in expanding, the other in compressing the bellows. The concertina (q.v.) is based on the same principle.

Accosted, in heraldry, a term often applied to a bend, chevron, or fess, placed between two cotises.

Account, a statement in writing of the debits and credits, or either, existing with respect to the transactions between persons, or associations of persons, or with respect to things of value, costs of operation of business enterprises or commercial or other undertakings, or the cost of production of goods or other things of value, or the rendering of service. An account is a record of transactions, acts, receipts, or payments involving things of value. See ACCOUNTANT; BOOKKEEPING.

Accountancy. See **Accountant; Bookkeeping; Cost Keeping; Public Accountancy.**

Accountant, a person trained and skilled in the science of accountancy. An accountant should be versed not only in the art of bookkeeping, but in the theory and practice of finance, commercial law, and in scientific principles of organization and business management. The degree of Certified Public Accountant (C.P.A.) is now conferred after examination by each of the States. See PUBLIC ACCOUNTANCY.

Accra, or **Akkra,** seaport, West Africa,

capital of the British colony of Gold Coast, the most important town on the coast. Rubber, cocoa, and ivory are exported; p. 72,977.

Accrescimento, in music, the prolongation of a note for another half of its value, by a dot placed after it.

Accretion, the addition made to riparian land by the gradual action of the water. The corresponding principle in law of personal property is termed 'Accession.'

Accrington (ancient *Akerington*), town, Lancashire, England. Industries include cotton spinning, weaving, calico printing, and manufacture of textile machinery; p. 43,610.

Accumulation is the increase of a fund through the periodical addition of the interest accruing thereto.

Accumulator. See **Electric Battery.**

Accumulator, Hydraulic. See **Hydraulic Machinery.**

Accusative Case. See **Declension.**

Aceldama, or **Akeldama** (Aramaic, 'the field of blood'), so named because it was bought with the money with which Judas had been bribed. It is traditionally identified with Hakk-ed-Dumm, near the Pool of Siloam, south of Jerusalem.

Acephalous, a rhetorical term applied, in scanning verse, to a line that is short of a syllable at the beginning. Thus, 'A sea that is stranger than death' would be called 'anapæstic trimeter acephalous,' because the first foot is an incomplete anapæst.

Acer, Acerraceæ. See **Maple.**

Acerra, (ancient *Acerræ*), town and episcopal see, Italy, province of Napoli. It has a cathedral, rebuilt in 1788 after an earthquake, and a seminary. There are sulphur springs; p. 21,937.

Acetabulum, the cavity of the os innominatum, or hip bone, which receives the head of the femur, called also the cotyloid cavity. Similar cup-like structures in animals and plants receive the same name.

Acetal, $C_2H_4(OC_2H_5)_2$, is a colorless liquid of an agreeable odor, and a flavor resembling that of the hazel nut. It is one of the products of the slow oxidation of alcohol under the influence of finely divided platinum, or of chlorine. Its specific gravity is 0.821, and it boils at 104° C.

Acetaldehyde, or **Acetic Aldehyde**, CH_3CHO, a volatile liquid produced by the oxidation of ethyl alcohol and theoretically, at least, by the reduction of acetic acid. Its greatest use is as an intermediate step in the manufacture of synthetic acetic acid and a number of other compounds, as the aldols.

Small amounts are used in the manufacture of certain dyes.

Acetamide, $CH_3CO.NH_2$, is a white crystalline solid prepared by the reaction of acetyl chloride and ammonia.

Acetanilide, Antifebrin, or **Phenylacetamide**, $CH_3CONHC_6H_5$, is prepared by boiling aniline with glacial acetic acid. It is a colorless crystalline powder, slightly soluble in water, and with a pungent taste. It is employed in medicine as an antipyretic and analgesic, in place of quinine, and is a common ingredient of so-called 'headache powders.'

Acetates, salts of acetic acid, consisting of the characteristic group of that acid, $CH_3.COO$, combined with a positive element or group—as $NaC_2H_3O_2$ (sodium acetate) or $C_2H_5C_2H_3O_2$ (ethyl acetate). They may be prepared by dissolving a metal, a metallic oxide, hydroxide, or carbonate in acetic acid, and evaporating to crystallization, or in the reaction of an alcohol and acetic acid in the presence of a dehydrating agent, as sulphuric acid.

Important metallic acetates are: *aluminum acetate*, used by dyers in mordanting; *calcium acetate*, largely used as a source of acetone; *basic copper acetate*, verdigris; *copper aceto-arsenite*, the chief constituent of emerald green, Paris green, or Schweinfurt's green; *lead acetate*, sugar of lead. Many organic acetates are found in nature, and a considerable number are manufactured as artificial fruit essences.

Acetic Acid, $CH_3CO.OH$, is formed by the oxidation of alcohol, but is chiefly prepared from the complex mixture obtained in the destructive distillation of wood, called *Pyroligneous Acid;* it is purified by neutralization with lime, and subsequent distillation of resulting calcium acetate with sulphuric acid. It is also made by exposing poor wine to the air, oxidation of the alcohol taking place in the presence of the micro-organism *Mycoderma aceti* ('mother-of-vinegar').

Acetic acid is a colorless liquid, having a penetrating odor, sharp sour taste, and caustic action on the skin. It mixes with water in all proportions. It is very stable, and acts as a monobasic acid, forming a series of salts called *Acetates* (q.v.).

Acetic acid is used in dilute water solution as vinegar, which contains 3 to 6 per cent.; as a solvent for gelatin, albumin, resins, oils, etc.; for the preparation of acetates; in the manufacture of acetanilide and of white lead; and in medicine.

Acetic Ether, or **Ethyl Acetate,** $CH_3\cdot CO.O.C_2H_5$, prepared by the reaction of sodium acetate, sulphuric acid, and alcohol, is a colorless liquid with a refreshing, penetrating, fruity odor. It is used as a solvent and flavoring agent, and in medicine as a stimulant.

Acetone, dimethylketone, $CH_3CO.CH_3$, is the simplest of the class of organic compounds called *ketones* (q.v.).

Acetone is a colorless, volatile liquid of penetrating, pleasant, ethereal odor; boiling point, 56.1° C.; specific gravity, .792 at 20° C. It mixes with water and alcohol, and is a useful solvent for gums, resins, fats, etc. It is used in the preparation of chloroform, iodoform, sulphonal, and smokeless powders.

Acetyl, CH_3CO, is a univalent group or radical, of which acetic acid, acetyl chloride, etc., are compounds; the former being the hydroxide (CH_3COOH), and the latter the chloride (CH_3COCl).

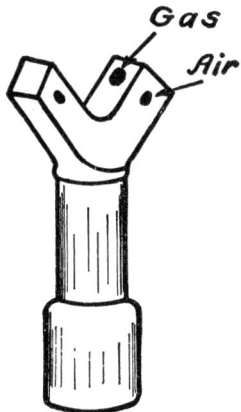

Acetylene Burner

Acetylene, C_2H_2, a gaseous hydrocarbon, discovered by Berthelot in 1862, is readily prepared by the reaction between calcium carbide and water, calcium hydroxide (slaked lime) being formed at the same time. The gas is colorless, and when pure has an ethereal odor which is not unpleasant; the disagreeable odor of the gas, as usually prepared, being due to small quantities of impurities. It is poisonous, and produces headache. For numerical properties, see GASES.

The flame of burning acetylene is luminous and smoky, but if burned from a jet of very fine aperture, with a proper admixture of air, an exceedingly luminous flame is produced, yielding nearly white light.

In the oxy-acetylene blowpipe the flame is produced by burning a mixture of oxygen and acetylene gases delivered under pressure. At the apex of the small central cone of this flame a temperature of about 3,000° C. is attained, which is sufficient to melt iron and steel. The instrument is therefore used for welding these metals; for welding alumi-

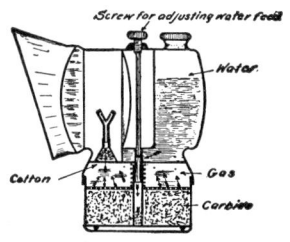

Acetylene Lamp

num castings; and for cutting steel beams in the repairing or wrecking of structures. The temperature of this flame (2,400° C.) is said to exceed that of any other blowpipe. (See OXY-ACETYLENE FLAME).

Achæi, or **Achæans,** a name applied by Homer to the whole of the Greek nation, and so used also by later poets. In historical times the name is restricted to the inhabitants of the north coast of the Peloponnesus (Achaia), who were united in a league of twelve towns, the ACHÆAN LEAGUE, which after 251 B.C. became the chief power of Greece. Finally, the league declared war against the Romans, and was crushed by them (146 B.C.). See GREECE, *History*.

Achæmenians, or **Achæmenides,** a dynasty of ancient Persia; it occupied the throne from about 730 B.C. to 333 B.C., and counted among its kings Cyrus the Great, Cambyses, and Darius the Great. In old Persian inscriptions Darius proudly traces his lineage back to Achæmenes, the founder of the line. See PERSIA, *History*.

Achaia, (1.) With Elis, a province (nomarchy) of modern Greece, extending from e. to w. along the s. side of the Gulf of Corinth; p. 361,845. The capital and port is Patras.

(2.) In New Testament times the southern province of Greece, the northern being Macedonia. Gallio was Roman 'deputy' or pro-consul of Achaia.

Achaquas, or **Achaguas,** a savage Indian tribe, of Arawakan stock, who formerly inhabited the waters of the upper Orinoco, on the boundary between Colombia and Venezuela.

Achar, used by Hindu philosophers to signify the all-in-all, the source of all matter, and the ultimate end to which matter will return—matter and all its phenomena being merely sensible manifestations of Achar.

Achard, Franz Karl (1753-1821), German chemist, was born in Berlin. He was the first to manufacture sugar from beet root (in 1801, at Kunern, in Silesia). Consult his *Europäische Zuckerfabrikation aus Runkelrüben* (1812).

Achard, Louis Amedée Eugène (1814-75), French novelist, was born in Marseilles. The chief of his fourteen novels are: *Belle Rose* (1847); *Madame de Sarens* (1865); *Marcelle* (1868); *La Cape et L'Epée* (1875).

Achates, the constant companion of Æneas in his long and varied wanderings. He is always styled by Virgil 'fidus Achates,' hence the name has become a synonym for a trusty companion.

Achelous, (modern name, **Aspropotamos**), largest river of ancient Greece, rises in Mount Pindus, and falls into the Ionian Sea opposite the Echinades Island, after a course of about 130 miles. In Greek mythology the god of this river was the oldest of the river gods.

Achenbach, Andreas (1815-1910), German painter of the Düsseldorf school, was born in Cassel. He was a leader of the realistic movement in German landscape painting—especially sea pieces.

Achenbach, Oswald (1827-1905), German landscape painter, brother of Andreas (q.v.). He has painted chiefly in the mountainous parts of Southern Europe.

Achensee, Lake, or **Achen;** 20 mi. n.e. of Innsbruck, Tyrol, Austria, at an altitude of 3,050 ft. It measures 5 m. by ½ m., and is surrounded by mountains 5,000 to 6,000 feet high.

Achenwall, Gottfried (1719-72), German statistician, was born in Elbing. He first formulated the treatment of statistics as a distinct science in *Abriss der neuesten Staatswissenschaft der Vornehmsten Europäischen Reiche una Republiken* (1749).

Achernar=a Eridani, a white star of 0.5 photometric magnitude, showing a spectrum intermediate between the Sirian and solar types. The small parallax of 0.043″, determined for Achernar by Sir David Gill of the Cape of Good Hope Observatory, corresponds to a light journey of seventy-six years, and implies that the star exceeds three hundred times the lustre of our sun.

Acheron, the name given to several rivers by the ancients, always with reference to some peculiarity, such as black or bitter waters, or mephitic gases.

Acheson, Dean Gooderham (1893-), U.S. diplomat, born at Middletown, Conn., educated at Yale, Harvard Law School. Was ensign in World War I; Asst. Secy. of State (1941-45); Under-Secy. of State (1945-47); Secy. of State (1949-).

Acheson, Edward Goodrich (1856-1931), American chemist and inventor, was born in Washington, Pa. In 1881 he invented the abrasive carborundum (q.v.); in 1899 he perfected his process for making 'Acheson-graphite,' and in 1907 invented 'Aquadag' and 'Oildag,' graphite lubricants. He has been awarded the Rumford Medal (1908) and the Perkin Medal in recognition of his services in applied chemistry.

Achievement, or **Hatchment**, in heraldry, the shield and accessories fully represented.

Achillas, Greek general and minister of Ptolemy Dionysius, king of Egypt. With L. Septimius he murdered Pompey (48 B.C.), and was assassinated by Ganymede, (47 B.C.).

Achillea, Milfoil, or **Yarrow**, hardy plants, two to four ft. high, with yellow, white, or pink flowers, widely naturalized in Europe and Asia.

Achilles, the hero of Homer's *Iliad*, was the son of the nereid Thetis and Peleus, son of Æacus, and king of the Myrmidons at Phthia in Thessaly. He led his Myrmidons in fifty ships to Troy. Homer's *Iliad* opens with his famous quarrel with King Agamemnon, who had robbed him of his cherished slave girl Briseis. He was mortally wounded in the heel by Paris. (See HOMER). In the *Odyssey* he is one of the heroes of the under world visited by Odysseus; and he is also one of the characters in Shakespeare's *Troilus and Cressida*.

Achilles Tendon. See **Tendon of Achilles**.

Achimenes, a genus of plants of the natural order Gesneraceæ (q.v.). The species are numerous, and are natives of tropical America.

Achish, probably a general title borne by certain rulers of the Philistines, but applied specifically to the king of Gath who sheltered David when he fled from Saul. A second Achish was contemporary with Solomon.

Achondroplasia, imperfect development of cartilage, with resulting stunting of bones; a disease of the embryo, in which the bones fail to develop, leading to excessive shortness of limbs and other deformities.

Achray, Loch, Perthshire, Scotland (1¼ m. by ¾ m.); 7 m. s.w. of Callander. Its beauties have been described by Scott, Coleridge, and Dorothy Wordsworth.

Achroite, a colorless variety of the mineral tourmaline (q.v.), found chiefly on the island of Elba.

Achromatic Lens. See **Achromatism.**

Achromatism, the property in virtue of which certain combinations of lenses, etc., refract a beam of light without producing colored fringes. Any arrangement of lenses or prisms which refract light without *dispersion* (q.v.) is achromatic. For example, by properly combining a convex lens of crown glass with a concave one of flint glass, a compound achromatic lens can be produced. The achromatism in the above arrangement, and in every other arrangement yet tried, is not absolutely perfect. The reason is that such media do not give exactly similar spectra (see SPECTRUM)—*i.e.,* the ratio of the distances between any two pairs of rays is not quite the same for the different media. A combination of three lenses, or prisms, gives a better approximation. See LENSES.

Achsah, daughter of Caleb. She was promised in marriage to whosoever would take Debir. Othniel performed the task, and received her hand.

Acidaspis, a genus of trilobites of rather small size, found in Silurian and Devonian strata. See TRILOBITE.

Acidimetry, the process of estimating the quantity of a free acid. Several methods of determination are in use. (1) When acids are mixed with water only, the strength may be determined by taking the specific gravity; (2) by measuring volumetrically the weight of alkali required to neutralize the acid; (3) by a gravi-metric process adapted to the particular acid; (4) by loss of weight, after expelling the acid—this method is generally applied in the estimation of carbonic acid. See ANALYSIS, CHEMICAL.

Acidity. The incomplete oxidation of organic substances in the body results in the production of various acids, such as lactic, oxalic, uric acid, etc. A healthy adult excretes by the lungs and skin about 28 ounces of carbonic acid daily, and the acids excreted by the kidneys are equivalent to about 30 grains of oxalic acid. The excess of acid in the body, or acidity, depends mainly on two causes—(1) excessive formation, the result of incomplete oxidation of the food and the tissues; and (2) deficient elimination of the acid formed. These result from overfeeding, insufficient exercise, sedentary habits, or disease. The skin and mucuous membranes are affected by acidity, which shows itself in the skin by attacks of eczema, urticaria, and erythema, and in the mucous membranes by catarrh. See DIGESTION; DYSPEPSIA.

Acids, in chemistry, a class of substances having the following characteristics: (1) The element hydrogen is a constituent of all acids; they are therefore sometimes called 'salts of hydrogen.' All organic acids, but a few, contain the group CO.OH (called *Carboxyl*). (2) If soluble in water—as most are—acids affect many coloring matters (called 'indicators'): *e.g.,* litmus, a purple dye obtained from certain lichens, is turned red. (3) Acids have a sour taste. (4) Acids react readily with bases, forming a salt and water; thus, sulphuric acid and sodium hydroxide react, and sodium sulphate and water are formed. Such a reaction is called *neutralization,* and the acid is said to neutralize the base, or conversely. (5) Acids react readily with some metals, hydrogen being frequently set free, and a salt forming; for example, sulphuric acid and zinc yield hydrogen and zinc sulphate. When applied superficially, the acid is said to corrode or 'eat' the metal.

Acids are found in nature, the sourness of fruits being due to their presence, as in the lemon, apple, currant, etc. Acetic acid, present to the extent of from 3 to 6 per cent., gives to vinegar its agreeable sour taste. Many acids are formed during fermentation, as lactic acid in sour milk. Hydrochloric acid, present in the gastric juice of the stomach, performs an important part in the process of digestion. Mineral waters frequently contain carbonic acid.

Acids find a wide field of usefulness. For example, the common sulphuric acid, or oil of vitriol, is used in almost all industries, and is required in large quantities in the manufacture of fertilizers, alkalies, dyes, explosives, and in the refining of petroleum. Etching depends upon the action of acids, nitric being used with metals, and hydrofluoric with glass. Gold is attacked by no single acid, but dissolves readily in *aqua regia,* a mixture of hydrochloric and nitric acids (3:1 by volume).

To counteract the injurious action of acids

on objects an alkali is applied. In case a large quantity is spilled, marble dust, whiting, slaked lime, or lime may be used. Ammonia water is best for the clothing or hands. A solution of sodium bicarbonate (baking soda) or sodium carbonate (washing soda) is a good antidote for internal administration. As used in *Medicine,* acids differ widely in their action. Externally applied, some of them, such as sulphuric, nitric, and hydrochloric acids, act as caustics, and are never given internally, except in a very diluted form. If swallowed pure—as they sometimes are in error—they act as corrosive poisons. (See POISONS). Internally, the above acids, much diluted, stimulate first the flow of saliva, and next that of the gastric juice, which itself contains hydrochloric acid. Nitric acid is also much used as a cholagogue. Insufficiently diluted, when not strong enough to act as corrosives, these acids are gastric irritants, and so interfere with digestion. Other acids, such as carbolic and sulphurous acids, are disinfectants. Carbonic and hydrocyanic acids are gastric sedatives, the latter being also the most rapid of poisons. Tannic acid is an astringent, coagulating albumin. Salicylic acid is a valuable antipyretic.

For information about individual acids, see the separate articles, as ACETIC ACID; BORACIC ACID; HYDROCHLORIC ACID; SULPHURIC ACID; etc.

Aci Reale, or **Acireale** (Sicilian *Jaci*), town and episcopal see, Catania, Sicily, at the foot of Mount Ætna. It has warm sulphur baths, and is visited for sea bathing. Linen, cotton, and filigree work are manufactured; p. 36,000.

Acis, a Sicilian youth, beloved by the nymph Galatea, was crushed under a huge rock by the Cyclops Polyphemus. His blood was changed by the nymph into the River Acis, at the foot of Mount Ætna. Handel composed an opera on the subject.

Ackermann, Konrad (1712-71), German actor, is generally regarded as one of the founders of German drama.

Ackermann, Rudolph (1764-1834), a native of Saxony, opened a print shop in the Strand, London, 1795, and introduced lithography as a fine art into England.

Acklin, or **Acklin's Island** (45 mi. by 1 to 2 m.), one of the South Bahamas.

Acknowledgment, in law, is the act of avowing before a proper officer or a court that one has executed a legal instrument, and of obtaining a certificate thereto appended which admits the instrument as evidence without further proof of its genuineness. A commissioner of deeds or a notary public is the regular officer before whom acknowledgments are made, though judges, clerks of court, mayors of cities, and in some States aldermen and justices of the peace, are sufficient for the purpose. In all cases the acknowledgment must be signed by the person in whose presence it is made.

Acland, Lady Christian Henrietta Caroline (1750-1815), commonly called LADY HARRIET, was famous for her devotion to her husband, Major John Dyke Acland, an English officer, during the Revolutionary War.

Acland, Sir Henry Wentworth Dyke (1815-1900), English physician, was born in Exeter, and was educated at Oxford, where he was Radcliffe librarian, and regius professor of medicine (1857-94). The formation of the Oxford University Museum was largely due to his labors. Among his works are: *Memoir on the Cholera in 1854; Village Health* (1884).

Aclinic Line, or **Magnetic Equator,** an irregular and varying line passing through those points on the globe at which there is no inclination or deviation from the horizontal position. See MAGNETISM; DIPPING NEEDLE.

Acne (according to Littré a corruption of the Greek word for 'a point') is a functional disturbance of the sebaceous glands and hair follicles of the skin (q.v.). The ducts of the glands become clogged by inspissated sebum, or by the action of invading micro-organisms. Their natural secretion accumulates within the glands, and there is at the same time a tendency to inflammation of the follicle and surrounding tissue. The characteristic eruption, either papular or pustular, usually appears upon the face, neck, back, or chest of young people at or near the age of puberty; and when once established, may persist for many years.

Two varieties of acne are usually described: *Acne vulgaris* or *simplex,* and *A. indurata.* In *A. vulgaris* the lesions may be either papular or pustular, but usually both are present at the same time. *Comedones* or 'Blackheads' may be few or many, but are usually part of the clinical picture. Comedones are collections of thickened sebaceous matter retained in the glands whose mouths are closed by black-topped plugs. They appear as pin-point papules in the skin, are not accompanied by inflammatory symptoms, and are spoken of as *acne punctata*. Sometimes deeper and larger areas of inflammation appear, and these are known as *A. indurata*. These areas usually suppurate, and may leave scars.

Treatment.—The primary cause must first be looked for in each case; and may be gastro-intestinal disturbance in one, anæmia and debility in another, or disease of sexual origin in a third. Treatment, both internal and local appropriate to the condition should then be instituted. Diet and hygiene will accomplish more than drugs. In recent years, the Roentgen rays and vaccine therapy (q.v.) have been employed with marked success. See ACNE ROSACEA.

Acne Rosacea is a reflex flushing of the central region of the face, due to vasomotor disturbance. This passive congestion of the region eventually results in a permanent redness, accompanied by dilatation of the blood vessels and a *secondary* acne of the sebaceous glands. Although commonly called acne rosacea, the disease is in no sense a true acne, and should better be called *Rosacea*. It is also known as *Gutta Rosea*.

Rosacea, in most cases, is limited to the middle third of the face, and usually first appears at or near the end of the nose, which in many cases is the only portion of the face involved. In others it may extend to the cheeks, forehead, and chin, and rarely over the whole face.

Rosacea has three stages. While the majority of cases never progress beyond the second stage, certain heavy drinkers, especially if much exposed to the cold, develop the third stage of the disease. In these cases the follicles on the nose become very large, and the tip and sides become converted into a lobulated mass of tissue, the hypertrophy in some cases being so great as to form pendulous tumors hanging down over the mouth. This condition is known as *Rhinophyme*. It may also occur in persons of regular habits of life.

In women, the disease is frequently associated with disorder of the menstrual functions.

Treatment should be both local and general, but the latter is the more important. The reflex cause must be found and corrected. The diet must be planned with great care, eliminating such articles as are found by experience to cause flushing. Alcohol should be strictly forbidden. Locally, the patient should protect his face from extremes of heat or cold, and cold water should never be put on the face.

In the first and second stages a calamine lotion, a mild ichthyol cream, or a powder such as cornstarch may be used. Dilated vessels are best destroyed by electrolysis. In the third stage, multiple scarification, or even better, a plastic operation to restore the nose to its original shape and size, gives most satisfactory results.

Acoemetae, or Acoemeti ('the Sleepless Ones'), communities of monks who in the fifth and sixth centuries, in Constantinople and elsewhere, carried on devotions without ceasing day or night. They were excommunicated in 534.

Acolytes, in the early Church, were youths in holy orders who assisted in the ritual of the Church. In the Roman Catholic Church, aspirants to the priesthood still pass through this order. See ORDERS, HOLY.

Aconcagua, a presumably extinct volcano, the highest summit of the Andes and of the New World, in the province of Mendoza, Argentina; lat. 32° 39′ s.; long. 70° w. Altitude, 23,080 ft.

Aconcagua, a central province of Chile, lying between the Pacific and the crest of the Andes. Area, 5,487 sq. mi.; p. 132,730. Capital, San Felipe.

A c o n i t e (*Aconitum*), MONKSHOOD, WOLFSBANE, or BLUE ROCKET, a genus of the order Ranunculaceæ, common in temperate regions. *A. napellus*, often cultivated in gardens, is a perennial plant from two to six feet high, and has dark green, deeply cleft leaves, and a long branched head of deep blue flowers; the sepals are petaloid, and resemble a hood, whence the popular name. All parts of the plant are very poisonous.

In medicinal doses it acts as an antipyretic, lessening the force, frequency, and volume of the pulse, and causing perspiration. It is also used externally and internally for neuralgia, lumbago, and rheumatic pains.

Aconitine ($C_{33}H_{43}NO_{12}$), the active principle of aconite (q.v.), is one of the most potent poisons known.

Acorn-shells (*Balanus*), a genus of Cirripedes, in the class Crustacea. They occur in abundance incrusting the rocks between high and low water mark, and are exceedingly familiar objects. The body is enveloped in a fold of skin, or mantle, which forms round about the animal a conical protective shell of six pieces, and a fourfold movable lid. When the animal is active (under water), six pairs of curl-like double legs may be seen alternately protruded and retracted through the valvular opening of the shell. These are borne on the thorax of the animal, and serve to brush the floating food down to the mouth, where it is seized and masticated by the three pairs of jaws.

The acorn-shells feed on small marine animals. They are attached not only to rocks, but to floating objects, and to other animals. See BARNACLE.

Acorus, a genus belonging to the order Araceæ. *A. Calamus,* popularly known as *Sweet Flag,* of wide geographic distribution in the north temperate zone.

Acosta, Gabriel or **Uriel d'** (1594-1640), a Portuguese of noble Jewish birth, was born in Oporto. Brought up a Roman Catholic, he early reverted to Judaism. His autobiography was published in Latin and German. Gutzkow made him the hero of a tragedy.

Acosta, Joaquim (1790-1852), South American explorer and geographer, was born at Guaduas, Colombia. He published: *Compendio Historico del Descubrimiento y Colonizacion de la Nueva Granada* (1848); *Semenario de la Nueva Granada* (1849).

Acosta, José d' (1539-1600), Spanish Jesuit and historian, was born at Medina del Campo. He was a missionary in Peru for several years. On his return to Spain in 1587 he became superior of the Jesuits at Valladolid, and rector of the Jesuit college at Salamanca. He wrote *Historia Natural y Moral de las Indias.*

Acoustics, strictly speaking, is the science of sound in relation to hearing. The conditions under which an aerial disturbance is audible as sound cannot be described with accuracy. If we confine our attention to musical sounds, or sounds of definite pitch, we know that the number of vibrations per second must lie between two limits; but the limits of hearing differ for different ears. Roughly speaking, the lower limit may be set at from 20 to 30 vibrations per second, and the upper limit at about 70,000.

The application of acoustic principles in the construction of a large hall is only partly understood. The quality of the acoustics of a room or hall is based upon the duration of the reverberation, or re-echoing, of the sounds produced. In turn, reverberation is dependent upon the cubic metres included in the room; the acoustic absorption, or the receiving of the energy of 'sound waves'; the materials of which the room is constructed, and with which it is furnished; the degree of intensity of the sound; and other considerations. Experience has led to the construction of rectangular halls.

For a discussion of the physical characteristics of the aerial vibrations which produce the sensation of noise, see SOUND; for the physiological side of the question, see EAR.

Lord Rayleigh's *Theory of Sound* is the most complete treatise on the subject of acoustics. Helmholtz' *Tonempfindungen,* or *Sensations of Tone* (Eng. trans.), is one of the classics of scientific literature, and discusses in a masterly manner many of the most profound problems connected with the sense of hearing. Consult also J. H. Poynting and J. J. Thomson's *Text Book of Science* (vol. II., 'Sound'); W. C. Sabine's *Architectual Acoustics* (1906); Alexander Saeltzer's *Treatise on Acoustics in Connection with Ventilation* (1908).

Acqui, town and episcopal see, province Alessandria, Italy, on the Bormida. It has hot sulphur springs; temperature 115°-167° F. The Gothic Cathedral dates from the twelfth century. Wine and silk are produced; p. 14,000.

Acquiescence denotes an important principle of equity otherwise known as 'laches' (q.v.), 'standing by,' or 'delay.' It is constituted by the fact that a person has by his conduct led others to believe that he has waived or abandoned his rights. This being so, he is precluded or 'estopped' by the principle in question from asserting those rights.

Acquired Characters. See **Heredity.**

Acquisition by a state usually comes about in one or other of three ways: (1) Occupation confers a title to newly discovered territory.

(2) Treaties and conventions may include the settling of frontiers and boundaries.

(3) Conquest (q.v.), which is the forcible appropriation by one nation of territory belonging to another, when followed by a declaration of annexation, vests the title of sovereignty in the conquering state.

Acquittal, the judgment of a court of criminal jurisdiction absolving a person accused of crime. An acquittal upon a verdict after a full trial is both at the common law and under the Federal and State constitutions of the United States a bar to a second prosecution for the same offence. See AUTREFOIS ACQUIT.

Acquittance, a written discharge of a debt or other money obligation.

THE GREAT ACHILLES, GREEK HERO AND FRIEND OF ULYSSES

Acre, a word (from Anglo-Saxon *æcer*) which is identical with Gothic *akr-s*, German *Acker,* Latin *ager,* Greek *agros,* Sanskrit *ajras*—a measure nearly corresponding to the quantity which one plough could plough in a day. The American and English statute acre consists of 4,840 sq. yds. The chain with which land is measured is 22 yds. long, and a sq. chain will contain 22 x 22, or 484 yds.; so that 10 sq. chains make an acre, or

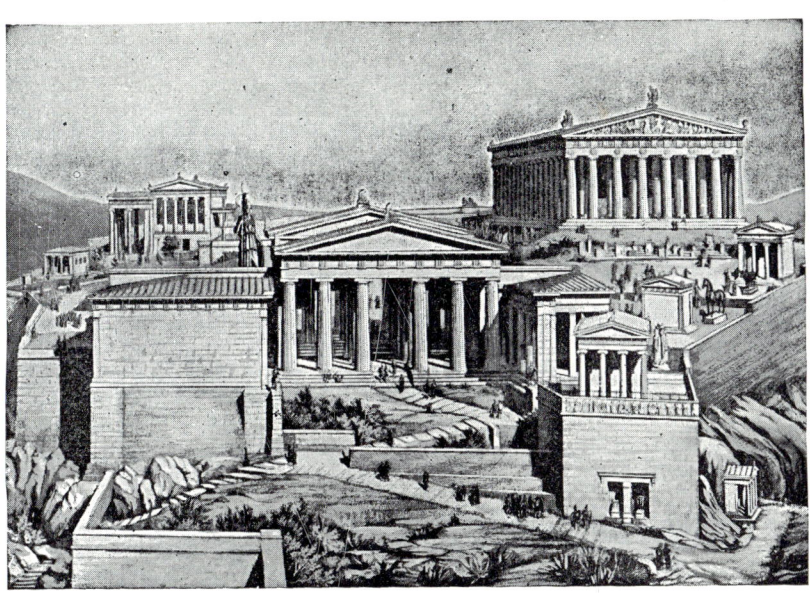

The Acropolis of Athens (as it was in the time of Pericles).

4 roods, or 160 perches, or 4,840 sq. yds. The old Scotch acre is larger than the English, the Irish than the Scotch.

The hectare (nearly 2½ acres; see ARE) of the French metric system has superseded on the Continent almost all the ancient local measures corresponding to the acre. See WEIGHTS AND MEASURES.

Acre, St. Jean d' (Turkish *Akka;* Old Testament *Accho;* New Testament *Ptolemais;* the *Ace* of Strabo), city and seaport, Syria, on a promontory at the foot of Mount Carmel. The older fortifications, much breached, may be traced outside later ones. p. 11,000 (8,000 Moslems; 3,000 Christians, Jews and others).

The city is famous for its many sieges: During the World War, Acre was captured from the Turks by the British in 1917, and is now under British mandate together with the whole of Palestine. It is planned to make this land a homeland for the Jewish people.

Acrisius, king of Argos, and father of Danaë, whom he shut up in a tower, because an oracle had foretold that her child would kill him. See DANAË; PERSEUS.

Acrobat, literally one who walks on tiptoe, but commonly applied to a person who practises feats of personal agility, such as tumbling, vaulting, and particularly walking, dancing, etc., on rolling balls, pyramids of chairs, etc., and especially on the slack or tight rope, a feat which was popular among the ancient Greeks and Romans. Consult Le Roux and Garnier's *Acrobats and Mountebanks* (Eng. trans.); *Tumbling for Amateurs* (Spalding's Athletic Library).

Acroceraunian, or **Ceraunian Mountains,** Albania, on the Adriatic coast; highest peak Tchika (6,300 ft.) ACROCERAUNIA is the modern Cape Linguetta or Glossa, 40 mi. n.e. of Otranto.

Acrolein, or **Acrylic Aldehyde,** C_2H_3-COH, is a colorless, limpid, strongly refracting liquid, lighter than water; boiling point, 52.4° C. It is the acrid constituent produced in the destructive distillation of fatty substances, and is in part due to the decomposition of glycerin.

Acroliths (Greek *akron,* 'extremity,' and *lithos,* 'a stone'), the oldest works of Greek plastic art, in which wood carving is seen in transition into marble statuary. The trunk of the figure is still of wood, but the head, arms, and feet, which are meant to appear outside the drapery, are of stone. See CHRYSELEPHANTINE.

Acromegaly, a disease causing general enlargement of the bones, and lasting for ten or twenty years before death. The cause is still uncertain, though disease of the pituitary body (q.v.) is generally found associated with it.

Acromion, the summit of the shoulder blade. It is commonly called the *Acromial Process.*

Acrophony, a term applied to a stage in the development of alphabetical writing—*viz.,* to the use of a picture of an object, or of a symbolical picture of an object, to represent the first syllable of the name of that object, and, later, to represent the first sound of that syllable.

Acropolis (Greek *akros,* 'lofty'; *polis,* 'a city') was the name given by the Greeks to the fortified eminences around which many of their towns were built. Among the most famous were those of Mycenæ, Tiryns, Argos, Corinth, Thebes, Pergamum, and in particular Athens, the last being generally referred to as *the* Acropolis.

The ACROPOLIS OF ATHENS (called also Cecropia, from its reputed Pelasgian founder, King Cecrops) is a rocky eminence, precipitous on all sides except the west, rising about 150 ft. from the Attic plain. Round the base to the hill, especially on the s., were grouped numerous temples and theatres. The whole area of the summit was occupied by a series of edifices, the most famous and the most important artistically in the history of the world. See ATHENS. Consult Penrose's *Principles of Athenian Architecture;* Burnouf's *L'Acropole;* Bötticher's *Die Akropolis von Athen.*

Acrostic, a verse or verses in which the initial letters of the lines, when read in order, spell a name, word, or phrase. Sometimes the final letters spell words as well as the initial, and this peculiarity may even run down the middle of the poem. Some sacred Greek verses, quoted by Eusebius, bishop of Cæsarea, in the fourth century, are written so that the initial letters spell the phrase 'Jesus Christ, the Son of God, the Saviour.' The first letters of the five Greek words of this phrase spell the word *ichthus,* 'a fish'; hence the use of the fish as a symbol for the Saviour.

Acroteria, or **Acroters,** small pedestals on buildings on which are placed statues or ornamental finials; also the statues or ornaments thus placed.

Act has various technical meanings, legal and other; frequently a document in writing, as when a person executing a legal instrument, declares it to be his *act and deed.* Or it may be the record of an act or proceeding of a public nature, as an Act of Congress. In the United States, an act signifies something done for which the person doing is responsible; something done by an individual in his private capacity, or as an officer; or by a body of persons, as an association, corporation, legislature, or court. An act indicates intention. An act is also an instrument in writing to verify facts. A *Public Act* is one that has public authority, made public by authority, or attested by a public seal, and one pertaining to the whole community; while a *Private Act* operates upon particular persons and private concerns.

In the Drama, an act is a distinct section of a play, in which a definite and coherent part of the plot is represented. It is generally subdivided into smaller portions, called *scenes.*

Actæon, in classic mythology a famous hunter, whom the goddess Artemis (Diana) changed into a stag, when he saw her bathing; in this form his dogs tore him to pieces.

Acta Pilati, or **Gesta Pilati** ('Acts of Pilate'), the name of an apocryphal work giving, by way of an official report purporting to have been drawn up under the orders of Pontius Pilate (q.v.), an account of the trial, crucifixion, and resurrection of Jesus.

Acte additionelle. *L'Acte Additionnel aux Constitutions de l'Empire* was issued by Napoleon on April 23, 1815, during the 'Hundred Days,' as a concession to Liberal politicians.

Actian Games, athletic contests and sea fights, were instituted by Octavius in commemoration of his great naval victory over Antony and Cleopatra (B.C. 31) at Actium.

Acting and Actors. See **Drama; Moving Pictures; Opera; Theatre.**

Actinic Rays, or **Ultra-violet Rays,** are those radiations which are found, by suitable means, as one passes from the red light through yellow, green, blue, and violet, on out into the region where no light is visible to the eye. They are of shorter wave length than the visible waves of light, have a greater frequency of vibration, and therefore are more refrangible. Being invisible to the eye, they must be detected by other means than vision. They were first observed through the photographic actions produced by them. Photographic plates which were known never to have been exposed to visible light were found to be 'light struck' when placed in the part of the spectrum beyond the violet, where nothing could be seen by the eye.

A more striking way of detecting and displaying actinic or ultra-violet light is by means of the phosphorescence which is brought about by such light in various substances, as uranium glass, salts like platinum-barium cyanide, certain ores like the zinc ores, Franklinite, Willemite, and sulphate of quinine. To accomplish this, a spectrum is produced by passing a ray of sunlight through a quartz prism; any of the several phosphorescent substances mentioned is placed in the several colors, beginning with the red, and then carried on into the region where there is no color at all. At once the substances begin to glow with ghostly colors, varying with the nature of the substance.

Still another means of detection is by means of the ionizing effect of ultra-violet rays. When Heinrich Hertz was carrying on the famous researches which led him to the discovery of the wireless telegraph in its earliest form, he made use of a small electric spark across a small gap. He found this very variable: sometimes he obtained sparks easily; again, under apparently the same conditions, he got none at all. He showed convincingly that the variations were caused by the variations of the ultra-violet light from the main spark. When these rays, the ultra-violet, illuminated the gap, sparks passed easily, but when the ultra-violet or actinic rays were cut off, sparks passed only with difficulty, if at all. If a beam of ultra-violet rays is made to fall upon an electrically charged body, the air will be ionized and made conducting, and will carry the charge off from the body.

Glass is transparent to visible light but quite opaque to the ultra-violet. Quartz is transparent to ultra-violet rays as well as to visible light. Therefore, for photographic purposes, the lenses will, with marked advantage, be made of quartz.

Red light has a wave length of about 7,600 Angström units; violet light has a length of about 3,800, while the ultra-violet rays have wave lengths down to about 2,000. Rays of shorter wave lengths are well known, but are not usually spoken of as actinic rays.

There are various sources of ultra-violet light, as sunlight, the electric arc between zinc or iron electrodes, and the mercury vapor lamp.

Actinic rays are now put to wide use in exposing frauds. Fake paintings and forged documents are detected by an ultra-violet ray lamp attached to the camera. In the case of counterfeit money, corresponding sections of the genuine and counterfeit bills are exposed at the same time to the rays, and the results compared. The authentic bill remains unaltered, the counterfeit is blurred. An ultra-violet ray desk lamp deciphers secret messages. The pioneer of this work was Dr. Loedwyk Bendikson of Los Angeles.

Actinotherapy.—Because of their germicidal and stimulative properties, the actinic rays have found important applications in the treatment of disease, and actinotherapy has become an accepted branch of therapeutics. The principal source of ultra-violet rays for medical application is the mercury vapor lamp, in which the essential feature is a quartz tube containing mercury vapor, through which an electric current is made to pass. The light produced by the mercury lamp contains about 28 per cent. ultra-violet rays as compared with 7 per cent. in ordinary sunlight, but this amount may be modified by dust, moisture, and organic matter in the air, as well as by the voltage of the current used.

The rays are beneficial in deep-seated localized infections, sluggishly healing wounds, sinuses, chronic ulcers, burns, almost all skin infections, simple anemia, and conditions which disturb metabolism. They should not be administered in diabetes, hemophilia, acute pulmonary tuberculosis, or in individuals with very sensitive skin.

William Firth Wells of Harvard reported in July, 1936, that he had destroyed influenza germs with actinic rays. The atmosphere in a large steel gas-insulated tank was sterilized by a mercury quartz lamp after germ-laden air was introduced. Ferrets exposed to the non-sterilized air contracted influenza, while ferrets within the chamber remained healthy. Some hospitals now irradiate the air in operating rooms.

See FLUORESCENCE; LIGHT; RADIANT ENERGY; SPECTRUM.

Actinium, a radioactive chemical element discovered by Debierne in 1899, soon after the discovery of polonium and radium.

Chemically, the element is associated with the group of rare-earth elements, and occupies, in the opinion of Auer von Welsbach, a position between lanthanum and calcium.

Actinograph, a self-recording actinometer (q.v.), in which the record is being made by the chemical effect of the sun's rays on sensitized paper.

Actinometer, an instrument for determining the amount of heat received from the sun on a surface of definite size in a given time. Sir John Herschel's actinometer was invented about 1824. The best modern instruments for measuring solar radiation are constructed on quite a different plan—the absorbing body being a blackened wire, whose change of temperature is measured

A View of Early English Stage, With Spectators on All Sides.

Actinolite, a variety of amphibole containing calcium, magnesium, and iron, and characterized by a dark green or gray green color. A hard dense sub-variety of actinolite, known as *Nephrite* (q.v.), which is included with a similar variety of pyroxene (see JADEITE) under the generic name of jade, is much used for carved ornaments and utensils throughout Eastern Asia.

by its change in electric resistance. The generic name for this type of instrument is *bolometer;* so called by Langley, who has used it with great skill in the measurement of solar radiation. See BOLOMETER.

Actinomycosis, a fungus disease of man and certain domestic animals, manifested by abscess formation and the production of inflammatory tissue, and characterized by the presence in the lesions of a vegetable parasite, *Actinomyces* bovis. Its frequent occurrence in the jaw and tongue has led to its being known in Great Britain as WOODY TONGUE, and in the United States as LUMPY JAW. The true nature of the disease had been overlooked up to 1876, when Bollinger accurately described and identified the characteristic micro-organism from which its name is derived. Modern treatment is by the Röntgen rays.

Action, as generally understood, means any civil proceeding in a court of justice. Formerly the term was applied solely to proceedings in the courts of common law, 'action at law' being contrasted with 'suit in equity.' In New York and a few other States it includes criminal proceedings also, and excludes non-litigious matters (termed 'special proceedings'), such as the probate or the interpretation of a will. In the action is embraced every step in the judicial procedure, from the service of the summons to the final judgment, but not the means subsequently taken for enforcing such judgment. See LAW.

Action, in physiology, a term used to include various forms of muscular movement. See PHYSIOLOGY.

Action Francaise, is the title of a French royalist faction which regards the Duc de Guise, head of the Bourbon-Orleans family, as the rightful King of France, to be designated as Jean III. The Camelots du Roi, or Henchmen of the King, is the name given to the students' group affiliated with the Action Francaise. The newspaper, *Action Francaise,* edited by Leon Daudet, son of Alphonse Daudet, is the official organ of the royalists.

Actium, a promontory on the west coast of Greece, at the entrance of the Ambracian Gulf, memorable for the naval victory of Octavian (afterward the Emporor Augustus) over Mark Antony and Cleopatra, which decided the fate of Rome and of the world (Sept. 2, 31 B.C.).

Act of God, as a legal expression, signifies any occurrence not caused by human negligence or intervention; such as storms, lightning, tempests, the consequences of which no party under any circumstances (independently of special contract) is bound to make good to another.

Act of Settlement, or **Succession Act,** settling the crown in the present royal family of Great Britain, was passed by Parliament in 1701. The act cut away the hereditary claim of the elder house of Stuart, and vested the succession in the house of Hanover. See CROWN.

Act of Union. See **Scotland,** HISTORY.

Acton, John Emerich Edward Dalberg, First Baron (1834-1902), English historian, was born in Naples. Lord Acton was a historian of almost incomparable learning, and had profound influence, as a liberal Catholic, upon English religious thought. His writings include: *The War of 1870; Wolsey and the Divorce of Henry VIII.; Lectures on the French Revolution.* He planned *The Cambridge Modern History* (1903 et seq.), written by several scholars in co-operation. After his death his vast library was bought by Andrew Carnegie, who presented it to Lord Morley, by whom it was handed over to the University of Cambridge. Consult *Letters of Lord Acton to Mary Gladstone* (1904); Gasquet's *Lord Acton and His Circle.*

Acton, Sir John Francis Edward (1736-1811), was born at Besançon, where his father (an Englishman) was a physician. He was generalissimo and prime minister at Naples during the French Revolution.

Actors' Equity Association, formed in 1917, was the first organization in the theatrical profession to protect the interests of the actor as a workman. In 1919 Actors' Equity called a strike which closed thirty-seven plays in eight cities and ended only when the Producing Managers' Association accepted Equity's standard contract which stipulates that in any theatrical company of which one member is a member of Equity, all must be.

Acts of the Apostles, the fifth book of the New Testament, and the most trustworthy source for the early history of the Christian Church. It is in form substantially a continuation of the Gospel of Luke, and both tradition and the majority of Biblical critics ascribe these books to the same author, who was the companion and friend of Paul. The book falls roughly into two parts; the first narrates the spread of the Church from Jerusalem outward to Judæa, Samaria, and Antioch, the central figure being St. Peter; while the second part carries the story to Asia Minor and Europe, being in the main a fragmentary biography of St. Paul, detailing his missionary labors in company with Barnabas, and subsequently with Silas and others.

The book is addressed to Theophilus, probably to inform him of the means by which the Gospel had been carried to the Gentiles. The probable date of its preparation is about 170 A.D., as indicated by the writings of Irenæus toward the close of the second century. See NEW TESTAMENT.

Acts of Uniformity, passed by the British Parliament to insure uniformity of public worship in the Church of England.

Actuarial Society of America, an organization for the promotion of actuarial science.

Actuary. In the roman empire the *actuarii* were clerks who recorded the *acta* or deeds of the senate and other bodies, and who kept the military accounts. At the present day, an actuary is an official in an insurance company whose duties are to deal with statistics, deduce therefrom rates of mortality, and, by combining these with rates of interest, to calculate premiums for all kinds of insurances; also to estimate the liability of the company under its contracts; and generally to perform calculations of all kinds, and advise on all questions of accounting and finance. See ANNUITY; INSURANCE; PROBABILITIES.

Acupressure, a method of closing a blood vessel. It is now rarely used.

Acupuncture, the insertion of needles into the body to a depth of one or two inches, generally until they pierce a nerve, where they are left for half an hour, to relieve lumbago and sciatica. It has been a specific surgical operation of the Chinese from very early times.

A.D., *Anno Domini*—in the year of our Lord—the chronological era now universally used in Christian countries, beginning with the supposed date of the birth of Christ.

Adagio, (Ital.), a slow or very slow movement or measure of time in music. The word is also used as the title of a piece of music, or as the name of a movement in a symphony or sonata, etc. See SYMPHONY.

Adair, John (1759-1840), American soldier, was born in Chester co., S. C. He served in the War of the Revolution; was U. S. Senator (1805-06), governor of Kentucky (1820-24), and Member of Congress (1831-3).

Adalbert (c. 1000-1072), German ecclesiastic, was appointed archbishop of Bremen and Hamburg in 1043 by the Emperor Henry III.

Adalbert, St., an early English saint (c. 700), son of Oswald, king of Deira.

Adalbert, St. (c. 950-997), the 'Apostle of the Prussians,' was a native of Prague, and was chosen its bishop in 982.

Adam, the first man. See **Adam and Eve.**

Adam, Adolphe Charles (1803-56), French musical composer, chiefly of comic opera, was born and died at Paris. Consult Pougin's *Adolphe Adam*.

Adam, Sir Frederick (1781-1853), British soldier. Made major-general (1814), he fought with great distinction and intrepidity at Waterloo.

Adam, Graeme Mercer (1839-1912), Canadian man of letters, was born at Loanhead, Midlothian, Scotland. His writings include: *The Canadian Northwest, Outline History of Canadian Literature.*

Adam, Juliette (1836-1936), French writer, born at Verberie, Oise. Under name of her first husband, 'MESSINE,' she published (1858) her *Idées Antiproudhoniennes sur l'Amour, la Femme, et le Mariage;* and thereafter, as 'JULIETTE LAMBER,' *Mon Village* (1860), and other works.

Adam, Lambert Sigisbert (1700-59), French sculptor, was born in Nancy. In 1723 he gained the Prix de Rome. His works, which are chiefly symbolic, adorned the gardens of St. Cloud and Versailles, and the Château de Choisy.

Adam and Eve, the first human pair, are represented in the well-known Biblical story as having been created by God and placed in the Garden of Eden, where they lived in a state of innocence until the Fall. It is now generally conceded that the narrative of Genesis is a combination of two accounts of the creation of man (see HEXATEUCH). The two writers diverge considerably in regard to the substance of the story. Both accounts, however, agree in representing man as the crown of creation, and imply that he possesses a community of nature with God, and a capacity for fellowship with Him.

Origin of the Paradise Story.—The story of the Garden of Eden, having been taken as the historical basis of the doctrine of sin, has become in consequence the objective of the most trenchant attacks from the side of modern science. Before proceeding to consider these attacks, or the place of the Fall in theology, let us ask what, if any, light is thrown upon the narrative by (1) philology, and (2) the study of comparative religion.

(1) The supposed proper name *Adam* is a generic term, applicable to both man and woman, in Gen. *i.*; but it is a proper name used with the article in ch. ii., iii., and iv. The origin of the name is usually connected with the Hebrew root *Adam*, 'to be red.' It is often derived from *Adamah*, 'the ground,' but this is taking the simpler from the more developed form. The Assyrian equivalent is

Adamu, 'man,' used only in a general sense, not as a proper name. Eve is the Hebrew *Havvah,* and means 'life.'

(2) It has been supposed that the Paradise story of Gen. ii. *ff.* is of Babylonian origin; but as yet investigators have not gathered from the cuneiform inscriptions any narrative sufficiently resembling the Biblical account to be deemed the source of, or even a fair parallel to, the latter. Hence, even if the parallels and analogies revealed by means of comparative religion were much more striking than they really are, the literature of Babylonia and Assyria has furnished as yet nothing to be compared, for richness of coloring or detail, with the Paradise story of Genesis. Nor have researches into other literatures brought to light any but obviously fortuitous resemblances to the Biblical narrative.

Later Developments.—The story of Adam and Eve has proved a fruitful theme for speculation in many directions.

Many of the later Jews explained the story as an allegory. Philo, the foremost writer of the Alexandrian school, explains Eve as the sensuous part, Adam as the rational part, of human nature. The serpent attacks the sensuous element, which yields to the temptation of pleasure, and next enslaves the reason. Augustine accepted the story as history, but admitted a spiritual meaning superinduced upon the literal; and his explanation was adopted generally by the Church.

Apocryphal literature is rich in themes drawn from Adam and Eve—*e.g.,* the lost Gnostic works, *Revelations of Adam, Penitence of Adam,* and *On the Daughters of Adam; The Ethiopic Book of Adam* (Eng. trans. by Malan); *Testament of Adam.* In art and poetry the beautiful Garden, as well as the innocence and the tragic experiences of its occupants, have proved fruitful themes for pictorial and literary treatment—*e.g.,* Michelangelo's beautiful fresco in the Sistine Chapel of the Vatican, and Milton's *Paradise Lost.* See GENESIS; CREATION.

Adamant, a term now used to express any substance of extraordinary hardness, chiefly a rhetorical or poetical word.

Adamawa, a Central African state. Its area is perhaps 100,000 sq. mi.; p. 3,000,-000, mainly Fulahs. Islamism is the dominant religion; the masses are pagan. Gum arabic, rubber, ivory, skins, kola nuts, and a few slaves are exported in exchange for cotton cloth, silk, copper, salt, sulphur and beads. The ruler is a native sultan. The territory of Adamawa has been divided by treaties between Great Britain, Germany and France without regard to natural boundaries or tribal divisions

Adam de la Halle, (1240-88), called 'LE BOSSU D'ARRAS' (Hunchback of Arras), author of *Le Jeu de Robin et de Marion,* the oldest French dramatic pastoral, or primitive comic opera.

Adamites, an Antinomian Gnostic sect in north Africa in the 2nd century, who professed to return to the innocence of Eden, abstained from marriage, and rejected clothing.

Adamnan (*c.* 625-704), Irish saint, and abbot of Iona (*Hii*)—was born in Donegal, a scion, like his great predecessor, of the powerful local tribe of the Neills or O'Donnells (the clan Domhnaill). The Latin *Life of Columba,* now generally accepted as Adamnan's, is almost the only record outside Bede's History of one of the most attractive portions of the life of the early church in Scotland. *Adamnan's Vision,* a professed account of his visit to heaven and hell, is preserved in an Irish MS. of the twelfth century.

Adam of Bremen (d. ?1076), born in Upper Saxony, missionary, traveller, and canon of Bremen. His principal work, *Gesta Pontificum Hammenburgensium,* c o n t a i n s this passage referring to America: 'Besides this, he [the king of Denmark] told of still another island that had been found by many in that ocean [the Atlantic]. It is called Wineland, because vines spring up there spontaneously, producing excellent wine.'

Adamic, Louis (1899-1951), writer, born in Blato, Yugoslavia. He came to the U. S. in 1913 and was naturalized in 1918. He served in the U. S. Army. In 1932 he won a Guggenheim Fellowship. He is the author of *Dynamite!* (1931), a study of class violence in the U. S.; *Laughing in the Jungle* (1932); *The Native's Return* (1934); *Grandsons* (1935); *Cradle of Life* (1936); *My America* (1938); *From Many Lands* (1940); *What's Your Name* (1942).

Adams, Abigail Smith (1744-1818), wife of John Adams and mother of John Quincy Adams, was born of Puritan stock at Weymouth, Mass. In 1764 she married John Adams (q.v.), and in 1785-8 accompanied her husband when the latter was 1st American Minister at the Court of St. James. Her letters, which were collected and published in 1840 by her grandson, Charles Francis

Adams, afford valuable glimpses of the life of that period.

Adams, Alvin (1804-77), founder of the Adams Express Company, was born in Andover, Vt.

Adams, Brooks (1848-1927), American lawyer and author, son of Charles Francis, brother of Henry Adams, was born in Quincy, Mass. His book, *The Law of Civilization and Decay* (1895), was republished in 1943.

Adams, Charles Follen (1842-1918), American humorous writer, was born in Dorchester, Mass. He wrote numerous verses in German dialect, which have been collected as *Leedle Yawcob Strauss and Other Poems* (1878) and *Dialect Ballads* (1887).

Adams, Charles Francis (1807-86), American diplomat, the son of John Quincy Adams, was born in Boston, Mass. His childhood was spent in Russia, his father having become U. S. Minister there in 1809, and in England, where he attended school. In 1825 he was graduated from Harvard. He then studied law under Daniel Webster; spent several years in private study, in writing for *The North American Review,* and in managing the business affairs of his father. An ardent opponent of slavery, he presided in 1848 over the National Free Soil Convention, and was the Free Soil candidate for Vice-President. During the Civil War period he represented the United States at London, with marked ability.

Adams, Charles Francis, Jr. (1835-1915), American lawyer and man of letters, son of Charles Francis Adams (1807-86), was born in Boston, Mass. In 1884-90 he was president of the Union Pacific Railroad; and in 1892-5 was chairman of the Massachusetts Metropolitan Park Commission. He was president of the American Historical Association (1901), and was a member of the American Academy of Arts and Letters. His works include *Railroads, Their Origin and Problems* (1878); *Lee at Appomattox, and Other Papers* (1902); *Autobiography* (1916).

Adams, Charles Francis (1866-   ), ex-sec. of Navy, the great-great-grandson of President John Quincy Adams, was born in Quincy, Mass. He was graduated from Harvard University in 1888, and was admitted to the Massachusetts bar in 1893. He was twice elected mayor of his native city and practised law in Boston after 1893. He has always been an enthusiastic yachtsman and in 1920 sailed the *Resolute,* the America's Cup defender which defeated *Shamrock IV.* In 1929 he was made Secretary of the Navy in President Hoover's cabinet. He served to March 4, 1933, and is now pres. of the Union Trust Co., Boston.

Adams, Charles Kendall (1835-1902), American educator, was born in Derby, Vt. He was president of Cornell from 1885 to 1892, and of the University of Wisconsin from 1892 until his death. He was editor-in-chief of Johnson's *Universal Encyclopædia* (1892-5).

Adams, Cyrus Cornelius (1849-1928), American geographer, was born in Naperville, Ill. He became a writer of geographical topics for the New York *Sun,* and in 1908-15 was editor of the *Bulletin* of the American Geographical Society, and wrote *David Livingstone, African Developer* (1902).

Adams, Edwin (1834-77), American actor, was born in Medford, Mass. He was one of the best light comedians of his day.

Adams, Ephraim Douglass (1865-1930), American historian, was born in Decorah, Ia. He was associate professor and professor of history at Leland Stanford Junior University. In 1919 he began the collection and organization in Paris, France, of the great American research library on the World War and Reconstruction known as the Hoover War Library, located at Stanford University. His publications include: *Great Britain and the American Civil War* (1925).

Adams, Frank Dawson (1859-1942), Canadian geologist, was born in Montreal. He was graduated from McGill University (1878) and Heidelberg (1892), and holds several honorary degrees. In 1924 he retired as Emeritus Dean and Vice Principal of McGill University. He has published numerous papers and books on researches in experimental geology.

Adams, Franklin Pierce (1881-   ), American humorous writer, was born in Chicago, Ill. He served on the editorial staff of the New York *Tribune* (1914-21), and the New York *World* (1922-1931), where he conducted, over his initials, a column of miscellaneous verse and prose, 'The Conning Tower.' Since 1931 he has been on the staffs of various New York newspapers. He has published *Tobogganing on Parnassus* (1910); *Half a Loaf* (1925); *The Column Book of F. P. A.* (1928); *Innocent Merriment* (1942).

Adams, George Burton (1851-1925), American historian, was born in Fairfield, Vt. His works include *Civilization During the Middle Ages* (1894); *Constitutional History of England* (1920); *Council and Courts in Anglo-Norman England* (1926).

Adams, Henry (1838-1918), American historian, son of Charles Francis Adams (1807-86), was born in Boston, Mass. In 1870-76 he edited *The North American Review*. His publications include *History of the United States, 1801-1817* (1889); *Historical Essays* (1891); *Mont Saint Michel and Chartres* (1904); *The Education of Henry Adams* (1906, printed privately but published after his death).

Adams, Henry Carter (1851-1921), American economist, was born in Davenport, Iowa. From 1887 until his death he was professor of political economy and finance at the University of Michigan. Besides numerous reports.

Adams, Herbert (1858-1945), American sculptor, was born in Concord, Vt. Besides honorable mention at the Paris salons of 1888 and 1889, he has received several medals. Among his works are the MacMillan Memorial Fountain, Washington; bronze doors, Library of Congress, and St. Bartholomew's Church, New York.

Adams, Herbert Baxter (1850-1901), American educator, was born in Amherst, Mass. He was professor of history at Johns Hopkins University (1883-1901), and edited

John Adams

an important series of monographs known as the *Johns Hopkins Studies in Historical and Political Science* and his books include *The College of William and Mary; History of the United States Constitution*.

Adams, James Truslow (1878-1949),

Am. historian; born Brooklyn, N. Y.; grad. Yale Univ. 1900; until 1912 member of a N. Y. Stock Exchange firm. In 1922, won the Pulitzer Prize for the best book on Am. history. His published works include *Jeffersonian Principles* (1928); *Hamiltonian Principles* (1928); *The Adams Family* (1930); *America's Tragedy*, (1934); *The American* (1943).

Adams, John (1735-1826), American statesman, 2nd President of the United States,

John Quincy Adams

was born in that part of Braintree, Mass., now known as Quincy, on Oct. 30, 1735. He was admitted to the Massachusetts bar in 1758. In 1764 he married Abigail Smith.

Throughout the period immediately preceding the outbreak of the Revolutionary War, Adams was one of the most influential leaders of the Whig or Patriot Party in Massachusetts, and from 1774 to 1777 he was one of the most conspicuous members of the Continental Congress. He was a member of the committee appointed to draft the American Declaration of Independence (q.v.), which document he signed. From 1785 to 1788 he was the 1st Minister of the United States to Great Britain, and at that time wrote his *Defence of the Constitution of the United States* (1787). On his return he became the 1st Vice-President of the United States, serving two terms (1789-97), **and** was one of the leaders of the new Federalist Party (q.v.). In 1797, he succeeded Washington in the Presidential chair, serving until 1801, during a period marked by critical relations with France, resulting almost in war.

Consult his *Works, with Life and Notes,* and *Familiar Letters of John Adams to His Wife,* both edited by Charles Francis Adams; Morse's *John Adams,* in the 'American Statesmen Series'; Chamberlain's *John Adams;* C. M. Walsh's *The Political Science of John Adams* (1915).

Adams, John (*c.* 1760-1829), seaman and mutineer, served on board H.M.S. *Bounty* (1789), where he took a prominent part in the famous mutiny (see BOUNTY, MUTINY OF THE). His real name was Alexander Smith. He afterward sailed with nine men to Pitcairn Island, which he governed with great wisdom and success. See PITCAIRN ISLAND.

Adams, John Quincy (1767-1848), American statesman, the 6th President of the United States, was born in that part of Braintree, Mass., which is now Quincy, on July 11, 1767, the eldest son of John Adams (q.v.), President in 1797-1801. His interest was primarily in politics, however, and he soon attracted attention by a series of articles opposing Paine's *Rights of Man,* arraigning certain aspects of the French Revolution, and urging the observance by the United States of strict neutrality in the European conflicts of the time.

In 1794 he received from President Washington the appointment of Minister Resident at The Hague; was afterward sent to the Court of St. James; was nominated by Washington as Minister to Portugal; and on the accession of the elder Adams to the Presidency, was appointed Minister to Prussia, where he negotiated (1799) a treaty of amity and commerce. From 1809 to 1814 Adams was Minister to Russia, and from 1817 to 1825 he was Secretary of State in the Cabinet of President Monroe, negotiating with Spain the treaty by which Florida was ceded (1821) to the United States, and being credited by many with the 1st formulation of what is now known as the Monroe Doctrine (q.v.).

As President (1825-9), Adams advocated internal improvements, and steadily refused, in spite of considerable pressure, to remove office holders for political reasons. He was not popular, however; and at the close of a troublous and comparatively uneventful term as President he was defeated for re-election (1828) by Andrew Jackson (q.v.).

Instead of retiring into private life, however, Adams returned to Washington in 1831 as a Representative in Congress, where he served continuously until his death, seventeen years later. This was in many respects the most noteworthy period of his career, and was marked by his long and finally successful fight (1844) to secure the repeal of the 'Gag Rules' (q.v.), which virtually took away the right of petition as regards slavery; and, in general, by his courageous and able fight against all measures (such as the annexation of Texas) in the interest of the institution of slavery.

John Quincy Adams' chief characteristics were his extreme independence, his unyielding courage, his conscientiousness and self-sacrificing devotion to duty, and his frequent indulgence in keen, biting invective. He was never really popular, had few intimate friends, and numerous and bitter political enemies; but his qualities everywhere compelled respect.

Adams kept an extensive diary, which is included in his *Memoirs,* and which constitutes a storehouse of valuable material for the period during which he was active in diplomatic and political life. Consult W. H. Seward's *Life;* Morse's *John Quincy Adams,* in the 'American Statesmen Series'; Quincy's *Memoir.*

Adams, Maude Kiskadden (1872), American actress, was born in Salt Lake City, both her parents being actors. In 1898 she became a star as Lady Babbie in *The Little Minister;* and in 1899 played Juliet to William Faversham's Romeo; appeared, 1905, in Barrie's *Peter Pan,* a great popular success: teaching drama at Stephens College, Columbia, Mo., 1939–.

Adams, Nehemiah (1806-78), American Congregational clergyman, was born in Salem, Mass. He antagonized the anti-slavery element by maintaining, in *A South Side View of Slavery,* that slavery heightened the religious character of the negroes.

Adams, Oscar Fay (1855-1919), American author, was born in Worcester, Mass. He is chiefly known for his *Dictionary of American Authors* (new ed., 1905), and his edition of *Through the Year with the Poets* (12 vols., 1886).

Adams, Samuel (1722-1803), American statesman, was born in Boston, Mass., on Sept. 27, 1722. He was graduated from Harvard (1740; A.M. 1743), and took up the study of law.

From 1765 until 1774 he was a member

of the lower house of the General Court; and during this period he was practically the leader of the opposition in Boston—and therefore in Massachusetts and the New England colonies—to the arbitrary measures of the British government. He was instrumental, after the so-called 'Boston Massacre' (q.v.) of March 5, 1770, in forcing the withdrawal from Boston of the two British regiments quartered there. He probably inspired the 'Boston Tea Party' (q.v.) of Dec. 16, 1773; and above all, by personal contact with his fellow citizens and by numerous articles in the press, he won over many waverers to the patriot cause, and greatly influenced the views of the colonists.

From 1774 to 1782 (excepting 1779) Adams was a member of the Continental Congress, and was a signer of the Declaration of Independence. He was secretary of State of Massachusetts; took an important part in drafting (1779-80) the 1st State constitution; and in 1782 was president of the State senate. At first opposed to the Federal Constitution framed at Philadelphia in 1787, he ultimately used his influence to secure its ratification. From 1789 to 1794 he was lieutenant-governor of the State; and from 1794 to 1797 governor. Bancroft calls him 'the type and representative of the New England town meeting.' Though not a great orator, he was always an effective speaker, and he was perhaps the most voluminous political writer of his time in America.

Consult W. V. Wells' *Life and Public Services of Samuel Adams;* J. K. Hosmer's *Samuel Adams,* in the 'American Statesmen Series'; H. A. Cushing's *The Writings of Samuel Adams* (4 vols., 1904-8).

Adams, Samuel Hopkins (1871), American journalist and author, born in Dunkirk, N. Y. Was special writer New York *Sun* (1891-1900); *McClure's Magazine* (1903-5). In 1906 his articles in *Collier's Weekly* on the patent medicine evil attracted wide attention. He has written *The Great American Fraud* (1905); *Average Jones* (1911); *The Clarion* (1914); *The Flagrant Years* (1929); *The Gorgeous Hussy* (1934); *Incredible Era* (1939); *Whispers* (1940), and the motion picture, 'It Happened One Night.'

Adams, Sarah, *née* **Flower** (1805-48), English hymn writer; author of the hymn, 'Nearer, My God, to Thee' (1840).

Adams, Suzanne (1873), American operatic soprano, was born in Cambridge, Mass. In 1898-9 she was a member of the Metropolitan Opera Company in New York City.

Adams, Thomas Sewall (1873-1933), American economist, was born in Baltimore, Md. His writings include: *Taxation in Maryland* (1900); *Labor Problems* (with H. L. Sumner, 1905); *Mortgage Taxation in Wisconsin and Neighboring States* (1907).

Adams, William (1807-80), American clergyman, was born in Colchester, Mass. He became, in 1853, the pastor of Madison Square Presbyterian Church, New York City. In 1873 he became president of the Union Theological Seminary.

Adams, William Davenport (1851-1904), English author, widely known as a literary and dramatic critic. His published works include: *Dictionary of English Literature* (1877); *Dictionary of the Drama* (1899).

Adams, William Taylor (1822-97), popularly known as 'OLIVER OPTIC,' American author of juvenile fiction, was born in Medway, Mass. He wrote over a hundred volumes of juvenile fiction, which included: *The Boat Club, Young America Abroad, The Starry Flag, Onward and Upward,* and *The Yacht Club.* He also edited *Oliver Optic's Magazine, Student and Schoolmate, Our Boys and Girls,* and *Our Little Ones.*

Adam's Apple, the popular name given to the projection in the fore part of the neck formed by the anterior extremity of the thyroid cartilage of the larynx (q.v.); so-called from the notion that it was caused by a bit of the forbidden fruit which stuck in Adam's throat.

Adams, Mount (5,805 ft.), one of the Presidential Range in New Hampshire, 4 mi. n.w. of Mount Washington.

Adamson, Patrick (1537-92), Scottish prelate, was born in Perth. He became minister of Paisley, chaplain to the Regent Morton, and regent to the archbishopric of St. Andrews. He was excommunicated for heresy by the General Assembly in 1588. Author of many religious works, he ranks high as a Latin poet.

Adamson, Robert (1852-1902), English educator, was born in Edinburgh. He was professor of logic at Aberdeen University, and at Glasgow. He wrote: *The Philosophy of Science in the Middle Ages* (1876); *The Philosophy of Kant* (1879); *The Development of Greek Philosophy* (1906); *A Short History of Logic* (1911).

Adam's Peak (7,420 ft.), called by the natives SAMANELLA, an isolated granite mountain on the s.w. edge of the central highlands, Ceylon, and a place of pilgrimage for Buddhists and Moslems.

Adana, capital of the Turkish vilayet of Adana (15,500 sq. m.; p. 425,000), in Anatolia, Asia Minor, 528 mi. s.e. of Constantinople. A place of importance in the time of the Romans; p. 72,600.

Adanson, Michel (1727-1806), French botanist, was born in Aix, Provence. He wrote: *Histoire Naturelle du Senegal* (1757); *Familles des Plantes* (1763); *Histoire de la Botanique et Plan des Familles Naturelles des Plantes* (2 vols., ed. by his son, A. Adanson, and Payer, 1864).

Adaptation. One of the most striking characters of living things is their fitness for their surroundings. This fitness is never absolute; but where it is specially marked in any species, the members of that species tend to increase in number, such increase being at the expense of other forms less well fitted for the given environment. Characters which obviously render an organism well suited to its peculiar environment are termed adaptive characters, or adaptations.

In general, it may be said that every organism possesses two sets of characters: (1) those whose use it is often difficult to define clearly, which it has inherited from its ancestors, and which are of supreme importance in classification; and (2) those which are adaptations to a particular mode of life, which have been acquired during the evolution of the stock, and which are of no importance in classification. See DARWINISM; ENVIRONMENT; EVOLUTION.

Adar, the twelfth month of the sacred (and the 6th of the civil) Hebrew year—end of February and beginning of March.

Addams, Jane (1860-1935), American social settlement worker, born in Cedarville, Ill., and was graduated from Rockford College (1881). In 1889, with Ellen Gates Starr, she opened Hull House settlement in Chicago. In 1909 she was made president of the National Conference of Charities and Correction, and in 1910 received the 1st honorary degree ever given by Yale to a woman. In 1912 she was prominent in the formation of the national Progressive Party, and was vice-president of the National Women's Suffrage Association. In April, 1915, she presided at the International Peace Conference of Women at The Hague and at various later meetings. In 1931 she shared the Nobel Peace Prize with Nicholas Murray Butler. She wrote: *Democracy and Social Ethics* (1902); *Newer Ideals of Peace* (1907); *Spirit of Youth and the City Streets* (1909); *Twenty Years at Hull House* (1910); *A New Conscience and an Ancient Evil* (1912); *The Long Road of Women's Memory* (1916); *The Second Twenty Years at Hull House* (1930); *The Excellent Becomes the Permanent* (1932). She was awarded the Bryn Mawr prize of $5000 "to an American woman in recognition of her achievements". She died in Chicago in 1935.

My Friend, Julia Lathrop was published posthumously in 1935.

Adder, the popular name for certain poisonous snakes of the viper family (see VIPER; PUFF ADDER), as well as of harmless snakes of the family Colubridæ.

Head of Adder.

In the United States, the name adder is applied to some poisonous snakes without rattles, as the Moccasin (q.v.) or Water Adder, and the Copperhead (q.v.) or Red Adder; also to the harmless Hognose (q.v.).

Adder's Tongue (*Ophioglossum vulgatum*), a small fern which forms annually one leaf, dividing into a flat, ovate, sterile portion, and an elongated, narrow, unbranched, spore-bearing part. It is found throughout the Northern Hemisphere, the Cape of Good Hope, and New Zealand.

Addicks, John Edward (1841-1919), American political leader, was born in Philadelphia, Pa. He made a fortune, by operations in gas properties, and gas-lighting companies. From 1895 to 1905 he was an important factor in the politics of Delaware.

Addicks, Lawrence (1878-   ), American metallurgical engineer, was born in Philadelphia, Pa. He has made a study of copper.

Adding Machines. See **Calculating Machines.**

Addis Ababa. See **Adis Ababa.**

Addison, Joseph (1672-1719), English writer and essayist, was born in Milston, Wiltshire, where his father was rector. He was educated at the Charter House and Queen's College, Oxford. In 1693 he began his literary career with a poetical address to Dryden; the next year appeared his *Account of the Greatest English Poets,* and a translation of the fourth book of the *Georgic.*

Addison

Addison's 1st preferment—a commissionership of appeal in the excise—came in 1704. Thus endowed, he entered upon the composition of *The Campaign,* which launched him on his career of state service—a career which, thanks to the magnanimity of Swift, whose close friendship he won when in Ireland as secretary to the lord-lieutenant (1709), was not altogether broken even by the Tory triumph in 1710. This Irish visit also marks the opening of Addison's true literary vein. He had just started for Dublin when (April 12, 1709) Steele began *The Tatler,* and in No. 18 his 1st contribution appeared. But it was with the more famous *Spectator* (March 1, 1711, to Dec. 6, 1712) that Addison really found himself, and left the imprint of his genius upon literature. Under George I., Addison again became secretary to the lord-lieutenant of Ireland; then a commissioner for Trade and the Colonies; and finally (1717) secretary of state, a post resigned in March, 1718, owing to ill health. From 1710 till his death he was M.P. for Malmesbury. On Aug. 3, 1716, Addison married Charlotte, Countess of Warwick. He died at Holland House, and was buried in Westminster Abbey.

Addison's writings fall under the heads of political journalism, verse, and miscellaneous prose. His political writings embrace *The Whig Examiner* (September-October, 1710); *The Freeholder* (55 numbers, 1715-16, etc., etc.); *The Old Whig* (1719), a reply to Steele's *Plebeian,* etc. As a light essayist he has no equal, and scarcely a 2nd, in English literature. The noble monument of his success is the *Spectator.* As an 'abstract and brief chronicle' of the manners of the time, it is incomparable.

Addison's works were 1st collected by Tickell (4 vols., 1721), and have since appeared in numerous editions. Reprints of the *Spectator* are also numerous. His *Life* has been written by Lucy Aikin and by Courthope. Consult Macaulay's 'Essay on

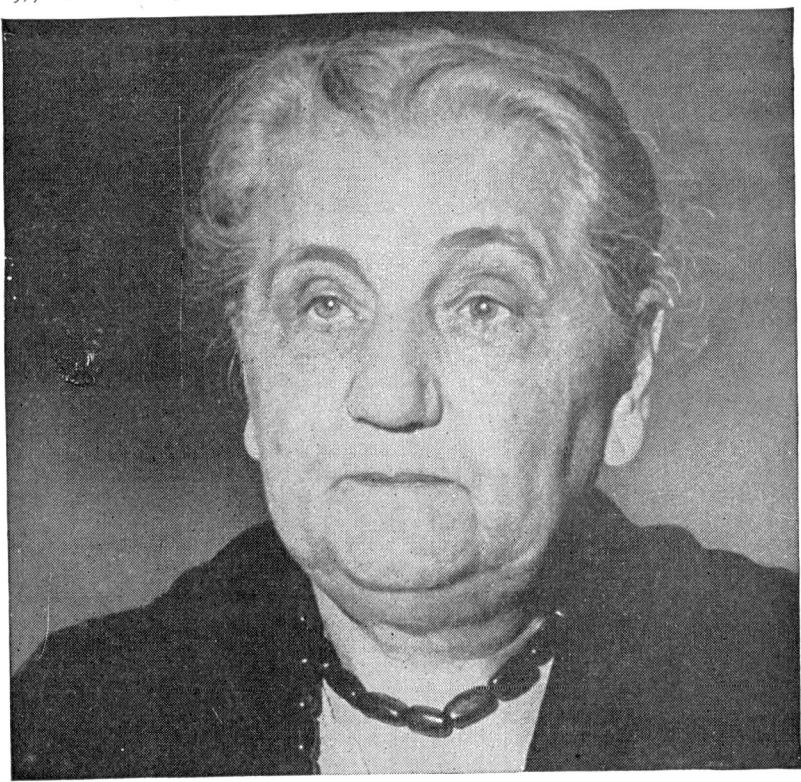

Jane Addams.

Addison,' and Johnson's *Lives of the Poets.*

Addison's Disease is associated with disease of the suprarenal bodies, usually of a tuberculous nature, and is characterized by weak heart, low blood pressure, gastric and intestinal irritation, anæmia, increasing muscular weakness, and generally, though not always, by discoloration or browning of the skin.

Addition, in arithmetic, is the uniting of two or more numbers in one sum total (see ARITHMETIC). In Algebra, it is the combining of quantities according to their algebraic signs.

Addled Parliament, name given to the second Parliament of James I. of England, which sat April 5 to June 7, 1614. It discussed the illegalities of the king so freely that it was dissolved before it had passed a single act.

Ade, George (1866-1944), American author and playwright, was born in Kentland, Indiana. Among his best-known books are: *Fables in Slang* (1899); *More Fables* (1900); *The Slim Princess* (1907); *Knocking the Neighbors* (1912); *Handmade Fables* (1920); *The Old-Time Saloon* (1931); *Thirty Fables* (1933). His plays include: *The Sultan of Sulu* (1902); *The County Chairman* (1903); *The College Widow* (1904); *Father and the Boys* (1907); *Nettie* (1914).

Adee, Alvey Augustus (1842-1924), American public official, was born in Astoria, N. Y. He took an active part in the diplomatic negotiations incident to the Chinese Boxer uprising of 1900; assisted in preparing the Treaty of Paris after the Spanish-American War; and in 1908 acted as Secretary of State *ad interim.*

Adelaer, Curt Sivertsen (1622-75), Danish admiral, was born in Brevig, Norway. In 1645 he entered the Venetian service, during that republic's warfare with the Turks. As admiral-general he took command in 1675 of the entire Danish fleet on the outbreak of the war with Sweden, but died before the expedition set out.

Adelaide, city, Australia, capital of South Australia. It was 1st settled in 1837, and named after the Queen of William IV. It stands on a large plain, bounded on the e. and s., at a distance of 4 to 8 mi., by the Mount Lofty Range (alt. 2,333 ft.). North Adelaide, the residential quarter, is separated from South Adelaide, the business quarter, by a park half a mile wide, through which runs the Torrens River, spanned by numerous bridges. Public buildings include the Government House, Parliament Houses, Town Hall, and Post Office; St. Peter's Cathedral (Anglican) and the Cathedral of St. Francis Xavier (Roman Catholic); the vice-regal summer residence at Marble Hill, 12 mi. from the city; and the Art Gallery, Museum, Meteorological Observatory, Public Library, and School of Mines. Besides the Botanic Gardens and Botanic Park (104 acres), and the Zoological Gardens (17 acres), the town is surrounded by a belt of reserved parklands half a mi. wide.

Among educational institutions the most important are Adelaide University (q.v.), St. Peter's (Episcopal) College, St. Barnabas' Theological College, and Prince Alfred (Wesleyan) College. The leading manufactures are woolen, leather, iron, and earthenware goods; but the city's chief importance depends on its being the great emporium for South Australia; p., with suburbs, 330,217.

Adelaide University, in the city of Adelaide, South Australia, was founded by act of Parliament in 1874. The institution was opened in 1876, and the present buildings occupied in 1882.

Adelbert College, the collegiate department of Western Reserve University.

Adeler, Max pseudonym of **Charles Heber Clark** (1841-1915), American author, born in Berlin, Md. He is best known for his works of fiction, which include: *Out of the Hurly Burly; Captain Bluitt* (1901); *In Happy Hollow; The Quakeress* (1905); *By the Bend of the River* (1914).

Adelochorda or **Hemichorda,** a subclass of the Chordata, embracing the wormlike Balanoglossus (q.v.), in which the spinal cord is very obscure. The lowest of vertebrates. See CHORDATA.

Adelphi College, a non-sectarian institution, coeducational, for higher education, located Garden City, N. Y. It awards in its own name its diplomas and degrees, and is an approved college of the University of the State of New York for the reception of the university scholars.

Adelsberg, (Slav., *Postojna*), town and summer resort, Carniola, Austria; 22 mi. n.e. of Trieste. Near it are caves, the most famous being a large stalactite cavern, the *Adelsberg Grotto.* This cavern, the largest in Europe, is divided into the old and the new grotto, the latter discovered in 1816.

Aden, peninsula and fortified port near the southwestern extremity of Arabia. It is a port of call for all P. & O. liners. Aden is a British possession, and comprises the peninsula of Aden proper (21 sq. m.), the peninsula of Little Aden (15 sq. m.), and the district of Shaikh Othman (34 sq. m.) on the mainland—or, including the hinterland Protectorate, some 42,080 sq. m. The peninsula of Aden is an irregular oval, connected with the mainland by a narrow, sandy isthmus; the peninsula of Little Aden is a mass of granite. Between them is the harbor, Aden West Bay. The climate is hot, but healthy.

Solyman the Magnificent fortified Aden, and it was afterward occupied successively by the Portuguese and the Turks, until it became a British possession in 1839. The imports, including coal, cotton and silk fabrics, live stock, grain, provisions, tobacco, are valued at $15,000,000 annually; the exports, coffee, gums, spices, ivory, ostrich feathers, hides, pearls, at $14,000,000. Aden is under the government of Bombay. Most of the natives are Arabs, and Somalis from Africa, all speaking Arabic; p. 100,000.

Aden, Gulf of, arm of the Arabian Sea, to the south of the Red Sea, between Southern Arabia and the Somali coast. Length, 500 mi.; breadth, 150 to 200 mi.

Adenia. See **Anemia**.

Adenitis, (Greek ἀδήν, a gland), and **Angeioleucitis** (Greek ἀγγειον, a vessel, λευκός, white) are the terms employed in medicine to indicate inflammation of the lymphatic glands and inflammation of the lymphatic vessels, respectively. The latter condition is more commonly known as LYMPHANGITIS. In most instances of inflammation in the lymphatic system, the vessels and glands are simultaneously involved. Depending upon the cause, this inflammation may be either Acute or Chronic. See GLANDS.

Adenoids are gland-like swellings on the roof and posterior wall of the naso-pharynx. They are most common in children or young persons, are by no means uncommon in adults.

The symptoms of this hypertrophy vary in kind and severity, depending upon the amount of nasal obstruction, but in the majority of cases are unmistakable. The child habitually breathes through the mouth, is dull and listless, with vacant expression, and is often deaf to a greater or less degree. The breathing of children affected with adenoids is noisy and snuffling, due to the nasal catarrh commonly present. At night the child snores. Surgical removal of these growths is common and is usually effective, as are often other forms of treatment.

Aderno, town, Catania, Sicily. It contains two Norman structures of Roger I.—a keep and a monastery (1157). It stands on the site of ancient *Hadranum;* p. 39,000.

Adersbach Rocks, labyrinthine group of sandstone rocks near the village of Adersbach, in Northeastern Bohemia. There are thousands of curious cones, peaks, and pinnacles (one over 200 ft. high), produced by the influence of rain, frost, and other atmospheric changes.

Adhesion, in Physics. See **Cohesion; Friction.**

Adhesion, in Pathology, a vital union between two surfaces of a living body which have been either naturally or artificially separated. After injuries to joints, adhesion frequently takes place between the injured structures and those adjoining, which may cause subsequent stiffness.

Adiabatic. See **Steam Engine; Thermodynamics.**

Adiabene, the ancient name used by Pliny for Assyria, lay between the Tigris, Lycus (Upper Zab), and Caprus (Lower Zab) Rivers. By the Aramæans it was called *Hadyab*. The capital of Adiabene was Arbela (q.v.), celebrated as the place where the Macedonians commanded by Alexander the Great defeated the Persian army under Darius (331 B.C.). Adiabene was conquered by Trajan in 116 A.D., who changed its name to Assyria; under Hadrian it enjoyed semi-independence; but it was again conquered by Septimius Severus in 195 A.D.

Adiantum, or **Maidenhair** (*Adiantum Capillus-Veneris*), a small, delicate, and graceful fern. It is supposed that the name maidenhair originated in the use of a mucilage made from this fern by women for stiffening their hair.

Adiaphora, (Greek, 'indifferent things'), in Ethics, are such actions as lie between the spheres of good and of evil. The Stoics gave currency to the word in this sense, and Cicero (*De Finibus,* iii. 16) translates it by '*indifferens.*' The Adiaphoristic controversy troubled the Reformed Church in Germany for a few years subsequent to 1548. It had to do with certain customs and tenets of the church, as the use of candles, pictures, hymns, and other forms of ritual.

Adige (ancient *Athesis,* German *Etsch*), after the Po the most important river in Italy, rises in the Rhætian Alps, in the

Tyrol (alt. 5,005 ft.), flows s. into Lombardy, and finally e. to the Adriatic. In its lower course the Adige is connected with the Po by canals. Length, 250 mi. During the World War it was the scene of heavy fighting, the Austrian advance into Italy being checked in 1916 at its banks.

Adigei (plural), a tribe formerly inhabiting the northern slopes of the Caucasus. In 1861 the Russian government compelled them to remove to the plains. Many of them thereupon settled in what is now known as Adigei, an autonomous area of 1,200 sq. mi. at the angle of the Caucasus and the Sea of Azov, whose chief city is Kraznodar; p. 155,000. Two hundred thousand members of the tribe went in 1861 to Turkey.

Adi Granth, the sacred books of the Sikhs. They consist in great part of poems and legends, and are exalted in ethical and intellectual tone.

Adipic Acid, $C_4H_8(COOH)_2$, is a dibasic acid of the oxalic series, obtained by the oxidizing action of nitric acid on oleic acid, suet, spermaceti, and other fatty bodies. It melts at 149° C.

Adipose Tissue consists of an aggregation of minute vesicles filled with fat or oil. Adipose tissue is widely distributed throughout the body. It occurs in the yellow marrow of bones; and a considerable layer is found under the skin, where, being a poor conductor of heat, it is specially valuable in retaining the warmth of the bodies of animals exposed to great cold, such as whales. It is also found surrounding large vessels and nerves, the kidneys, joints, etc., where it affords support, and protects from injurious pressure. Its utilization as a reserve supply of nutriment is well illustrated in hibernating animals like the hedgehog. See FAT.

Adirondack Park, an extensive area in the heart of the Adirondack region of New York State, was established in 1892. It comprises all of Hamilton co., and the adjacent portions of Essex, Franklin, St. Lawrence, Warren, and Herkimer counties, and contains 3,313,564 acres, of which the State owns 1,412,702. The region is mountainous, and much of it densely wooded, comprising large areas of virgin forest. It embraces over a thousand lakes and ponds, which are well stocked with game fish. At Saranac Lake (q.v.) there is a sanatorium for consumptives.

Adirondacks, specifically a group of mountains in Northeastern New York. The mountain section culminates in Essex co., the tallest peaks being Mount Marcy, the highest land in the State (5,344 ft), McIntyre (5,112 ft), Skylight (4,920 ft), Haystack (4,918 ft), and Dix (4,916 ft).

The geological formation of the Adirondacks consists principally of crystalline rocks —gneisses, labradorites, and syenites. The most important mineral deposit is iron ore of the magnetite variety. The largest lakes of this region are Lake Champlain, over 120 mi. long, and from 700 ft. to 15 mi. wide, and Lake George, 33 mi. long, and from $\frac{3}{4}$ mi. to 3 mi. wide. Others are Big and Little Tupper, Raquette, the Fulton Chain, Blue Mountain, Schroon, and Long Lakes. In the mountain region, Lake Placid and the Upper and Lower Saranac Lakes are noteworthy.

Much of the Adirondacks is heavily forested with red and black spruce, balsam fir, white pine, red Norway pine, hemlock, yellow and white ash, cedar, tamarack, soft maples, and other species. Above the forest line grow juniper, grasses, and mosses. The fauna include deer, hares, beaver, and partridges. In the streams and lakes are found black bass and brook trout. Salmon once lived in these waters, but is now extinct.

Consult the *Reports* of the New York State Geologist, State Botanist, and State Forestry Commission; *Bulletin* of the State Museum.

Adis Ababa, or **Addis Ababa** (*Finfini*), capital and chief city of Ethiopia, in the province of Shoa, and in the midst of mountains, near one of the sources of the Blue Nile (alt. 10,000 ft.). Here was signed the treaty of peace between Abyssinia and Italy (1896) after the latter's defeat by King Menelek; captured by the Italians in 1936, and by British, 1941; p. 65,000.

Adit (Latin *aditus,* an approach or access), a mining term for nearly horizontal passages opened for drainage purposes, entrance and exit, or ventilation.

Adjective (Latin *adjectivus,* 'added') in grammar defines and limits the noun to which it refers. See PARTS OF SPEECH.

Adjudication, in a general sense is the decision of a court of law on a question of law or fact arising in an action. See BANKRUPTCY.

Adjutant (*Leptoptilus argala*), a stork-like bird, common during summer in India. It stands about 5 ft. high, and measures 14 or 15 ft. from tip to tip of extended wings. The four-sided, pointed bill is very large;

the head and neck are almost bare; and a sausage-like pouch, sometimes 16 in. long, and apparently connected with respiration, hangs down from the base of the neck. While feeding largely on carcasses and offal about the towns, it also fishes for living food, and sometimes devours birds and small mammals.

Adjutant, a staff officer of a post, battalion, squadron, or regiment, whose duties are to assist the commanding officer in the details of military work. Consult *United States Army Regulations.*

Adjutant-General, staff officer to the commanding general, with the duty of assisting in all details of the command, such as issuing orders, receiving and executing orders, dealing with reports, and regulating the details of the service. See ARMY OF THE UNITED STATES.

Adler, Alfred (1870-1937), Austrian psychiatrist, was born in Vienna. He is best known as the promulgator of the theory of the inferiority complex which has received a wide currency not only in scientific circles but also in popular biography. Among his works that have been translated into English are: *The Theory and Practice of Individual Psychology* (1924); *Understanding Human Nature* (1927, 1928); *The Science of Living* (1929); *The Pattern of Life* (1930).

Adler, Cyrus (1863-1940), Orientalist, was born in Van Buren, Arkansas, and was graduated from the University of Pennsylvania (1883). From 1884 to 1893 he was at Johns Hopkins University. He was special commissioner of the Columbian Exposition to Turkey, Tunis, Algiers, and Morocco (1890-92); at the Smithsonian Institution (1892-1908), and at the U. S. National Museum (1888-1908). In 1908 he became president of Dropsie College in Philadelphia. He has written: *Told in the Coffee House* (with Allan Ramsey, 1898); *The Voice of America on Kishineff* (1904); *Jews in the Diplomatic Correspondence of the United States* (1906). He was also one of the editors of *The Jewish Encyclopædia;* editor of *The American Jewish Year Book* (1899-1905), and of *The Jewish Quarterly Review.*

Adler, Felix (1851-1933), American educator, was born in Alzey, Germany. He came to the United States in 1857, and was graduated from Columbia University (1870). He was professor of Hebrew and Oriental languages and literature at Cornell University (1874-6); established the New York Society for Ethical Culture in 1876; and became professor of social and political ethics at Columbia in 1902. His works include: *Creed and Deed* (1877); *The Moral Instruction of Children* (1892); *Life and Destiny* (1905); *Religion of Duty* (1905); *Marriage and Divorce* (1905); *An Ethical Philosophy of Life* (1918); and *The Reconstruction of the Spiritual Ideal* (1923).

Adler, Georg (1863-1908), German economist, was born in Posen. He was an opponent of radicalism in social policy, and published: *Karl Marxsche Kritik* (1886); *Internationaler Arbeiter-Schutz* (1888); *Staat und Arbeitslosigkeit* (1894); *Die Social-Reform in Altertum* (1898); *Geschichte des Socialismus und Communismus* (1900); *Die Bedeutung der Illusionen für Politik und Sociales Leben* (1904).

Adler, George Jakob (1821-68), German-American lexicographer, was born in Germany. He is best known for his *German-English Dictionary* (1848) and *German Grammar* (1868).

Adler, Hermann (1839-1911), Jewish rabbi, was born in Hanover, Germany. On the death of his father, Nathan, in 1890, Dr. Adler was unanimously chosen to succeed him as chief rabbi of the United Hebrew congregations of the British Empire. He also served as president of the Jews' College, London. He published: *Ibn Gabirol and His Relation to Scholastic Philosophy* (1864); *Jewish Reply to Dr. Colenso; Can Jews be Patriots?* (1878); *Anglo-Jewish Memories* (1909).

Adler, Jakob Georg Christian (1756-1834), Danish Orientalist. He was one of the best Arabic scholars of his day, author of the celebrated *Novi Testamenti Versiones Syriacæ* (1789).

Adler, Nathan Marcus (1803-90), chief rabbi, was born in Hanover, Germany. Having filled the office of chief rabbi of Oldenburg, and later of Hanover, he was in 1844 elected chief rabbi of London, where he performed an important part in the reunion of the English congregations. He published *Nethinah Lager,* a Hebrew commentary on the Chaldee paraphrase of the Pentateuch.

Adler, Samuel (1809-91), German-American rabbi, was born in Worms. For fifteen years (1842-57) he was rabbi of congregations in Rhine-Hesse, when he was called to Emanu-el Temple, New York City. His books include: *Jewish Conference Papers* (1880); *Benedictions* (1882).

Ad Libitum (in Italian *a piacere,* or *a*

piacimento) is a musical term which implies that the part so marked may be performed according to the taste of the performer.

Admetus, mythical king of Pheræ in Thessaly, married Alcestis, the fairest daughter of Pelias, king of Iolcos; Apollo becoming his obedient slave either because of affection simply, or by way of punishment for slaying the Cyclopes. See ALCESTIS. The story is the subject of Euripides' Alcestis.

Administration, in politics. See **Government; Local Government.**

Administration, in law, is the settlement of the estate of a deceased person. This is effected through the agency of one who is known as the personal representative, because he represents the person of the deceased in his legal relations. When designated by will, this representative is known as an *executor* (q.v.); when not so designated, as an *administrator* (q.v.).

Administrative Law (*droit administratif*) means in most European states that special body of rules which applies to the agents of the government. The doctrine of the separation of powers, as there understood, forbids interference on the part of the judiciary with officials of the executive in the performance of their duties.

The theory of the English common law, which has extended to the United States, is directly opposed to any such principle as that of *droit administratif*. In the United States and Great Britain the ordinary courts are competent to try all offences on the part of the government officials according to the ordinary law, though something corresponding to administrative law may be found in statutory provisions protecting executive officers from vexatious interference in the exercise of their official duties.

Administrator is the person appointed by a probate court to administer the estate of an intestate, or of a person who has made a will but has failed to appoint an executor. The husband of a deceased wife, or the wife of a deceased husband, has generally the first claim; failing whom, the next of kin of the creditors may receive the appointment.

The duties and liabilities of an administrator correspond closely to those of an executor.

Admirable Crichton. See **Crichton, James.**

Admiral (Arabic, *emir*, 'commander'), the title of a naval officer of the highest rank. It has been in use among maritime countries since the thirteenth or fourteenth century.

In the United States Navy, no rank above that of captain was actually conferred until 1862. In 1864 the rank of vice-admiral, and in 1866 that of admiral, were established, and in each case Farragut was the first to be promoted to the new rank. After their establishment the grades of admiral and vice-admiral were held special honorary rewards to which officers might be appointed for distinguished service in war. The officers who earlier attained the rank of admiral are David G. Farragut (1866-70) and David D. Porter (1870-91); those who held the rank of vice-admiral are David G. Farragut, David D. Porter, and Stephen C. Rowan. At their deaths those grades became extinct. For his distinguished services in the Battle of Manila Bay (May 1, 1898), George Dewey was promoted by Congress to the rank of 'admiral of the navy.'

In 1915, a naval appropriation bill provided that the commander-in-chief of the United States Atlantic fleet, the Pacific fleet, and the Asiatic fleet shall, while serving as such, have the rank of admiral. The admiral's flag has a navy blue background on which four stars are arranged like the points of a diamond. March, 1946, the U. S. Congress created the permanent rank of *admiral of the fleet* and the following admirals were promoted to it: Ernest J. King, William D. Leahy, Chester W. Nimitz and Frederick W. Halsey, Jr. See NAVY, U.S.

Admiralty, Board of, a government department which has the management of all matters concerning the British navy. It comprises six lords commissioners, who decide collectively on important questions.

Admiralty Courts. The English Admiralty Court (whose functions are now exercised by the Probate, Divorce, and Admiralty Division of the High Court of Justice, constituted in 1873-5) was created for the purpose of trying and deciding maritime causes.

In the United States, the court of original admiralty jurisdiction is the United States district court. From this court causes may be removed, in certain cases, to the circuit court, and ultimately to the Supreme Court. Its civil jurisdiction extends to cases of salvage, bonds of bottomry, seamen's wages, seizures under the law of imposts, navigation or trade, cases of prize or ransom, contracts of affreightment between different States or

© *British Information Service*

Admiralty. This is Whitehall outside the Admiralty building in London, England. It was in this building that Nelson lay in state when his body was brought home from Trafalgar.

foreign ports, contracts for conveyance of passengers, contracts with material men, jettisons, maritime contributions and averages, pilotage, surveys of ship and cargo, and generally to all damages and trespasses occurring on the high seas. Its criminal jurisdiction extends to all crimes and offenses committed on the high seas.

Admiralty Inlet. (1.) East arm of Puget Sound, Washington, connecting it with the Strait of Juan de Fuca. Greatest width, 10 mi.; navigable for largest ships. Seattle, Tacoma, and Port Townsend (q.v.) are upon this inlet. (2.) Northwest opening in Tierra del Fuego; 54° S., 70° W.

Admiralty Island lies off the coast of

© *Australian News and Information Bureau*

Admiralty Islands. Australian civil administration has taken over from the United States Navy at Manus Island, vast wartime base in the Admiralty Group, 250 miles north of New Guinea. Shown are members of the New Guinea native constabulary, serving on Manus Island with the Australian civil administration.

Southern Alaska, in 57° 30′ N. lat., and 134° 15′ W. long. It is about 90 m. long, well wooded and watered; and contains coal and copper. It is inhabited, and belongs to the United States.

Admiralty Islands, a group of forty islands in the Pacific Ocean, n.e. of New Guinea, about 2° s. lat. and 147° E. long. Their total area is 872 sq. m. They were annexed by Ger. in 1885, and later made an Australian mandate by the League of Nations. Occupied by the Japs in World War II; retaken by the Allies, March, 1944.

Admiralty Law. See **Maritime Law.**

Admiralty Sound separates Tierra del Fuego from the mainland of South America. It is 43 mi. long and 7 mi. wide, and constitutes a southern extension of Magellan Strait.

Admission, in criminal law, is any confession, tacit or express, made by an accused person of his guilt, or of any fact or circumstance relevant to the proof thereof. See CONFESSION; EVIDENCE.

Admonitionists, in English history, were the supporters of a Puritan memorial called *An Admonition to the Parliament,* issued by two clergymen about 1572; and also of a second document, which similarly urged the advantages of the Presbyterian method of ecclesiastical government as opposed to that of the Church of England.

Adobe, (Spanish; Anglicized into *doby,* plural *dobies,* in New Mexico), the sun-dried brick of Spanish America, first used by the Indians of Mexico and Peru, and introduced into the Southwestern United States by the Spaniards. The clay, with hay or dried grass sometimes added, is trodden to the proper consistency, moulded into bricks, and hardened by exposure to the sun. Similar brick, frequently mixed with straw, was used in ancient Egypt and Assyria.

Adolescence means the state of growing, and is used almost exclusively of human beings to denote the period of youth—that is, the period between puberty and full growth: for men, stretching from fourteen to twenty-five years of age; for women, from twelve to twenty-one. The development of the organs of reproduction which takes place during this period is commonly accompanied in both sexes by general physical and mental instability, due to new functioning of the body and the widening of the sphere of the feelings and desires. At this time, too, when the diseases of childhood are losing, and those of maturity are gaining, in power, the boy or girl is peculiarly liable to the lighter forms of both. Adolescence is the crucial period in the development of character, the whole future depending on how the newly acquired powers are organized and directed.

Adolphus, or **Adolph** (?1255-98), king of Germany, was elected king of the Romans on the death of Rudolph of Hapsburg (1292), but deposed in 1298, and killed in battle the following year.

Adoni, or **Adwani,** town, province of Madras, India; 64 mi. from Bellary. It has cotton and silk manufactures, especially carpets; p. 30,000.

Adonijah. (1.) The fourth son of David, king of Israel, was the next heir to the throne on the death of Absalom, but was set aside in favor of Solomon, who caused him to be put to death on the charge of conspiring for the crown. (2.) A Levite teacher to the Judæans. (3.) One of the 'chiefs of the people' after the Captivity.

Adonis, a beautiful youth beloved by Aphrodite. He was slain by a boar while hunting, and the goddess, coming too late to his rescue, changed his blood into flowers. Her grief was so great that Pluto, the god of Hades, allowed him to spend six months of every year on earth. A yearly festival was celebrated in honor of Adonis.

Adonis, a small genus of the Ranunculaceæ. *A. autumnalis* (Pheasant's Eye), found in European cornfields, has bright scarlet petals, the name coming from the legend that they were stained by the blood of Adonis.

Adoptianism, a heretical doctrine regarding the person of Christ, allied to the tenets of Nestorius, which, arising in a crude form in the fourth century, was recast toward the close of the eighth century, and maintained in Spain by Elipandus, archbishop of Toledo, and by Felix, bishop of Urgel. These held that Christ was the Son of God only in His divine nature; in His human nature He was, like the rest of humanity, but a child of God, becoming the Son by *adoption.* Charlemagne summoned various synods (Ratisbon, 792; Frankfort, 794; Aix-la-Chapelle, 799) to deal with Felix and his teaching, when this doctrine was condemned as heresy.

Adoption, in law, is the admission of a child, not the lawful issue of the adopter, to the legal rights and privileges of a son or daughter. In the United States, the common law makes no provisions for adoption, and the practice is therefore based on statutes in the several States. The regulations governing adoption vary considerably, requiring judicial proceedings, or at least an order of the court, in some States, while it may be effected by a deed of adoption in other States. In all cases, however, the status of the adopted person is substantially that of a child born in lawful wedlock. (See PARENT AND CHILD.)

Adoption, or the admission of an alien to the full rights and privileges of a *gens* or family, is a practice of very ancient date.

Adoration (Latin *ad*, 'to,' *os*, 'the mouth'), among the Romans, was the act of kissing the hand and waving it toward some person or object as a sign of deep reverence. The kissing of a sovereign's hand or of the cross on the Pope's slipper is the modern form of this practice. In our time, adoration denotes a mental attitude of worshipping devotion to God.

In the Roman Catholic Church *Adoration of the Host* is the supreme act in the celebration of the Mass. *Adoration of the Cross* is a special ceremony.

In Christian art and archæology an *Adoration* is a representation of the adoration of the Infant Jesus by the Magi.

Adrastus, king of Argos, whose daughter married Polynices of Thebes, who had been exiled from his native city by his brother Eteocles.

Adrenalin. One of the most important advances in pharmacology and therapeutics in recent years has been the discovery of adrenalin, the active principle of the suprarenal glands, located about the same time by a Japanese scientist, Takamine, and an American investigator, Abel.

The uses of adrenalin are many, and of very great value. It is a most valuable hemostatic, to check bleeding. On being shot directly into a dead heart it has started the muscle working again. A lack of adrenalin causes Addison's disease, which is marked by a bronze discoloration of the skin and nervous disorders, ending in coma and death. An overactive adrenal cortex exaggerates masculinity in either sex. It can change the sex of the unborn child from female to male. In 1935, Dr. Frank Humman of California reported that he had relieved such over-activity by snipping away part of each gland's cortex. See SUPRARENAL GLANDS.

Adria, town, Rovigo province, Italy, between the Rivers Po and Adige. It was an important seaport of the Etruscans, and was formerly on the Adriatic, to which sea it gave its name; p. 16,000.

Adrian, Emperor of Rome. See **Hadrianus.**

Adrian, the name of six popes of the Roman Catholic Church.

ADRIAN I. (772-95) obtained the help of Charlemagne against Didier, king of the Lombards.

ADRIAN II. (867-72) took part in the struggles between Louis II. and Charles the Bald. During his term of office the schism between the Eastern and Western Churches began.

ADRIAN III. (884-5) passed a decree restraining the Emperor Charles III. from interfering with the papal election.

ADRIAN IV. (1154-9), Nicholas Breakspeare, was the only English pope. He was born at Langley, near St. Albans. He became cardinal in 1146 and was made Pope in 1154.

ADRIAN V. (1276) held office only for a month.

ADRIAN VI. (1522-3) had held office as dean of the Church of Louvain, bishop of Tortosa, cardinal (1517), regent of Spain during the minority of Charles v.

Adrianople, vilayet, European Turkey. An agricultural region; p. 150,889.

Adrianople (Turkish *Edirnè;* ancient **Uskudama** or **Orestia**), city, capital of the vilayet of the same name, is an important centre of commerce; p. 34,669. The third city of European Turkey, it is located on the navigable river Maritza. It exports raw silk, cotton, opium, wine, fruits, attar of roses, and turkey red dye.

Adriatic Sea, an arm of the Mediterranean, extending from Venice for 460 mi. s.e. to the Strait of Otranto (less than 40 mi. wide), lies between the low, sandy beaches of Italy on the w. and the rocky cliffs, islands, and inlets of Dalmatia and Albania on the e. Its general breadth is about 90 mi.

The Italian coast is well populated. The Dalmatian coast is inhospitable. The fisheries of the Adriatic are rich, and industriously worked. The principal ports are Brindisi, Ancona, and Venice, Trieste, Pola, and Fiume, Corfu, Zante, Vostitza, Patras, and Kalamata. The annual wedding of the Doge to the sea on Ascension Day, a ceremony instituted in 1174, symbolized the maritime basis of Venetian prosperity. Consult F. H. Jackson's *The Shores of the Adriatic—The*

Italian Side (1906), *The Austrian Side* (1908).

Adularia, a clear, transparent, glassy form of potash feldspar which is found mainly in the crevices of crystalline schists and gneisses, often in perfect crystals. See FELDSPAR.

Adullam, a cave, or rather 'stronghold,' on the Philistine border of Judah, in which David and 400 refugees and outlaws took shelter.

Adullamites, a term applied to those English Liberals, who in 1866 seceded from Russell and Gladstone on the question of Parliamentary reform (q.v.).

Adult Education.—Public provision for education in a democratic state cannot be considered complete until adequate opportunity for study, research, and intellectual life is offered to all the people, irrespective of age, social or occupational status. England claims to have been the pioneer in the modern movement, with a history that can be traced at least to the 18th century.

The British Association of Adult Education was founded in 1921 by the World Association for Adult Education (founded in 1920). Its functions are inquiry, publicity and research, in collaboration with all organizations engaged in adult education. It also carries on educational work in prisons. The National Council of Labor Colleges, supported largely by the trade unions, represents another movement in adult education.

People's High Schools are a well-developed system for the education of adult young people in Scandinavia.

Educational societies, notably the Ligue de l'Enseignement, have fostered the movement in France.

The Government in Germany gave financial support to adult educational institutions. Political parties after World War I, founded educational institutions whose aim was propaganda for the party.

In Russia there is a well-thought-out system of adult education. Under the People's Commissariat of Education were the following institutions for adult education in 1929: 70 institutes of university standard where it is easier for adults to gain admittance than for others; 27 workers' universities, providing a four-year course, mainly in technical subjects; 62 workers' colleges, attached to and preparing for the universities and providing a four-year course; schools of elementary and secondary grade designed to raise the general level of intelligence of adults; peasant courses for poorer peasants, providing one or two years of study including agriculture. All but the universities are for part-time students. Nearly a quarter of a million adults are reached by these schools annually—a large proportion of them women.

In India the movement began at the end of the 19th century, but it can do little until compulsory education is adopted on a national basis.

In China mass education began as an effort to wipe out illiteracy by the introduction of a simplified form of writing—the famous thousand-character alphabet, invented by James Yen after World War I. The Chinese National Association of the Mass Education Movement was formed in 1923. In 1929, 5,000,000 were studying in the laboring classes and army.

In Austria the development of adult education as planned by those interested in the movement awaits financial improvement in Austria.

In 1929 Yugoslavia provided for compulsory education of adults who have not been to school, up to the age of 25.

In Czechoslovakia workers' education is carried on by the Central Workers' College, the organizing and study centre, and by the Workers' Academy, the cultural centre of the Social-Democratics.

No especial organization for the development of adult education exists in Italy.

War conditions since 1939 have disrupted adult education in many parts of Europe.

Remarkable progress in adult education was made in Japan between 1920 and 1940.

United States.—The United States ranks high among the nations in the support of adult education. The modern movement dates from 1907, when the University of Wisconsin began its plan of carrying information directly to the people of the State. In 1926 the American Association for Adult Education was formed as a clearing house for all activities in adult education. During 1932, the Association made studies of experiments in Opportunity Schools, which are experiments in occupational education. In 1933, the Adjustment Service of New York was established which would aid about 14,000 individuals with counselor aid and expert tests. The National Occupational Conference, with headquarters in New York City, was established in 1933 to serve as a clearing house for occupational information.

The public library, though not formally a part of this movement, is of very great importance. Some State library commissions maintain traveling collections to send to isolated regions without other access to books. The new conception of the functions of a public library includes adult education. The museums too reach out to the public by means of publications, exhibits, loans and classes.

Private correspondence schools as a method of adult education have enrolled as many as 1,500,000 new students annually.

University extension in the United States has grown steadily since 1900 and is the most important factor numerically in adult education in the United States. Adult education is also fostered by the large religious and social organizations.

The workers' education movement formed the Workers' Education Bureau of America in 1921, which became the agency of the adult education program of the American Federation of Labor.

Community organization, in order to shape its own adult education, is exemplified in the Adult Education Association of Cleveland, Ohio, the Buffalo Educational Council, and like associations in Chicago, Detroit, St. Louis, Brooklyn, Dallas, etc. A National Community Conference has been formed and the community movement for adult education is taking shape in larger towns and even in rural communities. The first community wide plan, using the entire school system and conducted by school officials was established in 1933 at Des Moines, Iowa, and was financed by the Carnegie Corporation of New York.

Bibliography.—Consult *Bulletins* and *The International Handbook of Adult Education* of the World Association for Adult Education; Yeaxlee's *Lifelong Education* (1929); Newman's *Some Notes on Adult Education in England* (1930); Cartwright and Ely's *Adult Education in the U.S.A.* (1929); Whipple's *Adult Education* (1931); Alderman, *Adult Education* (1928-30); C. H. Judd, *Problem of Education in the U. S.* (1933). The Division of Adult and Civic Education, Office of Education, was discontinued during World War II.

Adulteration (Latin *adulterare*, 'to debase,' 'to corrupt,' 'to render impure'), a term applied generally to the practice of adding cheaper substances to articles of commerce, or of abstracting from them one or more of their valuable ingredients for separate sale, with the purpose of making a greater profit. While all adulterations are to be condemned on the ground of fraud, the adulteration of food and drugs, as affecting health and nutrition of the community, is held to be the most serious offense.

In the United States practically nothing was done officially to prevent food adulteration until about 1880. In 1881 the Division of Chemistry of the U. S. Department of Agriculture began a series of investigations. In 1883 the first practical food inspection law was enacted by Massachusetts; and by 1906, when the national Pure Food and Drug Law (q.v.) was passed, 25 States had special regulations as to the purity and methods of labelling foods and drugs.

As the discovery of fraud and consequent exposure is often the most salutary form of punishment, the detection of food adulteration becomes highly important. In the United States this is effected mainly by two agencies, chemical analysis and microscopical examination, employed for the purpose by inspectors under the Pure Food and Drug Law, or State and local enactments.

All foods and drugs imported from foreign countries are required to fulfil the conditions laid down in the Pure Food and Drug Law.

The U. S. Department of Agriculture has established 'Standards of Purity' for all food products, which have been published in the Department's Circulars. See PURE FOOD AND DRUG LAW; MEAT, *Government Inspection;* PACKING INDUSTRY.

Consult Blyth's *Foods: Their Composition and Analysis* (a manual and a history) (1927); Brooks' *Critical Studies in the Legal Chemistry of Foods,* for chemists, food inspection officials, and manufacturers and dealers in food products (1927); Chase and Schlink's *Your Money's Worth* (1927); Kallet and Schlink's 100,000,000 *Guinea Pigs, Dangers in Everyday Foods, Drugs and Cosmetics* (1933); Liverseege's *Adulteration and Analysis of Foods and Drugs* (1932); Martin's *Practical Food Inspection* (2 vols. 1932).

Adultery is the voluntary sexual intercourse of one spouse with any person except the other spouse. It was punished severely by the Jewish and Roman laws, and under the canon law was held a good ground for separation, though the marriage itself was indissoluble.

Adultery is not a criminal offense at the common law either in England or America, though a number of States of the United States have by statute made it punishable with more or less severity. See DIVORCE.

Ad Valorem (Latin, 'according to value'), a phrase used in levying customs duties, when the duties on the goods are fixed, not according to weight, size, or number, but at rates proportioned to the value of the goods as estimated and sworn to by the owner and confirmed by customs authorities.

Advance Guard, a detachment of troops detailed from the main body to protect it on the march against sudden attack and to give time for deployment.

Advancement of Science, American Association for the, an organization formed to promote scientific research and the dissemination of scientific knowledge. The Association, formed in 1848, is one of the largest scientific bodies in the United States. It publishes *Science,* a weekly magazine.

Advance Note, a draft, generally for a month's wages, given to sailors by shipowners when they sign articles of agreement.

Advent (Latin *adventus,* 'the coming'), a season of preparation for the festival of Christmas. In the Greek Church, the Advent period comprises forty days; and similarly, in the earliest authentic note of Advent, a canon of the Council of Mâcon (581 A.D.), fasting three times a week is enjoined from the feast of St. Martin (Nov. 11) to the Nativity. In England, this forty days' fast was observed even after Bede's death (735), though Gregory the Great (590-604) had restricted the season to the four Sundays of Advent, now observed in the Roman Catholic communion and the Church of England. The ecclesiastical year commences with the First Sunday in Advent.

Advent, Second. While it was formerly held that the coming of Christ was fourfold—(1) at His Nativity; (2) to His disciples at His death; (3) at the fall of Jerusalem; (4) at the Day of Judgment—the term Second Advent is now usually restricted to the last mentioned, when He shall appear 'the second time without sin unto salvation.'

Adverb, a part of speech generally modifying verbs, adjectives, or other adverbs; frequently formed from the corresponding adjective by the addition of 'ly.' See PARTS OF SPEECH.

Adverse Possession, in law, designates the undisturbed occupancy of real estate by some one other than the true owner, for a specified term of years, the length of the term being fixed by statute—usually twenty years.

Advertising is defined as the application of the force of organized publicity to business. It is associated today mainly with printed forms, though oral advertising doubtless preceded the written or chiselled word, and was employed soon after barter began among men.

The public notice was a means of disseminating information as early as Babylonian times, and a clay tablet of Babylon bears an inscription of cattle and feed for sale. An Egyptian papyrus in the British Museum containing a notice of a runaway slave and of a reward offered for his apprehension is assuredly the first known advertisement on material which can be classed as paper. The Greeks and Romans painted signs on walls in public places, the announcements still to be observed in Pompeii and Herculaneum being distinctly of an advertising character. The crier was another means of calling the attention of the populace to wares for sale, in Greece and probably elsewhere.

The Middle Ages witnessed a great vogue of public criers. Posters were also painted, chiefly as the signs of the guilds, and signboards were much favored in France by innkeepers and shopkeepers. An ordinance of 1567 required the keeper of an inn to report his 'enseigne,' and a royal decree of 1616 limited the size of these devices, probably in the interest of public safety, so great was the rivalry among enterprising advertisers to engage attention by their signs. The trademarks of artificers to identify the origin of goods must also be regarded as advertising. Printing afforded the first means of broadcasting announcements, and the handbills which followed soon upon its invention were advertising.

In America, one of the earliest records of advertising was in John Campbell's Boston *News Letter.*

The idea of advertising was well recognized in the latter half of the 18th century, though the mediums for its expression were limited in their circulation and influence. The founding of daily newspapers naturally gave it a strong impetus, while the perfection of the cylinder press was a further aid, permitting the increasing of circulations to a point never before thought of.

It can hardly be denied that the first persons to appraise correctly the power of mass advertising were those who used it to mislead the public by extravagant language, for though the early announcements of local tradesmen were, in general, models of sober utterance, the patent medicine men, then as now, promised far more than their physicks could perform. Such extravagant claims brought the whole practice of advertising into a disrepute, in the eyes of many, from which it was long in recovering. But economic and business forces were at work which were to demand just such an aid to distribution as advertising afforded. It was soon realized that so potent an ally of business must be cleansed of its bad reputation, and the era of greater honesty in announcements began.

A strong factor in the spread of newspaper advertising was the influence, in the three decades after 1850, of such journals as the New York newspapers. The greatest increase in volume, however, came in the period of business expansion between 1880 and 1900, and has grown enormously since.

The annual total of advertising expenditure in America is broken up into many divisions, covering a great variety of mediums and methods, the newest of which are radio, also sky-writing.

There have been interesting shifts of emphasis and volume in advertising. Up to 1890 *outdoor, painted sign* advertising represented the largest volume; the fences and barns of millions of farmers carrying ads. Between 1890 and 1905 the *newspaper* carried the largest volume of advertising. Between 1905 and 1920 the *magazine* was the leader, if not quite in total volume, then in prestige and special advertising interest. Between 1920 and 1928 the newspaper swung back into a position of leadership—only to have its supremacy challenged in 1928 by radio broadcasting, which soon reached well over $100,000,000 annually. Advertising agencies set up radio divisions and developed special features which advertisers sponsored. National advertising during World War II, despite wartime uncertainties, did not decrease as greatly as had been expected.

America has distinctly led the world in the development of advertising, although in the creation of artistic posters (upon which Continental Europe heavily relies for advertising), France, Germany and Switzerland have been leaders. England is not a great distance behind America, and has in particular increased the vogue of modern advertising in recent years. Newspapers are extensively relied upon there; whereas the newspapers of Continental Europe are minor advertising factors. The magazine in all of Europe is secondary. The international advertising club conventions since 1919 have stimulated interest in advertising abroad. Some American advertising agencies maintain branch offices abroad to handle the foreign advertising of American concerns.

Bibliography.—Hollingsworth's *Advertising and Selling* (1913); D. Starch, *Principles of Advertising* (1923); J. G. Frederick, *Masters of Advertising Copy* (1925); Haase, *Advertising Appropriation* (1931); F. H. Young, *Advertising Layout* (1928); R. S. Durstine, *This Advertising Business* (1928); Haase and Keeler, *The Advertising Agency* (1930); Frederick, *Business Research and Statistics* (1923); Tobias, *Profitable Retail Advertising* (1930); Ramsey, *Effective Direct Advertising* (1921); *How to Get a Job and Win Success at Advertising*, by W. A. Lowen and L. E. Watson (1941).

Advocate (Latin *advocatus*) in its general sense includes any one who pleads for another in a court of law or other tribunal. In the days of the Roman Republic such a person was called *patronus* or 'orator,' and it was not until imperial times that the term *advocatus* was applied to him. In France the *avocat and avoué* correspond closely to the barrister and solicitor in England. In the United States, most of the British colonies, and some parts of Europe, the two branches of the legal profession are not kept separate. See BARRISTER; DISBAR; LAWYER; SOLICITOR.

Advocate, Lord. The Lord Advocate, or His Majesty's Advocate, is the chief law officer of the crown in Scotland, and one of the great officers of state. He represents the sovereign in all proceedings which affect the royal or public interest.

Advocates' Library, in Edinburgh, Scotland, is the largest and most important library in Scotland. It was founded in 1682, and in 1709 received the privilege of obtaining free a copy of every book published in the United Kingdom.

Ædiles, (Ediles), magistrates of ancient Rome, who were entrusted with the care of public buildings, streets, markets, weights and measures, etc.; fixed the prices of foodstuffs; were the custodians of the decrees of the senate and of the people; and maintained public order. The public games and spectacles were arranged by the ædiles.

Ædui, or **Hædui,** one of the most powerful tribes in Gaul at the time of Cæsar's arrival (58 B.C.). They formed an alliance with Cæsar, but joined the rest of the Gauls in the final struggle for independence. After his victory, Cæsar treated them leniently for the sake of their old alliance.

Æetes, or **Aeeta,** in Greek mythology, son of Helios and Perseis, was king of Colchis (Æa) when Jason, the leader of the

Argonauts, sought the golden fleece. His daughter Medea (called by the poets Æetis) assisted Jason to obtain the prize, and left Colchis as his wife. See ARGONAUTS.

Ægean Sea, the n.e. division of the Mediterranean, between Greece, Turkey, and Asia Minor. Its waters are relatively shallow, and studded with islands (the Greek Archipelago), and its shores are greatly indented. The greatest depth, between Samos and Chios, is only 640 fathoms.

Ægeus, in classic mythology, son of Pandion and father of Theseus, and king of Athens, where he introduced the cult of Aphrodite. When Theseus went to Crete to deliver Athens from the tribute to Minos, he promised his father he would hoist a white sail on his return, as a signal of safety. But in the intoxication of his victory he forgot his promise, and his father, perceiving the black sail, thought that his son had perished, and threw himself into the sea, which, from this event, received the name of the Ægean.

Ægina, a Greek island, now **Egina,** area 33 sq. m., in the Gulf of Ægina (the ancient *Saronicus Sinus*). It is mountainous, with deep valleys and chasms. The most ancient name of the island was Œnone, and the Myrmidons dwelt in its valleys and caverns. For a century before the Persian War it was prosperous, and the chief seat of Greek art. In the eastern part of the island stand the ruins of a temple of Pallas Athene. A series of statues excavated there are now the most remarkable ornaments of the Glyptothek at Munich. They probably date from about fifty years before Phidias. The considerable remains left of the ancient city attest its size and importance; p. 4,700.

Ægina, Gulf of, or **Saronic Gulf,** between the Greek peninsulas of Attica on the north and Argolis on the south.

Ægis, in mythology, the cloud surrounding the thunderbolts of Zeus, Apollo, and Athena. The word is now used as a symbol of protection or patronage.

Ægisthus, son of Thyestes and cousin of Agamemnon, mentioned by Homer, Sophocles and Euripides.

Ægium, town, ancient Greece, one of the twelve towns of Achaia, and its capital after the destruction of Helice (373 B.C.). According to legend, the birthplace of Zeus.

Ægyptus, son of Belus and Anchinoe, and twin brother of Danaus. He received Arabia from his father, and, conquering the land of the Nile, called it Egypt, after himself.

Ælfred Atheling, son of Æthelred II. and Emma; taken with his brother Edward (afterward the Confessor) to their uncle, Richard the Good of Normandy. In 1036, on the death of Canute, the claims of Ælfred and Edward to the English throne were set aside by the Witan. Ælfred landed at Dover with a force of Normans, but was attacked and captured by Earl Godwin, who cruelly blinded him; he died from his injuries at Ely.

Ælfric (called *Grammaticus*, 'the Grammarian'), a voluminous Old English writer about the close of the 10th century. His most important work is his collection of *Homilies*, eighty in number, edited by Thorpe for the Ælfric Society (1844-6).

Æmilian Way, a famous Roman road built in 187 B.C. by Marcus Æmilius Lepidus, Roman consul.

Æneas, the hero of Virgil's *Æneid*, was, according to Homer, the son of Anchises and Aphrodite (Venus), and ranked next to Hector among the Trojan heroes.

Æneas Silvius. See **Pius II.**

Æneid. See **Æneas; Virgil.**

Æolian Deposits, formations due to the action of the wind, such as the sandhills or dunes of many maritime regions, and the similar hillocks which occur in the Sahara, in Arabia, Utah, Arizona, etc.

Æolian Harp, a simple musical instrument formed by stretching eight or ten catgut strings of various thickness, all tuned in unison, over a wooden shell or box.

Æolian Islands. See **Lipari Islands.**

Æolian Mode in Music. See **Mode.**

Æolians, one of the principal races of the Greek people, who were originally settled in Thessaly, from which they spread and formed numerous settlements in the northern part of Greece and in the Western Peloponnesus. Their dialect was generally regarded as the oldest form of Hellenic speech.

Æolipile (Latin 'ball of Æolus'), a hollow metal ball. When the water in the globe is heated, and steam rushes out of the tubes, rotation is set up. It was invented by Hero of Alexandria about 120 B.C. See TURBINES, STEAM.

Æolotropy (from Greek words for 'changeful' and 'turning'), or ANISTROPY, is the opposite of *isotropy,* and implies change in the electrical, optical, or other physical properties of bodies in consequence of change of position. See ISOTROPY.

Æolus (Greek 'fleet'), in Greek mythology, the god of the winds and ruler of the Æolian (Lipari) Islands, where he kept the several winds immured in a cave.

Æon, a cosmological term signifying an age, an indefinitely long period of time, an era.

Æpinus, Franz Maria Ulrich Theodor (1724-1802), German physicist who discovered the electric properties of turmaline and devised many new experiments in electricity. He held the 'single fluid' theory of electricity.

Æqui, a warlike tribe of ancient Italy who inhabited the upper valley and hills to the southeast of the River Anio, on the eastern border of Latium. They waged constant warfare with Rome up to their final defeat in 304 B.C.

Aerated Bread is bread not fermented with yeast, but mechanically charged with carbonic acid gas, the gas being derived usually from carbonic acid water. See BREAD.

Aerated Waters, a name applied to the large class of beverages which are rendered sparkling by dissolving in them carbonic acid under pressure. The term does not include champagne or other carbonated beverage in which the carbonic acid gas is produced by the natural process of fermentation.

The temperance drinks, which include such favorites as lemonade, ginger ale, ginger beer, and tonic bitters, are made by putting the requisite quantity of flavoring syrup into a bottle, and filling up with simple aerated water.

Aeration, in plants, is the process by which interchange of gases takes place between the plant tissues and the surrounding medium.

Aerial Mail. See **Aeronautics.**

Aerodrome, the name proposed by S. P. Langley for flying machines with wing-like appendages, has been superseded by AEROPLANE. Aerodrome now signifies aviation grounds.

Aerodynamics, that branch of hydrodynamics which treats of air and other gases in motion. See GASES; HYDROKINETICS; HYDROSTATICS.

Aeroklinoscope, the name of an instrument used, principally in Europe, in connection with weather signals for exhibiting publicly the difference of barometric pressure at different observing stations.

Aerolites. See **Meteorites.**

Aeronautics, the science and art of flight, as distinguished from *aviation,* the operation of heavier-than-air aircraft (see Airplanes).

Aeronautics passed from the speculative era to an era of experimentation in 1783 when the Montgolfier brothers constructed their first balloons in France, the first man-carrying flight being on Oct. 15, 1783, with de Rozier the passenger. In all Europe, ballooning became a great fad and the object of scientific inquiry. The first American ascent was made in Philadelphia in 1793. Early in the 19th century, interest languished, due to increased accidents and also to unsettled political conditions on the European continent.

Military interest in the balloon was aroused early; by 1794 it had been used for reconnaissance by the French. During the U. S. Civil War, two balloons were similarly used by the Union forces. Until suitable engines became available, projects to develop a navigable balloon, i.e. *dirigible,* inevitably failed. Giffard in 1852 demonstrated control possibilities in France with a semi-rigid airship equipped with a three-bladed propeller powered by a 3-hp. steam engine. The first metal airship was built in 1897 in Germany by Schwarz and was powered by a gasoline motor. It was destroyed on its first flight. Santos-Dumont, the wealthy Brazilian, and Count von Zeppelin, the German, at the close of the 19th century, did much to further the dirigible (see BALLOONS).

Man's dream of flight goes back beyond the earliest days of history, and of the several ideas conceived to attain this goal the ornithopter, or flapping wing mechanism, is the oldest. Among early speculators were Bacon and da Vinci in the 13th and 15th centuries, respectively. Da Vinci also experimented with the helicopter, a vertically rising aerial machine. Cayley's work in England in 1809 forecast the possibilities of using rigid planes to support flight, and he has correctly been called the father of the airplane idea. He also was the first to succeed in the art of gliding.

During the 19th century many men sought to develop a practical airplane. Deserving of mention are: Henson and Stringfellow, whose work was climaxed in 1848 by a 120-foot flight of a 10-foot, powered model; Penaud for his study of equilibrium and other problems of flight in the '70's; Wenham and H. F. Phillips for research on wing sections after the midcentury, using crude wind tunnels; Ader for his "avion," which was a full scale '97 "good try" airplane, and Maxim for his work with wing sections, propellers and engines in the '90's. There were others, of course, including three whose work with gliders was most important, Lilienthal, Chanute, and the Californian, Montgomery.

Except for the efforts of the Wright Brothers, the work of Langley from 1886 to 1903 probably came closest to reaching the goal of man-carrying heavier-than-air flight. Progressively he conducted his research and experimentation until, after several successful flights with large, steam powered models, he undertook construction of a full-size, gasoline-engine-powered airplane in 1898 under U. S. War Department contract. Perhaps the outstanding aspect of this was development by Manly of an engine which had a weight per horsepower of only 2.4 lbs., phenomenally low for the time. Twice in the fall of 1903 his "aerodrome" was badly damaged in launching; after the second attempt, Langley gave up his work, a broken man.

First flight of an airplane.—The Wright Brothers, Wilbur and Orville, began their aeronautic experiments in 1896. First they studied and speculated. Then they tested their ideas with kites and gliders, and in a wind tunnel they built. Early in 1903 they felt ready to attempt the "real thing." They designed and built their own airplane. They designed and built their own engine. On December 17, 1903, they made history with their first powered, man-carrying flights of an airplane from the sands of Kitty Hawk, N. C.

Although the Wright Brothers had informed the press of their first flights and in 1904 had staged unsuccessful flight demonstrations of their second airplane before the press near their home at Dayton, Ohio, the public was slow to realize that man-made flight had been attained. The scientific world, to the contrary, was thrilled by the news and soon others were taking to the skies in fledgling, powered flight. Santos-Dumont had turned his enthusiastic interest from ballooning and in 1906 was the first to fly an airplane in Europe. In rapid succession he was followed by such designer-pilots as Blériot and Farman, and such pilots as Latham and Delagrange.

If the Wrights failed to gain early general recognition in the United States—it was not until 1907 that the War Department offered to buy one of their airplanes *providing* it could carry pilot and one passenger at least 10 miles at 40 mph—the Wright conquest of Europe in 1908 was as spectacular as it was complete. In the United States Glenn Curtiss flew in 1908 and in the same year made the first officially recorded airplane flight in America. The following year, '09, the Wrights earned a $5,000 bonus over the War Department offer of $25,000, by flying at 42 mph over the prescribed course. The airplane was establishing itself, and a host of expositions and air meets, both in America and in Europe, reflected popular interest.

It was in Europe rather than in the United States, however, that greatest emphasis was now placed on theory and design. First in France and not long after in all the major European countries, the mysteries of flight were probed for scientific information. Perhaps it was the realization that an improved airplane offered great possibilities as a military weapon; in any event, government support in the absence of commercial funds was provided for such research effort. In contrast, it was not until 1915 that the United States took steps to catch up, by establishing the National Advisory Committee for Aeronautics to conduct research in this field.

World War I impetus.—By the outbreak of World War I in 1914, the airplane and its engine had been improved to the extent that altitudes higher than 18,000 feet, speeds of more than 100 mph, and distance flights of more than 700 miles had been attained. The war impetus further speeded airplane development.

During the war years, aero engines were greatly improved; the Liberty 400 hp is a good example of what was accomplished. In addition to fighters with top speeds of more than 150 mph, other multi-engine airplanes were designed to perform such special purposes as bombing. The lumbering British Handley-Page, the German Gotha and the 4-motored Russian Sikorsky deserve mention. Seaplanes, too, were rapidly advanced, to the extent that when the war ended in 1918, the U. S. Navy proposed to fly its NC-series flying boats across the Atlantic. The NC-1 on Nov. 27, 1918, had set a record by carrying 61 men on a trial flight. On May 27, 1918, the NC-4, the only one of three to succeed in the attempt, became the first airplane to have flown the Atlantic. On June 15 of the same year, Alcock and Brown flew the ocean nonstop, from Newfoundland to Ireland.

It has been said that within the time of World War I was compressed aeronautical progress which normally would have needed 20 years. Certainly, at the end of the war, there was to be a period when aeronautical interest was relatively fallow. There were too many thousands of unused airplanes and engines to make attractive the financial risk involved in designing and manufacturing new airplanes and engines. Further, the airplane had not yet proven itself, except in a very limited way, as a vehicle of real commercial value. There were, of course, exceptions. Ambitious pioneers, operating with extremely limited funds, did continue their efforts to build other, more useful airplanes, and gradually, the airplane began to demonstrate that it had commercial possibilities.

In a very small way, regularly scheduled transport of mail by air had begun in the United States May 15, 1918, between New York and Washington, with the Army providing the service for the Post Office. The first American mail carried by commercial air operators went from Seattle, Wash., to Vancouver, B. C., beginning March 3, 1919, and on September 8, 1920, transcontinental air mail service was first provided. In 1924 this transcontinental service was established on a 24-hour basis with completion of lighted airways. The following year, 1925, passage of the first Air Mail Act provided for the transfer of air-mail operations to private air carriers. This carriage of mail by air did much during the twenties to encourage initial development of airplanes of higher performance, designed for commercial rather than military use.

Post-War Period.—Although the military services were greatly hampered by their lack of procurement funds, they did what they could to foster aeronautical development in the post-war period. One device was the constant effort made to keep the airplane in the public eye. This was accomplished by the determined attempts to establish new records for distance, load-carrying, altitude and speed. Some examples would include the world altitude record flight in 1920, when Maj. R. W. Schroeder reached 33,113 feet, the world endurance record of 26 hrs. plus, by "Eddie" Stinson and Lloyd Bertaud in 1921 (a record soon broken by Kelly and Macready who were in the air almost 37 hours; in 1923 Kelly and Macready flew nonstop across the continent). Perhaps the most spectacular of these flights was the first round-the-world flight made by Army pilots in 1924, from April to September 28. Of four Douglas biplanes, powered by a single Liberty engine, two completed the entire trip, a distance of 26,445 miles. They had taken 175 days, and been in the air 368 hours.

At what is now Wright-Patterson Field near Dayton the Army airmen in these years were busy seeking ways and means of improving aircraft performance at little cost. The Navy, too, was engaged in such work. So

were private individuals. Godfrey L. Cabot, then a Navy lieutenant, from 1918 to 1920 did considerable work with the problem of refueling in flight. In 1919 Leslie L. Irvin made a successful jump, using a manually operated parachute. Propellers, capable of being reversed, were tested. Leak-proof gasoline tanks were developed. Dr. Sanford A. Moss of General Electric developed a supercharger for aircraft engines. In engines, development of radial air-cooled engines, championed by Charles L. Lawrance, offered new power possibilities.

In the field of research, American scientists were laying the foundations which would enable the United States to gain world leadership in aeronautics. Especially in its fundamental research in aerodynamics and related subjects, the NACA's Langley, Va. Laboratory was making important contributions. The NACA, an unpaid committee of outstanding civil and government aeronautic authorities, gives direction to the activities of a corps of scientists and supporting personnel, working under civil service.

Even before World War I attempts had been made to establish commercial air travel service, but with one or two exceptions, until the private companies began carrying the mail in 1926 these ventures were little more than "air-taxi" operations. One such exception was the service provided from Chicago to Cleveland. In 1923 Henry Ford had come to the financial rescue of William B. Stout, whose development of an all-metal monoplane transport with thick wing interested the motor magnate. Later versions of this airplane were known as the Ford tri-motor, and some of them were in use as late as 1938, hauling heavy cargo. The Chicago-Cleveland service began April 3, 1925, without benefit of air mail contracts. These came later, when Ford's line was the first to carry air mail, under the Act of '25, beginning on February 15, 1926.

Then, as commercial air transport expanded —and also because the supply of war surplus equipment was nearly exhausted—there soon came a steady procession of airplanes especially designed for the carriage of passengers and mail. Fokker tri-motors, Curtiss Condors, Lockheeds and Boeing transports were among the best known and most widely used. Sikorsky and Consolidated built flying boats. The Douglas DC-2 and DC-3, destined to become standard equipment on air lines around the world, would not appear until 1934.

In Europe air-mail and passenger service between London and Paris had begun in 1919. The same year Ross McPherson Smith won a $50,000 prize, flying from England to Australia. European governments gave subsidy-support to both manufacturers and air transport companies in these post-war years. Despite a widespread feeling in America at the time to the contrary, there is little evidence of European superiority in this period except in isolated instances.

Autogiros and Helicopters.—One such instance was the success which the Spaniard Juan de la Cierva achieved with the autogiro. Designed in 1920, it consisted of a fuselage, landing gear, engine, and tractor propeller. Its fixed wings were so small as to appear vestigial. Above the fuselage, four struts converged to support a vertical drive shaft, coupled to the forward-located engine, which powered a four-bladed rotor system. Except during take-off, the blades rotated without engine power, providing adequate lift for flight. The autogiro first flew in 1923, and was demonstrated to the British Air Ministry in 1925. It approached hovering flight and could land almost vertically. It was built in limited quantity both in Europe and the United States, and might today be used except for the successful development of the helicopter.

For centuries, the thought of being able to ascend into the air vertically intrigued those who dreamed of flight. Even development of the fixed-wing airplane did not entirely cause this dream to fade. Both in the United States and in Europe, there were those who continued to seek this goal. In America Berliner, as early as 1908, was working with the helicopter idea, and by 1922 both he and de Bothezat had constructed full-size machines which, in demonstrations before Army officials, managed a few seconds of shaky flight during which they remained substantially stationary in the air, or climbed or descended vertically. But neither was improved to the point where it could be considered a practical flight vehicle. The first practical helicopter was the Focke-Achgelis, which in 1937 flew from Bremen to Berlin in Germany.

But the most positive helicopter success was scored by Igor Sikorsky, also known for his early work with large, multi-engine airplanes in Russia during World War I and before, and later, for his development of flying boats in the United States. As early as 1908, Sikorsky had investigated the helicopter principle, but soon turned his attention to other aeronautical problems. In the mid-thirties he resumed his work on the helicopter and by 1939 had constructed the first of a line of helicopters which he has since manufactured for both military and commercial use.

The Sikorsky helicopters utilize a single rotor system. So does the Bell helicopter, developed by that company during World War II as a private venture. The Bell machine, the first ever to be licensed for commercial use, incorporates a special stabilizing device. The Piasecki helicopter uses a tandem rotor system, and in 1951 was being built in large number for military use. Hiller, Kaman, McDonnell and Seibel are among other companies interested in the helicopter.

In 1947 inauguration of helicopter air mail shuttle service was authorized for the greater Los Angeles area, and later was established also in metropolitan Chicago. In both cities, over a period of years, the service provided by the helicopter has been successful. Other commercial uses of the helicopter include insect pest control, aerial crop seeding, forest fire fighting, aerial photography, etc. In the Korean conflict which began in the summer of 1950 helicopters gave outstanding performance in rescue and other close support work.

The Lindbergh Flight.—By the spring of 1927 public interest in America had been developing to a point where only some single exploit was needed to touch off a wave of great enthusiasm (see Post-War Period, above). Since May 30, 1919, the Orteig prize of $25,000 had been waiting for the first man to make a non-stop flight between New York and Paris. There had been unsuccessful attempts, but now other aviators made preparations for such a flight. Among such contenders for the prize were Commander Richard E. Byrd with a Fokker tri-motor; Clarence Chamberlin with a Bellanca monoplane, and Charles A. Lindbergh, with a Ryan monoplane. Only Lindbergh proposed to fly alone.

Lindbergh was first to take off from Roosevelt Field, leaving at 7.25 a.m. the morning of May 20, 1927. Early the same evening he flew over St. John's, N. B. For the first half of his flight he fought sleet and fog, but then the weather cleared. The next morning he sighted Ireland, and by mid-afternoon flew over England. His landing at Le Bourget airport, outside Paris, came 33 hours, 39 minutes after take-off; he had flown non-stop 3,605 miles.

Public response was immediate. The "Lone

Eagle" received immense praise and adulation. In the nearly 25 years since, Lindbergh's life has been full of accomplishment, and tragedy. He and his wife—Anne Morrow—blazed air trails across the Atlantic and Pacific which later became commercial routes. He served manufacturers and air lines in important consulting capacities. In the thirties, a son was kidnapped and murdered. Lindbergh became the object of national abuse and misunderstanding for his views about the German air force, prior to World War II, but subsequently he was largely vindicated for the realistic views he had taken. His work during the war years was also important, and the presentation, in 1949, of the Wright Award to him was by way of recognizing his services to the nation over many years.

Quickly following Lindbergh's Paris flight were others. Chamberlin flew non-stop 3,911 miles, landing 118 miles outside Berlin. The Byrd Fokker was beset by fog on its flight, landing on the beach at Ver-Sur-Mer in France. In 1927, three trans-Atlantic flight attempts ended in disaster. Amelia Earhart was a member of the crew of the "Friendship" which made the west-east crossing in 1928. By the following year most interest in this exploit had subsided.

Prevailing winds made the east-west Atlantic flight more hazardous, and numerous attempts failed. It was not until 1928 that the team of von Huenefeld, Koehl and Fitzmaurice succeeded in a German Junkers monoplane. Even their flight was marred by a crash landing at Greenley Island, Straits of Belle Isle, Labrador, after they had bucked heavy winds for 34 hours. The first Paris-New York non-stop flight was made in September, 1930, by Coste and Bellonte.

Other Atlantic Flights.—In 1931 Boardman and Polando flew a Bellanca monoplane across the Atlantic, establishing a non-stop distance record of 5,011 miles when they landed in Istanbul, Turkey. In 1932 Miss Earhart (see above) became the first woman to fly the ocean non-stop. Also in 1932, the 12-engine German Do-X flying boat crossed the North Atlantic, via the Azores. In 1933 Gen. Italo Balbo led a formation of 24 Savoia Marchetti seaplanes on a round trip, multi-stop flight from Italy to Chicago which was without accident. Flights across the Atlantic were becoming commonplace. In 1938 Douglas G. Corrigan won brief notoriety by his "wrong-way" flight from New York to Dublin, Ire. in a 9-year-old, single-engine Curtiss Robin monoplane.

After painstaking preparations and numerous survey flights, transatlantic air mail and passenger service from New York to London and Paris was inaugurated in May, 1939, by Pan American Airways, using Boeing 307 flying boats. The Germans had begun flying the shorter, safer South Atlantic route in 1934. In the years following World War II American air carriers competed with foreign lines, transporting tens of thousands of passengers across the Atlantic every 12 months. During the war, thousands of military aircraft were ferried over the ocean to speed up the time when they could be used in combat.

In 1948 jet fighters crossed the Atlantic, both ways. On September 22, Col. David C. Schilling crossed, non-stop, in a Republic F-84-E Thunderbolt, from Manston, Eng., to Limestone, Me., in 10 hrs., 2 minutes. The flight was remarkable because it involved three aerial refuelings, over Scotland and Iceland and, the third, between Labrador and Greenland. A second Thunderbolt, piloted by Lt. Col. William A. Ritchie, was crashed in Labrador, when the refueling device failed. Ritchie was unhurt. On January 31, 1951, Charles F. Blair, Jr., flying a World War II P-51 Mustang, flew non-stop from New York to London in 7 hrs., 48 min. The previous record was 8 hrs., 55 min.

Polar Flights.—Although proposals to engage in arctic exploration, using airplanes, had been made as early as 1914, it was not until 1925 that the first such flights were made by Lieut. Comdr. Richard E. Byrd and Donald B. MacMillan. Using Navy amphibians, some 700,000 square miles were surveyed that year. In May, 1926, Byrd and Floyd Bennett, the pilot, flew over the North Pole, from Spitzbergen, in a tri-motor Fokker monoplane. In April, 1928, Sir Hubert Wilkins with Carl B. Eielson, pilot, flew in a Lockheed Vega monoplane from Point Barrow, Alaska, to Spitzbergen in a 2,200 m. polar hop that passed near the Pole.

Byrd led an expedition to the antarctic in the fall of 1925, and in November, 1929, flew over the South Pole. Bernt Balchen was pilot of the tri-motor Ford monoplane used. Byrd led other antarctic expeditions in 1933-35, 1939-41, and 1946-47. Airplanes and a helicopter were used. In July, 1937, three Russian flyers crossed over the North Pole on a record-breaking 6,262-mile flight from Moscow to San Jacinto, Cal., in 62 hrs., 2 min. Following World War II, U. S. Air Force pilots flew over the North Pole hundreds of times on long-range weather flights from

Alaska. It must be presumed that Soviet pilots have been similarly engaged.

Transcontinental flights.—The first airplane crossing of the United States, from New York to California, was completed Nov. 5, 1911. Calbraith P. Rodgers had taken 49 days to cover the 3,390 m. Numerous accidents required virtual rebuilding of his plane, which was accompanied by a special train. The first non-stop flight, from New York to San Diego, Cal. was made in May, 1923, requiring 26 hrs., 50 min. for the 2,520 m. In June 1924, Lieut. Russell Maughan made the first dawn-to-dusk flight from New York to San Francisco in 18 hrs., 26 min. In the years that followed, the west-east flight from metropolitan Los Angeles to metropolitan New York became a popular yardstick of sustained speed. Prevailing high winds often aided the pilots in their attempts.

In April, 1930, Frank Hawks crossed from San Diego to New York in a glider towed by an airplane, making the 2,860 m. in 36 hrs., 47 min. John M. Miller made the transcontinental flight, with numerous refueling stops, in an autogiro in May, 1931. In September, 1933, Roscoe Turner flew west to east in 10 hrs., 4 min. In January, 1936, Howard Hughes lowered the time in a Northrop Gamma to 9 hrs., 27 min., and in January, 1937, lowered it again in a Hughes racer to 7 hrs., 28 min. In January, 1950, Paul Mantz flew a P-51 Mustang fighter the distance in 4 hrs., 52 min. Col. W. H. Council made the flight in 4 hrs., 13 min. in a jet-propelled F-80 Shooting Star, averaging 580 mph. In February, 1949, a B-47 6-jet bomber flew from Moses Lake, Was., to Washington, D. C., in 3 hrs., 46 min., 2,289 m., averaging 607 mph.

The records mentioned in the paragraph above were established by either racing or military airplanes. Beginning in the thirties, commercial transport airplanes began establishing records, too. In April, 1935, a TWA Douglas DC-2 made the transcontinental flight in 11 hrs., 5 min. By April, 1944, the record had been cut to 6 hrs., 58 min., this time by a TWA Lockheed Constellation. In February, 1949, this was again cut by a Constellation to 6 hrs., 17 min.

Pacific Flights.—The first flight from the West Coast to Hawaii was made in August, 1925, by a Navy flying boat under Comdr. John Rodgers, and came within 15 miles of success before crashing into the sea. In June, 1927, Lieuts. L. J. Maitland and A. F. Hegenberger succeeded in the Hawaii flight, covering 2,407 miles in 25 hrs., 50 min. in an Army Fokker tri-motor. In July, 1928, civilians Ernest Smith and Emory B. Bronte made the flight. Amelia Earhart made the first solo flight in January, 1935.

June 9, 1938, the "Southern Cross" monoplane, piloted by Kingsford-Smith and Ulm, completed the first flight from the United States to Australia, a distance of 7,300 miles. The following year, they completed a 'round-the-world flight. The first non-stop flight of the Pacific, from Japan to the United States, was made in 41 hours on October, 1931, by Clyde Pangborn and Hugh Herndon. By 1935, Pan American Airways had inaugurated air mail service, followed soon by passenger service, from San Francisco to Manila using Martin flying boats. In August, 1947, six B-29 Superfortresses made a record-breaking flight from Tokyo to Washington. In March, 1949, William Odom flew a single-engine light plane, the Beech Bonanza, 4,957 m. from Hawaii to New Jersey in 36 hrs.

Around - the - world flights. — The first 'round-the-world flight (see above, *Post-war period*) in 1924 required 175 days. On July 1, 1931, Wiley Post and Harold Gatty completed such a flight, having flown 16,500 m. in a single-engine Lockheed monoplane, the "Winnie Mae" in 8 days, 13 hrs., 51 min. Post, flying solo in the same plane, bettered that record in July, 1933, with the time of 7 days, 18 hrs.

In June, 1937, Amelia Earhart and Fred Noonan were lost near the Howland Islands in the Pacific. Howard Hughes, flying a two-engine Lockheed transport, set a new record when he and his crew made the flight in 91 hrs., 14 min. in July, 1938.

After World War II, 'round-the-world flights became commonplace. In September, 1945, the Military inaugurated regular service with a Douglas C-54 transport, making the flight in 149 hrs. It soon became possible to fly around the globe in almost as fast time using only scheduled, commercial air transport. William Odom, flying solo in a twin-engine Douglas A-26 light bomber, circled the earth in August, 1947, in 73 hrs., and the following November, Truman and Evans flew around the world in two Piper Cubs, small private-type monoplanes. The "Lucky Lady II," a B-29 Superfortress made the flight non-stop in March, 1949. Refueling four times in flight, it followed a longer route, traveling 23,452 m. in 94 hrs.

Distance and other flights.—In 1908, Wilbur Wright made history with a non-stop flight of 77.5 miles. In the years after World

NORTH AMERICA

LAMBERT AZIMUTHAL EQUAL-AREA PROJECTION

SCALE OF MILES
0 200 400 600 800

SCALE OF KILOMETRES
0 200 400 600 800

Capitals of Countries........ ★
International Boundaries....
Other Boundaries..........
Canals.....................
Railroads..................

Copyright by C.S. HAMMOND & Co., N.Y.

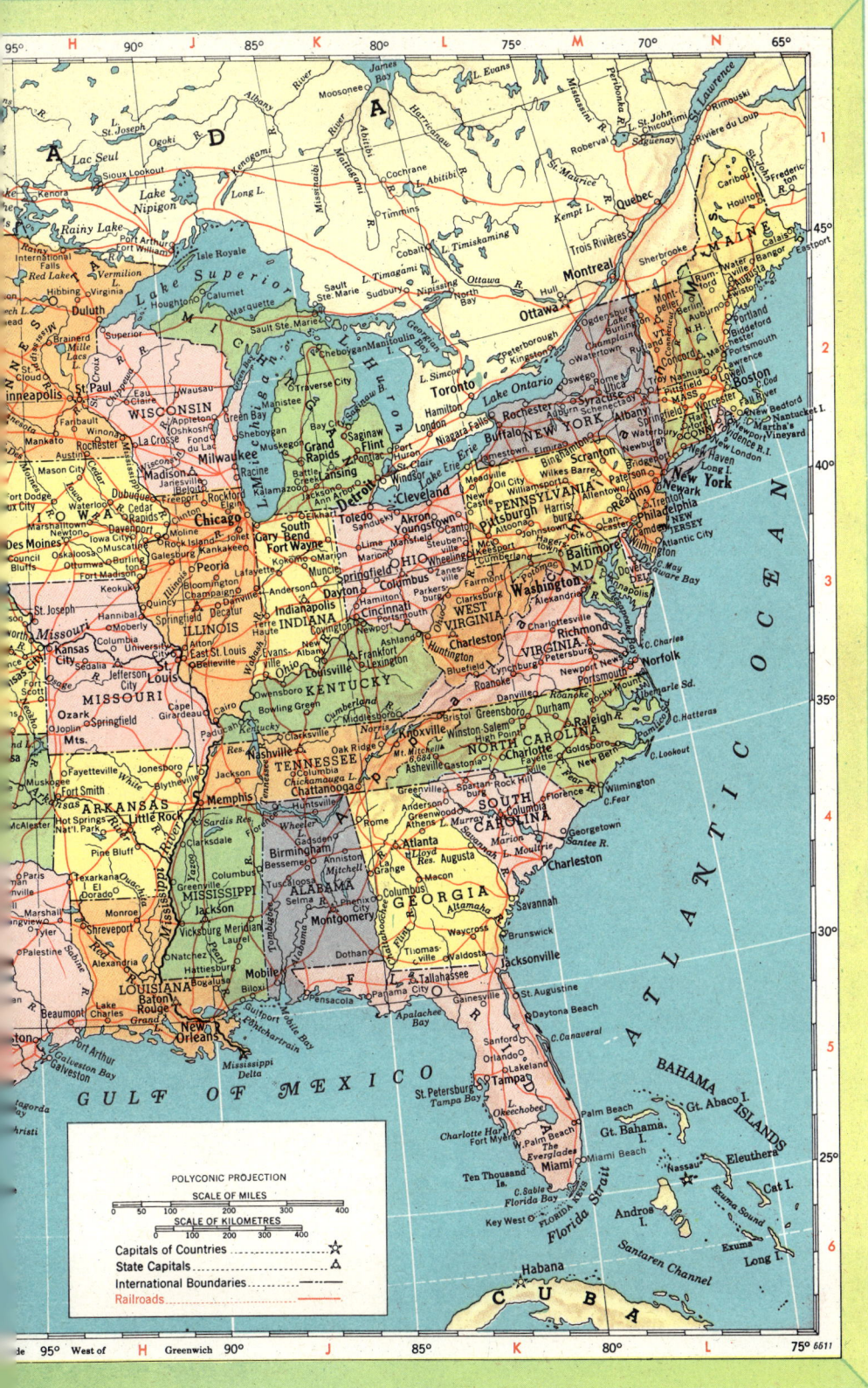

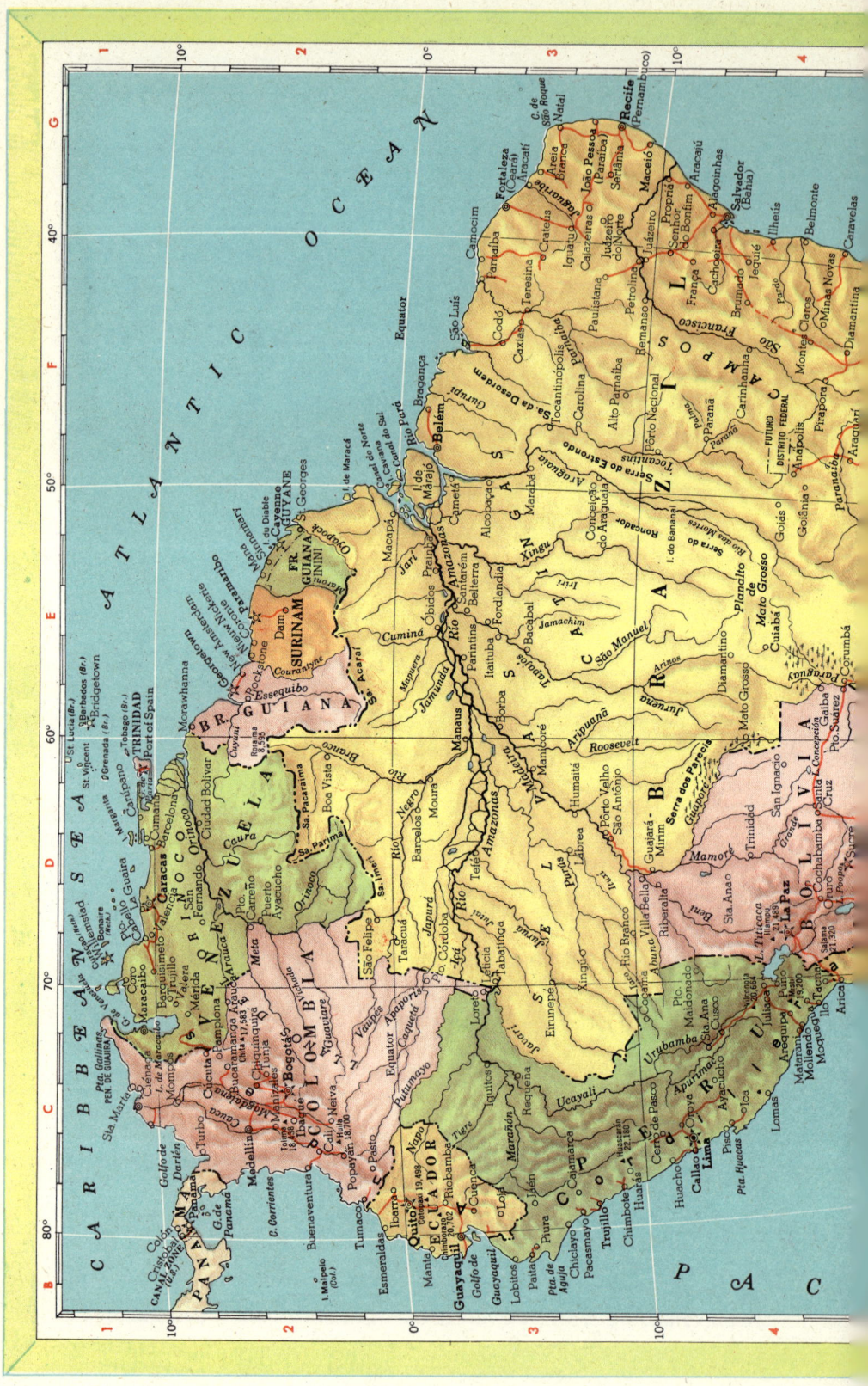

EUROPE

LAMBERT AZIMUTHAL EQUAL-AREA PROJECTION

SCALE OF MILES
0 100 200 300 400 500

SCALE OF KILOMETRES
0 100 200 300 400 500

Capitals of Countries............ ☆
International Boundaries........ -·-·-
Canals.................................
Railroads............................ ―――

Copyright by C. S. HAMMOND & CO., N.Y.

ASIA

LAMBERT AZIMUTHAL EQUAL-AREA PROJECTION

SCALE OF MILES
SCALE OF KILOMETRES

Capitals of Countries ....★   Canals ....
International Boundaries ....   Railroads ....
Elevations in Feet

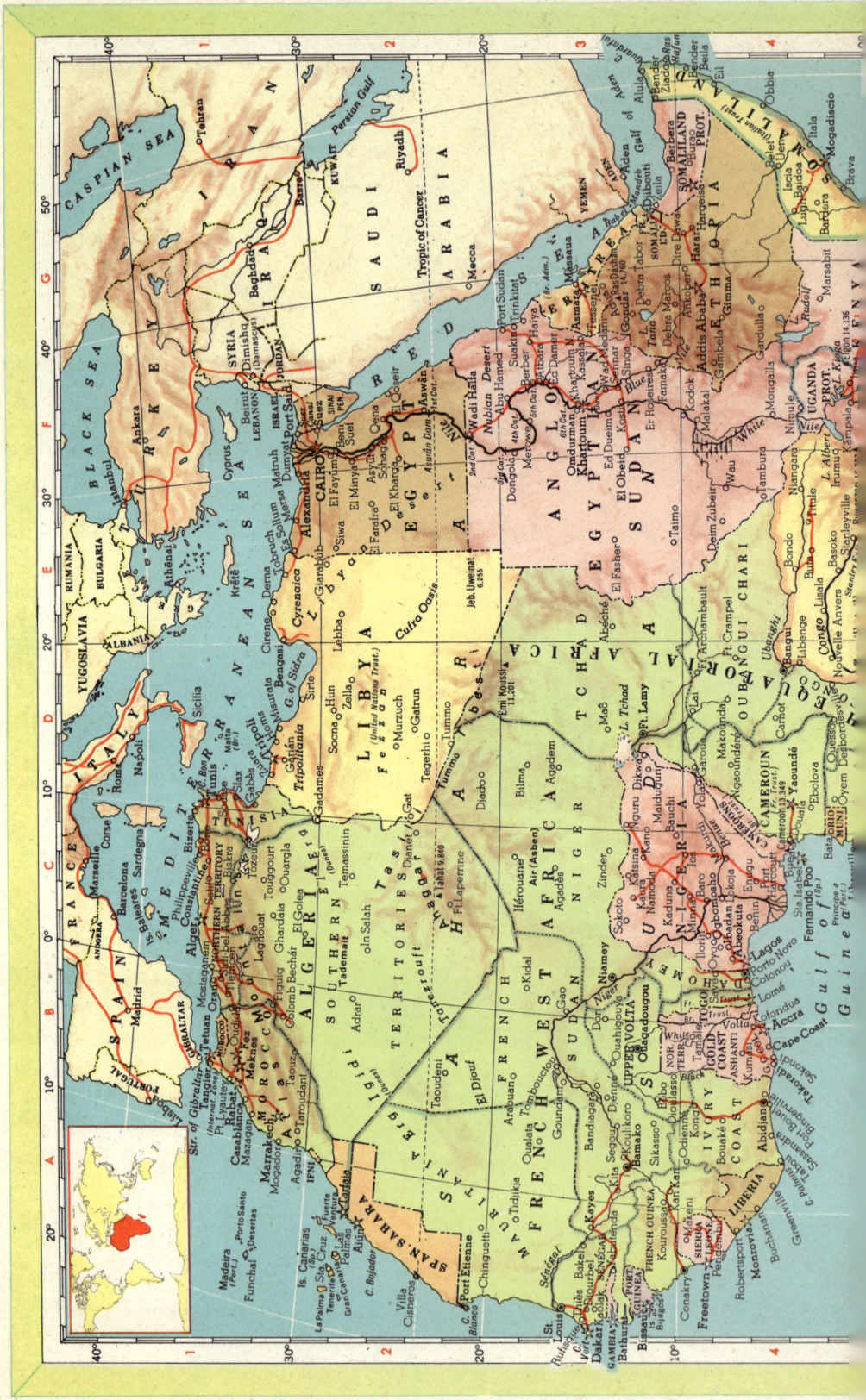

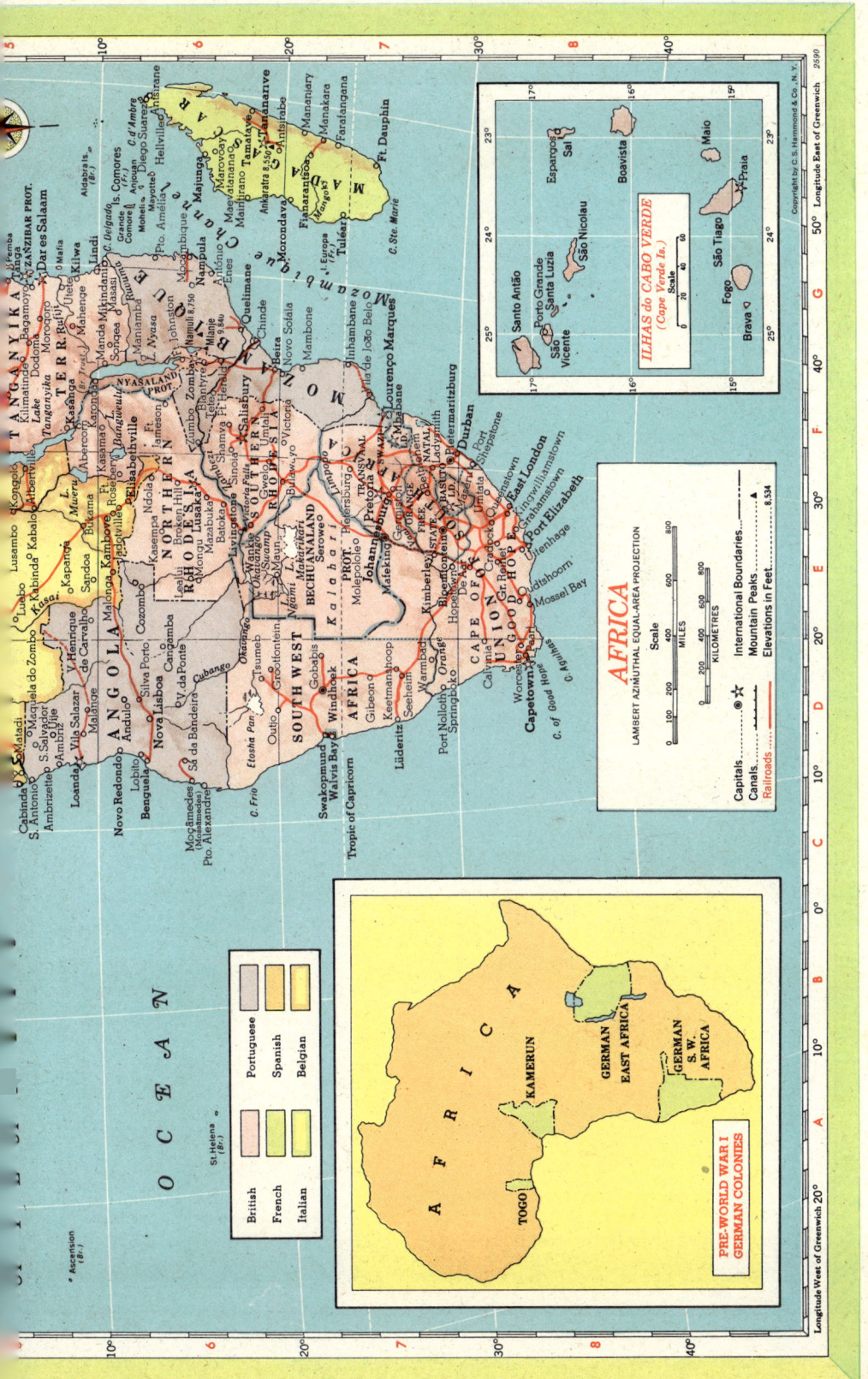

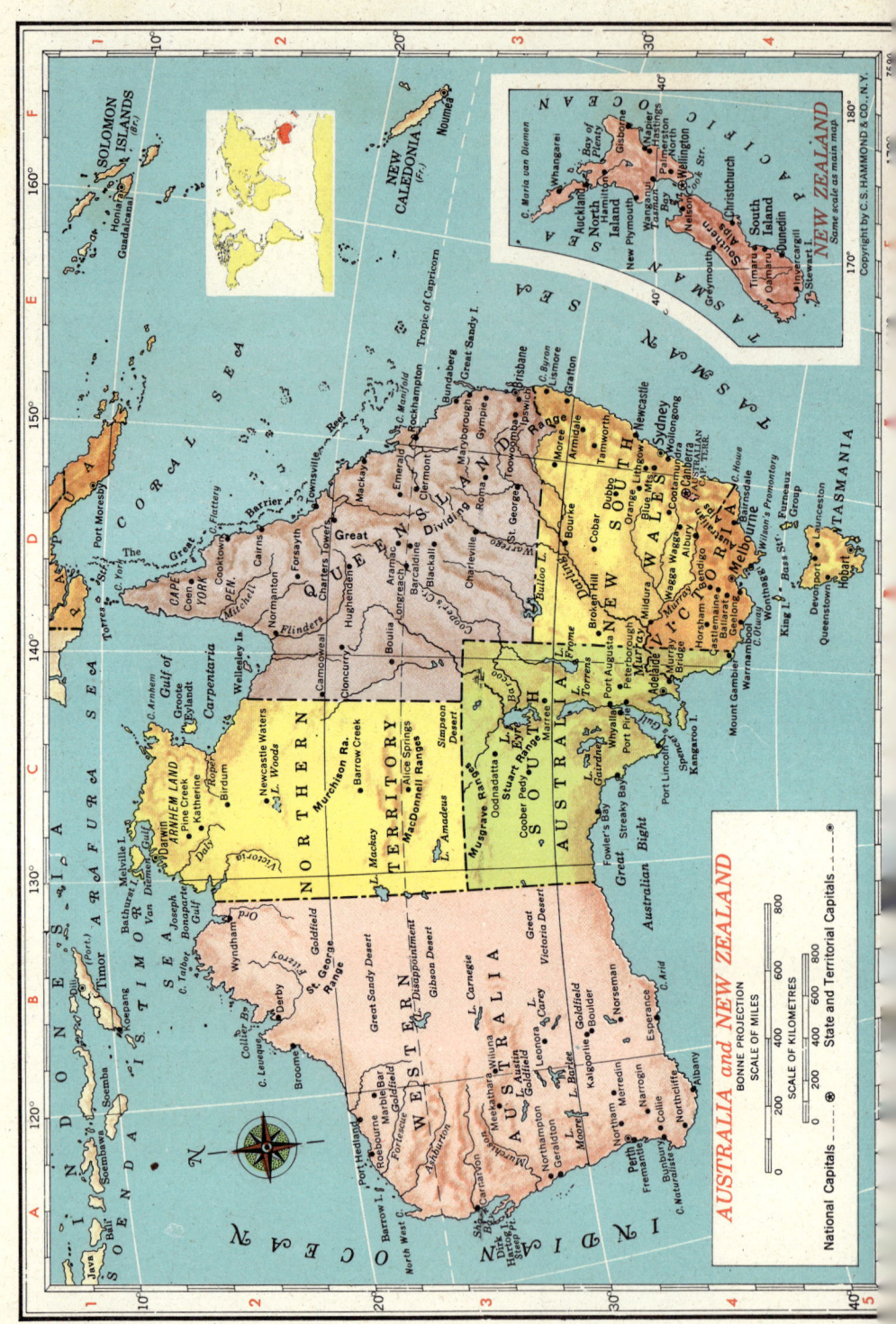

ANDROMACHE IN CAPTIVITY
From a Painting by Sir Frederick Leighton

War I the 2,000-mile mark was soon passed, and in 1923 Kelly and Macready flew 2,516 miles non-stop across the continent. In 1931 Boardman and Polando flew non-stop from New York to Turkey, 5,011 miles. In 1937, a Soviet team flew 6,262 non-stop miles from Moscow to California. The following year, November, 1938, a British non-stop flight from Egypt to Australia logged 7,158 miles. The World War II years saw no official records established. In November, 1945, however, a B-29 Superfortress, the "Dreamboat," flew 7,916 non-stop miles from Guam to Washington. At present (1951), the non-stop distance flight record is held by the Navy P2V Lockheed, the "Truculent Turtle." In October, 1946, it flew from Australia to the United States, a distance of 11,822 m., in 55 hours. All these flights were without refueling.

There is another type of endurance flight, the kind in which the airplane is refueled in mid-air. In August, 1923, Lieuts. Lowell Smith and Paul Richter stayed in the air 37 hours, using refueling. Beginning January 1, 1929, the "Question Mark" stayed up 150 hours. This flight is especially memorable because in the flight crew were men destined to become world famous, Carl Spaatz, Ira Eaker, and Elwood R. Quesada. Such endurance flights quickly became a fad, and the record was broken almost monthly. On July 13, 1929, Dale Jackson and Forest O'Brine started on a flight that lasted 420 hours. In 1930 Kenneth and John Hunter boosted the time to 553 hours. The Jackson-O'Brine team then went up again, this time for 647 hours, but now the craze had died down. The present world's record refueling flight was made in the spring of 1949 by Barras and Riddle, who flew an Aeronca light plane for 1,008 hrs. over California.

Other memorable flights include James A. Mollison's pioneering trip from England to South Africa in 1932, in 113 hours. In 1934, pilots from many nations entered the Mac-Robertson race from London to Melbourne, Australia. A British team, flying a racer-type de Havilland Comet made the 11,300 m. in 70 hrs., 54 min. to win.

Speed flights.—The Federation Aeronautique Internationale, known generally as the F.A.I., speed records, such as those which follow are official. In 1906, Santos Dumont had flown 25.6 mph. By 1913 Prevost had managed 126.7 mph. Lecointe raised that figure to 188 mph in 1920 and Bonnett was credited with 278.5 mph in 1924. In 1933, James R. Weddell officially flew 304.98 mph, only to have the Frenchman Delmotte make 314 mph the following year. All these statistics are for land planes. Seaplane racers in 1934 had flown 440 mph. In 1935 Howard Hughes raised the land-plane mark to 352 mph. A hint of what was to come in World War II was given early in 1939 when the German, Wendel, flying a Me-109-R, a specially groomed and powered Messerschmitt fighter, was clocked at 469.22 mph.

After World War II, the speed record was taken by jet-powered aircraft. In 1946, a British Meteor flew 616 mph. In June, Col. Albert Boyd flew a P-80-R Shooting Star 623.8 mph. In August, 1947, a Navy D-558-I, flown by Cmdr. T. F. Caldwell, flew 640.7 mph. The same month Maj. Marion Carl in the same airplane hit 650.6 mph. Sept. 15, 1948, Maj. Richard L. Johnson flew a North American F-86 Sabre 670.981 mph. There have been other planes which have flown faster, but not under the rigid regulations prescribed by F.A.I.

Altitude flights.—A record altitude of 361 ft. was established by Wilbur Wright in 1908; by 1914 and World War I, this had been extended to 25,755 ft. In the years after World War I, the U. S. Army sought to extend this figure and did so spectacularly. In 1920 Schroeder reached 33,114 ft. The following year Macready boosted this to 34,563 ft.

But here, European pilots took over, Lecointe, Champion, and Neuenhofen raising the mark year by year to 41,794 ft. in 1928. Lemoine of France recorded 44,819 ft. in 1933 and the Italian Donati reached 47,352 ft. in 1934. The current record was established in October, 1938, by Pettzi, who climbed his Italian Caproni to 56,046 ft. If other airplanes of 1950 vintage can do better, there is no indication of military eagerness to establish that fact.

For lighter-than-air records, see BALLOONS.

U. S. Air Transport from 1926.—In the section of this article, *"Post-War Period,"* above, the transfer of the air-mail carriage in 1926 to private companies was noted. This resulted in a rapid growth of transport companies, and also in the development of airplanes designed to carry both passengers and mail. Postmaster General Walter F. Brown, in the 1928-32 Hoover administration, vigorously worked for the growth of strong air-transport companies. He was bitterly criticized for the manner in which he reached this goal, but never was he charged with having acted except to strengthen commercial air transport in the United States.

The Roosevelt administration in February, 1934, cancelled the air-mail contracts with private companies and turned back to the Air Corps the job of carrying the mail. Flying unfamiliar routes in bitterly foul weather, the service pilots lacked even aircraft suitable for the task. By May, when new contracts were let with private companies, a dozen service pilots had been killed. Another action of the Roosevelt administration was breaking up the giant aviation companies which manufactured engines and airplanes and also operated the air routes. Example: In the United Aircraft organization were Boeing Airplane, United Air Lines, Pratt & Whitney Engines, Hamilton Standard Propellers, Chance-Vought Aircraft, and Sikorsky Aircraft. In such cases, the air lines were separated, and often the transport-plane manufacturers were divorced from the engine manufacturers.

Recovery from the troubles of 1934, despite the national depression, was rapid. Almost every year, the number of passengers and the pounds of mail carried was larger. In 1932, the domestic air lines flew 127,433,000 passenger miles (one passenger carried one mile). By 1937 this passenger-mile figure had increased to 481,116,000. In 1941, it was 1,506,303,000; in 1945, 3,408,290,000; in 1947, 6,307,690,000, and in 1950, estimated nearly 8,000,000,000 passenger miles. In 1939, only 12% of the first-class travel market was going by air. In 1949, 41% of this first-class travel market was air borne. In safety, too, the air lines were making great improvements. In 1935, there were 9.05 fatalities per 100 million passenger miles. In 1938, this safety index was down to 4.48. In 1945, it was 2.23. In 1948 and 1949 it was 1.3 each year. Between December 29, 1946, and November 29, 1949, American Airlines flew over 4.4 billion passenger miles without a single fatality.

In equipment, too, the air lines made rapid progress from 1925 on. First they used such 100-mph equipment as Ford and Fokker tri-motors and Curtiss Condors. Early in the thirties there came the Boeing 247 and shortly after, the Douglas DC-2, low-wing monoplanes which cruised at about 150 mph. The Douglas DC-3 which quickly followed the DC-2 was a 21-passenger plus crew airplane, and today is widely used around the world.

Just before the outbreak of World War II, both Boeing and Douglas introduced four-motored transport types, but except for a small number of Boeing Stratoliners, none was put into service until 1945. More recent transports were the post-war Douglas DC-6, the Lockheed Constellation, the double-deck Boeing Stratocruiser, the Martin 404, and the Convair 240, all 300-mph cruising transports.

Research and Development Progress.—Despite the fact that in Europe there was a greater amount of government support of aeronautics, the United States in the 1920's regained the lead in this race and held it almost to the outbreak of World War II. At the NACA's Langley Laboratory during this period a number of new wind tunnels were designed and built to enable conduct of pioneering research. Among these were a tunnel with a test section 30 by 60 feet which enabled testing full-size airplanes at speeds up to 150 mph. Another was the free-flight tunnel, in which models could be tested for stability and control. At yet another tunnel propellers could be tested at high speeds. The NACA cowl is but one benefit to have resulted from this work.

Industry, too, was working mightily to improve the American aeronautical position. As noted above, American radial, air-cooled engines were considered, rightly, to be without equal. First Wright Aeronautical and then Pratt & Whitney also continued to perfect the reliability, fuel economy and power output of this type engine. American interests, largely because of geography, were interested most in this type of engine to power long-range transports and bombers. In Europe, also largely because of geography, the emphasis was more on speed and the liquid-cooled, in-line engine was emphasized because of its greater promise here.

For the World War II story, see WORLD WAR II, *War in the Air.*

The United States at the end of the war led the world in aircraft production. Its bombers and fighters had successfully stood the test against the best efforts of the enemy. In jet propulsion, America lagged, but took vigorous steps to catch up. Even before the end of the war, the aircraft industry joined hands with the Military Services and the NACA to design and build a series of research airplanes to be used in probing the mysteries of transonic and supersonic flight (transonic, where air flow is part slower, part faster than sound). Among such airplanes to have been announced are the Bell X-1 and X-2, the Douglas D-558-I and D-558-II, Douglas X-3, Northrop X-4, and Convair XF-92.

On October 14, 1947, the X-1 was flown

Pan American World Airways

The Clipper America, largest commercial landplane in the world is shown above flying over San Francisco Bay. It holds 75 passengers and is the first airplane with a double deck. It was built by the Boeing Airplane Co. for Pan American World Airways.

faster than sound (160 mph at sea level; 660 mph at 35,000 ft.). Later, it was officially announced the X-1 had been flown "hundreds of miles" faster than sound. The D-558-II, it also has been announced, has been flown supersonically. Capt. Charles E. Yeager, USAF, made the first supersonic flight.

At the beginning of 1951, research in development in aeronautics in the United States was being carried on in an atmosphere of world crisis. The NACA, in addition to a Langley Laboratory greatly enlarged and modernized, was operating its Ames Laboratory, near San Francisco, in aerodynamic research, and its Lewis Laboratory in Cleveland in the study of propulsion problems. More than 7500 scientists and supporting personnel were engaged in this work seeking to hasten the day when supersonic flight would become commonplace.

Eastern Air Lines

The Douglas DC-3, a 21 passenger plus crew airplane, is in wide use around the world today.

Official Department of Defense

This is the U. S. Air Force's lance-shaped Northrop X-4. One of the smallest airplanes ever built for the Air Force, the semi-tailless X-4 is approximately 20 feet long, and has a wing span of about 25 feet. It is not designed to travel at rates in excess of the speed of sound, but is intended to explore flight characteristics in the subsonic zone.

Official Department of Defense

Shown during one of its early test flights is the Air Force's first jet fighter, the XF-91, designed specifically for interceptor missions by the Republic Aviation Corporation. As an interceptor fighter, the XF-91 is designed for local defense against high-speed, high-altitude enemy aircraft.

During 1950, a new word came into general use which may be indicative of the shape of things to come. The word is "hypersonic" and describes speeds five times, or more, faster than sound. One of NACA's newest tunnels has a speed potential 15 times that of sound. Propulsion research includes study of ram-jet, prop-jet, turbo-jet and rocket engines. Nuclear energy, as a possible aircraft propellant, also is being studied.

In every respect, aeronautics in the United States is expanding vigorously in 1951. The Military Services are placing multi-billion-dollar orders for new airplanes of improved performance. The industry is accelerating its production schedules, and the automotive industry is being called in to assist in this work. Both the Air Force and the Navy are adding personnel rapidly. The United States is determined to stay strong in the air, to lead in the air. See also **Airplanes**; **Balloons**.

Consult *The Aircraft Yearbook* (1919-); Jane's *All the World's Aircraft* (1909-); H. L. Smith's *Airways* (1942); Magoun and Hodgins' *History of Aircraft;* F. C. Kelly's *The Wright Brothers.*

WALTER T. BONNEY, *Information Specialist. National Advisory Committee for Aeronautics.*

Aeroscope, an apparatus for collecting microscopic objects (dust, etc.) from the air.

Aerostatic Press, a machine for extracting the coloring matter from dyewoods.

Aerostatics, that branch of hydrostatics which treats of the equilibrium and pressure of air and gases. See HYDROSTATICS.

Aerotherapeutics, the term applied to the treatment of disease by atmospheric air and specially prepared atmospheres.

Æschines, (389-314 B.C.), an Athenian orator, second only to his political rival, Demosthenes. He established a school of eloquence in Rhodes. Only three of his orations are extant.

Æschylus, the earliest of the three great Athenian tragic poets, was born in Eleusis, near Athens, in 525 B.C. He fought for Athens in the great Persian wars. He won thirteen first prizes in tragic competitions, but was defeated by Sophocles in 468 B.C. This may have induced him to leave and go to Sicily, where he died in 461 B.C. Out of some sixty plays ascribed to him, we have only seven extant.

Consult Wecklein's critical edition of the works of Æschylus, Paley's edition (with English notes), and numerous editions of single plays. There are translations by Potter, Blackie and Plumptre; Browning and Fitzgerald published translations of the *Agamemnon*, and Mrs. Browning of *Prometheus.*

Æsculapius, (Greek *Asklepios*), appears in Homer as the 'blameless physician,' of human origin; in the later legends he has become the god of the healing art.

The oath of Æsculapius, still seen in many physicians' offices, bound the Æsclepiades to preserve their medicinal secrets.

Consult Dyer's *The Gods in Greece;* Canton's *Temples and Ritual of Æsculapius at Epidaurus and Athens.*

Æsop, or **Æsopus** (probably 620-560 B.C.), a celebrated Greek fabulist. The general conclusion seems to be that Æsop was a real person—a Phrygian by birth, and a slave until set free by Jadmon of Samos. Consult Jacobs' *Introduction to the Fables of Æsop.*

Æsopus, Claudius or **Clodius,** a celebrated Roman tragic actor, a friend of Cicero.

Æsthesiometer, (Greek 'measure of perception'), an instrument used for estimating the sense of touch in any part of the body. See TOUCH.

Æstheticism is, primarily, attachment to the principles of æsthetics. The term is popularly applied to extravagant devotion to trifling forms of beauty, which frequently develops into whimsical absurdities. Among the promoters of a saner æstheticism were Ruskin, Leighton, Millais, and Morris.

Æsthetics. By æsthetics is meant primarily a theory of the beautiful as exhibited in works of art. That is to say, æsthetics, considered on its objective side, has to investigate, first, the function of art in general as expressing the beautiful, and the nature of the beauty that is so expressed; and, second, the special functions of the several arts, and the special aspects of the beautiful with which they are severally concerned. Esthetics, therefore, has to discuss, among others, such topics as these: the relation of art to nature and life; the distinction of art from nature; the distinction of beauty from truth, from utility, and from moral goodness—and so on.

The two most important contributions of classical antiquity to general æsthetic theory are the discussions in Plato and Aristotle. The most important single work on æsthetic theory in antiquity is Aristotle's *Poetics*. (See ARISTOTLE.)

In the modern period, the greatest and most continuous development of æsthetic theory has taken place in Germany. The valuable work of Lessing in his *Laocoön* and his dramatic criticism was followed in 1790 by Kant's epoch-making *Critique of Judgment*. Hegel's *Lectures on Æsthetics* is perhaps the greatest work on the whole subject, aiming, as it does, at determining the nature of the ideal or the beautiful, and exhibiting the manner of its concrete realization throughout the whole scope of art. Herbart and Fechner, again, seek to bring an exact psychology to bear upon the problems of æsthetic science; while in no philosophy is the place of art more exalted than in that of Schopenhauer. Later German writers on the subject have been Lotze, Carrière, and F. T. Vischer.

Most of the leading works above mentioned are translated (see, for example, LESSING, KANT, and HEGEL). Consult also Bosanquet's *History of Æsthetic*, with bibliography; Santayana's *The Sense of Beauty;* Baldwin Brown's *Fine Arts*.

Æstivation, in Zoology, a summer sleep, not uncommon in animals which inhabit climates where the summer is very hot and dry. See HIBERNATION.

Æestivation, in Botany, the arrangement of leaves in the bud with relation to one another. The term is applied chiefly to flower buds. See FLOWER.

Æt, abbreviation for *ætatis anno,* 'in the year of his age.'

Aëtas, or **Inagtas,** a Negrito people, woolly haired, dwarfish, and aboriginal, found in Luzon and other parts of the Philippine Islands. See NEGRITO.

Ætheling, or **Atheling,** in Anglo-Saxon times meant, at first, one of noble (*athel*) birth, and, later, from the ninth to the eleventh century, a prince of the blood royal.

Æther, in Greek mythology, son of Chaos and Darkness, one of the elementary substances out of which the universe was formed: in later times the wide expanse of heaven, the abode of the gods.

Æthrioscope, an instrument designed by Leslie in 1817 for the purpose of measuring changes of temperature produced by radiation.

Aetius, a Roman general, the last successful defender of the Roman Empire, was born in Mœsia. Consult Gibbon's *Decline and Fall* (chaps. xxxiii., xxxv.).

Aetius, surnamed 'the Atheist,' the leader of the Anomœan sect of Arians, who are sometimes called after him Aetians. His work *De Fide* was refuted by Epiphanius.

Ætolia, a district of ancient Greece, on the north coast of the Gulf of Corinth, bounded on the east by the Ozolian Locrians, south by the Corinthian Gulf, west by the Achelous River, and north by Epirus and Thessaly. In ancient times the inhabitants appear to have been equal in culture to the rest of the Greeks, and their chief city Calydon was famous in the legends. With Acarnania, Ætolia now forms the nomarchy Acarnania and Ætolia of modern Greece. Area, 3,034 sq. m.; p. 190,000.

Afanasiev, Alexander Nikolaievitch (1826-71), Russian author and scholar. His principal work, *The Poetical Views of the Slavs about Nature* (3 vols., 1865-9), is a rich storehouse of information concerning Slav mythology. He published also a large collection of Russian *Popular Tales* (1873).

Afer Domitius, of Nemausus (Nimes), a celebrated Roman orator; prætor A.D. 25. He gained the favor of Tiberius by accusing Claudia Pulchra, cousin of Agrippina, A.D. 26. By flattery he secured the consulship under Caligula (39), and is said to have died of over-eating.

Affection, a psychological term used to designate the consciousness of a general change in the tone of the nervous system. As such it is considered one of the two elements of consciousness (see SENSATION), and possesses two qualities, pleasantness and unpleasantness.

Affenthaler, a red wine named from a village in Baden.

Affettuoso, an Italian musical term indicating a tender and affecting style; it lies between *adagio* and *andante,* and is frequently joined with these terms. *Affetto* and *con affetto* are used in the same sense.

Affidavit (Latin, 'he hath sworn') is a written statement of facts made upon oath or solemn affirmation before a magistrate, or other person authorized by law to administer the oath.

Affidavits should set forth facts only, and not arguments or statements of the merits of the case. Generally, the matters dealt with should be within the knowledge of the deponent, but in some cases he is entitled to speak 'to the best of his knowledge and belief.'

Affiliation is the legal process whereby the father of a bastard child, upon the paternity being proved against him, may be rendered liable to contribute toward its maintenance and education.

Affinity (Latin, *affinitas*) is the tie which arises in consequence of marriage betwixt one of a married pair and the blood relations of the other. See CONSANGUINITY; MARRIAGE.

Affinity, Chemical, that property in virtue of which, when bodies are brought into contact, they react on each other, forming new bodies. The way in which chemical forces act has been extensively studied.

In 1935 Dr. Harold S. Booth and his co-workers at Western Reserve University succeeded in combining argon, one of the six supposedly "inert" gases, with boron trifluoride.

At present, in conformity with the 'electron conception of valence,' as developed by Sir J. J. Thomson and others, the belief is that the union of two atoms is brought about by the transfer of a negatively charged corpuscle from one atom to the other; the atom losing the corpuscle becoming charged positively, the one gaining the corpuscle becoming charged negatively. See ELECTRO-CHEMISTRY; ELECTROLYSIS; EQUILIBRIUM, CHEMICAL.

For the older views on chemical affinity, consult the article on 'Affinity' in Watts' *Dictionary of Chemistry;* for a more modern discussion of the subject, Sir J. J. Thomson's *Corpuscular Theory of Matter* (1907).

Affirmation, a solemn declaration made in the legal form as required by law. See OATH.

Afghanistan, inland country of Asia, bounded on the east and south by India and Baluchistan, on the north and northeast by the Russian and Chinese empires, and on the west by Persia. Area, about 250,000 sq. m.

As a 'buffer state' between the Russian and British empires, the precise limits of its territory have been settled by treaty and locally demarcated by several boundary commissions.

Physical Features.—The chief mountain range is the Hindu-Kush (q. v.), with its prolongation the Koh-i-Baba. To the east are the Sulaiman Mountains, forming the watershed of the Indus, and the Safed Koh, dividing the Kabul from the Kuram.

Hydrographically, Afghanistan may be divided into the three great river basins of the Oxus, the Indus, and the Helmund.

The climate is continental, with great heat in summer and severe cold in winter (above 5,000 feet), but the climate generally is considered healthful.

Agriculture and Trade.—The valleys and plains are exceedingly fertile, and with the aid of irrigation agriculture is extensively carried on.

Among the natural productions of Afghanistan is the plant yielding the asafœtida. The castor-oil plant and madder are everywhere grown in the district of Kandahar. The cultivated area round Herat produces magnificent crops of wheat, barley, cotton, grapes, melons, and the mulberry tree. Surrounding the villages, and in orchards, the ash, elm, apricot, apple, plum, quince, peach, and pomegranate are cultivated; the zizyphus is indigenous. In special localities are forests of pistachio the leaves of which are used in dyeing.

Domestic animals include camels, horses and ponies, cattle, goats, and dogs. A curious variety of fat-tailed sheep is of considerable economic value, its flesh furnishing meat, its wool wearing apparel, and its skin an important article of export.

Manufactures are limited. The industrial products are silk, chiefly for domestic use, carpets, felts, and fabrics from the wool of sheep, goats, and camels. The manufacture of *postins,* or sheepskins, is one of the most important of the industrial occupations.

Trade is carried on with Iran, Russian Central Asia, China, and India. The chief exports are wool, silk, sheepskins, timber, drugs, cattle, and fruits. The imports are cotton, silk, and woolen goods, coarse cloths, sugar, tea, indigo, drugs, arms, and metal goods. Oxen, camels, and horses are used for caravans. There are no railways, but there are some 200 m. of road fit for motor traffic.

People.—The population is about 12,000,000, the dominant race being the Afghans or Pathans, who number about 3,000,000. Non-Afghan races comprise the Hazáras, Aimaks, Arabs, Jews, Baluchis, and Kaffirs. The language is Pushtu, but Persian is in general use.

Government, etc.—The government of Afghanistan is a constitutional monarchy, with legislative and State assemblies and a cabinet. At its head is the king, who is assisted by a cabinet.

For administration purposes the country is divided into five provinces—Kabul, Kandahar, Herat, Afghan Turkestan, and Kataghan-Badakhshan. At the head of each province is a *hakim* or governor, under whom are the *kazis* or chief magistrates, assisted by *muftis* or mutaassibs.

The Afghan army is said to number about 90,000 in addition to large numbers of well-armed tribesmen.

The religion of the Afghans is (Sunni) Islam. Elementary education is free and compulsory. There are elementary and secondary schools throughout the country and two colleges at Kabul, besides various schools of fine arts, agriculture and telegraphy.

History.—Afghanistan is the gateway to India. Most historic invasions of that peninsula have been made through its passes from the days of Darius and Alexander (330-329 B.C.) to Moslem and Mogul times. After forming successively part of the Parthian and Sassanian empires, the country was at times partly subject to Persia, partly to the Mogul empire, and at times divided among small native dynasties.

The years from 1708 on were disturbed by domestic conflict, and anarchy, out of which after some complications which involved Russia, the British occupation emerged in 1839, marked for the next 60 years by many revolts.

Late in the century it was found necessary to have the northwestern boundary defined. An Anglo-Russian commission was appointed, and a protocol was signed at St. Petersburg in 1887. In 1910 an agreement was reached by the governments of Afghanistan and India to submit their disputes to a joint commission.

The virtual protectorate established by Great Britain in Afghanistan was resented by tribal chiefs and others and in 1919 Habibullah, who was blamed for the existing situation, was assassinated. His fifth son, Amanullah, succeeded him as ruler of the country. One of Amanullah's first acts was to vow publicly that he would liberate Afghanistan. In February, 1921, a permanent treaty was signed whereby Great Britain recognized the unqualified independence of Afghanistan.

Three weeks later Amanullah entered into friendly treaty relations with Great Britain's rival, Soviet Russia.

Amanullah aroused the fiercest opposition of the priesthood by his drastic reform decrees, such as the unveiling of women and the adoption of western clothing; free education for girls as well as boys; forbidding dervishes to perform in public; ordering beards to be shaved off but mustaches to remain, etc. The army remained loyal for a while, but when it turned against him the Amir was forced to flee with his family. A Persian usurper, calling himself Habibullah Ghazi, seized the throne; he was soon defeated by a former finance minister, who assumed royal power in 1929, took the title of 'Shah' instead of 'Amir,' and was recognized as such by the British Government. Nadir Shah proclaimed a new Constitution in 1932 which provides for an independent constitutional monarchy with Islam as the state religion. Primary education is compulsory. Assassinated Nov. 8, 1933, King Nadir Shah was succeeded by his son, Mohammed Zahir Shah.

Africa, a continent of the Eastern Hemisphere, forming the southernmost prolongation of the Old World, and a southwest extension of Asia. The greater bulk of its compact mass lies between the tropics; the Equator crosses it almost halfway between north and south. The distance from north to south is 5,000 miles, and from west to east (Cape Verde to Ras Hafun, south of Cape Guardafui) 4,650 m. Its shape roughly resembles that of a pear, bulging out in the north and tapering to the south, so that its breadth at 10° s. is only about 1,800 m. Total area, 11,513,000 sq. m.

The Mediterranean Sea separates Africa from Europe in the north, but the two continents approach to within 9 m. of each other at the Strait of Gibraltar. Africa is bounded by the Atlantic Ocean on the west, and by the Indian Ocean on the east. The coast line is 19,000 m.

Physical Features.—Africa is a massive platform rising out of deep seas. The continental ledge or shelf is everywhere narrow. The average elevation of the continent is 2,130 ft.

The *Northern Plateau* has an area of between 4,000,000 and 5,000,000 sq. m., and an average elevation of 1,500 ft. The north and centre of this region form the Sahara, a land of barren, stony plateaus and shifting sand dunes, crossed by a few dry valleys. The *Congo Basin* is a hollow in the Central Plateau formerly occupied by a great lake.

East Africa is bounded on the west by the Nile and the great lakes—Albert Nyanza, Edward Nyanza, Tanganyika, and Nyasa. Much of the plateau south of Abyssinia lies about 4,000 feet above the Indian Ocean, to which it descends by a series of terraces.

The *South African Plateau* has also a high average elevation, between 3,000 and 4,000 feet. This plateau is divided into four regions, each over 4,000 ft., by the valleys of the Zambezi, Limpopo, and Orange—the Congo-Zambezi Plateau in the north, the Matabele Plateau in the east, the High Veldt in the southeast, and the Damara Plateau in the west.

In its *geological* constitution. Africa presents the appearance of great stability and antiquity. Unlike those of other continents, the seaboard is subject to scarcely any movements of upheaval or subsidence. Earthquakes are confined mainly to the Atlas region.

Climate.—Three-fourths of Africa lies between the tropics, and here the days are of nearly uniform length, with almost twelve hours of light every day. At sea level the mean temperature of the coldest month is over 70° F., except near the extremities of the continent, where it falls to 55° F. Around the tropics the daily and seasonal ranges of temperature are great—over 30° F. between the warmest and coldest month; but in equatorial regions, and toward the north and south of the continent, where it is bordered by seas, the range is small. A narrow strip of the Southwest coast is kept cool at all seasons by an upwelling of cold water along the coast and by low fogs. At the equinoxes a belt of rising air and heavy rains is found near the Equator, and this moves north and south with the zenithal sun; so that around the Equator there are two rainy seasons, and in some regions almost constant rains, while at the tropics there are one wet and one dry season. The mean annual rainfall ranges from under 4 inches in the Sahara and about 10 in the Kalahari, to 60 and 80 inches about the Equator, and from 80 upward on the Guinea coast.

Hydrography.—Each climatic region has its own type of river, and most African rivers, where they leave the plateau, have their courses impeded by cataracts. The Zambezi and Limpopo, with the Rovuma, Rufiji, Juba, and other coast streams, flow to the Indian Ocean; the Nile, Niger, Congo, Orange, Senegal, together with the Cunene, Coanza, Ogowai, Volta, and Gambia, flow to the Atlantic, either directly or through the Mediterranean. Nearly all are obstructed by formidable falls and rapids, such as the stupendous Victoria Falls on the Zambezi; the Yellala and Isangila on the Lower, and Stanley on the Middle Congo; the so-called 'Six Cataracts,' the Ripon, Murchison, and many others.

The rivers of the equatorial rainy regions spread out into numerous channels or loops. The Zambezi and the Niger reach the sea across great deltas fringed with mangrove swamps. The Nile crosses all the climatic zones, and consequently is an epitome of African rivers. The Kagera, draining into the Victoria Nyanza, is the ultimate source of the Nile, which flows north 4,037 m. to the Mediterranean, and, next to the Missouri-Mississippi, is the longest river in the world. The Congo basin is the greatest in Africa and ranks next to the Amazon for volume.

Africa possesses a magnificent equatorial lake system, unrivalled elsewhere except by the Great Lakes of North America. They are grouped toward the east side of the continent, between 15° s. and 4° N. lat., and all stand on the south tableland, draining seaward through the Zambezi, the Congo, and the Nile. The Victoria, queen of African lakes, is next to Superior (31,200 sq. m.) the largest fresh-water basin (30,000 sq. m.) on the globe.

Minerals.—Gold was mined by the ancient Egyptians at Mount Elba, Red Sea coast, and is still the principal metal exported from Africa. Alluvial diamonds are found in South-West Africa, but 98% of the world's output comes from the open workings of the Kimberley region, in the basin of the Vaal. Coal is worked in many parts of the continent, principally in Natal, the Transvaal, Rhodesia, Katanga and Nigeria. The copper deposits of the Katanga district of the Belgian Congo are in full development, and American geologists have located ore containing 20,000,000 tons of copper near N'Kana, Northern Rhodesia. Iron is produced in Angola, the Transvaal and Natal, and radium in the Congo. Northern Nigeria and the Congo contain the principal tin fields of Africa, and phosphates are worked in Tunisia and Algeria.

Flora.—The regions with winter rains are characterized by heaths and other dry, scrubby plants; water-storing species, like mesembryanthemum; and thick-skinned plants, such as the agave. The deserts have a very poor flora, of even more spiny, leathery, or water-storing plants than the above. The most important grass lands are the savannas, which are continuous from the Upper Niger across the Sudan by the Eastern and the Matabele Plateaus; and the High Veldt, a branch running westward along the Congo-Zambezi divide. Flat-topped trees are dotted about the savannas, and form continuous woods along the river courses. The wet jungles of the equatorial forests cover the coastal plain of Upper Guinea, the lower part of the Congo Basin, and the east of Madagascar; they are characterized by the number of palms.

In North Africa are found the olive, date, fig, and cork, the oak and Atlantic cedar, and the eucalyptus, introduced from Australia. The papyrus still lingers in the Upper Nile, although in the Lower Nile the lotus and other characteristic plants have been largely replaced by cereals, cotton, tobacco, and other economic species. South of Egypt, the date gives place to the doom and deleb palms, wheat and rice to durra; in the forest regions of the Sudan and Guinea the mahogany is found and also baobab, banana, butter tree, ebony, oil palm, which yields the palm oil of commerce, bamboo palm, mangrove, acacias, mimosas, and other gum trees. Indigenous to Africa is the cotton plant, which, like indigo, is cultivated in Egypt, the Sudan, Nigeria, Uganda and Natal, and which grows wild in many places as far north as 19° N. lat.

Wheat, corn, coffee, flax and sisal are widely cultivated in East and South Africa, whilst peanuts are a growing export from Nigeria and Senegal, and cocoa from the Gold Coast and the islands of the Gulf of Guinea. The bulk of the world's supply of cloves comes from the little islands of Zanzibar, Pemba and Mafia on the east coast.

Fauna.—The savannas are very rich in animal life, the most numerous and characteristic being antelopes. On the borders of the forest, lions, elephants, buffaloes, leopards, hyenas, and giraffes are still found in great numbers. The okapi is peculiar to East Africa and in South Africa, alone, is found the Cape ant-eater (aardvark). The white rhinoceros still haunts the Lake Albert Edward region and the black double-horned variety is abundant on the grassy plateaus. The hippopotamus and crocodile are found in the rivers and lakes, which teem with fish. Among the birds, besides the ostrich, are the ibis, pelican, secretary bird, parrot, and guinea fowl. Reptiles and insects abound, among the latter being the tsetse fly, fatal to man and domestic animals alike; and the donderobo, which attacks the ass, goat, and sheep.

The gorilla, chimpanzee, and other monkeys, the hippopotamus and elephant, are among the most important mammals. Madagascar has the lemur and the aye-aye.

Peoples.—The population of Africa is estimated at about 155,000,000, or nearly 13 inhabitants per sq. m. These are distributed very unevenly over the surface, being massed somewhat densely in the Nile delta, in the Upper Nile valley, and generally throughout the Sudan; less thickly over the southern plateau, and very thinly on the northern and western coast; while large tracts, especially in the West Sahara, the Libyan and Kalahari wastes, are almost uninhabited.

Of the whole number, probably not more than 4,000,000 are *white* immigrants from Europe, settled chiefly in the extreme north (Egypt, Italian Libya, and French West Africa) and the extreme south (Union of South Africa, Rhodesia, and the former German colonies). About 34,000,000, of *Semitic* stock, are intruders from Asia, some in remote or prehistoric times (3,000,000 Himyars in Abyssinia and Harar from South Arabia), some since the spread of Islam (over 30,000,-000 nomad and other Arabs, chiefly along the Mediterranean seaboard, in West Sahara, and Central and East Sudan). All the rest may be regarded as the true aboriginal elements, which may be roughly divided into two great physical and linguistic groups—*Hamites* in the north, *Negroes* in the south, meeting and intermingling in the intermediate region of Sudan.

The Hamites in physical type are essentially Mediterranean, often characterized by extremely regular features, and in places even by blue eyes and fair complexion. The Negroes include, in addition to the true negroes, the diverse races of the Congo-Nile divide—the aberrant Hottentots, and a number of dwarf races, such as the Bushmen, the Obongos, the Akkas and the diminutive Batwas.

In its inhabitants, as well as its natural history, Madagascar forms a region apart (see MADAGASCAR).

Languages.—Various classifications of the African language have been proposed. Proceeding on the basis of racial difference, five main classes are distinguished: (1) *Semitic,* the tongues spoken by the Arabs and certain Abyssinian tribes. (2) *Hamitic,* including Libyan and various Abyssinian dialects. (3) *Negro,* a bewildering variety of dialects. (4) *Bantu,* spoken by all the black races south of a line running roughly eastward from the head of the Gulf of Guinea. Of this group the Zulu is the most perfect type. (5) *Hottentot-Bushman,* spoken by the Hottentots and Bushmen.

The Ki-swahili language of the eastern seaboard is the *lingua franca* used by whites and natives alike from 10° N. to 20° S. as far to the westward as the Belgian Congo. In the bilingual Union of South Africa, Afrikaans, or Cape Dutch, is, equally with English, the official language and is spoken by 60% of the white population.

Economic Conditions.—The majority of native Africans live by hunting and by superficial cultivation of the soil or pastoral pursuits.

The more effective administration of Africa by the European Powers amongst whom it is principally divided has resulted in a policy of vigorous development of the economic possibilities since the beginning of the century. Agricultural experimentation has led to the introduction of many crops of commercial value, such as cocoa and rubber on the West Coast, coffee and fibre plants on the East, and rustless types of wheat in Central and Southern Africa. The cultivation of indigenous crops has been vastly extended, peanuts and palm oil, notably, in West Africa, cotton in the Sudan, Uganda and Natal, and tobacco in Nyasaland and Northern Nigeria.

The mineral resources of the continent are in process of vigorous development by foreign capital with the aid of native labor, the low wages of which constitute, in some instances, a threat to the maintenance of world prices.

The result of the employment of the Africans in peaceful, profitable avocations has been the accumulation of wealth in native ownership and the creation of needs and desires which are providing a growing market for the manufactures of the world. The people have acquired a taste for civilized clothing, for better housing and for amusements and, with the widespread construction of roads, they are buying bicycles and automobiles. The backward condition of Africa is becoming a memory of the past and she is taking place with the other continents as an economic factor of account.

Religion.—Fully one-half of the continent has accepted the tenets of Mohammedanism, which on the whole have had a beneficent influence on the Negro. The all-prevailing fetishism of the past, intimately associated with the baneful practice of witchcraft, is giving way slowly before the influences of civilization and the confidence engendered by stable government. Christianity has made very great progress amongst the pagan tribes, though in some areas, notably in West Africa, it competes with difficulty against Mohammedanism, which does not conflict with the immemorial African habit of polygamy.

Communications. — Great developments have been accomplished since World War I in the communications of Africa by land and air. Railways have been pushed further into the interior from all coasts and motor roads have been developed as feeder lines through regions hitherto only accessible to hardy travellers. Nearly 30,000 miles of railway are now in operation, 9,000 of which cover the Union of South Africa and Southwest Africa. A scheduled service operates on a through ticket from Cape Town to Cairo in 45 days.

The first transcontinental railway in Africa was completed in 1931. From Tabora, on the Central Railway of Tanganyika Territory, an extension has been completed to Mwanza, on Victoria Nyanza, affording lake steamer connection with the Kenya-Uganda Railway, which is being extended into the Belgian Congo. In Northwest Africa the French Government was constructing (1938) a line across the Sahara Desert to join its colonial railway system on the West Coast and, in Eritrea, the Italians were making extensions.

The motor highways of Africa stretch throughout the interior and in Uganda and the Belgian Congo, in particular, the routes are open in all seasons. The roads of East Africa are well kept and make possible a regular passenger automobile service between Cape Town and Juba, a distance of over 5,000 miles. Native chiefs now own their cars, while primitive natives operate trucks in regions where lion and giraffe still roam abroad.

French air services cross the Mediterranean to North Africa and traverse the Sahara to Dakar, whence is a service to South America. Scheduled air lines have been established in the Belgian Congo from Boma along the River Congo to Elizabethville and from Leopoldville, the capital, to Coquilhatville. A British line now operates flying boats from Cairo up the Nile via Khartum, to Kisumu on Victoria Nyanza, and the route was extended, in January, 1932, by airplanes via Nairobi through Tanganyika and the Rhodesias to Cape Town, a total flying distance of 6,720 miles.

Exploration.—Although the Nile Valley was the earliest seat of human culture, Africa is still the least known division of the globe. Little was known of the seaboard till the fourteenth century A. D. General knowledge of the periphery was nearly completed toward the close of the next century, when Vasco da Gama doubled the Cape and skirted the eastern coast north to Magadosho in 2°

N. lat. (1497-8). Then followed 30 years of comparative inactivity.

The modern epoch of geographical research, apart from political or commercial considerations, begins properly with James Bruce, who discovered the Abai source of the Blue Nile in 1770, and whose adventures in Abyssinia stimulated the foundation of the African Association (1788). In 1802-5, Lichtenstein travelled in the district north of the Cape of Good Hope. In 1809 Burckhardt was sent out by the African Society. The labors of Oudney, Clapperton, Denham, and the Lander brothers, in the Sahara and Sudan, are memorable by the discovery of Lake Chad and the course of the Niger.

From 1843 to 1873 David Livingstone was engaged in trying to open the countries north of the Cape of Good Hope.

Burton and Speke, crossing the Border Mountains from Zanzibar, in 1857, discovered Lake Tanganyika; and the former, then journeying to the northeast, discovered the southern part of the Victoria Nyanza, which he supposed to be the head reservoir of the Nile. At Gondokoro, Speke and Grant were met by Sir Samuel Baker, who, accompanied by his heroic wife, pushed on to the south, and discovered in 1864, west of the Victoria, another great lake, which he called the Albert Nyanza.

Henry M. Stanley, after exploring the Shimiyu, farthest south head stream of the Nile, circumnavigated Victoria Nyanza, and discovered the Muta Nzige.

During the scramble for spheres of influence in Africa by the European Powers at the end of the nineteenth century, much valuable exploration was accomplished. The first man to cover the entire distance from the Cape to the Mediterranean was Major E. S. Grogan, who made the journey on foot, 1898-1900. Between 1926 and 1930, scientists of the American Museum of Natural History and of the Rockefeller and Smithsonian institutes studied the big game and ornithology of Africa, and British, French and German expeditions continued their explorations.

During World War II British and Axis armies fought for two years in North Africa. Nov. 7, 1942, U.S. army, navy and air forces joined the British, and Axis power was eliminated May 7, 1943.

African Oak, a heavy, hard timber used in shipbuilding, obtained from West Africa.

Africanus, a title of honor borne by the two great Scipios, in commemoration of their African victories. **Sextus Caecilius,** a famous Roman jurisconsult and orator, of the time of Antoninus Pius. **Sextus Julius,** a Christian writer of the third century.

Afridi, a tribe of Pathans or Afghans, dwelling on the northwestern frontier of India, in the neighborhood of Peshawar, the most powerful and independent of the border tribes except the Waziri. They number about 300,000.

Afrikaans the South African language (formerly known as the Taal) which has developed from the Netherlands tongue. Jointly with English, Afrikaans is the official language of the Union of South Africa, 60% of the white population being bilingual.

Afrikander, a native of South Africa descended from Dutch parents settled there.

Afrikander Bond, a South African association, formed (1879) for the furtherance and consolidation of Afrikander influence.

After-birth. See **Placenta.**

After-damp. See **Choke-damp.**

After-glow, the glow sometimes seen in the sky after sunset, illuminating the upper strata of the clouds, usually in shades of red and yellow; due to the presence of fine dust in the higher atmosphere.

After-images are representations to the mind of bygone impressions. They are sensations for which at the time of their occurrence there is no present external stimulus.

Aftermath, a second mowing of grass following one hay crop. It is used as a figure of speech for the results of tragedy.

Afzelius, Adam (1750-1837), Swedish botanist, founder of the Linnaen Institute at Upsala and professor of materia medica. In 1823 he prepared the biography of Linnaeus.

Afzelius, Arvid August (1785-1871), Swedish poet, translated the *Edda,* and edited a fine collection of ancient Swedish folk songs.

Aga, or **Agha,** a Turkish title borne by officers in the army under the rank of major and by various lower officials in the ministries.

Aga Khan I, His Highness The (1800-1881), spiritual head of the Ismailiah sect of the British Indian Mohammedans. The great influence he wielded over his co-religionists proved of immense value to the British.

Aga Khan III, (1875-   ). He was given an European education and has done much for the advancement of Mohammedan education in India. During the post-war years of treaty-making he used all his great influence to secure the continuance of a strong and free Turkey. In Sept., 1939, he issued a call to 10,000,000 Mohammedans to help Great Britain in the war against the Nazis.

Agades, Aghades, or **Agadez,** African town, capital of oasis of Aïr or Asben, Sahara. Once an important city of Central Africa, and still a great centre of the caravan route between the Sudan and Tripoli. In the sixteenth century it probably contained 60,000 Tuareg.

Agadir, town on the southern coast of Morocco, at the mouth of the Sus River, a caravan station on the route between Upper and Lower Morocco. In 1930 the port was opened to commerce; p. about 3,000.

Agag, the title of the Amalekite kings.

Agalamatolite, a hydrated aluminum and potassium silicate, which varies in composition and color, and which is of a soft, waxy consistency. It is used extensively by the Chinese for the carving of images, and is sometimes known as 'figure stone.'

Agamemnon, son of King Atreus, and brother of Menelaus. After his father's death he reigned in Mycenæ, and married Clytæmnestra, by whom he had three children—Iphigenia, Electra, and Orestes. When Paris carried off Helen, Agamemnon traversed Greece, exhorting all the leaders of the people to unite in an expedition against Troy. Agamemnon was appointed general-in-chief of the united forces assembled at Aulis in Bœotia. The *Iliad* gives an account of the war that followed. After the fall of Troy he was murdered by Clytæmnestra, with or without the aid of Ægisthus.

Agamogenesis, reproduction without sex, a process of multiplication by division, budding, etc., in which there is no union of sexual elements, but simply more or less discontinuous growth. See PARTHOGENESIS; REPRODUCTION; SEX.

Agaña, or **San Ignacio de Agana,** the capital of the island of Guam, one of the Ladrones; lat. 12° N., and long. 145° E. (See GUAM.); p. 18,620 including the military establishment.

Agapæ, (Greek *agape,* 'love') were love feasts, or feasts of charity, originally celebrated by the early Christians in connection with the Lord's Supper. Wealthy or well-to-do Christians brought the materials of the feast, in which the poorer brethren who had nothing to bring shared equally. The meetings closed with the 'holy kiss.' Consult J. F. Keating's *The Agape and the Eucharist.*

Agapemone, ('abode of love'), called also LAMPETER BRETHREN, the community of mystics, holding to a community of goods, and conventual in form, founded (1859) at Bridgwater, England, by Henry J. Prince, a former Anglican clergyman.

Agapetus I. (d. 536), a native of Rome, elevated to the papacy in 535. He was unsuccessful in a mission to Constantinople (536) with a view to making peace between Justinian and Theodatus, king of the Eastern Goths.

Agapetus II., a native of Rome, occupied the papal chair from 946 to 955.

Agar, or **Augur,** town, state of Gwalior, India. It stands on a rocky height, 1,600 ft. above the sea; p. 30,000.

Agar-agar, Agal-agal, Malayan names for a seaweed (*Plocaria lichenoides*), known also as CEYLON MOSS and JAFFNA MOSS. It forms an article of trade between China and the East Indies. Agar-agar is much employed by bacteriologists for the cultivation of bacteria.

Agardh, Karl Adolf (1785-1859), Swedish botanist, an authority on algæ whose most important work was *Systema Algarum.*

Louis Agassiz. See Page 80.

Agaricin, Agaric, Agaricic, Agaricinic, or **Laricic Acid,** a white powder obtained from *Polyporus officinalis,* used medicinally to check the night sweats of phthisis.

Agaric Mineral, a variety of calcite or calcium carbonate, very soft and light. usually pure white, and found either in the clefts of rocks or the bottom of lakes.

Agassiz, Alexander (1835-1910), American zoologist, only son of Louis Agassiz (q. v.), was born in Neuchâtel, Switzerland.

After serving as assistant in the U. S. Coast Survey, he became assistant in zoology, assistant curator, curator, and director (1902-10) of the Harvard Museum of Comparative Zoology. In 1875 he founded the zoological station at Newport, R. I. He assisted in the development of the Calumet and Hecla copper mines near Lake Superior, of which he became president.

Agassiz was especially distinguished for his studies in marine zoology—e. g., echinoderms, starfishes, and jellyfishes. His publications include: *Three Cruises of the U. S. Coast and Geodetic Survey Steamer 'Blake,'* 1877-80; *Coral Reefs of the Tropical Pacific*. Consult G. R. Agassiz' *Letters and Recollections of Alexander Agassiz* (1913).

Agassiz, Elizabeth Cabot (Cary) (1822-1907), American educator, was born in Boston. In 1850 she was married to Louis Agassiz. She accompanied him to Brazil, and on the *Hassler* expedition, besides taking a prominent part at Radcliffe College (president 1894-1900). She wrote: *A First Lesson in Natural History; Life of Louis Agassiz*.

Agassiz, Jean Louis Rodolphe (1807-73), Swiss-American naturalist was born in Motier, canton Fribourg. He was educated at the Universities of Zürich, Heidelberg, Erlangen, and Munich, receiving degrees in philosophy and medicine. He devoted much time to the study of natural history.

In 1832 he became professor of natural history in the University of Neuchâtel. In 1839 he issued the first part of his *Histoire Naturelle des Poissons d'Eau Douce de l'Europe Centrale*. In 1836 he commenced an examination of the glacial phenomena of the Alps. His theory of glacier motion (dilatation of water frozen in the crevasses) soon gave way, however, to that formulated by Forbes (gravitation *plus* plasticity).

In October, 1846, Agassiz visited America, and delivered a course of lectures *On the Plan of the Creation*. In 1848 he was elected to the newly founded chair of natural history in the Lawrence Scientific School at Harvard University. In 1858 he founded the Museum of Comparative Zoology at Harvard, for which a land grant had been made by Massachusetts and funds contributed by private individuals. He himself gave his collections, representing an outlay of $10,000.

In 1865, in consequence of ill health, Agassiz decided upon a trip to Brazil, which became one of the most important scientific expeditions of his life. His publications include: *Nomenclator Zoologicus; Contributions to the Natural History of the United States; The Structure of Animal Life*. Consult Mrs. Agassiz' *Louis Agassiz;* C. F. Holder's *Life;* Marcou's *Life, Letters, and Works*.

Agassiz Association, formed in 1875 by Harlan H. Ballard to encourage young people to emulate the example of Louis Agassiz by studying natural history.

Agassiz, Lake, name given to the basin of a large sheet of water that in the Glacial Period covered a considerable area in the Red River Valley of Minnesota, North Dakota, and Manitoba. The bed of the lake, now covered by a fertilizing silt produces rich grain. See GLACIAL PERIOD.

Agassiz, Mount, a peak in Utah. Height, 13,000 ft.

Agate, one of the many minerals consisting of cryptocrystalline silica, and included under the general name of chalcedony (q.v.). It occurs chiefly as rounded nodules with irregular surfaces, in cavities of igneous rocks into which silica, dissolved in water, has percolated. Layer after layer of siliceous matter is laid down within this cavity, the outermost and earliest being often a coating of green chloride or celadonite. The layers follow the outlines of the original cavity, and hence are mostly concentric. The commonest of these are the oxides of iron, producing red, brown, or yellow; but bands of other tints are often found. Carnelian, amethyst, common quartz, jasper, opal, and flint may occur as layers.

Because of its hardness, and because moist air and chemical fumes will not rust or tarinsh it, agate enters into the construction of certain scientific instruments—e. g., the knife edge on which the beam of a chemical balance is suspended. It is also used for mortars and pestles employed by chemists to pulverize hard substances.

The great centre of agate working has for centuries been Oberstein, in Germany. For many years the chief sources have been Brazil and Uruguay. Agate of considerable beauty is found in the Lake Superior region, particularly Agate Bay, and in the stream beds of Colorado. Montana and other Rocky Mountain regions furnish agate pebbles of various sizes.

Agatha, St., a noble Sicilian maiden of great beauty, who rejected the love of the Prefect Quintilianus, and suffered a cruel martyrdom (251.) She ranks among the saints of the Roman Catholic Church. Her festival is celebrated on Feb. 5.

Agathocles, tyrant of Syracuse (361-

289 B.C.), was born at Rhegium, in Italy. Having in 317 created an army of adventurers, he assembled about four hundred of the rich and influential citizens and killed them. During the ensuing two days four thousand people were slain, as many banished and their property confiscated, and Agathocles was proclaimed tyrant of the town.

By conquering nearly all of Sicily, Agathocles came into collision with the Carthaginians.

After concluding peace with the Carthaginians, Agathocles once more became master over Syracuse, and over most of the Greek cities in Sicily. His government was now marked by good laws and peaceful administration. In 289 he committed suicide, to escape the effects of poison administered by a slave at the instigation of one of his grandsons.

Agathon (*c.* 447-400 B.C.), Athenian tragic poet, contemporary of Euripides, Plato, Aristophanes, and Socrates. He was the first to write a play, *Anthos* ('the Flower'), with an invented plot.

Agau, a people belonging to the Hamitic race, believed to be the aborigines of Abyssinia.

Agave, a genus of plants, belonging to the order Amaryllidaceæ. There are a number of species, all natives of Mexico and Central America. They are often popularly confounded with the Aloe and *Agave americana* is generally known by the name of *American Aloe.* The agaves have either no proper stem, or a very short one bearing at its summit a crowded head of large, fleshy leaves, which are spiny at the margin. By macerating the leaves, coarse fibres can be obtained, known as *Maguey, Pita Hemp,* or *Tampico Hemp,* from which thread, twine, rope, and a coarse variety of paper may be made.

When the young flower bud has been cut out, the sap continues to flow into the cavity. This sap is termed *aguamiel,* and contains a considerable amount of sugar. It is collected daily, and after rapid fermentation furnishes the national beverage called *pulque.* This is milky, sour, and ill-smelling, resembling thin buttermilk; yet even Europeans find it agreeable and refreshing. In large quantities it produces a dull intoxication followed by heavy sleep.

Age, a historical period marked off by special characteristics. Thus, we speak of the Homeric Age, the Age of Pericles, the Augustan Age, the Elizabethan Age, to denote certain broad distinctions in literature and art. We also refer to certain ages as the Golden Age, the Iron Age, etc.—a form of reference originating with Hesiod, who divided the world's history into five periods: (1) *The Golden Age,* or reign of Saturn; of patriarchal simplicity, when the earth yielded her fruits spontaneously, and spring was eternal. (2) *The Silver Age,* or reign of Jupiter; a lawless time when troubles began, labor was imposed on man, and property began to be held. (3) *The Brazen Age,* or reign of Neptune; a period of lawlessness, war, and violence. (4) *The Heroic Age,* when men began to aspire to better things. (5) *The Iron Age* (Hesiod's own), from which justice and piety had disappeared. Ovid followed Hesiod, leaving out the Heroic Age. Varro recognized three ages: (1) *before the Deluge;* (2) *after the Deluge to the First Olympiad*—mythical period; (3) *after the First Olympiad*—historical period. Lucretius also noted three : (1) *the Age of Stone,* (2) *the Age of Bronze,* and (3) *the Age of Iron.*

Historians divide European history from the fall of the Roman Empire to the beginning of modern times into certain ill-defined periods. The *Dark Ages,* nearly coinciding in time with the Middle Ages, refer to the period of intellectual darkness from the decline of classical learning, after the establishment of the barbarians in Europe in the fifth century, till the Renaissance in the fifteenth century (or till about the eleventh century, by Hallam). *The Middle Ages,* or the thousand years between the fall of Rome (455) and the great movements of the fifteenth and sixteenth centuries. (See MIDDLE AGES.) *The Feudal Ages,* from the tenth to the sixteenth century.

The geological ages or periods will be found discussed at GEOLOGY; while the stone, bronze, and iron ages which archæological research has accepted, are treated under BRONZE AGE; IRON AGE; STONE AGE.

In the life of the individual, it is usual to speak of four ages—infancy, youth, manhood, and old age. For the biological consideration of length of life, see LONGEVITY.

Age, in Law, is that period in the life of a human being when he is deemed fully capable of exercising the rights and fulfilling the duties of ordinary citizenship. In Roman law boys up to the age of fourteen and girls to that of twelve were called pupils, and if their *paterfamilias* were dead had to be under a tutor. From fourteen or twelve to twenty-five they were in minority, and though generally capable of performing all legal acts, might be under the guidance of a curator.

In modern legal system (*e.g.*, that of Scotland) which maintain the Roman twofold division of a young person's life, minority generally ceases at twenty-one, instead of at twenty-five. In the United States, full age is generally attained on the day preceding the twenty-first birthday, though in some States women come of age at 18. Prior to that time they are termed infants.

Agence Havas. See **Havas Agency.**

Agenda (Latin *agere,* to do), used in theology to distinguish between practical duties and doctrinal beliefs.

Agenor, in Grecian mythology king of Phœnicia, son of Poseidon, and father of Cadmus, Europa, Cilix, and (according to some) Phœnix. When Europa was borne away by Zeus, Agenor commanded his sons to seek their sister, and not to return without her. Their search proving vain, Cadmus founded Thebes, while Phœnix became the ancestor of the Phœnicians.

Agent. See **Principal and Agent; Broker.**

Agent and Client. A person who employs a law agent or solicitor is entitled to expect from the latter competent professional knowledge and skill. See ATTORNEY.

Agent, Consular. See **Consular Service.**

Age of Reason, The, a period of the French Revolution (the winter of 1793-4) when Reason was deified as a goddess, and the Christian religion was tabooed by Hébert and his atheistical followers.

Ageratum, (*Eupatorium*), a genus of Compositæ, with white or lavender flowers; used as summer bedding plants, mostly in borders.

Agesilaus (445-360 B.C.), king of Sparta from 398 to 360 B.C. After the death of his brother he became king with the aid of the general Lysander. Although insignificant, ugly, and lame, he soon made his great abilities felt. At the time Sparta was at the height of her power, and Agesilaus resolved to attack the Persians. He invaded Asia, and defeated them in many battles, and in 396 gained a great victory at the River Pactolus. Agesilaus perished in a tempest while returning from his expedition, at the age of eighty-four years. Xenophon has written his *Life* in eulogistic terms; also Cornelius Nepos and Plutarch.

Agglomerate, or **Volcanic Agglomerate,** is a rock made up of a confused mass of angular and subangular blocks of all sizes.

Agglutinative Languages, those languages which may be roughly characterized as adding qualifying words as suffixes, instead of inflicting the principal word or allowing the qualifying word to stand alone. The principal languages of this group are Hungarian, Finnish, Turkish, Mongolian, and the Dravidian languages (Tamil, Telugu) of Southern India. See PHILOLOGY.

Agglutinins, protective substances arising in the blood serum after inoculation with a bacterial vaccine or during a period of specific infection, causing the bacteria directly concerned to coalesce into flocules. See VACCINE THERAPY.

Aggtelek, or **Agtelek** (Hungarian, *Baradlam*), Hungarian village to the northeast of Budapest, near one of the largest and most remarkable stalactitic caves of Europe.

Agha Mohammed Khan, (1720-97), shah of Persia, founder of the reigning Kajar dynasty. The son of Mohammed Hasan, chief of Astrabad, he raised the standard of revolt against Lutf Ali Khan, the last of the Zend dynasty, and gained the throne after a prolonged struggle in 1794.

Agincourt, Battle of, a most important battle in the Hundred Years' War between France and England, was fought on Oct. 25, 1415, near the site of the present village of Agincourt.

Agio, an Italian word, signifying rate of exchange between actual and face values of coinage or paper, or between the standards of different countries. See EXCHANGE.

Agis, three kings of Sparta (or four, counting the lengendary founder of the Agidæ dynasty). AGIS I.(II.) reigned 427-397 B.C.; several times invaded Attica, and defeated the Athenians and their allies at Mantinea (418), and besieged Athens (405).—AGIS II. (III.) reigned 338-331 B.C.; endeavored to crush the Macedonian supremacy in Greece during the absence of Alexander the Great in Asia.—AGIS III. (IV.), king from 245-241 B.C., sought to revive the institutions of Lycurgus, but was put to death by his suspicious subjects.

Agitato, a term used in music, generally along with *allegro* or *presto,* to denote a restless and emotional style.

Agnadello, Battle of, or **Battle of the Rivolta** (May 14, 1509). Here, after the League of Cambray, the French under Louis XII. defeated the Venetians.

Agnano, Lake of, Italy, filled the basin of an extinct crater, but was drained in 1870.

The carbon dioxide waters are now used in baths. Near it is the famous Grotto del Cane and the sulphurous baths of San Germains.

Agnates, or **Agnati,** in Roman law, blood relations on the father's side, tracing their descent exclusively through males—*e. g.*, one's father's brother's child, but not one's father's sister's child.

Agnel, a French gold coin struck during the reign of Louis IX., but not used after the time of Charles IX. So called because it had a figure of the paschal lamb (*Agnus*).

Agnes, St., a Roman Christian in the time of Diocletian, who, having in her thirteenth year repulsed the heathen son of the prætor, was publicly humiliated. A series of miracles could not save her from the executioner's sword. Her festival falls on Jan. 21. The eve is known as St. Agnes' Eve.

Agnosticism, a word introduced into the English language by Professor Huxley, in 1869, suggested to him by the Greek inscription ('To an Unknown God'), which the Apostle Paul saw on an Athenian altar. Agnosticism restricts our cognition to the manifestations and transformations of matter and energy, and disclaims all knowledge of spiritual existence, whether of God or man.

There are many shades and varieties of agnosticism, but all reasoned and systematic forms of it at the present day are based more or less overtly upon the speculations of Kant. See PHENOMENALISM; RELATIVITY OF KNOWEDGE. Consult Huxley's *Lectures and Essays*; Spencer's *First Principles*.

Agnus Dei (Latin 'Lamb of God'), a title of the Saviour (John i. 29). Also a prayer which since the sixth century has been used in the service of the Mass.

Agonic Lines, imaginary lines on the earth's surface connecting those points where the magnetic needle shows no declination. See MAGNETISM, TERRESTRIAL.

Agony Column, a column in newspapers devoted to personal advertisements, such as notices of losses, disappearances, mysterious communications, and such matters. These notices are often in cipher.

Agoo, pueblo, Luzon, Philippine Islands; in La Unión province. Sugar cane, cotton, corn, and rice are produced. East of the town is Mount Santo Tomás (7,406 ft.); p. 10,653.

Agoraphobia. (Greek 'fear of the public square'), a nervous disease characterized by fear in certain situations, usually large spaces. The patient suffers palpitation of the heart, trembling, coldness, and other symptoms of terror.

Agoult, Marie Catherine Sophie de Flavigny, Comtesse d' (1805-76), French author whose pseudonym was 'Daniel Stern,' was born in Frankfort-on-Main. In 1827 she married Count d'Agoult, but left him to live with Franz Liszt. To Liszt she bore three children, of whom Blandine married Emile

© F. Firth & Co. Ltd.
AGRA.—*The Taj Mahal, or 'Peerless Tomb'*

Ollivier, and Cosima married first Hans von Bülow and later Richard Wagner. Her published works include *Esquisses morales et politiques,* by which she is best known.

Agra, third city of the United Provinces of Agra and Oudh, India, and the capital of Agra district, is situated on the Jumna River. The native city originally covered 11 sq. m., about half of which is now occupied. To the south is the British cantonment, within which are the barracks, hotels, post office, banks, and public gardens.

Architecturally, Agra is one of the most remarkable cities of India, and some of the public buildings are on a scale of striking magnificence. Within the walls of the Fort, built by Akbar, are mosques and pavilions, including the Moti Masjid or Pearl Mosque, so called for its beautiful interior of white marble. About a mile to the east is the famous Taj Mahal, considered the most beautiful building in the world. See TAJ MAHAL. There are manufactures of shoes, pipe stems, gold lace, gold and silver embroidery, carving in soapstone, and of inlaid mosaic work, for which Agra is famous; p. 229,764.

Agra and Oudh. See **United Provinces.**

Agram, or **Zagreb,** city, the capital of Croatia-Slavonia, Yugoslavia, situated at the foot of a richly wooded range of mountains. Its industries include the manufacture of tobacco, leather, linen, porcelain, and silk. There is a good trade in grain and wine. Repeated shocks of earthquake in November, 1880, destroyed most of the public buildings. Until after World War I it was a city of Hungary; p. 185,581.

Agraphia a nervous complaint, in which the patient is unable to write what he means. See APHASIA.

Agrarian Laws, the term used to denote the legislation of the ancient Romans dealing with the *ager publicus* or public domain. These laws play an important part in Roman history, their object being to utilize the public lands for the greatest public good. As the Roman power was extended through victories over surrounding tribes and nations, large portions of territory were appropiated by the state. The use of these public lands came largely into the hands of the patrician families, who, by means of slave labor, were able to cultivate huge farms at infinitesimal cost.

The name Agrarian Laws was formerly associated with the idea of interference with private property in land, and with the application thereto of communistic principles. Thus the French Convention in 1793 passed an act punishing with death any one who should propose an agrarian law, in the sense of a bill for the equal distribution of the soil among all citizens. It has now been conclusively proved that the Roman laws of that name had reference solely to public or state lands, not to those held in private ownership. See LAND LAWS.

Agreda, Maria Fernande Coronel, Abbess of (1602-65), known to the convent as Maria de Jesus. She embodied her inspiration in a life of the Virgin, *Mystica Ciudad de Dios.* Translated into French, Italian, and German, her book is still read by upholders of the Immaculate Conception.

Agreement. See **Contract.**

Agricola, Cnæus Julius (37-93), a distinguished Roman of imperial times, was born in Forum Julii (now Fréjus in Provence). Having served with distinction in Britain, Asia, and Aquitania, he was in 77 A.D. elected consul, and in the following year proceeded as Governor to Britain. The jealousy of the Emperor Domitian caused his removal, and is supposed to have hastened his death (A.D. 93). His *Life* by his son-in-law Tacitus is regarded as one of the finest specimens of biography in literature.

Agricola, Johann (1492-1566) (originally SCHNITTER or SCHNEIDER, called also MAGISTER ISLEBIUS from his birthplace, Eisleben), was one of the most zealous founders of Protestantism. He took an active part in the drawing up of the Augsburg *Interim,* and wrote many theological books; but his collection of German proverbs gives him his best claim to lasting fame. Consult Kawerau's *Johann Agricola.*

Agricola, Rodolphus (1443-85), the foremost scholar of the 'New Learning' in Germany, was born near Groningen, in Friesland. His real name, Roelof Huysmann ('husbandman'), he Latinized into Agricola. He distinguished himself as a lecturer, a musician, and a painter.

Agricultural Associations are voluntary organizations of farmers and others, having for their purpose the advancement of agriculture and the mutual benefit of their members.

Agricultural associations, local, regional, and national in scope, are found in all the civilized countries of the world; and there is an International Institute of Agriculture, established in 1905. See CO-OPERATION; GRANGE; FARMER'S ALLIANCE.

Agricultural Experiment Stations are institutions or departments devoted to practical, systematic investigations in the science of agriculture. The first public experiment station was opened near Leipzig, Germany, in 1851, in connection with the University of that city. Such stations are now maintained in almost every civilized country, and are usually supported by the government.

United States.—Experiment stations are to be found in every State, as well as in Alaska, Puerto Rico, Hawaii, and Guam. These stations are maintained by the several States, and each station receives appropriations from the Federal Government under the Hatch Act, the Adams Act, the Purnell Act and the Bankhead-Jones Act. Certain sums are 'to be applied only to paying the necessary expenses of conducting original researches or experiments bearing directly on the agricultural industry of the United States.' The funds available to United States stations in the year ended June 30, 1938, totaled about $20,000,000, of which about $6,000,000 was contributed by the U. S.

With few exceptions the experiment stations are departments of the land-grant agricultural colleges, but in some instances the subsidy has been divided between two stations.

A vast amount of valuable research and experimental work has been accomplished at these stations; and the results have been published in special reports, bulletins, circulars, and press notices for free distribution. They also encourage private experiments, and publish the results, and give advice and information to farmers on application. The stations are represented in the U. S. Department of Agriculture by the Office of Experiment Stations.

Agriculture. In a broad sense, Agriculture includes Horticulture and Forestry, as well as what is ordinarily called Farming. The dividing line between these subjects cannot be sharply drawn, and in particular farming and horticulture overlap each other at various points.

The earliest definite knowledge of agriculture that we have is found in the history of ancient Egypt. The sovereign, priesthood, and military caste were the owners of the land and the live stock, while the people did the actual work. The Egyptians possessed cattle, sheep, goats, and swine, and produced wheat, barley, durra, and millet. They cultivated and irrigated the soil, using wooden ploughs and hoes, and rude harrows and rollers. They likewise cultivated flax for its fibre from very remote times; grew lentils, lupines, onions, garlic, and radishes, grapes, olives, figs, pomegranates, and dates; and cultivated watermelons and the castor-oil plant.

The Romans were the pioneer agriculturists of Europe. They loved their herds and flocks and well-tilled fields, and even during the decay of the empire their affection for their country estates remained strong. The Romans introduced their methods into the countries conquered by them. They brought wheat into Great Britain, and transplanted the vine from Sicily to France. They grew wheat, barley, millet, oats, and rye; alfalfa and vetches for fodder; hemp and flax for fibre; beans, turnips, and lupines; and a great variety of fruit They were also skilled in raising horses, cattle, sheep, mules, swine, and poultry, and made cheese and butter. They practised some sort of rotation, the land being allowed to lie fallow after grain, and made use of irrigation and land drainage. They utilized the sickle and flail, and the treading floor for threshing grain. Although much that they taught the world was lost when the Goths and Vandals overran Europe, the progress they made in agriculture and the dignity they attached to it must ever remain to their credit.

During the Middle Ages, agriculture in Europe owed its preservation to two agencies—the Saracens in Spain, and the church estates. The barbarians had trampled out nearly every vestige of Roman husbandry, and the feudal barons were more interested in devastating their neighbors' fields than in cultivating their own. The Saracens, however, introduced various plants from Asia and Africa; grew rice, cotton, and sugar cane; and brought Spain under a degree of cultivation then unknown in Europe.

The revival in agriculture first appeared in Northern Italy, where the waters of the Po traverse one of the most fertile regions of Europe, and in the Low Countries, where the industrious Dutch developed dairy farming and the Flemings became famous for their knowledge of farming and gardening. The discovery of America brought in three new products—tobacco, maize, and the potato; and the last two became in time the food of the poor with rye and oats.

The influence of Australia, New Zealand, South Africa, India, South America, and Eastern Asia is now felt in many directions, and is slowly readjusting the agricultural industries of the world. Brazil practically controls the world's coffee market, though excellent coffee is produced elsewhere. The wheat, wool, and meat products of Argentina, Australia, and South Africa, and the rice of India and Eastern Asia, are competitors with which the farmers of the United States and Canada must reckon. The increasing population of the civilized world must have cheap foodstuffs, and it is the mission of agriculture everywhere to provide them.

United States.—The early colonists were obliged to discard in great part the customs and practices of the mother country. They came from long-settled, thickly populated districts; they found before them a forest-covered region of unknown extent, occupied only by savages. The climate was new to them; there were puzzling variations in the fertility of the soil; they had no market for their products; and their colonies were separated by pathless forests. They found the natives cultivating maize and tobacco, and these became their staple productions. They also brought seeds from the old country, and in this way the New World received many of the productions that were destined to become prime sources of its incalculable wealth. Horses, cattle, sheep, swine, and poultry, all of them unknown to the New World, also came with the early settlers.

Under such conditions only a primitive type of agriculture was possible during the first century of our colonial life. Later on, the development of cotton production in the South and the discovery that rice could be grown there added two important products; while the enterprise of the sailors of New England developed new markets.

As the American settlers moved westward they found vast treeless plains with a deep alluvial soil—one of the richest agricultural regions in the world. They became extensive

Kansas Industrial Development Commission
WHEAT HARVEST
The modern machine harvesting wheat in a Kansas field.

producers of wheat, maize, hay, cattle, sheep, and swine, and in time their food products found a market in every port, and brought them wealth. In recent years the tide of emigration and settlement has flowed across the boundary line into the great Canadian Northwest.

American Crops.—In the Northern States and Canada, wheat is a staple article of export. In some exporting districts, wheat and red clover are grown as alternate crops. In Canada and the adjacent States and Territories, spring wheat is more profitable than the ordinary winter wheat. South of 42°, winter wheat is more commonly the standard crop. Wheat is the great staple in the northern half of the Mississippi Valley and on the

Pacific Coast. Between latitudes 42° and 39°, wheat is often grown alternately with maize or Indian corn, after the land has been under pasture for some years. Again, between latitudes 39° and 35°, the climate is better suited for maize than wheat, which becomes less productive. Below latitude 35°, maize is much less productive, and the climate becomes suitable for cotton. This plant furnishes the staple article of production from latitude 35° to the shores of the Gulf of Mexico.

Rice is a very profitable crop in some of the Southern States; but its culture is chiefly confined to swamps which can be flooded by fresh water. The sugar cane is chiefly limited to the rich alluvial lands near the Mississippi as far north as latitude 31°. Tobacco is a principal crop in several States. On the Pacific Coast the climate is characterized by mild winters and dry summers. On the great plains of the Western half of the Continent, and also in the Rocky Mountain region and in Texas, there are many extensive ranches for the pasturage of cattle and sheep. In the older Northern States and Canada, dairy products form leading articles of export.

The production of *Corn* or *Maize* ranks first among American agricultural industries. It is produced in every State, and the annual corn crop is more than three billion bushels.

Live Stock.—When the United States was first settled there were no domestic animals worthy of note; and of the early stock of horses, cattle, sheep, swine, goats, mules, and poultry brought here by the settlers, some were of good grade, some not. Since the early nineteenth century, however, a continuous stream of live stock of all kinds has been brought into the United States to upbuild and improve the native farm stock; so that practically every noted breed in Great Britain and Europe is now represented in America by superior animals.

Bibliography.—The publications of the U. S. Department of Agriculture, especially the *Experiment Station Record, Farmers' Bulletins,* and *Year Books,* as well as the reports of the State boards of agriculture, are invaluable to the progressive farmer.

Agriculture, U. S. Department of, is administered by the Secretary of Agriculture, who is a member of the Cabinet.

The work of the Department started in the Patent Office, then in the State Department, in 1836, when Henry L. Ellsworth, the Patent Commissioner, began distributing seeds and plants to farmers. In 1839 Congress authorized the Patent Office to spend $1,000 for agricultural purposes. In 1849, when the Department of the Interior was created, the Patent Office became a part of it, and an agricultural division was later established. In 1862 the Department of Agriculture was created by Act of Congress, but it was not until 1889 that the head attained Cabinet rank.

During the following years the work of the Department became divided into various sections and divisions. By 1951 the Department was divided into Program Agencies and Staff and Service Agencies. The Program Agencies then consisted of the *Agricultural Research Administration,* established in 1942, comprising the following: *Office of the Administrator,* which determined research policy and administered the over-all program; *Office of Experiment Stations,* which administered funds for agricultural research by State Agricultural Experiment Stations; *Bureau of Agricultural and Industrial Chemistry,* which operated four Regional Research Laboratories and a number of field stations; *Bureau of Animal Industry,* which devoted itself to the breeding, feeding, and control of disease among domestic animals; *Bureau of Dairy Industry,* which conducted research on milk production and manufacture of milk products; *Bureau of Entomology and Plant Quarantine,* which conducted research on the control of insects in agriculture; *Bureau of Human Nutrition and Home Economics,* which carried on research into the nutritive properties of foods and the best ways to cook and serve them; and the *Bureau of Plant Industry, Soils, and Agricultural Engineering,* which carried on research on crop, soil, machinery, storage, transportation, and housing problems of farming, forestry, and gardening. The *Commodity Exchange Authority* administered the Commodity Exchange Act to control prices; the *Extension Service* carried on educational programs on agriculture and homemaking in rural areas; the *Farm Credit Administration* provided a complete co-operative credit service for farmers; the *Farmers Home Administration* provided small farmers with credit; the *Federal Crop Insurance Corporation* developed and administered crop insurance programs; the *Forest Service* was responsible for promoting the conservation of forests; the *Production and Marketing Administration* consolidated the work of 12 former agencies of the Department; the *Commodity Credit Corporation* carried out price-support, foreign-supply, and other programs; the *Rural*

Electrification Administration financed the construction of electric-power facilities in unserved rural areas; and the *Soil Conservation Service* carried on a national service of physical adjustments in land use. The Staff and Service Agencies consisted of the *Bureau of Agricultural Economics*, which was the central statistical and economic research agency of the Department; the *Office of Budget and Finance*, a staff agency of the Department; the *Office of Foreign Agricultural Relations* handled the foreign demand for American agricultural products; the *Office of Hearing Examiners* held hearings in rule-making and quasijudicial proceedings; the *Office of Information* was responsible for the direction, integration and coordination of all USDA information activities; the *Library* served the Department and as the National Library of Agriculture; the *Office of Personnel* managed the personnel program of the Department; the *Office of Plant and Operations* was responsible for the housing of departmental activities; and the *Office of the Solicitor* performed all legal work for the Department.

Agrigentum (Greek *Akragas*), town on the south coast of Sicily. It was a colony of Gela—itself a colony of Rhodes—founded about 580 B.C. It is noted as the birthplace of Empedocles. On its site is the modern GIRGENTI (q.v.).

Agrippa I. and II. See **Herod**.

Agrippa, Marcus Vipsanius (63-12 B.C.), a Roman of obscure family, but raised to the highest position by his friend Octavius, afterward Emperor Augustus. He married Julia, Augustus' daughter, and had by her five children, one of whom, Agrippina, became the wife of Germanicus.

Agrippa, Menenius, a Roman patrician, who as consul (503 B.C.) defeated the Sabines and Samnites. He is a principal character of Shakespeare's *Coriolanus*.

Agua, a volcanic mountain of Guatemala, Central America. More than 12,000 feet high, it ejects its hot-water streams from a crater 90 ft. wide, and has twice destroyed the city.

Aguascalientes, ('warm waters'), state, Anahuac plateau, Mexico. p. 160,282.

Aguascalientes, town, Mexico, capital of the state of Aguascalientes. It stands on a plateau 6,000 feet above sea level, and is a prosperous commercial and manufacturing centre. p. 82,234.

Ague. See **Malaria**.

Aguirre, Lope de (1507-61), a Spanish adventurer. He saw the first rising of the Incas, and set out down the Amazon to discover El Dorado, but proved instead the connection between that river and the Orinoco. He killed the new king of Peru, and was defeated and killed at Barquisimeto.

Agur, a Hebrew sage, to whom is attributed the collection of wise sayings in Prov. xxx. See PROVERBS.

Agustina, (d. 1857), **Maria,** the Maid of Saragossa, who encouraged the Spaniards to defend Saragossa against the French during the sieges of 1808 and 1809. Consult Byron's *Childe Harold,* i. 54-56; and Southey's *History of the Peninsular War*.

Ahab, king of Israel (875-853 B.C.), was the son and successor of Omri, and the contemporary and ally of Jehoshaphat, king of Judah.

Ahasuerus, the title in Scripture of several kings of Media and Persia. The best known of these is Esther's husband (see ESTHER), who is probably the same as the Persian king Xerxes. Ahasuerus is also the traditional name of the Wandering Jew (see JEW, THE WANDERING).

Ahaz, king of Judah (c. 735-719 B.C.), the *Jauhazi* of the inscriptions, was the son and successor of Jotham.

Ahaziah. (1.) King of Israel (c. 853-852 B.C.), the son and successor of Ahab.

(2.) King of Judah (c. 843-842 B.C.), the son of Jehoram (of Judah) and Athaliah, and thus the nephew of the foregoing.

Ahimelech, twelfth high priest of Israel, who at Nob fed David with the shewbread, and gave him the sword of Goliath; and who was slain by Saul for his kindness to David.

Ahithophel, a Gilonite, one of King David's ablest and most trusted counsellors, who nevertheless joined the revolt of Absalom.

Ahlen, town, Westphalia, Prussia, on the River Werse. It manufactures linen and enamels; p. 10,673.

Ahmed I., or **Achmet** (1589-1617), sultan of Turkey, son of Mohammed III., whom he succeeded in 1603.

Ahmed II., or **Achmet** (1642-95), sultan of Turkey, succeeded his brother Solyman II. in 1691.

Ahmed III., or **Achmet** (1673-1736), sultan of Turkey, a brother of Mustapha II., whom he succeeded in 1703.

Ahmed IV. See **Abdul Hamid I.**

Ahmedabad, or **Ahmadabad,** principal city of Ahmedabad district, Bombay Presidency, British India, was founded in 1412 by Ahmed Shah. Architectural remains are splendid, and in extent and beauty rank next to those of Delhi and Agra. Ahmedabad is centre of trade; p. 591,267.

Ahmed Fuad II (1952-   ), King of Egypt and the Sudan.

Ahmednagar, or **Ahmadnagar**, district, Central division, Bombay prov. Wheat, Indian millet, and grain are its chief agricultural products; p. 1,142,229.

Ahmednagar, capital of the district. The chief industries are the manufacture of silk and cotton, and the making of copper and brass vessels; p. 54,193.

Ahriman, or **Arimanes**, was the supreme evil spirit of the ancient Persian religion (Zoroastrianism).

Ahuachapán, town, El Salvador, capital of the department of Ahuachapan. The department produces sugar cane, coffee, tobacco, cotton, and fruit; p. of town 13,505; of department, 103,198.

Aicard, Jean François Victor (1848-1921), French poet, was born in Toulon. He published several volumes of verse, several novels and many dramatic works.

Aïda, an opera by Verdi, first performed at Cairo, Dec. 24, 1871.

Aidan, St. (d. 651), a Columban monk of Iona, where he was consecrated bishop about 635, in which year he began his work of Christianizing Northumbria. Consult Fryer's *Aidan, the Apostle of the North*.

Aide-de-Camp, or **Aid**, an officer attached to the personal staff of a general officer. He carries all orders from the general in command to the commanding officers on the field of battle. In garrison and quarters the aide-de-camp superintends the general's household, and acts as his secretary.

Aigrette, the French name of the bird known as Egret, the lesser white heron. Hence the term has come to be used for its feathery crest, for feathers in a lady's head dress, or for a similar ornament of precious stones.

Aiguille, (French 'needle'), an instrument used by engineers to pierce a rock for the reception of gunpowder, when any blasting or blowing up is to be effected. The word is also used of the needle-like peaks of mountains, especially in the Alps. See ALPS.

Aiguillette, (diminutive of *aiguille*), an ornament of bullion cords or loops, attached to the shoulder of the uniform of certain military and naval officers.

Aigun, Aikhun, or **Sakhalin Ula**, town, Manchuria. The treaty which gave Russia the Amur region was concluded here in 1858; p. 38,112.

Aiken, city, South Carolina, county seat of Aiken county. Because of its mild climate, it is a noted health and pleasure resort; p. 6,168.

Aiken, Conrad Potter (1889-   ), American poet, was born at Savannah, Ga In later years he has made his home in England. He was class poet at Harvard and in 1930 received the Pulitzer Prize for his *Selected Poems*. His writings both in prose and poetry reveal a preoccupation with the melodic sound of words; he is master of the dying fall cadence. Works: Poetry: *Earth Triumphant; Bright Margins* (1936). Novels: *Blue Voyage, Great Circle, King Coffin* (1935); *The Conversation* (1939); *Ushant* (1952).

Ailanthus, a genus of large Asiatic or Australian trees of the natural order Simarubaceæ (the Quassia family). The best known species is the 'Tree of Heaven' (*A. glandulosa*).

Ailanthus Moth, a species of silk-spinning moth (*Bombyx or Philosamia cynthia*), which lives on the leaves of the ailanthus. Its silk, although inferior in quality to mulberry silk, is cheaper and more durable.

Aimak, a group of four Mongol tribes which, with the Hazáras, occupy the region of Afghanistan between Hérat and Kabul. Consult McGregor's *Central Asia;* Elphinstom's *Caubul*.

Aimard, Gustave, (1818-83), French novelist, was born in Paris. Shipping as a cabin boy to America, he spent ten years among the Indians of Arkansas and Mexico, where he gathered themes for a large number of stories of adventure. During the Franco-German War (1870-1), he organized the famous 'francs-tireurs'.

Ainmiller, Max Emanuel (1807-70), German designer of stained glass. Some of his best work is found in the cathedrals of Cologne and Glasgow and in St. Paul's Cathedral, London.

Ainsworth, William Harrison (1805-81), English novelist. His novel *Rookwood*, was published in 1834; 7 of his 39 novels were illustrated by Cruikshank. Consult S. M. Ellis' *W. H. Ainsworth and His Friends*.

Ain'-Tab, town, in Turkey, 60 m., n.e. of Aleppó. Chief trade is leather, hides, and cotton. It is a military post, and a centre of American missionary work; p. 57,314.

Ainu, or **Aino** (signifying 'men'), a primitive people inhabiting Yesso, the southern parts of Sakhalin, and the Kurile Islands as far as 48° N. lat. In former times they also occupied the main island of Japan. European in type, they are aptly compared to the Russian *moujiks;* their most striking physical characteristic is their hairiness of skin. They have affinities in speech and blood with the people of Kamchatka and the Amur district. The present number of the Ainu is about 15,000.

Most of the scientific works on the Ainu are included by Von Wenckstern in his *Bibliography of Japan.* Consult also Savage Landor's *Alone with the Hairy Ainu;* Batchelor's *Ainu and Their Folk Lore.*

Air, in music. See **Aria.**

Air, the mixture of gases constituting the substance of our atmosphere. Its chief properties are nitrogen and oxygen, with negligible amounts of aqueous vapor, argon, carbon dioxide, hydrogen, neon, xenon, helium, and krypton. Formerly, all aeriform fluids, now known as gases, were called 'airs'. See ATMOSPHERE; GASES; STORM; WINDS.

Air Beacons. Powerful lights for guiding aircraft at night.

Air Bladder, or **Swimming Bladder,** a sac, present in most fishes, arising dorsally from the alimentary canal; in the haddock, and in some other species, connection with the intestine, is not maintained throughout life. The sac may be double, constricted, or provided with side chambers. In the Dipnoi it serves as a lung, while in other fish its function is hydrostatic, although it may also be an accessory organ of respiration. The air bladder of fishes afford the finest isinglass.

Air Brake. See **Brakes.**

Air Brush, an instrument operated by compressed air to spray liquid color or paint. The nozzle is composed of two valves—a needle valve and an air valve, as on the familiar atomizer. The super air brush is a spray gun with an automatic pressure regulator and an electric motor belted to an air pump, usually mounted on wheels. Not only ordinary house paint can be used in the air brush, but also enamels, shellacs, varnishes, cellulose paints, lacquers, water colors, glues, spirit and water stains and cement mixtures. Consult S. W. Frazer and G. F. Stine, *Treatise on the Air Brush* (1930).

Air Cells, or **Air Spaces,** minute intercellular spaces in the stems or leaves of plants, which furnish the means for the interchange of gases necessary for their life. In terrestrial plants communication with the exterior occurs by means of the *stomata.* The buoyancy of many aquatic plants is due to the especially large and numerous air spaces which they contain (see AQUATIC PLANTS).

Air Compressors. See **Compressed-Air Motors.**

Air Conditioning, a term which came into use since 1927 to describe any process or device to maintain effective control of temperature, humidity, velocity and purity of indoor air, whether for human or animal health and comfort, or for the preservation or processing of materials. The rapid growth of engineering development in this field was due to the desire of people for more uniformly comfortable and healthful interiors, and the need of industry for new products with wide sales possibilities.

Egyptians 4,000 years ago rigged up fans propelled by slaves to condition the air in the palaces of kings and important personages. In 1757 Joseph Black discovered carbon dioxide, and in 1774 Rutherford and Cavendish discovered nitrogen and Priestley discovered oxygen. In 1862 studies of indoor air showed that oxygen content rarely falls below 20% and that carbon dioxide content rarely rises above 1%, so that the emphasis was shifted in study of indoor air from chemical content to *odors, temperature, circulation and humidity.* There is no proved toxicity of expired air.

The first public places to capitalize the advantage of air conditioning were theatres, using in early years various crude forms of air conditioning such as ventilating shafts, fan motors, etc. *Cooling* systems are, however, very new to man. One is the simple direct use of ice (air being passed over cakes of ice), or the indirect method of circulating ice water in pipes. Other air conditioning devices use air passed through a finely divided water spray. Still others cool through evaporation, on the well-known principle that evaporating water absorbs heat. Refrigerated water sprays are also used, or air passed over refrigerated coils. Many more claims that interiors are 'air-conditioned' are misleading (such as pumping basement air upward).

The control of humidity is especially conducive to human health and comfort. Nature intended that the mucous membranes of nose, mouth and lungs be moist, whereas, the old indoor heating systems dry out the atmosphere enormously and encourage pulmonary and germ ailments. Mere pans of water in a room are not sufficient; a surprising amount of moisture is needed for normal humidity. A cubic ft. of air at 90° **F**

Photo, Carrier Corp.
HOME AIR CONDITIONING
Latest small unit placed into window opening.

can hold 14.8 grains of moisture. A relative humidity of 65 is normal for the human organism—and at the same time does not warp doors, windows, furniture, pianos, etc., as excess dryness or humidity does. Mechanical refrigeration corrects excess humidity because air rapidly lowered in temperature is relieved of excess moisture. Change of air and circulation of air are also important factors in rooms and auditoriums.

Air conditioning equipment is rapidly spreading in theatres, professional offices, public buildings, business offices, hospitals, institutions, schools, restaurants, banks, hotels, factories, etc. The most recent developments (1941) were the air conditioning of railway trains and automobiles, several railroads advertising air conditioned train service.

Department stores are now frequently air conditioned. The White House has had this system installed, and included in New York, are the Bronx Zoo and Rockefeller Center. The greatest potential developments for air conditioning lie in the home. The home of the future, it is believed by many, will contain no movable window sashes, but will be ventilated and air conditioned mechanically. An outstanding engineering accomplishment in air conditioning engineering is the Holland Tunnel, under the Hudson River, used by 50,000 automobiles daily, and risking no lives through the deadly monoxide gas generated, which is eliminated to the extent of only one part to 10,000 parts of air. In fact the air is often purer inside than outside the tunnel.

In Nov. 1934, the Am. Society of Mechanical Engineers awarded its 1934 medal to Willis Haviland Carrier, accredited founder of the air-conditioning industry in the U. S. W. H. Stangle, *An Air Conditioning Primer* (1940); A. J. Rummel, *Practical Air Conditioning* (1941).

Aircraft. See **Balloons; Airplanes; Gliders; Aeronautics.**

Aircraft Carriers, a term applied to all modern naval vessels which carry aircraft as part of their equipment, but more specifically to ships at sea and in the air devoted principally to the operation of airplanes on scouting, bombing or combat missions. The giant airship U. S. S. *Macon* and her ill-fated sistership the *Akron* were designed to carry five airplanes within their hulls in a concealed hangar. The term is more often applied to those modern warships developed principally on lessons gained in World Wars I and II to permit the operation of fleets of airplanes from their decks.

The Washington Treaty for the Limitation of Naval Armaments recognized the important role which aircraft carriers might be expected to play in future warfare. The 5-5-3 ratio as applied to aircraft carriers limited the United States and Great Britain to 135,000 tons of carriers each and Japan to 81,000 tons. With expansion of the Limitation, the United States, before "Pearl Harbor," in 1941, had six aircraft carriers, and twelve others building; by 1945 it had 43.

The British have developed radio-controlled pilotless airplanes, capable of carrying bombs, which are catapulted from warship decks. The most recent development is the "pocket carrier" warship which carries seven or eight planes in pockets. They catapult the planes into the air, and pick them up on a canvas apron trailing from the stern. Since a long flat deck is unnecessary, they can be small, fast and maneuverable.

Aircraft Disasters. The first airplane fatality in the United States was on Sept. 17, 1908, when Lieut. Thomas E. Selfridge, U. S. A., was killed, and Orville Wright, who piloted the plane, was seriously injured.

The World War (1914-1918), reaped an enormous harvest of deaths among the flying men on both sides of the belligerents. The French alone suffered 7,555 air casualties, including 1,945 killed, 2,922 wounded, 1,461 missing, in the war zone, and 1,277 casualties outside of the war zone; 1,998 casualties were reported among American military aviators, serving with the American, British, French, and Italian armies overseas.

The first dirigible disaster occurred in 1897, near Berlin, when Wolfert's dirigible exploded, due to benzine vapor ignition, and two were killed. The destruction of the French dirigible *République*, on Sept. 25, 1909, due to faulty metal propellers, killing Captain Marchal, Lieutenant Chauré and two others, was the first of the disasters to large airships. The early accidents to Zeppelins were singularly free of human fatalities, even the score of passengers of the *Deutschland* escaping with their lives when she was caught in a storm without fuel to drive her motor and was partially wrecked June 28, 1910, on her seventh trip. Zeppelin No. 1 was dismantled after tests without accidents. No. 2 was destroyed by a storm Jan. 17-18, 1906, no lives lost. No. 3 was damaged and sank on Lake Constance, December 1907. No. 4 was destroyed by a thunder storm while at anchor Aug. 5, 1908. No. 5 was carried away by a storm at anchor, April 25, 1909, and wrecked on a hill. No. 6 burned in its shed. No. 7 was *The Deutschland,* already mentioned. No. 8, the second *Deutschland,* was battered against its shed and wrecked on May 16, 1918.

In the United States the first dirigible disaster was the explosion of the Goodyear dirigible *Akron,* built for Melvin Vaniman, which caused the death of Vaniman and his four assistants, July 2, 1912. On Aug. 25, 1921, the *R-38,* which had been named *Z R-2* by the U. S. Navy buckled, crumbled, and exploded while cruising over the town of Hull, only 4 out of 66 persons on board surviving the tragedy. The disaster to the *Roma, a* dirigible bought in Italy by the U. S. Army, occurred Feb. 25, 1922, and caused the death of 35 persons. The U. S. Navy dirigible *Shenandoah,* launched on Sept. 4, 1923, was destroyed in a storm near Caldwell, Ohio, on Sept. 3, 1925. All the officers and men in the control cabin, including the commander (Lt. Comm. Zachary Lansdowne) were killed. On May 25, 1928, the Italian dirigible *Italia,* crashed on an ice floe in the Arctic wastes after cruising over the North Pole for two hours. On Oct. 4, 1930, the British airship R-101, then the largest in the world, struck against a hill, crashed, exploded and burned. One of the most disastrous of airship tragedies was the loss of the great U. S. airship, *Akron* which crashed into the sea in flames off the New Jersey coast early in the morning of April 4, 1933. There were only three survivors. A report published in April, 1933, stated that the world's production of rigid airships had reached a total of 150. By far the greater part of these were the World War ships of Germany. Of the total, 145 used hydrogen as lifting gas, and about half of them were burned. Of the vessels using helium, one, the *Shenandoah,* was wrecked but not burned; the *Los Angeles* was decommissioned, and the *Akron* was wrecked.

The airplane *Southern Cross,* carrying Capt. Charles Kingsford-Smith and three companions, hopped off in Australia for England, March 31, 1929, but was forced down en route. A search party composed of Lieut. Anderson and Robert Hitchcock vanished with their plane; they grounded in the Taninie Desert and perished there. On March 17, 1929, a Ford plane of Colonial Western Airways, Inc., crashed into a freight car at Newark (N. J.) Airport, killing 14 persons. On June 18, 1929, near Dungeness, England, the British Imperial Airways liner *City of Ottawa* crashed into the Channel, killing seven; accident reported due to mental fatigue of pilot. Sept. 3, 1929, a tri-motored Ford passenger plane of the Transcontinental Air Transport (now TWA) crashed into a *mesa* jutting from the side of Mt. Taylor in New Mexico. All on board (8) were killed. On March 31, 1931, a tri-motored Fokker plane (Transcontinental Air Transport F-10) was flying between Kansas City and Wichita en route to Los Angeles when it crashed near Bazaar in southeast Kansas. Two pilots and six passengers were killed, among them Knute Rockne, the famous football coach. March 25, 1933, 14 persons were killed, one injured and three houses destroyed by fire, when a transport plane of the Varney Speed Lines crashed into a private residence between San Leandro and Hayward, California. March 28, 1933, near Dixmude, Belgium, a giant tri-motored plane, *City of Liverpool,* of the British Imperial Airways, crashed to earth in flames, killing all on board—fifteen. In May, 1935, the *Sky Chief* of TWA crashed in Missouri with thirteen on board; five were killed, including Senator Bronson Cutting of New Mexico. Forty-eight persons were killed when the Soviet airplane *Maxim Gorky,* largest in the world, crashed with another airplane near Moscow, May 18, 1935. In July, 1935, two Boeing planes crashed, with a loss of five lives. On August 15, of the same year, Will Rogers, American humorist, and Wiley Post, famous aviator, were killed when their airplane nose-dived less than 100 feet near Point Barrow, Alaska. In a plane crash near Troy, N. Y., on October 21, 1935, Ruth Nichols, a leading American aviatrix, was severely injured, and her co-pilot, Capt. Harry Hablitz, was killed. In 1935, the Australian flyer, Capt. Sir Charles Kingsford-Smith and Thomas Pethybridge disappeared in a monsoon off the coast of Siam.

In January, 1936, the *Southerner* crashed in Arkansas, killing 17. In the following April, the *Sun Racer* crashed, with 18 dead; then in August the *City of Memphis,* with 8 dead; and in December a Douglas ship with 14 dead. The same month a Western Air Express plane with seven on board en route from Los Angeles to Salt Lake City disappeared in a snowstorm. On December 23, near Dallas, Texas, a plane on a test flight crashed, killing six air-line employees.

In January, 1937, a Western Air Express transport crashed against a mountain near Burbank, California, killing four, including Martin Johnson, explorer, and injuring nine. Eleven persons were killed on February 9, 1937, when a large United Air Lines transport plunged into San Francisco Bay.

On May 6, 1937, the German dirigible *Hindenburg* blew up and burned at Lakehurst, N. J. Thirty-six were killed.

At Bogota, Colombia, July 24, 1938, an airplane crashed into a crowded grandstand; 53 killed, many injured. On August 24, 1938, at Tokyo, Japan, 58 were killed and 100 injured by two planes colliding and setting fire to buildings.

At Oklahoma City, 1939, a Chicago-Dallas air liner crashed; 8 killed, several injured.

At Rio de Janeiro, a Pan Am. clipper crashed into a dock, killing 13.

In March 1941, an Eastern Airlines plane crashed near Atlanta, Ga., 7 killed, including Congressman Wm. D. Byron of Maryland.

Aircraft, Jet Plane. See JET-PROPELLED PLANE.

Aird, Sir John (1833-1911), English engineer. He is best known for the building of the Assuan dam and the Assiut barrage.

Airedale Terrier, one of the largest and tallest of the terriers, originating in Yorkshire, England, and known for its 'all round' qualities. In color it is black or grizzled.

Air Engines, engines in which the motive power is obtained by the alternate heating and cooling of a quantity of air within a closed vessel, part of which may form the motor cylinder. It is seldom that a hot-air engine is now used save in the tropics where wood is cheap.

Ericsson Engine.—A successful type of hot-air engine was invented by John Ericsson, the builder of the *Monitor*, in 1833. Consult B. Donkin's *Gas, Oil, and Air Engines;* Ewing's *The Steam Engine and Other Heat Engines;* Carpenter and Diederich's *Experimental Engineering.*

Air Gun, a weapon for propelling bullets or darts by the force of compressed air, commonly made like a musket, with lock, stock, and barrel. Its range is short, owing to the comparatively small propulsive force of compressed air. See PNEUMATIC APPLIANCES.

Air Meter. See **Anemometer.**

Airplane. Airplane is the name for any mechanically driven aircraft, heavier than air, fitted with fixed wings, and supported by the dynamic action of the air. It has a fuselage or body, where pilot, passengers and cargo are carried, and to which the wings and control surfaces are attached; a power plant driving one or more propellers, to propel the craft through the air, and landing gear, equipped with wheels, floats or skis for taking off from land, water, or ice.

Landplanes are airplanes designed to rise from and alight on the land. Seaplanes are airplanes designed to rise from and alight on the water.

Helicopters are those aircraft whose sole support in the air is derived directly from the vertical component of the thrust produced by rotating airfoils. Powerless flying machines include gliders, which are similar to airplanes, but contain no power plant.

Metal construction had, by 1929, almost entirely superseded the wood-and-wire structures of the war-period. Fuselages were con-

Wreck of the Hindenburg

structed of welded steel tubing of high tensile strength, and the light alloys, principally duralumin (an aluminum-copper-manganese alloy) were employed wherever possible. Fabric covering was still employed in small craft, but the use of duralumin sheet for wing- and fuselage-covering was becoming more prevalent.

The air-cooled radial engine was developed to high standards of performance, low weight per horsepower, and extreme reliability, and, except in military airplanes, where high speed was the objective, has almost swept the field. American companies or licensees have produced the Ford Trimotor, with 14-

passenger cabin; the Fokker F-32, with accommodations for 32 passengers; the Keystone 'Patrician'; the Lockheed Vega, the Loening cabin amphibian; the Consolidated 'Admiral'; and the Boeing 18-passenger transport. By 1943, transport planes existed with accommodations for 75 persons, and by 1945, for more than 160. (See page 64.)

Light airplanes, with low-powered engines, have been built in large quantities for private ownership; and many astounding flights have been made in them. Señor de la Cierva, a Spanish engineer, produced a novel experimental type, the 'Auto-giro,' in which the main supporting surface took the form of four airfoil blades rotating horizontally about a pivot secured to a conventional fuselage. Marked lateral stability and high lift featured the machine, which can rise after a very short run, and descend almost vertically. In 1931 the Collier Trophy was awarded to Harold F. Pitcairn for his development of the autogiro. In World War II autogiros were used as Army planes. The theory of the airplane is essentially that of the flying kite or the sail boat. The force of the wind acting on a surface obliquely is resolved into two components. In the sail boat, one component tends to capsize the craft, and must be resisted by stable design and ballast, while the other tends to push it forward; in the flying kite, one component acts in a vertical direction, and the other against the pull of the string. In the case of the airplane a wind blowing from beneath a plane would act to overturn it were not its stability maintained by its construction or balancing. The airplane uses the air as a cushion which supports it for an instant, as the water supports a skipping stone. When the force of the moving air acts on the surfaces inclined at an angle to its direction, it is resolved into two components—one known as lift, a force which acts at right angles to the direction of the wind, and the other known as drag, which is in the general direction of the wind. In normal flight there is a positive pressure on the lower surface of the plane, and a negative pressure on the upper, due to the flow of air around the wing. Obviously, the intensity of the lift component must depend to some extent upon the density of the air, the power of the engine, and the thrust of the propeller. Speed is also more or less proportional to the weight of the machine and motor, as the more powerful the engine the greater the weight, under ordinary conditions.

It will be apparent that two primary considerations are involved—namely, the supporting surfaces and the power plant. A curved or cambered wing is superior to a flat plane as it not only supports more weight, but affords less resistance to forward motion. The term span is usually applied to the width or extreme spread of wings, while their narrower dimension is referred to as the chord. The amount and nature of the supporting surface depend upon the speed of motion, and therefore on the power of the propeller and engine. If a machine is designed to fly slowly it requires a larger surface than one with engine and propeller capable of driving it at high speed. With no power, if he maintains his equilibrium, it is possible for the aviator to glide or volplane in safety to the ground from a considerable height.

Given the supporting surfaces, the next consideration is to diminish the amount of head resistance. Accordingly, the central portion, carrying the pilot and power plant, has been reduced in recent designs, and is now usually enclosed in a car or fuselage so as to offer minimum resistance to the air. All of the various factors connected with the airplane are susceptible of mathematical analysis. The importance of research in the development of sound engineering practice has nowhere been so well understood as in the field of aircraft construction, and much effort and money are being devoted by governmental and private agencies to the provision of proper laboratory facilities. High-speed and variable-pressure wind tunnels capable of testing the efficiency of large scale models of airplanes have resulted in important improvements in design and construction.

At Langley Field, Va., there is a vertical free-spinning tunnel 27 feet high with a 15 foot inside diameter. Air is drawn up this tube by suction, and small model airplanes of balsa wood hover and spin freely in this upward current. Controls are guided by a clockwork mechanism directed by remote control. By varying controls it is possible to bring the model plane under observation out of varying degrees of spin. From such data it is possible to learn more about the dreaded spin than by risking the lives of pilots in full-size planes.

Hand in hand with the advance in speed has come the extension of range. In 1929, the French pilot Coste flew more than 5,000 miles in a closed circuit at Marseilles.

In 1946, a U. S. Navy P2V flew 11,236 miles non-stop, from Australia to Ohio.

The use of the light alloys of aluminum,

and of high tensile-strength steels, as well as of plastics and plywood, has made it possible to construct airplanes whose useful load approximates 50 per cent. of their gross weight. The improvement in construction methods, and the design of more efficient wing-sections have aided in this advance, and made the airplane an economical vehicle for transporting passengers, mail, and express.

Engines.—The airplane imposes many requirements on its engine, including not only extremely light weight in proportion to the power developed, but the ability to run without failure for long periods of time, unattended, at high power, and with the least possible consumption of a generally available fuel. Compactness, with the minimum frontal area, is required, in order that head resistance may be kept low. Simplicity and accessibility are essential in order that inspection and repair may be facilitated. While the modern aircraft engine is an outgrowth of the automotive industry, it was not long before the design and construction of aircraft engines became the highly specialized field which it is today. Multiple power plants have been used in most modern commercial and military types of large size, to secure the advantage of a reserve of power for use in case one or more engines should fail, as well as to permit flying with throttled engines, which greatly increases their life.

Aircraft engines are classified, according to the system of carrying away the heat received from the hot gases of combustion, as *air-cooled* or *water-cooled*. Airplane engines are also classified by the arrangement of their cylinders. The number of cylinders depends principally upon the power of the engine, although to a less degree on the type. In very small engines, as few as two or three cylinders may be used, but where it becomes necessary to avoid vibration, as in medium and large sizes, the number of cylinders is increased, and they are so arranged as to balance each other. Airplane engines usually have cylinders of less than $6\frac{1}{2}$ in. bore and 8-in. stroke. Among the more important types of airplane are the following:

Vertical Engine.—An engine having its cylinders arranged vertically above or below the crankshaft, in a single row.

V Engine.—An engine having its cylinders arranged in two rows, in the form of the letter V, both rows of cylinders being connected to the same crankshaft.

W Engine.—An engine having its cylinders arranged in three rows, all connected to the same crankshaft, the three rows of cylinders, when viewed from the front, forming a figure similar to the letter W.

X Engine.—An engine having four rows of cylinders, in the form of the letter X when viewed from the front and all connected to the same crankshaft.

Radial Engine.—An engine having stationary cylinders arranged radially, *i.e.,* like the spokes of a wheel, around a common crankshaft. The usual type is a single-row radial, but radial engines may be made in more than one row, *i.e.,* one 'wheel' of cylinders behind another. Among water-cooled engines, the V and W types are most common, although X engines have been built in small numbers.

Jet Engine.—The jet engine came into use during World War II. The turbo jet model had units with more than 5,000 pound thrust. Being more dense, the fuel which was utilized in the jet engine occupied less space than gasoline.

Seaplanes.—In general, a seaplane is an airplane designed to rise from and alight on the water. Two distinct types have appeared, the float type, in which a pontoon or float is attached to the fuselage by struts, and the boat-type, in which the fuselage is itself transformed into a boatlike hull, which serves as shelter for the passengers and furnishes the buoyancy required to support the airplane on the water. Amphibious airplanes have appeared, and attained great success. In these, wheel-type landing gear is so mounted on a float or boat-type seaplane as to permit its extension or retraction by gearing or an hydraulic mechanism under the pilot's control. The adaptability of such an airplane renders it of great value in undeveloped territory, where prepared landing fields do not exist, but where lakes or rivers afford excellent landing places for a seaplane.

Propellers.—Airplane propellers are manufactured in various types, sizes, and methods of mounting, and are constructed of different materials. Wood is not completely satisfactory for propellers, due to its limited strength and the adverse effect of hot and cold climates. Other materials have been used, among them *micarta*, a fabric impregnated with bakelite. Successful metal propellers have been manufactured in great quantity in the last few years, and are superseding propellers of other materials. In adjustable-pitch propellers, which are universally of metal construction, the pitch may be altered while the engine is in operation and the airplane in flight, by a mechanism under the pilot's control. The propeller can thus be made to hold the engine down to its rated speed at sea-level, but the angle of attack, and with it, the thrust, can be increased as the airplane climbs. Gearing between the engine and the propeller has been widely used, in the form of spur- or epicyclic-gears. The engine speed may thus be high, with consequently high power output, while the propeller speed may be kept in the lower ranges, where propeller efficiency is higher.

Landing-gear.—The landing-gear of landplanes has been standardized to such an extent that two wheels, with or without a cross-axle, and a tail-skid, which may be either the sliding type, or a smaller wheel, are almost universally used. Wire wheels, with pneumatic cord tires are most common, although very small disc wheels, with exaggerated balloon tires containing air at extremely low pressures, are meeting great favor in commercial and sporting airplanes.

Shock-absorbing mechanisms, introduced between the axle and the fuselage, have been much improved, and are now commonly of the oleo-hydraulic type. Brakes are fitted on all modern airplanes, and are actuated by pedals controlling the left and right brakes independently, or simultaneously as desired. They permit easier manœuvering on the ground, and shorten the landing run.

Wings.—Wing construction consists generally of two main spars or girders running the length of the wing, connected by transverse ribs to give the wing its desired shape. Over this framework is stretched cotton cloth, or to it is applied the sheet metal covering. Fabric covers are held in place by stitching with heavy thread, which passes completely around the ribs, and are then shrunk to the required degree of tautness by painting with 'dope,' a cellulose derivative which fills interstices of the cloth, and stretches it to form a smooth, tight envelope. Metal covering, commonly corrugated for stiffness, is attached by riveting. Wood spars are cut from single pieces of spruce, or are box girders built up with spruce flanges and ply-wood webs. Metal spars are of duralumin in rolled or extruded shapes; built-up girders of duralumin sheet, riveted together; or of steel tubing joined in Pratt- or Warren-trusses by welding. The laminar flow wing, 1939, reduced drag.

Fuselage.—Wood-and-wire fuselages are giving place to metal fuselages of steel or duralumin tubing, welded into a rigid framework covered with fabric or veneer; or monocoque metal fuselages, in which the metal covering is given the desired shape by steel or duralumin ribs spaced along its length. The fuselage usually supports the engine and propeller, houses the pilot and passengers or cargo, and carries the control surfaces. To it are attached the wings and the landing-gear. In commercial passenger types, it takes the form of a well-appointed cabin, often containing sleeping berths, culinary and toilet facilities, and a separate baggage compartment.

Controls.—The control and steering of the airplane are accomplished by the movement of small auxiliary surfaces mechanically connected to the control apparatus in the pilot's cockpit. There are three fundamental systems which control the motion of the airplane about three axis; the elevator, which regulates the rate of ascent or descent, and determines the angle of the flight path to the horizontal; the rudder, which regulates the steering, or motion about the vertical axis, and the ailerons, which overcome rolling, and regulate banking. The elevator and rudder are carried at the rear or tail of the fuselage, or on out-rigger booms extending aft from the wings. The ailerons are mounted in cut-outs at the trailing edge of the ends of the wings, and are so connected that when the aileron of one wing-tip is depressed, the opposite aileron is elevated above the surface of the wing to which it is attached. The depressed aileron raises the wing to which it is hinged, and with the application of rudder toward the side of the depressed wing, banks and turns the airplane toward the latter's side.

The devices used to operate the manual controls vary in detail, but are essentially the same in all airplanes. The rudder is actuated by a rudder bar, or pedals, upon which the pilot's feet rest. The elevators are moved by the fore-and-aft motion of the control column. In large aircraft, the ailerons are moved by a wheel much like an automobile steering wheel, mounted on top of the control column; in small aircraft, by the lateral motion of the control column itself, which is referred to as the 'stick.' The engine throttles, spark controls, and carburetor mixture controls, as well as the supercharged controls where fitted, are actuated by hand-levers in the pilot's cockpit. Engine starters of various types are fitted in modern airplanes. Some have compressed air or gas as a prime mover and others are electrically operated.

Application of Airplanes.—The value of airplanes in modern warfare has been thoroughly demonstrated, and their varied duties have led to the evolution of distinct types, each supreme in its particular field. *Pursuit* airplanes are usually single-seaters of great speed, able to climb rapidly to altitudes approaching 30,000 feet. Their objective is the destruction of enemy aircraft. *Attack* airplanes are two-seaters of great speed and heavy armament, with machine-guns and bombs so mounted as to permit their use against troops on the ground. *Bombing* airplanes are multi-engined machines of slow speed, but with great lifting capacity and inherent stability. They have long range, and are used to bomb enemy vital areas behind the front lines. *Observation* airplanes are usually two-seaters of high speed and good climb, with a high degree of visibility for the observer, and fair defensive power. They are used for scouting, artillery regulation, photography, and communication. *Transport* airplanes are large-capacity passenger carriers. *Naval* aircraft perform many of the functions listed above, but are designed to operate over the sea, and from aircraft carriers, whose decks serve as floating landing fields from which they may rise and upon which they may land.

In the field of commerce, new uses for airplanes are discovered daily. Aside from their accepted tasks of transporting mail, passengers and express, they are used for mapping, by photography, areas which are of such extent or character as to render older methods of topography too slow or too expensive; for eradication of insects menacing to health or destructive to growing crops, a service which they perform by expelling poisonous dusts as they fly back and forth over the region to be treated; for exploration in regions where other methods of transport are slow, or, indeed, impracticable; for forest fire patrol and firefighting; for advertising and for many other purposes.

There is a vast potential market for flivver planes to sell for $1000 or less. Fundamental here is the problem of engine weight and fuel cost. Several attempts have been made to adapt automobile motors (Ford, Plymouth) to aircraft use. These engines, however, average 5 pounds per horsepower, and they must be redesigned to a lower weight. The French flivver plane *Pou de Ciel* (Sky Louse) attracted much attention. It costs about $800, takes off in 150 feet, lands in 100 feet, and cruises at 65 miles an hour.

The Federation Aeronautique Internationale was founded in October, 1905, with headquarters in Paris. Its American representative is the National Aeronautic Association, which superseded the earlier Aero Club of America. While the F. A. I. continues to license pilots for sporting events, the examination and licensing of pilots for commercial aviation have become a function of Federal governments in all large countries. In the United States, by the Air Commerce Act of 1916, this power was vested in the Secretary of Commerce, who administers it through the Aeronautics Branch of the Department of Commerce. The requirements for licensing are strict, and licenses are issued in categories as follows:—Private, Limited Commercial, and Transport. Many States in the United States require State examination and licensing of airplane pilots operating within their borders.

Operating.—The operation of an airplane requires considerable skill, but is within the capability of any person, with normal vision and in good physical condition who possesses ordinary manual dexterity and has no nervous disorders. Military fliers are required to undergo lengthy training in navigation, gunnery, bombing, and other military branches before they are brevetted as pilots. Commercial pilots are required to demonstrate their proficiency before licenses are issued by the appropriate governmental agency, and are examined periodically to insure their physical well-being and their skill.

Sir George Cayley, an English inventor, was the first known person to plan dynamic flight on a scientific basis. He planned an aeroplane built with slightly oblique planes, resting on a wheeled chassis, fitted with propellers, motors, and steering devices. Samuel Henson, another English inventor, in 1843, patented what was designated as an 'aerial steam carriage.' Another English scientist, F. H. Wendham, improved on Henson's idea, and in 1867 developed a multiplane. This model was taken up by J. Stringfellow, who reduced the number of planes to three, making a triplane, which he fitted with a tail and two propellers, and which he showed at the exhibition of the Aeronautical Society of Great Britain in 1868.

In 1872, a French inventor Alphonse Penaud, constructed a small monoplane. It was only a toy—two flimsy wings actuated by a twisting rubber—but it had fore-and-aft stability, something that most of the creations of the time lacked. Louis Pierre Mouillard, a Frenchman, constructed a number of gliders, built on the principle of bird wings, and experimented with gliding. In 1881 he published a valuable work entitled 'L'empire de l'air,' which inspired many of the later experimenters. The next generation, which came toward the close of the 19th century, was divided into two schools. The first sought to achieve soaring flight by means of large kite-like apparatus, which enabled them to soar in the air against winds, their machines being lifted up and supported by the inertia of the air as kites are. The second sought to develop power flight, that is, to send their kite-like machines through the air at high speed, being tracted or propelled by revolving screws actuated by motor power.

The most eminent experimenters in the first schools were Otto Lilienthal, who was the chief expounder of gliding flight; P. L. Pilcher, an English follower of Lilienthal; Octave Chanute, an American follower of Lilienthal and J. J. Montgomery, also an American. Lilienthal, a German, was the first to make gliding flight a science, being the first also to define the value of arched wings, and to determine the amount of pressure to be obtained at various angles of incidence. The leaders of the second school, who actually built and tried power-driven airplanes, were Clement Ader (1890-1897), Sir Hiram Stevens Maxim (1890-1894), and Samuel Pierpont Langley (1895-1903). Clement Ader was the first to construct an airplane large and powerful enough to carry a man. Samuel Pierpont Langley, in America, was employed by the Board of Ordnance and Fortification of the U. S. Army to construct the 'Aerodrome' of his own invention, Congress having appropriated $50,000 for the purpose. Langley's machine was a tandem monoplane, 48 ft. from tip to tip and 52 ft. from bowsprit to the end of its tail. It was fitted with a 50-horsepower engine and weighed 830 pounds. Two attempts were made to launch it, Oct. 7, and Dec. 8, 1903, but on both occasions the aerodrome became entangled in the defective launching apparatus, and was thrown headlong in the Potomac River and Congress refused to appropriate money for further experiments.

Wilbur Wright and his brother Orville Wright began their experiments with a glider in the fall of 1900 at Kitty Hawk, North Carolina. There, on the barren sand dunes, these two intrepid investigators took all the theories of flight and tried them one by one—until they had, at last, developed a glider wonderfully exact, which, when fitted with a light motor, also built by them, made initial flights on December 17, 1903, of from 12 to 59 seconds' duration.

The Wrights did not make their achievements public at the time; in fact, until 1908 they flew only in private. But the report of their wonderful achievement went far and wide, stimulating those who had given up experimenting and inspiring others to take up the work. Octave Chanute, in 1902, went to France and related the early successes of the Wrights with their glider, and described the general shape of the Wright machine. As a result half a dozen enthusiasts, including Louis Blériot, Captain Louis Ferber, Ernest Archdeacon, and later the Voisin Brothers and Alberto Santos-Dumont, took up the work, thus founding the French school which has increased so greatly and accomplished so much. The first of this school to succeed was Santos-Dumont, the Brazilian aeronaut sportsman. He constructed a machine of original design, and in 1906 made short sustained flights of from 50 to 700 ft. in straight line, which created a world-wide sensation. In 1908 some American enthusiasts combined under the auspices of Mr. Alexander Graham Bell, the inventor of the telephone, and Mrs. Bell, and organized the Aerial Experiment Association. Glenn H. Curtiss, one of the experimenters, developed a suitable type of airplane, and in 1908-09 became proficient in piloting it, and founded a school which did much in the following years to popularize and develop aviation in America. The more important developments in the history of flying may be followed year by year.

On Sept. 15, 1904, Orville Wright, flying the Wright bi-plane near Dayton, Ohio, made the first turn. On Sept. 20 he made the first circle; on Oct. 4, 1905, he made the first flight of over half an hour, the flight having lasted 33 minutes and 17 seconds. In 1905 also were founded the Aero Club of America and the International Aeronautic Federation.

In 1906 Alberto Santos-Dumont, the Brazilian inventor and pioneer in aeronautics, made the first public flight ever made. James Gordon Bennett presented the Gordon-Bennett International Aeronautic Trophy for free balloons, the contest for which was held from Paris in 1906. In 1907, the U. S. Army issued specifications for a military airplane, becoming the first country in the world to recognize the value of airplanes for military purposes. In 1908 the Wrights brought out their biplanes and practically taught the world to fly. Glenn H. Curtiss made the first public flights ever made in the United States. In 1900-10 two score of professional aviators toured the world giving public exhibitions, which aroused much enthusiasm at first, but which cost the lives of a multitude of aviators. Blériot crossed the English Channel.

In 1911 a number of long-distance airplane races took place. Glenn H. Curtiss made the first successful flight ever made with a hydro-aeroplane. The year 1912 was entirely a military year, practically every effort in European countries being given to developing and constructing military aircraft. In 1913 all the European nations continued to add to their aerial forces, and at the end of that year they all had large fleets of airplanes and dirigibles. Cross-country flying also developed rapidly, scores of aviators making long flights across many countries, including flights from Paris to St. Petersburg and return, 60 flights from Paris to London and return, and many flights of from 500 to 1,300 m. carried out in a single day. An average of 200,000 passengers were carried in flights monthly. Another most important innovation was the use of airplanes for carrying mail in France.

The records at the close of 1913 were as follows:—Speed: 125 m. an hour, for over an hour. Endurance: Fourteen hours without stopping. Touring: From Paris to St. Petersburg and back, and from Paris to Cairo, 3,500 m., with one passenger, in a land airplane; 3,000 kilometres (1,875 m.) in a hydroaeroplane. Altitude: 20,295 ft., for aviator alone; 16,270 ft. for aviator with one passenger. Greatest distance covered in 24 hours: 1,376 m. Greatest distance covered in one day by aviator and one passenger: From Berlin to Paris. Weight carrying: Seven passengers on a two-hour flight; thirteen passengers for a short flight. Flying over water: Two flights across the Mediterranean Sea; half dozen across the Baltic; a score across the Great Lakes. Licensed aviation pilots numbered 6,000 in Europe. In America little progress was made outside of marine flying, but in that branch of aeronautics progress was great. The year 1914 promised to bring about the application of aircraft for utilitarian purposes. Airship passenger lines were in operation in Germany; airplane mail-carrying tests were being made in France, England, and Algeria. Aero Clubs of the world were coöperating with the Panama-Pacific Universal Exposition in arranging a round-the-world airplane race; and aviators all over the world were piling up new records.

Before World War I airplanes were built in a more or less haphazard way, and there was little aeronautic engineering data available. In 1912-18 courses in aeronautical engineering were established at a number of American universities. The greatest work in aeronautic engineering in the United States was done at the U. S. Army Aeroplane Engineering Department at Dayton in 1918-19, and at the largest airplane factories. Their work was, however, limited to some extent by the exigencies of war, which confined them to the analysis and construction of those types of aircraft which were being considered for production. The year 1927 was one of epochal long distance flights, which captured popular fancy the world over, and in the United States, resulted in the revitalization of the aircraft industry, and its enormous expansion.

In 1945, 7,502,538 passengers were carried 214,959,855 miles by 17 transport companies employing 414 planes. Over 87 million pounds of freight were carried. The number of passengers carried in the first half of 1946 was 5,225,299; over 151,000,000 miles flown.

From 1919 to 1923, little improvement was made in airplane performance. In the United States, the growth of commercial aviation was slow, but a wise policy of governmental support brought about sound private financing, and prepared sound foundations for future growth. A transcontinental air-mail service was inaugurated by the Post Office Department, and was operated with marked success.

On May 9, 1926, Commander Richard E. Byrd, U. S. N., and Aviation Machinist Floyd Bennett, U. S. N., flew from Kings Bay, Spitzbergen, to the North Pole and back, in a three-engined Fokker monoplane. On June 4, Clarence Chamberlin and Charles Levine flew from New York to Eisleben, Germany, a distance of 3,905 air line m. in 42 hours and 45 minutes, a world's record for uninterrupted flight. On June 28, Lieutenants Maitland and Hegenberger, U. S. Army Air Corps, after 25 hours and 50 minutes in the air, over 2,400 m. of open ocean, landed in Honolulu after taking off from Oakland, California. The year 1928 saw a continuation of notable long-distance flights, the first of which, by Captain George H. Wilkins and Lieutenant Carl B. Eilson led across 2,200 m. of frozen Arctic polar wastes, from Point Barrow, Alaska, to Green Harbor, Spitzbergen.

On July 3-5, 1928, Captain Arturo Ferrarin and Major C. P. del Prete, Italian aviators, made the record non-stop distance flight of the year from Rome, Italy, to Touros, near Natal, Brazil, a distance of 4,466 m. in

51 hours, 59 minutes, in a Savoia-Marchetti airplane. The outstanding accomplishment of the year came in midyear on May 31; Squadron-Leader Charles E. Kingsford-Smith, with Flight-Lieutenant Charles T. P. Ulm, Lieut. Comdr. Harry W. Lyon and James W. Warner took off from Oakland, California, and in eight and a half days flew to Brisbane, Australia, with stops at Honolulu, Hawaii, and Suva, Fiji Islands. Their airplane, a Fokker three-engined monoplane, the *Southern Cross* covered a total distance of 7,400 m. in 83 hours 15 minutes, flying time. With Wilmer Stultz, pilot and Louis Gordon, mechanic, Miss Amelia Earhart, an American social-service worker and licensed pilot, flew, on June 17-18, 1928, from Trepassey Bay, Newfoundland, to Burryport, Wales, in her Fokker monoplane *Friendship*.

Other notable flights in recent years include that of Boardman and Polando in 1931 from New York to Istanbul, a distance of 5,011 m. in 49 hours; Mrs. Amelia Earhart Putnam's solo flight in 1932 from Harbor Grace to Ireland, the first trans-Atlantic solo flight by a woman; and Capt. James Allan Mollison's flight, also in 1932, from Ireland to New Brunswick, the first East to West trans-Atlantic solo flight.

In 1934 Amelia Earhart Putnam flew from Mexico City to Newark, N. J., first solo trans-continental flight by a woman. Her time was 14 hours 19 minutes, average speed of 151 miles per hour. Laura Ingalls in 1935 flew from New York to Los Angeles in 18 hours 23 minutes. In the same year she broke Miss Earhart's West-East record by almost an hour.

Eddie Rickenbacker flew the first Douglas transport plane cross country Feb. 19, 1934. Overnight passenger service on the transport plane Sky Chief was initiated August 1-2 on the same year. Fourteen passengers were carried from New York to Los Angeles in 18 hours.

H. F. Broadbent made a solo flight in 1935 from Croydon, England, to Port Darwin, Australia, in 6 days 21 hours 18 minutes; Lieut.-Commander Hebrard and Pilot Lieut. Deilliere combined in a non-stop seaplane flight in 1935 from Cherbourg, France, to Ziguinchor, Senegal, West Africa, June 22-23, establishing a world record for seaplanes. There was also Mollison's flight in 1936 from Harbor Grace, Newfoundland, to Croydon, England, in 13 hours 17 minutes; the first trans-Pacific flight of the *China Clipper* from San Francisco to Manila (8,200 miles) 1936, which inaugurated six-day passenger service. Howard Hughes circumnavigated the world 1938, in 3 days, 19 hours and 8 minutes and this record held until 1947. Then W. P. Odom made a round-the-world solo flight in 73 hours 5:11 minutes, breaking the Wiley Post solo record of 1933. See **Aeronautics; Globester; Jet-propelled Plane.**

Bibliography.—Consult Chatfield and Taylor's *The Airplane and Its Engine;* Studley's *Practical Flight Training;* Jones' *Practical Flying; Aircraft Year Book;* Clark's *Aeronautical Engines;* Kinnert's *America's Fighting Planes in Action* (1943).

Airport, as defined by the Air Commerce Act of 1926 is 'any locality either on water or land which is adapted for the landing and taking off of aircraft, and which provides facilities for shelter, supply, and repair of aircraft, or a place used regularly for receiving or discharging passengers or cargo by air.'

Air Pumps, any apparatus for removing air from a given space. Pumps for forcing atmospheric air into closed pressure chambers, or for furnishing a supply at various pressures above atmospheric, are commonly known as *compressors* and *blowers,* as distinguished from Air Pumps, which work at pressures below the normal atmosphere (see COMPRESSED-AIR MOTORS; BLOWING MACHINES). Air pumps may be divided into two broad classes—*displacement and impulse.*

Many improvements and varieties have been devised since the air pump was invented in 1650.

Very small hand compressors, such as tire inflaters, are also commonly called air pumps. The inflator consists of a tube in which works a loosely fitting piston faced with a leather cup-shaped valve. When the piston is pulled out, air passes the leather valve and fills the tube; and when the piston is pushed in, the cup expands, preventing the escape of air past the piston, and compelling it to make its way through the tire valve. On the piston being pulled out again, the tire valve is closed by the pressure of the air in the tire, the amount of air within it being increased by a definite quantity at every stroke.

The mechanism of the usual form of laboratory air pump is essentially the same open in the opposite directions, so that the as that just described, except that the valves action is reversed. As a general rule, the vessel or space to be exhausted of air is in permanent connection with the tube and piston by which the exhaustion is effected. It is enclosed in a glass bell-shaped jar, called the receiver, which rests on a perfectly plane plate, the junction being made air tight by means of a layer of lard. From the centre of the plate a tube passes to the piston chamber, and brings the space within the receiver into communication with the space through which the piston works. This piston may be single or double acting. In the latter arrangement the valves are so adjusted as to bring into continuous communication the receiver and the end of the piston chamber which is being evacuated by the piston. During the return stroke this air is pushed out into the open air through an outward opening valve, while the valve through which the air from the receiver previously passed closes. Thus at every half stroke the receiver loses a definite fraction of the air contained within it, the fraction being the proportion of the volume of the piston chamber to the combined volume of the receiver and piston chamber.

An improved style of *wet vacuum pump* contains only one set of valves—namely, stationary discharge valves at the head of the pump barrel. As the air lies on top of the water and is discharged ahead of it, no air is left within the pump barrel, which is an advantage, as such air would re-expand during the ensuing downward stroke, and thereby diminish the effective capacity of the pump to take in a new charge of water and vapor from the condenser. In condenser practice it is sometimes desired to withdraw the air and water separately, in which case recourse is had to what is known as a rotative dry vacuum pump, or *dry-air pump*.

A series of *rotary jet pumps*, built upon the principle of the aspirator and injector have become of great importance in recent years. The first of the rotary jet pumps was invented by M. Leblanc, of France, and introduced into America by George Westinghouse. With this a vacuum has been realized of about 99 per cent. ideal.

A still further improvement in apparatus for producing high vacuums in steam-condenser work is represented by the Radojet vacuum pump. It operates on the dry-air principle and may be used to replace any other type of air pump.

Mercurial Air Pumps. — To obtain very low pressures—or high vacua, as they are called—recourse is had to mercury air pumps.

An Army Airport—Mitchel Field, Long Island.

In these, mercury pistons fall through glass tubes much as water slugs in the Leblanc pump discharge. The two chief types are described in the article VACUUM.

Air Sacs, in birds, are thin-walled chambers communicating with the lungs.

Air Ships. See **Aeronautics; Balloons.**

Air Space. See **Ventilation.**

Air Transport Routes. Air transportation was welded as an integral part of the world's network of transportation facilities between 1927 and 1930 with more than 125,000 m. of civil airways in regular use by commercial airlines. The United States and Germany each had services over more than 40,000 m. of airways. Latin America, including American and European owned lines, had about 25,000 m. of regularly flown routes, with the remainder in Australia and Asia. While Germany led the world in the development of air lines during the early years of transport development, the United States took the lead in 1929.

By the end of 1935 the country had services over nearly 60,000 miles of airways and the Newark, N. J., airport was, in number of arrivals and departures, the busiest in the world.

Huge tri-motored or twin-motored planes, seating from 10 to 50 passengers besides their crews, were favored on the exclusive passenger lines. Smaller planes for from five to eight passengers were used on lines feeding the trunk systems. The major transport lines developed their own air terminals and intermediate landing fields on routes where public facilities were not available; installed weather reporting systems; and perfected radio communication from station to station and with planes in flight.

The Federal Government now directly supports such aids to air navigation as weather reports, radio range beacon stations, radio marker beacons, and revolving beacons.

The first regular night passenger service with Boeing tri-motored transports was inaugurated May 1, 1929 on the line between Oakland and Salt Lake City.

An act of Congress in June 1938, transferred control of civil aviation to a new 5-man independent, quasi-judicial body,—the Civil Aeronautics Authority. Reorganized in 1940, it was divided into the Civil Aeronautics Board, and the Civil Aeronautics Administration which included the Administrator and his staff.

New York, Rio and Buenos Aires Line inaugurated the first mail and passenger service over a transcontinental air line in *South America* September 1, 1929, when the route between Buenos Aires and Santiago, Chile, was opened.

The China Clipper, the pride of Pan-American Airways, took off Oct. 7, 1936, on an 8,200-mile flight for Manila. This was the fifty-second crossing of the Pacific since survey flights were started in 1935. Weekly six-day passenger service was soon after initiated. On May 22, 1939, the Pan-American Airways' *Yankee Clipper,* carrying mail from New York, alighted in Marseille, France, on the first regular scheduled transport service flight between North America and Europe; passenger service was inaugurated on June 28, when the *Dixie Clipper* took off from Port Washington, N. Y., on a successful flight, carrying 22 fare-paying passengers, a crew of 11 and a mail cargo.

Prior to the outbreak of war in Europe in 1939, commercial air transport was well established in all of the foremost countries of Europe, particulariy in Austria, France, Germany, Great Britain and Italy. The war greatly disarranged and in some countries practically disrupted all service.

Since 1940 operations have been largely restored within Germany and the German dominated countries, and schedules flown from Berlin to the principal German cities and to Stockholm, Oslo, Budapest, Rome and Lisbon. Air lines were also more or less active from Italy, Spain, Portugal, Switzerland, Hungary, Sweden and Russia.

Lisbon became the most important airport in Europe by reason of being the junction point for transatlantic service and lines to Great Britain and various continental European countries, as well as for planes of the British Overseas Airways. Except for those countries most badly devastated by the Germans, Europe in 1941 saw more attention paid to air transport generally.

Meanwhile air service was established between the United States and New Zealand and between the United States and Alaska. In 1942-45 the U. S. air lines flew over 2,500,000,000 passenger miles overseas for the Army and Navy; 16-hour passenger service began between London and U. S.

During the year 1946 United States airlines made 36,370 transatlantic commercial flights, and in these flights they carried 104,980 passengers.

Aisle, the lateral subdivision of a church parallel to the choir, nave, or transept. The word is also popularly applied to the passage in a church or hall between the pews or seats.

Aislé, in heraldry, used when the wings are blazoned of a different tincture from the animal.

Aisne, department, Northern France, comprising parts of Picardy, Brie, and the Isle of France and forming for a few miles the French frontier toward Belgium. Capital, Laon. See AISNE, BATTLES OF.

Aisne, river (ancient *Axona*), rises in the department of Meuse, traverses the departments of Ardennes, Aisne, and Oise, passing through Vouziers and Soissons, and joins the Oise near Compiègne. Length, 175 m. See AISNE, BATTLES OF.

Aisne, Battles of the, a name given to a number of engagements in the Great War of Europe. *First Battle.*—On Sept. 12, 1914, following the retreat of the First Battle of the Marne (see MARNE, BATTLES OF), the Germans occupied the line of positions on the Aisne and the Suippe which they had previously prepared against such an emergency, a line which is one of the strongest defences in Europe.

Von Kluck, with the First German Army, held the western section from the Forest of the Eagle to the plateau of Craonne, and the Saxon troops were joined to Von Buelow's forces. Against Von Buelow was ranged Foch's 9th French Army. On Sept. 11 and 12 the Allied armies had believed the enemy to be in full retreat. General Joffre decided to make a frontal attack.

The first fighting was an affair of advanced Allied cavalry and strong German rearguard action. By the close of the day, Sept. 13, most of the Allied armies had crossed the Aisne. During the next five days there was a series of attacks and counter-attacks. Sept. 18 is known as the end of the First Battle of the Aisne, as it marked the conclusion of the attempt of the Allies to break down the German positions by a frontal attack. The past five days convinced the Allies that this was no rearguard action but a long-thought-out defence of an army ready and willing for battle. The forces were too evenly matched to produce anything better than stalemate. Not less than 50,000 Germans were put out of action in this battle, while the Allied loss was considerably less.

Second Battle.—On April 1, 1917, (see SOISSONS, BATTLE OF), with the exception of the front at Troyon, the Germans occupied the dominating positions. Gen. Nivelle, of Verdun fame, was in command of the French armies on this front. His plan was to force the Aisne heights in one bold assault. The French armies were divided into three main groups—the Eastern, under De Castelnau; the Central, under Pétain; and the Northern, under D'Esperey. A fourth group, a reserve, was under Micheler. It was the largest front of attack on the West since the Marne, and the divisions of assault employed were three times those which Haig had used at Arras.

On the German side the Army Group of the Crown Prince extended from the Oise to Verdun. The front was defended by not less than 350,000 infantry, and by a great mass of artillery and machine guns. But as Nivelle did not gain his objective—the road to Laon was as firmly barred as ever—in the time calculated, discouragement and dissatisfaction arose throughout France, resulting in the revival of the office of Chief of the General Staff in the French War Ministry to which Pétain was appointed. He ordered the resumption of the limited objective tactics. Finally on May 15, in conformity with the new trend of events, Pétain succeeded Nivelle as Commander-in-chief of the French armies of the north and northeast, and Foch succeeded the former as Chief of the General Staff in Paris. From then until May 20 the French action was mainly for the improvement of their lines, which they held against violent German counter-attacks on May 21, 23, and 24.

The Second Battle of the Aisne lasted a little more than a month. It did not achieve the aim of the French High Command, which was the dislocation of the southern point of the Siegfried Line, and to that extent may be written down a failure, but it was far from barren of results. It engaged and destroyed a large number of German divisions; it used up a quantity of the best German 'shock-troops'; and it cost the enemy positions which were essential to his comfort, and ultimately, to his security. The Second Battle of the Aisne, as far as the main operations were concerned, finished with the capture of the California Plateau on May 5, but it continued to drag out with sharp and costly fighting for more than 100 days.

Following the successes at Verdun during August and September, Pétain launched a second autumn battle against the Germans. He chose that part of the Aisne where the enemy still had a foothold, the western end of the Chemin-des-Dames between Allemant and Malmaison, his aim being to clear the enemy wholly off the heights and to advance to the banks of the Ailette. Success was immediate and unbroken. That day an advance of $2\frac{1}{2}$ miles was made on a four-mile front with 8,000 prisoners and many guns. The Germans were in a position in which they could not remain. Presently the two armies faced each other across the marshy valley bottom. The Germans were in sore straits. After six months' battle the Heights of the Aisne, on which the Germans had, for three years, been entrenched, were again in the hands of the French.

Third Battle.—The success of Von Hindenburg's armies in the West during April and May, 1918, keyed the German people to a high pitch of confidence. The Germans still had a superiority in numbers over the Allies; they also had the strategic initiative and the advantage of interior lines. Ludendorff still aimed at the separation of the British and French armies, and for him the vital terrain was still the Somme. But he did not consider that the time was ripe for the final blow, and he resolved to repeat his Lys experiment, and strike first in a different area —this time the Aisne—with the object of exhausting Foch's reserves and stripping bare his centre.

On Sunday, May 26, 1918, all was quiet in the threatened area; although the first news of an impending attack came from a prisoner taken by the French that day. At 1 A.M., May 27, a sharp bombardment began everywhere from the Ailette to the suburbs of Rheims. At 4 o'clock the infantry advanced, and in two hours had swept the French from the crest of the ridge. By nightfall the Germans had crossed the Aisne. The battle now reached the district of the Tardenois, that upland which is the watershed between the Aisne and the Marne. It was Ludendorff's desire to push for the Marne at his best speed; but the difficulty lay with his flanks. So long as Soissons and Rheims held he would be forced by every day's advance into a narrower salient. On May 28 he succeeded in forcing back the containing Allied wings. That day the first U. S. Division, brigaded with the Third French Army, attacked in the Montdidier section and took the village of Cantigny, along with 170 prisoners. Three furious counter-assaults failed to retake the place. On May 29 the broadening of the salient began in earnest, and Soissons fell. By the close of May 30, the Germans had advanced over 30 m. in the past 72 hours and occupied 10 m. of the Marne from Dormans to just east of Château-Thierry. The next day the German right made considerable advance. The situation was very grave. Consequently the French brought up fresh reserves.

The American troops had been brought into action on the western and southern side of the salient, and counter-attacked with success west of Torcy, and defeated an attempt to ford the Marne at Jaulgonne. The French and the Americans took Neuilly-la-Poterie and Bouresches, and the French captured the important Hill 204 above Château-Thierry on June 7. On Sunday, July 9, Von Hutier attacked the Allies on the Montdidier-Noyon front, on most of which he failed. The battle front was now gigantic, not less than 100 miles from Mesnil St. George to Rheims. For the rest of the month there was a nip-and-tuck struggle without any advantages to either side. Having failed on his right flank, the Crown Prince now made an effort on his left. On June 18, Von Below, under-rating the defence of Rheims, used only three divisions in a futile attack on that front. Although encircled on three sides, the city of Rheims stoutly held.

Last Actions on the Aisne.—In the Second Battle of the Marne (1918), Mangin with the Tenth French Army struck at dawn on Thursday, Aug. 1, and by 9 A.M. took Hill 205. That hill was a key position which was now held against two counter-attacks. Von Boehn admitted defeat as his front was turned between the Ourcq and the Vesle and his hold on Soissons was fatally loosened. Then followed a retirement of the German Seventh Army while Mangin continued the advance.

All was quiet on the Aisne until 6 A.M., Sunday, Aug. 18, when Mangin's Tenth Army struck between the Oise and the Aisne. It was a strictly limited operation on a 10-m. front. Von Boehn, much harassed by requests for reinforcements everywhere, disregarded the business as only a local attack. He withdrew his troops there to the battle zone and waited. The next day Mangin, by cunningly varying his hour of attack to the confusion of the enemy, pressed in on a broader front. On Aug. 20, he had established himself firmly on the western part of the Heights of the Aisne, and threatened alike the German line on that river and their line west of the Oise, and Von Boehn and the Crown Prince had every man they could muster involved in its defence.

Mangin gained ground, and Sept. 5 found him well north of the Ailette, while his right wing was moving eastward along the Chemin-des-Dames, and the French and Americans of the Sixth and Fifth Armies had driven the Germans from the Vesle, and stood on the crest between that stream and the Aisne. By Sept. 24 Mangin had fought his way to the edge of the Chemin-des Dames. On Oct. 1 Mangin had regained the western part of the Chemin-des-Dames. The Tenth and Fifth French Armies occupied the whole of the Chemin-des-Dames and the Germans were soon in full retreat all along the line. On Oct. 14 Laon and LaFère were taken by Mangin; this with the captures of Cambrai and St. Quentin completed the demolishment of the key positions of the famous Hindenburg line.

Aitken, Robert Grant (1864), American astronomer, was born in Jackson, Cal. He discovered some 3,000 double stars, and in 1906, was awarded the Lalande Prize by the French Academy of Sciences.

Aitken, Robert Ingersoll (1878-1949), American sculptor. For the Panama-Pacific Exposition (1915) he executed 4 titanic figures—Fire, Air, Water, and Earth—and the Fountain of the Earth. He was a member of the National Academy of Design and of the National Institute of Arts and Letters.

Aix-la-Chapelle, or **Aachen,** city, Prussia, in the Rhineland, capital of Aachen district. Its Cathedral dates from the time of Charlemagne; p. 165,710. Nov., 1918, in accordance with the Treaty of Versailles, it was occupied by Belgian troops. It was bombed and seized by the Allies, Oct., 1944.

Aix-la-Chapelle, Congress of, a meeting held in 1818, to regulate the affairs of Europe after the Napoleonic wars.

Aix-la-Chapelle, Treaties of. The first Peace of Aix-la-Chapelle (1668) ended the war carried on between France and Spain for the possession of the Spanish Netherlands (see LOUIS XIV.).—The second Peace of Aix-la-Chapelle (1748) concluded the War of the Austrian Succession.

Ajaccio, capital of Corsica, was the birthplace of Napoleon I., and the 'Casa Bonaparte' (Bonaparte's House) is now national property; p. 37,146.

Ajalon, the modern **Yalo,** town of the Levites in ancient Palestine, northwest of Jerusalem.

Ajax The Greater, son of Telamon. He sailed against Troy with twelve ships, and is represented by Homer as, next to Achilles, the bravest and handsomest of the Greeks.

Ajax The Less, son of Oïleus, king of the Locrians. He was famous for swiftness of foot and skill in hurling the spear.

Akbar (*i.e.,* 'the Great') (1542-1605), properly JELAL-UDDIN-MOHAMMED, *Mogul* emperor of India, the greatest Asiatic monarch of modern times. He conquered and conciliated all the independent Mohammedan and Hindu princes of Northern India from Cashmere to Behar. Consult Malleson's *Life.*

Akeley, Carl Ethan (1864-1926), American naturalist and explorer. While on an expedition to Uganda he died in Kabale, Nov. 29, 1926. Akeley was known for his invention of the Akeley camera, and for his sculptures, particularly those of elephants. He was the author of *In Brightest Africa* (1923).

A Kempis, Thomas. See **Kempis.**

Akenside, Mark (1721-70), English physician and poet born in Newcastle. His arrogance provoked Smollett to satirize him in *Peregrine Pickle.* His *The Pleasures of Imagination* was published in 1744.

Akers, Benjamin Paul (1825-61), American sculptor. He executed portrait busts of Milton, Longfellow, and Edward Everett.

Akins, Zoe (1886-   ), playwright and poet, was born at Humansville, Missouri. She won the Pulitzer Prize for the best play of 1936 with *The Old Maid.* She was educated at Monticello Seminary, Godfrey, Ill., and at Hosmer Hall, St. Louis. She began contributing poetry and criticism to *Reedy's Mirror,* St. Louis, at an early age, and then to leading national magazines. She is a member of Poetry Society and American Dramatists and Composers Society. *The Old Maid* was an adaptation from a story by Edith Wharton. Miss Akins is the author of *Interpretations* (poems), *Declasse, Footloose, The Greeks Had a Word For It, The Human Element,* an adaptation from a story by W. Somerset Maugham.

Akita, department, northern part of Hondo, or Honshu, Japan. Area, 4,502 sq. m.; p. 1,211,962.

Akita (*Kubota*), seaport, capital of Akita department, Japan; p. 101,009.

Akka, or **Akoa** (called *Tikki-Tikki* by their Niam-Niam neighbors), a dwarf people of Equatorial Africa, discovered by Schweinfurth in 1870. See DWARFS. Consult Schweinfurth's *Heart of Africa;* Stanley's *In Dark-*

est Africa; Quatrefages' *Les Pygmées* (English trans.).

Akron, city, Ohio, county seat of Summit co. It is a prosperous, modern city. Akron is the largest rubber manufacturing centre in the world; it also contains some of the greatest cereal mills and fishing tackle factories in the country. There is a large printing industry, and many manufactures; p. 244,791.

Arabic, as alcohol, alembic, almanac, alchemy, etc.

Alabama (the 'Cotton State'), one of the Gulf States of the United States. It has Tennessee on the n., Georgia on the e., Mississippi on the w., and Florida and the Gulf of Mexico on the s. It has a total surface of 51,998 sq. m., including 719 m. of inland waters.

Topography.—The Appalachian Mountains

The Akron.

Akron, largest airship ever built until 1931, was constructed at the Municipal Airport of Akron, Ohio. *Akron* was the first of two airships authorized by Congress in 1926. Dr. Karl Arnstein of the Zeppelin works in Germany designed the craft, his 71st dirigible. Lieutenant Commander Charles E. Rosendahl, U. S. N., of the *Los Angeles,* was appointed commander. Loss of the *Akron* on April 4, 1933, with 73 officers and men, was one of the greatest peacetime disasters in naval history. Subsequent investigations by a Navy Court of Inquiry, showed the loss due to no fault in design or construction.

Al, or **El,** the Arabic definite article, a first syllable in English words derived from

extend from Tennessee and Georgia into the northeastern part of Alabama, and terminate near the central part of the State, where they break into foothills and ridges, among which are large deposits of iron and coal. Nearly three-fourths of the State is wooded, and the 'forest belt' on the lower coastal plain produces large quantities of long-leaf pines. Alabama possesses unusual advantages for inland navigation. The principal streams are the Tombigbee, the Alabama, and the Chattahoochee, which flow southward, and the Tennessee, which crosses the northern part of the State in a westerly direction. The coast line is short and contains one good harbor—Mobile Bay, an estuary 10 to 15 m. wide and 25 m. long.

Climate.—The uplands, particularly in the n.e., are cool and healthful The thermometer rarely records 95°, even in the lowlands; but the continued heat of the summer is somewhat enervating. In the s., winds from the Gulf relieve the heat. The swampy districts are unhealthful in summer.

Geology.—Extending from Chilton co., in the center of the State, n.e. to the Georgia line, there is a belt of metamorphic rocks. The series includes crystalline limestones, slates, schists, gneisses, and some that are of igneous derivation; surrounded by limestones, shales, sandstones, and conglomerates, which occupy the remainder of the Appalachian highland. On the South the coastal plain is floored by loosely textured Cretaceous and Tertiary deposits. The inner portion of the plain has a dark, rich, soil adapted for cotton raising, and is known as the 'black prairie.' The lower and outer portion is the sandy 'forest belt.'

Mining.—In Annison, about half of the cast-iron pipe supply of the United States is made. Gold has been mined on a small scale in Randolph co. In marble, building stones, clay materials and rock asphalt the State is well-endowed. It ranks fourth in coke production. Iron, coal, cement and clay products are the principal minerals of the State.

Agriculture is the most important industry of the State. Of cotton, the leading crop, the greater part is grown in the strip extending across the south central portion, the 'Cotton Belt.' Other products: corn; white and sweet potatoes; sugar cane; hay; fruit; peanuts.

Stock Raising.—Farm animals are being raised in decreasing numbers.

Manufactures.—Alabama possesses excellent water-power. Another aid to industry is the fact that the cost of living is moderate, thus allowing for a low wage rate. The principal industries are cotton goods, iron and steel works, timber products, coke.

Transportation.—Birmingham is the most important railway center. All parts of the State are accessible either by paved or by gravel roads. At the southern terminus of the entire river system of Alabama the State has one of the most modern dock systems in the world. The State has 1,488 m. of navigable waterways.

Commerce.—Mobile, the only port of Alabama, is well located to reach export trade with South America and the Pacific Coast.

Population.—The Federal census of 1940 showed a population of 2,832,961, of which 855,941 were urban and 1,977,020 were rural. The population of the principal cities was as follows: Birmingham, 267,583; Mobile, 78,720; Montgomery, the capital, 78,084; Gadsden, 36,975.

Education.—The chief executive of the public school system is the Superintendent of Education, assisted by a State Department of Education, and a State Board of Education. The principal institutions for higher learning include the University of Alabama, at University; Alabama Polytechnic Institute, at Auburn. A famous institution for colored students is Tuskegee Normal and Industrial Institute, at Tuskegee.

Government.— The present constitution went into effect Nov. 21, 1901. According to its provisions, all who served in the armies of the United States or the Confederacy, and all descendants of such persons (the so-called 'Grandfather Clause'), and all persons of good character who comprehended the requirements for citizenship, might register as life electors before Dec. 20, 1902. Additional qualifications were provided after Jan. 1, 1903, including the ability to read and write any article of the Constitution, and the pursuit of some lawful occupation or profession. The ownership of a certain amount of property by the voter or his wife is acceptable in lieu of the other requirements. The usual restrictions as to residence in the State, county, and precinct are also in force. By these requirements a large percentage of the Negro population is disfranchised. Montgomery is the State capital. In 1931 an act conferred upon municipalities power to facilitate aerial navigation by the establishment of airports, etc. A child labor law was passed in 1931 and a law to levy inheritance taxes.

History.—The State takes its name from the Alibamo Indians, found in the Gulf country by Hernando De Soto in 1540. Not until 1682 was this territory visited by white men when the Frenchman La Salle took formal possession of the country in the name of his king and named it 'Louisiana.' During the French and Indian War, the Creek and Chickasaw Indians of this region were allies of the English. The French lost post after post; and finally, in 1763, all of Louisiana e. of the Mississippi passed to the English. In 1779 the southern half of Alabama was seized by Spain, but the greater part of it was relinquished to the United States in 1795. Alabama and Mississippi were at that time regarded as part of Georgia; but in 1798 the Territory of Mississippi was created, and made to include a part of what is now Alabama. The War of 1812 gave the lower Creeks encouragement to rise against the Americans. Punishment was meted out to them by General Jackson at Talladega (1813), and at Horseshoe Bend (1814). In 1817 the Territory of Alabama was formed of part of the Territory of Mississippi. Huntsville was the temporary capital. A convention assembled here in July, 1819, which drew up a constitution, and Alabama became a State on Dec. 19 of that year. In 1830 the Choctaws, and in 1832 the Creeks, ceded their lands to the United States, and removed to reservations in the West. The Cherokees followed in 1835. In 1847 the capital was removed to Montgomery. On Jan. 11, 1861, Alabama passed the secession ordinance, and on Feb. 4 the Provisional Congress of the seceded States met at Montgomery. In 1862 Federal troops took possession of the Tennessee Valley, and on Aug. 5, 1864, a Federal fleet, under Farragut, ran past Forts Morgan and Gaines, which defended Mobile Bay, and destroyed the Confederate fleet. The forts, surrounded by a land force, surrendered.

In the Great War Alabama was the scene of much industrial activity. A large shipbuilding plant was established at Mobile and a Federal nitrate plant at Muscle Shoals on the Tennessee. Visited in the southern part by the Mississippi River flood in 1927 and by drought in the Tennessee River and other sections in 1930, Alabama has held her own to a remarkable degree. Power production at strategic points is a factor in this progress. Alabama experienced a notable expansion of her steel industry in 1941.

Bibliography.—Consult Owen's *History of Alabama and Dictionary of Alabama Biography* (4 vols. 1921); and *Our State, Alabama* (1927); Harper's *Resources of Southern Alabama* (1920); Boyd's *Alabama in the Fifties* (1931); Abernethy's *The Formative Period in Alabama* (1922) and Brannon's books (1929-   ); Fleming's *Civil War and Reconstruction in Alabama*; McBain's *How We Are Governed in Alabama*.

Alabama, The, a celebrated Confederate cruiser during the American Civil War. She was originally known as 'No. 290,' was a wooden, barkentine-rigged screw steamer of 1,040 tons, with a speed under steam of about eleven knots. On July 29, 1862, the vessel, under pretext of making a trial trip, slipped out to sea. She made for the Azores; and on Aug. 24 was commissioned by Captain Semmes, of the Confederate navy, as the *Alabama*. Cruising in the neighborhood of the Azores, she had by Sept. 14 captured ten U. S. ships, all of which were destroyed. During her short existence, the *Alabama* captured one steamer and no less than 67 sailing vessels. For the damage done by the *Alabama* and several other cruisers, claims were made by the United States against the British government for breach of neutrality. The arbitrators upheld the claims for damage done. The award (signed Sept. 14, 1872) fixed the indemnity at $15,500,000.

Consult Semmes' *Cruise of the Alabama;* Haywood's *Cruise of the 'Alabama';* Porter's *Naval History of the Civil War;* Scharf's *History of the Confederate States Navy;* Balch's *Alabama Arbitration*.

Alabama Claims. See **Alabama, The**.

Alabama, University of, a co-educational institution at University, Ala.

Alabaster, the name given to two minerals.—True alabaster is a form of gypsum, pure white or tinted, resembling marble but much softer. It is quarried in Italy, England, France, and, to a lesser extent in the United States and Canada. 'Oriental alabaster,' known also as 'onyx marble,' is a variety of marble. It is harder than true alabaster. It is found in Egypt, Algeria, Persia, Italy, and Mexico. Both forms are used for building purposes, sarcophagi and statues. Consult Renwick's *Marble and Marble Working*; Crook's *Economic Mineralogy* (1921).

Alacoque, Marguerite Marie (1647-90), a nun, founder of the devotion of the Sacred Heart. She was beatified in 1846. Consult *Lives* by Barry, Tickell, and Bougaud.

Aladdin, hero of the 'Arabian Nights' tale entitled *Aladdin* or *The Wonderful Lamp*. Aladdin, a poor boy in China, becomes the owner of a magical lamp and obtains anything he wishes through its slaves, the powerful djinns.

Alaman, Lucas (1792-1853), Mexican statesman and historian, author of *Disertaciones sobre la Historia Mejicana* (1844-49) and *Historia de Mejico* (1849-52), both works of high authority.

Alamanni, Luigi (1495-1556), Italian poet, was born in Florence. Detected in a conspiracy against Cardinal Giulio de Medici, he escaped to Venice, and thence to France (1522), where he enjoyed the favor of Francis I. Among his works were *La Coltivazione* (1546), a didactic poem on agriculture (his principal work, and one of the best of its kind in Italian literature).

Alameda, city, Alameda county, California, on San Francisco Bay; p. 35,033.

Alamo, The, a building or group of buildings, San Antonio, Texas, (q.v.) of historical interest because of its stubborn though unsuccessful defence by Texans against a vastly superior force of Mexicans under Santa Anna in 1836, during the Texan struggle for independence. Consult Ford's *Origin and Fall of the Alamo;* De Zavala's *History and Legends of the Alamo* (1917).

Alamos, ('poplar trees'), mining town, Sonora, Mexico. The mines of the vicinity (gold, silver, and lead) were famous in Spanish days; p. 18,715.

Alamosa, town, county seat, of Alamosa co., Colorado, 7,545 ft. above sea level Gold and silver are mined in the neighborhood; p. 5,107.

Aland Islands, an archipelago including 300 islands, of which 80 are inhabited, situated at the mouth of the Gulf of Bothnia. The inhabitants are chiefly of Swedish origin, and the principal occupations are hunting, fishing and agriculture.

In 1920, Finland granted the islands autonomy but denied separation. As a result of invoking the Council of the League of Nations, Finland's sovereignty was upheld but specific guarantees to the islands were included in the 1920 autonomy law; p. 27,093.

Alarcon, Hernando de, Spanish navigator, sailed from Acapulco in 1540, and disproved the idea that California was an island.

Alarcon, Pedro Antonio de (1833-91), Spanish author, was a native of Guadix in Granada. His work is notable for freshness and vigor, its national spirit, and a humorous yet sincere tone.

Alarcon published four long novels; two shorter novels, one being, *El sombrero de tres picos* (1874; Eng. trans., *The Three-Cornered Hat,* 1918); and volumes of short stories, travel, essays, and verse.

Alarcon y Mendoza, Juan Ruiz de (1581-1639), Spanish dramatist, was born in Mexico. In 1611 he went to Spain, where he remained until his death. Editions of his works have been published at Madrid by Hartzenbusch (1848-52), and by Garcia Ramon (2 vols., 1884).

Alaric I. (*c.* 375-410), king of the Visigoths or Western Goths, was a scion of the noble family of the Balthings. He overran Greece. He invaded Italy in 400, and again in 409, plundering Rome in 410. The Empire of the West was almost within his grasp, when he died suddenly at Cosenza. See GOTHS.

Alaric II. (*c.* 484-507), eighth of the Visigothic kings of Spain, succeeded to the throne in infancy in 485. Clovis inflicted a crushing defeat on the Visigoths near Poitiers, in 507, when Alaric was slain. He compiled *The Breviary of Alaric II.* See GOTHS.

Alarm, or **Alarum** (from Ital. *all' arme,* 'to arms'), originally a call to arms; as now commonly used, a mechanical or electrical device to give warning of danger.

The most familiar example of an alarm is probably to be found in the common alarm clock. Other examples are the bell and whistling buoy (see BUOY); the alarm whistle attached to a boiler; automatic fire alarms; the alarm funnel attached to a cask which is being filled; and certain types of burglar alarm. For the numerous varieties of *electric alarms,* see ELECTRIC BELLS AND ALARMS.

Alarodian Languages, a term sometimes applied to the Caucasian languages, of which Georgian is the chief division. Consult Sayce's *Introduction to the Science of Language.*

Ala-Shan, province, Southern Mongolia. Vegetation is almost absent; and the fauna is poor—the wolf, fox, hare, crow, crane, lizard, and serpent. The province was annexed to the empire of China in 1636; p. 20,000.

Alashehr (ancient *Philadelphia*), walled city, Asia Minor. Mineral springs in the vicinity attract many visitors; p. 25,000. Philadelphia is said to have been one of the Seven Churches of Asia referred to in Revelation.

Alaska, a territory of the United States, comprises the northwestern extremity of North America, west of the 141st meridian, together with a strip of coast extending south to 51° N. lat. and the adjacent islands, and the Aleutian Archipelago with the exception of Bering and Copper Islands. Its area is 590,884 sq. m., including both land and water. Point Barrow, the most northerly land of Alaska, lies more than 300 m. n. of the Arctic Circle, and is without the sun for 40 days during the winter season.

Topography.—The shores of the Arctic Ocean and Bering Sea are comparatively low and flat—with few places where a ship may closely approach the shore. The Pacific Coast, however, is extremely mountainous. In the North are vast plains with lakes and mountains here and there. In South Central Alaska is Mt. McKinley, the highest peak in North America (20,300 ft.). Mount Wrangell is an active volcano. The great Yukon River is the principal stream, and has a course of about 2,300 miles in Alaska and Canada. The Yukon is the natural highway of Alaska, its waters being navigable in summer, and its smooth ice coating in winter affording an unequalled sled road.

Glaciers.—The largest glaciers outside of the Polar regions are in Alaska, 170 being of sufficient importance to have names. The Muir Glacier has a front of 3 m., 300 ft. in height, and moves forward at the rate of about 6 ft. per day, tumbling its bergs into the sea with an almost continuous roar. This glacier is said to have retreated over 3 m. in the past 15 years.

Climate—With its lofty mountains, snow fields, and glaciers, its broad expanses of mossy tundra, and wide areas of valley lands, Alaska presents a great variety of climate, controlled largely by the principal mountain ranges and the modifying effect of the Japan current. In the interior the climate may reach 90° above zero in summer and 60° below in winter.

Southeast Alaska, is marked by heavy rainfall and moderate temperature, the average temperature for the three winter months being much like that of New York and Boston. The ports of this region are open to commerce throughout the year. The total annual precipitation—including the snowfall—ranges from 7 inches, at Point Barrow, to 84 inches at Unalaska.

Flora and Fauna.—The Alaskan flora includes a considerable number of timber trees, (see section on *Forestry*). Flowering plants and shrubs are abundant in the valleys, and

Juneau, the Capital City of Alaska.

gentians, saxifrage, lady slippers, cyclamines, asters, etc., cover the lower mountain slopes, merging into mosses and lichens in the loftier altitudes. There are broad areas of grass land in Southwestern Alaska and in the Copper and Yukon River valleys.

Alaska is a vast natural game park. Walrus and polar bears; caribou herds; giant moose, mountain sheep and mountain goats, Sitka deer, fur seals and sea lions; brown, black, glacier, and grizzly bears in a dozen varieties are abundant. Ducks, geese, swans, and sand hill cranes breed in the numberless ponds, and there are myriads of shore birds; the ptarmigan is everywhere; and there are five species of grouse. Alaska's game is protected by strict game laws, a substantial revenue being received from hunting licenses.

Mining.—In 1896-7 the discovery of rich gold placers in the Klondike region of the upper Yukon Valley was followed by a rush of immigration, which led to the discovery of productive workings elsewhere. In addition to placer mining, a large number of lode mines are worked. The output of gold in 1940 was valued at $23,279,000. Silver in 1938 was valued at $287,000. Copper mining dates from 1901. Because of the low price of copper in recent years, the amount mined in Alaska has shown a decrease. In 1923 the output was valued at $12,630,335. The value had diminished to $2,932,000 in 1938.

As railroad construction makes the coal mines more accessible, production shows a steady increase. In 1939 Alaska produced about 146,000 tons of coal. There are also great fields of lignite, and peat is widely distributed, the great tundras appearing to be underlaid with peat deposits. Petroleum has been developed in the Cook Inlet and Controller Bay districts. The total mineral production of Alaska for the year 1940 was valued at about $25,300,000. In addition to gold, silver, and copper, lead, petroleum, marble, gypsum, platinum, tin, and antimony are produced; also oil of high grade.

Forestry.—The most valuable trees are the western hemlock, Sitka spruce, western red cedar, and yellow cedar in the coast forests, and the white spruce, white birch, poplar, balsam poplar, black cottonwood, and aspen in the interior. About fifty million board ft. of timber are cut annually. The Federal Forest Service estimated that Alaskan forests can produce a billion ft. a year perpetually. The Tongass National Forest alone can continually provide a third of the newsprint needed by the United States.

Fisheries and Furs.—The fisheries of Alaska are exceedingly rich. Salmon and halibut fishing is carried on off the shores of Southeastern Alaska; codfish banks, said to be the most extensive in the world, are located along both shores of the Alaska Peninsula and herring abound. Whales are also caught, these and herring being used for the manufacture of oil and fertilizer. In 1944, fish products yielded over $60,000,000, Alaska's chief source of income.

Alaska has long been an important source of furs, the most important of these being the pelts of the fur seals. Indiscriminate killing did much to reduce the seal herds, but under the present laws all sealing is carried on under the authority of the Secretary of Commerce. Sealskins are a very important produce. An arrangement was made whereby Japan and Great Britain were each entitled to 15 per cent. of the sealskins obtained each year.

Other valuable Alaskan furs are fox, bear, ermine, muskrat, mink, lynx, marten, and otter. Fur farming is now considered to be upon a permanent basis in Alaska. In 1939 land fur shipped from Alaska were valued at $1,892,968. The killing of all fur-bearing animals is under strict government regulation.

Agriculture and Stock Raising.—Only a relatively small part of the land is actually cultivated. In Southern Alaska thrive vegetables and small fruits such as grow in New England. Further north, grain, potatoes, and root crops are successfully cultivated. Hay and forage are the leading agricultural products.

The reindeer industry was established by the government. Reindeer meat is being produced in quantity for export to the United States. The development of quick-freezing processes have given promise of benefit to Alaska meat-products industries.

Manufactures.—Alaska leads all the States and Territories in the production of canned and preserved fish. There are approximately 100 establishments devoted to the industry.

Transportation and Communication.—The development of Alaska has been greatly hampered by inadequate transportation facilities. There are about 1,000 miles of railroad; also river steamers, wagon roads, sled roads, and trails. Aviation has made accessible in a few hours places formerly reached only after weeks of difficult travel by dog sled. A military highway was opened in 1942 connecting Seattle, Wash., with Fairbanks and the port of Valdez.

Postal service is maintained throughout the interior the year round. There is telegraph connection between Alaskan towns and with the United States and Canada. A constant service of steamships is maintained between the Puget Sound ports and Southern Alaska; but Nome, St. Michael, and the Kuskokwim River ports can be reached only between July and September.

Commerce.—The commerce of Alaska is confined principally to the United States and Canada. For the fiscal year ending June 1937 exports to the United States were valued at $62,363,327 and imports from the United States at $42,860,774.

Finance.—Alaska has no provision for taxing real or personal property, except in municipalities, where personal property and real estate may be taxed 2 per cent. for municipal purposes only. The revenues come from licenses to conduct various businesses. The Territory has no funded debt. Government revenue, 1937, was $2,710,973; and expenditures $2,503,216.

Population.—The population of Alaska in 1940 was 73,000; in 1943, 100,000. The native stock includes about 16,000 Eskimos, 11,000 Indians and 5,000 Aleuts.

Education.—Schools are maintained in all the incorporated towns. They are supported by local license fees and appropriation from the territorial treasury, augmented by approximately $50,000 from the Alaska fund. Provision is made in these schools for industrial training. The churches provide additional educational facilities. Approximately one-fourth of the population is illiterate. The Alaska Agricultural College and School of Mines was opened in September 1922.

Government.—By Act of Congress of August 24, 1912, organized territorial government was granted to Alaska. The Territory may be said to be governed jointly by the local legislature and Congress at Washington. The governor is appointed by the President, and has the power of veto, which may be over-ridden by a two-thirds vote of both houses. The Territory has one delegate, without vote, in Congress.

History.—The earliest historical date connected with Alaska is 1648, when Deshneff navigated Bering Strait. But the discovery of Alaska is generally accredited to Vitrus Bering in 1741. The first permanent settlement was made at Three Saints' Bay, on Kodiak Island, by a Russian trading company in 1783. In 1867 the United States purchased Alaska from Russia, for $7,200,000 in gold. The government has aided in the development of the Territory by conducting experiment stations, under the direction of the Department of Agriculture. The Coast, Geological, and Geodetic Surveys have also done valuable work, including the extension of the lighthouse system and important explorations.

Alaska Coal Lands Dispute.—Considering its abundant resources, the growth of Alaska has been somewhat disappointing. One of the principal causes has been the lack of transportation facilities, the other the restrictions placed on the development of the coal lands and other great natural resources. After the discovery of the great coal fields of Alaska, the U. S. Government passed regulations (1904) which permitted individuals to enter claims of 160 acres each. Most of the claims passed into the hands of a few large groups of syndicates, so that grave fears of a monopoly were entertained. In view of this contingency, President Roosevelt in 1906 withdrew all coal lands from further entry, and withheld the patents on those claims already filed. An act providing for lease of the lands, under heavy restrictions, was passed in 1914.

In 1934 the Federal Government established the Matanuska Colony, in the Matanuska Valley of Alaska, as a New Deal project. The colonists were some 200 families from drought-stricken mid-central states of the United States. The Alaska Highway (q.v.), a road extending from the State of Washington to Alaska, was completed in 1942, and telephone communications with the United States were opened. Consult Driscoll, *War Discovers Alaska* (1943); Potter, *Alaska Under Arms* (1943). See ALASKA BOUNDARY DISPUTES; ALEUTS; ESKIMOS; SEAL FISHERIES; TLINGIT; YUKON GOLD FIELDS.

Alaska Boundary Dispute, a dispute regarding the respective boundaries of Alaska and Canada between Mt. St. Elias and the Portland Canal. The matter was not called in question till about 1888, when the Canadian claims were disputed by the United States, and in 1903 a tribunal of three British (including two Canadians) and three American jurists sat in London to settle the meaning of the treaty. The decision practically sustained the United States claims. Canada lost the sea coast north of 54° 40', but was awarded the main entrance to Portland Canal.

Alaska Highway, built in 1942, is 1630 m. long, extends from Dawson Creek, B. C. to Fairbanks; cost $138,000,000.

Alaska-Yukon-Pacific Exposition. See **Exhibitions; Seattle.**

Alastor, the name given to Zeus as the avenging deity, to the Furies, and to one of Satan's ministers.

Alatri, town, Italy, in the province of Rome. It is remarkable for its remains of Cyclopean walls, and for the church of Santa Maria Maggiore, which contains specimens of wood carving of the 12th century. The chief industry is the manufacture of cloth and tapestry; p. 16,413.

Alava, Don Miguel Ricardo de (1771-1843), Spanish general. At first a supporter of Joseph Bonaparte, he deserted to the winning side in 1811, and attracted the notice of Wellington, who made him a general of brigade. He was appointed ambassador to London (1834) and Paris (1835).

Alb, or **Albe** (Latin *albus,* 'white'), a white linen vestment worn by the priest and his assistants at the Holy Communion. It has narrower sleeves than the surplice, and is bound about the waist by a cincture.

Alba (ancient *Alba Pompeia*), town and episcopal see, Italy. The Cathedral dates from 1486; p. 14,213.

Albacid, a halogen derivative of albumen discovered by Gans, 1898.

Alba Longa, the most ancient city of Latium, situated on a rocky ridge about 20 miles east of Rome. According to legendary history, it was built by Ascanius, the son of Æneas, about 300 years before the foundation of Rome.

Alban, St., according to legend the first British martyr, was born at Verulamium in the third century. The modern St. Albans is near Verulamium.

Alban Hills, or **Mountains,** in Italy, a volcanic range, 15 to 20 m. e. of Rome. The summits are crowned with numerous small towns.

Albani, Roman family which in the 15th century was driven by the Turks from Albania, and took refuge in Italy. It produced many celebrated persons, including Pope Clement XI.

Albani, Madame (*née* **Marie Louise Emma Cecile Lajeunesse**) (1852-1930), soprano vocalist, was born in Chambly, Canada. Her stage name, *Albani,* was suggested by her teacher, Lamperti, and was not derived from Albany, N. Y. as often stated. She published *Forty Years of Song* (1911).

Albani, or **Albano, Francesco** (1578-1660), Bolognese painter. His 12 children were of extraordinary beauty, and served him as models for his Venuses, Galateas and angels' heads. His works are in the Louvre, and in Florence, Dresden, London, Milan, Turin, and Petrograd (Leningrad).

Albani, Matthias (1621-73), celebrated Tyrolese violin maker, a native of Bolzano. The tone of his instruments is more remarkable for power than for quality. His son, MATTHIAS, gained experience under the great violin makers of Cremona. His best violins are hardly inferior to those of the celebrated Amatis.

Albania, a republic, since Jan. 1946, of S. Europe, the principal industries of which are agriculture and stock raising, the chief products of the land being tobacco, wool, olive oil, timber and cattle. Albania is said to possess rich mineral deposits, notably copper, coal, silver, gold and lead, but these resources are undeveloped. The population of Albania is 1,003,124. The inhabitants (called by themselves *Shkipetars* and by the Turks *Arnauts*) are for the most part mountaineers who, until recent years, were given to intertribal feuds and bridandage. Formerly Christian, fully two-thirds of them have become Mohammedan. Area 10,629 sq. m.

The Albanian language is an ancient tongue, belonging to the Indo-European family of languages, with a comparatively recent intermixture of Slavonic words.

History.—In antiquity Albania was a part of *Illyria,* which in the second century B.C. became a Roman province. At the end of the sixth century A.D., the invading Slavs seized and settled what later became Serbia, Montenegro, Bosnia, Herzegovina, and Dalmatia, but were unable to conquer the Shkipetars, who fled to the mountains. Albania's status was fixed November, 1921, when the Council of Ambassadors set the boundaries of the country, assigning to Albania the disputed provinces of Scutari, Koritza, and Arghyrocastro. In 1925 Ahmed Bey Zogu, a native Albanian, was elected president of the new republic, but in September, 1928, he was proclaimed king and generally known as Zog I. In 1939 Albania was forcibly seized by Italy, and Albania ceased to exist as an independent country until 1944. The Greek Army occupied part of Albania until driven out by the Germans in 1941. Guerrilla troops were organized and succeeded in expelling the Germans by the end of 1944.

Albano, or **Albano Laziale,** a town in Italy, is an episcopal see and a favorite summer resort of the wealthy inhabitants of Rome; p. 8,826.

Albany, city, Georgia, county seat of Dougherty county. It is an important railroad centre, and makes large shipments of cotton and other agricultural products; p. 19,055.

Albany, city, capital of New York State, and county seat of Albany county. At the junction of several great railroads, at the head of navigation for large steamboats on the Hudson River, and the terminal point of the Erie Canal, Albany is a distributing centre for a great body of commerce, a passenger junction of importance, and a centre of varied and numerous manufactures; p. 130,577.

History.—Albany is one of the oldest chartered towns in the United States, having been incorporated as a city in 1686. Early in the 17th century the site of the present city was occupied as a trading post by the Dutch. During the era of the Revolution, Albany was the meeting place of delegates from the Colonies in 1754, when the Albany Convention passed resolutions in favor of a union for security and defence; and it was the object against which Burgoyne's campaign was directed in 1777. In 1797 it became the capital of the State of New York.

Albany's prosperity began with the completion of the Erie Canal in 1825.

Albany Convention an intercolonial convention which met at Albany, N. Y., on June 19, 1754. Twenty-five commissioners, representing the colonies of New York, Massachusetts, Connecticut, New Hampshire, Pennsylvania, Rhode Island, and Maryland, as well as delegates from 'the Five Nations' (the Iroquois Indians) assembled. A plan of intercolonial union, drafted by Benjamin Franklin, was adopted, providing for a comparatively centralized government, administered by a president-general appointed by the Crown, and a Grand Council, composed of representatives chosen by the assemblies of the several colonies.

State Capitol, Albany, N. Y.

Albany Regency, a title generally given to a group of Democrats of Albany, N. Y., who from 1820 to about 1850 controlled the nominating conventions, and had great influence not only in State, but in national affairs. Their motto was 'To the victors belong the spoils.' Among the group were Martin Van Buren, W. L. Marcy, Silas Wright, and John A. Dix.

Albatross, a large marine bird belonging to the family Diomedea, closely resembling the gulls and petrels. The albatross is one of the largest water birds in existence and has marvellous power of flight. The albatross is extremely voracious; it feeds on fish, cuttle-fish, jellyfish, and even carrion.

Albedo, a term used in astronomy to signify the proportion of incident light reflected by a non-luminous surface.

Albemarle, town county seat of Stanley county, North Carolina. Cotton mills are the main industry; p. 4,060.

Albemarle, The, an ironclad ram of the Confederate navy. On April 19, 1864, she attacked singlehanded the Federal squadron at Plymouth, sinking the *Southfield*. She was sunk on Oct. 27, 1864, by Lieut. W. B. Cushing.

Albemarle Island, or **Isabella Island,** the largest of the Galapagos Islands.

Albemarle Sound, an inlet on the east coast of North Carolina.

Alberi, Eugenio (1817-78), Italian historian, was born in Padua. In 1839 he published *Guerre d' Italia del Principe Eugenio di Savoia*, which was much admired for its scholarship. His last work was *Il Problema dell' Umano Destino* (1872).

Alberich. In German myth, a vassal of the Nibelungen kings, who is the spirit of darkness in Wagner's *The Ring of The Nibelung*.

Alberoni, Giulio (1664-1752), Spanish cardinal and statesman, was born in Firenzuola, Parma, the son of an Italian gardener. Consult Rousset de Missy's *History of Cardinal Alberoni;* Bianchi's *Giulio Alberoni e il suo secolo*.

Albert (1490-1568), son of the margrave of Ansbach and nephew of Sigismund, king of Poland, became last grand master of the Teutonic Order in 1512. He threw himself into the cause of the Reformation, made a treaty with Sigismund, and became hereditary duke of Prussia under the Polish crown, with the right of succession to the estates of the Teutonic Order.

Albert (1559-1621), archduke of Austria, surnamed 'The Pious,' sixth son of the Emperor Maximilian II. Brought up at the Spanish court, he entered the church, and became cardinal (1577), archbishop of Toledo (1584), and viceroy of Portugal (1594). In 1596 he was appointed stadtholder of the Netherlands.

Albert I. (1875-1934), king of Belgium, was born April 9, 1875, second son of Philippe, Count of Flanders, and of the Princess Mary of Hohenzollern-Sigmaringen (sister of King Carol of Roumania); and nephew of Leopold II. His father having renounced his own succession, Albert became heir apparent at the age of 17, on the death of his elder brother. From the beginning of his reign King Albert was an earnest advocate of more adequate measures of national defence, and during the Great War (1914-19) his unflinching determination to maintain Belgian neutrality and the unfailing courage and patriotism with which he commanded the Belgian forces in the face of tremendous odds won the respect and admiration of the world. He died February 17, 1934, while mountain climbing. (See BELGIUM.)

Albert I. (1250-1308), archduke of Austria and emperor of Germany, was the eldest son of Rudolph of Hapsburg. His arrogant claim to the throne on the death of his father in 1292 was met by the election of Adolphus of Nassau, who was deposed in 1298, and in the same year, defeated and slain by his rival. Albert was thereupon elected and crowned (1298).

Albert III. (1414-86), surnamed ACHILLES, and also ULYSSES, third son of Frederick I., elector of Brandenburg, whom he succeeded (1440) in the principality of Ansbach. He inherited the principality of Bayreuth from his brother John in 1464; and in 1470 received the electorate of Brandenburg from his brother Frederick II.

Albert III. (1443-1500), duke of Saxony, surnamed 'The Bold,' was the younger son of the Elector Frederick (1411-1464). On their father's death, the brothers Ernest and Albert ruled Saxony in partnership; but subsequently, by the agreement of Leipzig (1485), Ernest received Thuringia, and Albert Meissen. He was the founder of the Albertine Line.

Albert V. (1490-1545), archbishop of Magdeburg and elector of Mainz, commonly known as ALBERT OF BRANDENBURG, was the second son of the elector, John Cicero of Brandenburg. He entered holy orders. He was one of the principal adversaries of the Reformation, and Luther attacked him in a pamphlet, though at first Albert had tried to bring about reconciliation between the two parties.

Albert, Alexandre Martin (1815-95), French political leader, a mechanic by trade, played an active part in the revolution of February, 1848.

Albert, Eduard (1841-1900), Austrian surgeon, was born in Senftenberg, Bohemia. Results of his important researches appear in his *Beiträge zur Geschichte der Chirurgie;*

Beiträge zur operativen Chirurgie; Lehrbuch der Chirurgie; Diagnostik der chirurgischen Krankheiten; Zur Theorie der Skoliose.

Albert, Eugen Francis Charles d' (1864-1932), pianist and composer, was born in Glasgow, the son of a French musician. His compositions include the operas *Ghismonda; Die Abreise; Kain; Tiefland; Flötensolo; Der Geborgte Ehemann; Liebesketten.*

Albert, Francis Charles Augustus Emanuel (1819-61), Prince Consort, husband of Queen Victoria of England, was the younger of the two sons of Ernest, Duke of Saxe-Coburg-Gotha. Consult Sir T. Martin's *Life of the Prince Consort; Letters of Queen Victoria;* Strachey's *Queen Victoria.*

Albert, Frederick Rudolf (1817-95), archduke of Austria, son of the Archduke Charles, was born in Vienna. He married the daughter of Ludwig I. of Bavaria.

Albert, Heinrich (1604-55 or 56), musical composer, was born in Lobenstein, Vogtland. His hymns were set to music by himself, and include *Gott des Himmels und der Erde; Zum Sterben ich bereitet bin.* His secular poems are noted for their grace and lightness. They are collected in *Poetisch-musikalischen Lustwäldlein.*

Albert, Joseph (1825-86), German photographer, began his professional career at Augsburg in 1850, and in 1858 settled at Munich. He produced a large number of copies of famous pictures and drawings by what is called the Albertype Process. See PROCESS WORK.

Alberta, province of the Dominion of Canada, includes the former district of Alberta, the western half of Athabasca, and a strip of the former districts of Assiniboia and Saskatchewan. Area, 255,285 sq. m.

Topography.—Topographic conditions divide the province into a southern region of open rolling country, treeless except along the streams and foothills of the Rocky Mountains, and a northern region of timbered country, broken here and there by patches of prairie.

The rivers of Alberta run for the most part from west to east, in conformity with the general slope of the province. The highest peak in Alberta is Mount Columbia (alt. 14,000 ft.). There are 40 other mountain peaks in the province exceeding 10,000 ft.

Climate and Soil.—On account of the great size of the province and the varying meteorological factors, the climate of Alberta is far from uniform. For the most part, the soil is a rich alluvial loam, so fertile that manure and artificial fertilizers are unnecessary for many years after first cultivation.

Flora and Fauna.—In the south, where not cultivated, the province is clothed in a mantle of short grass in the summer season. The northern part is more thickly wooded, and is crossed by the forest belt. In the mountainous part of the western portion of Alberta bears and panthers are still found, together with moose and deer and other wild animals.

Fisheries.—The fishing industry in Alberta is not important, owing largely to the fact that the northern part of the province is still thinly populated.

Mining.—It is estimated that 87 per cent. of the coal reserves of Canada are located in this province. Gold is found in the banks and bars of most of the great rivers, but not, as a rule, in paying quantities. Natural gas is abundant, and is used extensively.

Agriculture.—For agricultural purposes the province may be divided into three parts. The southern part, is practically all rolling prairie, with little timber, and an average altitude of 2,500 ft. Central Alberta is open prairie country, interspersed with stretches of poplar and spruce, and is suitable for mixed farming, though all grain crops yield abundantly. Clover and timothy are grown here. The soil is a rich dark loam and produces wheat of the best quality.

Stock Raising.—The ranges of Southern Alberta have long been famous for the low cost at which cattle can be raised, and the excellence of the beef produced.

Transportation.—Many of the large rivers —such as the North and South Saskatchewan and the Athabasca—are used for transportation purposes; but railways will continue to be more and more important as instruments of transportation.

Population.—The population of Alberta, according to the latest census taken, is 788,393. In 1901 it was 73,022; in 1921 it was 588,454. The increase, therefore, in the 43 years was over 700,000.

Education.—There are some three thousand public schools of elementary and secondary grade. The provincial university is in Edmonton (see ALBERTA, UNIVERSITY OF).

Government.—The chief executive of Alberta is a Lieutenant-Governor appointed by the Dominion Government, who holds office for five years, and exercises his powers with the advice and consent of the provincial cabinet. The Legislative Assembly consists of 61 members. The province is represented in the

Alberta

Dominion Senate and in the House of Commons.

History.—Alberta was first discovered and partially explored and colonized by the French in 1752. Somewhat later, Alexander Mackenzie, after following up the course of the North Saskatchewan River to the height of land, explored the river which now bears his name. He also succeeded in reaching the Pacific Coast through the Peace River Pass, being the first white man to cross Canada from ocean to ocean. Alberta was proclaimed a province on Sept. 1, 1905.

Legislation of 1937 to carry out the spectacular financial policies of Provincial Prime Minister Aberhart's Social Credit government, was declared unconstitutional by the Dominion Supreme Court, in 1938.

Bibliography.—Consult *Canada and Its Provinces,* edited by Shortt and Doughty.

Alberta, University of, a provincial, non-sectarian university, founded and supported by the government of Alberta, Canada.

Albert Edward Nyanza (now known as EDWARD NYANZA), a lake in the upper part of the Nile basin, Central Africa, of nearly circular form, lying just south of the Equator, about 2,900 ft. above sea level, between Ankole (Uganda Protectorate) and the Congo.

Alberti, Leone Battista Degli (1404-72), Italian writer, architect, sculptor, painter, and scholar of the Renaissance. His great work in literature is *Della Famiglia* (1437-41), which contains a picture of Italian life at the time. He is accredited with the invention of the camera obscura. Consult Mancini's *Vita de Leon Battista Alberti.*

Albertine Line, the younger of the two dynasties of the German (Saxon) family of Wettin. It was founded in 1485. See ERNESTINE LINE.

Albertite, a solid bitumen, black in color, and with a brilliant lustre, found in Canada.

Albert Nyanza, a lake in British East Africa, Uganda Protectorate, in the basin of the Nile, extending northeast to southwest from about 2° 20′ to 1° 10′ N. lat. It is about 110 m. long by about 20 to 25 m. broad. Together with Tanganyika and Edward Nyanza, it occupies the western rift-valley of Eastern Equatorial Africa.

Albertus Magnus (1193-1280), Dominican monk, afterward (1260) archbishop of Ratisbon. He was a celebrated teacher of science, theology, and philosophy in the University of Paris (1230), and at Cologne,

Albumin

where he died. His knowledge brought on him the accusation of wizardry.

Albertype Process. See **Process Work.**

Albigenses, a sect of heretics living in the south of France; probably derived from the town Albi. They believed in the existence of two principles, good and evil, equally eternal; and they denied the incarnation, passion, and resurrection of our Lord. They condemned the procreation of children. The Albigenses were destroyed by the so-called crusade against them promoted by Innocent III., headed by Simon de Montfort, directed principally against Raymond VI., Count of Toulouse. That part of France was utterly devastated. The struggle lasted 20 years (1209-29). Consult Donais' *Les Albigeois;* Peyrat's *Histoire des Albigeois.*

Albinism, the absence of pigment in man or animals. In the human albino the skin is transparent, white and pink; the hair white; the iris a pinkish gray, or, in negroes, blue; the pupil contracted and bright red.

Albion, an ancient name, in use (probably) among the early Celtic inhabitants for *Britain.*

Albion College, a Methodist Episcopal co-educational institution, located at Albion, Mich.

Albion, New, the name given to the n.w. coast of America by Sir Francis Drake.

Albite, a soda feldspar. See FELDSPAR.

Albocarbon, a name for naphthalene, $C_{10}H_8$, when used to enrich coal gas. See NAPTHALENE.

Alboin (reigned 561-572 or 574), the Lombard conqueror of Italy. He twice defeated the Gepidæ (551 and 566)—on the second occasion slaying their king, Kunimond, whose daughter, Rosamond, he then made his queen. The story has been much used by dramatists, from the *Rosmunda* of Rucellai (1525) through Swinburne's *Rosamund, Queen of the Lombards.*

Album (Latin 'white'), among the Romans, was a white tablet overlaid with gypsum, on which were written the *Annales Maximi* of the pontifex. At the present day, it generally refers to a book for holding photographs, etc.

Albumazar (805-85), celebrated Arabian astronomer.

Albumen (Albumin), as a botanical term, is applied to the store of various reserve nutritive materials laid up for the use of the embryo within the seed.

Albumin (Albumen), $C_{72}H_{112}N_{18}SO_{22}$, is one of the simpler proteids present in

Albuminoids animal protoplasm. The form in which it is most widely known and easily experimented with is *egg albumin,* which, together with globulin (see GLOBULINS), forms the white of egg.

Albumin and Digestion.—In digestion, egg, lact, and serum albumin, all of which are present in an ordinary diet, go through the same stages. In the stomach they first change to *acid albumin* and to *albumoses,* through the action of pepsin, with the help of hydrochloric acid. From acid albumin and albumoses, albumins change to *peptones,* under the prolonged action of pepsin, before they leave the stomach. Peptones are distinguished from the earlier stage of albumose by being readily diffusible through an animal membrane (and therefore prepared for assimilation). Most of the albumin which enters the stomach passes into the small intestine in the form of the readily diffusible peptones, and is so absorbed. See PROTEIN; DIGESTION; FOOD.

Albuminoids, or **Scleroproteins,** compound organic nitrogenous substances chemically allied to proteids. *Gelatin* is the most important of the albuminoids. *Collagen* forms the white fibres of connective tissue; *elastin,* the yellow fibres. *Ossein* is the chief organic constituent of bone, and in chemical composition is similar to collagen. *Keratin* occurs in nails, hair, horns, and hoofs. *Chitin* is peculiar to the exo-skeleton of any invertebrate animals. The vegetable substance *Gluten,* prepared from wheat flour, and as a by-product in the manufacture of starch, is of a similar character to the animal albuminoids (see GLUTEN).

Albumoses. See **Albumin.**

Albumosuria, or **Propeptonuria,** is a morbid condition in which albumoses are present in the urine.

Albuquerque, city, New Mexico, county seat of Bernalillo co., and largest city of the State. It is the seat of the University of New Mexico; p. 35,449.

Albuquerque, or **Alburquerque,** town, Spain, in the province of Badajoz, 27 m. northwest of Badajoz, near the Portuguese frontier. It has an ancient castle and walls dating from the thirteenth century. Cattle fairs are held here in May and September; p. 10,000.

Alburnum, or **Sapwood,** is that portion of the wood of a dicotyledonous or coniferous tree which lies between the heartwood and the bark.

Alcæus, (*c.* 600. B.C.), of Lesbos, one of the greatest of Greek lyric poets, who gave his name to the metre called Alcaic. Horace employs Alcaics in his favorite form known as 'Horatian Verse.' Tennyson imitates the stanza in his *Ode to Milton.*

Alcala de Henares, town, Spain, in the province of Madrid, on the River Henares; 21 m. n.e. of Madrid. It is the garrison town for the province, and was the seat of a famous university founded by Cardinal Ximenes in 1508. Birthplace of Cervantes and Catharine of Aragon; p. 11,800.

Alcala Zamora, Don Niceto (1877-), the first President of the Republic of Spain, was formerly a royalist and active opponent of the Spanish dictatorship under Primo de Rivera. He was imprisoned for high treason on charges of subversive activities against the monarchy in 1930, but was liberated by the revolutionists in 1931 and inaugurated President same year. He resigned, 1936.

Alcalde, Spanish official title of the President of the municipal government.

Alcantara, town in Spain. Named from the Arabic, because of bridge built 105 A.D.

Alcantara, Order of, a religious order of Spanish knighthood, founded in 1156 to defend Estremadura against the Moors.

Alcatraz Island, in San Francisco Bay, California, is where the United States Government established in 1934 an 'escape-proof' prison for incorrigibles. One of the first of the notorious criminals incarcerated there was Alphonse 'Scarface' Capone.

Alcazar, name given to any palace built by the Moors in Spain. The Alcazar of Seville ranks second only to the *Alhambra* in architectural beauty.

Alcestis, wife of Admetus, king of Pheræ in Thessaly. Alcestis is the subject of a noble tragedy by Euripides, which Browning has translated as *Balaustion.*

Alchemy—the early form of *chemistry*—was occupied chiefly with the supposed art of making gold and silver from the baser metals. Tradition points to Egypt as the birthplace of alchemy; and Hermes Trismegistus is represented as the father of it. From the Arabs, alchemy found its way through Spain into Europe generally. The earliest authentic works on European alchemy now extant are those of Roger Bacon (1214-94) and Albertus Magnus (1193-1280). Consult Rodwell's *Birth of Chemistry.*

Alcibiades, (*c.* 450-404B.C.), the Athenian son of Clinias, was brought up after the death of his father (447) by his kinsman Pericles, the great statesman. The Athenians feared that he might attempt to overthrow their constitution and make himself despot of the city, and their distrust prevented them from making full use of his genius; and so, according to Thucydides, led to their own ruin.

Alcibiades was a favorite pupil of Socrates. He induced Athens to fight with Argos against Sparta at Mantinea (418), and to undertake the great expedition to Sicily (415), of which he and Nicias and Lamachus were commanders. Implicated in the religious scandal caused by the mutilation of the busts of the Hermæ, he was summoned to trial, but escaped, and took refuge in Sparta. He induced the Lacedæmonians to form an alliance with Persia and to support the people of Chios against Athens. But Agis and other leading Spartans, jealous of Alcibiades' success, ordered their generals in Asia to have him assassinated. Discovering the plot, he fled to Tissaphernes, a Persian satrap. He then secured the favor of the Athenians by detaching the Persian satrap Tissaphernes from the Spartan side, and in 407 returned to Athens, where he was appointed commander-in-chief. But next year, in his absence, his lieutenant Antiochus lost the battle of Notium, and the Athenians superseded him. He went into voluntary exile in Bithynia, and after three years of inactivity was assassinated in Phrygia. Consult *Life* by Plutarch; Plato's *Symposium*.

Alcmæon, physician and philosopher (sixth century B.C.). He is said to have been a disciple of Pythagoras, and is chiefly distinguished as discoverer of the optic nerve and the Eustachian tube.

Alcmæonidæ, a celebrated family at Athens, from which Cleisthenes, Pericles, Alcibiades, and other great Athenians were descended.

Alcohol (Arabic), a generic term in chemistry for a number of compounds which are the hydroxides of hydrocarbon radicals (see ALCOHOLS), but usually applied to one member of the series—*viz.,* Ethel Alcohol, C_2H_5OH, the active principle of intoxicating liquors. Alcohol may be formed synthetically from its elements carbon, hydrogen, oxygen, but in practice it is always produced by the fermentation of solutions containing sugar. Originally the juice of the grape was used, as it still is in the preparation of wine and brandy; but the alcohol of commerce is now made from malt and one or other of the following raw materials: wheat, corn, rice, millet, potatoes, molasses, glucose, cane or beet sugar, honey, milk, apples, peaches, blackberries, and cherries. The manufacturing operations, the details of which vary in different countries are divided into three distinct stages: (1) the preparation of the saccharine liquid or *wort;* (2) the fermentation of the wort, producing what is technically known as *mash;* and (3) the distillation of the mash.

Fusel oil and *furfurol* are important by-products of distillation. They are difficult to remove entirely, and are responsible for many of the objectionable qualities of alcoholic drinks. Small quantities of other alcohols, of greater toxicity in proportion to their greater atomic weight, are also often found mixed with ethyl alcohol. Alcohol may be made by the fermentation of any liquor containing sugar. Frequently the source gives the name to the alcohol. (See DENATURED ALCOHOL).

Alcohol is the characteristic component of rum, brandy, whiskey, gin, beer, and other beverages, being present in approximately the following percentages: rum, 43 per cent.; whiskey, 43; brandy, 43; gin, 37; port, 25; sherry, 21; champagne, 10-15; claret, 9; bottled beer, 7-8; lager beer, 4 per cent. It is used in the manufacture of chloroform, chloral, ether, essences, tinctures, alkaloids, liniments, and lotions; as a solvent for oils, fats, resins, and gums; in making transparent soap; and for heating and illumination. It is used, also, to a large extent as a motor fuel for internal combustion engines either alone or mixed with other fuels, as gasoline, benzene, etc. It is the most valuable of industrial solvents except water. Chemically, alcohol forms a series of esters with organic acids, such as ethyl acetate, ethyl propionate, ethyl butyrate, etc.

Medical Action and Uses.—When applied to the skin and allowed to evaporate, alcohol cools the surface of the body, and causes contraction of the local vessels, with diminution of the secretions. It may therefore be employed as a refrigerant and astringent. Taken internally, alcohol is completely oxidized in the body; none of it is retained or stored up, nor does it produce any body that may be stored up. Its food value is only its combustion value. It is a stimulant in small doses, and a depressant in larger doses. When taken immoderately over a long period, alcohol induces serious structural changes in many important organs, notably the brain, blood vessels, heart, liver, kidneys, and stomach. (See ALCOHOLISM.)

Alcoholism

See ALCOHOLS; DENATURED ALCOHOL; METHYL ALCOHOL; ALCOHOLISM; BREWING; BRANDY; WHISKEY; WINE.

Alcoholism, a morbid condition due to the excessive use of alcohol.

Acute alcoholism is caused by the rapid absorption of alcoholic beverages, and is characterized by unusually sharpened sense perception, animation and exaltation, impairment of judgment, and increase or perversion of emotion. Later, locomotion and all the muscular movements become disordered and difficult, and speech becomes thick.

Chronic alcoholism may follow several experiences of acute alcoholism, or may be caused by continuous tippling, 'moderate drinking,' in those who have never appeared to be intoxicated. The lesions of the central nervous system vary, but usually result in a deterioration of personality, increasing inevitably in intensity.

Recently, Dr. Richard Steinback of Germany reported a new approach to the problem of alcoholism. On the theory that increased brain pressure caused most of the delirium, he tried draining the spinal fluid. In 1936, Drs. Pline and Coleman, of Valhalla, N. Y., reported a modification of Steinback's technique. They drew off half the patient's spinal fluid and administered dehydrating agents. This procedure cut deaths in half.

See ALCOHOL; DRUNKENNESS; INTOXICATION.

Alcoholometry, the determination of the percentage of alcohol in a liquid. In liquors containing substances other than alcohol, such as beer, the strength can be determined only after the alcohol and water have been separated by distillation.

Alcohols, any one of a large class of compounds in organic chemistry which are formed by the substitution of one or more hydroxyl radicals for an equal number of hydrogen atoms in the original hydrocarbon. Alcohols are classed chemically according to the number of hydroxyl groups they contain. Thus there are monatomic or monohydric alcohols; diatomic or dihydric alcohols, triatomic or trihydric alcohols. The monohydric alcohols may be further classified, according to the products obtained by oxidation, as primary, secondary, and tertiary.

Alcorn, James Lusk (1816-94), American legislator, was born in Golconda, Ill. He was a member of the Mississippi legislature, 1846-65; governor of the State 1868-71, and U. S. Senator, 1871-7. He was the founder of the Mississippi levee system.

Alcott, Amos Bronson (1799-1888), American transcendentalist, writer, and teacher, was born in Wolcott, Conn. As a teacher he introduced educational methods considerably in advance of his time.

Removing to Boston and then to Concord he was made dean of the Concord School of Philosophy. His chief works are: *Concord Days* (1872); *Table Talk* (1877). Consult Sanborn's *Life* (with W. T. Harris).

Alcott, Louisa May (1832-88), American writer for the young, was born in Germantown, Pa., daughter of A. B. Alcott. Her life as a volunteer hospital nurse during the Civil War furnished material for her *Hospital Sketches* (1865), *Little Women* (1868; second part, 1869), which was followed by *Little Men* (1871), with its sequel, *Jo's Boys* (1886). Other works are: *Rose in Bloom* (1876); *Under the Lilacs* (1878). Consult *Lives* by Cheney and Moses and *Invincible Louisa* by Cornelia Meigs (1933).

Alcudia, Duke of. See GODOY.

Alcuin, or **Albinus** (735-804), surnamed FLACCUS, whose early name in English was EALHWINE, a noted scholar of the eighth century, confidant and adviser of Charlemagne, was born in York. In 781, Alcuin met Charlemagne and was persuaded by the Emperor to settle in France. His chief fame is from the school in which he had as his pupils Charlemagne, and his sons, his sister and other court ladies and nuns. In 796 he settled in Tours as abbot and head of the great school. There he died in 804. His works include treatises on grammar, orthography, rhetoric, and dialectic, and the discourse *de Virtutibus et Vitiis*. The best edition of Alcuin's work is that of Frobenius. Consult Lorenz' *Life* (Eng. trans.); Gaskoin's *Alcuin, His Life and Work;* Bishop Browne's *Alcuin of York;* Page's *The Letters of Alcuin* (1911).

Alcyonaria, a subdivision of the Anthozoa, including *Alcyonium* or Dead Men's Fingers, Sea-Pens (*Pennatula*), Red Corals (*Corallium*), and numerous other beautiful forms. See CORALS.

Alcyone, or **Halcyone (Halcyon),** in Greek legend the daughter of Æolus and Enarete or Aegiale, and the wife of Ceyx. According to legend the gods turned the pair into kingfishers, and gave them calm weather for their breeding season. The kingfisher, or halcyon, as a matter of fact, breeds very early, and its breeding season is supposed to bring fine weather. Hence, the expression *halcyon days*.

Alcyone, the brightest star in the Pleiades.

Alda, Frances (1885-1952), operatic soprano, was born in Christchurch, New Zealand, and was educated in Melbourne, Australia. In 1908 she made her début in the United States at the Metropolitan Opera House, New York City, in the rôle of Gilda in *Rigoletto*. In 1911 she was married to Giulio Gatti-Casazza, divorced in 1928.

Aldebaran, Tauri, a standard first magnitude star of a light red color, showing a spectrum of type K5. The name signifies the 'follower' (of the Pleiades), and an alternative Arabic appellation, *Ain-at-Thaur*, means the 'eyes of the bull.'

Aldehydes, a generic term applied to a class of organic compounds which are produced by the partial oxidation of the primary alcohols, and which contain a group CHO. They are intermediate compounds between the alcohols and acids; by reducing agents they are converted into alcohols and by oxidizing agents into acids. Aldehydes are characterized by a penetrating odor. See ACETALDEHYDE; ACROLEIN; ALMONDS, OIL OF; fORMALDEHYDE.

Alder, Kurt (1876-), German chemist. Received jointly the 1950 Nobel Prize in chemistry for work in 1927-28 with Otto Diels which discovered the Dien synthesis.

Alden, Henry Mills (1836-1919), Amercan author and editor, a descendant of John Alden, was born in Mount Tabor, Vt. From 1869 until his death was editor-in-chief of *Harper's Magazine*. His published works include *God in His World* (1890); *Magazine Writing and the New Literature* (1908).

Alden, Isabella Macdonald ('Pansy') (1841-1930). American author, was born in Rochester, N. Y. She edited the juvenile periodical *Pansy* (1873-96), and is the author of about 75 books for young people.

Alden, James (1810-77), American naval officer, was born in Portland, Me. He served in the Wilkes expedition to the Antarctic (1838-42). He took part in the capture of New Orleans (April 24, 1862), and in the engagement at Mobile Bay (Aug. 5, 1864). In 1871 he was made rear admiral commanding the European squadron.

Alden, John (1599-1687), one of the Pilgrim fathers who signed the compact in the cabin of the *Mayflower*. His wooing of Priscilla Mullens is the subject of Longfellow's *Courtship of Miles Standish*. He lived at Duxbury, Mass., after his marriage; was a magistrate for fifty years.

Alder, any shrub or tree of the genus *Alnus*, of the order *Betulaceæ* (the Birch family). The Alders are natives of cold and temperate climates.

The *Common European Alder*, or *Black Alder* (*A. glutinosa*), is found in North America, Great Britain.

The *Gray Alder* or *Speckled Alder* (*A. Incana*), a native of North America, and of many parts of Continental Europe and Kamchatka, differs from the common European alder in having acute leaves, downy beneath. The bark is used in dyeing. The name Alder is also bestowed on various trees and shrubs that do not belong to the genus *Alnus*. Of these may be mentioned the North American *Black Alder* or *Winterberry* (*Ilex verticillata*), one of the Holly family; the *Dwarf Alder* or *Alder Buckthorn* (*Rhamnus*) of the Buckthorn family; and the American *White Alder*, of the Heath family.

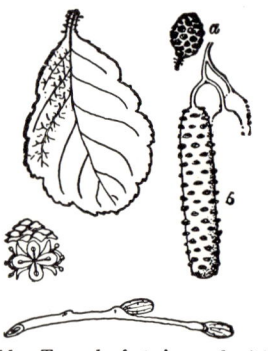

Alder Tree; leaf, twig, male (b) and female (a) catkins, and flower

Alderman, a title derived from the Anglo-Saxon *ealdorman*, compounded *of ealdor* ('older') and *man*. The term, originally applied to a Teutonic head of a privileged family, seems to refer to a primitive constitution, in which the chief authority was held by the oldest member of a tribe. In cities of the United States the aldermen, forming the city council, usually constitute a legislative body with limited powers, as in matters of local ordinances and appropriations, police regulation, the care of streets and sewers, etc. See also LOCAL GOVERNMENT.

Alderman, Edwin Anderson (1861-1931), American educator, born in Wilmington, N. C. In 1904 he became president of the University of Virginia. He was a member of the American Academy of Arts and Letters. His publications include *Life of Wil-*

liam Hooper; *The Spirit of the South; The Growing South; The Growth of Public Education in America*. He was editor-in-chief of the *Library of Southern Literature*.

Alderney, (French *Aurigny;* ancient *Riduna*), the most northerly of the Channel Islands. Agriculture and grazing are the leading industries, Alderney cattle (see CATTLE), a small but handsome breed.

Aldershot, town, England, in Hampshire. The largest permanent military camp in England is situated here.

Aldhelm, (Ealdhelm), St. (*c.* 640-709), Saxon ecclesiastic, was educated at Malmesbury and Canterbury; became abbot of Malmesbury about 673, and bishop of Sherborne in 705. He built the little church still standing at Bradford in Wiltshire. He wrote Latin treatises, letters, and verses, besides English poems that have perished.

Aldine Editions, the name given to the works that issued (1490-1597) from the press of Aldus Manutius and his family in Venice. They are distinguished for their beautiful and accurate typography, and are highly prized by book collectors. The Aldine Press continued for 100 years and printed 908 different works.

Aldobrandini, a celebrated Tuscan family settled in Florence about the end of the twelfth century. Among its chief members are: SILVESTRO ALDOBRANDINI (1499-1558), juris-consult, banished from Florence for opposing the Medici, entered the service of the papal court.—IPPOLITO ALDOBRANDINI, son of Silvestro, became pope under the title of Clement VIII. (1529-1605).—GIOVANNI ALDOBRANDINI, son of Silvestro, became a cardinal (1570). — PIETRO ALDOBRANDINI (1572-1621), was archbishop of Ravenna.

Aldred (Ealdred) (d. 1069), was English bishop (of Worcester); in 1060 elected archbishop of York. He crowned William the Conqueror.

Aldrich, Nelson Wilmarth (1841-1915), American public official, was born in Foster, R. I. For thirty years (1881-1911) he was U. S. Senator from Rhode Island. The Aldrich-Vreeland Currency Law of 1908 was largely his creation (see BANKING IN THE U. S.); His name is also given to the Payne-Aldrich Tariff Act of 1909 (see TARIFF).

Aldrich, Thomas Bailey (1836-1907), American poet, editor, and author, was born in Portsmouth, N. H. He held editorial positions with the Willis' *Home Journal,* and the New York *Illustrated News* and *Every Sat-* urday until 1874. He was editor of *The Atlantic Monthly* from 1881 to 1890.

T. B. Aldrich is best known for his graceful and artistic poetry. Among his prose works are: *The Story of a Bad Boy* (1870); *Marjorie Daw* (1873), one of the best American short stories. Consult E. C. Stedman's *Poets of America;* F. Greenslet's *Life* (1908).

Aldrovandi, Ulysses (1522-1605), Italian naturalist, was born in Bologna. He established the Botanical Garden at Bologna in 1567, and formed a museum of natural history. The first volume of his great work on natural history appeared in 1599. Six others appeared during his lifetime, seven after his death.

Ale, the current name in England for all malt liquor before the introduction of hops from the Netherlands (1524). As now used, *ale* is distinguished from *beer* chiefly by the greater percentage of alcohol and sugar. See BREWING.

Alemanni, or **Alamans,** a fusion rather than a confederation of Teutonic tribes who rose into prominence during the later years of the Roman Empire, with which they were almost constantly at war during the third, fourth and fifth centuries. From their name comes the French *Allemand* and *Allemagne,* applied to the whole of Germany.

Alembic, an apparatus for distillation used by the alchemists. See RETORT.

Alençon, capital of department Orne, France. The manufacture of the famous Alençon point lace (*point d'Alençon*) employs barely a 10th part of the 20,000 hands that once engaged in it (see LACE); p. 17,378.

Aleppo (Turkish *Haleb-es-Shabba;* ancient *Berœa*), city of Northern Syria. European schools and churches have been established by various religious orders. Aleppo was formerly the principal emporium of trade between Europe and Asia, and supplied a large part of the East with fabrics of silk, cotton, and wool, gold and silver stuffs. The city is one of great antiquity, Egyptian monuments testifying to its existence 2,000 years B.C. It was conquered by the Saracens (636 A.D.); sacked by Tamerlane (1402); captured by the Turks (1517); devastated by earthquakes (1170 and 1822); and ravaged by plague (1827) and cholera (1832); under the League of Nations mandate, France took possession of Syria in 1920; p. 177,313.

Alessandria, fortified town and episcopal see, capital of Alessandria province, Piedmont, Italy. It was built (1168) by the Lombard League as a bulwark against Frederick Barbarossa; the citadel was built in 1728. There are a cathedral (rebuilt 1823), palace, old castle, and barracks; p. 75,687.

Aleutian Islands, or **Catherine Archipelago,** a bow-shaped chain of small islands in the Northern Pacific, extending west from Alaska toward Kamchatka for nearly 1,000 m., between lat. 52° and 55° N., and long. 172° E. and 163° W. There are about 70 islands and 85 islets. Only a few of the islands are inhabited. At the time of their discovery by Vitus Bering, in 1741, there were many thriving villages and a population of about 17,500; but disease and other causes reduced their number. June 3, 1942 the Japanese attacked Dutch Harbor and seized the western islands. Attu was recovered May, 1943.

Aleuts, a tribe closely related to the Eskimos, inhabiting the Aleutian Islands and the Alaskan peninsula.

Alexander, the name of eight popes of the Roman Catholic Church.

ALEXANDER I. (106-15) is believed to have died a martyr.

ALEXANDER II. (1061-73) was born in Baggio, in Milan.

ALEXANDER III. (1159-81), Orlando Bandinelli, one of the greatest popes of the Middle Ages, was born in Siena. In 1179 he summoned the Third Lateran Council, which conferred on the pope alone the right of canonization, and drew up the laws under which the election of the popes is still governed.

ALEXANDER IV. (1254-61), Rinaldo de Conti, formerly bishop of Ostia, was of weak character, and in his struggle against Manfred, natural son of Frederick II., was defeated and compelled to fly to Viterbo, where he died.

ALEXANDER V. (1409-10), Pietro Filargi, was pope only 10 months.

ALEXANDER VI. (1492-1503), Rodrigo Borgia, whose memory is one of the most abused in history, was born in 1431 in Játiva, Valencia, Spain. The beautiful Vanozza Catanei, his mistress, bore him four sons and a daughter, two of whom were the notorious Cæsar and Lucrezia Borgia. He showed himself an able administrator and politician, a patron of the arts and sciences, and a friend of the people. He apportioned the New World between Spain and Portugal. Savonarola was condemned by him to be burned as a heretic.

ALEXANDER VII. (1655-67), Fabrio Chigi, was born in Siena in 1599.

ALEXANDER VIII. (1689-91), Pietro Ottoboni, born in Venice (1610), was bishop of Brescia, and was elected pope in 1689. He assisted Venice in her struggle against the Turks.

Alexander I. (?-330 B.C.), king of Epirus, son of Neoptolemus, came to the throne in 342 B.C., through the assistance of Philip of Macedon, whose daughter Cleopatra he married (336 B.C.).

Alexander I (1888-1934), King of Yugoslavia. Born the second son of the exiled Prince Peter of Serbia, he became Crown Prince of Serbia after the recall of his father and the renunciation by his elder brother of the rights of succession. He led the Serbian troops in the World War and was crowned King of Yugoslavia in 1921, proclaiming himself dictator in 1929. In 1934 he was assassinated at Marseilles with Louis Barthou, French Foreign Minister. His twelve-year-old son, Peter, succeeded to the throne.

Alexander I., Paulovitch (1777-1825), tsar of Russia, the eldest son and successor of Paul Paulovitch. His reign synchronizes with the stormy period of Napoleonic conquest, aggrandizement, and decay. He was present at the Battle of Austerlitz, where Austria and Russia were defeated. This enlightened ruler founded universities and schools; fostered trade; abolished torture, the secret tribunal, and the transference of peasants as mere chattels, whether by sale or by gift; and reconciled church and people. Nevertheless, his closing years were marked by reactionary measures. Disappointed and broken in spirit, he took refuge in dissipation, alternating with fits of religious mysticism. He died at Taganrog, on the Sea of Azov. Consult Joyneville's *Alexander I.*

Alexander II., Nicolaevitch (1818-81), tsar of Russia, known as the 'Tsar Liberator,' was the eldest son of Nicholas I., whom he succeeded on March 2, 1855. His reign is marked by two great wars—the Crimean War, which was going on at the time of his accession, and the war with Turkey in 1877-8. The emancipation of the serfs in 1861 was due to the initiative of Alexander II.; and he also took a keen interest in advancing internal reforms in Russia, especially the reorganization of the judiciary and the army. The most remarkable feature of the second half of Alexander's reign was the struggle of the Russian autocracy with the Nihilists. On March 13, 1881, he was fatally injured by a bomb thrown at him near his palace. Consult *Lives* by Laferté (pen name of his morganatic wife) and Tatistshev.

Alexander III., Alexandrovitch (1845-94), tsar of Russia, second son of Alexander II., succeeded to the throne on the death of his father; but fear of assassination caused his coronation to be postponed till 1883. His home policy was reactionary. Consult Lowe's *Life*.

Alexander III. (1241-86), king of Scotland, succeeded his father Alexander II. in 1249, and till 1261 was beset by regencies of English and Scottish nobles; renowned for his fine architecture, wise administration of justice, and defeat of Haco of Norway at Largs, 1263, uniting the Hebrides to Scotland.

Alexander, Eben (1851-1910), American educator; professor of ancient languages (1873-86) and of Greek (1886-1910), Univs. of Tenn. and of N. C.; U. S. Minister to Servia, Roumania, and Greece (1893-7).

Alexander, of Tunis, Viscount Harold R. L. G. (1891-), Brit. general, b. in Ireland; served in World War I. In World War II, commanded Brit. forces at Dunkirk; led retreat from Burma; led Allies in N. Africa and Sicily; military governor in Sicily; commander, 1944, in the Mediterranean area. Gov. General of Canada, 1946-

Alexander, John Henry (1812-67), American physicist, born in Annapolis, Md., and educated at St. John's College; served with the geological survey of Maryland, and was later professor of physics at St. John's College and at the University of Pennsylvania.

Alexander, John White (1856-1915), American artist, was born in Allegheny, Pa. Though influenced by Whistler and by Japanese art, Alexander's work reveals marked individuality. He is especially happy in the portrayal of feminine grace. Among his best-known canvases are: portraits of Walt Whitman (Metropolitan Museum of Art); *The Pot of Basil* (1897, Boston Museum); *The Engagement Ring* (Metropolitan Museum of Art).

Alexander, Stephen (1806-83), American astronomer, was born in Schenectady, N. Y. He served as professor of mathematics and astronomy (1834-54), and professor of astronomy (1854-78), at Princeton University. In 1860 and 1869 he conducted expeditions to Labrador to observe solar eclipses.

Alexander, William (1726-83), American Revolutionary soldier, known as LORD STIRLING, was born in New York City. He captured a British transport ship at Sandy Hook in January, 1776, for which exploit he was made a brigadier-general. In the Battle of Long Island (Aug. 27, 1776) his division met the first British advance; but ultimately attacked in the rear by Lord Cornwallis, it was almost destroyed, and Alexander himself was captured. Subsequently exchanged, he became a major-general in February, 1777, and afterward took part in the Battles of Brandywine, Germantown, and Monmouth. Consult W. A. Duer's *Life*.

Alexander, William (1824-1911), Irish prelate, was born in Londonderry, and was graduated from Oxford University (1847). After holding various benefices he served as bishop of Derry and Raphoe from 1867 to 1893, and attained wide recognition as an eloquent preacher.

Alexander Karageorgevitch, (1806-85), prince of Servia, was born in Topola. He served in the Russian army, and in 1842 was chosen prince; but he was deposed in 1858. In 1868 he was sentenced to prison for 20 years as one of the conspirators in the murder of Prince Michael.

Alexander Land, in the Antarctic Ocean, in lat. 68° 43' S. and long. 73° 10' W., was discovered by Bellingshausen in 1821.

Alexander of Aphrodisias (c. 200 A.D.), so called from his birthplace in Caria, was styled the 'Second Aristotle' as being the greatest expositor of the peripatetic school. He was the head of the Lyceum at Athens, and author of numerous commentaries on the philosophy of Aristotle.

Alexander of Hales, (d. 1245), English scholastic theologian (*Doctor Irrefragabilis*).

Alexander Severus, Roman emperor (208-235), was born in Arca, Syria. He was adopted by his cousin, Heliogabalus; and on the murder of the latter was proclaimed emperor by the Prætorians (222). He was murdered (235) by Maximinus on the Rhine.

Alexander the Great (356-323 B.C.), son of Philip II. of Macedon and Olympias, daughter of Neoptolemus of Epirus, was born at Pella. In 336 B.C. Alexander ascended the throne, and found himself surrounded by enemies—the Greeks, the Thracians, the Illyrians and Attalus. With marvellous rapidity he met and conquered his foes in turn, and then prepared for his conquest of Asia. In 332 B.C. Alexander subdued the cities of Phœnicia—Tyre only after a seven months' siege. The fall of Gaza opened the road to Egypt, which he entered in November, 332. The country at once submitted, and Alexander was crowned king. The conquest of Syria and Egypt destroyed the sea power of Darius, and left Alexander free to advance against

Persia. He did so in 331, and in September of that year gained the decisive victory of Gaugamela (generally known as Arbela). His foes are said to have numbered a million of men. As a result of the victory, Babylon and Susa submitted.

The year 328 was spent in securing the recent conquests. In 327 he returned to Afghanistan, and prepared to invade India, which he reached through the Khyber Pass. In 326 he crossed the Indus, and advanced to the Hydaspes (Sutlej), where Porus, an Indian king, resisted stoutly, but was finally defeated after the third of Alexander's three great battles. Porus received his kingdom back from Alexander.

In the spring of 324 Alexander went to Ecbatana. At the end of the year he returned to Babylon. His next purpose was to conquer Arabia, for which he began to make preparations (323 B.C.). When all was in readiness for the expedition, after a banquet to Nearchus followed by two nights of carousal, he was attacked by a fever. The report spread among the Macedonians that he was dead, and they forced their way into the palace, and passed his couch in single file; he was able to greet them with a movement of his head and by signs. He died a few days later, in the 32nd year of his age and the 13th of his reign.

In 12 years Alexander made himself master of Western Asia, and left a mark upon it which centuries could not efface. That he spread Greek civilization even beyond the Euphrates was the most enduring monument of his fame. As soldier and statesman, in brilliancy of strategy, rapidity of movement, grasp of detail aud breadth of organization, Napoleon alone among men can compare with him, and Napoleon's work perished almost entirely when he died.

Alexandra, Caroline Marie Charlotte Louise Julie (1844-1925), queen-mother of England, was born in Copenhagen, the eldest daughter of Christian IX. of Denmark. Her marriage to Albert Edward, Prince of Wales, was solemnized on March 10, 1863. On her husband's accession as Edward VII. (q.v.), in 1901, she became queen of England.

Alexandra Nile. See **Kagera.**

Alexandrescu, Grigorie (1812-86), Roumanian author and statesman, who won great popularity by his political satires.

Alexandria, one of the most famous cities of antiquity, was founded in 332 B.C., by command of Alexander the Great. The plan of the city was the work of the architect Dinocrates. At the east end, in the quarter called the *Brucheion* or *Basileia,* stood the royal buildings, the Museum, for centuries the focus of the intellectual life of the world, and the famous Library (see ALEXANDRIAN LIBRARY). Here also stood the two Cleopatra needles (sixteenth century B.C.), one of which is now in London (since 1878), and the other (the Obelisk) in New York City (since 1880); the Temple of Poseidon; the palaces of the Ptolemies; the mausoleum of Alexander the Great and of the Ptolemies.

From the time of its foundation, Alexandria was the Greek capital of Egypt. After the death of Alexander the Great it became the residence of the Ptolemies, who made it, next to Rome and Antioch, the most magnificent city of antiquity, as well as the chief seat of Greek learning and literature (see ALEXANDRIAN SCHOOL). It also rose to be a mighty trading centre, with a mixed population of about 750,000, consisting of Greeks, Egyptians, Jews, Romans, and a sprinkling of other nationalities. It was famous for its glass, paper, and fine textiles, and was the emporium of the world's commerce, especially for wheat. Even when Egypt became a Roman province, after its conquest by Cæsar (B.C. 48), Alexandria continued to be the greatest seaport of the empire. The misrule of the Turks (who took the city in 1517), the discovery of America and of the sea route to India and the East, completed the temporary ruin of Alexandria, until toward the end of the eighteenth century it had only about 6,000 inhabitants.

In 1806 Alexandria began to revive under Mehemet Ali; and with the returning prosperity of Egypt, in modern times, it has acquired fresh importance. In 1798 the city was taken by storm by Napoleon; but in 1801 it was wrested from him by the British. In 1882, during the rebellion of Arabi Pasha, the British fleet under Admiral Seymour bombarded and destroyed the harbor forts.

Modern Alexandria (Turkish *Iskanderieh* or *Skanderieh*) is the chief port and second town of Egypt, and is the station of the Egyptian fleet. Alexandria has two harbors. The eastern or Great Harbor is now accessible only for fishing craft; the western harbor, covering more than 2,000 acres, and protected by a two-mile headwater, is the chief shipping centre. About nine-tenths of the entire trade of Egypt passes through Alexandria. Exports include grain, cotton, beans, sugar, and rice. The city is joined to the Rosetta branch of the Nile by canal, and has rail connection with Cairo; p. 699,400.

Alexandria, city, Minnesota, county seat of Douglas co. The principal industries are the manufacture of furniture, wagons, plows and cutlery; p. 5,051.

Alexandria, city, Virginia, in Arlington co., was first settled in 1695, and was formerly called Bellehaven. Here in 1775 Braddock established his headquarters. During the Civil War it was the capital of the loyal section of Virginia; p. 33,523.

Alexandria, town of Ukraine, U. S. S. R. in the former Russian government of Kherson. Its industries are: leather, soap, candles and trading in cattle; p. 29,000.

Alexandria Bay, a village in Jefferson co., N. Y. It is a summer resort, surrounded by the Thousand Islands; p. 1,952.

Alexandrian Age. During the third century B.C. Alexandria became the centre of science and literature under the direction of the Ptolemies, who used their wealth to attract poets, scholars, and artists to their capital.

Alexandrian Codex (*Codex A*), one of the authoritative Greek texts of the Holy Scriptures, dating probably from about 450 A.D. It was presented to Charles I. of England in 1628, by Cyrillus Lucaris, patriarch of that city, who had taken it thither on his removal from Alexandria. Since 1753 it has been in the British Museum.

Alexandrian Library. This remarkable collection of books, the largest of the ancient world, was founded by the first Ptolemy (*c.* 300 B.C.), and fostered by his son. There were two libraries—the 'Great' in the Museum, and the 'Daughter' in the Serapeum. The Great Library and Museum were destroyed during Cæsar's wars (B.C. 48-47); but was partly replaced by the collection of Pergamum, which was presented to Cleopatra by Mark Antony. The Daughter Library and Serapeum were destroyed by command of Theodosius (A.D. 389).

Alexandrian School. After liberty and intellectual cultivation had declined in Greece, Alexandria in Egypt became the home and centre of science and literature. The thousand years over which the influence of the Alexandrian School extended falls into two periods, the Grecian (B.C. 332-30), and the Neo-Platonist, merging into the Christian (B.C. 30-A.D. 641). The influence of the Alexandrian school upon Latin literature in the Augustan Age must not be forgotten. We find it in all the contemporary poets, notably in Virgil, the greatest of the group.

Still more active than the poets were the grammarians, to whom it is mainly due that we now possess the masterpieces of Greek literature. In science also we are their debtors. Euclid the geometrician, Eratosthenes and Ptolemy the geographers, and Hipparchus the astronomer here laid the foundations and extended the borders of their respective sciences. Alexandria was also the seat of Jewish learning, a school of thought which came under the influence of Greek ideas, and of which the most illustrious teacher was Philo.

Alexandrian Philosophy is characterized by a blending of the philosophies of the East and of the West, and by a general tendency to *eclecticism,* as it is called, or an endeavor to reconcile conflicting systems of speculation, by bringing together what seemed true in each. The most famous representatives of this school were the Neo-Platonists.

Alexandrine Liturgy, called also the LITURGY OF ST. MARK, who is said to have composed it for the use of Egyptian Christians. Still used in the church of Alexandria.

Alexandrine Verse is an iambic metre consisting of twelve syllables. The name is derived from the old French romance of *Alexandre le Grand,* composed about 1180 by Lambert li Court and Alexandre de Bernay, in which the measure is first used. It is the standard measure in French epic and heroic poetry. According to the rules of scansion in French, the cæsura must always fall after the sixth syllable; but this rule has been neglected by most English poets who have employed the metre. The only long English poem in which this metre is exclusively employed is Drayton's *Polyolbion* (1612-22), and the result shows how little it is adapted to the genius of our language.

Alexandrovsk-Grushevski, town, province Don Cossacks, Russia. It is the centre of a rich coal region; p. 45,000.

Alexei (Alexis), called **Michailovitch** (1629-76), 2nd tsar of Russia, of the house of Romanoff, succeeded his father, Michael Feodorovitch, in 1645. By his 2nd wife he was the father of Peter the Great.

Alexei (Alexius), called **Petrovitch** (1690-1718), eldest son of Peter the Great, was excluded from the Russian succession because of his opposition to his father's reforms. He died (or was executed) in prison. His son became Peter II.

Alexeiev, Mikhail Vasilevich (1855-1918), Russian general. During the World War was appointed chief of general staff.

Alexinatz, or **Aleksinac,** town, Serbia, capital of the province of same name. It is the centre of a tobacco-growing district; p. 5,500.

Alexis, Nord (c. 1810-1910), Haitian soldier, who rose to the rank of general. See HAITI, *History*.

Alexius Comnenus (1048-1118), nephew of the Emperor Isaac Comnenus, and one of the ablest of the Byzantine emperors.

Alfa, or **Halfa,** the Arabic name, now naturalized in French, for esparto grass, particularly for the varieties *Stipa tenacissima* and *Stipa arenaria.*

Alfalfa, the Spanish name for the *Medicago sativa,* or lucerne, a leguminous plant highly valued for pasture and forage. Its original home was in Southwestern Asia, whence it has been carried to all parts of the world. In the sixteenth century it was introduced by the Spaniards into Mexico and South America.

Alfalfa or Lucerne.

Alfalfa is a deep-rooted, long-lived plant of the clover family, bearing violet clover-shaped flowers in oblong racemes, and small, slightly hairy pods, coiled spirally, enclosing several kidney-shaped seeds. Its most characteristic feature is the long tap root extending fifteen ft. or more into the soil, enabling the plant to draw upon food stores beyond the reach of most field crops, and to withstand extremes of drought. Alfalfa is one of the most highly nutritive and palatable of feeding stuffs. See FEEDING STUFFS; HAY.

Alfarabi, or **Farabi** (d. c. 950), Arabian philosopher, was born in Farab, beyond the Oxus. He popularized among the Arabs the theories of Aristotle, and was the master of Avicenna. The subjects of his writings embrace almost every known science. He was the first to attempt the compilation of an encyclopædia, the MS. of which is in the Escurial.

Alfieri, Vittorio, Count (1749-1803), Italian poet and dramatist, was born in Asti, Piedmont. Alfieri's own *Memoirs* (Eng. trans.) give an excellent picture of his character. Alfieri published twenty-one tragedies, six comedies, and one 'tramelogedia'—a name invented by himself. The most successful of his dramatic works is *Abele,* a mixture of tragedy and opera. After his death appeared his *Misogallo,* a memorial of his hatred of French anarchy. Consult Vernon Lee's *Countess of Albany;* Bertana's *Vittorio Alfieri.*

Alfonso I. (*El Conquistador,* 'the Conqueror') (1110-85), earliest king of Portugal, was the son of Henry of Burgundy, conqueror and first count of Portugal. He died at Coimbra.

Alfonso I. (1104-34), surnamed 'the Victorious,' king of Aragon and Navarre, succeeded his brother Pedro I. in 1105. The victor in twenty-nine engagments, he was mortally wounded during the siege of Braga.

Alfonso I. of Castile and **VI. of Leon** (1030-1109), son of Ferdinand of Castile and Leon, ascended the throne of Leon in 1065. He carried on a long and sanguinary warfare with his brother Sancho, king of Castile; and on the assassination of the latter, in 1072, obtained his kingdom. He won New Castile from the Moors, but ultimately sustained a crushing defeat at their hands in 1108.

Alfonso V. of Aragon and **I. of Sicily and Sardinia** (1385-1458), 'the Magnanimous,' was the son of Ferdinand the Just, whom he succeeded in 1416. He was an enlightened ruler, and gave asylum to many scholars who fled from Constantinople when it was captured by the Turks.

Alfonso X., king of Leon and Castile (1226-84), surnamed 'the Wise,' or 'the Astronomer,' succeeded Ferdinand III., his father (1252). He was successful in his wars with the Moors, and his victories over them enabled him to unite Murcia with Castile. He was a patron of literature; completed the codification of the laws, *Leyes de las Partidas,* which in 1501 became the universal law of the land. To improve the Ptolemaic tables he assembled at Toledo upward of fifty of the most celebrated astronomers of that age, who prepared the Alphonsine Tables (q.v.). By his command the first complete history of Spain was written in the Castilian tongue, and the Old Testament was translated into Spanish.

Alfonso XII. (1857-85), king of Spain, son of the exiled Queen Isabella, was chosen by the provisional government to succeed Amadeus of Aosta in 1874.

Alfonso XIII. (1886-1941), king of Spain, posthumous son of Alfonso XII., was proclaimed king on the day of his birth (May 17). His mother, Queen Maria Christina, with the help of Canovas and Sagasta, ruled during his minority (1886-1902), the chief event of which was the loss of Cuba and the Philippines to the United States. On April 14, 1931, Alfonso quit Madrid without formally resigning the throne, and a republic was proclaimed under the provisional presidency of Niceto Alcala Zamora at Barcelona. Later, a popular election was held, a Republican Parliament (Cortes) was organized, Zamora was chosen president and a constitution established. The Roman Catholic Church was disestablished and the Jesuit Order was outlawed. See SPAIN, *History.*

Alford, Henry (1810-71), English scholar and poet. He is remembered chiefly for his *Greek Testament.* Consult *Life* by his widow.

Alfred the Great (849-901), king of the West Saxons in England, was born at Wantage in Berkshire. He was the youngest son of King Ethelwulf; but when his brother Ethelred died, in 871, Alfred was declared king by universal consent in the midst of a Danish invasion. He practically founded the British navy; reorganized the national defences; raised public buildings and reclaimed waste lands; and revised all existing laws, combining those which he found good into a single code. He established schools, encouraged literature in the native tongue, and improved the services of the church.

Alfred's principal writings are as follows: A translation of the *Universal History* of Orosius; a translation of Bede's *Ecclesiastical History;* a translation of the *De Consolatione Philosophiæ* of Boëtius, and a close translation of Gregory's *Cura Pastoralis* and *Dialogues.* There are *Lives* of Alfred by Asser, Reinhold Pauli, Thomas Hughes, Plummer, and Draper. Consult also Turk's *Legal Code of Alfred the Great;* Snell's *Age of Alfred* (1912).

Alfred University, a non-sectarian and co-educational institution at Alfred, N. Y., established in 1836, and chartered as a university in 1857.

Alfreton, market town, Derbyshire, England; p. 20,485.

Alfuras, or **Harafuras,** the original inhabitants of Celebes, but found also in Buru, Ceram, Jilolo, the Sula Islands, and Northwest New Guinea. They are apparently of Malay descent, greatly modified by Papuan blood.

Algæ, a large group of simple cryptogamous plants, including Seaweeds and the filamentous and microscopic forms which are found in stagnant pools and on moist surfaces exposed to the air, such as damp soils, stones, and the bark of trees. Though they vary greatly in complexity— algæ never possess true roots, stems, or leaves, however closely these structures may be simulated. They come, therefore, under the general division of the Cryptogamia known as *Thallophytes.* They are distinguished from the Fungi, which are also Thallophytes, by the possession of chlorophyll, the substance by means of which new material is assimilated under the influence of sunlight; and by their power of building up their organic materials out of elementary inorganic substances. They are also distinguished from Lichens, which consist of algæ and fungi living together in an intimate nutritive relation—a high form of Symbiosis.

Algæ are the simplest in organization of all plants, being composed of but one class of cells. Algæ are usually classified in three orders, based on the coloring matters present: (1) CHLOROPHYCEÆ (green); (2) PHÆOPHYCEÆ (brown); and (3) RHODOPHYCEÆ or FLORIDEÆ (red); to which some authorities add a fourth, CYANOPHYCEÆ (blue-green).

Consult A. F. Arnold's *The Sea Beach at Ebb Tide;* G. Murray's *An Introduction to the Study of Seaweeds;* Wolle's *Fresh-Water Algæ of the United States.*

Algardi, Alessandro (1602-1654), born at Bologna, ranks next to Bernini among Italian sculptors of the seventeenth century. His most important work is a colossal relievo, in St. Peter's, Rome, of *Pope Leo Restraining Attila from Marching on Rome.*

Algarotti, Count Francesco (1712-64), Italian scholar and critic, was born in Venice. His *Neutonianismo per le Donne* (1732; translated into several languages) was praised by Voltaire. His *Saggi* (essays) on art (1769) were influential in Italian literature.

Algarve, the smallest and southernmost province of Portugal; p. 280,000.

Algebra, that branch of pure mathematics which makes it possible, by means of letters and other symbols to simplify and generalize the solution of arithmetical questions. Algebra is an outgrowth of arith-

Statue of Alfred The Great, Erected at Winchester in 1901.

metic, and is governed by the same fundamental laws, but differs from that branch of mathematics in a number of important points. In the first place, the operations of algebra and their results are more general than those of arithmetic. In arithmetic, quantities are represented by particular numbers, which do not vary in value, and the results obtained apply only to particular questions.

The most striking difference between algebra and arithmetic is the use, in the former, of negative and imaginary numbers, which cannot be entertained in arithmetic. In its widest sense algebra may be said to include the theory of numbers (see NUMBERS), the theory of equations (see EQUATION and QUADRATIC EQUATION), infinitesimal calculus and the calculus of variations (see CALCULUS, and VARIATIONS, CALCULUS OF), the theory of functions (see FUNCTION), and multiple algebras, including quaternions, and other vector analyses (see VECTOR).

Historical.—The earliest treatment of algebra is found in an Egyptian MS. of 1700 B.C. Egyptian algebra, however, was undoubtedly rudimentary, and no trace of it has been discovered among the ancient Greeks, who seem to have been acquainted with the solution of equations in geometrical form only.

The oldest work in the West on algebra is that of Diophantus of Alexandria, who lived in the fourth century A.D., and whose *Arithmetica* presents some methods of simplifying equations which are still in use. The development of algebra among the Hindus and the Arabs seems to have preceded any further advances in European countries.

The Italian mathematicians led in the renaissance of mathematics in Europe. In 1494 Lucas Paciolus, a Minorite friar, published the first important work on the subject, and in 1505 Scipio Ferro discovered the solution of one case of quadratic equations.

An important epoch is marked by the work of Vieta of France (1540-1603), who first used letters for all quantities, known and unknown. Harriot, in England (1631), and Girard, in Holland (1629), carried this work still further. Descartes was the first to apply algebra to geometry, and to represent the nature of curves by means of equations. In more recent years the development of algebra has been largely along special lines. Consult Merriman and Woodward's *Higher Mathematics;* K. Fink's *History of Mathematics;* Smith's *Teaching of Elementary Mathematics.*

Algeciras, or **Algeziras,** town, province Cadiz, Spain. It has a busy export trade in leather, charcoal, cork, and grain. Here, on April 7, 1906, the *Algeciras Convention,* an international agreement concerning Morocco, was concluded by the European Powers (see MOROCCO, *History*); p. 19,417.

Alger, Horatio (1834-99), American author, was born in Revere, Mass. He is well known as the writer of books of juvenile fiction, which still maintain their popularity —most of them included in the *Ragged Dick, Tattered Tom,* and *Luck and Pluck* series.

Alger, Russel Alexander (1836-1907), American soldier and lawyer, was born in Lafayette, O. He served as governor of Mich.; Secretary of War in President McKinley's Cabinet and was U. S. Senator. He was the author of *The Spanish American War* (1901).

Algeria, or **L'Algérie**, French colony in N. Africa, occupies the central part of the former Barbary States. Area 847,818 sq. m.

Physical Features.—The coast line is steep and rocky. The country is marked off into three distinct regions: in the n., the *Tell*—mountainous, cultivated land, with fruitful valleys; in the middle, the region of Steppes —mountainous plateaus, traversed from w. to e. by a chain of brackish lakes or marshes called *shotts;* farther s. the Algerian Sahara, a rock table land with cultivated tracts or oases. Algeria has no navigable rivers, though there are numerous streams, some of which are valuable for irrigation. There are many lakes, most of them impregnated with salt, and extensive salt marshes.

The *climate* of Algeria belongs to the Mediterranean zone, characterized by the division of the year into two seasons—the rainy or cold season, and the dry and hot season. The climate fluctuates between the humidity of the Mediterranean and the aridity of the Sahara.

The *flora* and the *fauna,* like the climate, are Mediterranean. The trees and shrubs are chiefly evergreens, the olive being characteristic. The forests are composed mainly of cork trees, evergreen oaks, Aleppo pines, cedars, elms, ashes, maples, and cypresses; the steppes are covered with alfa or esparto grass and salt-loving plants; the date palm is the characteristic tree of the Sahara. Jackals, hyenas, Algerian apes, wild boars, antelope, red deer, and wild goats are found. Birds are numerous, and scorpions abound in the arid regions.

The country's mineral wealth is considerable. There are copper, zinc, iron, lead, antimony, and mercury mines, and petroleum springs.

Industry and Trade.—Algeria is essentially an agricultural country. The principal products are cereals and wines. Olives are cultivated extensively, and the production of olive oil is an important industry. Cotton, tobacco, flax, silk, maize, potatoes, beans, dira, and a great variety of fruit, including the orange, date, mandarin, citron, banana, pomegranate, almond, and fig, are also grown.

Fishing is of importance. Sardines, allaches, anchovies, sprats, and tunny are caught.

Mining is poorly developed.

Peoples.—The population of Algeria in 1936 was 7,600,000, of whom about 1,000,000 were Europeans. Of the native inhabitants, the Berbers predominate. The Arabs inhabit the plains and steppes, principally in the western portion of the country; are mostly nomadic or semi-nomadic; Mohammedan, and polygamous. There are some Turks, Negroes, and Moors, and a sprinkling of Algerian Jews.

Government, etc.—The government and administration of Algeria are centralized at Algiers under the authority of the Governor-General, who directs all departments except the non-Mussulman services of Justice, Public Instruction and Worship, and the Treasury, which are under a separate ministry.

The Algerian Sahara is administered separately, and has a separate budget, but is under the Governor-General.

Northern Algeria is divided into the three departments of Oran, Algiers, and Constantine. Among the Mohammedans, justice is administered by the cadis (see CADI), with appeal to the French courts.

Education is supported by the State.

History.—The history of Algeria, the ancient Numidia, is one of successive conquests forced in turn upon the old Berber stock. Passing under Roman sway at the close of the Punic Wars (145 B.C.), the country attained a high degree of prosperity and civilization. But its conquest by the Vandals (about 440 A.D.) threw it back into a state of barbarism, from which it only partially recovered after the Mohammedan immigrants had established their dominion (about 650 A.D.). In 1492, Moors and Jews, driven out of Spain, settled in Algeria. (See BARBARY STATE). In 1901 the conquest of the French Algerine Sahara was completed. In 1942 Algeria was occupied by the U. S., to be preserved for return to France. It played a central role in the Allied drive against the Axis and the restoration of French independence.

Bibliography.—Consult Shoemaker's *Islam Lands;* J. F. Fraser's *Land of Veiled Women;*

Algerine   132   **Alias**

J. C. Hyam's *Illustrated Guide to Algiers and Algeria;* R. Humphreys' *Algiers, the Sahara, and the Nile;* D. Pember's *Aspects of Algeria;* M. D. Stott's *Real Algeria.*

Algerine War. See **Barbary Pirates.**

Alghero, seaport and episcopal see, on the northwestern coast of Sardinia; coral fishing is carried on; and wine and olives are produced; p. 11,799.

Algiers (French *Alger;* Arabian, *Al-jez-air,* 'the islands'), capital and chief port of Algeria; an important trade centre, coaling station, and favorite winter resort for Europeans, especially those suffering from pulmonary diseases. Nov. 8, 1942, American forces entered the city, and a day later it surrendered; p. 252,321.

Algin, or **Alginic Acid,** a substance resembling albumin, but not coagulated by heat, is obtained from seaweed, chiefly the genera Fucus and Laminaria, as a precipitate after boiling with sodium carbonate and adding hydrochloric acid. It is used as a dressing for fabrics, and as a thickening for soups and jellies.

Algol, Persei, was catalogued by Ptolemy as the *Lucida* of the Gorgon. It is the model 'eclipse star,' varying in brightness. The light changes of Algol, noticed by Montanari in 1669, were methodically observed and explained by Goodricke in 1783; and his occultation hypothesis, discussed by Pickering in 1880, was spectroscopically verified by Vogel in 1889. It gives a helium spectrum, and is now purely white. Al-Sûfi classed it in the tenth century as a red star.

Algoma, mining district, Northwest Ontario, Canada. Copper, silver, and nickel abound; p. 74,294.

Algonkian System, in geology, comprising the earliest of the sedimentary rocks, lies below the Cambrian formation and above the Archæan System. With the latter it is sometimes classified as the pre-Cambrian. The Algonkian consists of slates, quartzites, gneisses, and other rocks. See GEOLOGY.

Algonquins, a name applied originally to a small tribe of American Indians in the province of Quebec; and now used also to indicate one of the main linguistic divisions of the North American Indians.

Linguistically, the Algonquins fall into four main divisions: the *Blackfeet,* the *Arapahoes,* the *Cheyennes,* and the *Eastern-Central tribes,* including Crees, Montagnais, Sauks, Foxes, Kickapoos, Shawnees, Ojibways, Pottawatamies, Ottawas, Algonquins, Peorias,

Naticks, Delawares, Micmacs, Malecites, Passamaquoddies, Penobscots, and Abenakis. See separate articles on the various tribes. Consult T. Michelson's 'Classification of Algonquin Tribes' (*Twenty-Eighth Annual Report* of the American Bureau of Ethnology); Hodge's *Handbook of American Indians.*

Alguazil, (Sp. *Alguacil*), an inferior officer of justice in Spain, intrusted with the duty of seeing the decision of a judge put into execution.

Al-Hakim II., succeeded his father Abdur-Rahman III. as calif of Cordova (961-76). During his reign the Moors in Spain were at the height of their power, and Al-Hakim is remembered for his encouragement of the arts and sciences.

Alhama (Arabic, *Al Hammám*), town, province Granada, Spain; is a resort for invalids; and has been famed for its medicinal springs since Roman times; p. 8,000.

Alhambra, (Arabic, *Kilaat el-Hamara,* 'Red Castle'), the palace of the Moorish kings of Granada, was erected between the years 1248 and 1350. The Emperor Charles v. (1515-56) destroyed part of it, in order to build a newer palace, and Philip v. (1700-46) further defaced it. In 1812 the French under Sebastiani blew up eight of the towers, and an earthquake in 1821 did serious damage. Its restoration was commenced by Queen Isabella in 1862, but it was again damaged by fire in 1890, by a landslide in 1915, and by the great civil war, 1936-39. Even in its present condition, it is the most characteristic example of Moorish architecture and ornamentation in Spain. See ARABESQUE. Consult Washington Irving's *Alhambra;* Murphy's *Arabian Antiquities of Spain;* Calvert's *The Alhambra,*

Alhambra, city, Los Angeles County, California; p. 38,935.

Al-Hazan, or **Al-Hazen** (965-1039), Arab astronomer and optician. He wrote a treatise on optics, published at Basel in 1572, under the title *Opticæ Thesaurus.* His account of the power of lenses is the earliest and he is credited with the first suggestion of spectacles.

Ali, (d. 661), cousin and son-in-law of Mohammed, was the first to believe in the mission of the Prophet, whom he served as an intrepid soldier and able vicegerent. He was succeeded, on his assassination, by his son Hassan.

Alias, in common usage, that part of an indictment describing a prisoner who goes under one or more feigned names, from the Latin words formerly used in the indictment, *alias dictus* ('otherwise called').

Ali Baba, the hero of the story of 'Ali Baba and the Forty Thieves' in the *Arabian Nights Entertainments* (q.v.).

Alibi (Latin 'elsewhere'), a defence resorted to in criminal prosecutions when the accused tenders evidence that he was elsewhere at the time the offence was committed.

Alicante, province, Southeastern Spain, part of the ancient kingdom of Valencia, area, 2,185 sq. m. It is one of the most fertile districts of Spain. The wine of Alicante is highly esteemed; p. 529,934.

Alicante, capital and chief city of Alicante province, Spain, on a small bay of the Mediterranean. Alicante is strongly fortified, and has an excellent harbor, protected by two moles. It ranks third among the seaports of Spain, with export trade in wines, raisins, tropical fruits, vegetables, oil, licorice, and esparto grass. It has large tobacco manufactures. The climate is hot in summer and mild in winter, and the city has become a popular resort for invalids; p. 67,775.

Alien, a person resident in a country to which he does not owe allegiance as a subject or citizen. The status of the alien is usually fixed by treaties and international custom and by the law of the land in which he is a resident. The public rights usually granted to aliens include: individual liberty; security of person and property; liberty of conscience and worship; freedom of the press, within certain limits; freedom of association and assembly, though this may be denied if for political purposes; liberty to carry on commerce and trade, with certain exceptions; instruction in the public schools.

Aliens may not, as a rule, exercise the franchise, occupy public office, or practise professions requiring an oath of allegiance, such as that of judge or attorney-at-law; and in some states of the United States their employment on public works is restricted. An alien becomes a citizen or subject by naturalization (see NATURALIZATION).

Alien Enemies.—When a state of war exists between the country in which an alien resides and that to which he owes allegiance, he becomes an *alien enemy,* and his rights and privileges are greatly restricted, though, generally speaking, he is allowed to remain in the country as long as he conducts himself as a friend. Following the entrance of the United States into the Great World War in April, 1917, measures were taken by the Federal Government to regulate the activities of alien enemies within its jurisdiction. Any German or Austrian subjects, not conducting themselves as prescribed, were liable in addition to all other penalties under the law, to restraint, or to give security, or to remove and depart from the United States as prescribed in the Revised Statutes and in regulations, promulgated by the President.

Internment of Enemy Aliens.—Undesirable aliens might be interned for the period of the war. There were three principal internment camps located at Hot Springs, N. C., and at Forts McPherson and Oglethorpe, Ga. Up to August, 1918, between 3,500 and 4,000 enemy aliens had been interned in the United States.

Alien Property.—In order to prevent the property of alien enemies from being used in the service of the enemy or in any way detrimental to the best interests of the United States, the Trading with the Enemy Act approved Oct. 6, 1917, provided for the appointment of an Alien Property Custodian with power to receive all money and property in the United States due or belonging to any enemy or ally of the enemy, as defined by the act, and to hold, administer, and account for the same under the general direction of the President. Under the terms of the Act and supplementary proclamations and orders, all persons holding enemy property, or any interest therein, were required to report such fact to the Custodian.

For all property which came into his hands the Custodian had all the powers of a Common Law trustee except in the case of money, which was deposited with the Secretary of the Treasury and invested by the latter in Government bonds or certificates of indebtedness. All property other than money was deposited with banks and trust companies as depositaries for the Alien Property Custodian. To the end of July, 1918, over 25,000 reports of enemy property had been received containing 22,500 trusts; 13,000 active trust accounts had been opened on the books of the Custodian; and $430,000,000 in money and property had been taken over by the Custodian. Among the properties thus taken over were: six large German-owned New Jersey woolen mills of more than $70,-000,000 total valuation; a company in New York State, entirely enemy-owned, with a capital stock of $2,400,000; and a large lumber company in Florida, with a total value of $3,000,000, the president of which was interned for the period of the war.

Alien property in patents was also governed by the Trading with the Enemy Act. By its terms any American citizen or corporation might make application to the President of the United States for a license to use a 'patented invention, trade mark, print, label, or copyrighted matter' owned by an enemy (or ally of enemy), and the President had authority to grant such license (exclusive or non-exclusive) if he deemed that the request was a bona fide one and that the granting of a license would be conducive to the public welfare. When the war ended and until one year thereafter, the original owner might file a bill in equity against the licensee for recovery from the license, 'for all use and enjoyment,' of the patent, copyright, or other such property. It was estimated that these regulations affected some 20,000 patents, many of them of great importance to American industry. In March, 1928, President Coolidge signed the bill introduced into Congress to restore German property seized during the War. The bill authorized the expenditure of not more than $100,000,000 for this purpose.

See ALLEGIANCE; CITIZEN; EXTRADITION; IMMIGRATION; NATURALIZATION. Consult E. M. Borchard's *The Diplomatic Protection of Citizens Abroad* (1915).

Alien and Sedition Acts, four acts passed by the U. S. Congress and signed by President John Adams in June and July, 1798. (1) The first of these, the Naturalization Act of June 18, 1798, raised the period of residence in the United States from five to fourteen years in the case of alien immigrants seeking citizenship. This act was repealed in 1802. (2) The Alien Act of June 25, 1798, empowered the President to order out of the country all such aliens as he should judge dangerous to the peace and safety of the United States; to remove forcibly any aliens who might disregard his order, or to cause their imprisonment. This act expired in 1804. (3) The Alien Enemies Act of July 6, 1798, empowered the President, in case of war, to remove or detain as alien enemies all male subjects of a hostile nation. This act is still substantially in force. (4) The Sedition Act of July 14, 1798, provided for the punishment by fine and imprisonment of any persons conspiring against any measure

Alhambra, the famous Court of the Lions.

of the government of the United States, impeding the operation of any U. S. law, or uttering any malicious statement against U. S. officials. This act expired in 1801.

The Alien and Sedition Acts were passed at a time when war with France seemed imminent, and when the Federalist administration was being denounced in the Republican press. Though President Adams did little to enforce these acts, they were attacked with great bitterness by the Republicans. They led to the passage of the Virginia Resolutions and Kentucky Resolutions; and hastened the downfall of the Federalist Party. See UNITED STATES, *History*.

Alienation, in law, a transfer of the title to property from one person to another, by conveyance, and not by inheritance. See REAL PROPERTY.

Alienation of Affections, the act of making one of a married couple averse to the love and affection of the other. In the case of such estrangement by a third party, the following points have been established at law. A husband is entitled to compensation for the enticing away of his wife. It has been claimed, however, that a woman has no right, either at common law or under the statutes that grant her the right to sue, to take action against one who entices her husband away from her. See HUSBAND AND WIFE.

Alien Immigration. See **Immigration; Contract Labor.**

Aligarh, or **Alighur,** district, Meerut division, United Provinces, India, between the Ganges and the Jumna; p. 1,200,000.

Aligarh, or **Alighur,** town, India, capital of Aligarh district; p. including Koil (1921), 66,963.

Alignment, in general, implies arrangement in or adjustment to a straight line. In engineering, alignment denotes the ground plan of a railroad, fort, or field work, as distinguished from the gradient.

Alikhanoff, General (1846-1907), Russian soldier, whose real name was ALI KHAN AVASKI, was born in Baku. His severe treatment of the Armenians is believed to have been the cause of his assassination in 1907 at Alexandropol.

Alimentary Canal, or **Alimentary Tract,** the principal part of the digestive apparatus, extends from the mouth to the anus, having, in man, an average length of about 30 ft. It consists of certain distinct and important divisions, as follows: mouth, pharynx, œsophagus, stomach, small intestine, and large intestine; the entire passage being lined with a mucous membrane, on a foundation layer of muscles and fibres. In vertebrates, the canal is never in the form of a straight and simple tube, but always has its regional differentiations, each region, or division, having its particular physiological function, mechanical or chemical, and differing from the others, also, in size and shape. Some of the parts are long, narrow tubes, and others are short sacs, but in some instances different regions blend into one another with very little in the way of boundaries to mark them. The whole digestive system, except for a few auxiliary organs (teeth, tongue, jaws, etc.), develops from a simple embryonic tube, by means of a process of lengthening, enlargement, folding, etc. From the upper or forward part of the canal, in the embryo, develops the respiratory system, closely related to the digestive system. See DIGESTION; MOUTH; ŒSOPHAGUS; STOMACH; INTESTINES.

Ali Mirza, Mohammed, (1872-1925). shah of Persia, was educated in Europe. He was governor-general of Azerbaijan until he succeeded his father on the throne in 1907. In July, 1909, he was deposed by the new Nationalist Assembly, which chose his 11-year-old son, Ahmed Mirza, to be his successor. (See PERSIA, *History*.)

Alimony, in the law of the United States and England, is the allowance which a wife is entitled to receive out of the estate of her husband during divorce proceedings, or upon a judicial decree of separation or divorce. The granting of alimony to the husband out of the wife's estate is also allowable, but instances of it are rare. The obligation is created by order of the court, usually as an incident of the proceedings for divorce. Alimony terminates with the death of either party. Remarriage on the part of the wife does not of itself release the husband from payment, though he may in such case apply to the court for an order vacating the original decree. In England permanent alimony is due not after divorce, but when the parties are judicially separated. See DIVORCE.

Ali Pasha (1741-1822), Turkish leader surnamed *Arslan*, 'the Lion,' was born in Tepeleni, a village of Albania. Appointed lieutenant to the Derwend Pasha, an officer charged with the suppression of brigandage, he rendered the highroads more insecure than ever, sharing in the plunder of the *klephts* (robbers). He did such good service to the

Turks in their Austro-Russian war of 1787, that he was named pasha of Trikala in Thessaly. In 1820, Sultan Mahmoud sentenced him to be deposed. He was put to death, February 5, 1822. Consult Davenport's *Life*.

Aliquot Part, a number which divides another exactly without remainder. Thus 1½, 2, 3, 4, 6 are aliquot parts of 12, being contained therein respectively 8, 6, 4, 3 and 2 times.

Alison, Sir Archibald (1792-1867), British lawyer and historian. His *History of Europe* passed through numerous editions, and was translated into several languages. Consult his *Autobiography*.

Alizarin, or **Dioxyanthraquinone,** $C_{14}H_9O_2(OH)_2$, is the principal coloring matter of the madder root, but is now almost entirely prepared synthetically by the following series of reactions: Anthracene from coal tar is first oxidized to anthraquinone, which, after purification, is converted by fuming sulphuric acid into sulphonic acids. The latter are neutralized by sodium carbonate, and then heated under pressure with sodium hydroxide and sodium chlorate, alizarin being precipitated from the product by hydrochloric acid. See DYEING.

Alkahest, or **Alcahest,** the universal solvent of the alchemists. See ALCHEMY.

Alkalies. The term alkali is now chiefly applied to the hydroxides of the 'alkali metals'—*i.e.,* sodium, potassium, and the rarer elements lithium, rubidium and cæsium, and the radical ammonium; but the carbonates of these elements, as well as ammonia and the compound ammonias or amines, are included. The hydroxides are deliquescent, and very soluble in water. The solutions neutralize acids, forming salts in which the peculiar properties of both acid and alkali are generally destroyed; act corrosively on animal and vegetable substances (*i.e.,* are caustic and poisonous); and change the tint of vegetable coloring matters, or are said to have an *alkaline reaction*. See ALKALI MANUFACTURE.

Alkali Lands. See **Alkali Soils.**

Alkali Manufacture. The principal alkali is *Sodium Carbonate*. Sodium carbonate is manufactured in the United States by four processes: the Leblanc or Black Ash, the Solvay or Ammonia Soda, the Cryolite (only to a slight extent), and the Electrolytic.

LEBLANC PROCESS.—The older, or Leblanc, process of manufacture is divided into three stages: 1. The preparation of *salt cake,* in which sulphuric acid is heated in iron pots with common salt. Hydrochloric acid is evolved, and collected in 'scrubbers,' or condensing towers, in which a descending stream of water absorbs the ascending gas. The mixture is then heated more strongly in a reverberatory furnace, from which the product, salt cake, containing 95 to 98 per cent. of sodium sulphate, is withdrawn. 2. The preparation of *black ash,* in which chalk or limestone (30 cwt.), slack or powdered coal (20 cwt.), and salt cake (30 cwt.) are mixed and introduced into a large revolving iron cylinder. The cylinder is heated by a furnace, or by a Siemens gas producer; the mass fuses, and then is emptied into iron trucks. 3. The *lixiviation* of the black ash, or solution of the sodium carbonate, which is effected in vats, fresh water being used to wash the nearly exhausted ash, afterward passing on to fresh ash; in this way all the sodium carbonate is extracted with a minimum quantity of water, and a strong liquor is obtained. The tank liquor is boiled down to obtain sodium carbonate, which is sold in three strengths— (1) soda crystals or washing soda ($Na_2CO_3 \cdot 10H_2O$); (2) 48 per cent. alkali, crystal carbonate, or refined soda ash; (3) alkali or soda ash. The first two are preferred for scouring wool and for domestic use; but the 58-per-cent. alkali has now largely superseded them for all other purposes.

Caustic soda (NaOH) is prepared from the tank liquor by boiling it with slaked lime.

SOLVAY PROCESS.—In this process water is first saturated with common salt and then with ammonia; the resulting ammoniacal brine is filtered, cooled, and pumped into tall iron cylinders, divided into a number of compartments by perforated horizontal shelves. Up this tower a stream of carbon dioxide is forced, bubbling through the liquid in numerous streams through the holes in the shelves, with the result that it is absorbed, and sodium hydrogen carbonate formed, $NaCl + NH_3 + H_2O + CO_2 = NaHCO_3 + NH_4Cl$. The sodium hydrogen carbonate separates in the form of fine crystals, so that, when the resulting sludge is drawn off through filters, the crystals are retained and the solution of ammonium chloride passes on. The crystals are dried and heated, by which they are converted into sodium carbonate, $2NaHCO_3 + Na_2CO_3 + H_2O + CO_2$. The ammonium chloride is heated with lime, reforming ammonia to be used again, $2NH_4Cl + Ca = CaCl_2 + 2NH_3 + H_2O$; while the carbon dioxide from the lime kilns provides the necessary carbon dioxide for the main reaction of the process.

In the CRYOLITE PROCESS, cryolite, a double sodium and aluminum fluoride, is heated with lime, whereby calcium fluoride and sodium aluminate form. On passing carbon dioxide into the solution of the latter, sodium carbonate is formed and alumina is deposited. From the latter, common alum is made. This process is gradually giving way to other methods, owing to the difficulty in securing cryolite.

ELECTROLYTIC PROCESSES.—In these, common salt, either in solution or fused, is decomposed by an electric current, $2NaCl = 2Na + Cl_2$, and the resulting sodium is converted, as a rule simultaneously, into *caustic soda* (sodium hydroxide) by water, $2Na + 2H_2O = 2NaOH + H_2$, or into sodium carbonate by water and carbon dioxide, $2Na + H_2O + CO_2 = Na_2CO_3 + H_2$. All of the electrolytic processes are represented by two general types: (1) Castner-Kellner, Rhodin, and Hargreaves-Bird, in which a solution of salt is electrolyzed in a cell divided by a porous diaphragm to separate the products formed (in this class also is the Aussig Bell Process, in which the separation of the products is accomplished by gravity instead of a diaphragm); (2) those in which the sodium set free is collected in a metallic solvent, such as mercury for a solution of salt, or molten lead (Acker Process) if fused salt is employed, this being subsequently removed as caustic soda by the action of steam. For a detailed description of the electrolytic processes, see ELECTRO-CHEMISTRY.

Alkalimetry, the quantitative estimation of the amount of alkali, is usually carried out by adding an acid solution of known strength to a given weight of the substance, until the color of litmus, or some other indicator, shows the solution to be neutral, when from the measured amount of acid that has been required the amount of alkali can be calculated.

The *alkalimeter* is used for this purpose. It consists of a graduated glass tube, filled with dilute sulphuric acid, and containing as much absolute sulphuric acid as would neutralize a given weight—say 10 grams of potassium carbonate. Then 10 grams of the article to be judged of is dissolved in water, and sufficient acid is gradually added to it from the tube to neutralize the solution—*i.e.,* take up all the alkali.

Alkali Soils, or soils containing an excess of soluble salts, are the natural result of a rainfall insufficient to leach out of the land the salts formed in it by the constant weathering of the rock powder of which all soils are largely composed. The alkali content of such soils consists, in the main, of sodium chloride, sodium sulphate, and sodium carbonate. Evaporation of the soil moisture holding these salts in solution brings them to the surface, where they accumulate in *alkali spots,* or more extensive tracts known as *alkali deserts.* Any considerable quantity of alkali in the soil retards germination, exerts a toxic influence on the crops, and except in the case of specially resistant plants, often renders vegetation impossible. Alkali soils are rich in plant food, however, especially lime an l potash, and for that reason their reclamation is of great economic importance.

The *alkali lands* of the United States lie west of the 100th meridian, and cover some 850,000 acres, or about one-tenth of the irrigated land of that section. See SOILS. Consult C. W. Dorsey's *Reclamation of Alkali Soils,* and *Alkali Soils of the United States* (U. S. Bureau of Soils, *Bulletins Nos. 34* and *35,* 1906; E. W. Hilgard's *Soils;* T. H. Kearney's *The Choice of Crops for Alkali Lands* (U. S. Department of Agriculture, *Farmers' Bulletin No. 446,* 1911).

Alkaloids, or **Plant Bases,** form an important class of substances discovered by modern chemistry. They may be divided into two classes—*natural* and *artificial.* The natural alkaloids are found in plants and animals, and are often designated *organic bases.* Examples of artificial alkaloids are antipyrine, kairine, thalline, and acetanilide or antifebrine. Most of the alkaloids give an alkaline reaction, have an acrid, bitter taste, and are sparingly soluble in water, more freely so in alcohol. The following list contains the names of the chief alkaloids, with the plants from which they are obtained:

ALKALOID.	SOURCE.
Aconitine	Aconite.
Atropine ⎱ Belladonnine ⎰	Belladonna.
Beberine	Greenheart.
Berberine .... ⎰	Barberry.
⎱	Calumba.
Caffeine or Theine ⎰	Coffee.
⎱	Tea.
Cocaine ⎱ Ecgonine ⎰	Coca Leaf.
Colchicine	Colchicum Root.
Conine	Hemlock.
Curarine	Curare.
Cytisine	Cytisus.
Delphinine	Stavesacre.

ALKALOID.	SOURCE.
Emetine } Cephæline }	Ipecacuanha.
Ergotine	Ergot.
Eserine or Physostigmine	Calabar Bean.
Hyoscyamine	Henbane.
Jervine	Hellebore.
Laburnine	Broom.
Lupuline	Hops.
Morphine .... } Codeine .... } Narcotine .... } Thebaine or Paramorphine }	Opium.
Muscarine	Amanita Muscaria.
Nicotine	Tobacco.
Pilocarpine	Jaborandi.
Piperine	Black Pepper.
Quinine ..... } Quinidine .. } Cinchonine . } Cinchonidine }	Cinchona.
Sinapine	Mustard.
Solanine	Bittersweet.
Strychnine } Brucine . }	Nux Vomica.
Theobromine	Cocoa Bean.
Veratrine	Veratrum.

See separate articles on the principal alkaloids.

Al-Kindi, Abu Yusuf, mathematician and philosopher, was born at Basra in the ninth century. The Arabs, who call him *the philosopher,* look upon him as the founder of their philosophy.

Alkmaar, town, province North Holland, Netherlands. The Town House and the Church of St. Laurence (15th century) are notable; p. 22,000.

Allah (from Ar. *al,* 'the'; and *ilah,* 'worthy to be adored'; *cf.* Hebrew *Eloah*), the word used by the heathen Arabs to denote their chief god, and adopted by Mohammed as the name of the one true God. The word forms the substance of the battle cry of Mohammedans—'Lā Ilāha Illallāh!' ('There is no God save Allah'). See MOHAMMEDANISM.

Allahabad ('City of God'), city and capital of the United Provinces, India, occupies the fork of the Rivers Ganges and Jumna; 390 m. s.e. of Delhi. The fort, which dates from 1575, is of red stone, and is approached by a handsome domed gateway. Within are the ancient Palace of Akbar, part of which is now the Arsenal, and the famous Pillar of Asoka (240 B.C.). With the exception of a few ancient monuments of elaborate workmanship, the native part of the city consists of mean houses and narrow streets. The European quarter is much superior, with handsome residences and broad avenues of trees. The position of Allahabad renders it naturally a centre of commerce and civilization. The situation of Allahabad, at the confluence of the holy streams of India, renders it a much-frequented place of pilgrimage for the purposes of religious ablution; p. 171,697.

Allan, Sir Hugh (1810-82), Canadian ship owner. In 1853 he organized the Allan Line of steamships.

Allan, Sir William (1782-1850), Scottish historical painter, was born in Edinburgh. Among his works are: *Peter the Great Teaching His Subjects Shipbuilding* (painted for the Tsar); *The Stirrup Cup* (National Gallery, Edinburgh).

Allantoin, $C_4H_6N_4O_3$, a crystalline substance occurring in the allantoic fluid, in fœtal urine, and in the urine of many animals shortly after birth. It may be obtained chemically.

Allantois, an important fœtal membrane by means of which the embryos of reptiles and birds breathe, while in most mammals it is converted into the *Placenta* (q.v.), the organ by which the developing young both feed and breathe. At a very early stage in the embryo of reptile, bird, and mammal, the allantois appears as a bud from the posterior part of the food canal; and rapidly increasing in size, grows out of the embryo into a space provided for it by the amnion. It becomes richly supplied with blood vessels, and in birds and reptiles comes to lie close beneath the egg shell, through whose pores the respiratory interchange occurs. See EMBRYOLOGY.

Allegan, city, Michigan, county seat of Allegan co. Industries include planing, paper, and flour mills, and carriage, furniture, and casket factories; p. 4,526.

Allegation, in law, the formal declaration or statement, by a party to a suit, of the issue which he undertakes to prove. See PLEADINGS.

Alleghany Mountains, a range of the Appalachian system, traversing Pennsylvania, Maryland, West Virginia, and Virginia in a southwesterly direction, and forming the watershed between the Atlantic and the Mississippi. In the northern portion the Alleghanies have an elevation of about 2,000 ft.;

gradually increase toward the south; and reach a height of 4,500 ft. in Virginia. They are composed of stratified rocks of the Silurian, Devonian, and Carboniferous ages, and are rich in timber and minerals, especially coal and iron. The name Alleghanies is sometimes applied to the entire Appalachian system. See APPALACHIANS.

Alleghany Plateau, the westernmost division of the Atlantic highlands, including several of the Eastern and Middle States, and extending from the centre of New York southward into Alabama and westward into Ohio and Kentucky. The Plateau is well wooded, and is rich in bituminous coal, oil, and natural gas.

Allegheny, former city of Pennsylvania, since 1907 a part of the city of Pittsburgh (q.v.). See PITTSBURGH.

Allegheny College, a co-educational institution located at Meadville, Pa., founded under Presbyterian auspices in 1815, and controlled by the Methodist Episcopal Church since 1832.

Allegheny Observatory, one of the principal astronomical observatories in the United States, was founded in 1859, in Allegheny, Pa. It possesses a 30-inch photographic refractor, the most efficient instrument of its kind in the world.

Allegheny River, one of the head streams of the Ohio River (q.v.), rises in Potter co., Pa., nearly 2,000 feet above sea level. It follows a general southwesterly course for about 325 miles, and unites with the Monongahela (q.v.) at Pittsburgh to form the Ohio. It is navigable for nearly 200 m. above that city, whence by the Ohio and the Mississippi navigation reaches the Gulf of Mexico. Drainage area, 11,000 sq. m.

Allegiance, in the strict legal sense, is the duty of every subject to submit to the authority of the government under which he lives, or his sovereign, in return for the protection which he receives. The right of a person to change his allegiance at will is admitted by England and the leading European states, (see NATURALIZATION).

See ALIEN; CITIZENSHIP; NATURALIZATION.

Allegory (Greek *allos,* 'other'; *agoreuo,* 'I speak'), a form of composition in which one series of events or qualities is treated as typical of another series of events or qualities expressed or understood. As a rule, allegory is used in order to impart some human interest to metaphysical and abstract subjects. Some of the parables of Christ are allegories of the highest type, as that of the Prodigal Son; but others, such as the picture of the Pharisee and the publican who went up to the Temple to pray, are merely vivid transcripts of contemporary or universal life and character.

The origins of allegory may be found in the writings of Plato, who used it in its simpler forms in order to provide his pupils with a convenient means of passage from the world of appearance to the world of ideas or of reality. But the real flourishing of allegory dates from the time of the *Romaunt of the Rose.*

Meanwhile, however, Langland, in his *Vision of Piers Plowman* (1362), had adapted allegory to the purpose of moral and social satire. The form next passed under the hands of Spenser, who, in his *Faërie Queene* (1590), applied it to the description of Aristotle's 12 virtues. Allegorical figures had always appeared in the *miracle play* (q.v.), and the separation of the allegorical from the historical elements in these resulted in the *morality play* (q.v.) of the early Elizabethan era. The morality in turn, when its brief course was run, handed over its allegorical machinery to the *masque* (q.v.), with such changes as the transition from moral teaching to court compliment rendered indispensable.

Since the decay of the Spenserian school there has been no regular English school of allegory; but numerous independent works have appeared, embracing some of the finest compositions of this class. We have the allegory of religious experience in Bunyan's *Pilgrim's Progress* (1678), and his *Holy War* (1682); the allegory of political satire in Dryden's *Absalom and Achitophel* (1681), and of religious debate in his *Hind and Panther* (1687); and the allegory of scholastic and ecclesiastical satire, respectively, in Swift's *Battle of the Books* and *The Tale of a Tub* (1704). Tennyson's *Idylls of the King* is meant to contain beneath its appearance of a heroic poem a representation of the eternal war between flesh and spirit in human life. Maeterlinck's fairy play, *L'Oiseau Bleu* ('The Blue Bird') (1909), which represents man in his search for human happiness, assisted by the material necessaries of life, such as bread, sugar, milk, etc., who take an active part in the play—as opposed to the elemental forces of nature, who hinder him in his quest—is one of the most beautiful examples of the allegory in modern literature. Consult Courthope's *History of English Poetry* (vol. i.); Saintsbury's *Flourishing of Romance and Rise of Allegory.*

Allegretto, a musical term indicating a tempo slower than *allegro* (q.v.), but not so slow as *andante* (q.v.).

Allegro, (Italian, 'lively'), the fourth of the five principal degrees of movement in music, implying that the piece is to be performed in a quick or lively style, nearly intermediate between *andante* and *presto* (qq. v.).

Allemande, a German national dance. The name has also been used for an orchestral composition in slow and measured time.

Allen, Charles Grant Blairfindie (1848-99), English author, better known as GRANT ALLEN, was born in Alwington, near Kingston, Ontario, Canada. He wrote a number of works intended to convey scientific instruction in a popular style. He also published more than 30 novels. Consult E. Clodd's *Life.*

Allen, Edward Patrick (1853-1926), American Roman Catholic prelate, was born in Lowell, Mass. In 1897 he became bishop of Mobile, Ala.

Allen, Elisha Hunt (1804-83), American diplomat, was born in New Salem, Mass. He was U. S. consul at Honolulu (1852-6); chief justice of the Hawaiian Islands (1857-76); and minister from Hawaii to the United States.

Allen, Ethan (1739-89), American Revolutionary patriot and soldier, was born in Litchfield, Conn. About 1769 he moved to the region known as the 'New Hampshire Grants,' now Vermont. When the governor of New York claimed jurisdiction over that territory, and issued new grants to the land, Allen became the leader of those who resisted the encroachments of the New York claimants. Defeated in a land suit at Albany (1771), the original settlers determined to defend their claims by force, and organized the 'Green Mountain Boys,' with Allen as commander. Hostilities resulted, the New York governor declared him to be a felon and an outlaw, and a price was set for his arrest. (See VERMONT, *History*).

At the beginning of the Revolution Ethan Allen offered his services to the American cause, and on May 10, 1775, at the head of the Green Mountain Boys, surprised and captured Fort Ticonderoga, forcing the commander to surrender 'in the name of the Great Jehovah and the Continental Congress' (see TICONDEROGA). Subsequently he served under General Schuyler. He joined Montgomery's expedition to Canada; was captured by the British near Montreal (Sept. 25, 1775); was sent a prisoner successively to England, Halifax, and New York; and was not exchanged until May, 1778.

Allen, Florence Ellinwood (1884-   ), first American woman judge of a court of appeals. In 1920 she was elected Judge of the Cuyahoga County, Ohio, common pleas court at Cleveland, and in 1922 and 1928 was elected a Justice of the Supreme Court of Ohio.

Allen, Fred Hovey (1845-1926), American author, was born in Lyme, N. H. He brought to America the art of artistic reproduction of paintings, produced the first photogravure plates made in America.

Allen, Hervey (1889-1949), American poet and novelist, born in Pittsburgh, Pa., was the author of a biography of Poe, *Israfel;* the volumes of poetry entitled *Wampum and Old Gold, Earth Moods,* and *New Legends;* and the novels *Toward the Flame, Anthony Adverse* and *Bedford Village. Anthony Adverse* is an important novel.

Allen, Horace Newton (1858-1932) American diplomat, was born in Delaware, O. He was U. S. consul-general, minister resident, and plenipotentiary in Korea (1897-1905). His published works include *Korean Tales* (1889); *Things Korean* (1908).

Allen, Horatio (1802-89), American civil engineer, was born in Schenectady, N. Y. He invented the swiveling truck.

Allen, Ira (1751-1814), American Revolutionary soldier and patriot, was born in Cornwall, Conn. He was one of the founders of Vermont and was associated with his brother Ethan Allen (q.v.) in the land grant disputes between New Hampshire and New York (see VERMONT, *History*). He was the founder of the University of Vermont (1789), and delegate to the State constitutional convention in 1791. From 1795 to 1801 he was imprisoned in London and in Paris on the charge of furnishing arms to Irish rebels.

Allen, James Lane (1849-1925), American author, was born near Lexington, Ky. Among his many works, which deal chiefly with Kentucky life, are: *Flute and Violin* (1891); *The Blue Grass Region of Kentucky* (1892); *The Emblems of Fidelity* (1919).

Allen, Joel Asaph (1838-1921), American naturalist, was born in Springfield, Mass.; in 1871 he became assistant in ornithology, Museum of Comparative Zoology, Harvard; and in 1885 a curator in the American Museum of Natural History, New York. He wrote numerous scientific works.

Allen, Thomas (1849-1924), American artist, was born in St. Louis, Mo. His canvases, which are largely devoted to landscape and animal studies, include: *Maplehurst at Noon*, and *O'er All the Hilltops Is Rest* (City Museum, St. Louis); *Mission of San Jose* (Boston Museum of Fine Arts).

Allen, William (1784-1868), American educator, was born in Pittsfield, Mass. He was assistant librarian at Harvard; pastor of the Congregational Church at Pittsfield (1810). He was president of Dartmouth College (1817); and president of Bowdoin College (1820-39). His *American Biographical and Historical Dictionary* (1809) was the earliest American biographical work.

Allen, William (1806-79), American public official, was born in Edenton, N. C. He became prominent in the Northwest Boundary Dispute (q.v.), and is said to have originated the political cry of 'Fifty-Four Forty or Fight.' He was governor of Ohio, 1873-5.

Allen, Zachariah (1795-1882), American inventor and author, was born in Providence, R. I. He invented the automatic cutoff valve for steam engines (1833).

Allenby, Edmund (Henry Hynman), Lord Allenby of Megiddo (1861-1936), British general. In World War I (1914-18) he won honor and distinction as Commander-in-Chief of the British Third Army, contributing in no little degree to the Allied victories on the Somme and the Aisne. In 1919 General Allenby was made High Commissioner of Egypt and held the post until 1925. In his later years he became a philosopher and pacifist. In April, 1936, he was appointed Lord Rector at Edinburgh University. He died in May, 1936.

Allentown, industrial city, Pennsylvania, county seat of Lehigh co. on the Lehigh River. The city is one of the leading producers of furniture and of silk in the United States; p. 96,904.

Aller River, in Germany, rises 20 mi. w. of Magdeburg, flows northwest, and empties into the Weser (q.v.) near Verden. Length, 155 m.

Allerton, Isaac (c. 1583-1659), one of the Pilgrim Fathers (q.v.) who came to America in the *Mayflower*. His daughter Mary is reputed to have been the last survivor of the *Mayflower* band.

All Fools' Day, the first of April, when it is customary to play tricks on one's friends, such as sending them on fruitless or impossible errands. In Scotland the victim is called a *gowk* (cuckoo), in France *un poisson d' Avril* (an April fish). The custom is of unknown antiquity.

Allgemeine Zeitung, a daily newspaper, one of the most widely reputed in Germany, published at Munich. It was founded at Stuttgart in 1778 by J. F. Cotta.

All-Hallows-Tide. See ALL SAINTS' DAY.

Alliaceous Plants, a name applied to members of the genus Allium (onion, leek, shallot, garlic), or plants nearly allied to that genus, notable for their characteristic odor and taste, due to the presence of an essential oil. See ALLIUM.

Alliance, a union between nations, contracted by specific agreement, for purposes of defence or offence, or both. The United States under the existing Constitution has never made a treaty of alliance. The treaty of alliance with France, made by the Continental Congress, was declared by act of Congress passed Jan. 7, 1798, as no longer obligatory upon the United States.

In 1914, at the beginning of the World War (see EUROPE, GREAT WAR OF), the principal European Powers were allied as follows: Germany, Austria and Italy were leagued together in the Triple Alliance, Russia and France formed a Dual Alliance, and England, by virtue of separate treaties with France (1904) and Russia (1907), was combined with them to form the Triple Entente. Italy refused to join Germany and Austria in prosecuting the war on the ground that her alliance with them was for defence only; and later broke with the Triple Alliance and entered the war on the side of England, France, and Russia, under the terms of the Treaty of London (April 26, 1915).

The Little Entente was entered into in 1921 between Czechoslovakia, Yugoslavia and Roumania. See BALANCE OF POWER; EUROPE, HISTORY; LEAGUE.

Alliance Israélite Universelle, a society founded in Paris, in 1860, for the religious, intellectual, and political improvement of Jews in general, but devoted chiefly to the interests of the Jews in the Orient.

Allibone, Samuel Austin (1816-89), American bibliographer, was born in Philadelphia. His best known work is the *Critical Dictionary of English Literature and of British and American Authors* (3 vols., 1854, 1870-1).

Allier, department of Central France, contains some of the most fertile districts of that country. Area, 2,850 sq. m.; p. (1921) 370,950.

Alligator, a member of the reptilian sub-class Crocodilia, which includes also the true crocodile and the gavial (qq.v.).

The alligator family comprises three genera—the Alligator, the Caiman, and the Jacaré—that differ from crocodiles in their shorter and broader head; the presence of pits on the upper jaw, which receive the first and fourth lower-jaw teeth; the limited extent of the union between the two lower jaws; and the separation between the scales of neck and back. Generally, however, they resemble crocodiles both in habit and structure—e.g., in the lizard-like body, with powerful tail and short legs; the body armature of the skin; the abundant teeth fixed in sockets; the large head, with very solid skull and nostrils at the end of the snout; the double ventricle of the heart. Their feet are less webbed and their habits less perfectly aquatic, though they are powerful swimmers.

Of the true alligators there are only two species—the American or Florida alligator (*A. mississippiensis*), found in the rivers and swamps from Southern North Carolina to the Rio Grande, and a little known Chinese species (*A. sinensis*).

At birth the alligator is about 8 inches long, glossy black or dark brown, with orange stripes ringing the tail and body. Under favorable conditions the rate of growth averages about one foot a year for the first 10 years, the male reaching a length of 12 or 13 ft., the female seldom exceeding 7 or 8 ft. The brightly colored rings disappear with age, and the color becomes a dull, greenish black. Alligators feed on fishes, birds, mammals, and sometimes on their own young. They are exceedingly shy, and seldom attack man except in self-defence. After the mating season the female constructs a compact conical or rounded nest of sand and flags or marsh grass, in which she lays between 100 and 200 eggs. The heat of the sun and the warmth and moisture generated by the decaying vegetation complete the process of incubation in about 60 days.

Alligators are hunted chiefly for their hides, which are used extensively for bags, portfolios, etc., and also for their teeth, which are of fine ivory. Many live and stuffed animals are sold to tourists, and thousands have been destroyed merely for sport. The eggs are eaten, and the flesh is sometimes used as food. Their numbers have thus been greatly reduced, although the State of Florida has enacted laws for their protection.

Alligator Apple. See **Custard Apples.**

Alligator Fish (*Podothecus acipenserinus*), a species of fish belonging to the order Agonidæ, found in the Strait of Fuca, Puget Sound, and other inlets along the Northeast Pacific Coast.

Alligator Gar (*Lepidosteus tristœchus*), a species of gar-pike found in the waters of Central America, Mexico, Cuba, and the Gulf States of the United States. See GAR-PIKE.

Alligator Lizard, any species of the genus Sceloporus, family Iguanidæ, which includes a number of small forms common in the warmer parts of America.

Alligator Pear, or **Avocado,** known also as Midshipman's Butter and Vegetable Marrow, is a juicy, edible fruit obtained from a small tree of the order Lauraceæ, native to subtropical America. It varies in shape and size, but resembles a large pear.

Alligator Turtle, or **Terrapin.** See **Snapping Turtle.**

Alligator Wood, the timber of the West Indian tree, *Guarea grandifolia*.

Allingham, William (1824-89), Irish poet, was first a bank clerk and then an officer of the customs. In 1870 he retired from the civil service to become sub-editor of *Fraser's Magazine*. His longest poem was *Laurence Bloomfield, or Rich and Poor in Ireland* (1864). Allingham had early and close associations with most of the pre-Raphaelite Brotherhood, with Browning, Clough, Carlyle, and other literary figures. Consult *Letters of D. G. Rossetti to William Allingham* (ed. by Birkbeck Hill); *Diary* (ed. by H. Allingham and D. Radford).

Allison, William Boyd (1829-1908), American public official, was born in Perry, Ohio. His name was given to the Monetary Act of 1878, and he was U. S. representative at the Brussels Monetary Conference of 1892.

Alliteration is the recurrence of the same letter at the beginning of several words in a composition. As a method of procuring emphasis it has been much favored among Teutonic and Finno-Ugrian peoples, and constantly recurs in English popular phrases like 'kith and kin,' 'bed and board,' etc. In all old Teutonic poetry alliteration is the prevailing metrical distinction, as in ancient Gaelic poetry it is combined with assonance.

Allium, a genus of Liliaceæ, including about 250 species, natives chiefly of the temperate and colder regions of the Northern Hemisphere. They are perennial, or more rarely biennial, herbaceous plants, with bulbous roots, flat linear or cylindrical leaves, and flowers on a central stem—sometimes accompanied by bulbils, arranged in dense heads or umbels, which may fall off and develop new plants. Garlic, Onion, Leek, Shallat, Chive, and Rocambole (qq.v.) are species of this genus in common cultivation. They possess a sulphurous volatile oil, to which the acrid taste and characteristic odor of the genus are due.

Allman, George James (1812-98), Scottish zoologist.

All-mouth, a fish. See **Goosefish.**

Alloa, seaport on the River Forth, in county Clackmannan, Scotland; 35 mi. n.w. of Edinburgh; p. 11,893.

Allobroges, a tribe of ancient Gaul who dwelt between the Rhodanus (Rhone) and the Isara (Isère), as far n. as the Lacus Lemannus (Lake of Geneva). Their chief town was Vienna (Vienne). They were conquered in 121 B.C., but not finally pacified until Julius Cæsar settled the country.

Allocution, the formal address or exhortation by a Roman general to his soldiers; hence the public addresses of the pope to his clergy or to the Church generally.

Allodial, a legal term denoting strictly the independent ownership of land as distinguished from feudal tenure. Prior to the establishment of Feudalism (q.v.) all lands were allodial. In the United States, the title to land is essentially allodial, every tenant in fee simple having unqualified dominion over it; and though technically the land is said to be in fee, implying a feudal relation, actually no such relation exists. In some States the lands have been formally declared to be allodial. See PROPERTY; REAL PROPERTY; TENURE.

Allogamy, cross fertilization in plants. See FLOWER; SEX.

Allopathy (Greek, *allos*, 'other,' *pathos*, 'disease'), a mode of curing diseases by producing a condition of the system opposite to that characteristic of the disease; a name invented by Hahnemann to indicate the standard system of medical treatment, as opposed to homœopathy (q.v.).

Allori, Cristofano (1577-1621), Florentine painter. His chief work, *Judith with the Head of Holofernes,* in which the beautiful Judith is the portrait of his mistress, and the head of Holofernes that of himself, is in the Pitti Gallery, Florence.

Allotment, the distribution among subscribers of the shares of stock of a corporation or of corporate or other bonds (see STOCK).

Allotropy, the faculty possessed by certain chemical elements of existing in forms that possess entirely different properties while still being composed of the same kind of atoms. Phosphorus, sulphur, carbon, silicon, and oxygen exhibit this property in a striking degree. Two kinds of phosphorus are well known—one a colorless, wax-like solid, exceedingly poisonous and spontaneously inflammable; the other a red powder, neither poisonous nor spontaneously inflammable. Each can be converted into the other without adding to or taking from it; they are both composed only of phosphorus; and when burned, equal weights of them yield the same weight of phosphorus pentoxide. Lampblack, graphite, and diamonds consist solely of carbon; yet they all appear very different.

Allotropy is believed to be due to a difference in the arrangement of the atoms in the molecule; this is known to be the case in the intimately related oxygen and ozone, of which the former molecule contains two atoms (O_2), the latter three (O_3). There is also a varying energy content, as different forms give out a different amount of heat when burned.

Alloway, village, near the mouth of the River Doon, parish of Ayr, Ayrshire, Scotland. It contains the cottage, now converted into a museum, in which Robert Burns was born. The 'haunted kirk,' now in ruins, where Tam o' Shanter saw the dance of the witches, stands a quarter of a mile from the poet's birthplace.

Alloys. An alloy is usually a mixture or compound of two or more metals (see METALS); although in some cases the mixture of a metal and a non-metal—*e.g.,* steel and carbon—is also called an alloy. Some alloys, especially of the precious metals, occur in nature—as gold, which is never found pure, but contains silver or copper; and platinum, which always occurs with one of its associated elements, as iridium. Alloys are usually prepared artificially, by fusing the components together in order to impart special properties, such as to increase hardness, fusability, or toughness, to alter color, or to give a definite electrical resistance. Thus, carbon and manganese harden iron; tin and bismuth lower the melting point of lead; arsenic toughens copper, and aluminum increases its tenacity. Sometimes a second metal makes the first cast sounder; thus, aluminum is added to steel, and phosphorus to copper.

Alloys are either (1) mechanical mixtures which may be considered to be solidified solutions of one or more components in each other; (2) definite chemical compounds; or

(3) mixtures of these two classes. Some metals unite with evolution of heat, others with absorption: aluminum-copper, platinum-tin, and bismuth-lead belong to the former class; lead-tin to the latter. When mercury is mixed with another metal, the compound is termed an *amalgam* (q.v.).

Important Alloys.—The most useful alloy in the arts is *brass*. Several kinds are made, varying in composition from equal parts of copper and zinc, to 5 parts of copper with 1 of zinc. (See BRASS.)

German silver (q.v.) is an alloy composed, in its best quality, of 2 parts of zinc, 4 of copper, and 1 of nickel. An alloy formed of 9 parts of platinum and 1 of iridium is employed for the standard metre measures by the International Bureau of Weights and Measures, as well as for the standard metre itself, deposited in the Bureau des Archives of France in Paris. A copy of the latter is also preserved in the office of the U. S. Geodetic and Coast Survey at Washington, D. C.

Iron and Steel Alloys.—Iron and manganese unite in all proportions: steel with 14 per cent manganese is very hard, tenacious, and ductile; ferro-manganese is cast iron with 30 to 85 per cent. manganese.

Gold and Silver Alloys.—The proportion of alloy in gold and sterling silver coin and plate is regulated by law. *Sterling silver* consists of 11 oz. 2 dwt. of silver and 18 dwt. of copper in the troy pound—*i.e.*, it contains 7.5 per cent. of copper. When gold is to be used for coins, jewelry, or plate, it requires to be alloyed with copper or silver, or with both, in order to harden it. There are five legal standards for articles made of gold—*i.e.*, alloyed gold, apart from coin. These are commonly 22, 18, 14, 12, and 10 carat gold. These figures represent the number of parts of pure gold in every 24 parts of the alloy used by the goldsmith or jeweller. In Germany, Italy, and the United States, standard gold for the coinage is 21.6 carats.

In the United States, it is declared by law that the standard for both gold and silver coins shall be such, that of 1,000 parts by weight, 900 shall be of pure metal, and 100 of alloy. That is to say, the gold coins and the silver coins consist respectively of 900 parts of either gold or silver, with 100 parts of copper alloy, which may contain a certain negligible amount of silver.

See METALLURGY; ELECTRO-METALLURGY; SOLDERING AND BRAZING.

Consult Hiorns' *Mixed Metals;* Roberts-Austen's *Introduction to Metallurgy;* Thurston's *Treatise on Brasses, Bronzes, and Other Alloys;* Howe's *Iron, Steel, and Other Alloys;* Findlay, *Chemistry in Service of Man* (1939).

All Saints Bay, province of Bahia, Brazil, is an excellent harbor, guarded by the island of Itapasica (18 m. long, 3 wide). The town of Bahia (q.v.) is on the northern side.

All Saints Day (Nov. 1), **All-Hallows-Tide, All Hallows,** or **Hallowmas,** a church festival, dedicated to all the saints collectively, which originated in the seventh century when the Pantheon at Rome was consecrated as the Church of the Blessed Virgin Mary and All Martyrs (608). The festival was finally authorized by Gregory IV. in 835. See HALLOWEEN.

All Souls College. See **Oxford.**

All Souls' Day (Nov. 2), a festival of the Roman Catholic Church, that has for its object to assist souls in purgatory by prayers and almsgiving. It was first instituted in 993 at the monastery of Cluny, from which the observance quickly spread everywhere.

Allspice, the dried, unripe berry of a species of Pimento (q.v.), an evergreen tree of the order Myrtaceæ, native to the West Indies, and chiefly cultivated in Jamaica.

Allspice, with Flower and Fruit.

Allston, Washington (1779-1843), American painter and author, was born in Waccamaw, S. C. He studied art under Benjamin West at the Royal Academy, London, at Paris, and at Rome. Among his important canvasses are: *Dead Man Revived* (1810, Academy of Fine Arts, Philadelphia); *St. Peter Liberated by the Angel; The Prophet Jeremiah* (Yale College); *The Flood,* and *A Spanish Girl* (Metropolitan Museum, New York City); portraits of Benjamin West (Boston) and S. T. Coleridge (National Portrait Gallery, London). Consult J. B. Flagg's *Life and Letters.*

Alluvion takes place where land is gained

from the sea by the washing up of sand and earth.

Alluvium, in Geology, any earthy material deposited by the ordinary operation of water. See DELTA; DENUDATION.

Alma, city, Gratiot co., Michigan, on Pine River. It is the seat of Alma College. Chief industries are flour mills, beet sugar factories, and the manufacture of furnaces, auto trucks, gas engines, and lumber products; p. 7,202.

Alma, river in Russia. Scene of engagement in 1854 during the Crimean War (q.v.).

Almack's. About the year 1763 a Scotsman named M'Caul opened a gaming club in Pall Mall, London, known as Almack's Club.

Alma College, a coeducational institution located at Alma, Mich., established in 1887 under the auspices of the Presbyterian Church.

Almada, town, Estremadura province, Portugal, on the Tagus River, opposite Lisbon. The fortress of San Sebastian occupies the heights above the town; p. 8,000.

Almaden, town, province Ciudad Real, Spain. It is noted for its rich quicksilver mines; p. 8,500.

Almagest, the Arab title of the principal work of Ptolemy (q.v.), the Alexandrian astronomer. This monumental treatise, composed between 140 and 150 A.D., is divided into thirteen books. The *Almagest* is the great codex of Greek astronomy.

Almagra, the Arabic name of an ochreous earth of a fine deep red color, used, under the name of Indian red, as a paint, and as a powder.

Almagro, town, Ciudad Real province, Spain. Important lace manufacture; p. 8,000.

Almagro, Diego de (?1475-1538), Spanish conquistador, whose name is derived from the town near which he was discovered as a foundling. He emigrated to America in 1514, and lived in turn at Darien and Panama. He accompanied Pizarro on his successful expedition to Peru (1526-33), when the wealth of the Incas was won (see PIZARRO, FRANCISCO). In 1535 the Emperor Charles v. made Almagro governor of the region which is now occupied by Chile, then called New Toledo. Consult Prescott's *Conquest of Peru.*

Alma Mater (Latin 'nourishing mother') is a name given to a university or higher school by those who have derived instruction from it.

Almanac, a word probably derived from the Arabic *al-manah,* 'the sun dial,' was originally applied by Roger Bacon in 1267 to permanent tables showing the apparent movements of the heavenly bodies. In general usage, Almanac refers to a year book of dates and tables giving a calendar of days and months, and usually including ecclesiastical fasts and feasts, the age of the moon, the tides, the exact time of the sun's rising and setting, dates of eclipses, and the position of the planets throughout the year. The oldest known copy of such a work, preserved in the British Museum, dates back to the times of Rameses the Great of Egypt (1200 B.C.).

Tables of this kind were undoubtedly used by other ancient peoples, and the Roman *fasti* (q.v.) were in many respects akin to the almanac of to-day. The first printed almanac was published in Vienna in 1457 by Purbach. The first almanac printed in *England* was Richard Pynson's *Kalender of Shepardes* (1497), translated from the French. It was soon followed by others, and in the later years of Henry VIII. almanacs were in common use.

In *France,* prophetic almanacs were especially popular, particularly after the prediction of the death of Henry II. in the almanac of Nostradamus.

In *Germany,* the *Almanach de Gotha,* published annually at Gotha by the great geographical house of Perthes, has a cosmopolitan character. It was begun in 1764, in the German language, in which it was continued until Napoleon v. became emperor, when it was changed to the French language. Since the Franco-German War (1871) it has been published in both tongues.

United States.—The first almanac printed in the United States was that of Captain William Pierce, issued in 1639; while the oldest almanac of which there is a copy extant was Samuel Danforth's, printed by Matthew Day in 1646. In 1732 Benjamin Franklin (q.v.) published the first issue of *Poor Richard's Almanac,* which was continued for twenty-five years, and which was justly celebrated for its wit and wisdom. Since the beginning of the nineteenth century the number of almanacs has increased rapidly. The most important and comprehensive present-day almanacs are issued by the large newspapers.

Nautical Almanacs.—Of great scientific importance and indispensable information in astronomy and navigation are the official almanacs published by many of the national governments.

Almansa, city, province Albacete, Spain.

Here was fought the great battle (April 25, 1707) which practically decided the war of the Spanish Succession; p. 12,000.

Al-Mansur, ('the Victorious'), title assumed by ABU-JAFAR (*c.* 707-775), second calif (754) of the dynasty of the Abbasides. He removed the seat of government to Bagdad, which he built (764) at immense cost. He caused the *Elements* of Euclid to be translated from the Syriac, and the fables of Bidpai from the Persian.

Alma-Tadema, Sir Lawrence (Laurens) (1836-1912), English painter, was born near Leeuwarden, Netherlands. His early pictures were mainly illustrative of Frankish life, and his first important works were *Clotilde at the Tomb of Her Grandchildren* (1858) and *The Education of the Children of Clovis* (1861). In 1863 he turned to Egyptian subjects; and a few years later devoted himself to depicting ancient Greek and Roman life. In 1870 he removed to London; became a naturalized British subject (1873); was elected a member of the Royal Academy (1879); and was knighted (1899).

Consult *Lives* by G. M. Ebers, P. C. Standing, and Zimmern; W. C. Monkhouse's *British Contemporary Artists;* R. Dirck's *The Later Work of Alma Tadema* (1910).

Almeh, Alme, or **Almai** (Arabic *ālim,* 'wise,' 'learned'), a class of Egyptian singing girls in attendance at festivals, entertainments, or funerals. See NAUTCH GIRLS.

Almeida-Garrett, Joao Baptista da Silva Leitao d' (1799-1854), Portuguese poet, was born in Oporto. He played an active part in the liberal movement of 1820, and subsequently devoted himself to the high task of founding a national and romantic drama. He is the author of some of the best dramas of modern Portuguese literature— *e.g., Auto de Gil Vicente* (1838); *Frei Luiz de Sousa* (1844); *Camoens* (1825); the epic *Dona Branca* (1826); *Romanceiro* (3 vols., 1851-3), a collection of Portuguese folk tales; *Folhas Cahidas* (1852), a volume of lyrics, and his finest production.

Almería, capital of Almería province, Spain, and an important Mediterranean port. It is a bishop's see, and has a Gothic cathedral built in 1524. On the hills to the west of the city are the ancient castle of San Cristobal and the old Moorish *alcazaba*. The harbor is large (177 acres) and well fortified.

Almería, reached its highest prosperity under Moorish dominion in the Middle Ages, being the great port of traffic with Italy and the East; p. 45.198.

Almohades, or **Muwahhadis,** a dynasty of Berber princes who expelled the Almoravides (q.v.), and who reigned over a large part of Northwest Africa and the southern half of Spain during the twelfth and thirteenth centuries. Consult Ibn-Khaldun's *Histoire de Berbères* (French translation); Dozy's *Histoire des Almohades* (French translation).

Almond, the name applied both to the tree and the fruit of a genus (*Prunus amygdalus*) of the order Rosaceæ, native to Western Asia and Northern Africa, but now found growing throughout Southern Europe. The almond tree, which is similar to the peach tree, is from 20 to 30 ft. high; its flowers are similar to peach blossoms; its leaves lanceolate with serrated edges; and it has a peach-like fruit. The wood of the almond tree is hard and of a reddish color, and is used by cabinet makers.

Almond.
a, Flower; *b,* fruit.

In the United States, almonds are cultivated chiefly in California, where they are grown by budding into seedlings of either the bitter or sweet variety. Large quantities are also imported from France, Spain, Italy, and the Levant. The *Dwarf Almond* (*A. nana*) is used as an ornamental shrub.

Almonds, Oil of. The *fixed oil of almonds* is prepared from either bitter or sweet almonds by crushing and pressing. That prepared from sweet almonds is similar to olive oil, and is used as a substitute.

It is employed as a flavoring agent, and in the manufacture of perfumes and dyes. A large proportion of the oil of bitter almonds now used in commerce is prepared artificially from *toluene*, obtained from coal tar.

Almoner, an official charged with the dispensing of gifts and alms. Of monastic origin, the office afterward extended to the house-

Almora holds of sovereigns, feudal lords, etc., and to public institutions such as hospitals.

Almora, chief town, Kumaun division, Northwest Provinces, India. For centuries it was the stronghold of native rulers. Ramsay College is located here; p. 11,000.

Almoravides, or **Murabtis,** a Berber dynasty which reigned over North Africa and Southern Spain during the eleventh and twelfth centuries. Consult Ibn-Khaldun's *Histoire des Berbères* (French translation by Slane); Dozy's *Histoire des Musulmans d'Espagne* (English translation by F. G. Stokes as *Spanish Islam,* 1913).

Almshouse, an institution for the charitable support of persons suffering from old age or poverty.

Almucantar, or **Almacantar,** an astronomical instrument consisting of a small telescope carried by a float swimming in a tank of mercury, and revolving round an imaginary perpendicular axis, so as to describe a small horizontal circle passing through the pole of the heavens.

Almy, John Jay (1815-95), American naval officer, was born in Newport, R. I.; assisted in the capture of Vera Cruz (1847). During the Civil War he was commander of the South Atlantic squadron. Subsequently he was commander of the Pacific squadron. He was promoted commodore (1869) and rear-admiral (1873), retiring in 1877.

Alnus. See **Alder.**

African Aloe, showing inflorescence and section of flower.

Aloe, a genus of Liliaceæ, of about 100 species, native to the Mediterranean region, Western Asia, and South Africa, and extensively naturalized in all warm countries.

Aloes are much cultivated as decorative plants, especially in public grounds and gardens. Their chief value, however, lies in their medicinal properties. For AMERICAN ALOE see AGAVE.

Aloes, the juice of the leaves of various species of aloe (q.v.). It is a stimulating, purgative drug with an intensely bitter taste.

Aloes Wood, Agila Wood, or **Eagle Wood,** called also **Lign (Lignum) Aloes,** is the heart-wood of certain species of Aquilaria—trees related to the laurel, and native to Eastern Asia. It contains a dark-colored, fragrant, resinous substance, and when burned diffuses a sweet aromatic odor for which it is highly valued.

Aloidæ, Aloeidæ, or **Aloadæ,** in Greek mythology, the sons of Iphimedia and Poseidon. They made war on the gods.

The Alpaca.

Alopecia, (Greek 'fox mange'), the technical term for baldness.

Alopecurus. See **Foxtail Grass.**

Alora, town, province Malaga, Spain; 20 m. n.w. of Malaga. A fruit centre, especially famed for its Manzanilla olives; p. 20,839.

Alost, (Flemish *Aalst*), fortified town, province of East Flanders, Belgium. It contains the fine Church of St. Martin; p. 37,380.

Aloysia. See **Verbena.**

Aloysius, St. See **Gonzaga, Luigi.**

Alpaca (*Lama pacos* or *Auchenia pacos*), a South American animal, a semi-domesticated relative of the llama (q.v.). The alpaca is a native of the Andes, from the Equator to Tierra del Fuego, but is most frequent in the high mountains of Peru and Chile. In form it somewhat resembles the sheep, but differs from that animal in its longer neck and the erect carriage of the head. Although occasionally used as a beast of burden, the alpaca is chiefly prized for its long, fine fleece, which is of a silken texture, and of an uncommonly lustrous, almost metallic appearance. The fabric manufactured is cool, light, and durable.

Alpargata, a kind of footwear used by the laboring classes of Spain and Central America.

Alp Arslan, 'Valiant Lion' (1029-72), second sultan of the Seljuk dynasty of Persia, whose name, Mohammed-ibn-Daoud, was assumed on his conversion to Islam.

Alpena, city, Michigan, county seat of Alpena co., on Lake Huron. Manufactures include saw, shingle, and veneer mills, machine shops, cement and paper factories, and tanneries; p. 12,808.

Alpenhorn, a long bugle horn made of wood, used by Swiss peasants.

Alpes-Basses. See **Basses-Alpe.**

Alpes-Hautes. See **Hautes-Alpes.**

Alpes Maritimes, the most southeasterly department of France, on the shores of the Mediterranean and known as the French Riviera. One of the most mountainous districts of France, its climate varies according to locality, the genial winter of the coast contrasting greatly with the severity of the highlands a few miles inland. Large herds of sheep are pastured in the Alps in summer; olives, vines, and fruits are cultivated on the littoral; in the Plaine de Grasse large quantities of flowers are grown for the manufacture of perfumes. The tunny, anchovy, and sardine fisheries are important. Capital, Nice; p. 356,338.

Alph, 'the sacred river' of Coleridge's *Kubla Khan,* is an imaginary stream, although placed by the poet in a real locality.

Alpha and Omega, the first and the last character of the Greek alphabet, a name applied to the Deity.

Alphabet (so called from *alpha* and *beta,* the first two Greek letters) means a set of graphic signs, denoting sounds by whose combination words can be visibly represented. It is distinguished from other systems with such signs by having no pictures or *ideograms* (see HIEROGLYPHICS) intermixed. The common parent—of all living alphabets—is Semitic, which as Phœnician is found well developed by about 900 B.C.

The oldest fairly datable alphabetic monument is the Moabite Stone (q. v.), 900-850 B.C.

History.—The Phœnicians were close neighbors and trading partners of the Semitic peoples. They might well use and remodel the system of any. But it is certain that what they did use about 1400 B.C. was the Assyro-Babylonian cuneiform, in which they sent all official and private correspondence to Egypt, and were answered in the same. The Greeks must have learned the alphabetic system from Phœnician traders in the Ægean as early as the ninth century B.C. The forms underwent little change at first, and writing was probably right to left; before 600 B.C. the more natural left-to-right was adopted. By 550 B.C. the Greek alphabet, in all essential respects, had attained its final development.

The primitive alphabet of Italy, from which the English is derived, belonged to the Western Greek type. Roman scripts are the sources of our printed capitals and types. Through Scotland this alphabet was introduced into Northumbria by Irish monks. In the English alphabet the order of the letters does not differ greatly from the Phœnician arrangement. The Greek alphabet was the source not only of the Latin, but of the other national alphabets of Europe. See ORTHOGRAPHY; PRONUNCIATION; and the separate articles on the letters of the English alphabet. Consult Clodd's *Story of the Alphabet.* The best monograph on the origin of the alphabet is Dr. J. P. Peters' last article in *Journal of the American Oriental Society* (1907).

A script found near Jerusalem, at Tell Duweir, in 1936, contains inscriptions in an alphabet which is believed to antedate the Phœnician alphabet. It may be a connecting link between the Phœnician and the Serabit alphabet, which is the oldest known. Earlier evidences of this intermediate alphabet were discovered in the same vicinity in 1930. This latest find was made by J. L. Starkey.

Alpha Rays. See **Radioactivity.**

Alpheus, in Greek mythology, the god of the River Alpheus, the chief stream of the Peloponnesus, Olympia to the Ionian Sea. The legend of Alpheus' love for the nymph Arethusa and their transformation into springs of water is found in Ovid's *Metamorphoses* v. 572 and is the foundation of Shelley's poem *Arethusa.*

Alphonsine Tables, or **Alfonsine,** improved astronomical tables drawn up by fifty celebrated astronomers at Toledo in 1252, first printed in 1483.

Alphonso. See **Alfonso.**

Alpine Clubs. See **Mountaineering.**

Alpine Plants, a name given to plants found at elevations approaching the limit of perpetual snow in the Alps, and other mountainous regions, whose natural place of growth is near snows that are never melted.

The small spaces clear of snow in these high regions possess a characteristic flora, the plants of which are distinguished by a low diminutive habit, and an inclination to form a thick turf; frequently, also, by a covering of woolly hairs, while their stems are often either partly or altogether woody, and their flowers are in proportion remarkably large, of brilliant colors, and in many instances very odoriferous.

Alps, the great European mountain system that extends in the form of a crescent from the Gulf of Genoa, westward to the French frontier, northward on the borders of France and Italy, and n.e. through Switzerland and Western Austria. It is bounded on the n. by the hilly ground of Switzerland and the upper plain of the Danube; on the e. by the low plains of Austria; on the s. by the Adriatic Sea, the plains of Lombardy, and the Gulf of Genoa; and on the w. by the plains of Provence and the valley of the Rhone. The Apennines (q. v.) join it at its western extremity, separated only by the Pass of Altare (*Col d'Altare*), while the Dinaric Alps (q.v.), on the e., link it with the Balkan range. The Alpine system is about 650 m. in length, and varies in width from 30 m. to 160 m. Total area, 90,000 sq.m.

Divisions.—In describing the manifold ranges of the Alpine system, three main divisions are commonly distinguished: (1) the Western Alps, extending from the Mediter-

Development Based on Phœnician 22-Letter Alphabet.

ranean coast to the Simplon Pass; (2) the Central Alps, stretching from the Simplon Pass to Reschen Scheideck and the Stelvio Pass; and (3) the Eastern Alps, comprising the remainder of the system.

(1) The *Western Alps*. The chief ranges are the Maritime Alps, near the Mediterranean coast; the Cottian Alps, the Dauphiné Alps, the Graian Alps, forming the boundary between Savoy and Piedmont, and the chain of Mont Blanc and the Pennine Alps, which include most of the loftiest peaks of the entire system, among them Mont Blanc (q.v.), 15,782 ft., Monte Rosa (q.v.), 15,217 ft., and Matterhorn (q.v.), 14,781 ft.

(2) The *Central Alps* include the Bernese Oberland, from Lake Geneva to Lake Lucerne, the Furka Pass, and the Reuss valley, with the Finsteraarhorn, 14,026 ft., Aletschhorn, 13,721 ft., and Jungfrau (q.v.), 13,669 ft.; the Lepontine or Helvetian Alps, from the Simplon to St. Gothard to the Splügen Pass; the Rhætian Alps, and the Alps of n.e. Switzerland.

(3) The *Eastern Alps* include the Alps of Bavaria, the Ortler, Oetzthal, and Stubai ranges to the Brenner Pass; the Lombard Alps, from Lake Como to the Adige valley; the Central Tyrolese, Dolomites of South Tyrol, and the Southeastern Alps.

Railways and Tunnels.—Besides the great trans-Alpine systems, there are ten principal Alpine railways with their branches. Light railways ascend the Rigi, Uetliberg, Pilatus, Generoso, Salvatore, Brienzer Rothhorn, Rochers de Naye, Grand Revard, Salève, Stanserhorn, Gornergrat, and Gurten. The Jungfrau railway rises from 6,772 ft. to the top of the peak at 13,428 ft.

The highest carriage roads pass over the Stelvio from Austria to Italy, Col du Galibier, Umbrail from Switzerland to Italy, Great St. Bernard, and Furka.

Railway tunnels have been pierced under a number of the passes. Three of these afford communication with Italy: the Col de Fréjus, 17 m. w. of Mont Cenis, and generally known as the Mont Cenis tunnel (see CENIS); the St. Gothard, between Lakes Lucerne and Maggiore (see GOTHARD); and the Simplon (q.v.), between the Upper Rhone Valley and Lago Maggiore. A 4th trans-Alpine railroad leading into Italy passes over the Brenner. The Arlberg (q.v.) tunnel joins Switzerland and Austria, and the Wocheiner, with those beneath the Pyhrn and Hohe Tauern Passes, makes possible direct communication between Vienna and Trieste. The Lötschberg tunnel (q.v.), opened in 1911, along with the Simplon, furnishes a direct through route from Milan to Berne, and thence to Calais. (See TUNNELS AND TUNNELING.)

Mountaineering and Health Resorts.—The chief mountain-climbing centers are Grindelwald, Chamonix and Zermatt. See MOUNTAIN CLIMBING. Among the most frequented *health resorts* are Davos-Platz, St. Moritz, Pontresina, Engelberg, Mürren, Grindelwald, Interlaken, Lugano, Vevey, Lausanne and Yverdon (qq.v.).

Climate.—The climate of the Alps is characterized by cold winters, pleasant summers, and disagreeable springs, with f r e q u e n t cyclonic storms. The average annual temperature on the *northern border*, at 1,500 ft. is about 40° F.; average summer temperature, about 65° F. A maximum of 90° F. is not uncommon in summer, and zero is often reached in winter.

Geology.—The geological history of the Alps is one of successive periods of upheaval, due to pressures from n.w. and s.e., which have folded, broken up, and in some cases overturned the strata of the earth's crust. Precious stones are found in abundance among the crystalline rocks of the central ranges. Mining and smelting become more and more productive as we advance e. Mineral springs, hot and cold, are innumerable.

Glaciers, Rivers and Lakes.—In every part of the Alps, *glaciers* occur, from the Maritime Alps at one extremity to the Dolomites at the other; and these form a striking feature of Alpine scenery. The total number of glaciers is said to exceed 1,100, while their combined area is estimated at about 1,500 sq.m. The largest and longest is the Great Aletsch, in the Bernese Oberland. There are also the Unteraar and Fiescher, the Gorner, in the Pennines, and the Mer de Glace (q.v.), at Chamonix. (See GLACIERS.)

The Alpine system is the center of radiation for some of the largest *rivers* of Europe. See RIVERS and Individual Names.

A chain of *lakes* encircles both the northern and southern bases of the Alps. Among the last are Lucerne (q.v.), Brienz (q.v.), Walenstadt, and Thun. To the s. are Maggiore, Lugano, Como, Iseo, and Garda (qq.v.); and on the northern borders are Geneva, Zürich, Constance, Chiemsee, Königssee and Hallstatt (qq.v.).

Fauna.—The Alpine Mountains present many peculiarities worthy of note in the animal kingdom.

Salmon and trout are sometimes caught in ponds 6,000 ft. above the level of the sea. The lofty mountains are inhabited by eagles, hawks, and various species of owls. Among quadrupeds are the steinbok or ibex, chamois, bear, wolf, lynx, wildcat and marmot. For the flora of the Alps, see ALPINE PLANTS.

See BERNESE OBERLAND ALPS; COTTIAN ALPS; DAUPHINÉ; DOLOMITES; GRAIAN ALPS; LEPONTINE ALPS; MARITIME ALPS; ORTLER GROUP; PENNINE ALPS; RHÆTIAN ALPS; SOUTHEASTERN ALPS.

Alpujarras, (Arabian *Al-Busherat*), mountain chain in the province of Granada, Spain. In its fastnesses the Moriscos (q.v.) of Granada found their last refuge.

Alruna, name given to a witch or prophetess by ancient Teutonic tribes.

Alsace-Lorraine, French province, from **early 1871 to 1918 an imperial territory of** *Reichsland* of the German Empire, to which it was ceded by France at the close of the Franco-German War (see *History*). It covers an area of 5,605 sq.m. (Alsace, 3,202 sq.m.; Lorraine, 2,403 sq. m.) Alsace embraces the western half of the Rhine Valley and the eastern half of the Vosges Mountains and their valleys. Agriculture is the chief occupation, 50 per cent. of the area being cultivated, and 15 per cent. meadow and grass land. The production of wine is important. Lorraine possesses rich mineral resources, especially iron and coal fields. Transportation facilities include a canal system, 5,000 m. of roads, and over 1,300 m. of railway.

The *population* of Alsace-Lorraine is 1,-795,100. The prevailing religion is Roman Catholic.

History.—In Cæsar's time *Alsace* was occupied by Celtic tribes. From the 10th century it formed part of the German empire, till a part of it was ceded to France at the Peace of Westphalia (1648), and the rest fell a prey to the aggressions of Louis XIV., who seized the free city of Strasbourg (1681). By the Peace of Ryswick (1697) the cession of the whole was ratified. *Lorraine* was also included in Charlemagne's empire; was constituted a kingdom under Lothair II.; and was divided in 959 into the duchies of Upper and Lower Lorraine, of which only the former retained its name. This passed to France in 1766. In 1871, by the Treaty of Frankfort at the close of the Franco-German War (q.v.), Alsace and Lorraine were ceded to Germany. The policy of Germany in Alsace-Lorraine was one of alternate coercion and conciliation.

The use of the French language was greatly restricted.

In 1911 a new constitution was granted, which provided for legislative autonomy and representation in the Federal Council. Early in World War I (1914-18) French forces invaded Alsace-Lorraine, and throughout the war the provinces were openly regarded by Germany as enemy territory. By the peace treaty the territories ceded in 1871 by France to Germany were restored to France with their frontiers as before 1871—to date from the signing of the armistice, Nov. 11, 1918. Dominated by Germany 1940-45. See EUROPE, GREAT WAR OF; PEACE CONFERENCE.

Alsegno, (Italian 'to the sign'), in musical score, directs the musician to turn back from the bar thus marked to the sign :S: and begin again at that place, continuing to the first double bar.

Alsen, a fertile island in the Baltic Sea. Formerly Danish, it was united to the Prussian province of Schleswig-Holstein in 1864. Area 120 sq.m.; p. 28,000, mostly Danish speaking.

Al Sirat, in Mohammedan teaching the bridge to Paradise, over the abyss of Hell.

Alsop, Richard (1761-1815), American author, was born in Middletown, Conn. He was one of a group of writers known as the 'Hartford Wits.' He was the chief contributor to *The Echo*, a series of pamphlets issued by them between 1791 and 1795, satirizing the public papers and political fads of the day.

Alsop Claim. See **Chile**, *History*.

Alstrœmeria, or **Alstromer's Lily**, a genus of Amaryllidaceæ (q.v.), cultivated for its flowers and curiously twisted leaves.

Alt, a term applied to the notes of the octave above the treble stave, beginning with G.

Altai Mountains, or **Kin-Shan** ('golden mountains'), one of the principal mountain systems of Central Asia, lies between lat. 45° and 54° N., on the borders of Mongolia, Zungaria, and Siberia. The Altai region is alpine in character, having deep and wild gorges, immense glaciers, beautiful lakes, such as Teletsk (1,600 ft. above sea level), fertile valleys, and valuable mineral deposits. The outskirts or steppes have been colonized by Russian agriculturists. The chief centre of administration is the town of Barnaul.

Altair, Aquilæ, a white star of 0.74 photometric magnitude. It is approaching the sun with a velocity of 24 m. a second (Vogel).

Altamaha River, in Georgia, is formed

by the junction of the Oconee and Ocmulgee Rivers in Montgomery co., whence it flows s.w. into the Atlantic Ocean. Length 155 miles.

Altamura, town, province of Bari, Italy. It has a Norman cathedral dating from 1220; p. 26,000.

Altar (Latin *altare,* 'a high place'), a raised structure on which sacrifices (see SACRIFICE) are offered, in use by man since the dawn of religious worship. The altars used in pagan times were of two types: those which stood low before the images within the temple, that the worshipper kneeling thereon might offer up his supplication; and those used for burnt offerings, which were placed before the temple door. Among both Jews and pagans the altar provided a protection to fugitives and slaves, which it was sacrilege to violate (see SANCTUARY).

The *altar piece,* a picture or framed sculpture in relief of a religious nature, placed on or near the altar, was one of the earliest forms of Christian art; and some of the most famous works of art are altar pieces. In the *Church of England,* at the time of the Reformation, Archbishop Laud caused the altar to be replaced from the body of the church, where it had been transplanted, to the upper end of the chancel. In the churches of other Protestant denominations the form of the altar and its use are determined by the manner in which the Lord's Supper is observed. See COMMUNION; EUCHARIST; HIGH PLACE; BALDACHIN; REREDOS. Consult M. Jastrow's *Religion of Babylonia and Assyria;* G. G. Scott's *Essay on the History of English Church Architecture;* W. Lowrie's *Monuments of the Early Church* (1906); H. C. Bowerman's *Roman Sacrificial Altars* (1913).

Altar Piece. See **Altar.**

Altazimuth, or **Altitude and Azimuth Instrument,** essentially a large theodolite (q.v.) for determining the altitudes and azimuths of the heavenly bodies, invented by Olaus Römer of Copenhagen in 1690.

Altdorf, or **Altorf,** capital of Swiss canton of Uri. The town is associated with the legend of William Tell, of whom it has a fine statue; p. 2,837.

Altdorfer, Albrecht (*c.* 1480-1538), painter, architect and engraver. He has been called the father of landscape painting. The most important of the twenty-five known paintings by him is the *Battle between Alexander and Darius* (Munich).

Altenburg, city, Germany, capital of the duchy of Saxe-Altenburg. The ducal castle (14th century, rebuilt 1865-70) crowns a steep rock above the town. The town was the scene of the 'Prinzenraub'—*i.e.,* the attempted abduction in 1455 of the Saxon princes Albert and Ernest by Kunz von Kaufungen; p. 39,977.

Altenstein, a summer castle of the dukes of Saxe-Meiningen, s.e. of Eisenach, Thuringia. It is historically associated with the seizure of Luther in 1521 when returning from Worms.

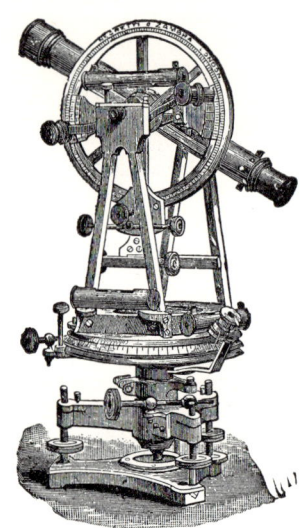

Altazimuth or Universal Transit Instrument.

Alteration. Generally speaking, any change in a written legal instrument which in effect substitutes a different legal instrument for the original one voids it at common law as against a party not assenting thereto. See NEGOTIABLE INSTRUMENTS; CANCELLING OF DEEDS.

Alteratives, in medicine, a term applied to remedies that 'improve the nutrition of the body without exerting any very perceptible action on individual organs' (Lauder Brunton).

Alter Ego, expressing an intimate friend, was officially employed in the kingdom of the Two Sicilies to designate the administrative plenipotentiary or general vicar of the king.

Alternating Current. See **Electricity, Current; Dynamo and Motor.**

Alternating Motion, a term used in mechanics to indicate motion backward and for-

Alternation   153   **Altötting**

ward, as opposed to rotation. See HARMONIC MOTION.

Alternation of Generations, common to both plant and animal life, is the alternate occurrence in one life history of two or more forms differently produced.

Plants.—A period arrives in the life of every plant when single cells become detached from the organism with which they have hitherto been identified, and enter upon a phase of independent development. Cells of this character are known as *reproductive cells,* and the plants resulting from them as *generations.* Only in the lowest plant forms, however, are the successive generations alike. Even in certain algæ and fungi, and in practically all mosses and ferns, the generations that proceed from one another are dissimilar: gametophytes, in which sexual reproduction takes place, alternating with sporophytes, in which reproduction is accomplished by means of asexual unicellular spores. The fertilized egg of the gametophyte develops into a sporophyte, from whose spores in turn gametophytes arise. In flowering plants the same law of alternating generations holds true; although the sexual generation lies concealed within the spore-bearing plant.

Animals.—Among animals alternation of generations is of common occurrence, especially in the lower forms. See BIOLOGY; REPRODUCTION; PARTHENOGENESIS; SPORE. Consult Steenstrupp's *On the Alternation of Generations* (Eng. trans.).

Alternator, Electric, or **Alternating-Current Dynamo,** is a machine designed to supply electrical energy in the form of an alternating electric current, in exchange for some form of mechanical energy supplied to it. See DYNAMO AND MOTOR.

Altgeld, John Peter (1847-1902), American public official, was born in Germany. He became judge of the Chicago superior court (1886-91), and governor of Illinois (1893-7). While governor he pardoned the Chicago anarchists Fielden, Schwab, and Neebe. He published: *Our Penal Machinery and Its Victims* (1886); *Eight-Hour Movement* (1890); *Live Questions* (1899).

Althæa, a genus of the Malvaceæ, including the Marsh Mallow, Hollyhock, and Rose of Sharon (qq.v.).

Althing, the Icelandic parliament. See ICELAND.

Althorn, or **Tenor Saxhorn,** a valve bugle in E *b* or F, used in military bands. See SAXHORN.

Altin-Tagh, or **Altyn-Tagh,** range of mountains in Central Asia. Highest known altitude, 14,000 ft.

Altitude, in astronomy, is the height of a heavenly body above the horizon. Altitudes are taken in observatories by means of a telescope attached to a graduated circle, which is fixed vertically. The altitude thus observed must receive various corrections—in order to determine the true altitude. At sea observations of altitude are made with the sextant. The correct determination of altitudes is of great importance in the problems of astronomy and navigation. See SEXTANT; ALTAZIMUTH; LATITUDE AND LONGITUDE.

Altman, Benjamin (1840-1913), American merchant, art collector, and philanthropist. He was an art collector of exquisite taste, and at his death left his remarkable collection to the Metropolitan Museum of Art.

Alto, a musical term, strictly applicable to the male voice of the highest pitch, counter tenor, but also used to denote the lowest range of the female voice, contralto (q.v.).

Alt-Ofen. See **Budapest.**

Alton, city, Illinois, Madison co., on the Mississippi River. The city occupies an elevated and picturesque situation. It is a railroad and manufacturing centre. The first settlement was made at Alton by the French, in 1807; p. 31,255.

Altona, city, in the southern part of Schleswig-Holstein, immediately west of Hamburg. North of the city lies Stellingen, containing Hagenback's Zoological Park, one of the famous animal collections of the world. Altona has a fine harbor accommodating large ocean-going craft, and there are extensive docks. In 1901 a free harbor was opened; p. 242,006.

Altoona, city, Blair co., Pennsylvania; 117 m. e. of Pittsburgh. The famous Horseshoe Bend on the Pennsylvania Railroad is four m. w. of the city. The chief industries centre in the extensive shops of the Pennsylvania Railroad, which cover 200 acres and employ over 12,000 workmen; p. 80,214.

Altoona (Allatoona) Pass, in Bartow co., Georgia, the scene of a hard-fought battle in the Civil War.

Alto-relievo, or **Alto-rilievo** ('high relief'). See SCULPTURE.

Altorf. See **Altdorf.**

Altötting, town, Bavaria, Germany; 60 m. n.e. of Munich. It possesses a chapel with a black wooden image of the Virgin (the Black Virgin), dating from the 8th century, which has attracted pilgrims for centuries; p. 5,408.

Altruism, a term brought into use by Comte (*altruisme*), and introduced into English by his Positivist followers, denoting (1) the social, as opposed to the egoistic, impulse in human nature; (2) this instinct or impulse raised to the rank of a conscious principle—the ethical principle which makes the good of others the paramount end of human action. See ETHICS.

Alum, Common Alum, a double salt, sulphate of potassium and aluminum, $KAl(SO_4)_2.12H_2O$, may be had in the form of glassy, colorless, octahedral (sometimes cubical) crystals, or as a white powder obtained by pulverizing these. It tastes first slightly sweetish, then distinctly sour, with noticeable astringent action. Alum is used as a mordant (especially for delicate colors). Other applications are in the tanning of glove kid and other light leather, in the sizing of paper, in the purifying of water, in medicine as an astringent and hæmostatic, in fireproofing fabrics and hardening plaster of Paris, and in making inferior baking powders. In most of its uses it is being replaced by aluminum sulphate.

Burnt alum is a white, anhydrous, slightly basic substance. *Chrome alum,* potassium chromium sulphate, $KCr(SO_4)_2.12H_2O$, is used in photographic fixing or hardening baths. *Concentrated alum* is aluminum sulphate (q.v.). *Neutral alum,* a basic compound $KAl_2(OH)_3(SO_4)_2$, is used as a mordant and in clarifying water. *Roman alum,* common alum as produced at the extensive works in the vicinity near Rome, occurs in crystals slightly orange red, an impurity easily removed by recrystallization.

Alumina, Aluminum Oxide, Al_2O_3, a compound of aluminum (53.0 per cent.) and oxygen, of great technical importance. It is found in nature in many forms: (*a*) as *corundum* (q.v.), (*b*) as *ruby,* (*c*) as *sapphire,* (*d*) as *emery.* It is colorless, yielding a white, tasteless powder insoluble in water. Alumina is little susceptible to chemical action. When made from the hydroxide by moderate heat it is soluble in acids, but when strongly heated it is hard, fusible with difficulty (melting point about 1,880° c.), and extremely resistant to the action of acids. When it is fused with caustic alkalies or acid sulphates, soluble aluminum compounds are formed. Alumina is the indirect source of the metal *Aluminum.* The principal source of this metal is bauxite. (See ALUMINUM; ALUNDUM).

Alumina is the principal material for the preparation of synthetic or artificial rubies and sapphires, an industry which is assuming importance. It is always one of the products formed in the Goldschmidt aluminothermic process for the reduction of oxides.

Aluminum or **Aluminium** (Al, 27.0), a soft, silvery white metal, extremely malleable, and of high ductility. With a specific gravity of only 2.70, it is the lightest metal in common use. It melts at 659° c (1185° F). The tensile strength of cast aluminum is 11,000-14,000 pounds per square inch; working by rolling will double this value, but on annealing the worked material the strength drops to about the cast value; in the form of wire the values are somewhat higher, and in small sizes of hard-drawn wire the strength may go to 55,000 pounds. The strength of the metal may be materially increased by allowing up to 33,000 pounds for cast metal, and certain types of alloys, by working and heat-treating, may be brought up to 80,000 pounds per square inch.

About half of the aluminum produced is used in the pure form, as sheet, wire, bars, rods, tubes, foil, or powder, while the other half goes into the various types of alloys, chiefly as castings. The largest consumer of aluminum is the automobile industry; modern cars have been made much lighter by the extensive use of aluminum in body construction, engine parts and fittings. Current development in aircraft construction has been largely dependent on the development in the use of high-strength aluminum alloys. Aluminum and its alloys are extensively used in the manufacture of cooking utensils, for apparatus in the dairy industry and in certain branches of the chemical industry; in steel metallurgy, aluminum is used as a deoxidizer for the liquid steel; aluminum foil is widely used to replace lead or tin foil in the wrapping of tobacco, chocolate, and the like; aluminum powder is used as a paint pigment and as grains, in the precipitation of gold and silver in the cyanide process (see GOLD and SILVER), and in the reduction of metallic oxides by the thermite process (q.v.); in the form of wire and cable, aluminum is a serious competitor of copper as an electrical conductor for high-tension transmission lines; and besides these there are innumerable other uses where the light weight and permanent character of the metal make it specially applicable.

The properties that contribute particularly to the metal's usefulness are: lightness; color; ability to take high polish; ability to form alloys of high strength; ductility;

malleability; good resistance to oxidation; resistance to corrosion by nitric acid and practically all organic acids; high electrical conductivity; ease of working and machining. Aluminum was first isolated by Wöhler in 1827, but the first attempts at the commercial production of the metal were not until 1854, when Ste. Claire Deville developed the process of reducing aluminum chloride by means of metallic sodium. His efforts laid the foundations of the aluminum industry, and this process was used for 30 years, until the development of the present electrolytic process.

Alloys.—While the light weight of aluminum is of great value in its technical applications, its low tensile strength is a disadvantage; to overcome this, numerous alloys have been developed in which the strength is materially increased. The chief alloying agents are copper, silicon and zinc, particularly for casting metal, iron, nickel, manganese, magnesium, and other metals are also frequently introduced. The alloy most used for rolling, forging and heat-treating is duralumin.

Compounds.—The compounds of aluminum of greatest commercial importance are the oxide and sulphate. (See ALUMINUM; ALUM). Though never occurring in nature in the metallic form aluminum is one of the most abundant of the chemical elements, being exceeded only by oxygen and silicon. Although it is mostly found as a silicate, as in clays, or feldspars, the only source from which the metal is commercially recovered is bauxite (q.v.). Aluminum is produced commercially by the electrolysis of a solution of the purified oxide, alumina, in fused cryolite.

Statistics.—The world's production and consumption of aluminum has grown rapidly during recent years. In 1897 the world's production was 3,200 metric tons; in 1939 it was about 675,000 metric tons. Of this total production the United States produced about 22 per cent., and Canada about 11 per cent., about 60 per cent. being produced in Europe, chiefly in Germany. Definite figures since 1939 are not obtainable but it is known that the stimulation of war requirements has greatly increased production. Consult Corson's *Aluminum* (1926); Holmes' *Out of the Test Tube* (1943).

Aluminum Bronze. This gold-like alloy contains from 5 to 10 per cent. of aluminum, and is very strong. For many years it has been manufactured into watch chains, pencil cases, and other small ornamental articles.

Alum Root, a name given in the United States to two native plants, very different from each other, but agreeing in the powerful astringency of their roots, which are used medicinally—*Geranium maculatum* (see GERANIUM) and *Heuchera americana,* a plant of the natural order Saxifragaceæ.

Alundum, an artificial crystalline oxide of aluminum (Al_2O_3), used as an abrasive and a refractory. Its resistance to high temperature and corrosion is valuable.

Alunite, or **Alumstone,** a hydrous sulphate of aluminum and potassium. Extensive deposits are mined near Rome, Italy, in Tuscany, Hungary, and New South Wales, and deposits have recently been found in Utah and Nevada.

Alunogen, a fibrous aluminum sulphate, found in volcanic *débris,* clays, feldspathic rocks which contain pyrites, and often as an inflorescence on walls of mines and caves.

Alva, or **Alba, Ferdinand Alvarez de Toledo,** Duke of (1508-82), Spanish general and prime minister, was descended from one of the most illustrious families of Spain. He entered the army a mere youth, and became a commander-in-chief at thirty years of age. His skilful defence of Navarre and Catalonia gained him his rank as Duke of Alva. Alva died at Thomar, Jan. 12, 1582, at the age of seventy-four. Alva had a haughty carriage, a hard voice, and a dark and gloomy countenance. He was cruel, avaricious, and a fanatic. It has been said of him that during sixty years of military service he never lost a battle, and never allowed himself to be surprised. Consult Motley's *Dutch Republic.*

Alvarez, Luis (1841-1901), Spanish painter, was born in Madrid. He first attracted notice by his picture *Caesar's Wife, Calpurnia,* which is now in the Royal Palace at Madrid. He also painted large historical canvases and devoted himself with success to genre painting—*e.g., A Funeral, The Heir's Picture.*

Alwar, or **Alwur,** native state in Rajputana, India; p. 791,688. Its capital is ALWAR, about 85 m. s.w. of Delhi; p. 60,000.

Alyattes, King of Lydia (reigned *c.* 617-523 B.C.). His tomb, situated n. of Sardis, near Lake Gygæa, was one of the wonders of antiquity.

Alypius, a Greek writer on music, who flourished at Alexandria in the middle of the 4th century A.D. His works, under the title *Introductio Musica* contain the key to scales and modes of Greek music.

Alyssum, a genus of cruciferous, European plants. *A. maritimum* is the fragrant annual known as **Sweet Alyssum.**

A.M., abbreviation of (1) *Anno Mundi*, 'in the year of the world'; (2) *Ante Meridiem*, 'before noon'; and (3) *Artium Magister*, 'master of arts.'

Amadavat, one of the weaver birds (q.v.), a native of East India, but found in captivity in all parts of the world. The amadavat should receive the same care as the canary.

Amadeus, the name borne by several princes of the house of Savoy, of whom the most notable are: AMADEUS V. (1249-1323), —AMADEUS VIII. (1383-1451).

Amadis, a much-used name in the chivalric poetry of the Middle Ages, chiefly associated with the adventures of AMADIS OF GAUL. A Frenchman, Duverdier, at the beginning of the seventeenth century, brought the history of Amadis and the series of about 50 vols. to a close in his *Roman des Romans*.

Amadou, or **German Tinder**, a fungus, *Polyporus fomentarius*, growing on trees, is cut into slices and beaten into a felt; it has been used to plug wounds and stop bleeding. The felt steeped in saltpetre forms German tinder.

Amager or **Amak**, an island off the east coast of Zealand. It is the most densely populated part of Denmark; p. 20,000.

Amakosa, or **Ama-Xosa**, an important branch of the Bantu nation, inhabiting the Transkei, Tembuland, and Pondoland. See BANTU.

Amaldar, the governor of a province under the Mohammedan rule in India.

Amalekites, a nomadic Arab people of great antiquity, inhabiting the desert region southwest of Palestine. See Gen. XXXVI. 12; outside the Old Testament we have little reliable information concerning them.

Amalfi, seaport and archiepiscopal see of Italy, Salerno province, 22 m. s.e. of Naples. The Cathedral of S. Andrea dates from the eleventh century, and was restored in 1891. At the present time it has manufactures of macaroni, soap, and paper; p. 7,500.

Amalgam, an alloy of mercury. All metals except iron and platinum form amalgams—some, like sodium and potassium, combining with great energy; while others, like lead, bismuth, and tin, require the application of heat See GOLD; METALLURGY. Copper amalgam is used in dentistry; silver and tin amalgams for silvering metals and mirrors; and zinc amalgam in the manufacture of frictional electrical machines. See ALLOYS.

Amalia, Anna (1739-1807), duchess of Saxe-Weimar-Eisenach. She is specially remembered as a patron of art and letters whose court was frequented by the most distinguished writers of the day, including Herder, Goethe, Wieland, and Schiller.

Amalthæa, in Greek mythology, the nurse of Zeus, most frequently represented as a goat.

Amana Community. See **Communism**.

Amanita, a genus of fungi, nearly allied to the mushrooms (*Agaricus*). Several of the species are edible, notably the delicious Orange (*A. Cæsarea*), but the majority are poisonous.

Aman-Jean, Edmond François (1860-1936), French portrait painter, was born in Chevry-Cossigny. He is essentially a decorative designer and portrait painter. The Carnegie Institute of Pittsburgh has his decorative panel *La Vasque*.

Amaranth (*Amaranthus*), the leading genus of Amaranthaceæ. *A. caudatus* ('Love-Lies-Bleeding') whose spikes are sometimes several feet in length. *A. speciosus, A. hypochondriacus* ('Prince's Feather'), and other species, are common annuals. The plant has been employed from early times as an emblem of immortality.

Amarapura, ('city of the gods'), a former capital of Upper Burma, 9 m. n.e. of Ava. A colossal bronze statue of Buddha is its chief feature; p. 8,500.

Amara-Sinha, or **Amara-Simha**, Sanskrit grammarian, who flourished, probably in the fifth century A.D. His only surviving work is the *Amara-Kosha*.

Amari, Michele (1806-89), Italian historian, Orientalist, and statesman, was born in Palermo. In 1834 he published *Fondazione della Monarchia dei Normanni in Sicilia*. Other works are *La Sicile et les Bourbond; Altre Narrazioni del Vespro Siciliano*.

Amarillo, city, Texas, county seat of Potter co., 300 m. n.w. of Fort Worth. The city is in a rich agricultural and stock-raising district, and in the midst of rich oil and natural gas fields; p. 51,686.

Amarna Tablets. See **Tell-el-Amarna**.

Amaryllidaceæ, or **Amaryllideæ**, a natural order of petaloid monocotyledons. See AGAVE; AMARYLLIS; ALSTRŒMERIA; BLOOD FLOWER. NARCISSUS.

Amaryllis, a genus of bulbous-rooted plants of the order Amaryllidaceæ, formerly including many species now assigned to other genera.

Amasis, or **Aahmes**, the name of two ancient Egyptian kings, reigning about 1600 B.C. and 570-526 B.C.).

Amateur, in sports, according to the Intercollegiate Association of Amateur Athletics of America, 'one who engages in sport solely for the pleasure and physical benefits he derives therefrom, and to whom sport is nothing more than an avocation.' Basketball, billiards, boxing, fencing, gymnastics, handball, hurdleracing, jumping, lacrosse, pole vaulting, putting the shot, throwing the discus and weights, running, swimming, tugs of war, walking, and wrestling in the United States are under the jurisdiction of the Amateur Athletic Union. Into such sports as curling, quoits, polo and canoeing, the spirit of professionalism seldom enters. Others, such as bicycle racing in America and football in England, are dominated by professional interests which in recent years have also entered into American football and lawn and indoor tennis.

Amati, a famous family of violin makers, who resided in Cremona.

ANDREA (c. 1520-1611), founder of the Cremona school of violin making.

ANTONIO (1550-1635) and GERONIMO (1556-1630), sons of Andrea, worked together for many years, and produced a large number of beautiful and highly prized instruments.

NICOLA (1596-1684), the great man of the family, son of Geronimo, followed his father's model until about 1625, when he designed a model—since known as the 'grand Amati'—which has not been excelled in grace and elegance of form, exquisite workmanship, and sweet and responsive tone. He had many pupils, of whom Antonius Stradivari was the most famous.

Amatitlan, department, Guatemala, Central America, contains LAKE AMATITLAN (area, 20 m.), on which the capital AMATITLAN, 15 m. s.w. of the city of Guatemala, is situated; p. 37,000.

Amato, Pasquale (1878-1942), Italian opera singer, was born in Naples. He sang in many cities of the United States.

Amaurosis (Greek 'a darkening') is total loss of vision caused by diseases not directly involving the eye. See AMBLYOPIA.

Amazon, the largest river of South America, and in the volume of its waters and the extent of its basin the greatest in the world. It rises in the Peruvian Andes, crosses the continent in a northeasterly direction, and empties into the Atlantic Ocean after a course of about 3,300 miles. The main stream is seldom more than three or four degrees from the Equator, which it reaches at its mouth. Its course lies chiefly in the northern half of Brazil. With its tributaries it is said to afford over 25,000 m. of waterway suitable for steam navigation. The fall of the Amazon after it emerges from the Andes is slight. The current is generally placid, averaging about $2\frac{1}{4}$ miles an hour, though it may be as much as 5 m. an hour in the more contracted channels during times of flood. Between Tabatinga and Manaos the river has a breadth of $2\frac{1}{2}$ to 4 m., and it gradually widens as it approaches the sea, until at its mouth it is 50 m. across. The Atlantic tides ascend the Amazon for a distance of more than 400 m., (see TIDES). The fresh water of the river is perceptible 180 m. out into the Atlantic.

For the greater part of its course the Amazon flows through level, densely wooded lowlands, which are intersected in all directions by stagnant backwaters, narrow side channels, or *furos*, and shallow lagoons. Islands are numerous, especially in the lower river, where they are formed by narrow cross streams connecting the tributary rivers. Many of these islands are thickly wooded.

The river begins to rise in November, and, swollen by heavy tropical rains, continues to increase in volume until June, when it reaches an average maximum depth of 120 ft. During this period the adjoining country is inundated, many of the islands disappear completely, and the scattered lagoons and sluggish *furos* are united in a great inland sea. In its lower course the river is seldom less than 150 ft. deep, even in periods of low water.

The climate of the Amazon basin, though hot and very damp, is greatly mitigated by trade winds which blow from the east with little interruption throughout the dry season. The average temperature is 84° F., and the average annual rainfall is about 100 inches. Dense forests, almost impenetrable on account of the enormous growth of lianas, or woody vines, of countless species, cover the greater part of the valley. Tall grasses, willows, and trumpet trees abound on the river borders, and rubber trees, palms, dyewoods, and valuable timber trees grow in profusion beyond.

The Amazonian fauna is exceedingly rich. In the river and its tributaries are fish of many species, alligators, turtles, and manatees. The forests abound in insects and birds, and in mammals, notably tapirs, monkeys, ant-eaters, capybaras, agoutis and sloths. Boa constrictors are among the reptiles found, and there are several varieties of lizards.

chief among which is the iguana. The mouth of the Amazon was discovered in 1500 by Vicente Vañez Pinzon (q.v.). See BRAZIL; SOUTH AMERICA.

Amazonas, the northernmost and largest of the states of Brazil, occupying a large part of the basin of the Amazon River. The greater part of the state is covered with forests; p. 275,000.

Amazonas, a department of Peru, in the Amazon basin. Cap. Chachapoyas; p. 60,000.

Amazonas, territory of Venezuela; p. 50,000.

Amazons, according to Greek legend, a warlike race of women, who lived in the neighborhood of the Caucasus, and invaded Asia Minor, Thrace, Greece, Egypt, and other countries. They were governed by a queen, and once every year met a neighboring race of men, the *Gargareans,* to propagate their race; they retained only female children, the males being killed, or handed over to the Gargareans. Consult F. M. Bennett's *Religious Cults Associated with the Amazons* (1912).

Ambassador, the highest rank of diplomatic agents between states. Their grades were officially settled by the Congresses of Vienna in 1815 and Aix-la-Chapelle in 1818 as (1) ambassadors, including the papal nuncio; (2) envoys extraordinary or ministers plenipotentiary; (3) *chargés d'affaires.* The name ambassador is still withheld from envoys to any but important states. The United States never used it till 1893, when Congress authorized the President to accredit ambassadors to any state represented by that grade at Washington. The rank is now given

Scene on the Amazon River.

its ministers to Argentina, Australia, Belgium, Bolivia, Brazil, Canada, Chile, China, Colombia, Costa Rica, Cuba, Czechoslovakia, Dominican Republic, Ecuador, Egypt, El Salvador, France, Great Britain, Greece, Guatemala, Haiti, Honduras, Iceland, Iran, Italy, Mexico, Netherlands, Nicaragua, Norway, Panama, Paraguay, Peru, Poland, Philippines, Portugal, Turkey, Union of Socialist Soviet Republics, Uruguay, Yugoslavia, Venezuela. Before declaring war, a state usually recalls its own ambassador and dismisses the other state's ambassador; but the severing of diplomatic relations is not always followed by war. *Ambassadors extraordinary* are special envoys, usually to make some treaty. See DIPLOMACY; DIPLOMATIC SERVICE.

Amber, a fossil resin, arises from the exudation of coniferous trees. It is of a clear brownish-yellow color, varying in shade, and is often clouded with irregular streaks. When rubbed it is negatively electrified, and from this property, which was well known to the ancients, the word 'electricity' has been derived (Greek *elektron*, 'amber'). Amber is used principally in the manufacture of mouthpieces for pipes and cigar holders, beads, necklaces, and ornaments. It is soluble in alcohol, and forms the basis of certain varnishes. A large part of the amber of commerce is artificial. Amber is found chiefly on the shores of the Baltic, and on the shores of Pomerania, West Prussia, Schleswig-Holstein, and Denmark. Amber beads have been found in the royal tombs of Mycenæ in Greece, in Scandinavian relics of the Stone Age, in the ancient pile dwellings of Switzerland, and in Etruscan ruins. Amber was well known to the Romans, and is described by Pliny.

Amber-fish, any of several carangoid fishes (genus *Seriola*), allied to the pompano (q.v.), and of graceful form and a color suggesting amber.

Amberg, ancient capital of the Upper Palatinate, Bavaria, on the River Vils. It has iron mines and iron works, and manufactures of earthenware, ironware, and firearms (state factory); p. 27,000.

Ambergris, a fatty substance often found floating in the sea, or cast up on tropical beaches in lumps of from half an ounce to a hundred pounds in weight, and highly valued for making perfumes. Its nature and origin were formerly uncertain, but it is now known to be a concretion, similar to bezoar (q.v.), formed in the stomach and intestines of sperm whales, from whose bodies it has frequently been saved.

Ambidexterity. See **Right-Handedness.**

Ambler, James Markham Marshall (1848-81), American surgeon, was born in Fauquier co., Va. In 1879 he accompanied G. W. De Long (q.v.) as surgeon to the *Jeannette* Arctic Expedition, and the whole party succumbed to starvation in 1881.

Ambleside, market town, Westmoreland, England, beautifully situated near the northern end of Lake Windermere; p. 2,553.

Amblyopia (Greek 'dim sightedness'), defective or diminished vision. Scientifically, the term is supposed to apply only to those

War Ambulance—World War I.

cases which cannot be more strictly classified after ophthalmoscopic examination.

Amblyopsis, a bony fish, found in the Mammoth Cave (q.v.) of Kentucky, and interesting as illustrating in the rudimentary condition of its eyes the effects of darkness and consequent disuse. It measures only a few inches in length, is colorless, and has its small eyes covered by the skin. See BLIND FISH.

Amblypoda, an order of extinct ungulate mammals which flourished in the Eocene (q.v.) period, but which left no descendants. Many were as large as an elephant.

Ambo, in early Christian churches, a reading desk or pulpit from which the lessons were read or the sermon preached at the regular services.

Amboise, (ancient *Ambatia*), town,

France, department Indre-et-Loire, on the River Loire. The town possesses an ancient castle, in which Charles VIII. was born and died; p. 4,284.

Amboise, Georges d' (1460-1510), cardinal, and Prime Minister of Louis XII. of France, was born near Amboise. He was made cardinal by Pope Alexander VI., after whose death he aimed at the popedom, and, failing to secure it (1503), became strongly opposed to the Popes.

Amboyna, or **Amboina,** an island in the Dutch East Indies, one of the smallest, but one of the most important, and though hot, the most healthy of the Moluccas group. The town of Amboyna, p. 8,000, has a good harbor; it is the principal fortified post of the Dutch in this part of the East Indies. See MOLUCCAS.

Ambracia, ancient town of Greece, on the north of the Ambracian Gulf (Gulf of Arta), in Epirus.

Ambrine, a preparation of wax, paraffin, and resin for the treatment of burns and wounds, was discovered by Barthe de Sandfort, a French surgeon, about 1900, and came into extended use during the Great War.

Ambrose, St. (c. 340-397), patron saint of Milan, and one of the most famous of the ancient fathers of the Christian Church. He was born in Gaul, but went when young to Rome. On the death of Bishop Auxentius in 374, Ambrose, though a layman, was elected to the vacant see of Milan. In the theological conflicts that raged over the question of Christ's divinity, Ambrose took up a resolute position against Arianism. On the assassination of Valentinian and the usurpation of Eugenius in 392, Ambrose fled; but when Theodosius defeated the usurper he returned to Milan, and continued there till his death, in 397. His most valuable legacy to the church is his hymns, and the improvements he introduced into the service. (See AMBROSIAN CHANT.

Ambrose Channel, the main ship channel entering New York harbor, is 40 ft. deep, 7½ m. long, and from 1,850 to 2,000 ft. wide. The channel was opened to vessels of 29 ft. draught and over, or 600 ft. or more in length, in 1907, and to all steamers not having tows, in 1909.

Ambrosia, in Greek mythology the food of the gods, which bestowed immortal youth and beauty upon all who partook of it.

Ambrosia Beetles, a name applied to the timber-boring beetles of several genera and a large number of species, common throughout North America. They are small, elongate insects, dull brown in color, with compact cylindrical bodies and short legs, and differ from the bark beetles (q.v.) in that they penetrate deeply into the wood of forest and fruit trees and feed upon ambrosia, a coating of certain minute fungi propagated on the walls of their borings.

Ambrosian Chant, the choral music introduced from the Eastern to the Western Church by St. Ambrose (q.v.), bishop of Milan, in the fourth century. It was used till Gregory changed it, in the sixth century, for the less monotonous Gregorian chant.

Ambrosian Library, a celebrated collection in Milan, made possible by the munificence of Cardinal Borromeo, archbishop of that city. Founded at the beginning of the seventeenth century, the library was afterward enriched by the acquisition of the manuscripts of the Pinelli Collection. It contains about 230,000 printed books and 15,000 manuscripts.

Ambulance, a vehicle or other means of transport used for the conveyance of the sick and wounded.

Army ambulances are fully equipped for the care and tranportation of sick and wounded soldiers; and in the U. S. Army are organized into a corps for each division, under specially designated ambulance officers.

In the Great War (1914-19) the Motor Ambulance was used with marked success, under innumerable difficulties, to carry the wounded from the front to the rear, where they might receive the careful attention their condition demanded. The typical and durable American military ambulance used in the war established a remarkable record for itself, being successful in the mud of Flanders, as well as in the mountains of the Vosges, where it replaced the mule in the transportation of the wounded. This type of car has a light body, constructed of canvas and tough wood, and is capable of accommodating several stretchers, on the floor and suspended from the roof.

The American Ambulance, which rendered invaluable aid in the war, did not at first include a field service for the Allied armies, but did most efficient hospital work at the bases and in Paris itself. In April, 1915, however, the French gave American Ambulance sections a trial at the front and the end of April, 1915, saw the American Ambulance Field Service well under way. After that time it rendered distinguished service, many of its drivers being awarded the *Croix de*

Guerre. See **Hospitals**; **Medical Department**; **Red Cross**.

Ambur, town, Madras, India, on the Palar River, 100 m. s.w. of Madras; with fort commanding an important pass into the Carnatic; p. 16,000.

Ambush, or **Ambuscade,** the disposition of troops who conceal themselves in a suitable locality with the object of lying in wait for an enemy and falling upon him unawares.

Ameer. See **Emir.**

Amelanchier, a genus of small, hardy trees of the Rosaceæ. They have simple leaves, racemes of white flowers, and small, juicy fruit. *A. botryapium,* an American variety, is sometimes called June Berry, from its early ripening. Other popular names for different species are Service Berry, Shad Bush, and Sand Cherry.

Amelia Island, off the coast of Florida, and opposite the estuary of St. Mary's River. The island was settled by General Oglethorpe (1736), and saw the first struggle of the English war with Spain (1739-48).

Amélie-les-Bains, watering place, France, department Pyrénées-Orientales. It has hot mineral springs, known since the time of the Romans. Until 1840 it was known as Bains d'Arles; p. 1,484.

Amen, a Hebrew word signifying 'firmly' or 'surely,' from *aman,* 'to prop or support.' The use of the word, has become a characteristic of Christian worship, and has passed into the liturgical diction of Mohammedanism.

Amen. See **Ammon.**

Amende Honorable, (French 'honorable compensation'), in France in the ninth century was a public and humiliating confession made by traitors and other offenders in court, kneeling, and with a rope around their neck. The phrase is now used figuratively of a full and open apology.

Amendment. In parliamentary procedure, the object of an amendment is to effect such an alteration in a proposal or motion as will render it more acceptable to a certain party or group. (See **Parliamentary Law**.)

Amendment in legislation is the alteration or modification, by legislative action, of laws already on the statute books. (See **Constitution**.)

Amendments to the State constitutions are passed upon by the State legislatures, and referred to the electorate for adoption (see **Referendum**).

Amenemhat, the surname of four kings of Egypt who ruled during the twelfth dynasty. (1.) Amenemhat I., king from about 2130 B.C. to about 2100 B.C., brought order out of chaos. (2.) Amenemhat II. ruled from about 2066 B.C., for 35 years. For a few years before his death, he and his son, Usertesen I., reigned together. (3.) Amenemhat III. held power from about 1986 to 1942 B.C. (4.) Son of Amenemhat III., reigned from about 1940 to 1932 B.C.

Amenhotep (Amenophis) the name of four Pharaohs of Egypt of the eighteenth dynasty. (1.) Son of Amasis I., reigned for about ten years (*c.* 1570 B.C.). (2.) Son of Thothmes III., reigned twenty-five years, from about 1450 B.C. (3.) Son of Thothmes IV., reigned thirty-six years, from about 1410 B.C. He erected the great temples at Thebes, of which only the ruins of the Temple of Luxor, and the two colossi, one of which was known in classical times as 'the Vocal Memnon,' now remain. (4.) Son of the last named, reigned eighteen years, from about 1375 B.C. See **Egypt**.

Amenorrhœa. See **Menstruation.**

Amentaceæ, or **Amentalos,** a collection of orders of dictoyledonous plants whose flowers, devoid of corolla, and often of calyx, are grouped into unisexual inflorescences, called aments (amentums) or catkins.

Amenthes, the name for the unseen world of the ancient Egyptians, the Hades of the Greeks, who borrowed their ideas about the lower world from Egypt. See **Egypt**.

Amentum. See **Catkin.**

America, or the **New World,** is the second largest continent on the globe. The New World and the Old World are separated by Bering Strait, abut 50 m. wide. The mainland lies between 71° N. and 54° S. lat., and between 35° and 168° W. long. The meridian of 80° W. divides it approximately into a w. and n. and an e. and s. mass, which are connected by the narrow Isthmus of Panama. These two masses of North and South America have several common characteristics. They are broad at the n. and taper toward the s.; the western part consists of a belt of lofty mountain chains enclosing extensive plateaus; the centre is a great lowland, continuous from n. to s., and drained by great rivers, the Mackenzie and Mississippi in the n., and the Orinoco, Amazon, and Rio de la Plata in the s. The e. is a highland broken by the St. Lawrence in the n. and the Amazon in the s.

The total area of America is estimated to be about 14,800,000 sq. m., with adjacent islands, about 16,125,000 sq. m. The popu-

AMERICA'S CUP RACE
The American yacht, in foreground.

lation of the New World is approximately 280,000,000. The native peoples of North and South America alike would appear to have been all of one race. Further notice of the red men and of their ancient centres of semi-civilization is contained in the article AMERICAN INDIANS.

The present population of North America contains a copious element of the Indian stock, but by far the largest share of the North American people are English in language, if not in descent. The aboriginal population of South America is noticed in the article AMERICAN INDIANS. The white population is largely Spanish in language and descent, except in Brazil, where Portuguese is spoken. For detailed information, see the separate articles on NORTH AMERICA and SOUTH AMERICA; CENTRAL AMERICA; WEST INDIES.

America, a national hymn for patriotic ceremonies, composed by the Rev. Samuel F. Smith in 1832, and set to an eighteenth century tune ascribed to Henry Carey (1742), which is also adopted in 'God save the King,' the national anthem of Great Britain.

America Cup, or **America's Cup**, an international yachting trophy. The competition for this cup is of British origin, having arisen out of a Royal Yacht Squadron contest, for which a prize, called the Queen's Cup, was offered, the course being around the Isle of Wight. The cup having been carried off by the U. S. schooner *America* (1851), the winners conveyed it by deed of gift in 1857 to the New York Yacht Club, to be held by

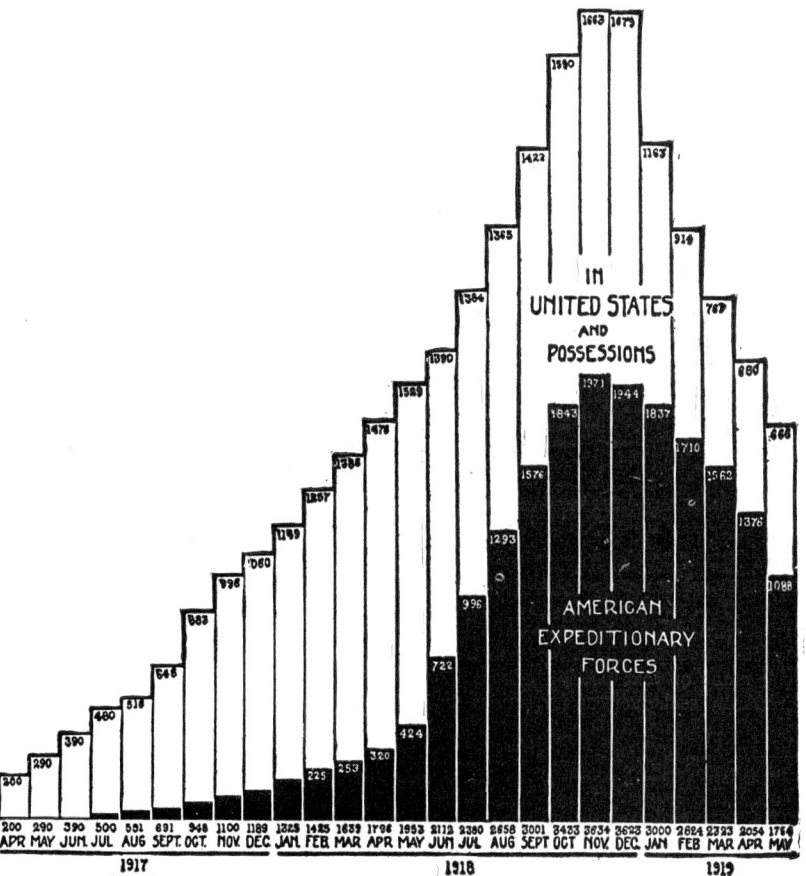

Thousands of Soldiers in American Army on the First of Each Month—World War I

that club against all challengers as an international trophy. In 1870 and 1871, Great Britain challenged and was defeated. A similar fate befell Canadian challengers in 1876 and 1881, and further British challengers in 1885, 1886, 1887, 1893, and 1895. Among all the British challengers the most notable and the most persevering has been Sir Thomas Lipton. In 1899 his Clyde-built *Shamrock* was pitted against the *Columbia*, and defeated. In 1901 Sir Thomas was again defeated. In 1903 Sir Thomas made a third unsuccessful attempt with the *Shamrock III*. In 1913 he again challenged. The races were held in July, 1920, between *Shamrock IV*, and the *Resolute*, designed by N. G. Herreshoff and built in Bristol, R. I. Five races were run; *Shamrock IV* won the first two, but the last three went to the American *Resolute*. In 1930 Sir Thomas Lipton challenged with the *Shamrock V*, and was defeated by the American yacht *Enterprise*. He died in 1931, having won the great admiration of the American public as a perfect sportsman. In 1934, T. O. M. Sopwith, the British challenger, was defeated by Harold Vanderbilt who sailed the *Rainbow;* the *Rainbow* winning four and the *Endeavour* winning two, all closely contested races. Mr. Sopwith challenged again in 1936 and the races were sailed in July-August 1937; the contestants being Mr. Sopwith's *Endeavour II* and Mr. Vanderbilt's *Ranger;* all four races were decisively won by the *Ranger*. See YACHT.

American Aloe. See **Agave.**

American Expeditionary Forces, the official name of that portion of the United States Army sent overseas for service during World Wars I and II. (q.v.).

On April 6, 1917, when the United States issued its declaration of war on Germany, the Army numbered about 200,000 men, two-thirds of that number belonging to the Regular Army and one-third to the Federalized National Guard. During the course of the War this number was increased to 4,000,-000 men, fifty per cent. of whom were in overseas service. Of the total, more than 500,000, or 13 per cent. came in through the Regular Army; almost 400,000, or 10 per cent. through the National Guard; and the rest, constituting 77 per cent. through conscription or enlistment (see CONSCRIPTION).

The average member of the American Expeditionary Forces received six months of training in camps and cantonments in United States and two months overseas training before entering the battle line, with an additional month in a quiet sector before going into heavy fighting. Training was for the most part in the division (q.v.), which was the typical combat unit, consisting of about 1,000 officers and 27,000 men. The First and Second Divisions, composed almost wholly of Regular Army men, were organized in France; the Twenty-sixth, Forty-second, and Forty-first reached France within three months, or less, of the date of organization; while the remaining divisions underwent comparatively extended periods of training in the United States.

The first troops were shipped within a few weeks of the entrance of the United States into the War. Early in 1918 negotiations were entered into with the British Government by which three of its big liners and four of its smaller troop ships were definitely assigned to the service of the U. S. Army. Before the end of October the second million men had sailed from our shores. No such troop movement as that of the summer of 1918 had ever been contemplated, and no movement of any such number of persons by water for such a distance and such a time had ever previously occurred. The record has been excelled only by the achievement in bringing the same men back to the shores of the United States. The return of troops was begun shortly after the signing of the Armistice. Large quantities of food and equipment had also to be transported to support the forces abroad. During the whole period of active hostilities the Army lost at sea only 200,000 deadweight tons of transports. Of this total 142,000 tons were sunk by torpedoes. No American troop transport was lost on its eastward voyage.

Active Service.—Of the 42 divisions that reached France, 29 took part in active combat service, while the others were used for replacements or were just arriving during the last month of hostilities. The battle record of the U. S. Army in the War is largely the history of these 29 combat divisions. Seven of them were Regular Army divisions, (1st, 2d, 3d, 4th, 5th, 6th, 7th); 11 were organized from the National Guard (26th, 27th, 28th, 29th, 30th, 32d, 33d, 35th, 36th, 37th, 42d) and 11 were made up of National Army troops (77th, 78th, 79th, 80th, 81st, 82d, 88th, 89th, 90th, 91st, 92d). The 93d division, while not listed as a combat division, because it was at no time complete as a division, was brigaded with the French, with whom it also saw active service.

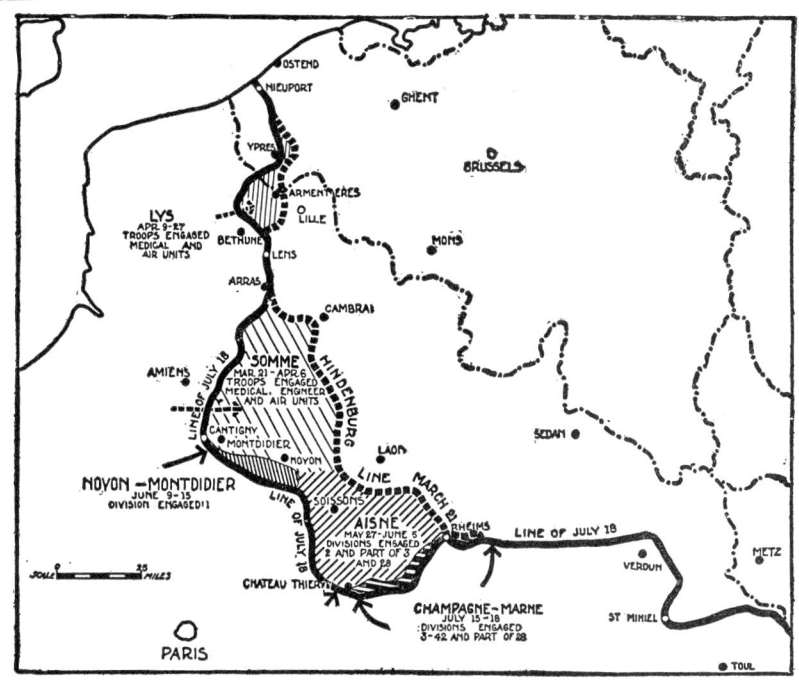
The Five Great German Offensives of 1918.

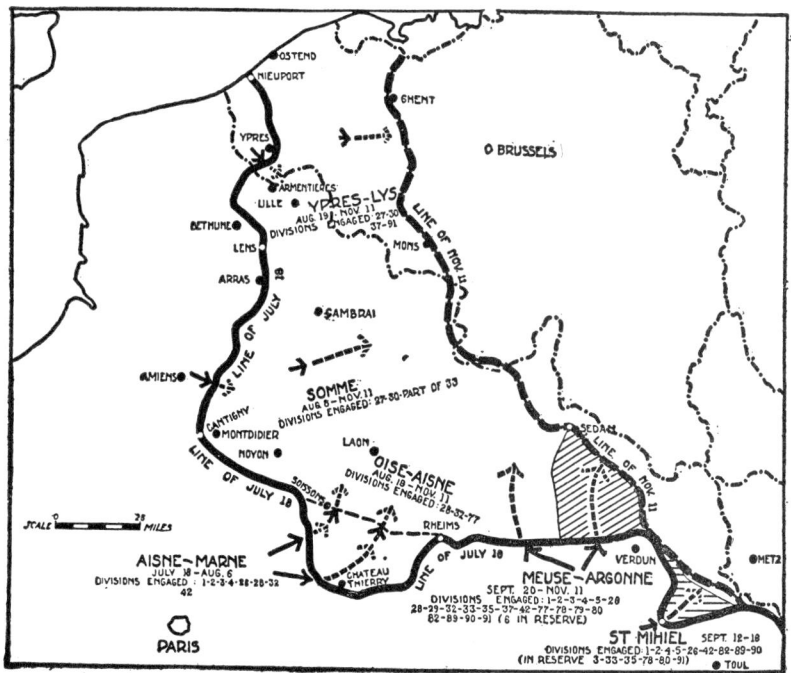
The Allied Offensives of 1918.

AMERICAN PARTICIPATION IN WORLD WAR I

American combat divisions were in battle for 200 days, from the 25th of April, 1918, until the signing of the armistice. During these 200 days they were engaged in 13 major operations, of which 11 were joint enterprises with the French, British, and Italians, and 2 were distinctively American.

The first major operation was the Cambrai battle at the end of the campaign of 1917. The other major operations were the five great German offensives (Somme, Lys, Oise, Noyon-Montdidier, and Champagne-Marne) from March 21 to July 18, 1918; the Allied offensives (Aisne-Marne, Somme, Oise-Aisne, Ypres-Lys, St. Mihiel, and Meuse-Argonne from July 18 to Nov. 11; and the Battle of Vittoria-Veneto (Oct. 24-Nov. 4, 1918) on the Italian front. The two distinctively American actions were the Battle of St. Mihiel (q.v.) and the Battle of the Meuse-Argonne (see ARGONNE). For further details, see the article EUROPE, GREAT WAR OF, and on the individual actions.

Battle Casualties in the A. E. F. were as follows: Killed in action, 34,180; died of wounds, 14,729; severely wounded, 80,130; slightly wounded, 110,544; wounded, degree undetermined, 39,400; missing in action, 2,913; taken prisoner, 4,434; making a total of 286,330 battle casualties, of which 48,909 were deaths either in action or from wounds. In addition to this number, there were 27,790 deaths from disease and other causes.

In **World War II,** American expeditionary forces were sent to Iceland, England, Ireland, France, the Philippines, Australia, New Caledonia, Solomon Islands, and other undisclosed points. Consult *The War with Germany; A Statistical Summary,* by Leonard P. Ayres; *History of the A. E. F.* issued by the War Department.

American Federation of Labor, a confederation of self-governing trade unions in the United States, Canada, Porto Rico, and Panama comprising 5 departments; the building trades, metal trade, union label trade, railway employees and mining. Samuel Gompers was president of the Federation for forty-three years 1881-1924; William Green 1924-52; George Meany 1952- . In 1925 the Federation organized the Union Labor Life Insurance Company. At its annual convention in 1932 the Federation went on record as favoring compulsory unemployment insurance under State auspices and shorter working hours. It also adopted a resolution calling upon Congress to repeal the Eighteenth Amendment. In 1933 the Federation demanded a thirty-hour-week for federal employees and compulsory Federal and State old age pensions. In 1939 it called for revision of the National Labor Relations Act. See UNITED STATES, NEW DEAL.

American Indians, the aborigines of the New World, so called from the original delusion of Columbus, who supposed that the land discovered by him was India, and its inhabitants the Indians, of the Eastern Hemisphere. While great uncertainty exists as to the time of man's appearance in America, it is considered safe to assume that it was some tens of thousands of years ago.

Physical and mental characteristics are much the same, from the Arctic Ocean to Fuegia. The Eskimo of the far North alone differs widely in appearance and habits from the so-called 'Red Indian'; but they both agree in having a polysynthetic language. Their physical characters are a certain tallness and robustness, with an erect posture of the body; a skull narrowing from the eyebrows upward; prominence of the cheek bones; the eyes black and deep set; the hair coarse, very black, and perfectly straight; the nose prominent or even aquiline; the complexion usually of a reddish, coppery, or cinnamon color, but with considerable variations in this respect. The men are usually expert in war and the chase, but inactive in other pursuits. In many tribes, both sexes take part in athletic games. They often excel in horsemanship, and, as a rule, sight and hearing are wonderfully acute. The old-time Indian had courage, dignity, self-respect, and hospitality, and not one of these qualities has entirely disappeared from the Indian of the present day.

In Peru, Colombia, Central America, Yucatan, and Mexico, there were tribes five hundred years ago who had attained a relatively high degree of native civilization. In New Mexico and Arizona, the rather numerous *pueblos* or native Indian towns are the relics of what may have been a northern extension of the Mexican civilization. The Mexicans and Peruvians excelled in architecture. Neither of them had iron; both had native or other copper and gold, and the Peruvians seem to have had cutting tools of bronze.

In the United States, the Indians waged many bitter wars against the whites. The greater spirit and vindictiveness of the Northern Indians have involved them in ruin; but the Mexican Indians, contented to belong to a subject race, have multiplied more rapidly than the conquering people.

In Mexico, the Indians consider themselves a *gente sin razon,* 'people without reason,' while the Spanish Americans constitute a superior *gente de razon,* or 'people of reason.' In Peru, many of the priests and monks are of Indian race. In Brazil, where the Portuguese language prevails in towns, the speech of the Tupi-Guarani tribes has been adopted as a kind of *lingua franca* throughout the interior. In Paraguay, the same language has nearly displaced the Spanish, even among the whites. Each one of the countless tribes of America has its own language.

Rejecting the Aleuts and Eskimos from the category of 'Indian' peoples, the principal stocks or recognized families of North America are as follows: (1) The Athabascans (Tinné), including many tribes of Alaska and North Canada, as well as the Apaches, Navahoes. (2) The Algonquins once covered a large part of the Atlantic slope from Labrador to Virginia, and westward to the Rocky Mountains. Here belong the Abnaki, the Delawares, the Crees, the Chippeways, and many now historic tribes. Some authors assign the Cheyennes, the Arapahoes, and even the Blackfeet to this stock. (3) The Iroquois, formerly dwelling for the most part in the St. Lawrence Valley and what is now New York State. It includes the Cherokees, Mohawks and Senecas. (4) The important Siouan family, including the great Dakota group, and the Omahas, Osages, Winnebagoes, Crows, Catawbas, and others. (5) The Muskhogeans, including the now extinct Alibamas, Apalachis, Choctaws, Creeks, Chickasaws, and Seminoles. (6) The Caddoan family, including the Pawnees, Arickarees, Wichitas, and Caddos. (7) The tribes of the Northern Pacific Coast, among which are the Tlingit of Alaska, and many tribes of Western Canada and the United States. (8) The Yuman family, in the valley of the Colorado River and California, including the Maricopa. (9) The Shoshones, with whom are classed the Utes, the warlike Comanches and the half-civilized Moquis, and many of the degraded Diggers. They live mostly among or near the Rocky Mountains. (10) The Pueblo Indians of New Mexico and Arizona, a composite division, including the Zuñi and the Keresan family. (11) In the Mexican tribes are placed the celebrated Aztecs, the Toltecs, and the civilized Nicaraguans. (12) The Maya stock of Mexico and Central America, and (13) a number of independent Central American and Isthmian stocks.

A comprehensive classification of the South American tribes is much more difficult. In the mountainous district of the northwest belong the Chocos, Chibchas, Paniquitas, and Paezes, the tribes of Cauca and Antioquia, and the Coconuca, Barbacoa, and Mocoa stocks. The linguistic stocks of the Peruvian region include the Quichuas, Aymaras, Puquinas, Yuncas, Atacameños, and Changos. The Amazonian Indians are grouped in a great number of bands or tribes. They include the Tupi-Guarani stock, the Tapuyas, the Arawaks, the Caribs and Orinoco Indians of many tribes, and the Indians of the Upper Amazonian basin and the Bolivian highlands. In the Pampean region are the linguistic stocks of the Gran Chaco, the Charruas, the nomadic Pampean tribes, the Araucanians, the Patagonians, and the degraded tribes of the Fuegiana family.

The number of Indians in the United States is about 334,000.

For a detailed account of the History, Population, and Customs of the Indians in the United States, see the article UNITED STATES, section on *American Indians.* See also the separate articles on the principal Indian tribes, as ALGONQUINS; DAKOTAS; FUEGIANS; IROQUOIS; PUEBLOS, etc.

Consult *Bulletins* of U. S. Office of Indian Affairs; *Annual Reports* of the Bureau of American Ethnology; *Journal of American Folklore;* S. G. Drake's *Aboriginal Races of North America;* F. W. Hodge's *Handbook of American Indians;* J. K. Dixon's *The Vanishing Race;* W. K. Moorhead's *The American Indian in the United States;* C. A. Eastman's *The Indian Today.* For Indian linguistics, consult J. W. Powell's *Indian Linguistic Families of America;* F. Boas' *Handbook of American Indian Languages.*

American Iron and Steel Institute, an association of the larger manufacturers of iron and steel through which the policies of the industry are given expression. A major activity of the institute, 1941, is co-operation with various governmental agencies in the national defense program.

American Ipecac. See **Gillenia.**

Americanisms, a term applied by the members of other English-speaking communities to certain words or locutions peculiar to the English speech of the United States. These are mainly of three sorts. The first consists of absolutely new words introduced into the English language in the United States. The second consists of words or phrases current also in the British Isles, but to which a new meaning has been attached on this side of the

Atlantic. The third consists of obsolete words, or words used in senses once more or less familiar in the British Isles, but now discontinued there.

The vast mass of so-called Americanisms consists of slang usages applied to combinations of existing English words. Some of them are Americanisms only by virtue of the relatively greater frequency with which they are employed. In many instances Americanisms proceed from the desire for brevity. See SLANG.

Consult Farmer's *Americanisms Old and New;* De Vere's *Americanisms;* Clapin's *New Dictionary of Americanisms.*

Americanists, a name applied to persons making a special study of American ethnology, archæology, etc.

Americanization is the educating and training of newly arrived immigrants in the United States before they are admitted to citizenship. It embraces their instruction in the history, achievements, institutions, aims, and ideals of the country. Consult Dixon's *Americanization;* Bogardus' *Essentials of Americanization;* Talbot's *Americanization;* Berkson's *Theories of Americanization;* Roberts' *The Problem of Americanization.*

American Knights, Order of. See **Knights of the Golden Circle.**

American Legion, The, a national organization of American veterans of the World Wars organized in Paris. The American Legion is non-partisan and non-political, a civilian organization, neither military nor militaristic, composed principally of men and women who were civilians before the World Wars and returned to resume their civilian life. The organization makes no distinction of rank and no distinction between overseas service and service in the United States. Any soldier, sailor, or marine who served honorably is eligible for membership, as are women who were regularly enlisted, enrolled, or commissioned for active duty in any of the branches of the American forces. In 1946, the membership was 2,887,743.

American Line, a line of Atlantic steamers growing out of the International Navigation Company.

American Literature. See **United States, Literature of.**

American Merchant Marine. See **Shipping, Merchant.**

American Museum of Natural History. See **Museums.**

American Party, the name given at different times to three political parties which flourished for a brief term and disappeared.

American Red Cross. See **Red Cross.**

American Revolution. See **Revolution, American.**

American River, California, flows through picturesque canyons, where some gold is to be found.

American University, a co-educational institution for higher learning in Washington, D. C.

American University of Trade and Applied Commerce, an educational institution in Philadelphia, Pa., was opened in 1916. It embraces the existing educational activities of the John Wanamaker Store; offers to its employees opportunity for further education.

American Veterans of World War II, organized in 1944. Called AMVETS.

Americus, city, Georgia, county seat of Sumter co. The city is located in a productive agricultural region, and is the seat of the State Agricultural College, p. 9,281.

Amerighi, Michelangelo. See **Caravaggio.**

Amerigo Vespucci. See **Vespucci.**

Amerind, and **Amerindian** or Amerindic, terms invented by members of the Anthropological Society of Washington, D. C., to denote, in scientific treatises, the aboriginal tribes of the American continent and adjacent islands, including the Eskimos.

Amerling, Friedrich (1803-87), Austrian painter, was born in Vienna. He executed about a thousand portraits, and a number of historical pictures, including *Moses in the Desert* and *Dido on the Funeral Pyre.* Consult Frankl's *Life.*

Ames, Adelbert (1835-1933). American soldier, was born in Rockland, Me. He served with distinction in the Civil War; was brevetted major-general of volunteers; and became a lieutenant colonel in the regular army. He was U. S. Senator from Mississippi (1870-73), and was elected governor of that State in 1873.

Ames, Edgar (1868-1944), American shipbuilder, b. St. Louis, developed Seattle Harbor, and built 25 steel ships for the U. S. government during World War I.

Ames, Fisher (1758-1808), American public official and orator, was born in Dedham, Mass. His advocacy of a strong government won him recognition, and soon he rose to a position of eminence in the Federalist Party. In 1789 he was elected to Congress, where he served four terms, supporting Washington's administration. Consult *Works,* edited by his son, Seth Ames.

Ames, Herman Vandenburg (1865-1935), American educator, was born in Lancaster, Mass. He was the author of *The Proposed Amendments to the Constitution of the United States,* which was awarded the prize of the American Historical Association in 1897; *Outline of Lectures on American Political and Institutional History during the Colonial and Revolutionary Periods,* and a number of historical monographs and papers.

Ames, James Barr (1846-1910), American educator, was born in Boston, Mass. Besides his articles in legal periodicals, he published a number of compilations of cases connected with various branches of the law. In 1895 he became dean of the Harvard Law School.

Ames, Joseph Alexander (1816-72), American portrait painter, was born in Roxbury, Mass. In 1848 went to Rome, where he achieved sufficient prominence to paint the portrait of Pope Pius IX. Among his well known portraits are those of *Rachel, Rufus Choate, Seward, Webster,* and *Emerson.*

Ames, Joseph Sweetman (1864-1943), American physicist, and university administrator, was born in Manchester, Vt. He was president of Johns Hopkins Univ. (1929-35), and the author of numerous articles.

Ames, Mary Clemmer (1839-84), American author, was born in Utica, N. Y. She prepared biographies of her friends, Alice and Phœbe Cary, and published several novels, *Ten Years in Washington,* and a volume of *Poems.* Consult *Life* by Edmund Hudson.

Ames, Oakes (1804-73), American legislator and manufacturer, was born in Easton, Mass. He was one of the capitalists who built the Union Pacific Railroad.

Ames, William (1576-1633), known also as AMESIUS, English Puritan divine, was born in Ipswich. His works include *Medulla Theologiæ,* a student's handbook; the famous *Coronis ad Collationem Hagiensem; De Conscientia, Ejus Jure et Casibus;* and *Bellarminus Enervatus.* Consult *Life* by Nethenus.

Ames, Winthrop (1871-1937), American theatrical manager, was born in North Easton, Mass. He built and managed the Little Theater (1912) and the Booth Theater (1913), both in New York City. In 1929 he retired as an active producer.

Amesbury, town, Massachusetts, in Essex county. It is an old historic town, the birthplace of Josiah Bartlett, and for many years the residence of John Whittier; p. 10,862.

Amesha Spenta (modern *Amshaspends*), the 'immortal holy ones' of the later Avesta, are the principal spirits who assist Ormuzd in his work of creation. They are seven, including Ormuzd. See ZEND-AVESTA.

Amethyst, a variety of quartz distinguished by its beautiful violet-blue or deep purple color. The presence of a small amount of manganese has been regarded as the origin of the characteristic color. It is one of the most esteemed varieties of quartz, and is much employed for pins, rings, and necklaces. The finest specimens are found in India, Ceylon, and Brazil. It is a common mineral in Europe, and occurs in the United States. Not to be confounded with this mineral is that sometimes called the *Oriental amethyst,* which is a variety of spinel. It has an amethystine color, and is a valuable gem.

Amfortas, or **Anfortas,** king of the Holy Grail, in Wolfram von Eschenbach's *Parzival* and Wagner's opera of *Parsifal.*

Amhara, ('highlands'), the central division of Abyssinia. The name is also given to the 'happy valley' in Dr. John's *Rasselas.*

Amharic Language, the official language of Abyssinia spoken in its central province of Amhara. Like Ethiopic, it is a Semitic tongue, and is written from right to left.

Amherst, town, Massachusetts, in Hampshire co. The town was settled early in the eighteenth century, and is rich in historic associations; p. 6,410.

Amherst, a district of Tenasserim, Burma; p. 417,910.

Amherst, Jeffrey (1717-97), created BARON AMHERST (1776), British soldier, was born in Riverhead, Kent. He was made governor-general of the British provinces in North America, but he proved unable to deal effectively with the conspiracy of Pontiac (q.v.), and in 1763 returned to Great Britain. Consult Mayo's *Jeffrey Amherst.*

Amherst, William Pitt (1773-1857), created EARL AMHERST OF ARAKAN (1826), British diplomat, nephew of Jeffrey Amherst. After a brilliant diplomatic career he became governor-general of India, and carried the first Burmese war to a successful conclusion.

Amherst College, was founded in 1821 at Amherst, Mass., and was incorporated by the State in 1825. It has confined its work to purely collegiate instruction, and has no technical or professional schools. The college has a number of valuable scientific collections, notably the Adams collection of shells, a part of Audubon's celebrated bird collection, the

Shepard meteorite collection, the Hitchcock ichnological collection, and a mineralogical collection of about 25,000 specimens.

Amice, a flowing cloak formerly worn by priests and pilgrims. Also a strip of fine linen, worn upon the shoulders by priests.

Amicis, Edmondo de (1846-1908), Italian writer. He wrote a series of books of travel, *La Spagna* (1873), *Ricordi di Londra* (1874), *L'Olanda* (1874), *Marocco* (1876), *Constantinopoli* (1877), *Ricordi di Parigi* (1879), *Sull' Oceano* (1889). In fiction De Amicis' greatest success was the sentimental *Il Cuore* ('The Heart of a Boy'), primarily intended for young people.

Amides, compounds derived from ammonia (NH_3) by the substitution for one or more atoms of hydrogen of a corresponding number of atoms of a metal or a compound radical. More recently, the term Amide, as distinct from Amine, has been restricted to those compounds derived from ammonia in which one or more atoms of hydrogen are replaced by an acid radical. The amides are classed as Primary, Secondary, or Tertiary, according as one, two, or all three of the atoms by hydrogen are replaced by an acid radical.

Amidogen, or **Diamide,** NH_2—NH_2, was till lately looked upon as a hypothetical body, to which the formula NH_2 was assigned. Curtius has, however, recently produced the sulphate of amidogen, from which amidogen itself is obtained by the action of an alkali. It is a gas.

Amiel, Henri Frédéric (1821-81), Swiss author, best known by his diary, *Fragments d'un journal intime* (Eng. trans. by Mrs. Humphry Ward).

Amiens, city, France, capital of the department of Somme, on the River Somme. The old town is separated from the new by eight boulevards on the site of the ancient fortifications. The Cathedral (1220-88) is one of the finest examples of pure Gothic architecture in Europe. Amiens is one of the principal manufacturing centres of France. Textile products include linens, woolens, silks and velvets. Other industries are the making of chemicals, shoes, and machinery, dyeing, and iron founding.

Previous to the Roman occupation Amiens was known as *Samarobriva.* It was taken by the Franks in the fifth century, and was ceded to the French crown in 1185. It was held by the dukes of Burgundy from 1435 to 1477; captured by the Spaniards in 1597; and recaptured by Henry IV. Until 1790 the city was the capital of Picardy. During the Franco-German War it was taken by the Prussians (1870). During the Great War of Europe, Amiens was of special importance because of its strategical position. In the German advance of August, 1914, as Von Kluck's army swung southwards from Brussels, the line of advance was on Amiens by way of Arras and the town was occupied Aug. 30, 1914. (See ARRAS, BATTLES OF.)

Amiens was again the German objective in March, 1918. (See SOMME, BATTLES OF.) See also AISNE, BATTLES OF; EUROPE, GREAT WAR OF. The Germans occupied it in May 1940; bombed by the RAF in March, 1944.

The *Treaty of Amiens* (March 27, 1802), between Great Britain and France (with Spain and the Batavian Republic) brought a truce in the Napoleonic struggle.

Amines, or **Ammonia Bases,** are organic compounds derived from ammonia (NH_3) by the substitution of hydrocarbon radicals—for example, ethyl (C_2H_5)—for hydrogen in the ammonia, as *ethylamine* ($NH_2C_2H_5$). They are called Primary, Secondary, or Tertiary, according as one, two, or three of the hydrogen atoms of the ammonia have been replaced by hydrocarbons of alkyl groups. The reactions of the amines differ to some extent according to the nature of the substituting alkyl groups, so that they may be further classed as follows: (1) pure *aliphatic amines;* (2) mixed *aliphatic* and *aromatic amines*—(a) with the nitrogen attached to the aliphatic residue, as in benzylamine, and (b) with the nitrogen attached to a carbon atom of the benzene ring, as in methyl aniline; and (3) pure *aromatic amines,* as aniline and its homologues.

As to the properties of the amines, those of the *aliphatic* series are volatile, inflammable substances, the lower members being either gaseous or liquid with low boiling points and very soluble in water. They have an ammoniacal and fishy odor, and a basicity considerably greater than that of ammonia. The higher members are solids. The *aromatic amines* have similar properties, but are less basic in character, while the *aromatic aminocompounds* are even less basic than ammonia.

Diamines are derived from two molecules of ammonia by replacement of two hydrogen atoms. Similarly, there are *triamines, tetramines,* and *pentamines,* which are, however, but little known.

Amirante Islands, or **Admiral Islands,** a group of small coral islands in the Indian Ocean. They belong to Great Britain.

Amiens Cathedral, the finest example of Gothic Architecture.

Amleth, or Amlet, king of Jutland about the second century B.C. Shakespeare's tragedy of *Hamlet* is founded on his story, although its authenticity is not credited by Danish historians.

Ammanati Bartolomeo, (1511-92), Italian sculptor and architect. He was the architect of Cosimo de' Medici in Florence.

Ammann, Othmar Hermann (1879-), American civil engineer, born Switzerland, was assistant chief engineer on Hell Gate Bridge, N. Y., and in 1925 became chief engineer of bridges, superintending construction of the George Washington Bridge, from New York City to Fort Lee, N. J., opened 1931. He is chief engineer of the Triborough Bridge, East River, N. Y. C., and a member of several engineering societies. He won the Thomas Rowland Fitch Prize for civil engineering.

Ammeter, or **Ampere Meter,** a commercial instrument for measuring electric current in terms of amperes (see AMPERE).

Ammon, Amun, or **Amen** ('the Unrevealed'), a deity of the ancient Egyptians, represented as a ram with downward-branching horns, the symbols of power; as a man with a ram's head; and as a complete man with two high feathers on his head, bearded, sitting on a throne, and holding in his right hand the scepter of the gods, in his left the handled cross, the symbol of divine life. After the eighteenth dynasty we find in hieroglyphics the name *Amun-Ra* frequently inscribed, indicating a blending of Ammon with the sun-god Ra. The colossal ruins of his temple still stand at Karnak.

Ammon, Otto (1842-1916), German anthropologist. He was the author of *Ammon's law,* that the immigrants from country to town tend to group themselves in two divisions—a 'roundheaded' division following commercial and industrial pursuits and a 'long-headed' division recruiting the ranks of the learned and official classes.

Ammonia, NH_3, an important gaseous compound of nitrogen and hydrogen, takes its name from a related compound, *sal ammoniacum,* which was prepared in ancient times in Egypt, in the neighborhood of the temple of the sun god Ra Ammon. The term Ammonia, or *Ammonia Water,* is also applied to a water solution of this gas. In modern times ammonia was obtained by Priestley in 1774, while its exact composition was demonstrated by Berthollet in 1785.

Ammonia, under normal atmospheric pressure, is a colorless gas above $-32.5°$ C., a liquid between the temperatures $-32.5°$ and $-77°$ C., and a white crystalline solid below the latter temperature. In minute quantities, diluted with air, it has an agreeable odor; in moderate quantities, pungent; in larger quantities, irritating to nose and eyes, and suffocating when inhaled. Ammonia is noticeable in the air about stables, being formed by the action of putrefying bacteria in the decay of animal and vegetable matter.

There are several methods of preparing ammonia. It may be prepared by heating organic substances containing nitrogen, as bones, hoofs, horns, etc., an old custom, which gave the water solution the name *Spirits of Hartshorn.* It is conveniently prepared in small quantities by heating ammonium hydroxide, which yields the gas readily, or by heating a mixture of ammonium chloride (sal ammoniac) and calcium hydroxide (slaked lime), in about the ratio 53:37 by weight, which should yield about 17 parts of ammonia gas. Nearly all the ammonia of commerce comes from the ammoniacal liquors obtained from the destructive distillation of coal.

Ammonia is synthesized on a commercial scale by the direct combination of hydrogen and nitrogen at high pressures and temperatures, in the presence of a catalyst. Still other reactions for obtaining ammonia are the action of steam and cyanamide, which gives a very large yield, and has commercial possibilities, and the reaction of water and a metallic nitrate, as magnesium nitride.

Ammonia is extremely soluble in water, which takes up about 800 times its volume at ordinary temperatures, and more at lower temperatures, following Henry's Law, approximately. Ammonia may be decomposed into its constituents, two volumes yielding one volume of nitrogen and three of hydrogen. When ammonia dissolves in water, some ammonium hydroxide (NH_4OH) forms, which is a base, and turns pink litmus blue. Moist litmus paper may therefore be used as a test for ammonia. Ammonia combines with acids to form salt.

When one gram of gaseous ammonia is condensed to liquid ammonia, 316 calories of heat are liberated. Conversely, when one gram of liquid ammonia passes into the gaseous state, an equal quantity of heat is taken in. In the ammonia process for manufacturing *artificial ice,* gaseous ammonia is compressed by a pump in a system of iron pipes until it liquefies, and the liberated heat is removed by streams of water pouring over the pipes. In a tank of brine (a water solution of calcium chloride) are immersed cans of the shape of the blocks of ice desired, filled with distilled water (about 200 lbs.), and surrounded by a second system of pipes, called an expansion coil. The liquid ammonia is allowed to escape into the expansion coil; and the pressure being reduced, the ammonia passes into the gaseous state, taking in heat, which is given up by the nearest body at a higher temperature—namely, the brine on the outside of the expansion coil. The brine being cooled below the freezing point of water, heat passes to it from the water in the cans, which then freezes. (See REFRIGERATION.)

Ammonium salts, as the sulphate and chloride, are valuable fertilizers.

Aromatic Spirits of Ammonia (see SAL VOLATILE), is used medically as a stimulant in cases of fainting, for the relief of dyspepsia, and as an expectorant.

Household Ammonia, a dilute solution of the gas, is supposed to contain 8 per cent., but sometimes as little as 2 per cent. is present. Liquid ammonia is brought into the market in steel cylinders.

Bibliography.—Consult Lunge's *Coal Tar and Ammonia* (1909); Lange's *By-Products of Coal Gas Manufacture* (1915); Maxted's *Ammonia and the Nitrides* (1921).

Ammoniacum, or **Gum-Ammoniac,** a gum resin obtained from *Dorema ammoniacum* (Umbelliferæ). It is used medicinally as an expectorant and disinfectant and externally as a counter-irritant.

Ammonite. See **Explosives.**

Ammonites, a Semitic race occupying the region to the east of the lower Jordan north of Moab.

Ammonites, a group of animals belonging to the Cephalopoda, now extinct. Their spirally coiled shells, like the shell of the living nautilus, were divided into a series of separate chambers by transverse partitions.

Ammonoidea, a totally extinct group of mollusca, of which no less than 5,000 fossil species have been discovered. A monograph of the U. S. Geological Survey, *The Carboniferous Ammonoids of America* (1903), by James P. Smith, lists, describes, and illustrates, where possible, the Carboniferous ammonoid genera and species; it contains an extensive bibliography.

Ammonoosuc, Lower, a river of New Hampshire, rising in the western slopes of the Presidential Range.

Ammonoosuc, Upper, a river of New Hampshire, rising in the Randolph Range.

Ammophila, a genus of perennial grasses common to sandy beaches. The most important species, *A. arenari,* is popularly known as 'Sea Reed,' 'Sand Reed,' 'Beach Grass,' or 'Mat Grass'.

Ammunition, a term formerly including all the military stores of an army in the field, but now confined to projectiles (q.v.) and the various agents necessary for their effective employment. The term includes the *missile* (bullet or projectile); the *propelling charge* and its container, for projecting the missile from the cannon; the *primer,* for igniting the propelling charge; the *bursting charge,* for breaking the missile into fragments; the *fuse,* for igniting or detonating the bursting charge; and *grenades* and *bombs* thrown by hand or other means.

Ammunition for cannon is classified as *fixed* or *separate loading,* depending upon whether or not the projectile is attached to the cartridge case. Modern projectiles for cannon, according to their use, are classified into: armor-piercing shot; armor-piercing and deck-piercing shell; common shell; and shrapnel. Propelling charges for cannon of most of the Great Powers consist of some form of nitro-cellulose smokeless powder; but some use nitro-glycerine powder. The powder is made up into grains or sticks, which increase in size with the calibre of the gun, on the theory that all the powder should not be consumed until just before the projectile leaves the muzzle. (See EXPLOSIVES.)

The percussion primer is used in modern field artillery cannon, and in seacoast cannon using metallic cartridge cases; the electric primer, in seacoast cannon of calibre of 5 inches and upward using separate ammunition. The friction primer is still used in the older models of field and siege cannon, such as the 3.2-inch and 5-inch guns and 7-inch howitzer; and in seacoast cannon for drill and for emergency when the electric firing circuit fails. (See FUSES AND PRIMERS.)

Bursting charges for most modern projectiles are some form of high explosive. In the United States, Explosive D is used for shot and shell for seacoast cannon. Black powder is still employed in the shrapnel, but trinitrotuluol, or 'trotyl,' is coming into use for field artillery shells and the new universal shrapnel. The ammunition for small arms rifles is fixed.

During the sixteenth and seventeenth centuries, when the range of muskets was short, the use of hand grenades, particularly in siege warfare, was general. The explosive was gunpowder, and was set off by a burning fuse which was lighted before the grenade was thrown. When the range of small arms was increased beyond the distance to which hand grenades could be thrown, their use was discontinued. During the Russo-Japanese War they came into use again in the trench warfare, but charged with high explosive and set off by a percussion fuse. Since that time the hand grenade has been developed into a very powerful short-range instrument of destruction. It is made of forged steel, as a rule, and filled with high explosive. It is set off upon impact by a percussion fuse, and usually carries some form of vane or tail to insure that the fuse shall be struck. Most of the powers engaged in World Wars I and II used grenade throwers.

The aeroplane bombs developed during World War I were similar in principle of action and construction to hand grenades, but they were much larger and more powerful. Gas bombs contain some substance which develops poisonous fumes upon explosion. Incendiary bombs are of numerous types. Flame throwers were revived in World War II. They produce terrific heat and deadly carbon monoxide gas. Fragmentation bombs are dropped by parachutes to delay their explosion.

In World War II the bazooka rocket gun (British counterpart, PIAT–Projector, Infantry Anti-tank) made its appearance. The rocket is two feet long and finned; its head contains a high explosive and its body a propelling charge. June 15, 1944, the German robot attack on London opened. The robot (V-1, vengeance weapon No. 1) is a flying bomb carrying an explosive charge of about a ton. V-2 followed, a long-range rocket 40 ft. long and 5 ft. in diameter, soaring 60-70 m. high, having a range of 250-300 m. and a velocity of about 4,000 m.p.h.

See PROJECTILES; CARTRIDGES; EXPLOSIVES; GUNPOWDER; GUNNERY; GUNS, ARSENAL; ORDNANCE DEPARTMENT, U. S. Consult publications of the U. S. Navy Department; pamphlets of the U. S. Ordnance Department.

Amnesia, (Greek 'forgetfulness'), loss or defect of memory; loss of memory of spoken words. Amnesia is due to cerebral conditions which may be temporary or permanent. See APHASIA; MEMORY.

Amnesty is a general pardon, applying to a whole class of offenders, whereas an ordinary pardon is special. An amnesty is generally offered at the conclusion of a war. In the United States the power to grant amnesty for past offences against the Government and its laws is vested by the Constitution in the President, though it has been held by the Supreme Court that the power resides also in Congress.

Amnion, a fœtal membrane which surrounds the embryo in mammals, birds, and reptiles, but not in amphibia, fishes, or lower vertebrates. See ALLANTOIS; CAUL; EMBRYOLOGY.

Amœba, (Greek 'changing'), a genus of Protozoa, or simple unicellular animals; but the term is also used in a more general sense to designate any protozoön which structurally resembles a true amœba. Amœbæ are found in fresh water or in mud, and occasionally in damp earth (*A. terricola*). As to size, a diameter of a hundredth of an inch is not uncommon, but some amœbæ are

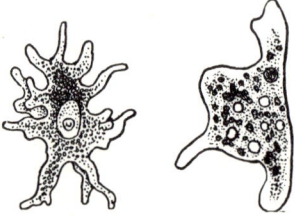

Typical Forms of Amœba, Showing Pseudopodia. (Greatly magnified.)

much larger than this. The life history of amœba is very simple. It grows until the limit of advantageous size is reached, and then divides through the nucleus to form two amœbæ. Two amœbæ sometimes flow together and fuse in a manner which may be fairly regarded as an incipient form of sexual union. (See CONJUGATION). This simple organism thus exhibits within small compass all the usual animal functions. See CELL.

Amorites, a name applied generally to the primitive inhabitants of Canaan, sometimes also to the Canaanites.

Amorphous, a term applied to substances devoid of characteristic shape. Glass, glue, opal, obsidian may be cited as examples.

Amortization, the reduction or extinction of a debt; also the payments made for that purpose. In law, the act of conveying lands or tenements to a corporation in mortmain.

Amos, one of the twelve Minor Prophets,

Amoy, city and treaty port, province of Fu-kien, China, is situated on the island of Amoy or Haimun, at the mouth of the Lung-kiang (Dragon River). It is in almost daily steamship communication with Hong-kong and was formerly one of the great tea centres of China. In 1841 Amoy was captured by the British, and was thrown open to British trade by the treaty of Nanking (1842). It was later opened to all **nations; p. 219,974.**

and the earliest of the prophets whose writings are extant.

Ampere, the practical unit of electric current, is theoretically defined as equal to 10^{-1} c.g.s. electro-magnetic units of current. It is practically defined as the amount of a constant current which deposits 1,118 milligrams of silver per second out of a specific solution of silver nitrate.

Amphibia.—Anura: 1. Surinam toad; 2. Green frog. Urodela: 3. Proteus; 4. European spotted salamander. Gymnophiona: 5. Siphonops; 6. Cæcilia.

Ampère, André Marie (1775-1836), French physicist and mathematician. Professor of physics at the Collège de France in 1824. His fame rests on his physical researches, especially on his development of electro-dynamics and his original demonstration of the relations between magnetism and electricity. He was the inventor of the astatic needle, and he first propounded the theory that currents of electricity in the earth attracted the magnetic needle. The measure of electricity called the ampere was named for him.

Amphibia (Greek 'double-lifed,' as living on both land and water), or BATRACHIA, a class of vertebrates between fishes and reptiles. The term was used by Linnæus to include reptiles, amphibians, and some fishes, but the content of the term was later narrowed, and the amphibia were separated on the one hand from the reptiles, which never breathe by gills, and on the other from the fishes, which, with the exception of the Dipnoi, never breathe by lungs. The amphibia include four orders: (1) Forms like the newt and salamander, with long smooth bodies and persisting tails termed *Urodela* (Greek 'tail distinct') or *Caudata*. (2) Forms like the frog and toad, with short, broad, naked bodies, and without tails in adult life, are included in the order *Anura* (Greek 'without tail'). (3) The third order of amphibia includes the few snake-like, limbless forms technically known as *Gymnophiona* or *Apoda*. (4) The numerous extinct *Labyrinthodonts* or *Stegocephali* of the Trias, Permian, and Carboniferous periods mostly resembled the Urodela in form, but some were snake-like. They were well provided with skin armor on the breast and ventral surface, and sometimes attained a large crocodile-like size. Compared with these the modern amphibia are a diminutive race. The amphibia, such as the common newts and frogs, are readily distinguished from higher vertebrates by the gills borne by the embryo, and sometimes persisting throughout life; by the absence of an amnion, and of an allantois save in so far as this is represented by the urinary bladder; by the two condyles of the skull; and by other peculiarities in the skeleton. On the other hand, they closely approach the double breathing fishes and are strictly distinguishable from the fish class only in the absence of fin rays, and in the general possession of fingered limbs as in higher animals. The majority of amphibia are much more at home in water than on land, though in some cases the adaptation to terrestrial life is complete, and has even modified the ordinary course of development. Even among exclusively lung-breathing forms, the majority prefer to remain in the vicinity of water.

The life history of a form like the frog is of considerable interest as an abbreviated recapitulation of the history of the race, and may be briefly noted. In the Anura, the eggs are fertilized by the male as they leave the oviduct; while in others such as salamanders, the fertilization is internal. They are laid in gelatinous masses in water. When the tadpole is hatched, it is at first enclosed in the gelatinous *débris* of the egg case. It grows for a short while longer at the expense of the yolk, which in a few forms is seen as a distinct external sac. Soon, however, the tadpole acquires a mouth and arms, and begins to feed. As the tadpole grows, the suckers behind the mouth disappear, the gut becomes much longer, and the lungs appear as outgrowths from the œsophagus. The limbs appear as minute buds, but the front pair become free first. The tail is absorbed, and the mainly vegetarian tadpole gradually assumes all the characters of the carnivorous frog.

Consult H. Gadow's *Amphibia and Reptiles,* and his treatise on 'Amphibia' in the *Cambridge Natural History* (VOL. VIII.).

Amphibole, a name applied to a large group of minerals which are essentially silicates of lime and magnesia, though these bases are often partly replaced by alumina and oxides of iron and manganese. They occur, like the pyroxenes, to which they are closely allied, in igneous and sedimentary rocks.

Amphibolite, a name applied to a group of metamorphic rocks having some member of the amphibole group as the sole essential constituent, and containing such accessory minerals as feldspar, mica, garnet, augite, quartz, pyrite, etc.

Amphibrach, a metrical foot of three syllables, the first and the last short or unaccented (⌣), and the middle one long or accented (-).

Amphictyonic Council, a celebrated council of the states of ancient Greece. An *amphictyony* was an assemblage of deputies of tribes dwelling around any important temple, gathered together to manage the affairs of that sanctuary. Twelve tribes, with their colonies, composed the Amphictyony of Delphi. To the two annual meetings, in spring and autumn, each tribe sent two wardens with voting powers, and several deputies who might speak but could not vote. They bound themselves to observe certain intertribal principles of right, and thus the amphictyony became a political force. The amphictyonic council continued, with limited powers, under Roman sway, the last mention of it occurring in the second century A.D. See DELPHI.

Amphicyon, a genus of large fossil Carnivores, found in the Lower and Middle Miocene rocks of Europe and India. It combines the characteristics of dogs and bears, and to it are traceable the modern bears.

Amphimacer, a metrical foot consisting of three syllables, the first and last long (-), and the middle one short (⌣).

Amphineura, an order of marine molluscs including a number of primitive forms, of which Chiton is the most familiar. See MOLLUSCA.

Amphion, son of Zeus and Antiope, and twin brother of Zethus. Their family was connected with Thebes. His story is told in Ovid's *Metamorphoses*.

Amphioxus, or **Lancelet** (*Amphioxus lanceolatus*), is a small, pointed creature (length, 1½ to 2 inches), interesting as being one of the most primitive of vertebrates. Though exceedingly simple in structure as compared with higher vertebrates, amphioxus is in some respects specialized, possessing characters not represented in higher forms.

Amphipoda, an order of diminutive Crustacea. Many species are known, usually plainly colored, including the familiar Sandhopper; the Gammarus of running water; and the quaint Spectra or Skeleton Shrimp (*Caprella*). See CRUSTACEA.

Amphipolis, ancient city, Macedonia. Once an important commercial city, and the centre of a region rich in gold, silver, and timber. Under the Romans Amphipolis was the capital of one of the four districts into which the province was divided in B.C. 167. Now a Turkish town occupies the site.

Amphisbæna, one of a family of serpentiform lizards, found for the most part in subtropical America.

Amphitheatre, the structure, usually oval in its ground plan, surrounding the arena which, in ancient Rome, was the scene of gladiatorial and other combats. The finest specimen of all, the lavian Amphitheatre at Rome, known as the *Colosseum* from its colossal size, was begun by Vespasian and finished by Titus 80 A.D. On the occasion of its dedication by Titus, 5,000 wild beasts were slain in the arena, the games lasting nearly a hundred days. The open space in the centre of the amphitheatre was called *arena*, the Latin word for sand, because it was covered with sand or sawdust during the performances. (See COLOSSEUM.)

Amphitrite, a sea goddess in Greek mythology, daughter of Nereus, or of Oceanus, and wife of Poseidon (Neptune).

Amphitryon, in Greek mythology, a king of Tiryns, son of Alcæus, and husband of Alcmene. The story has been treated by Molière in his *Amphitryon*.

Amphiuma, a genus of American tailed amphibians, including long, eel-like forms, with minute, two or three toed, widely separated limbs.

Amphora, among the Greeks and Romans, a large vessel, usually made of clay, with a narrow neck and two handles, chiefly used for preserving various liquids.

Amplification, in rhetoric, the elaboration of a statement or discourse.

Amplitude, in astronomy, is the distance of a heavenly body, at the time of its rising or setting from the east or the west point of the horizon. When the sun is in the Equator, at the time of either equinox, he rises exactly east, and sets exactly west, and therefore has no amplitude.

Amputation is the operation of cutting away a portion of the body, generally a limb, for the safety of the patient or to prevent the spread of disease. (See ARTIFICIAL LIMB.) Amputations of limbs are broadly divided into the 'flap' and the 'circular' operation, modified to meet the necessities of the case. The flap operation is the most favored, but choice depends upon the site of operation. The question when amputation of a limb is necessary is often one of the most difficult in surgery. See SURGERY.

Amraoti, (*Oomrawutti*), town, India, capital of Amraoti district; an important centre of the cotton trade, and celebrated for its temples—one of them, the Temple of Bhawani, built a thousand years ago; p. 36,000.

Amravati, town, Madras, India. It was one of the centres of the Buddhist kingdom of Vengi, and has ruins of a great Buddhist tope.

Amritsar, town, India, capital of Amritsar district, in the Punjab. The island on which it stands is reached by a marble causeway. The town is noted for the manufacture of cashmere shawls, silks, and carpets; p. 264,840; of the district, 929,374.

Amru, Ibn el-Aas (?600-663 A.D.), Arab general, who at first opposed Mohammed, but later became a convert, joining the prophet in his refuge at Medina. He is thought by many to be the greatest Arabian poet, and was the author of the first poem in the collection called the Muallokat.

Amsterdam, chief seaport and largest city of the Netherlands, in the province of North Holland, is situated at the influx of the Amstel River into the Ij or Y, an arm of the Zuider Zee. It is intersected by the Amstel and numerous canals, which divide it into 90 small islands connected by more than 300 bridges.

Amsterdam presents a fine appearance when seen from the harbor, or from the high bridge over the Amstel. Church towers and spires, and a forest of masts, relieve the flatness of the prospect. In the older central parts the more conspicuous buildings are constructed of brick, in the Dutch style of the sixteenth and seventeenth centuries. Among other buildings are the Church of St. Nicholas (1885-6); the Nieuwe Kerk (1408), where the sovereigns of Holland are crowned; the Oude Kerk (c. 1300), containing fine stained glass and carvings. Farther south are three large museums. One of these, the Rijks Museum, erected 1877-85, is **the most important** art depositary in the Netherlands. It includes a valuable picture gallery, containing works by the most famous Dutch artists of all periods. The others are the Museum Fodor (1860) and the Municipal Museum (1892-5), both containing paintings by modern Dutch artists. The city has zoölogical and botanical gardens of high reputation.

The defences of Amsterdam are comprised in a row of detached forts, and in the sluices, several miles distant from the city, which, in a few hours, can flood the surrounding land. Amsterdam is connected with the North Sea, 15 m. to the west, by the North Sea Canal, which gives access to the largest vessels. It is the headquarters of Dutch finance and of the ship-owning interest, was the principal market for the produce of the Dutch East Indies, especially rice, coffee, sugar, tobacco, and spices. Prominent industries are diamond cutting and polishing and the manufacture of chocolate, glass, porcelain, jewelry, cottons, woolens, leather, liquers, and other products; p. 746,746.

The origin of the city is ascribed to Giesebrecht II. of Amstel, who built a castle there in 1204. Its greatest development was due to the Treaty of Westphalia (1648), which closed the Scheldt to the rival port of Antwerp. In 1808 the city was chosen as the capital of the Netherlands by Louis Bonaparte. The present epoch of prosperity dates from the opening of the North Sea Canal in 1876. Distinguished natives are Spinoza (1632), Swammerdam (1637), and the poet Bilderijk (1750).

Amsterdam, city, New York, in Montgomery co., on the Mohawk River, is a busy manufacturing center. and makes woolen and cotton goods, carpets, etc.; p. 33,329.

Roman Amphitheatre, Arles.

Amsterdam, or New Amsterdam, a volcanic, wooded islet, in the Indian Ocean, midway between the Cape of Good Hope and Tasmania. It is under French control.

Amtorg, the commercial agency in the United States for Soviet Russia. Established in 1924, its volume of trade reached a peak of $138,000,000 in 1930, having mounted from $50,000,000 in 1923. In 1932 the total turnover was $24,000,000 and in 1934 approximately the same.

Amuck, or **Amok,** a Malay term denoting a sudden frenzy which seizes an individual, causing him to rush about armed.

Amu Daria, Oxus or **Jihun,** one of the largest rivers in Russian Central Asia, formed by two streams which rise on the Little Pamir near the Indian frontier—the Ak-su ('white water'), from which, perhaps, the ancient name Oxus is derived; and the Panj, the sources of which flow from the glaciers of the Hindu-Kush, northwest of the Kitik Pass. It enters the Sea of Aral by a large delta 327 ft. above sea level. It is useful for irrigation purposes.

Amulet. In architecture, a ringlike moulding on a column. In decorative art, a band painted in relief around a vase or similar object. In heraldry, a ring borne as a charge, being a mark of cadency.

Amulet, any object worn as a charm. It is often a stone, or a piece of metal, with an inscription or figures engraved on it, and is generally suspended from the neck, and worn as a protection against sickness or witchcraft The ancient Chaldæan and Egyptian amulets were inscribed with magic letters or signs and sometimes formed necklaces. The use of amulets passed into the Christian Church, but in 721 the wearing of amulets was solemnly condemned.

Amundsen, Roald (1872-1928), Norwegian explorer, the discoverer of the South Pole, was born in Borges. In 1910 Amundsen sailed for the Antarctic, and on Oct. 19, 1911 with four others, he started on a dash for the South Pole, which was reached on Dec. 14, 1911. (See ANTARCTIC EXPLORATION). In 1918-20 he made the Northeast Passage in the *Maud*. In 1925, with Lincoln Ellsworth, an American, he made an aeroplane flight over the North Pole, and the following year they two, accompanied by Umberto Nobile, an Italian, made a second flight in a semi-rigid airship over the Pole. (See ARCTIC EXPLORATION). In June, 1928, on the report that Nobile's expedition to the Arctic had met with disaster, Amundsen set forth from Tromsö to rescue him and was never heard from again.

Captain Amundsen is the author of *The Northwest Passage* (1908); *The South Pole* (1913); *The Northeast Passage* (1921); *My Life as an Explorer* (1927).

Amur, a province of Eastern Siberia, lying between the Amur River and the Stanovoi range on the north. The greater part of the country is mountainous and covered with forest, especially in the west, and the broader valleys are marshy. The wet summer and the cold winter with no snowfall, are unfavorable to farming. Gold is extracted from the riverbeds and coal is found in considerable amount. Immense tracts are uninhabited. Of the inhabitants, 88 per cent. are Russians; the remainder is made up of Manchus and of Tungus nomads who live by the chase. Area 154,795 sq. m.; p. 230,200.

Amurath, or **Murad,** the name of five sultans of Turkey: AMURATH I. (1319-89), son of Orkhan, succeeded his father in 1359. He was the first Turkish sultan to make great headway in Europe, and the chief events of his reign center round his invasions of the Balkan peninsula. AMURATH II. (1403-51), succeeded his father Mohammed I. in 1421. He is chiefly noted for his wars with Janos Hunyadi, the Hungarian hero. AMURATH III. (1546-95), son of Selim II., succeeded to the throne in 1574. A weak ruler, his reign marks the first deterioration of the powers of the sultans. AMURATH IV. (1611-40), son of Sultan Ahmed I., succeeded his uncle Mustapha I. in 1623. He was noted for his severity; many victims are said to have perished through his orders. AMURATH V. (1840-1904), the son of Sultan Abdul Medjid, was proclaimed sultan in 1876, and ruled for but three months.

Amur River, one of the most important rivers of Asia. It is formed by the union of the Shilka and the Argun. The total length is about 2,760 m. On its course the Amur breaks through the Great Khingan and Little Khingan ranges, and from the mouth of the Ussuri is forced northward by the Sikhota-alin Mountains, entering the Sea of Ohkotsk at Nikolaievsk, not far from the northern end of Sakhalin Island. The total length of navigable waterways is nearly 8,400 m. Consult Holmes' *Down the Amur.*

Amygdalin, $C_{20}H_{27}NO_{11}3H_2O$, is a crystalline principle existing in the kernel of bitter almonds, the leaves of the *Prunus laurocerasus,* and various other plants, which, by distillation, yield hydrocyanic acid. See ALMONDS, OIL OF.

Amygdaloid, a name given to igneous rocks, usually old lava flows, full of almond-shaped cavities which have been filled up with secondary minerals, such as calcite, agate, or the zeolites. Amygdaloidal rocks are chiefly noted in America for their occurrence at Keweenaw Point, Lake Superior, where the cavities are filled with native copper, and are important as a source of that metal.

Amyl, C_5H_{11}, is the fifth in the series of alcohol radicals whose general formula is C_nH_{2n+1}, and of which methyl and ethyl are the first two members. It is obtained by heating amyl iodide with an amalgam or zinc in a closed tube at a temperature of about 177° C., and is one of the natural products of the distillation of coal. See FUSEL OIL.

Amyl Nitrite, $C_5H_{11}NO_2$, a valuable drug which may be prepared by the action of nitric acid on fusel oil (amyl alcohol).

Amylopsin, the diastatic ferment in the pancreatic secretion. See PANCREAS; DIGESTION.

Amyot, Jacques (1513-93), French scholar, celebrated as the French translator of Plutarch's *Lives.* His translation (1559, 1572) marks an epoch in the history of French style. North translated it into English, and so came to give materials for the Roman plays of Shakespeare.

Anabaptists (from Greek *anabaptizein,* 'to baptize again'), a term often applied to those Christians who reject infant baptism and administer the rite only to adults. It is properly applied to the adherents of a movement which appeared in many parts of Europe, particulary in Germany, Switzerland, and the Netherlands, during the Reformation. Consult Heath's *Anabaptism from Its Rise at Zwickau to Its Fall at Münster.*

Anabasis, the name of two historical works, The *Anabasis of Cyrus,* written by Xenophon, which gives a narrative of the unfortunate expedition of the younger Cyrus against his brother, the Persian king Artaxerxes, and of the retreat of his 10,000 Greek allies under the command of Xenophon, after the Battle of Cunaxa, 401 B.C. The *Anabasis of Alexander,* written by Arrian, and giving an account of the campaigns of Alexander the Great.

Anableps, a genus in Agassiz' cyprinodont family of bony fishes with open-air bladders. They are specially noteworthy for their projecting eyes, which are divided into an upper and a lower portion.

Anabolism, the constructive processes within the protoplasm, by which food or other material passes through a series of ever more complex and unstable combinations, till it is finally worked up into living matter. See METABOLISM.

Anachronism, the erroneous reference of a circumstance or custom to a wrong date. Anachronisms may be made in regard to mode of thought and style of writing, as well as in regard to mere events.

Anacoluthon, a term employed both in grammar and rhetoric, to denote the absence of strict logical sequence in the grammatical construction.

Anaconda, a large South American water snake of the Python family, closely related to the boa constrictor. See BOA; PYTHON.

Anacreon, one of the most esteemed lyric poets of Greece, was born about 500 B.C. at Teos, an Ionian city in Asia Minor.

Anæmia is a comprehensive term commonly employed to denote a deficient quantity or quality of the blood. Deficiency in quantity is evidenced by an absolute reduction in the amount of blood in the body; in qualitative deficiency there is a reduction in the number of the red corpuscles, or their contained hæmoglobin. The causes of anæmia, following Osler, may be divided into two groups, according as they act upon the blood directly, or upon the blood-forming structures. Great advances have recently been made in the treatment of secondary anæmia through careful attention to diet.

Three United States physicians were jointly awarded the 1934 Nobel Prize for their discovery that a diet of animal livers is a specific remedy for pernicious anæmia. They were: Dr. George Hoyt, Dean, University of Rochester School of Medicine and Dentistry; Dr. George Richards Minot and Dr. William Parry Murphy, Professor and Instructor in Harvard Medical School, respectively. See also CHLOROSIS.

Anæsthesia (Greek 'absence of sensation'), loss of sensation, local or general, due to disease or induced by artificial means chiefly as an adjunct to surgical procedures. The term is commonly used as synonymous with analgesia, which refers to absence of sensibility to pain only, with retention of consciousness.

General anæsthesia is induced by the inhalation or intravenous administration of certain drugs, chief among which are ether, chloroform, ethyl chloride, and nitrous oxide. Ether is given, also, in an oil medium by rectal injection. Other less common anæsthetics are ethylene, acetylene, and carbon dioxide. All these drugs act by producing a progressive paralysis of the central nervous system with suspension of the vital functions except respiration and circulation. The anæsthetic properties of the various agents are improved by combination with oxygen.

Regional (local) anæsthesia is the production of insensibility in any given region of the body. There are two distinct procedures by which this is accomplished: (1) Field block consists in making fanwise injections of the anæsthetic drug in certain definite planes of the body, so as to soak all the nerves supplying the operative field, thus creating a wall of anæsthesia which blocks pain transmission. (2) Nerve block consists in injecting the nerves individually or reaching them *en bloc* by a single injection. *Spinal anæsthesia* is in reality an extensive nerve block resulting from the injection of the roots of the spinal nerves in the subarachnoid space. Local analgesia is produced by the use of various freezing mixtures, such as ethyl chloride, in the form of a spray. The drug of choice for inducing regional anæsthesia is novocaine.

Refrigeration (Crymo) anesthesia was developed during World War II and provided for bloodless and shockless amputations. Continuous caudal analgesia was introduced in 1943 to relieve the pain of childbirth.

Symptomatic Anæsthesia.—Loss of sensibility occurs naturally as the result of disease or injury of the nervous system involving the sensory end organs.

Anagram (Greek, *ana,* 'backward,' and *gramma,* 'a letter of the alphabet'), the transposition of the letters of a word, phrase, or short sentence, so as to form a new word or sentence.

Anahuac, (a term signifying, in the old Mexican language, 'near the water'), the original name of the ancient kingdom of Mexico.

Analcite, a mineral of the zeolite group; hardness, 5 to 5½; specific gravity, 2.25. It is found, as a rule, lining amygdaloidal cavities in basic volcanic rocks.

Analecta, or **Analect** (Greek, 'things gathered'), a literary collection or anthology.

Anal Glands, pouches from the end of the intestine beside the anus. See GLANDS; MUSK GLANDS; BEAVER; CIVET; SKUNK.

Analogy, a term which signifies an agreement or correspondence in certain respects between things in other respects different. It makes a resemblance of relations, as in the phrase, 'Knowledge is to the mind what light is to the eye.' Euclid employed it to signify proportion, or the equality of ratios, and it has retained this sense in mathematics; but it is a term little used in the exact sciences, and of very frequent use in every other department of knowledge and of human affairs.

Analogy, in biology, is used to denote physiological, independent of morphological resemblance. Organs are *analogous* to one another, or are *analogs,* when they perform the same function, though they may be altogether different in structure; as the wings of a bird, and the wings of an insect. See HOMOLOGY; MORPHOLOGY.

Analysis (Greek, 'taking apart') and its converse Synthesis ('putting together') are now generally used to designate two complementary processes, the correlatives of each other, employed in chemistry, logic, mathematics, and philosophy. Analysis is the resolution of a whole into its component parts, the tracing of things to their source, and so discovering the general principles underlying individual phenomena. The Analysis of Infinites comprehends the Differential Calculus, the Integral Calculus, and the Calculus of Variations (see the several articles). The analysis of the ancient mathematicians was entirely different, and consisted simply in the application of the analytic method, as opposed to the synthetic, to the solution of geometrical questions. The invention of it is ascribed to Plato; but of the works of the ancients on geometrical analysis none are extant, except some portions of those of Euclid, Apollonius of Perga, and Archimedes.

Analysis, Chemical, is the term applied to that department of experimental science which has for its object the chemical disunion or separation of the constituents of a compound substance, such as the resolution of water into its components hydrogen and oxygen; salt into chlorine and sodiums. Chemical analysis is of two kinds—qualitative analysis, which determines the quality or nature of the ingredients of a compound, without regard to the quantity of each which may be present; and quantitative analysis, which calls in the aid of the balance or burette, and estimates the exact proportion, by weight or volume, in which the several constituents are united. (See ELECTRO-CHEMISTRY.)

The divisions of Inorganic and Organic Chemistry have led to a corresponding classification of chemical analysis into *inorganic* analysis, comprehending the processes followed and the results obtained in the investi-

Analysis

gation of the atmosphere, water, soils, and rocks; and *organic* analysis, treating of the modes of isolation, and the nature of the ingredients found in or derived from organized structures—plants and animals. Both these departments afford examples of what are called *proximate* and *ultimate* analysis.

Several other terms are in use in chemical treatises: thus, *Gas* analysis is applied to the processes employed in the separation by absorption of the various gases (see GASES); *Metallurgic* analysis includes the reduction of metallic ores (see ASSAYING); *Agricultural* analysis is restricted to the examination of manures, feeding stuffs, and soils; *Medical* or *Physiological* analysis, to the investigation of blood, urine, and other animal fluids and juices, and the examination of medicinal compounds; *Commercial* analysis is the term used where great accuracy or nicety of detail is not required in an analysis, but where the commercially important constituents alone are determined (see ANALYSIS, COMMERCIAL).

CRYSTALLO ANALYSIS is really a method of identification, not analysis in the strict sense. It is in process of formulation by Prof. E. C. Fedoroff of St. Petersburg. See ASSAYING. Consult Fresenius' *Qualitative Analysis* and *Quantitative Analysis;* Sutton's *Volumetric Analysis;* Hempel's *Gas Analysis;* Blyth's *Foods: Composition and Analysis* (4th ed.); Allen's *Commercial Organic Analysis* (2 vols); Rockwood's *Introduction to Chemical Analysis* (1913); Treadwell's *Analytical Chemistry* (1913).

Analysis, Commercial, or **Pharmaceutical Analysis,** differs from inorganic or organic analysis, pure and simple, in dealing usually with complex mixtures to which it is impossible to apply tests having a definite value as to the information they afford. To such a mixture it is necessary to apply many physical processes, in the hope that these will so separate the constituents as to render it possible to recognize them either by appearance, odor, or specific test. Thus it comes about that a knowledge of experimental physics, no less than of chemistry, is essential to the successful analyst. Among the most important physical processes are—Distillation (See DISTILLATION); Solution (See SOLUTIONS); Rotation of the polarized ray (See POLARIZATION OF LIGHT); Fluorescence (See FLUORESCENCE); Melting point (See MELTING); Sublimation (See SUBLIMATION); Microscopical examination (See MICROSCOPE AND SPECTROSCOPE).

In the examination of an unknown substance many or all of these methods must be tried, the ingenuity of the chemist having here unbounded scope. Numerous precautions are of course necessary to make sure that no substance remains undetected.

Analysis, Spectrum. See **Spectrum.**

Analytical Geometry. See **Geometry.**

Anamalai, or **Annamally** ('Elephant Mountains'), is the part of the Sahyadri range, or Western Ghâts, which lies in the Coimbatore district, Madras Presidency, and the Travancore State, India. The lower range (2,000 ft.) is well wooded. The higher range (6,000 to 8,000 ft.) consists of open grassy hills. Here is the peak Anamudi (8,850 ft.). The hill tribes are keen hunters, and are called Kaders ('lords of the hills') and Malassers.

Anambas Islands, a group of small islands in the Dutch East Indies, between Borneo and the Malay Peninsula; p. 3,000.

Ananchytes (*Echinuscorys*), 'irregular' or heart-shaped sea urchin, a common and characteristic fossil of the Upper Chalk.

Ananias, the husband of Sapphira. The pair, pretending to surrender to the church treasury the whole proceeds of a possession which they had sold, retained a part.

Ananias, a disciple at Damascus, who baptized Saul.

Ananias, the high priest before whom Paul was brought by Claudius Lysias.

Anapæst, a reversed dactyl; a metrical foot consisting of two short or unaccented ($\smile$) syllables, followed by one long or accented (-) syllable.

Anarchism (Greek, *an,* 'not,' and *archē,* 'rule') properly means the negation of government. In its ordinary sense, anarchy is a state of society without any regular government. The acknowledged father of anarchism, as a form of recent and contemporary socialism, is Proudhon. After Proudhon, the philosophy, is Proudhon. After Proudhon, the most prominent expounders of the anarchist theory are the Russians Bakunin and Kroviews, but the following are the leading points: They desire complete liberty for all men; common ownership and free agreements. They object to all authority. As the essential means for bringing about this new evolution of society, they insist on the universal diffusion of knowledge. Natural laws being recognized by every man for himself, he cannot but obey them, for they are the laws also of his own nature; and the need for political organization and administration will at once disappear.

Anarchism has also come to have another

aspect—that with which it is now usually identified—war on human society as at present constituted, hatred of the *bourgeois* and propertied classes as such, and a systematic effort to establish, especially by means of explosives, a terrorism such as was formerly associated with extreme Russian Nihilism and the Irish dynamiters' attempts. See NIHILISM; SOCIALISM. Consult Proudhon's *What Is Property?*; Lombroso's *Anarchists: a Study in Criminal Psychology and Sociology;* Kropotkin's *Anarchy* and *Memoirs of a Revolutionist.*

Anascarca, a general diffusion of serous fluid into the subcutaneous connective tissues. See DROPSY.

Anastasius, St., or **Astric** (954-1044), a monk of Rouen, made bishop of Coloeza by Duke Stephen of Hungary.

Anastasius I. (430-518 A.D.), Emperor of Constantinople.

Anastasius I. (d. 401), Pope, held the supreme office from 398. There were three other Popes of this name—ANASTASIUS II. (496-8), ANASTASIUS III. (911-13), ANASTASIUS IV. (1153-4).

Anastasius II., Emperor of Constantinople, deposed (715) in favor of Theodosius.

Anastomosis, the union of the vessels which carry blood or other fluids; also the junction of nerves.

Anatase, also known as octahedrite, a mineral form of titanium dioxide.

Anathema (Gr., 'a thing set up or hung up'), a word originally signifying some offering or gift to the gods, also signifies a thing devoted to destruction. In the Roman Catholic Church, anathematizing is the extreme form of denunciation. See EXCOMMUNICATION.

Anatidæ, the family of birds which includes the swans, geese and ducks. See ASIA MINOR.

Anatolia. See **Asia Minor.**

Anatomy (Greek, 'a cutting up or dissecting') is the science of the form and structure of organized bodies, and is practically acquired by separation of the parts of a body, so as to show their distinct formation, and their relations to each other. The science of structure, both in the animal and in the vegetable kingdom, is properly called morphology, and the word anatomy is usually restricted to the more special investigations, particularly of the human subject.

It is probable that from the earliest times some persons took advantage of favorable circumstances to acquaint themselves with the study of anatomy. Hippocrates, born at Cos about 460 B.C., though the father of medicine, is less justly regarded as the father of anatomy, as his views of the structure of the human body are very superficial and incorrect. Aristotle, born 384 B.C., is really the founder of the science. He seems to have based his systematic views of comparative anatomy on the dissection of animals, but does not appear to have dissected men. He first gave the name *aorta* to the great artery. No real progress in human anatomy was made, owing to the researches being confined to animals, till the time of Erasistratus (250 B.C.), who was the first to dissect human bodies—the bodies of criminals. Celsus (63 B.C.), in his De Medicina, wrote much on anatomy. Galen (131 A.D.) dissected apes, as being most like human subjects, though he occasionally obtained bodies of persons found murdered; and his writings show a knowledge of human anatomy.

Thomas Vicary, in 1548, is said to be the first who wrote in English on anatomy; he published *The Englishman's Treasure, or the True Anatomy of Man's Body.* In the 17th century, progress was rapid. William Harvey, in 1619, discovered the circulation of the blood, and the microscope was employed to detect the structure of minute vessels. Aselli, in 1622, discovered and demonstrated the existence of the lymph vessels. Willis (1622-75) gave the first systematic description of the brain and its ventricles. The glandular organs were investigated by Wharton. Eminent names in the history of anatomy are numerous in the 18th century.

COMPARATIVE ANATOMY, the investigation and comparison of the structures of two or more animals, was first treated systematically as a distinct science by Cuvier and his pupil, Meckel the younger. Huxley, Turner, and Flower may be named as eminent contributors to this branch of science. See MORPHOLOGY. GENERAL ANATOMY, also styled STRUCTURAL and ANALYTICAL ANATOMY, gives a description of the elementary tissues of which the systems and organs of the body are composed. It also investigates their laws of formation and combination, and the changes which they undergo in various stages of life. In our day, microscopic investigation has been successfully applied to the study of elementary textures (see HISTOLOGY). SPECIAL ANATOMY, or DESCRIPTIVE ANATOMY, treats of the several parts and organs of the body in respect to their form, structure, and systematic connection or relation with each other.

Special anatomy may also be treated by an arrangement made in accordance with natural divisions, or by imaginary lines dividing the body into several regions—as the head, the trunk, and the extremities. Again, the trunk may be subdivided into neck, thorax, and abdomen; and in each of the main regions several subdivisions may be made. The necessity of a union of theory and practice has led to the study of PATHOLOGICAL or MORBID ANATOMY (the dissection and study of structures as modified by disease). The origin of this branch of anatomy may be traced back to ancient times in Egypt; and among the Greeks some anatomico-pathological observations are found.

SUPERFICIAL or ARTISTIC ANATOMY is studied with reference to the effects produced by internal structure on the external form, and describes the organs, especially the muscles and tendons, not only in a state of rest, but also as modified by passion, action, and posture. PRACTICAL ANATOMY includes *Dissection* and the making of *Preparations*. Preparation consists in dividing parts or organs, so that their respective forms and positions may be clearly shown. Organs or parts thus treated are styled *Anatomical Preparations* of bones, muscles, vessels, nerves, etc.

The anatomy of the various parts and organs of the body will be found described under their appropriate titles. Some of the more important articles are:

Abdomen	Leg
Arm	Liver
Artery	Lungs
Bile	Lymphatics
Blood	Man
Bone	Muscles
Brain	Nervous System
Cartilage	Palate
Circulation of the Blood	Pelvis
	Pericardium
Digestion	Peritoneum
Eye	Placenta
Fœtus	Ribs
Glands	Skeleton
Hair	Skin
Heart	Skull
Intestines	Stomach
Joints	Teeth
Kidneys	Trachea
Larynx	

See BIOLOGY; EMBRYOLOGY; PHYSIOLOGY; TERATOLOGY. Consult *The Reference Handbook of the Medical Sciences* (vol. i.); Gray's ANATOMY.

Anaxagoras (500-428 B.C.), one of the most eminent Ionic philosophers, went to Athens in 480, where he became intimate with Pericles; was banished for impiety (*c.* 430)—he asserted that 'the sun was a red-hot mass larger than the Peloponnesus'—and retired to Lampsacus, where he died. He arrived at some tolerably accurate conclusions regarding the cause of the moon's light, of eclipses, earthquakes, meteors, of the rainbow, of wind, and of sound. His great contribution to ancient philosophy, however, was his doctrine as to the origin of all things. He held that all matter existed originally not in the form of the so-called elements, but in the condition of atoms, or molecules, in modern terminology. Anaxagoras marks a great turning point in the history of speculation. His most notable work, *On Nature*, has survived only in fragments.

Anaximander (611-547 B.C.), a Greek mathematician and philosopher. He is said to have discovered the obliquity of the ecliptic, and he certainly taught it.

Ancestor Worship is of very ancient origin, and so widespread that it may be traced throughout the world. It arises naturally from the primitive conception of a soul during life animating the body and exercising influence over it, and after death retaining its power, continuing into the unseen world the life and social relations of the living world. The dead chief goes on protecting his clan and receiving service from them, and continues to keep the same temper as in mortal life. So that it is not mere family affection, but actual fear, that impels this reverence among the North American Indians, the ancient Aztecs, the negroes in Guinea, and other races. In China it is the dominant religion. Ancestors still have their temples and family shrines. The universality of ancestor worship led Herbert Spencer to the opinion that it was the origin of religion everywhere. See ANIMISM; RELIGION.

Anchises, the king of Dardanus on Mount Ida, to whom Aphrodite bore the illustrious Æneas. Homer's *Iliad*, the *Homeric Hymn to Aphrodite*, and Virgil's *Æneid* give his story.

Anchor, the iron or steel instrument by which ships hold fast to the bottom of the sea. A common anchor has a **shank, stock,** ring, and two arms, at the **extremities of**

which are flukes or palms. All large ships carry several anchors. When an anchor of ordinary type is holding properly, one of the flukes is imbedded in the mud and the other sticks up. As the ship swings around, the chain may catch on the upper fluke, pulling the anchor out of the mud and letting the ship drag—perhaps into danger or disaster. To avoid this difficulty many patent anchors have been invented in the past fifty years. The first iron anchors are supposed to have been used by the Greeks. As originally made, the anchor had only one fluke or arm for penetrating the ground, and no stock.

Anchorage. A sheltered position in which vessels may anchor. See MOORINGS.

Anchorage, largest town in Alaska, located 375 m. below the Arctic Circle, is of increasing military interest; p. 15,000.

Anchorite, a recluse or hermit. The term is specifically applied to the Christian ascetics of the 3d century, who established themselves in caves and lonely places in Egypt and in the adjacent deserts. St. Antony was the most illustrious. See HERMIT.

Anchovy (*Engraulis enchrasicholus*), a small bony fish of the herring family (Clupeidæ), of some importance as a food luxury. They are salted, and used for sauces, etc. See SARDINE.

Anchovy Pear, the fruit of a tree of the myrtle order, native of the West Indies. The fruit is edible, with a flavor like that of mango.

Ancient Demesne. Lands which formed a part of the royal estates of the English crown under William the Conqueror.

Ancient Mariner, poem by S. T. Coleridge, published in *Lyrical Ballads* (1798).

Ancona. (1.) Province, Italy, in the Marches, between the Central Apennines and the Adriatic, with an area of 756 sq.m.; p. 302,460. (2.) Town and episc. see, cap. of above province, situated on the Adriatic, is the only good port between Venice and Brindisi. There is a United States consular agency here; p. 89,198.

Ancona, Alessandro d' (1835-1914), Italian man of letters and philologist, born at Pisa. He edited a number of early and rare Italian texts and wrote studies on the Italian drama.

Ancren Riwle, or **The Rule of Nuns,** a manual of religious instruction and observance written about 1210.

Andalusia, or **Andalucia** (corruption of *Vandalusia,* so called from the Vandal invasion), the largest of the ancient divisions of the south of Spain. Its chief towns are Cordova, Seville, and Cadiz. It is one of the most fertile portions of Spain. It is drained by the Guadalquivir. The attire of the people is very picturesque, and the women are renowned for their grace and beauty. In the 5th century the province was invaded by the Alans, Vandals, and Visigoths, who conquered the whole of Spain. In 711 it was subdued by the Moors. Here they founded the caliphate of Cordova, which reached the height of its power under the Ommiades. During this period Andalusia was a flourishing and thickly-populated province. Cordova was one of the chief centres in Europe for the arts and sciences; p. 3,562,606. See SPAIN.

Andalusite, a mineral consisting of silicate of alumina, crystallizing in gray or pink rhombic prisms, usually coarse and nearly square in form. Andalusite is rarely transparent and well colored, but fine specimens come from Brazil, and are polished and used as gems. It is also found at Standish, Maine, and at Litchfield, Conn.

Andamans and Nicobars, two groups of British islands in the Bay of Bengal, about 400 m. e. of India. Only a small proportion of the aborigines are civilized. Andamanese are typical *negritoes:* Nicobarese are *mongoloid.* All are small of stature, of the pygmy type.

Andante (It. 'going'), in musical score, the name of an individual composition or of a movement; also used as a time indication signifying a slow degree of *tempo.* ANDANTINO, being a diminutive of andante.

Andersen, Hans Christian (1805-75), Danish author, son of a shoemaker at Odense. He wrote brilliant books of his travels in Greece, Sweden, Spain (novels); all of which have been translated into English. The first portion of the immortal *Fairy Tales* (*Eventyr*) came out in 1835 and they continued to appear, at irregular intervals, until the last were published in 1871-2, by which time they had won a world wide reputation. Among the best known of the Tales are 'The Fir-Tree,' 'The Ugly Duckling,' 'The Tinder-Box,' 'The Red Shoes,' 'The Snow Queen'.

Anderson, city, Indiana. The historic mounds of the 'mound builders' are near the city; p. 41,572.

Anderson, town, South Carolina; county seat of Anderson co., industries include cotton and lumber mills, machine shops, foundries, and factories for the manufacture of spring beds, mattresses, towels, and hosiery. The surrounding district is rich in cotton and other agricultural products; p. 19,424.

Anderson, Alexander (1775-1870), American wood engraver, was born in New York City. Among his best known works are illustrations to Bell's *Anatomy*, Shakespeare's *Plays*, Webster's *Spelling Book*, and Josephus' *History*. First wood engraver in America.

Hans Christian Andersen.

Anderson Carl David (1905-), American physicist at the California Institute of Technology. Received the Nobel Prize in Physics in 1936 for his discovery of the positive electron or positron in 1932.

Anderson, Clinton Presba (1895-), American public official, was born in Centerville, S. D., and educated at the Univ. of Mich.; in Congress (1941-47); Secy. of Agriculture (1945-48); in Senate (1949-).

Anderson, John Jacob (1821-1906), American author and educator, published many historical works, including *Pictorial School History of the United States* (1863) and *A School History of England* (1870).

Anderson, Larz (1866-1937), American diplomat. He was Envoy Extraordinary and Minister Plenipotentiary to Belgium (1911-12), and to Japan (1912), resigning in 1913.

Anderson, Marian (1908-), American contralto, born in Philadelphia, won the Spingarn medal (1939) for 'highest achievement' for one of her race; Bok Award, 1940.

Anderson, Maxwell, (1888-), American playwright, born at Atlantic, Pa. He was educated at the U. of North Dakota and Stanford U., and taught in both schools. He was on the staff of various newspapers and editorial writer on the *New Republic*.

His best known plays are: *What Price Glory* (with Laurence Stallings); *Saturday's Children; Elizabeth the Queen; Night Over Taos; Both Your Houses; Mary of Scotland; Valley Forge; Winterset* (1935); *High Tor* (1936); *Key Largo* (1939); *Anne of the Thousand Days* (1947).

Anderson, Melville Best (1851-1933), American educator, has translated and edited numerous classical works and published *Representative Poets of the 19th Century* (1896); *The Happy Teacher* (1910); *The Great Refusal* (1916).

Anderson, Rasmus Björn (1846-1936), American author and educator, the author of *Norse Mythology* (1875); *Viking Tales of the North* (1877); *The Younger Edda* (1880); *First Chapter of Norwegian Immigration, 1821-40* (1895).

Anderson, Sherwood (1876-1941), American author. His published works include *Windy McPherson's Son* (1916); *Winesburg, Ohio* (1919); *Dark Laughter* (1925).

Anderson, William (1842-1900), British surgeon, professor of anatomy and surgery at Tokyo (1872-1880). He is the author of *Catalogue of Collection of Japanese and Chinese Pictures in the British Museum* (1886).

Andersonville, village, Georgia, in Sumter co., notable as the site of a Confederate prison maintained during the Civil War. The prison site and adjoining graveyard have been made a national cemetery.

Andersson, Karl Johan (1827-67), Swedish African explorer. See his *Notes of Travel in S. Africa* (1875), ed. by Lloyd.

Andes, a mountain system stretching along the w. side of the continent of S. America, from Tierra del Fuego to the Caribbean Sea. Throughout most of its length the system is composed of two or more parallel ranges or Cordilleras, enclosing lofty plateaus. Its total length is considerably over 4,000 m.

The Andes are built up of Archæan, Palæozoic, and Cretaceous rocks, with some Jurassic strata and porphyritic rocks in the w. range. They appear to have been folded in Tertiary times, the Cretaceous rocks being involved in the folds. Probably the West Cordillera is more recent than the East Cordillera. Many volcanoes are still active. Andesite lavas fill the basins of Ecuador, where the grandest group of volcanoes in the whole chain is found, among which are Cotopaxi (19,613 ft.), Sangay (17,460 ft.), and others. These lavas also compose the large mass of Aconcagua, which rises to 23,080 ft., the highest point of the South American continent. Many of the highest peaks are covered with perpetual snow, and glaciers are still found in the south.

In Peru the West Cordillera forms a formidable barrier to traffic, while farther s., between lat. 23° and 32° s., there is no pass lower than 12,000 ft. In lat. 32° 33' is the Uspallata Pass, between Argentine and Chile, or La Cumbre (12,605 ft.), now crossed by the railway tunnel (alt. 10,468 ft.) between Buenos Ayres and Valparaiso; and at 36° the Planchon (10,000 ft.) In Ecuador and South Colombia the passes are of about the same height. The Guayaquil and Quito Railway crosses the Andes at an altitude of 10,800 ft. at 2° s. lat. This railroad connects the port of Guayaquil with Quito, the capital of Ecuador, and after climbing the Andes extends on the plateau for about 200 m., prepared to tap the agricultural and mineral wealth of Ecuador and South Colombia when extended still farther n. Consult Whymper's *Travels Amongst the Great Andes* (1892); Enoch's *The Andes and the Amazon* (1907).

Andesite. A volcanic rock of porphyritic or compact texture, composed of plagioclase feldspar and a dark silicate, either hornblende, mica, or augite. See TRACHYTE.

Andes, Los. A territory of Argentina; p. 2,250.

Andes Tunnel and Railway. The distance from Buenos Ayres in Argentina to Valparaiso in Chile is given, for the sake of easy remembrance, as 888 m. The project of tunnelling the Andes had been seriously discussed ever since the railway was constructed, because it had from the first seemed impossible to carry the line in the open across the higher pass used by foot passengers, or animals, on account of both engineering and climatic difficulties. This Uspallata Pass has an elevation of 12,605 ft. (3,841 meters), and is practically at the boundary between Argentina and Chile, at which point is situated the famous statue of 'The Christ of the Andes,' dedicated by the two nations as an emblem of peace in March, 1904. The Transandine Tunnel was first pierced by the workmen on Nov. 27, 1909. On April 5, 1910, the formal opening of the tunnel took place. The actual tunnel begins at Caracoles in Chile, passes under the frontier, and ends at Las Cuevas. Its length is 10,385 ft.; height 18 ft.; width 16 ft.

Andijan, town, Russian Central Asia, famous for its gardens and for its cotton manufactures; p. 20,000.

Andira, a genus of about 30 species of tropical American and African trees.

Andirons, or **Fire-Dogs,** the supports on which are laid the logs of wood burned in open hearths.

Andocides, (439-389 B.C.), one of the ten Attic orators.

Andorra, a small independent republic on the Spanish side of the Pyrenees. The Andorrans, about 6,000 in number, are of Spanish race. The republic of Andorra is under the joint suzerainty of France and the Spanish bishop of Urgel.

Andover, town, Massachusetts, the seat of Phillips Academy for boys, and Abbot Academy for young ladies; p. 11,122.

Andrada e Sylva, Bonifacio José de (1765-1838), one of the founders of Brazilian independence, was born in Santos, near Rio Janeiro.

Andrassy, Count Gyula (1823-90), Hungarian statesman, was born in Zemplin. In 1871 he became minister of foreign affairs for Austria-Hungary. He resigned in 1879 but until his death retained great popular influence.

Andrassy, Count Gyula (1860-1929), Hungarian statesman, son of Count Gyula Andrassy. His published works include *The Development of Hungarian Constitutional Liberty* (1908); *The Antecedents of the World War* (1925).

André, John (1751-80), British soldier, was born in London of Swiss parents. In 1771 he joined the British Army, and in 1774 ordered to America. He was apprehended at Tarrytown as a spy, was found guilty and hanged at Tappan, N. Y., Oct. 2, 1780.

Andrea del Sarto, (1487-1531), the name usually given to ANDREA D'AGNOLO, from his father's trade (*sarto,* a tailor), Florentine painter, the greatest colorist of the Florentine school. A full conception of Andrea's power can be best obtained by a study of the fine series of frescoes in Florence, in the Church of l'Annunziata. Most of his best known panel paintings are in the galleries of Florence, Dresden, Berlin, London, Paris, and Madrid. Consult Vasari's *Life* (translated by Blashfield and Hopkins).

Andreæ, Laurentius (1480-1552), Swedish reformer, lived some time in Rome and in Leipzig.

Andrée, Salomon August (1854-97). Swedish aeronaut and explorer. See ARCTIC EXPLORATION.

Andrew, Saint, the first called of Christ's disciples, was the brother of Peter.

Andrew, Saint, Brotherhood of, an organization of men and boys in the Episcopal Church, founded in 1883 in Chicago.

Andrew, Saint, Cross of. See **Flag.**

Andrew, Saint, Order of. See **Orders of Knighthood.**

Andrew, the name of several kings of Hungary, ANDREW I. (1046-61); ANDREW II. (1175-1234); ANDREW III. (?-1301).

Andrews, Charles McLean (1863-1943), American educator, was born in Wethersfield, Conn. His published works include: *The River Towns of Connecticut* (1889); *The Old English Manor* (1892); *The Colonial Period of American History* (1912); *Fathers of New England and Colonial Folkways* (1919); *The Colonial Background of the American Revolution* (1924).

Andrews, Elisha Benjamin (1844-1917), American educator, was born in Hinsdale, N. H. His publications, in addition to text-books on history and economics, include: *History of the United States* (2 vols. 1894); *History of the Last Quarter Century of the United States* (2 vols. 1896); *The United States in Our Own Times* (1904).

Andrews, Ethan Allen (1787-1858), American educator, published a Latin grammar and several Latin textbooks, and edited a *Latin-English Lexicon* (1850), based on Freund.

Andrews, Lorrin (1795-1868), American missionary, eventually entered the service of the Hawaiian government. He compiled a dictionary of the native language, made studies in Hawaiian literature and antiquities, and translated part of the Bible into Hawaiian.

Andrews, Mary Raymond Shipman (1884-1936), an American short-story writer. Her works include: *The Perfect Tribute* (1906); *The Militants* (1907); *Better Treasure* (1908); *Joy in the Morning* (1919); *His Soul Goes Marching* (1922); *Lost Commander* (1929).

Andrews, Roy Chapman (1884-), naturalist, explorer, was born in Beloit, Wis. He is chief of division of Asiatic exploration and director American Museum of Natural History, N. Y., and was the leader of the Museum's series of Asiatic expeditions ending in 1930. These were the largest land expeditions ever to leave the U. S., and by their researches in some of the richest fossil fields in the world, proved Central Asia to be one of the chief centers of the origin and distribution of the world's reptilian and mammalian life. Author of several books and many scientific papers. In 1935, he was made director of the American Museum of Natural History, and has directed many of its scientific explorations.

Andrews, Stephen Pearl (1812-86), American author and propagandist. While in England, (1843), Mr. Andrews learned phonography and introduced it into America.

Andria, town and episcopal see, Italy. Nearby is the Castel del Monte, built by Frederick II., for years the prison of Manfred's son.

Andro, or **Andros,** most northerly of the Cyclades Islands; p. 16,895.

Androclus, or **Androcles,** a Roman slave, who, according to Aulus Gellius, was thrown into the arena, where a lion appeared to recognize him and licked his hands. Inquiry showed that Androclus had previously taken pity on the animal in the forest, extracting a cruel thorn from its paw.

Andromache, in Greek legend, the daughter of Eëtion, king of Cilician Thebes, and the wife of Hector, to whom she bore Astyanax.

Andromeda, in Greek legend the daughter of Cepheus, king of Æthiopia, and Cassiopeia. After death she was placed among the stars.

Andromeda, one of the ptolemaic constellations, forming with Cepheus, Cassiopeia, and Perseus, a group of prehistoric antiquity. Three stars of about the second magnitude —Alpheratz, Mirach, and Almaach—mark severally the head, the girdle, and the foot of the mythical heroine.

Andromeda, a monotypic genus of plants belonging to the order *Ericaceæ*.

Andronicus, Livius, the earliest Roman poet, was of Greek birth, the slave of Livius Salinator, who later restored him to freedom.

Andronicus, of Rhodes, a Greek peripatetic philosopher, who lived in Rome about 58 B.C.

Andronicus Cyrrhestes, Greek architect, the builder of the famous octagonal tower at Athens generally known as the Tower of the Winds.

Andros, Sir Edmund (1637-1714), English colonial administrator in America, was born in London. He was governor of New York and nominally of the Jerseys from 1674 and 1681, and subsequently was governor of Virginia, of Maryland, and of the Island of Guernsey. See *The Andros Tracts* (3 vols. 1869-72), containing a memoir by Whitmore.

Androscoggin, a riv. in Maine and New Hampshire.

Androsphinx, a sphinx with a male instead of a female head—the sphinx of Gizeh.

Anemia, or **Anaemia,** q.v.

Anemochord, a stringed instrument, invented by Schnell in 1789, in which the strings were made to vibrate by currents of air directed upon them.

Robinson's Cup Anemometer.

Anemometer, an instrument for measuring the pressure or velocity of the wind. The best-known form is the hemispherical cup anemometer invented 1846 by Robinson, consisting of four hemispherical cups which rotate horizontally with the wind, and a combination of wheels which record the number of revolutions in a given time. The Robinson anemometer is the one most generally employed and is the standard form of the United States Weather Bureau, where Professor C. F. Marvin has made important investigations dealing with its construction and use. See Marvin's *Anemometry* (1900); and id. *Anemometer Tests* (1900).

Anemone, the 'wind-flower' genus of Ranunculaceæ, includes nearly one hundred species widely spread throughout the temperate regions.

Anemone, Sea. See **Sea Anemone.**

Anemophilous Flowers. See **Fertilization of Plants.**

Aneroid, the barometer invented by Vidi of Paris, 1843, consists of a metal box from which the air is exhausted, or 'vacuum chamber,' and a steel spring in the form of a double leaf. As these instruments are graduated experimentally, they have frequently to be compared with a mercurial barometer. Although very sensitive, they are liable to get out of order owing to rusting, or to alterations in the force of the springs, so that if an instrument has been long in use its scale alters. It is thus rarely used for accurate meterological observations, but, owing to its lightness, is a handy instrument for the traveller. After subjection to a low pressure, as in a mountain ascent, an aneroid does not at once recover its readings for normal pressures. See Marvin's *Barometers and the Measurement of Atmospheric Pressure* (1901); See BAROMETER.

Anesthesia, or **Anaesthesia,** q.v.

Aneurin, a Welsh poet, who flourished during the 6th century, later took refuge at the court of King Arthur, and wrote the *Gododin,* an epic poem, translated by E. Davies in his *Mythology and Rites of the Brit. Druids* (1809).

Aneurism, the local dilatation of an artery, varying greatly in size, and affecting the whole or part of the vessel's circumference. A cure of aneurism is rarely effected. Some surgeons have advocated electrolysis, fine silver wire being inserted and coiled within the aneurism and an electric current being passed through it. Meanwhile the general aim is to lessen strain by lowering blood-pressure, moderate diet, and rest.

Angamos, Battle of. A naval fight off Angamos Point, n. of Antofagasta, Chile, on Oct. 8, 1879. See Clowes's *Four Modern Naval Campaigns* (1902).

Angara, riv., Siberia. Dangerous for steam navigation because of rapids.

Angel. The word angel is formed from the Greek *aggelos,* which represents the Hebrew *mal'ak,* and though now restricted to super-human beings, had originally the general meaning of 'messenger.' At first the ethical character of the divine messengers does not come into consideration, but as the idea of Satan develops he becomes positively wicked in himself, the adversary not only of men but of God, the existence of moral and physical evil being frequently traced to him, and to the hierarchy of demons of which he is the head. The notion of a 'guardian angel' is found, not only in the 'princes' of the nations spoken of in Daniel, but may also be justified by statements of Jesus. It may not be out of place to warn the reader against a tendency to identify the 'angelophanies' in the Old Testament with the second Person of the Trinity; we must guard against foisting upon the early Hebrew consciousness ideas which emerged only in sub-apostolic times.

See ARCHANGEL, CHERUBIM, SERAPHIM; 'Excursus on Angelology,' etc., by Fuller, in Speaker's *Apocrypha* i. p. 171 *f.*; H. Schultz's *O. T. Theology* ii. p. 214 *ff.* (1892).

Angel, or **Angel-Noble**, a gold coin struck in England in 1465. The issue ceased in the reign of Charles I.

Angel-Fish, a name given fancifully to many unrelated fishes which seem to be 'winged.' British fishermen give this name to a small harmless shark called on the American coast 'monk-fish.'

Angeli, Heinrich von (1840-1925), Austrian painter, born in Oedenburg. Among his historical pictures are, *Mary Stuart on Her Way to the Scaffold* (1857); and among his genre pictures, *The Avenger of his Honor* (1869).

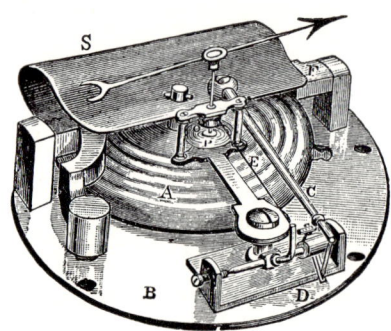

Construction of the Aneroid Barometer.

Angelica. A genus of the carrot family, so called from its carminative and reputed healing powers. The Indians on the n.w. coast of America also eat the raw sweetish-aromatic stalks of the indigenous species.

Angelica Tree. See **Aralia**.

Angelico, Giovanni (1387-1455), 'Il beato Fra Giovanni Angelico da Fiesole,' a celebrated Florentine painter. His most notable work is the remarkable series of frescoes he executed in the cells, cloisters, and chapel of San Marco, Florence. Among his chief works are *The Adoration of the Magi; The Coronation of the Virgin*, in the Louvre; and *The Resurrection*, in the National Gallery, London. Consult biographies by Goodwin (1861), and Douglas (1902).

Angelic Salutation. See **Ave Maria**.

Angell, James Rowland (1869-1949), American educator, was born in Burlington, Vermont, son of Dr. James B. Angell. He was president of Yale University 1921-1937. He wrote *Psychology* (4th ed. 1908); *Introduction to Psychology* (1913); *American Education* (1937). He edited *Psychological Monographs* (1912-22).

Angell, Sir Norman (1874-   ), Eng. author politics and economics; received Nobel Peace Prize 1933; lectured in U. S. 1940; autobiography *After All* 1952.

Angeln, district of Schleswig-Holstein, Prussia, the original seat of the Angles.

Angelo, Michael. See **Michelangelo**.

Angelus Bell, a bell rung thrice daily in Catholic countries.

Angelus Silesius, Johannes (1624-77), German mystic, whose real name was JOHANN SCHEFFLER. His philosophy has much in common with that of Schopenhauer.

Anger, a fundamental, aggressive emotion. In common with fear, bodily pain, and amorous passion, anger is characterized physiologically by the innervation of the sympathetic division of the autonomic nervous system, and biologically by resultant bodily changes that contribute to the efficiency of the organism in the vigorous action appropriate to emotion. Sympathetic stimulation inhibits the contractions and secretions of the stomach and intestines; even the mouth is dry. It also diminishes the blood supply to the digestive tract and to the surface of the body. These changes are interpreted biologically as meaning that the resources of the organism are placed at the command of voluntary action at the expense of digestion and other functions that are not essential to a biological emergency. That this picture of sympathetic and adrenal action is also the picture of emotion has been shown experimentally by the observation that dogs and cats in anger and fear exhibit all these bodily changes. Experiments also show that, in angry human beings, there is an increase of sugar in the blood. See EMOTIONS.

The distinction of anger from fear and other strong emotions is not entirely clear. See FEAR. In animals anger is elicited by the instinctive mechanisms that lead to attack. In infants anger, fear, and amorous passion seem to be the three emotions recognizable by bodily attitudes at birth. The stimulus to anger in an infant is a constraint of the limbs that robs of free motion. In human adults anger is most often elicited by situations which the angry subject considers to be derogatory to himself. Anger has, however, an important social function in civilization as the most compelling motive for action. Not only does war depend upon anger, but aggressive action that furthers human weal in the intellectual, social, and religious spheres, is due to its compelling force.

For the bodily expression of anger as bearing upon the biological argument, consult Darwin's *Expression of the Emotions in Men and Animals;* for the modern physiology of anger, W. B. Cannon's *Bodily Changes in Pain, Hunger, Fear and Rage,* 1915; on rage as an instinctive primitive response, J. B. Watson's *Psychology* (1924).

Angermanland, a district of Sweden, forming part of the province of Vesternorrland.

Angermünde, town, Prussia; p. 8,200.

Angers, town and episcopal see, France. Features of special interest are the Cathedral of St. Maurice, a Gothic structure of the 12th century, with the bishop's palace adjoining; the Museum; the Castle; and the Hôtel de Pincé, dating from the 16th century.

Angevin Line, the dynasty of English kings which began with Henry II., 1154 and ended with Richard III., 1485.

Angilbert, St., (c. 740-814), poet, historian and diplomatist; secretary and friend of Charlemagne, whose daughter, Bertha, he married.

Angina, a general term for any disease characterized by spasmodic attacks with symtoms of suffocation. See ANGINA PECTORIS; VINCENT'S ANGINA.

Angina Pectoris, or **Angina Cordis,** sometimes known as HEART STROKE, a disease or symptom of disease, characterized by spasmodic pain originating over the heart, and often radiating to the left shoulder, the arm, and even the finger tips. It occurs most frequently in men, over forty, frequently giving a history of long continued business strain, or of excessive eating, drinking, or smoking. Of immediate causes physical exertion is the most important. Other exciting factors are mental strain, emotional stress, and cold. In true angina the tendency is for attacks to recur, with increasing severity. A quiet, regular life, with avoidance of mental excitement and physical strain is of the utmost importance in therapy.

Angioma, a tumor consisting chiefly of blood-vessels or lymph-vessels. Tumors of this type are divided into two classes, according as they contain an excess of blood vessels —hemangioma—or of lymph vessels—lymphangioma.

Angling.

Hemangiomata are seen most frequently as congenital, flat, reddish areas on the skin, known as nævi or as 'port-wine marks.'

Lymphangiomata are of much rarer occurrence than hemangiomata. They may be flat, like the simple hemangiomata, may consist of large cystic cavities, or may form firm tumors.

Angiosperms, a sub-group of flowering plants.

Angkor, ancient ruined city of Cambodia, more correctly known as ANGKOR THOM, the capital of the Khmer kings. The city and the temple, Angkor Wat, a short distance to the s., are among the most magnificent ruins in the world. Consult Candee's *Angkor the Magnificent* (1924).

Angle, in plane geometry, the figure made by two lines drawn from a point called the vertex. It is measured by the difference in direction of the two lines. When the lines are perpendicular to each other the angle is a right angle. An angle less than a right angle is an acute angle; one greater than a right angle is an obtuse angle. Acute and obtuse angles are often called oblique angles. A straight angle is an angle whose measure is two right angles. The right angle is sometimes used as a unit of measure, but the most common units are the degree, or 1/90th part of a right angle, and the radian. The radian, much used in scientific work, is the angle subtended as its centre by the arc of a circle equal to its radius; 180 degrees equal 3.14159 radians.

Angle Iron, a rolled iron beam with an L-shaped cross section.

Angler. See **Goose Fish.**

Angles, a Germanic tribe which in early times occupied the district of Anglen, in Schleswig. From them the name England is derived.

Anglesey, an island, 23 m. long by 21 m. wide, lying n.w. of the Welsh coast. The island was a stronghold of the Druids previous to its subjugation by the Romans. It was harassed in turn by English, Irish, and Danes, and eventually conquered by Edward I., 1272; p. 51,695.

Anglesey, Henry William Paget, FIRST MARQUIS OF (1768-1854), English soldier and administrator, was born in London. The Irish Board of Education was founded through his efforts.

Anglesite, ($PbSO_4$), an ore of lead occurring in the upper oxidized zones of veins of lead ore, the result of the alteration of galena.

Angle Worm. See **Earthworm.**

Anglia, East, a kingdom in the e. central part of England founded in the sixth century by the Angles. The modern see of Norwich is approximately the successor of East Anglia.

Anglican Church, Anglican Orders. See **Church, Anglican.**

Anglin, Margaret (1876-), American actress, played many celebrated roles with James O'Neill, E. H. Sothern, Richard Mansfield, Henry Miller. She produced *Elektra* at the Metropolitan Opera House, New York, 1927. She won the Laetare Medal of the U. of Notre Dame. In 1936 she starred in *Fresh Fields.*

Angling, a term commonly restricted to fishing with hook and line as a sport or pastime and not for commercial purposes. Angling is of great antiquity, although in earliest times it was doubtless pursued as a means of procuring food rather than as a recreation. Mention of fishing is often made in the Bible, and the Greeks and Romans are said to have practised fly fishing.

The modern angler's equipment comprises rod, reel, hooks, lines, and bait. The rod may be of light wood or of steel. Reels for shortening and lengthening the line have been in use since the beginning of the seventeenth century. Fish hooks have been in use from prehistoric times, but the carefully shaped and tempered article of today originated in England in the eighteenth century. Hooks in great variety are now found on the market, differing in some slight degree, as in length of shank or shape of point. In general there are two distinct styles: the spear point and the hollow point. Several styles of hooks have no barb, but are made with a peculiar bend which prevents the fish from shaking it out. Many anglers prefer the barbless hooks as being less harmful to the fish and allowing the small ones to be returned to the water uninjured. Double hooks are made by forming hooks on both ends of a piece of wire and bending it in the centre. For lines horsehair was used exclusively up to the time of Sir Izaak Walton, in the seventeenth century, and is employed even now in some rural districts. Generally lines are of cotton, twisted and braided, linen, and silk, and of combinations of these. Bait used in angling comprises artificial flies, artificial bait other than flies, and natural bait. Artificial bait other than flies includes imitations, in wood, metal or rubber, of minnows, frogs, grasshoppers, worms, crickets and other insects.

Natural bait includes earthworms or angleworms, minnows, frogs, salt pork, and crickets. In most countries stringent laws regulate methods of fishing, prescribe closed seasons, and specify the size of fish which may be taken. The pastime of angling has called forth a large and interesting collection of literature. Among the earliest of English printed books was Dame Juliana Berners' or Barnes' *Treatyses pertenynge to Hawkynge, Huntynge, and Fysshynge with an Engle,* which issued from the press of Wynkyn de Worde in 1486. Barker's *Art of Angling* (1651) preceded by two years the most famous work on fishing ever published, *The Compleat Angler* of Izaak Walton, which established its author for all time as *vates sacer* of the craft.

In 1883, Westwood and Satchell in their *Bibliotheca Piscatoria,* enumerated 3,158 editions and reprints of 2,148 works on fish and fishing. Since that time the output has shown no symptom of slackening. Among the more notable contributions to literature by anglers may be mentioned Sir Humphry Davy's *Salmonia, or Days of Fly-Fishing* (1828); Captain Lloyd's *Field Sports of the North and Scandinavian Adventures;* W. C. Stewart's *Practical Angler;* Francis' *A Book on Angling.* Consult, also, Brooks' *Science of Fishing* (1912); Holden's *Streamcraft* (1919); Cox's *A Sportsman at Large* (1922).

Anglo-Israelitish Theory. See **Lost Tribes.**

Anglo-Japanese Treaty. See **Japan.**

Anglomania, a tendency towards imitating English social customs, dress, etc. Conversely, ANGLOPHOBIA is hatred of Great Britain.

Anglo-Saxon Chronicle. See **Chronicle.**

Anglo-Saxon Language, Literature, and Race. See **England and Wales; English Language; English Literature; Great Britain.**

Angola, or **Portuguese West Africa,** the general name for the Portuguese territory between the Belgian Congo on the n. and n.e., Rhodesia on the e., and Southwest Africa on the s. The climate is variable; near the coast the damp soil and mangrove swamps render it unhealthful; the interior plateaus are cooler and drier. Big game is abundant and if properly conserved would prove a valuable asset. Iron was once worked, malachite abounds, and there are deposits of copper, salt, gold, and petroleum. Rubber, coffee, sugar, tobacco, cotton, vegetable oils, and cocoanuts are produced. Trade is chiefly with Portugal. Coffee, rubber, dried fish, and ivory are exported. Area, 484,729 sq. m.

The population is estimated at between 3,500,000 and 4,000,000, of which 60,000 are white. The colony is ruled by a Governor General, resident in Loanda. Besides Loanda, the capital, the chief ports are Benguela and Mossamedes.

The entire coast line of Angola was discovered during the period 1482 to 1486, by Dioga Cam, the Portuguese explorer. Benguela was settled in 1617, from which time Portugal has held indisputed sovereignty over the Angola coast country, except for a brief period of Dutch partial control during the middle of the seventeenth century. Consult Chatelaine's *Angola;* M. H. Kingsley's *West African Studies;* Statham's *Through Angola* (1922).

Angoniland, a plateau between Lake Nyasa, the Zambezi River, and the Loangwa River, in Northern Rhodesia. The Angoni are said to be of Zulu origin.

Angora, now known as **Ankara,** in Asia, capital of Turkey since 1920, celebrated chiefly for its breed of goats whose long, fine, silky hair is employed in the manufacture of textiles. It was a place of importance during the Byzantine period. Modernized after it became the seat of the Turkish Nationalist government; p. 74,789.

Angora Cat, Angora Goat, etc. See **Cat, Goat,** etc.

Angora Wool, the silky wool of the Angora goat, known in commerce as mohair. See GOAT.

Angostura Bark, or **Cusparia Bark,** the aromatic bitter bark of *Galipea cusparia,* a native of Venezuela. A medicinal remedy, largely supplanted by quinine.

Angoulême, town, France, capital of the department of Charente. Site of the Cathedral of St. Peter, one of the most interesting Romanesque Byzantine churches in France; p. 34,895.

Angra Pequena, on the coast of Southwest Africa; the chief center of the diamond diggings. It was formerly a German colony; since the Great War it has been occupied by the British; p. 5,000.

Angular Motion is the motion of a line, fixed at one end, in one plane, relatively to a stationary line passing through the centre of rotation—the movement of the hand of a clock relatively to any fixed line on the face of the clock. See DYNAMICS.

Anhalt, formerly a sovereign duchy of the German Empire, declared a republic in

1918. Agriculture is the principal occupation, more than 60 per cent of the surface being cultivated. The chief industries are the manufacture of sugar and brewing and distilling. The population chiefly Protestant, numbers 331,258.

Anharmonic Ratio, or **Cross Ratio.** If a line AB is divided at two points C and D, the ratio of the two ratios AC:CB and AD:DB is called an anharmonic ratio.

Anhydride, an oxide of an element or organic radical, capable of combining with water to form an acid.

Anhydrite, a mineral consisting of anhydrous sulphate of lime, common in Austria, Switzerland, Bavaria, and Nova Scotia, and in parts of New York, Kansas, and Tennessee.

Anhydrous, the term applied to a chemical substance free from water.

Ani, or **Savanna Cuckoo,** a bird of the cuckoo family belonging to the genus Crotophago, found throughout the Southern United States, and in the West Indies and Northern South America.

Aniline, or **Anilin, amido-benzene,** $C_6H_5NH_2$, an aromatic base occurring in coal tar and similar products of the distillation of nitrogenous bodies. Formerly obtained from indigo, it is now prepared exclusively from the benzene of coal tar. See Sadtler & Matos' *Industrial Organic Chemistry*, (1923), and Groggins' *Aniline and Its Derivatives*, 1924.

Animalculæ, a term popularly applied to all minute forms of animal life.

Animal Heat, the heat constantly being generated in the body, the ultimate source of which is the oxygen consumed in the food and inhaled in breathing. The normal temperature varies throughout the animal kingdom, and bears a fairly close relationship to the activity or sluggishness of the animal. In man the normal temperature is 98.6° F., in birds, 100°–112° F., while in fish and reptiles it differs little from the air or water they inhabit.

Animal Kingdom, one of the three great divisions—the other two being plants and minerals—into which natural objects were at one time classified. Modern research has shown the close connection between simple plants and simple animals, and thus destroyed the basis of this primitive classification. The prime difference between animal and plant is the difference of diet. A green plant can in sunshine form its own carbohydrates, and, if supplied with water and salts, can build up protoplasm under these conditions. An animal must have its carbohydrates ready made, and is incapable of existing unless also supplied with proteids in some form—while a plant requires only simple food which it absorbs in solution, an animal requires complex food, usually taken in solid form. But some simple forms contain the green coloring matter chlorophyll, and are capable of feeding like plants.

The following are the chief groups of the animal kingdom given in an upward scale:—

A. Invertebrata: animals with ventral nervous system, with no backbone or notochord, and no gill slits. (1) Protozoa; (2) Sponges; (3) Cœlenterata, or hollow-bodied animals; (4) Unsegmented worms; (5) Annelids or segmented worms; (6) Echinoderms (starfish, sea urchins, etc.); (7) Arthropods (crustacea, insects, arachnids, etc.); (8) Molluscs, or shell-fish.

B. Vertebrata: animals with (*a*) a dorsal tubular nervous system; (*b*) a dorsal axis, known as the notochord, which in the higher forms is replaced at an early stage by the backbone; (*c*) gill slits, or their equivalents, the visceral clefts, which are openings from the mouth cavity to the exterior. (9) Adelochorda; (19) Tunicates, or Ascidians; (11) Amphioxus; (12) Cyclostomes; (13) Fishes; (14) Amphibians; (15) Reptiles; (16) Birds; (17) Mammals.

Animal Magnetism. See **Hypnotism.**

Animal-Power, the amount of work done in traction, or in working a machine, by animals or men. The standard horsepower, fixed by Watt at 33,000 ft. pounds per minute, is above what a good horse will do for a day of 10 hours.

Animals, Cruelty to. See **Cruelty.**

Animal-Worship. The deification and worship of certain of the lower animals, a usage traceable in most ancient religions, and still practised by many living races. The religion of ancient Egypt was permeated with these ideas. Cats were held sacred in the cities of Bubastis and Beni-Hassan; cat cemeteries existed in both these cities. In Herodotus' time bulls were worshipped. Serpent-worship forms a separate phase of this question; with which totemism, animism, and ancestor-worship are also involved. See Meyer, *Scarabs* (1894); Linforth, *Epaphos and the Egyptian Apis* (1910); Erman, *Handbook of Egyptian Religion* (1907).

Animism, a term originally used to denote the theory of the German chemist Stahl, who early in the eighteenth century developed and modified the classical theory which identified the vital principle with the soul, attributing to it the functions of ordinary animal life in man, while the life of other creatures was assigned to mechanical laws. It was applied by Dr. Tylor, in his work on *Primitive Culture,* to express the doctrine which attributes a living soul, not merely to human beings, but also to the lower animals, and to inanimate objects and natural phenomena generally.

The highest development of animism is in dualism or monotheism; for, to sum up, animism is, as Dr. Tylor says, 'the groundwork of the philosophy of religion, from that of savages up to that of civilized men.' See E. B. Tylor's *Primitive Culture; Researches into the Development of Mythology, Philosophy, Religion, Art, and Custom* (1871; 3d ed. 1891).

Animuccia, Giovanni (*c.* 1500-71), composer, born at Florence. His friend and confessor, San Filippo Neri, requested him to compose *Laudi Spirituali* (2 vols 1565 and 1570), to be interspersed throughout his sermons; these hymns were the origin of the oratorio.

Anise. The fruit of an umbelliferous plant of South Europe, cultivated in Egypt, Spain, Germany. 'Anise seed' is used in the preparation of liquers and by confectioners.

Anjou, anc. n.w. prov. of France. The title of Comte d'Anjou was revived in 1246, and bestowed by Louis upon his brother Charles, head of a new house of Anjou.

Ankara, modern name of **Angora,** q.v.

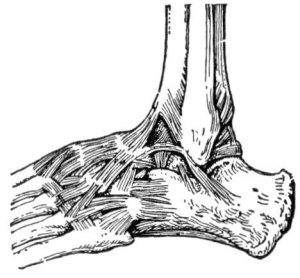

The Ankle Joints and Ligaments.

Ankle, The, is a hinge-joint, the bony surfaces of which are covered with cartilage, and are bound together by ligaments. The movements of the joint are mainly those of flexion and extension, but a certain amount of lateral motion is possible when the foot is extended. From its position the ankle is a frequent seat of sprains, fractures, and dislocations. See JOINTS.

Ankylosis, the partial or complete rigidity of a joint.

Ankole, or **Ankori,** a dist., Uganda Protectorate, British E. Africa. A land of thorny scrub in the e., traversed by ranges of about 5,000 ft.; fertile and well cultivated in the w.; has iron ores.

Ann, Cape, on the coast of Mass., about 30 m. n.e. of Boston. In the vicinity are many well known summer resorts.

Anna, an Indian coin, the sixteenth of a rupee.

Anna Ivanovna, Empress of Russia (1693-1740), daughter of Ivan, half-brother of Peter the Great. On the death of Peter II., 1730, she succeeded to the throne, declared herself autocratic, and gave supreme power to her favorite, Biron, who ruled the empire with intolerable tyranny and oppression. At her death Anna left the throne to Ivan, son of her niece, Anna Carlovna.

Annals. See **Records, Public.**

Annam, a kingdom of Indo-China, formerly comprising the whole of Tongking and Cochin-China. Annam is now conterminous on the n. with Tongking; on the w. it is separated from Siam by the 'neutral zone' which follows the r. bk. of the Mekong R. southwards to Lower French Cochin-China, and its trib. Sebang; on the e. and s.e. the China Sea, with a coastline of 800 m., forms the boundary. The area is 56,973 sq. m.

Agriculture is the chief occupation. Rice, cotton, sugar cane, tobacco, maize, tea, fruits, cinnamon, and vegetables are produced; and there are valuable forests of teakwood, ironwood, dyewoods, and bamboo. Hué is the capital and the chief ports are Tourane and Qui-nhon. The largest town is Binh-Dinh; p. 74,400. The population of Annam is 6,211,228. The inhabitants belong almost exclusively to the Southern division. The masses are Buddhists; the lettered classes call themselves Confucianists. Annam is a French protectorate, governed, theoretically at least, by a king, assisted by a council of six members. The French government is represented by a resident superieur.

Annapolis, city, capital of Maryland, and county seat of Anne Arundel co., on the Severn River, 2 m. from Chesapeake Bay. Among its public buildings are the Governor's House, the State House, the U. S. Naval Academy and St. John's College. A company of Puritans from Virginia made the first settlement here in 1649. It was named Annapolis in honor of Queen Anne; p. 13,069.

Annapolis Convention, a convention which met at Annapolis, Md., Sept. 11, 1786. A report, drafted by Hamilton, was adopted suggesting a new convention of delegates from all the States to consider what measures were advisable 'to make the Constitution of the Federal Government adequate to the exigencies of the Union.' This suggested convention—the famous Constitutional Convention—met at Philadelphia in the following year. Consult Volume 1 of the *Documentary History of the Constitution of the United States of America,* issued by the U. S. Government.

Annapolis Royal, formerly Port Royal, town, Nova Scotia, Annapolis co., on Annapolis River. The town was founded in 1604 and was the first European settlement made in North America n. of the Gulf of Mexico. It was fortified by both the French and the English, passing into the hands of the latter in 1713; p. 826.

Ann Arbor, city, Michigan, county seat of Washtenaw co., the seat of the University of Michigan; p. 29,815.

Annates. See **First-Fruits.**

Annatto, or **Arnotto,** a coloring matter obtained from the seeds of an evergreen plant, *Bixa orellana,* from Brazil; its principal use is to color butter, cheese, and varnishes.

Anne (1454-85), queen of Richard III. of England, younger daughter of the Earl of Warwick, the 'king-maker,' born in Warwick Castle, was married to Edward, Prince of Wales in 1470, and after his death to Richard of Gloucester, 1473. On Richard's usurpation of the crown, 1483, she became queen.

Anne (1665-1714), Queen of Great Britain and Ireland, second daughter of James II., then Duke of York, and his first wife, daughter of the Duke of Clarendon. Like her elder sister, Mary, she was brought up a member of the Church of England, to which she always maintained a loyal devotion. She was married, at eighteen, to Prince George of Denmark, brother of King Christian V. The death of Mary, on Dec. 28, 1694, without an heir, and thereafter the death of William, 1702, left the succession to the throne to Anne, and she was crowned on April 23, 1702. Although she bore many children none of them survived. The chief events of her reign were the union of the Parliaments of England and Scotland in 1707, the Jacobite rebellion of 1715, and the War of the Spanish Succession. Her reign was notable, also, for literary and scientific achievement and has been styled the Augustan age of English literature. Consult Ashton's *Social Life in the Reign of Queen Anne.*

Anne of Austria (1601-66), daughter of Philip III. of Spain, married Louis XIII. of France (1615). After his death (1643) she was regent for her son, Louis XIV., until he was proclaimed king at 13 (1651), but the actual management of the affairs of the kingdom she entrusted to the strong hand of Mazarin. Consult Freer's *Regency of Anne of Austria;* Matteville's *Memoirs.*

Anne of Bohemia (1366-94), daughter of the Emperor Charles IV. of Germany, sister of King Wenceslas of Bohemia, was born in Prague. In 1382 she married Richard II. of England. She was greatly beloved by her people, by whom she was known as 'good Queen Anne.'

Anne of Cleves (1515-57), daughter of John, Duke of Cleves, and fourth queen of Henry VIII. of England. The marriage was annulled.

Anne of Denmark (1574-1619), daughter of Frederick II. born to Skanderborg. In 1589 she was married to James VI. of Scotland. She was crowned with him in Westminster in 1603.

Anne, St., according to tradition, mother of the Virgin Mary, was born in Bethlehem and became the wife of Joachim. Tradition represents Mary as the only child of this marriage. A church was built in her honor in Constantinople by Justinian in 550, but it was not till 1584 that the observance of her festival (July 26) was enjoined on the Roman Catholic Church. See Baring-Gould's and Butler's *Lives of the Saints.*

Annealing, the process of rendering glass or metal less brittle. When glass is rapidly cooled, it easily cracks and flies to pieces if exposed to variations of temperature or when scratched. After rapid cooling, the outer surface, which solidifies first, is in a state of strain differing from that of the inner layers; but slow cooling makes the mass homogeneous.

Anne Boleyn. See **Boleyn.**

Annexation. The process by which a state extends its jurisdiction over territory not previously belonging to it. Though usually an act of aggression and frequently the result of successful war, annexation may be peaceful and not unfriendly, as in the taking over of territory voluntarily ceded with the consent of the inhabitants or in bringing newly-discovered lands under the flag. The Louisiana purchase and the acquisition of Alaska are illustrations of peaceful and friendly annexation by the United States, while the annexation of California, of Porto Rico and the Philippines illustrate territorial expansion by force. Annexation is thus the legal act of incorporating new territories, however acquired, whether by conquest, cession or discovery, in the domain of the state.

Anniston, city and county seat of Calhoun co., Ala., situated in a productive coal and iron district; p. 25,523.

Anno Domini, Anno Hejiræ, Anno Mundi, Anno Urbis Conditæ. See **A.D., A.M., A.U.C.**

Annuals, plants which complete their life-history in one growing period. The seed germinates in spring; the plant flowers, fruits, and dies before the end of the year.

Annuals, popular illustrated books intended as Christmas gift-books, published during the early 19th century. The most important of modern annuals are the reference year-books.

Annuity. A right to receive a fixed annual income perpetually or for life or for a definite term of years. An annuity may be a general obligation of the person or corporation creating it or it may be specially charged on certain funds or lands. In the United States annuities are frequently purchased upon the lives of two persons, such as husband and wife. The payments may be made either yearly or at shorter intervals.

An annuity certain is one where the status is a fixed number of years, and if the payment is to be continued forever, it is called a perpetuity. When the annuity is not to commence until after a certain term, it is said to be deferred for that term. When the first payment is to be made immediately, the annuity is called an annuity due. A life annuity may either cease with the last annual and half-yearly or other periodical payment falling due before death, or it may include a proportional payment for the time between the last periodical payment and the day of death. In the United States the business of selling annuities has been carried on principally by the life insurance companies, and has assumed important dimensions only within the last twenty years.

It has long been a well-recognized fact that annuitants as a class are longer lived than the average. This arises partly from the fact that annuitants usually lead quiet and retired lives, and partly from the fact that no person in bad health is likely to invest money in the purchase of an annuity. A process of selection, or choosing out the best lives, is thus gone through, with the result that the 'expectation of life' of annuitants is considerably greater than that of the average population. It should be observed that the 'expectation of life' cannot be used to find the value of an annuity. A common error is to suppose that a life annuity is equivalent to an annuity certain for a term equal to the expectation of life; the actual fact being that the latter is always greater than the former, and the true value of a life annuity can only be obtained by a lengthy calculation involving the theory of probabilities.

Annular Eclipse. See **Eclipse.**

Annunciation, the appearance of the angel Gabriel to the Virgin Mary to announce to her the incarnation; is now a church festival on March 25, or Lady Day. The subject has been a favorite one in religious art.

Annunzio. See **D'Annunzio.**

Annus Mirabilis, a poem (1667) by Dryden. The year referred to is 1666, when the English fleet destroyed the maritime power of the Dutch. In the same year occurred the Great Fire of London.

Anoa, or **Sapi-utan,** the small native buffalo of Celebes Island, the most diminutive of wild cattle. It is hardly larger than a goat, and has short, triangular, somewhat rough and flattened horns, which extend backward, slightly diverging, from the crown of the head.

Anode, the positive pole of a battery or source of current, as distinguished from the cathode, or negative pole. See ELECTROLYSIS.

Anodynes, or **Analgesics,** drugs which relieve pain. Opium and morphine are the most powerful.

Anointing. See **Extreme Unction.**

Anomalistic Year. The earth is in perihelion when it is at the point in its orbit nearest to the sun. This point is not fixed, but has a slow eastward motion; hence the next return to perihelion occupies a longer period than a complete revolution. This period is the anomalistic year.

Anomaly, irregularity or departure from the common rule. In astronomy, the angle subtended at the sun by the portion of its orbit through which a planet, at a given instant, has moved from its perihelion.

Anomodontia, an order of fossil reptiles, often of considerable size. The order has many structural resemblances to mammals.

They flourished in Europe, India, and Africa during Triassic and early Jurassic eras, and in America their remains have been found in the Permian.

Anonymous, a term applied to a work published without its author's name. Where an assumed name is used, the work is said to be pseudonymous. See Halkett and Laing's *Dict. of Anonymous and Pseudonymous Lit.* (1881-8); Cushing's *Anonyms* (1889).

Anopheles. See **Mosquito; Malaria.**

Anquetil-Duperron, Abraham Hyacinthe (1731-1805), Orientalist, was born in Paris. In 1754 he proceeded to India to study the works of Zoroaster. He published the first European translation of the *Zend-Avesta* (1771), and *Oupnek'hat* (1801-2), a Latin translation of the *Upanishads.*

Anschluss, a German term translatable as 'to connect,' but in political usage having reference to the union of Austria with Germany. This was early a major objective of the Hitler regime in Germany, but was powerfully resisted by other Powers. After cultivating Italian friendship, Germany accomplished it by rapid action when Austria was annexed, 1938, no resistance being offered to the overwhelming force of Germany.

Anselm (1033-1109), prelate and scholastic philosopher, was born at Aosta. 'As a thinker, a Christian leader, and a man, he was one of the most remarkable and most attractive characters of the middle ages.' Anselm came to England in 1092, and became in 1093 Archbishop of Canterbury. Anselm's later life was a long struggle in behalf of the spiritual against the temporal power. His fame as a theologian excels even his fame as a churchman. His great book is *Cur Deus Homo* (Eng. trans. by Prout, 1887). Besides this, he wrote *Monologion and Proslogion* (Eng. trans., with the *Cur Deus Homo,* by Deane, 1903). His *Letters* are collected by Gerberon (Paris, 1675). The best-known books on Anselm in English are by Möhler (Eng. trans. 1842), Hasse (1842-53; Eng. trans. 1850), Dean Hook (*Lives of the Archbishops of Canterbury,* 1860-76), and Dean Church (1870).

Anstey, F., pseudonym of THOMAS ANSTEY GUTHRIE (1856-1934), born at Kensington. His first book, *Vice Versâ: a Lesson for Fathers,* attained a great success. Mr. Anstey has contributed to *Punch,* and many of his papers have been reprinted. He also wrote the play, *The Man from Blankley's.*

Ant. Ants are social insects of the order Hymenoptera, to which bees and wasps also belong. The name is sometimes also given to the termites. The peculiarity which specially distinguishes the true ants, is the shape of the body, the abdomen being connected with the thorax, or anterior region, by a very mobile joint. This gives great power of movement, and frequently is associated with the presence of a sting.

Other characteristics of the ants are, first, the arrangement of the mouth parts. The mandibles (see INSECTS) are so arranged that they can be used for various industrial purposes without their movements affecting the maxillæ and lower lip, the true feeding organs. Further, ants are also characterized by the existence in each species of at least three types of individuals—males, females, and workers, the last type being often divided into castes. The young are helpless maggots, requiring to be fed and tended by the workers. When full grown, these maggots pass into a quiescent pupæ stage, from which the perfect insect emerges after an interval.

In conformity with their social habits and instincts, ants always live in communities, and construct nests specially devoted to the purpose of rearing their young. Ants are specially sensitive to dryness, and usually construct subterranean galleries and chambers, with the apparent object of obtaining moisture; but the shape and situation of the nest are subject to great variation. A remarkable peculiarity of ants, and one that has always attracted attention, is the slave-making practised by many species. The large red ant, Formica sanguinea, an inhabitant of both Europe and North America, a courageous and warrior-like species, at times makes raids on other ants, carrying off their pupæ to its own nest. This association of different species of ants as masters and slaves is paralleled by the habit which many display of living in association with totally unrelated insects. The fact that ants domesticate aphids has long been known; but modern research is greatly multiplying the number of kinds of insects which may be found in ant-nests.

Ants are so numerous that one or two typical forms only can be mentioned here. The large American black ant, Formica pennsylvanica, constructs loosely-built, moundlike nests, sometimes reaching three ft. in height, in which forty to fifty species of guests have been described. The tropical American leaf-cutting ants (Atta), are among the most destructive of insects. They gather an enormous amount of material in the shape of pieces of leaves, and utilize this with much skill to form 'fungus-beds,' on which they grow singularly pure cultures of a fungus which constitutes their main food supply. The wandering ants, Eciton, are interesting South and Central American forms, which are usually blind, and do not make permanent nests, but wander from place to place. The driver ants, Anomma, of West Africa are related forms, which travel in vast hordes, overwhelming everything on their path. For a general account of ants, see the Text-books of Entomology by P a c k a r d, Comstock, or Sharp; Lubbock's *Ants, Bees, and Wasps;* White's *Ants and Their Ways.*

Antacids, medicines which counteract acidity by combining with the acid. The acids formed in the stomach during digestion, such as lactic acid and butyric acid, are neutralized by antacids given after meals.

Antæus, according to Greek tradition, a Libyan giant of invincible strength as a wrestler, until overcome by Hercules.

Antagonism, in anatomy, the opposition of one set of muscles to another.

Antalcidas, Greek statesman born in the 4th century B.C. As admiral of the Spartan fleet, he conducted the war against Athens, by which all the cities and islands of Greece except Imbros, Lemnos, and Skythos were declared independent, and all the Greek cities of Asia Minor were annexed to the Persian empire.

Antananarivo, capital of Madagascar. See TANANARIVO.

Antar, or **Antara, ibn Sheddad al-Absi,** celebrated Arabian warrior and pre-Islamic poet of the 6th century, author of the *Moallakat* (Eng. trans., *Seven Arabic Poems,* by Johnson). *Antar: a Bedouin Romance.*

Antarctica, the name given to that part of the earth's surface which surrounds the South Pole.

Antarctic Exploration. The story of Antarctic exploration in the restricted sense of the area beyond the Antarctic Circle begins January 17, 1773. On that day Lieutenant James Cook crossed, for the first time in human history, the line that divides the South Temperate from the South Frigid Zone. On January 30, 1774, he reached in Longitude 106° 54′ w. and Latitude 71° 10′ s., the farthest s. attained in the 18th century. The honor of having sighted the first land within the Antarctic Circle belongs to Captain Fabian

"Little America." Admiral Byrd (inset).

von Bellingshausen. He led a Russian expedition in 1819 and in 1821, naming two islands, Peter I, and Alexander I.

While sailing eastward Bellingshausen encountered Captain Nathaniel B. Palmer, a Connecticut sailing master who had skirted the coast of a land lying s. of Bransfield Strait. The expedition of major note was that of James Weddell, who sailed into the sea that now bears his name, and there, on February 20, 1823, reached the farthest s. up to his day. After Weddell came John Biscoe, in 1831 and in 1833 a British skipper named Kemp. The honor of first recognizing Antarctica as a continent and of the longest tracing of its shore line belongs to Lieutenant (afterward Admiral) Charles Wilkes of the United States Navy, 1840. Wilkes christened the continent 'Antarctica,' and named Cape Hudson and Termination Land, Longitude 97° 37′ e., where he headed n. and ended his cruise.

The next major explorer in the Antarctic was Captain J. Clark Ross, R.N. He found open water in what is now Ross Sea and followed the western shore of that sea, landing on Possession Island. There, unable to reach the mainland, he named that mainland Victoria Land. He reached the Barrier in Longitude 161° 27′ w., a few degrees n.e. of Commander Byrd's Little America. A fruitful but very short expedition to the Antarctic was that of February 16, 1874 made by the *Challenger*, the first steamship to cross the Antarctic Circle. But with some of the ablest scientists aboard that ever set foot in polar areas she brought back a wealth of material.

Antarctic exploration for a quarter of a century was limited to the normal activities of whaling ships. But in 1898, a Belgian expedition under Lieutenant Adrien de Gerlache discovered more than a hundred islands in De Gerlache Strait. This expedition was the first that ever wintered in the Antarctic. During the same period C. E. Borchgrevink led an expedition to the Ross Sea area. February 17, 1899, his ship, the *Southern Cross* dropped anchor at the foot of Cape Adare, the first anchor ever dropped within the Antarctic Circle. After putting 10 men and supplies on shore, the ship, on March 2, departed for New Zealand. The hardships of this first Antarctic night on shore were indescribable. Finally the *Southern Cross* returned, finding the party January 28, 1900. This party reached 78° 50′ s. Latitude and breaking the previous record of poleward travel.

In 1901 Captain Robert F. Scott, accompanied by Lieutenant Ernest H. Shackleton, sailed for the Antarctic in the *Discovery*. They entered the pack ice January 1, 1902, landed at Cape Adare. Sailing eastward along the Barrier they discovered King Edward VII. Land. February 10, they found a harbor in McMurdo Bay. Here the *Discovery* was anchored, huts were built on shore, and the Antarctic night came apace. With the following summer Scott and Shackleton reached 82° 17′ s., the farthest s. The ice never broke sufficiently to release the *Discovery*. Lieutenant Shackleton was invalided aboard the *Morning* which had come out on a relief expedition. Scott explored Victoria Land. January 5, 1904 the *Morning* and the *Terra Nova* appeared at the edge of the ice with peremptory orders to bring the Scott party back to England even if the *Discovery* had to be abandoned. The ice fortunately broke up and February 18, 1904 the three ships headed homeward. In February, 1902, a German Antarctic expedition, under Erich von Drygalski, discovered new land, which was named Kaiser Wilhelm II. Land.

A Swedish expedition in the *Antarctic*, 1901-1903, under Otto Nordenskjöld, had its ship, the *Antarctic*, crushed by ice; but all the party, having wintered on Bouvet Island, were rescued by an Argentine gunboat commanded by Captain Irizar. A Scottish national Antarctic expedition, led by Dr. W. S. Bruce, in the *Scotia*, 1902-04, explored 4,000 m. of ocean, reached the southeastern extremity of the Weddell Sea, and discovered that a great barrier of ice, believed to be part of the Antarctic continent, was 600 m. n. of its supposed position. The expedition also dredged in Ross' Deep. In 1904-05 and 1908-1910, a French expedition under Dr. Jean Charcot, explored the Palmer Archipelago and discovered Charcot Land. One of the most successful of all Antarctic expeditions was that of Lieutenant (afterward Sir) E. H. Shackleton in the *Nimrod*, which returned in 1909, after a journey of 1,700 m. Shackleton reached 88° 23′ S., or within 111 m. of the South Pole, on January 9, 1909. Shackleton located the South Magnetic Pole, January 16, 1909, at 72° 25′ s. and 155° 16′ e. He also climbed Mount Erebus, 13,500 ft. high.

The year 1911 brought the final triumph over the forbidden areas of the Antarctic. In August, 1910, Captain Roald Amundsen left Christiania (now Oslo), Norway, headed for the Bay of Whales. There February 10, 1911, he began to prepare for his dash to the South

Pole. Amundsen got under way on his drive to the Pole October 19. November 17, the party was at the foot of the mountains and began the ascent to the Divide between the coastal area and the Polar Plateau. The party reached the greatest height, 10,750 ft., on December 6. From this point a flat plain extended to 88° 25', thus confirming Shackleton's observations at his last camp (88° 23'). With ideal sledging and beautiful weather each day 15 nautical m. were covered, until on December 14 the South Pole was attained.

The Pole was located upon a vast white, snow-covered plain. The mean temperature at the Pole was 15° below zero Fahrenheit, and the lowest on the journey thither, 34° below. During the greater part of the 4 days near the Pole the sun shone clear, and the wind was light. The tent was left standing, with the Norwegian flag flying. To the plateau was given the name King Haakon VII., and to the mountain extending from the Barrier far inland, and possibly an Antarctic extension of the Andes, Queen Maud's Range.

The journey back to Framheim, the base station, was made in 39 days, ending January 25, at an average of 19-20 m. per day. The world hailed with many honors the achievement of Captain Amundsen and his indomitable associates. While Captain Amundsen was making his way to the South Pole, another great explorer was setting out a little further to the w. in his 2d quest of the same objective. Captain Robert F. Scott reached Cape Evans, 14 m. n. of the headquarters of his previous *Discovery* expedition. He, like Amundsen, wintered on the shores of Ross Sea for an early march in the Antarctic spring of 1911. He left his base on November 2, fourteen days after Amundsen started. The motor party turned back at 81° 15'; and after most difficult traveling in snow Scott's party reached 83° 24' on December 4. On December 14, the day that Amundsen reached the South Pole, Scott was beginning his ascent of Beardmore Glacier. The 86th parallel was crossed on Christmas Day.

On January 3, 1912, when 150 m. from the Pole, 87° 32' s. Latitude, the last supporting party, under command of Lieutenant Evans, was dispatched northward. From that point he went forward with a party of five—Dr. Wilson, Captain Oates, Lieutenant Bowers, and Petty Officer Evans—with a month's provisions—expecting to reach the Pole in less than a week. They traveled the remaining 150 m. in 26 days, and on January 29, 1912, reached the Pole. From Amundsen's hut, at the Pole, Scott took the records and a letter to the King of Norway. Returning from the Pole everything went well until they passed the Beardmore Glacier. Then disaster after disaster overtook them. On February 17, Petty Officer Evans, thought to be the strongest man in the party, died from concussion of the brain, the effects of a fall on the ice. Captain Oates also suffered severely from frost bite and weakness; and on March 17, made desperate by his own condition and the delay he was causing his comrades, he walked from the tent, remarking, 'I'm going outside—I may be some time.' He never was seen again.

Scott, Wilson, and Bowers pushed on to within 11 m. of One Ton camp, 155 m. from Hut Point. There they were forced to make camp, March 21, with fuel for one hot meal and food for two days. The gale confined them to the tent for four days, on the last of which Scott wrote his thrilling and memorable message to the public, reciting briefly the arrival at the Pole, and declaring that the disastrous results were due not to faulty organization, but to misfortune in all the risks which had been undertaken. 'For my own sake, I do not regret this journey, which has shown that Englishmen can endure hardships, help one another, and meet death with as great fortitude as ever in the past. But if we have been willing to give our lives to this enterprise, which is for the honor of our country, I appeal to our countrymen to see that those who depend on us are properly cared for. Had we lived, I should have a tale to tell of the hardihood, endurance, and courage of my companions which would have stirred the heart of every Englishman.'

Ten months later, a party from Cape Evans, under Surgeon Atkinson, found Scott's last camp, recovered the records, and buried the bodies under a cairn, over which a cross was erected. Great Britain recognized generously and spontaneously the heroism of Scott and his comrades. In welcome contrast to the tragic fate of Captain Scott was the successful return to Hut Point of Lieutenant V. L. A. Campbell's northern party, which had arrived in safety at Cape Evans on November 7, 1912.

Closely following Amundsen, the *Aurora* carried Sir Douglas Mawson's Australian expedition to the Barrier. The expedition sought to ascertain what may be the resources of the Antarctic in mines and fisheries. It discovered and named George V. Land and surveyed hundreds of m. of coast. During this period there was a Japanese expedition in the Antarctic under the leadership of Captain Shirase.

Lieutenant Ernest Shackleton decided to try again to conquer the Antarctic, this time by crossing it via the South Pole from Weddell Sea to Ross Sea. In the *Endurance* he entered the ice pack December 7, 1914. Beset by the ice he pushed his way southward. On January 18, 1915, the *Endurance* became frozen into the ice. Crushed October 27, the *Endurance* remained afloat until November 21. Meanwhile Shackleton and his men had established themselves on an ice floe. Forced to take to their boats, the party of 28 succeeded in reaching Elephant Island. Here a camp was built, and Shackleton, with five men, undertook, in a whaleboat, to reach South Georgia, 750 m. away. This they succeeded in doing to the accompaniment of almost unbelievable hardships.

On August 30, 1916, Sir Ernest succeeded in reaching the 22 men he had left on Elephant Island on the previous April 15. Home again, Sir Ernest began making plans for another expedition, but at South Georgia he died of angina pectoris, January 5, 1922. His body was carried to Montevideo *en route* back to England. But cables from Lady Shackleton intercepted the party with instructions to carry the dead hero back to South Georgia and bury him at the base of the mountains he had been the first to cross. There today stands a great cairn surmounted by a cross.

Once again the Antarctic was left to its own to be reached next by explorers of the air, Richard E. Byrd of the U. S. Navy, back from a flight over the North Pole, and Captain Sir Hubert Wilkins, who arrived in 1928 with two monoplanes. His flight took him across the Antarctic Circle and gave him the honor of being the first aviator to fly in the South Frigid Zone. Between the 1st and 2d flights of Wilkins, Commander Byrd arrived at the Barrier in Ross Sea, with the best equipped and most completely staffed expedition that ever ventured into the Antarctic. It was on the 17th anniversary of Amundsen's discovery of the North Pole that the *C. A. Larsen* and the *City of New York* entered the ice packs.

The base at Little America was established January 6, 1929. During January and February Byrd made several important flights, discovering a great area which he named Marie Byrd Land, and charting a range of mountains which he called the Rockefeller Range. On January 27 he flew over King Edward VII. Land, saw 14 mountain peaks. On February 18 Commander Byrd discovered a 10,000-ft. peak and two mountain ranges, and claimed 40,000 sq. m. of territory for the United States. Thereafter the Byrd expedition settled down to winter life and preparation for the great assault on the South Pole in the following Antarctic spring. On November 19, 1929 Commander Byrd flew the *Floyd Bennett* to the last depot toward the South Pole, at the base of the Queen Maud Mountains, carrying a stock of gas and provisions to be used in emergencies.

At length on November 28, 1929 the big trimotored cabin monoplane, *Floyd Bennett*, weighing with its load, 15,000 pounds, took off with Commander Byrd; Bernt Balchen, pilot; Captain Ashley McKinley, aerial surveyor; and Harold I. June, radio operator. Then came the test of tests, the crossing of the mountains with the heavy load. McKinley and his aerial camera with the necessary emergency equipment and rations reduced the ship's ceiling 1,000 feet. Below them stretched the rugged crevassed ice of Liv's Glacier. To the right and left rose rugged cliffs and icy walls. There was no room to turn; they must rise or perhaps perish in that terrible area. Success was not assured until two 125-pound bags of concentrated food had been cast overboard and the plane thereby given several hundred feet more of ceiling. Then, with barely a few feet to spare, a few minutes brought the plane out on the great Polar Plateau, ranging from 7,000 to 11,000 ft.

Onward the *Floyd Bennett* flew, every minute adding to airplane records in the Antarctic. Finally the sun compass told them that they were above the bottom of the world. Dead reckoning and sun compass reading were checked with sextant observations and were corroborated. When they reached the point where the first turn was made, all hands stood at attention and four flags were dropped: a silken American flag, weighted with a stone taken from the grave of Floyd Bennett, a Norwegian flag in honor of Captain Roald Amundsen, the Union Jack, let down in memory of Captain Robert F. Scott, and the tricolor of France.

These ceremonies over, the dash back to Little America began, the *Floyd Bennett* reaching there at 10:10 A.M., November 29. One of the results of the Pole flight was the mapping, with Captain McKinley's aerial camera, of an area of about 160,000 sq. m.

of territory. The fall of 1929 saw Sir Hubert Wilkins returning for another series of flights. A third expedition in the Antarctic in 1929-30 was that of Sir Douglas Mawson.

The Byrd 1929 expedition accumulated data which it will take years to correlate fully with all the branches of science there studied. A second expedition which went out in 1933 made further scientific studies and geographical surveys of hitherto unknown regions of the earth's surface. Noteworthy in this expedition is the period of five months during the summer of 1934 spent by Rear Admiral Byrd taking metereological and other observations at a solitary outpost 123 miles south of the main base. In spite of illness which put his life in peril he refused to summon a rescue party at risk to their own lives. Consult Scott's *Voyage of the Discovery; The Heart of the Antarctic,* by Sir E. H. Shackleton and others (1909); Mawson's *The Home of the Blizzard* (1915); Markham's *The Lands of Silence* (1921); Hurley's *Argonauts of the South* (1925); Brown's *Polar Regions* (1927); Nordenskjöld and Mecking's *The Geography of the Polar Regions* (1928); Byrd's *Little America* (1930); *The National Geographic Magazine.*

In Nov., 1935, Lincoln Ellsworth, with pilot Hollick-Kenyon, left Dundee Island in fourth attempt to cross Antarctica. A third of the way out their radio stopped. After two-months search they were found safe in Little America. March, 1939 Capt. Ritscher claimed for the Reich land previously claimed by Norway. 1939-41 and 1946-47, expeditions under Adm. Byrd explored Antarctica. In 1947, he reported 845,000 sq. m. mapped. In Mar. 1951, Chas. F. Blair made first solo trip across North Pole in a single-engine plane: a 3,300-mi. flight from Bardufoss, Norway, to Fairbanks, Alaska in 10 hrs. 29 mins.; reached New York 3,450 mi. away in 9 hrs. 31 mins. May 30.

Antarctic Ocean, one of the great water divisions of the globe, the antithesis of the Arctic Ocean. The Antarctic consists of a central mass of land, covered with a thick and presumably unbroken ice cap causing huge table-topped icebergs projecting 150 to 200 feet above the surface of the sea, and descending 1,200 to 1,500 feet below.

Meteorologically, the South Pole area is one of low pressure; climatic conditions depend largely upon the wind; from the south it is clear and cold; from opposite directions, fogs and cloud and a rise of temperature. There is continuous daylight from November to January. In regions higher than 40° s. lat., the Antarctic plankton, or organic life of the surface, is characterized by an abundance of diatoms. Pelagic animals, such as molluscs, amphipods, copepods, and other marine organisms, are plentiful down to 1,000 fathoms, and are not at all scarce at 2,700 fathoms. The most characteristic birds are the penguins, especially the emperor and the Adélie; the petrels, especially the ice, giant, and Antarctic petrels; and the Antarctic skua.

See also the article on ANTARCTIC EXPLORATION, and Bibliography cited there.

Antares, *a* Scorpii, a red star of 1.5 magnitude. As the star has a very minute parallax—the measured value is 0".009, it must have the enormous diameter of something like 400 million m. With a volume 100 million times that of the sun, its density can be only one-millionth that of the sun or 1/900 that of air.

Ant-Bear, either of two large, furry, termite-eating animals: the great ant-eater of South America; or the Cape ant-eater of Africa.

Ant-Birds, tropical birds of various kinds which feed partly upon ants or termites, (white 'ants'). All belong to a large family of small South American insect-eating birds characteristically named Formicariidæ.

Great South American Ant-eater.

Ant-Eater, a term applied to several unrelated mammals of similar habits and diet. The true ant-eaters are members of the order Edentata, and are confined to South America. The largest, the great ant-eater or tamanoir (*Myrmecophaga jubata*), reaches a length of 4 ft. exclusive of the large, bushy tail, and has a face prolonged into a long, tubular snout. It is terrestrial and lives in dense forests, but does not burrow; and its long claws and great strength make it a formidable antagonist. Related forms are the arboreal tamandua and the little ant-eater, *Cycloturus*. The scaly ant-eater or pangolins are members of the same order; as is also the African aard-vark, ant-bear, or Cape ant-eater. The term spiny ant-eater is applied to *Echidna*, and banded ant-eater to *Myrmecobius fasciatus*, a curious little Australian marsupial mammal.

Antecedent, in grammar, the subject to which a succeeding pronoun refers; in logic, the premise from which a 'consequent' proposition is inferred; in mathematics, the first element in a ratio as $2:4=3:6$.

Antelope, one of a group of agile, swift-footed ruminants (Bovidæ), which cannot be definitely regarded as either sheep, goats, or oxen. They are characterized by having slender, usually cylindrical horns. Some of these, as the Alpine chamois, are structurally near the goats, and others, as the African genus Alcelaphus, are far removed from them. Antelopes are typically plains animals, and are therefore specially at home in Africa, but their migration thither from the north is recent in a geological sense. No true antelope belongs to America, its so-called 'antelope' being a prong horn. See also articles on the African gnu, the hartebeest, the gensbok, and the eland. Consult Sclater and Thomas, *The Book of the Antelopes*.

Ante Meridiem. See **A.M.**

Antennæ, or feelers, are sense organs, generally tactile, borne on the head in crustaceans, myriapods, and insects. See INSECTS; CRUSTACEA.

Antenor, the Trojan counsellor who urged the Trojans to restore Helen to Menelaus.

Ante-Nuptial Agreement. An agreement made by a man or woman, with each other or with third parties, in contemplation of their marriage with one another.

Anthelia, colored circles, usually three or four in number, which surround the shadow of the observer's head when projected on a fog.

Anthelmintics, remedies which kill or expel intestinal worms.

Anthem, a form of musical composition set to sacred words and used in the service of the church. See ANTIPHONY.

Anther, the male organ in flowering plants. It contains the pollen. See FLOWER.

Antheridium, the male reproductive organ in the fern and moss groups, and in some species of Algæ.

Antherozoid, the free-swimming male element or cell in the sexual reproduction of the lower plants. See REPRODUCTION; SEX.

Anthology (Gr. 'flower-gathering'), a term meaning a series of select extracts, generally poems, chosen from the works of various authors, and complete in themselves. Probably the most important is the Greek anthology. The earliest compilation of any note was the *Stephanos* ('garland') of Meleager of Gadara, put together early in the 1st century B.C. Other similar collections were edited by Philippus of Thessalonica during the reign of Nero, by Strato of Sardis (the *Paidike Mousa*) under Hadrian, and by Agathias of Constantinople (*c.* 550 A.D.). The range of the Greek anthology is from the 6th century B.C. to the 10th century A.D.

Latin anthologies, in imitation of the Greek, were published by Scaliger (1573), Pitthöus (1590), Peter Burmann (1759; ed. Meyer, 1835), and Riese and Bücheler (1894-7). The Chinese *Shi-King* (Book of Songs), attributed to Confucius, and said to be the oldest anthology in the world, has been translated into German by Rückert.

The standard English anthology of modern times is F. T. Palgrave's *Golden Treasury* (1861); other well known collections are Trench's *Household Book of English Poetry* (1868); Stedman's *Victorian Anthology* (1895), and *American Anthology* (1900); Louis Untermeyer's *Modern American Verse* (new ed. 1929); Mark Van Doren's *Anthology of World Poetry* (1928).

Antholysis is the formation of double flowers, in which the stamens and carpels become leaf-like.

Anthon, Charles (1797-1867), American classical scholar and writer, was born in New York City. Besides editing an edition of Lemprière's *Classical Dictionary* (1822), he published in 1841 a *Classical Dictionary* and a *Dictionary of Greek and Roman Antiquities* (1843).

Anthony, Henry Bowen (1815-84), American publicist, journalist, and legislator, was born in Coventry, R. I. He was twice (1849-50) governor of Rhode Island.

Anthony, John Gould (1804-77), American conchologist, was born in Providence, R. I. He accompanied Prof. Agassiz on his productive expedition to Brazil. He published *A New Trilobite* (1831).

Anthony, St. See **Antony, St.**

Anthony, Susan Brownell (1820-1906), American reformer and prominent advocate of woman suffrage, was born in South Adams, Mass., the daughter of a Quaker. In 1868-71 she published *The Revolution*, a journal devoted to the woman's rights cause; she also organized, in company with Mrs. Stanton, the National Woman Suffrage Association, and with her and Mrs. Gage published a volume, *History of Woman Suffrage*

(1881-1902). Consult Harper's *Life and Work of Susan B. Anthony* (2 vols., 1898).

Anthony, William Arnold (1835-1908), American physicist, was born in Coventry, R. I. He published: *Manual of Physics* (with C. F. Brackett, 1898); *Theory of Electrical Measurements* (3d ed. 1908).

Anthony's Nose, a promontory on Hudson River, between Peekskill and West Point. Said to have been named for Anthony Van Corlear, 47 m. n. of New York.

Anthophyllite, a fibrous orthorhombic mineral of the amphibole group. See AMPHIBOLE.

Anthozoa, or **Actinozoa,** an order of the Cœlenterata. See CŒLENTERATA; CORAL; SEA ANEMONE.

Anthracene ($C_6H_4C_2H_2C_6H_4$), a white crystalline solid with blue fluorescence, is an aromatic hydrocarbon formed when certain carbon compounds are exposed to a high temperature. It was discovered in 1832 by Dumas and Laurent. In 1866 Limpricht prepared it by synthesis, and Berthelot showed its formation from coal tar. See ALIZARIN.

Anthracite, a grade of coal distinguished by its hardness, its high proportion of carbon, and the intense heat given out in burning. Anthracite is brilliant and even metallic in appearance, often with a curious iridescence, like that of a peacock's feather. In burning, there is little flame, and no caking. The greatest anthracite mines are those of Pennsylvania, and it is also mined in the Rocky Mountain region, Western Canada, Wales, Silesia, Westphalia, France, and Russia; while in the Chinese province of Shansi are said to be the largest deposits in the world. See COAL; COAL MINING.

Anthracnose, a fungous disease that attacks many plants. See BEAN; COTTON, *Diseases*.

Anthraquinone, $C_{14}H_8O_2$, a yellow crystalline solid obtained from anthracene, used in the manufacture of alizarin (q.v.).

Anthrax (French *charbon*), an infectious disease occurring primarily in herbivorous animals, as cattle or sheep, in which it is known also as SPLENIC FEVER; and transmitted to man in a number of industrial pursuits, especially those involving the handling of hides and skins. The most acute type, *apoplectic* or *fulminant anthrax,* occurs chiefly in cattle or sheep. *Anthrax fever,* or *internal anthrax,* differs from the fulminant form chiefly in its duration.

The principal form of *anthrax in man* is the so-called *malignant pustule,* due to inoculation. *Pulmonary anthrax,* known also as *wool sorters' disease* and *ragpickers' disease,* is due to the inhalation of the spores of the anthrax bacillus in the dust from infected wool and rags. It is comparatively rare, but usually fatal. Consult *Bulletin 137,* U. S. Bureau of Animal Industry (1911); *Farmer's Bulletin 439.* U. S. Department of Agriculture (1911); *Bulletin 205,* U. S. Bureau of Labor Statistics (1917).

Anthropoid Apes, or **Simiadæ,** form, with the exception of man himself, the most specialized members of the primates. There are four living kinds of anthropoid apes—the gibbon, orang, chimpanzee, and gorilla. In all the tail is absent, and there are no cheek pouches. The fore limbs are much longer proportionately than in man, and the sternum is broad. See APE. Consult Hautmann's *Anthropoid Apes;* Huxley's *Man's Place in Nature.*

Anthropological Societies. See **Anthropology.**

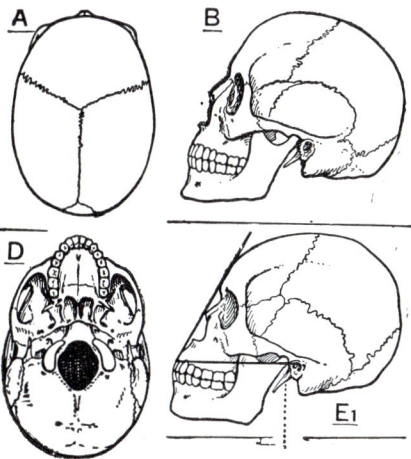

Anthropology—Craniometry.—A. Norma verticalis. B. Norma lateralis. D. Norma inferior. E. Dolichocephalic type (negro).

Anthropology, the Science of Man, embraces all those subjects which deal with man as a social animal. It is the most widely related of the sciences, for it includes or is allied to Ethnology, Archæology, Ethnography, Sociology, History, Physical Geography, Economics, Philology, the Useful and Fine Arts, Ethics, Religion, Physiology, Psychology, and many other subjects. The study of the natural history of social life, or the investigation of peoples in respect of the present state and the evolution of their culture, is known as *Ethnology*.

The earlier history of man is known as *Archæology*, which is essentially a department of ethnology. *Ethnography* is a general term, and signifies a description of the races of men, their material and mental culture, etc., in the geographical groups in which they are found, without reference to their origin, laws of development, and other scientific problems. *Sociology* traces the rise of communities, and their evolution to the complex civilizations of ancient and modern times. *History*, in the ordinary meaning of the term, deals with the later phases of this development. The *Physical Geography* of a country, including its climate, vegetation, and animals, affect profoundly the life of the inhabitants.

An essential condition of culture is that art of communication which has developed into language and into writing; and the study of the language of a people, or *Philology*, illustrates the stage of culture which has been reached, and may give a clue to the peoples with whom the race has previously come into contact. (See PHILOLOGY.) The communication of ideas by visual signs begins with *Picture Writing*, in which maps may be included, and ends with our alphabet. Finally, there are the universal languages of definite signs, of which mathematics, music, and to a certain extent chemistry, afford the best examples.

The *Useful Arts* may be next considered. The progress in the improvement of tools and mechanical appliances has been spasmodic. The greatest ingenuity is usually shown in weapons of offence; war has proved a great stimulus to invention, and the wit of the hunter has been sharpened in the continual attempt to circumvent his quarry. Certain crafts, such as agriculture, pottery, and weaving, are essentially women's work, as hunting and fighting form that of men. Clothing, house building, travel, transportation, weights and measures, etc., are also studied. See METALLURGY; WEAVING; BUILDING; etc.

The arts which do not appeal to mere utility, but have been most important factors in the mental development of man, are those which are investigated in the study of *Æsthetics* or the *Fine Arts*. The temporary decoration of the person by paint or ornaments, and its permanent embellishment by tattooing and deformation, are, at least in many cases, associated with some social or religious concept. Pantomimic dances, music, and feasting have played an important part in social development. Stories about the origin of the world and its creatures, and legends of heroes and races, are the beginnings of literature—at first traditional and oral, later recorded in writing. The rhythmic form, associated with a wealth of simile and allusion, leads to poetry as we know it. See POETRY; DRAMA; etc.

Man's social habit gives rise to customs, and then rules, which make for security and good fellowship in the community. Actions were early distinguished as good or evil, according as they were social or anti-social. These distinctions lie within the field of *Ethics*, and their sanctions within that of *Comparative Religion*. (See ETHICS; RELIGION.)

Physical Anthropology, or *Anthropometry*, is the comparative study of the structure of the human body in the various races of mankind. In the case of living persons, such characteristics as the color of the skin, hair, and eyes, as well as the general proportions of bodily stature and facial features, are available for examination; but the detailed study of the skeleton constitutes the most exact part of the science. The word *race* is used to designate distinct physical types of mankind, from the intermingling of which *peoples* or *nations* are developed; and it is necessary in the study of peoples to analyze the physical factors which have been derived from separate sources. Physical characters may be acquired under varying geological and geographical conditions, from climate and temperature, from food and exercise; clothing modifies the color of the skin; bones are influenced by habits and posture; and acquired and ancestral characters are transmissible from one generation to another.

The most important anthropological measurements are those of the SKULL. In the skull, the cranium is distinguished from the face. The former is the box which contains the brain. An estimate of its dimensions is formed by measuring its capacity, its circumference in different directions, segments of its circumference, and the chords which subtend them. The face consists of the apparatus for mastication, and of the parts surrounding the organs of sight, smell, taste, and hearing. Its dimensions, either as a whole or in reference to its parts, may be obtained by measurement.

The capacity of the normal human cranium varies from 1,000 to 1,800 cubic centimeters. In striking averages, it is preferable to compare crania of the same sex, because the mean capacity of female crania is 10 per cent. less than the mean of male crania. On this basis crania have been classified as: *Mi-Crocephalic*, below 1,350 c.c.—extinct Tasmanians, aboriginal Australians, Bush people, Andamanese, many Melanesians, Veddahs and Hillmen of India; *Mesocephalic*, from 1,350 c.c. to 1,450 c.c.—Negroes, Malays, American Indians and Polynesians; *Megacephalic*, above 1,450 c.c.—Eskimos, Europeans, Mongolians, Burmese, and Japanese.

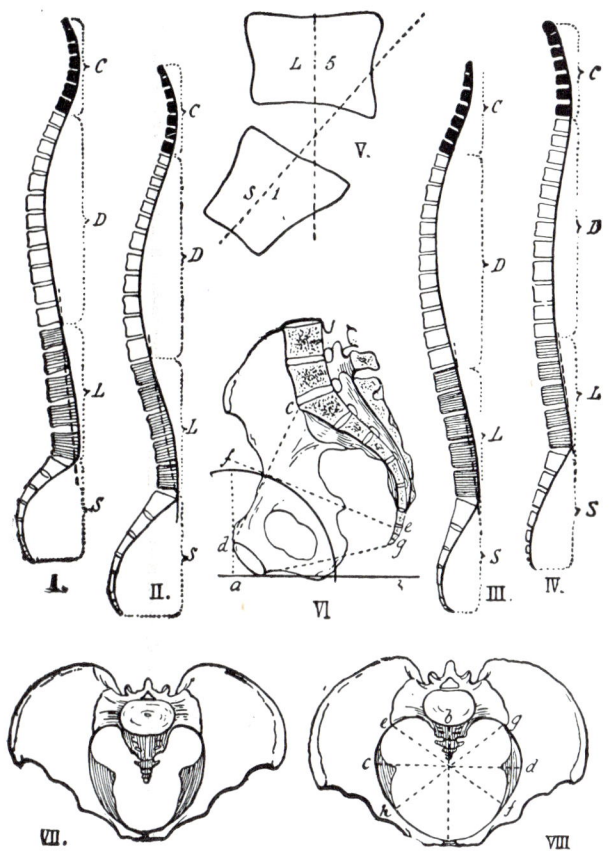

Anthropology.—*Spinal Column and Pelvis.*

Figs. I.-IV., *Spinal Curves.*—I. European (male). II. European (female). III. Hottentot—bushman. IV. Orang. (c, cervical; D, dorsal; L, lumbar; s, sacral vertebræ.)

Fig. V., *Lumbo-Sacral Angle.*—L5, fifth lumbar vertebra; s1, first sacral.

Fig. VI., *Inclination of the Brim of the Pelvis and its Axis in the Erect Posture.*—ab, horizontal line; cd, line of inclination of the brim of the true pelvis; ef, axis of interior outlet; g, diameter of inferior outlet.

Fig. VII., *Male Pelvis (European).*

Fig. VIII., *Female Pelvis (European).*—ab, antero-posterior or conjugate diameter; cd, transverse or widest diameter; ef, gh, oblique diameter.

The mean capacity among Europeans is about 1,500 c.c. A great gap separates man from the nearest of the anthropoid apes, in which 500 c.c. is the maximum capacity. Sex and general bodily stature undoubtedly influence the capacity of the cranium, and thus the weight of the brain. Manouvrier calculates that the cranial capacity multiplied by 0.87 gives the weight of the brain with reasonable exactness.

The current classification of skulls by a linear index, (length and width), is the following: *hyperdolichocephalic,* below 70; *dolichocephalic,* from 70-75; *mesaticephalic,* 75-80; *brachycephalic,* from 80-85; *hyperbrachycephalic,* above 85. These divisions are quite arbitrary, and unnecessarily minute. It may serve to indicate the general result of this classification to state that Eskimos, Fuegians, African Negroes, Veddahs, Australian aborigines, Fijians, and certain races of N. Europe are typically dolichocephalic; while aboriginal Americans, Malays, Mongols, Sandwich Islanders, Lapps, Finns, Poles, Tyrolese, etc., provide illustrations of brachycephalic skulls. The mesaticephalic crania are found among Japanese, Chinese, Greeks, French, Germans, Danes, British, etc.

The FACE is of peculiar interest, because it is modified more rapidly than the cranium in the process of evolution. To define its limits is not so simple as it might appear. Popularly, the face includes the forehead, and extends to the tip of the chin; anatomically, the forehead, being part of the cranium, is not included in the face. Most Europeans have high, narrow, faces; but Mongols, Eskimos, etc., have low or broad faces. The skeleton of the nose varies greatly; and the marked contrast between the Grecian nose and the squat bridgeless nose of the aboriginal Australian or extinct Tasmanian is chiefly due to a difference in the size of the nasal bones.

The SPINAL COLUMN of the infant consists of 33 distinct vertebræ. Of these, 24 remain separate in the adult, while 5 fuse to form the sacrum, and 4 to form the coccyx, or concealed and rudimentary tail. During life the adult vertebral column of man presents 3 well-marked curves—cervical, dorsal, and lumbar, of which the cervical and lumbar have their convexity, while the dorsal curve has its concavity, forwards. These curves are directly associated with man's bipedal gait and his erect attitude, in which the weight of the head requires to be poised upon the summit of the vertebral column.

The curves are therefore most distinct in civilized man, but the difference between him and primitive man is only one of degree. Quadrupeds do not possess these curves, and the anthropoid apes show them only to a modified extent.

The SACRUM is very wide in relation to its length, and the percentage proportion between these measurements is expressed by a *sacral index.* Width predominates in white races, but among many black races the length is the greater—the normal condition in lower animals.

The PELVIS, or basin, consists of the sacrum and the two haunch bones articulated together. It ranks next to the skull in anthropological importance, and possesses peculiar interest both because of modifications due to the erect attitude and because of sex characters associated with its obstetrical functions. Compared with that of animals, the human pelvis presents great breadth and shallowness, while the capacity of what is called the 'true pelvis' is also great.

The LOWER LIMB consists of the *haunch;* a *shaft,* divisible into thigh (of which the femur forms the skeleton) and leg (containing the tibia and fibula); and the *foot.* This limb is used for support and locomotion; only to a very slight extent can the foot be used for grasping. The femur presents many distinctive human characters directly associated with the erect attitude. Among Europeans its length is about 18 in. in males, and 17 in. in females.

The UPPER LIMB is primarily adapted for grasping (prehension), and in a minor degree for support and locomotion. The *clavicle,* or collar bone, merely presents variations in length and thickness, due to stature and muscularity. The *scapula,* or shoulder blade, is plate-like and triangular. Its anatomical features are believed to be considerably modified by muscularity, depending upon habits and occupation. In man (unlike quadrupeds) the length exceeds the width.

The *humerus,* or upper arm bone, is a typical long bone. The *radius* and *ulna* are the outer and inner bones of the forearm. According to an index relating the length of the *humerus* and these smaller bones of the forearm, the Lapps and the Eskimos, who have the shortest forearms, have an index about 71; Europeans, 74; aboriginal Australians, 77; Negroes, 79; Andamanese, 81; the chimpanzee, 90; and the gorilla, 100. This index is higher in the infant than in the adult. Indices are also employed to represent the relative length of the humerus and femur, the latter being taken as 100.

The fullest exposition of these details is known as *Bertillonage,* from M. Bertillon, who aims at establishing the identity of individuals by careful tabulation and classification of the data obtained by measurements. For this purpose actual measurements and not indices, are employed—standing height; sitting height; span of arms; length and breadth of ear, of nose; length of fore-

Specimens of Finger Prints (enlarged).

arm and hand, of foot, of fingers, etc. The color of the eyes—of the iris—and the nature and direction of the opening between the eyelids are also observed and noted. Similar attention is paid to the color of the skin (whether black, brown, yellow, copper color, fair white, or dark white), and to marks upon it such as tattooing or scars resulting from wounds. The natural structure of the skin, as seen in the palm of the hand and sole of the foot, where it shows fine alternating ridges and furrows, has led to elaborate methods of recording, classifying, and interpreting the finger-print patterns. Lastly, the hair is studied in regard to its color, and the shape which it presents on section. Among Europeans and American Indians it is circular, in transverse section; among aboriginal Australians, ovoid; among Hottentots, laterally compressed; among Papuans, kidney-shaped. Huxley classified mankind as *leiotrichi* (smooth-haired) and *ulotrichi* (crisp or woolly haired). A recently developed field for the physical anthropologist has been in the study and classification of types of blood. There are in human beings four main types of blood which may be classified as types I, II, III, and IV. Type III will mix with either type I or II without coagulating, but types I and II when mixed together do coagulate. It is necessary in blood transfusions to test the blood of the donor and the recipient to make sure that such coagulation does not occur. Statistical studies show that pure blooded American Indians are nearly all of type III, while pure blooded Mongolians consist largely of type II. Further statistical studies will be important, therefore, in tracing the racial relationships of various peoples.

In 1936 it was found that by subjecting the bones of Egyptian mummies to special tests the blood types of these mummies could be determined and classified, offering a splendid opportunity for tracing racial origins.

Dr. E. A. Hooton of Harvard, early in 1936, suggested that several problems of medicine could be more readily solved by a closer cooperation between physicians and physical anthropologists. A start in this direction has already been made by the Brush Foundation, founded in Cleveland in 1929. Dr. Ales Hrdlicka, of the Smithsonian Institution, unearthed a skull in the Aleutian Islands with the second largest cranial capacity of any human skull found yet. See MAN.

Recent books on anthropology: Benedict, *Race: Science and Politics* (1940); Chapple and Coon, *Principles of Anthropology* (1942); Mead, *Keep Your Powder Dry* (1942).

Anthropomorphism (Gr. 'in the form of man'), usually defined as the ascription to the Deity of qualities which properly belong to human beings, really denotes a more generic tendency to represent all things under conceptions derived from man's personal experience. Thus, the child instinctively attributes feelings like its own to inanimate objects. Many of our most important conceptions are, in varying degrees, transcripts of the nature of the self, and therefore anthropomorphic. Anthropomorphism is most prominently exemplified in religious thought. It is impossible for the religious mind to formulate the relations between God and man save by attributing to Him a nature akin to its own.

Antibiotics, name invented by Dr. Selman Waksman for those substances that check the development of microbes. New drugs which destroy bacteria include penicillin and streptomycin.

Antichlor, a name given by bleachers and papermakers to any substance used to neutralize small quantities of free chlorine which the paper retains. Hyposulphite of soda and sulphite of soda are the principal antichlors.

Antichrist. In the New Testament the word occurs only in the Epistles of John. It may mean either a false claimant to the Messiahship or an antagonist to the true Messiah. Of the former aspect we have illustrations in the discourses of Jesus, while the Johannine passages noted above furnish examples of the latter. In the view of the early eschatologists, the antichrist is a definite personality, a Jewish pretender of the Messiahship who is to appear, rebuild Jerusalem, and gain the allegiance of the world.

Anticlimax, a rhetorical figure in which the expressions after rising in intensity, suddenly fall to a lower level.

Anticline. Through a flexure of the earth's crust the rocks, which normally lie horizontal with the older rocks below, may be elevated into an upward fold or arch known as an anticline.

Anticline, denuded (diagrammatic section).

Anti-Corn Law League, an organization formed in 1838-9, to effect the repeal of the British corn laws. See CORN LAWS.

Anticosti, island, in the Gulf of St. Lawrence, Canada, which it divides into two channels. It is about 140 m. long, with an average breadth of $27\frac{1}{2}$ m., and has several lighthouses and important fisheries.

Anticyclone, an area of high barometric pressure surrounded by nearly circular isobars. See CYCLONE; WEATHER.

Anticyra, or **Anticirrha,** the name of three towns of ancient Greece—one in Phocis, on a bay of the Gulf of Corinth; one in Locris, also on the Corinthian Gulf; and one in Thessaly. All were famous for the production of hellebore.

Antidiphtheritic Serum. See SERUM.

Antidote, any substance which prevents or counteracts the effects of poison, either by its chemical action or its physiological effects.

Antietam Creek, a narrow but deep stream rising in the Alleghany Mountains, Pennsylvania, and flowing south into the Potomac River near Sharpsburg, Md. On its banks was fought on Sept. 16 and 17, 1862, one of the most hotly contested battles of the Civil War, between the Federal Army of the Potomac, numbering about 87,000, under Gen. G. B. McClellan, and the Confederate Army of Northern Virginia, numbering about 55,000 under Gen. Robert E. Lee. The Union loss in killed, wounded, and missing was about 12,400; that of the Confederates about 11,100, the combined losses making it, according to Longstreet, 'the bloodiest single day of fighting of the war.' The battle has been called a strategical victory for the Federals; tactically, however, neither side can be said to have been victorious. In the North the battle was regarded as a Federal victory both strategically and tactically, and it led President Lincoln to issue his preliminary emancipation proclamation of Sept. 22, 1862.

Antifebrin, the trade name for ACETANILIDE or PHENYLACETAMIDE, $CH_3CONHC_6H_5$, prepared by boiling aniline with glacial acetic acid.

Anti-Federalists, in American political history, a name first applied to those who in the various States opposed the ratification of the Federal Constitution in 1787; and afterwards to those who, in the early years of the National Government, insisted on a strict rather than a liberal construction of the Constitution and, in particular, vigorously opposed the centralizing measures of Alexander Hamilton, the leader of the Federalists. See DEMOCRATIC PARTY; FEDERALISTS; HAMILTON, ALEXANDER; UNITED STATES, *History*.

Anti-fouling Compositions, substances for application to the under-water parts of ships to prevent the adherence of seaweeds, barnacles, etc.

Antigo, city, county seat of Langlade co., Wisconsin. It is the centre of a rich agricultural region, and has numerous industrial establishments; p. 8,610.

Antigone, in ancient Greek legend, the daughter of Œdipus by his mother Jocasta. Antigone is represented as a maiden of noble and unselfish character. See SOPHOCLES.

Antigonish, formerly **Sydney** or **Sidney,** seaport town, Nova Scotia, capital of Antigonish co.; p. 1,787.

Antigonus, known as CYCLOPS or the ONE-EYED, one of the generals (381-301 B. C.) of Alexander the Great of Macedonia. After the latter's death Antigonus became ruler of much of Asia Minor, but was eventually defeated by Lysimachus at Ipsus, in Phrygia (301), and fell in the battle.

Antigua, British island, the most important of the Leeward group of the West Indies. The island is the seat of government of the British colony. Population, including the dependent islands of Barbuda and Redonda, 39,036. Antigua was discovered in 1493 by Columbus. It was first settled by a few English in 1632. It has suffered severely from earthquakes and hurricanes.

Antilles. See **West Indies.**

Anti-Loafing Laws, a name applied to a number of State laws enacted in 1917 and 1918, whereby every able-bodied man in the State is required to engage in some useful occupation.

Antilochus, one of the heroes of the Trojan War, son of Nestor and friend of Achilles, renowned for beauty and bravery; fell in battle while trying to save the life of his father, but was revenged by Achilles.

Anti-Masonic Party, a short-lived political organization in the United States, based, in its origin, on opposition to the Free Masons, but soon becoming essentially an anti-Jacksonian party. The occasion for its organization was the sudden and mysterious disappearance (1826) of William Morgan, of Batavia, N. Y., a Mason, who had threatened to divulge the secrets of his order. The new party elected many State officers and State legislators and a number of Congressmen, and even entered national politics. It disappeared after 1835. Consult McCarthy's monograph *The Anti-Masonic Party Annual Report* of the American Historical Society (1902).

Anti-Monopoly Party, a short-lived American political organization, formed at Chicago, May, 1884, to regulate commerce among the States. Consult Stanwood's *History of the Presidency.*

Antimony (Sb. 121.8), a metallic element, which represents a product intermediate between metals and non-metals, occurring native in rare instances, but derived almost exclusively from *stibnite* or gray antimony ore (Sb_2S_3), which has been known since very early times. It also occurs in *kermesite* or red antimony ($Sb_2S_3Sb_2O_3$), *valentinite* or white antimony (Sb_2O_3), *senarmontite* (Sb_2O_3), *cervantite* ($Sb_2O_3Sb_2O_5$), and certain ores of lead, silver and gold.

Antimony is an extremely brittle metal of a flaky, crystalline texture, tin-white color, and high metallic luster. Its specific gravity is 6.6, hardness, 3 to 3.5, melting point, 630.5° c. The principal compounds of antimony are the sulphides, chlorides, and tartar emetic. Antimony is produced in commercial quantities mainly in China. France, Algeria, Austria, Mexico, Bolivia, Canada, Australia, Japan, Italy, and Spain also produce small quantities. The output of the United States is limited.

Antinomianism, the doctrine, recurring from time to time in the history of the Christian Church, that Christians are freed by faith from obligation to observe the moral law laid down in the Old Testament.

Antinous, (d. 122 A.D.), a youth of extraordinary beauty, a native of Claudiopolis, in Bithynia, the favorite of the Emperor Hadrian, and his companion in all his journeys. He was drowned in the River Nile, and the Emperor Hadrian erected many monuments to him.

Antioch (modern *Antakieh*), town of Syria, on the Orontes River, 14 m. from the sea, first the Syrian and afterward the Roman capital; a great city of Bible times, ranking in importance next after Rome and Alexandria. Built by Seleucus Nicator about 300 B.C., the city reached its greatest glory in the time of Antiochus the Great, and under the Roman emperors of the first three centuries. At that time it contained 500,000 inhabitants, and vied in splendor with Rome itself.

Chosroës, king of Persia, destroyed Antioch in 538; but it was rebuilt by Justinian, and called by him *Theupolis.* After a gradual decline it was almost destroyed by an earthquake in 1872, but has since recovered, and has now a population of 30,000 (Mohammedans, Greeks, and Armenians).

Antioch, in Pisidia, founded also by Nicator, was declared a free city by the Romans in the second century B.C., and made a *colonia* under Augustus, with the name Cæsarea. It was visited by Paul and Barnabas.

Antioch College, a coeducational, nonsectarian institution at Yellow Springs, Ohio, organized in 1853.

Antiochus, the name borne by most of the kings of Syria belonging to the family of Seleucus, who founded the dynasty.

ANTIOCHUS III., THE GREAT, (reigned 223-187 B.C.), in the early part of his reign carrier on unsuccessful war, first with Egypt, then with Parthia. In 198 B.C. he conquered Palestine and Cœle-Syria, and afterward became involved in war with the Romans. In 192 he crossed into Greece, and the next year was defeated by the Romans at Thermopylæ, and forced to return into Asia.

ANTIOCHUS IV., EPIPHANES, son of Antiochus the Great, succeeded his brother, Seleucus Philopator in 175 B.C. and reigned till 164. From 171-168 B.C. he successfully waged war against Egypt. He is notorious for his oppression of the Jews and their religion.

Antiope. See **Amphion.**

Antioquia, a department of Colombia, South America, bounded by the departments of Bolivar on the north, Santander on the east, Tolima on the south, and Cauca on the west; area, 22,752 sq. m. It is occupied by branches of the Cordilleras. Minerals, leather, coffee, rubber, and Panama hats are exported; p. 840,000.

Antiparos (ancient *Oliaros*), one of the middle Cyclades in the Ægean Sea, close to Paros (q.v.). Its wonderful stalactite grotto is 312 ft. long, 98 wide, and 82 high, and is covered with stalactite and stalagmite formations.

Antipas. See **Herod.**

Antipater (*c.* 400-319 B.C.), a general highly trusted by Philip and Alexander the Great, regent of Macedonia when he crossed over into Asia in 334 B.C.

Antipater (d. 43 B.C.), the father of Herod the Great, was a favorite of Julius Cæsar who appointed him procurator of Judæa in 47 B.C.

Antipater, the son of Herod the Great by his first wife.

Antipathy, a term applied to a class of cases in which individuals are disagreeably affected by, or violently dislike, things innocuous or agreeable to the majority of mankind.

Antiphlogistine, a trade name for *cataplasma kaolini* (N.F.). It is used externally in inflammation.

Antiphon (480-411 B.C.), the earliest of the ten Attic orators in the Alexandrine canon, was born in Rhamnus. He belonged to the oligarchical party at Athens, and to him was mainly due the establishment of the government of the Four Hundred in 411 B.C. Only fifteen of his orations have come down to us.

Antiphony, a piece of sacred music sung in alternate parts replying to each other. Antiphonal singing has been practised from earliest times in the Hebrew Church, and many of the Psalms were intended to be sung in this manner. See **Anthem**; **Motet.**

Antipodes, a word of Greek origin, signifying, literally, those who have their feet over against each other. As applied in geography, it means the inhabitants of any two opposite points of the globe.

Antipope, a pontiff elected in opposition to one canonically chosen. The first antipopes were Felix, during the pontificate of Liberius, 352-66; Ursinus, against Damasus, 366-84; and Laurentius, against Symmachus, 498-514. During the Middle Ages several emperors of Germany set up popes against those whom the Romans had elected without consulting them. The election of Urban VI. in 1378 occasioned 'the great schism of the West,' which divided the church for fifty years. He was elected by the Romans, who demanded an Italian pope after the death of Gregory XI. The French cardinals withdrew to Provence, and elected a new pope under the name of Clement VII., who was recognized by France, Spain, Savoy, and Scotland; while Italy, Germany, England, and the north of Europe supported Urban VI. For thirty-eight years these two popes, one at Avignon, another at Rome, anathematized each other. Such disputes ceased after 1455. See **Papacy.**

Antipyretics are agents which lower temperature in fevers.

Antipyrin, Phenazone, or **Analgesin** ($C_{11}H_{12}N_2O$), a white, crystalline, inodorous solid with a slightly bitter taste. It is a prompt and usually efficacious antipyretic.

Antiquarian Society, American, an organization with headquarters at Worcester, Mass., founded in 1812. It has published semi-annual *Proceedings* since 1849, and *Transactions* since 1820.

Antiquities. See **Archæology.**

Antiquities, American. See **Archæology in America.**

Anti-Saloon League of America, a non-partisan, non-sectarian organization, having for its object the extermination of the beverage liquor traffic; founded in 1895 by the coalition of the Anti-Saloon League of the District of Columbia, the Anti-Saloon League of Ohio, and forty-five other State, national, and local temperance bodies. It was for long a major force in American politics, particularly during the post-war decade, but its influence waned rapidly as national sentiment turned to repeal. After 1935 it functioned chiefly in local option campaigns, though still urging the return of national prohibition and other temperance legislation. Consult E. H. Cherrington's *History of the Anti-Saloon League* (1913).

Antisana, a snow-covered volcanic cone of the Andes (19,335 ft.), in Ecuador. It is now dormant.

Antiscorbutics, drugs counteracting scurvy. See **Scurvy.**

Anti-Semitism, the modern form of anti-Jewish prejudice, began in Germany after the

Franco-Prussian War and played an important part in fascist preparation for World War II. After Hitler announced extermination of European Jews, 1942, 11 of the United Nations officially condemned 'this bestial practice.' See **Jews.** Read 'Anti-Semitism' in Janowsky, *The American Jew* (1942).

Antiseptics, in surgery, those substances which prevent sepsis or wound infection from pyogenic organisms, either by destroying such organisms or arresting their development. The employment of such agencies is known as *antisepsis;* and the system of treating surgical wounds by their use, as *antiseptic surgery.* Strictly speaking, antisepsis and antiseptic surgery are to be distinguished from asepsis and aseptic surgery, the latter terms implying the total exclusion of germs from the operative field rather than their destruction or inhibition. In modern surgical practice, however, the two methods are so closely combined that they may be properly considered together.

Modern antiseptic surgery dates from about 1867, when Lord Lister, realizing that putrefactive processes—sepsis—constitute the chief danger which the surgeon has to combat in dealing with accidental and operative wounds, introduced his method of treatment based upon the fact that certain chemical substances have the power to destroy or inhibit the action of those germs by which fermentative processes are induced. By the use of carbolic acid as a germicide he reduced the death rate after major operations from 45 per cent. to 15 per cent. in his wards at Glasgow; and later, when he had further developed his method, to about 12 per cent. in his wards at Edinburgh. In 1881 Koch of Berlin drew attention to the germicidal properties of bichloride of mercury, and his suggestion of its use in 1-1,000 aqueous solution was almost universally adopted. The number of antiseptics now in use is very large. In 1915 it was announced that Drs. Alexis Carrel and Henry D. Dakin had discovered a new antiseptic of great value, much used in World War I. A similar discovery was made independently by a British scientist, Professor Lorrelin Smith. In *medicine* antiseptics are used for their effect on the alimentary, respiratory, or genito-urinary tract. In the *arts* antiseptics include all substances which prevent or arrest putrefacton and analogous fermentative changes. See DISINFECTANTS.

Anti-Slavery. See **Abolitionists; Slavery.**

Anti-Slavery Society, American, an organization advocating the immediate and total abolition of slavery in the United States, was formed at Philadelphia in 1833 under the leadership of William Lloyd Garrison. In 1840 a majority of the Society's membership, who favored concerted political action, withdrew and helped to found the Liberty Party. The Society continued in existence until 1870. See ABOLITIONISTS; SLAVERY.

Antisthenes (*c.* 445-370 B.C.), founder of the Cynic school of philosophy, was a friend and follower of Socrates, and died at Athens at the age of seventy. Antisthenes held that virtue mainly consists in voluntary abstinence from pleasure, and in a stern contempt of riches, honors, and even learning. He attracted many imitators, among them Diogenes; from his school possibly the Stoics sprang. See CYNICS.

Antistrophe, in poetry, a portion of a poem following a strophe and corresponding to it. In rhetoric, the repetition of the same word at the conclusion of successive clauses—as, 'Wit is dangerous, eloquence is dangerous, everything is dangerous that has efficiency and vigor for its characteristics.'

Antithesis (Gr. *anti,* 'against,' and *thesis,* from *tithēmi,* 'I place'), an opposition or contrast of ideas expressed by bringing words that are the natural opposites of each other close together so as to produce a strong contrast. 'He dazzles more, but pleases less.' Antithesis, when it is naturally and moderately employed, gives liveliness to style; but becomes wearisome when too often repeated.

Antitoxins. See **Serum; Serum Therapy.**

Anti-Trust Legislation. See **Trusts.**

Antium, (modern **Anzio**), an ancient city of Latium, built on a rocky promontory. Stronghold of the Volscian pirates who fought Rome bitterly; later a favorite resort of the wealthy Romans. Among the ruins of their villas and palaces were found the Apollo Belvedere and the Borghese Gladiator. It was the birthplace of the Emperors Caligula and Nero.

Antivari, (Montenegrin *Bar*), town, Montenegro, on the Adriatic coast; 18 m. n.w. of Scutari. The port is at Prstan. Antivari was assigned to Montenegro by the Treaty of Berlin in 1878. During the Great War it was bombarded by the Austrians in January, 1916; p. 2,200.

Anti-Vivisection. See **Vivisection.**

Antlers, bony outgrowths from the frontal bones of almost all the members of the deer family. Except in the reindeer they are restricted to the males, and are secondary sexual characters used as weapons in fighting for possession of the females. They appear as a pair of knobs covered with dark skin, from which the bony tissue is developed. In the year after that of birth, the antlers remain unbranched conical 'beams.' In the following spring, the previous growth having been meanwhile shed, the antlers grow to a larger size, and form their first branch or 'brow.' Year by year the number of branches or 'tines' increases, and more than sixty have been counted on some magnificent heads. The soft hairy skin which secures their rapid annual growth is known as the 'velvet,' and its accidental injury affects the development of the antlers. The antlers are shed, in many cases at least, annually, after the breeding period. Antlers being of very tough, hard material and convenient form, they have been utilized by both savage and civilized men for many purposes.

Antlia Pneumatica, 'the Air Pump,' a southern constellation, placed by Lacaille, in 1752, between Argo and Hydra.

Ant-lion, the larva of an insect (*Myrmeleon*) of the order Neuroptera, remarkable for the ingenuity of its insect-catching habits. Some species are common in North America. The ant-lion feeds upon the juices of insects, especially ants, in order to obtain which it cleverly excavates a funnel-shaped pitfall in sandy ground, and lies in wait at the bottom, often with all but its mandibles buried in the sand. When insects approach too near to the edge of the hole, the loose sand gives way, so that they fall down the steep slope. If they do not fall quite to the bottom, but begin to scramble up again, the ant-lion throws sand upon them by jerking its head, and thus brings them back.

Antofagasta, a town and port, Chile, in Antofagasta province, connected with the

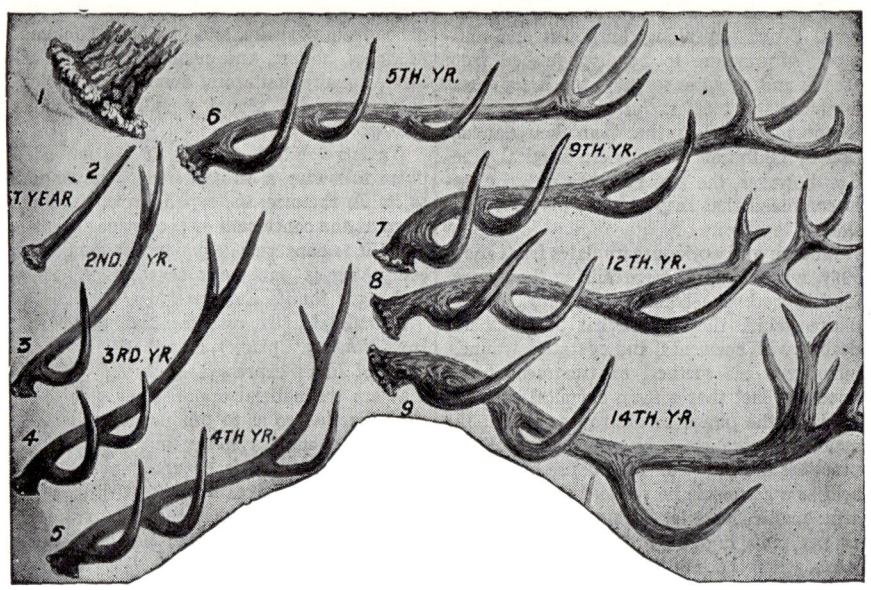

Typical Forms of Antlers.—Nos. 1-9, Red deer (1, burr enlarged).

rich silver fields of Caracoles and Huanchaca; p. 36,114.

Antofagasta, largest province of Chile, lies within the great Atacama desert. Silver, lead, manganese, iron, borax, guano, and salt-petre are the principal commercial products. The capital is Antofagasta. Area 46,408 sq. m.; p. 172,330.

Antokolski, Mark Matveyevitch (1843-1902), Russian Jewish sculptor, born in Vilna, achieved his greatest success by his statue of Ivan the Terrible. His important works include *Christ Before the People,* 1874; *Mephistopheles,* 1881; *Death of Socrates,* 1876, and portrait statues of famous contemporaries.

Antomarchi, Francesco (1780-1838), Italian surgeon, was born in Corsica. He studied medicine at Pisa and had acquired some celebrity as an anatomist, when he was induced in 1818 to go to St. Helena as physician to Napoleon I. He wrote *Les derniers moments de Napoléon,* 1823.

Antonelli, Giacomo (1806-76), Italian cardinal and statesman, was born at Sonnino; he was raised to the dignity of cardinal in 1847 by Pius IX., and was made premier in 1848 in the liberal cabinet which framed the famous *Statuto* or Constitution proclaimed in 1848.

Antonine Column, a column erected at Rome in 176 A.D. in commemoration of the victories of Marcus Aurelius.

Antonine Itinerary, a work giving a survey of the principal land and sea routes in the Roman empire, published in the reign of the Emperor Antoninus Caracalla, but based upon a survey made between the consulship of Julius Cæsar (44 B.C.) and the reign of the Emperor Augustus.

Antonine's Wall, a Roman rampart erected between the Firths of Forth and Clyde, Scotland, in 140-142 A.D., during the reign of Antoninus Pius, to restrain the encroachments of the northern tribes. Following the earlier line of Agricola's forts (81 A.D.), it extended some 40 miles.

Antoninus Pius, Titus Aurelius Fulvus Boionius Arrius (86-161 A.D.), Roman Emperor (138-61), was born during the reign of Domitian of a family originally from Nemausus, now Nîmes, in Gaul. In 138 he was adopted by the Emperor Hadrian, and in the same year came to the throne. His reign was proverbially peaceful and happy, forming, along with those of his immediate predecessors, Trajan and Hadrian, and that of his successor, Marcus Aurelius, the Golden Age of the Roman Empire. In his private character he was simple, temperate, and benevolent; while in public affairs he acted as the father of his people.

Antonio de Sedilla, (c.1730-1829), Spanish missionary priest, was sent to New Orleans in 1779. By his numerous charities, he greatly endeared himself to the people by whom he was popularly known as Père Antoine.

Antonius, the name of several distinguished Romans.

Marcus Antonius (143-87 B.C.), called *Orator,* was prætor in 104 B.C., governor of Cilicia in 103 B.C., and consul in 99 B.C. He figures in Cicero's *De Oratore.*

Gaius Antonius, surnamed Hybrida, son of the above-named, was expelled from the Senate in 70 B.C., but was Cicero's colleague as prætor in 65, and as consul in 63.

Marcus Antonius (83-30 B.C.), the famous Mark Antony of the Second Triumvirate, son of Marcus Antonius Creticus and Julia, sister of L. Julius Cæsar, was brought up in the house of Lentulus, a fellow-conspirator with Catiline. He became consul with Cæsar in 44 B.C., and on the latter's assassination, so wrought upon the passions of the people by his famous funeral oration that the conspirators were forced to flee from Rome, leaving him in possession of almost absolute power. Antony's claims were disputed, however, by Octavianus, the great-nephew and adopted son of Cæsar, who afterwards became the Emperor Augustus, later the Second Triumvirate—Octavianus, Antony, and Lepidus—was formed. A new division of the Roman world was arranged, Antony taking the East, and Octavian the West, while Lepidus had to be content with Africa.

The character of Antony is vividly portrayed in Shakespeare's *Julius Cæsar* and *Antony and Cleopatra.* Cicero's *Letters* and *Philippics* give contemporary but biased evidence as to his career. There is also a *Life* by Plutarch.

Antony, Mark. See **Antonius, Marcus** (3).

Antony, or **Anthony, St., of Padua** (1195-1231), was born in Lisbon. He is credited with many miracles, and is usually represented as the patron saint of the lower animals. In the Roman calendar his feast is June 13. Consult biographies by Hilaire, Beale, and Mrs. A. Bell.

Antony, or **Anthony, St., of Thebes,** known also as Antony the Great (?251-356), founder of Christian monasticism, was born at Coma in Upper Egypt. He founded a monastery, at first merely a group of scattered and separate cells, near Memphis. His immediate following at his death numbered 15,000. His festival is on Jan. 17. The temptations of St. Anthony, and other incidents of his life, many of them legendary, have afforded numerous subjects for sacred art.

St. Antony's Fire was the name given to a pestilential epidemic, also called the *sacred fire,* which in 1089 swept off great numbers, especially in France; it being held that many sufferers had been cured through the intercession of St. Antony. The disease was commonly supposed to be erysipelas, which is still frequently known as St. Antony's Fire. See Erysipelas.

Antraigues, Emanuel Louis Henri de Launay, Count d' (1755-1812), French diplomat, was born in Villeneuve, department of

Ardèche. In 1788 he published *Mémoires sur les Etats-Généraux*, which, by its advocacy of liberty, helped to bring on the French Revolution. Consult *Life* by Pingaud.

Antrim, maritime county in the n.e. of Ireland, province of Ulster, including Loughs Neagh and Beg in the s. and s.w. It is 57 m. long, 28 m. wide, and has 90 m. of seacoast. The area is 1,192 sq. m. Here is the Giant's Causeway, one of the finest examples of columnar basalt in the world. There are many peat bogs, but more than three-fourths of the area of the county is under cultivation, in tillage and pasture This county is the center of the Irish linen industry; cotton goods and coarse woolens are also manufactured, and much beautiful hand embroidery is made and sold by the householders.

Antwerp (Fr. *Anvers;* Flem. *Antwerpan,* 'on the wharf'), city, Belgium, capital of the province of Antwerp. The layout of the city includes three 'rings' or circles of forts, upon which the heavy German siege guns wrought terrible havoc in the fall of 1914. The most noteworthy of the city's buildings is the six-aisled cathedral, 1352-1518, one of the noblest Gothic structures in Belgium. It is a cruciform structure, 284 ft. long, 212 ft. wide, and 130 ft. high, and has an exquisite spire, in which hangs a splendid carillon of ninety-nine bells. The interior of the cathedral is ornamented with paintings by Rubens, including the famous 'Descent from the Cross' and the 'Assumption.' Before the invasion of Belgium by Germany in 1914, Antwerp carried on a flourishing trade and commerce. The history of Antwerp extends back as far as the 7th century, when it was known as a market town. During the first part of the 16th century, it was the commercial capital of the world. In 1576, during the 'Furie Espagnole,' Spanish soldiers seized the town, killed some 8,000 persons, and burned hundreds of buildings. From 1794 until 1814 Antwerp was held by the French. The union of Belgium with Holland, in 1815, gave an additional impetus to the commercial development of Antwerp, which had a wonderfully prosperous career from 1863 until 1914, when the German invasion took place. Some of the greatest masters of painting had their homes there—among them, Van Dyck, Rubens, Cornelius de Vos, Jordaens, and the two Teniers.

A new interest attaches to Antwerp because of the part the city played in the defense of Belgium during the invasion by the Germans in the fall of 1914. The German forces poured across the Belgian border on Aug. 4, 1914; between Aug. 15 and Aug. 17, the seat of the Belgian government was transferred to Antwerp; and on Aug. 19 the principal Belgian army, accompanied by King Albert, retired thither before an overwhelming drive of German troops. For the next five weeks the city was comparatively quiet, but on Sept. 25, heavy German guns were brought up, and by Sept. 28 these had been put in place and brought to bear with terrible effect upon the fortifications of the town. British reinforcements arrived on Oct. 3 and 5, but it soon became clear that retirement alone could save the Belgian army. The work of transferring the base at night to Ostend was splendidly carried out, and on the nights of Oct. 5 and 7 the Belgian army began its retirement to Ghent and the seacoast. At the same time, while Antwerp was undergoing intense bombardment, practically the entire civilian population of about 400,000 men, women, and children, withdrew from the beleaguered city. See EUROPE, GREAT WAR OF. It was again seized by the Germans, 1940; p. 277,929.

Anu, a Babylonian deity, supreme god of heaven.

Anubis, an Egyptian deity, usually represented in the form of a man with the head of a jackal or dog. He was the god of embalming, and the assistant of Osiris in weighing the hearts of the dead. The Greeks identified him with Hermes, and he was worshipped in Rome as Mercury.

Anura, an order of Amphibians characterized by absence of the tail in the adult, and including the frogs and toads. See AMPHIBIA; FROGS; TOAD.

Anus, the external opening of the rectum. See RECTUM.

Anvari, or **Anwari, Auhad uddin Ali,** a celebrated Persian poet who flourished during the 12th century, was born in Khorassan. His verses exhibit consummate skill and great satirical powers.

Anzacs, a term composed of the initial letters of the words Australia New Zealand Army Corps, and used to designate the Australasian military forces in the Great War (1914-1918). The name was coined by the troops while they were in the Levant.

On the morning of Aug. 5, 1914, Australia and New Zealand received the news that England had decided to stand with France, against Germany. Although the Australian Parliament was at the time dissolved, the Prime Minister with full popular consent immediately offered Great Britain a first contingent of 20,000 men. By the end of November 1914, the first Anzac contingent of about 30,000 infantry, cavalry, and artillery sailed for Egypt. It was in the spring of 1915, however, during the Dardanelles campaign, that the Anzacs first made themselves famous. From that time on they played a distinguished part in the war.

Aoki, Viscount Siuzo (1844-1914), Japanese statesman, first Japanese ambassador to the United States 1906-07.

Aorist (Gr. 'indefinite'), a tense of the Greek verb expressing indefinite past time.

Aorta. See **Heart.** The chief diseases of the aorta are atheroma, fatty degeneration, calcification, and aneurism.

Aosta (anc. *Augusta Prætoria*), tn. and episc. see of Italy. The walls are in great part those constructed by the Romans. Birthplace of Anselm; p. 7,554.

The VAL D'AOSTA is one of the most charming valleys of the Piedmontese Alpine country. Cretinism is common among the people.

Aoudad, Aoul, or **Arui,** a wild sheep (*Ovis tragelaphus*) inhabiting the mountains of northwestern Africa and familiar in menageries.

Apaches, N. American Indians, who formerly ranged over the southwestern parts of the United States, and the northern provinces of Mexico, but are now confined to reservations in New Mexico and Arizona where, with their Navajo kinsmen, they numbered (1903) about 6,090. *Handbook of American Indians* (1907).

Apaffi. (1.) Michael I., prince of Transylvania (1632-90); (2.) MICHAEL II. (1667-1713), son of above, also a prince of Transylvania.

Apalachicola. (1), River in southeast part of the U. S. (2) Town and port of entry, Florida; p. 3,065.

Apar, an armadillo of the genus Tolypeutes, especially the three-banded armadillo, which defies its enemies by quickly rolling into a ball.

Apatite is a phosphate of lime with fluoride or chloride of lime, or more usually a mixture of these last two ($FCa_5P_3O_{12}$). It has various forms, but always crystallizes in hexagonal prisms. It is soluble in dilute nitric acid, and with ammonium molybdate the solution gives a yellow precipitate (test for phosphates). Apatite is the principal natural phosphate of the crystalline rocks. As phosphoric acid is an essential constituent of the food of both plants and animals, vegetable and animal life are dependent on the existence of apatite in the earth's crust. The phosphates in sedimentary rocks and in soils are derived from the apatite set free by the disintegration of the older crystalline rock masses. The lime phosphate known in commerce as apatite contains many impurities.

Apatornis, one of the primitive toothed birds, closely allied to Ichthyornis (q.v.).

Ape, a term sometimes used to designate the anthropoid apes only, and sometimes quite indefinitely for the monkeys, baboons, and their allies of the order Primates.

Anthropoid apes are those of the largest size, most advanced organization and attainments, include the chimpanzees, gorillas, orang-utan and gibbons. They are entirely of the Old World, and differ more widely from the American than from the Old World branch of the Primates. Though arboreal for the most part, when they come to the ground they walk more erect than do the baboons or monkeys, and rest their weight upon the outside of the closed fingers, not upon the palm of the hand. None of the anthropoids has a tail, any cheek-pouches or ischial callosities, except the last, of small size, in the gibbons. The hair is more scanty—an approach to man. The placenta differs in detail from that in the lower apes and is exactly like that of man, and they have a vermiform appendix. The gorilla is regarded as the most advanced and manlike, and the gibbons as nearest to the lower apes. Consult Hartmann, *Anthropoid Apes* (1886); Haeckel, *The Last Link* (1898); and see CHIMPANZEE; GORILLA; ORANG; GIBBON.

Apeldoorn, tn., Netherlands. Near it is Castle Loo, the summer residence of the royal family; p. 25,761.

Apelles, the most celebrated painter of ancient Greece, contemporary of Alexander the Great, his patron. Two of his greatest pictures were, *Alexander wielding a Thunderbolt*, in the temple of Artemis in Ephesus; and *Aphrodite Anadyomene* (*i.e.* rising out of the sea), in the temple of Æsculapius in Cos. See Wustmann's *Apelles' Leben und Werke* (1870), Woltmann and Woermann, Eng. Trans. vol. I. (1886).

Apelt, Ernst Friedrich (1812-59), professor of philosophy (1840-59), Jena, author of philosophical works.

Apennines (anc. *Mons Apenninus*), one of the principal mountain ranges in Europe, running the entire length (some 750 m.) of the Italian peninsula, and continued through Sicily. The Apennines are, as a rule, bare and picturesquely rugged in their higher altitudes, but their lower slopes are clothed with forests. The system is poor in minerals, but is especially rich in marble. The Romans made roads over the Pietra Mala Pass between Florence and Bologna; the Furlo Pass, flanked by rocky walls over 1,500 ft.; the Via Salaria, between the Sibillini Mountains and the Gran Sasso; and the Caudine Forks, between Naples and Benevento. Railways now unite the two coast belts. See Partsch's '*Die Hauptketten des Centralen Apennins*,' in *Verhandl. d. Gesch. f. Erdkunde zu Berlin* (1889); and *L'Appenino Modenese* (1895).

Aperients, or **Laxatives,** are the mildest class of purgatives, intended to assist the natural action of the bowels. As examples of 'natural aperients,' one may instance hot or cold water taken on an empty stomach, ripe fruits generally, whole-meal bread, oatmeal biscuits. See CONSTIPATION; also MINERAL WATERS.

Apex (in Mining Law). The end of a mineral vein or lode which projects above the enclosing bed-rock. In the American law of mines it has come to be the accepted doctrine that the owner of a mining claim which includes the apex of a vein may follow that vein on the dip even into and through the land of another. This doctrine has been a source of

Apes—Anthropoid.—Upper Left, Hoolock Gibbon. Middle Left, Chimpanzee. Upper Right, Orang-utan. Lower Right, Gorilla.

great confusion in mining rights and consequently of much litigation.

Aphasia (Gr. 'absence of speech'), total or partial loss of the power of speech, either spoken or written. Some extend the meaning, and include the misunderstanding of what is said (word-deafness), and inability to read words (word-blindness). Aphasia, in any of these cases, is the term used only when consciousness is unaffected, and the intellect otherwise normal. See also AMNESIA.

Aphelion (Gr. 'away from the sun'). The planets revolve round the sun in elliptical orbits; and the sun is situated, not at the centre of these orbits, but at one of the two points known as the foci. The greater axis of each ellipse is the line passing through the centre and the foci. At one extremity of this axis the planet is at its greatest distance from the sun, and at the other extremity at its least distance. The former is known as the aphelion, the latter as the perihelion.

closely resemble their surroundings. They are greatly relished as food, not only by birds and other insect-eaters, but also to a much greater extent by other insects, notably 'ladybirds' (beetles). The cottony threads of 'American blight' (*Schizoneura lanigera*), and the shell-like shields of various bark-lice, are instances of a great variety of protective coverings formed by aphids, giving the name 'scale-insects' to many of the best-known fruit-pests (*Phylloxera vastatrix*). Consult Howard, *Insect Book* (1901), and authorities mentioned under special heads.

Aphonia (Gr. 'voicelessness'), loss of voice, sometimes due to disease of the larynx or vocal cords. sometimes to nervous disorders. See VOICE.

Aphorism, a concise statement of some truth, generally more or less abstract, such as, 'Wisdom is knowledge in action.'

Aphrodite, called VENUS by the Romans, the goddess of love and beauty. As her name

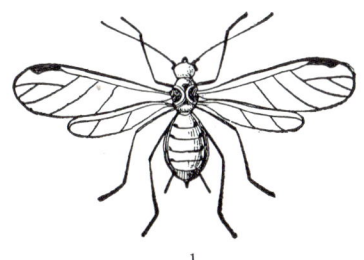 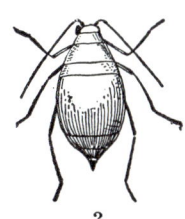

1   2
Aphids.
1.—Winged male of greenfly.   2.—Wingless form.

Aphids are the minute bugs known to gardeners as plant-lice, green-fly, etc., which feed by puncturing plants and sucking the juices, and in some instances they are so destructive as to become ruinous pests, owing to the enormous rapidity with which they reproduce, and the elaboration of the arrangements by means of which they migrate from one host to another, or from one region of the same host to another. Most aphids secrete a sugary substance which exudes through two tube-like apertures near the hinder end of the body, and forms a sweet food upon which the young are at first fed. Of this ants are extremely fond, and they will assiduously attend upon and arrange to protect aphid colonies in order to get it, promoting the secretion by stroking the aphids. They also carry aphids to their nests, and care for them like herds of cows, in order to maintain a constantly accessible supply of the honey. In color aphids

indicates, she sprang from the sea-foam, though in the *Iliad* Zeus and Dione are said to be her parents. By the famous judgment of Paris, described in Tennyson's *Œnone*, she was declared the most beautiful of the goddesses. Her girdle had the miraculous power of granting invincible charms to others. In works of art she is constantly represented with her son Eros (Cupid). Of the statues which remain may be mentioned the celebrated Venus of Milo in the Louvre, found in 1820 on the island Milos. Compare also VENUS.

Aphthæ, small gray and yellow catarrhal patches, occurring singly or in groups, on the mucous membrane of the mouth.

Apios. See **Ground-nut.**

Apis (in the hieroglyphics *Hapi*, 'the hidden'), a sacred bull worshipped by the Egyptians at Memphis. He was not allowed to live more than twenty-five years. If he died before his allotted span, he was buried in the temple of Serapis, called the Serapeum. After his death he became an Osiris or Osiris-Hapi, whence by corruption came the name of Serapis, which the Greeks and Romans gave to the Egyptian god. Mariette's discoveries of the Serapeum at Memphis (1856) threw much light upon the cult of Apis. See Mariette's *Le Sérapéum de Memphis* (1882).

Aplanatic, a combination of lenses so arranged as to bring parallel rays to a focus without spherical or chromatic aberration.

Apnœa (Gr. 'breathlessness'), strictly applied only to that form of breathlessness which is caused by hyperoxygenation of the blood, when breathing, for the time, has become unnecessary; but also applied to cessation of breathing from any cause.

Apocalyptic Literature, a peculiar type of Jewish literature which originated in the time of Israel's oppression by the Syrians, and furnished a consolatory forecast of the future of the nation. These apocalyptic writings, of which the Book of Daniel is the earliest example, did much not only to quicken the Messianic hope, but also to produce among the people that political unrest which culminated in the revolt against the Romans in A.D. 66. They were largely the compositions of Jewish Christians. For these works, see Charles's article in the *Ency. Biblica,* and Porter's *The Message of the Apocalyptical Writers* (1905).

Apocarpous, in botany a term used to designate fruits made up of separate carpels, the product of a single flower.

Apocatastasis, the return at length of all lost souls and fallen angels to divine forgiveness.

Apocrenic Acid, a compound in soil containing rotting vegetable substances, and in the yellow deposit of chalybeate waters.

Apocrypha (Grk. *apo* 'away' and *kruptein* 'to hide,' 'hidden away'). In its earlier use applied to books 'hidden away' either (1) to keep knowledge from the uninitiated or (2) from the initiated but unlearned. The Apocrypha proper include the following, arranged in the order of the English Bible: 1 Esdras; 2 Esdras; Tobit; Judith; the Additions to Esther; the Wisdom of Solomon; Ecclesiasticus; Baruch; the Song of the Three Holy Children; the History of Susanna; Bel and the Dragon; the Prayer of Manasses; 1 Maccabees; 2 Maccabees. Two other so-called books of Maccabees—3 Maccabees and 4 Maccabees—are contained in some important MSS. of the Septuagint.

The books may be classified critically as genuine, legendary, pseudepigraphic, or supplementary additions to canonical books, or ethnologically as Persian-Palestinian, pure Palestinian, and Jewish-Alexandrian. But it is simpler to arrange them according to their literary character as narrative, including (a) historical and (b) legendary, prophetic, including apocalyptic, and didactic. Most of them belong to the first class. Only 1 Maccabees, however, can rank as history. It furnishes an authentic record of the 40 years from the accession of Antiochus Epiphanes to the death of Simon (B.C. 175-135). 2 Maccabees covers only the period B.C. 176-161, and is by comparison inaccurate and highly colored.

Although some of these books (*e.g.* Ecclesiasticus and 1 Maccabees) were originally written in Hebrew, none of them ever found a place in the Jewish canon. But the Jews of Alexandria, unlike their Palestinian brethren, drew no sharp distinction between prophets and the later Scriptures, and did not scruple to include in the Septuagint other sacred writings besides the 24 books of the Hebrew canon. As the Greek Bible remained practically the Bible of the Christian Church for centuries, the place given by it to the Apocrypha conferred upon some of these books an exaggerated importance. But in relation to Jewish history, and apart altogether from the question of canonicity, the apocryphal books as a whole are of singular interest and value. Except the writings of Josephus, who was largely indebted to them, the Apocrypha form the only important source of information for the period between the Testaments. In this connection, 1 Maccabees, as a trustworthy record, is of priceless worth; and most of the other books afford significant glimpses into the internal condition and religious feelings of the people. Generally speaking, and in spite of the chilling influence of a rigid Pharisaism, they mark an advance in the religious life of the Jews as compared with the position reached in the time of Nehemiah. There is reflected in them a deeper reverence for the law, a purer monotheism, a stronger Messianic hope, and a clearer apprehension of a future life. Some of them also present an interesting combination of Jewish thought and Greek philosophy, especially the Book of Wisdom.

The Apocrypha are, however, inferior to

the canonical Scriptures in originality and strength. Instead of the freshness and simplicity of the earlier literature, we have the mechanical stiffness, the artificial and florid verbiage, and the imitation of older models which show that the nation had begun to live on its past. That books should have been issued under assumed names was perhaps a necessity in times of persecution; but such distortions of Old Testament narratives as sometimes occur as well as the introduction of ostensibly genuine but really fabricated official documents indicate that these writings are on a lower plane than the canonical books.

Besides the O. T. Apocrypha proper, 'an unspeakable quantity of apocryphal writings' were current in the early centuries of our era. The great value of these in tracing the development of thought from the Old to the New Testament is increasingly recognized. Hardly a doctrine of the N. T. exists which is not either expressed or implied in these books. Those that survive group themselves naturally into two divisions, according as they link themselves on to the Old or to the New Testament. See Fabricius, *Codex Apoc. N. T.* (1719; 2nd ed. 1743); James, *Apocrypha Anecdota* (1897). For an English translation of the apocryphal Gospels, Acts, and Revelations, based on Tischendorf's edition of these writings, see vol. XVI. of Clark's *Ante-Nicene Christian Library* (1897).

Apocynaceæ, an order of plants represented in America chiefly by the cultivated creeping blue periwinkles, and the dogbanes. Among the most important species are several producing india-rubber, trees yielding dita and other medicinal barks, cow-tree of Demerara, and ordeal-nut tree of Madagascar.

Apodictic, or **Apodeictic** (Gr. 'proving'), in logic, a term applied to judgments which admit of no contradiction, their truth being implied in the nature of thought or reason.

Apogee (Gr. 'away from the earth'), that point in its orbit at which the moon is farthest from the earth—the point where it is nearest the earth being known as *perigee*.

Apol, L. F. H. (1850-   ), Dutch painter. His *January Evening in the Hague Wood* is in the Amsterdam Museum.

Apollinaris, a spring in the Prussian prov. of Rhineland. It became known for the well-known alkaline Apollinaris water.

Apollinaris. (1.) The Elder, native of Alexandria (4th century A.D.), was associa-ted with his son in an attempt to reproduce the Old Testament in the form of classical poetry, and the New in the form of the Platonic dialogues. (2.) THE YOUNGER (d. 390 A.D.), bishop of Laodicea, son of the above, a controversial theologian upon whose teaching a sect, the Apollinarians, founded their creed.

Apollo, one of the great gods of the Greeks, and next to Zeus the most widely worshipped; son of Zeus and Leto (Latona), and twin-brother of Artemis. He was born in the island of Delos. He was worshipped as the god of punishment; as the god of prophecy; as the god of song and music, the patron of poets and the leader of the choir of the nine Muses, and as the god of the Sun—that is, the god of spiritual light. The wolf, swan, raven, hawk, cock, and crow were all sacred to him. The APOLLO BELVEDERE, the most famous statue of the god, discovered in 1495, among the ruins of ancient Antium, and now in the Vatican, Rome, is perhaps the noblest representation of the human form.

Apollo of Rhodes. See **Colossus of Rhodes.**

Apollodorus. (1.) Greek painter, born in Athens (fl. B.C. 400). He is considered as the inventor of *chiaroscuro*, for he was the first to succeed in blending tones and in handling light and shade. (2.) Greek poet (300-260 B.C.), born at Carystus in Eubœa, writer of 47 comedies. (3.) A Greek grammarian of Athens (fl. *c.* 140 B.C.); wrote many works, all lost except the *Bibliotheca*. It has been edited by Heyne (1803) and by Bekker (Teubner Series, 1854). (4.) APOLLODORUS of Damascus, architect in Rome during the reigns of Trajan and Hadrian. He is the author of a book about war-machines, entitled *Poliorcetica*, republished in Wescher's *Poliorcétique des Grecs* (1867).

Apollonia. (1.) An important ancient town in Illyria. (2.) Ancient town of Thrace, a colony of Milesia; it held a famous statue of Apollo.

Apollonius. (1.) Pergæus (3d century B.C.), known in his own age as the 'great geometer,' passed his life in Alexandria, at the time when the Ptolemies IV. and V. were kings of Egypt. Of his many books, only the *magnum opus* on conic sections and the *De Sectione Rationis* have come down to us. (2.) RHODUS (*c.* 240-180 B.C.), born at Alexandria, was famous both as poet and scholar. His only surviving work is an epic poem in four books, the *Argonautica*, describing the adventures of the Argonauts. It is the first love poem of antiquity; and may perhaps be considered the remote parent of the modern novel. Eng. prose trans., E. P. Cleridge (1889). (3). MOLON Greek rhetorician of the 1st century B.C. (4) TYANEUS 'of Tyana' (c. 4 B.C.-96 A.D.), a Pythagorean philosopher. He certainly was a man of remarkable powers and influence, and many notable sayings are attributed to him. None of his writings are extant. See PHILOSTRATUS. (5.) DYSCOLOS ('bad-tempered'), originator of scientific grammar; born in Alexandria. Bekker edited his works in 1817, the most notable of these being that *On Syntax*.

Apollonius of Tyre, a Latin romance of the 3rd or 4th century, is undoubtedly derived from a lost Greek original. The story forms the foundation of Shakespeare's *Pericles* (1609).

Apollos, a Jew of Alexandria, who, embracing Christianity, became noted, first in Ephesus and afterwards in Corinth, as an eloquent preacher of the gospel.

Apollyon, a Greek word signifying 'destroyer,' employed to translate the Hebrew word *Abaddon*.

Apologetics is the science of the Christian *apology* or 'defence.' Four subdivisions may be named:—

1. Independently of the Christian revelation, it may be held that reason, or conscience, proves the being of God, the existence of a soul, freedom of will, and immortality. (See THEISM.)

2. Passing now to the Christian revelation proper, apologetics involves the truth of the broad outlines of New Testament history. This is sometimes spoken of as historical evidence.

3. External evidence. The miracles, as a divine seal, are held to prove that the message spoken by Christ, or by His authorized representatives, is to be received as from God. Along with miracles, prophecies are also relied on.

4. Internal evidence. See Bruce's *Chief End of Revelation* (1881); R. Mackintosh's *First Primer of Apologetics* (1900); F. S. Beattie's *Apologetics* (3 vols. 1903).

Apologia pro Vita sua, religious autobiography by Cardinal Newman (1864).

Apologue (Gr.), a fictitious narrative used to convey moral lessons; it is a general term of which fable, parable, etc., are the varieties. For the differences between apologue and allegory, see ALLEGORY.

Apomorphine, Hydrochloride of, is the most powerful and certain of all emetics, and may be given hypodermically.

Aponeurosis, a broad, fibrous expansion of a tendon, attaching a muscle at its origin or insertion.

Apophysis, a prominent elevation or process of a bone which has no independent centre of ossification, being thus distinguished from an *epiphysis*. In botany, a swelling under the base of the spore-case of some mosses.

Apoplexy, the state of insensibility caused by the rupture of a cerebral vessel, or the blocking of one by an embolus or a thrombus. The attack is more or less sudden in its onset. The patient may fall down suddenly, utterly motionless and unconscious; or he may feel powerlessness and lethargy slowly creeping over him. He may have a convulsion. The patient may die at once or he may recover, with impaired powers. There are several other conditions with which apoplexy may be confounded: for instance, drunkenness, other narcotic poisoning as by opium, epilepsy, syncope or fainting, and uræmic convulsions, all have their points of likeness. Unequal pupils are strong evidence in favor of apoplexy.

Aposiopesis (Gr.), an abrupt breaking away from a sentence, and leaving it unfinished, for the sake of greater effect.

Apospory. See **Fern**.

Apostasy, originally a soldier's desertion in war; later, in early Christian times, the desertion or perversion from the discipline of church or order.

A posteriori. See **A priori**.

Apostle (Gr. 'ambassador'—*i.e.* not merely the *messenger* but also the *representative* of the sender) was the name applied by Jesus to those disciples whom He specially commissioned to preach the gospel and heal the sick. They received a second commission after the resurrection. Their number, twelve, corresponding to the twelve tribes of Israel, does not seem, after Christ's departure, to have been regarded as fixed. In their apostolic labors their field was the world. See Lightfoot's *Comm. on Galatians* (10th ed. 1890).

Apostles. Teaching of the Twelve.

Apostles' Creed. See **Creeds**.

Apostles' Islands, or **The Twelve Apostles**, a cluster of 27 islands, in Lake Superior, covered with valuable timber.

Apostle Spoons, spoons which terminated in an image of one of the apostles, usually made in sets of thirteen.

Apostolic Fathers, a name applied to the

authors of an important group of writings dating from the transition period between the apostles proper and the theological apologists of the 2nd century A.D. See Donaldson's *Apostolic Fathers* (1874) and translations in *The Ante-Nicene Christian Fathers*, i. (1887).

Apostrophe. (1.) A grammatical sign (') denoting the omission of a letter or letters in a word—ne'er, don't. In the genitive singular of nouns it is used to indicate the suppression of the vowel in the old termination *es*—son's in place of sones. The apostrophe in the genitive plural (as in sons') has no etymological justification. (2.) A rhetorical figure of speech by which the speaker addresses his remarks directly to the object of them.

Apothegm, or **Apophthegm** (Gr. 'from a word'), a short, pithy, and sententious saying, as distinguished from a maxim, which is a truth useful for practical guidance in life, and from an aphorism, which contains a statement of some abstract truth. The most famous collection in our literature is Bacon's *Apophthegms New and Old* (1625).

Apotheosis, the deification of mortals. Originating in ancestor-worship, its later development among the higher races, was due to the desire of men in power to add divine attributes to their honors.

Appalachian Mountain Club, an organization, which dates from 1878, whose object is to preserve mountain and forest lands in New England.

Appalachians, the easternmost mountain system of N. America, separating the basin of the Mississippi from the streams flowing directly into the Atlantic. It extends from S.E. Canada in a s.w. direction through the United States as far as N. Georgia and Alabama, a distance of some 1,300 m. The average elevation may be given at about 2,500 ft. The more important ranges are the Adirondacks of New York; the Taconic Range and the Berkshire Hills of Massachusetts; the Green Mts. of Vermont; the White Mts. of New Hampshire, culminating in Mt. Washington (6,293 ft.); the Blue Ridge, stretching s. from Maryland, and broadening in N. Carolina into a plateau that bears irregular ranges such as the Great Smoky Mts. and the Black Mts., the latter having Mt. Mitchell (6,684 ft.), the highest point e. of the Rockies. The Alleghany Mts. are three parallel ranges s. of New York, and their name is often applied to the Appalachian system as a whole. See A. Guyot, *The Appalachian Mountain System*.

Appanage, more correctly APANAGE, originally, in French feudal law, grants made to the sons of the sovereign for their support.

Apparitions. See **Psychical Research.**

Appeal. The judicial process whereby a judgment, order or decree of a court of justice is carried up to a higher court for review. The appeal is an ancient institution in all legal systems and has been greatly favored in the United States, where it has in certain classes of cases become a serious menace to law and justice. This is particularly true in those jurisdictions where as many as three or four appeals to higher and still higher courts are allowed in a single case. See APPELLATE COURT.

In the legal procedure of the middle ages an appeal was a formal charge of felony whereby the accuser (appellant) offered to make good the charge 'on his body,' *i.e.* by offering battle. In this sense the term survived until the final abolition of trial by battle early in the last century.

Appeal, Court of. In the reformed judicial system of Great Britain, that branch of the High Court of Justice which hears appeals from the several divisional courts. See APPELLATE COURT.

Appeals, Court of. The title of various courts of appellate jurisdiction in the United States, usually courts of last resort. See APPELLATE COURT.

Appearance. See **Phenomenon.**

Appearance. The submission of the defendant in a lawsuit or other legal proceeding to the jurisdiction of the court. Failure to appear within the time limited therefor is default and entitles the plaintiff to the judgment, order or decree demanded by him.

Appellate Court. A court empowered to review the judgments, orders or decrees of another court or judge. In our legal system the court organized for the trial of causes in the first instance is usually composed of a single judge, whereas an appellate court consists of a 'bench' of three, five, seven, nine or more judges sitting together. An appellate court may be an intermediate tribunal, whose decisions are themselves subject to revision, or it may be a 'court of last resort.'

UNITED STATES. The multiplicity of appellate jurisdictions in the United States renders it impracticable to describe them in detail. In the federal judicial organization a Circuit Court of Appeals is provided to hear appeals from decisions of the Circuit and District Courts of the United States. This is a court of last resort for certain classes of cases, but in many others a further appeal lies to the Supreme Court of the United States. In a few jurisdictions the descriptive phrase 'Court of Errors' or 'Court for the Correction of Errors' has been employed to describe the ultimate court of appeal. Most of the American states, however, are still satisfied with a single system of appeals and a single appellate court.

Appendant. See **Appurtenances; Common.**

Appendix and **Appendicitis.** The appendix vermiformis is a slender, round, tapering process given off from and opening into the inner and back part of the cæcum, near the ilea-cæcal valve in the human intestine. It is usually 3½ in. long, though it varies greatly; its diameter is about equal to that of a goose quill. It is a rudimentary organ; hence its vitality is low, and it is liable to infection. Appendicitis occurs at all ages, most frequently between twenty and thirty. The usual symptoms are pain and tenderness. Early operative treatment for removal of the appendix is generally necessary. Appendicitis is always a surgical disease and should always be referred as soon as suspected to a surgeon; he should decide if or when operation must be performed.

Appenzell, canton in n.e. of Switzerland. In 1597, owing to religious disputes, it was divided into half cantons—Inner Rhodes being Romanist and pastoral; and Outer Rhodes Protestant and industrial. Both halves are practically entirely German-speaking, and have preserved their primitive democratic assemblies, which meet annually. The largest town in Outer Rhodes is Herisau; p. 13,497.

Apperception, as a psychological term signifies the process of mental assimilation, the process in which a new presentation receives significance by virtue of being referred to already existing knowledge—*e.g.,* certain motions of a flag become a signal for one who knows the code. A few years ago the definition and application of the apperceptive process was the most important topic of discussion in pedagogical circles and still constitutes one of the chief principles of Herbartian Pedagogy. See Lange's *Apperception;* Wundt's *Outlines of Psychology;* De Garmo's *Essentials of Method;* Baldwin's *Dictionary of Philosophy and Psychology.*

Appert, François (1797-1840), French technologist, who discovered a food-preserving process without the use of chemicals. It is the now familiar one used in canning.

Appiani, Andrea (1754-1817), a famous Italian fresco painter; born and died at Milan. His best works are a series of frescoes (*Amor and Psyche*) at Monza, and those in the Royal Palace at Milan.

Appianus, or **Appian,** the historian of Rome, was born at Alexandria, but lived in Rome about 100-140 A.D. His history was written in Greek, and gave a separate account of each district until it became part of the Roman empire. Editions: Text, Bekker 1852-3), Mendelssohn (1879-81)—both German; the latter trans. by H. White (1899).

Appian Way (Lat. *Via Appia*), Italy, an ancient Roman military road which connected Rome with Alba Longa, and thence led on to Capua, Beneventum, and Brundusium. It was begun in 312 B.C. It was carefully and solidly built, paved with blocks of hewn stones laid on cement, and was of an average breadth of 20 ft. Parts have been excavated and found in an excellent state of preservation. The new Appian Way runs from Rome to Albano, parallel to the above; it was made by Pope Pius VI. in 1789. Beside it stand the ruins of the basilica of St. Stephen (4th century), and the Acqua Santa baths.

Apple, the fruit of a tree (*Pyrus malus*) which grows wild throughout Europe except in the extreme north, Asia Minor, and Persia. All cultivated varieties have been derived from the wild (or crab) apple. Its cultivation has spread over the whole world, except where extremes of heat and cold prevent its growth. The tree flowers in May, and after the flowers have been fertilized by bees the anthers and petals fall, and the fleshy receptacle swells up to form the main part of the fruit, enclosing the ovary, which becomes the core of the apple. After numerous experiments a coreless and seedless variety has been developed in Colorado.

North America is the greatest apple-growing country in the world. Apples are propagated by means of seeds, grafts, and cuttings. The cultivated tree is at its prime when about fifty years old, but bears fruit considerably longer. See FRUIT; ORCHARDS. Consult Bailey's *The Apple Tree* (1922); *Farmer's Bulletins* (U. S. Department of Agriculture) and reports of the State Experiment Stations.

Apple of Sodom, or **Dead Sea Apple,** the fruit of a tree said to grow on the site of Sodom; according to Josephus and other ancient writers, it turned to ashes when plucked.

Appleton, Daniel (1785-1849), American publisher, founder of the house of 'D. Appleton and Co.,' was born in Haverhill, Mass. Having associated with him his son, William H. Appleton (1814-99), he began the publication of books on his own account in 1831. WILLIAM H. APPLETON was made a partner in 1838, and the firm assumed the name which it has continued to bear.

Appleton, Nathan (1779-1861), American merchant. Was instrumental in introducing into the United States the use of the power-loom for the manufacture of cotton cloth.

Appleton, Samuel (1766-1853), American merchant and philanthropist.

Appleton, Thomas Gold (1812-84), American author and a noted wit. His publications include: *Syrian Sunshine* (1877). Consult his *Life and Letters*, edited by Susan Hale.

Appleton, William Henry. See **Appleton, Daniel.**

Appoggiatura, an ornamental note in musical score used to embellish a melody, is a small note prefixed to a principal note, and may be long or short; in the latter case it is generally termed an *acciaccatura*, and has an oblique line across the end of its stem.

Appointment, the designation by proper authority of a person to hold an office of trust or honor.

Appomattox, village, formerly Appomattox Courthouse, Virginia. Here, on April 9, 1865, General Lee and the main Confederate army surrendered to General Grant; p. about 992.

Apponyi, Albert Georges, Count (1846-1933), Hungarian statesman.

Apportionment, the division of a rent, common, contract, incumbrance, etc. into parts. Thus, if a lessee be partially evicted under title paramount from a demised estate, the entire rent of which is due from every separate part, } ˋ becomes liable to pay only a rent apportioned to the value of the remainder of the estate from which he has not been evicted. The Apportionment Acts in the United States and England have made the principle of accrual from day to day general, so that now in nearly all instances of recurring payments apportionment is the rule (see ANNUITY).

Appraisement, the valuation of property, real or personal, by persons appointed pursuant to law or agreement for the purpose.

Apprehension. See **Arrest.**

Apprentice, a person bound to service in some trade or occupation during minority or for a definite term of years. An apprenticeship, though created by contract, is a species of domestic relation in which the master stands in a parental relation to the apprentice, with the obligation of supporting him, of caring for him in illness, and of instructing him in the master's trade, the apprentice on his part being bound to serve the master diligently and to render him due obedience.

In modern industry apprenticeship has lost much of its importance, and an apprenticeship is now a matter of special agreement. The term apprenticeship is also applied to the system of enlisting minors between the ages of fifteen and seventeen for service in the navy of the United States and for training in the duties of seamanship.

Appropriation, the application of specific sums of money to a particular purpose. The term is most frequently employed of the application of payments made by a debtor. In Constitutional Law *acts of appropriation* are measures by which the legislature sets apart sums of money for the use of the different departments of the executive.

Approximation, in mathematics, denotes a result which, though not rigorously accurate, is sufficiently accurate for the end in view. See GRAPHIC METHODS.

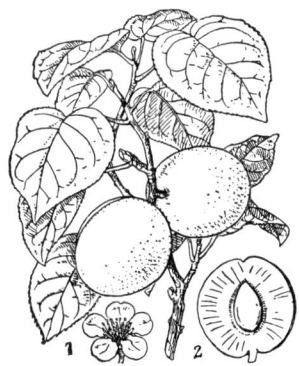

Apricot in Fruit.—1, Flower; 2, Section of fruit.

Appurtenances, rights in or over another's land which are regarded by law as attaching to another parcel of land for whose benefit the rights have been created.

Apraxin, Fedor, Count (1671-1728), Russian admiral, often considered the founder of the Russian navy.

Apricot (*Prunus armeniaca*), a species of the plum division of the Rosaceæ. The fruit is variable, but smaller than a peach, single-stoned, with a sweet or bitter kernel (seed) and golden or orange flesh, and a velvety skin of similar color, with pink or red on the sunny side. A distinct shallow groove runs down one side.

April, Month of. See **Year**.

April Fools' Day. See **All Fools' Day**.

A priori and **a posteriori.** The expression *a priori* is commonly applied to any knowledge which is general in its character, and thus independent of particular verifications: a general proof of the impossibility of squaring the circle makes it needless to examine particular attempts to solve the problem. *A posteriori* knowledge, on the other hand, must be referred to particular experience for its proof—as the proposition, 'Arsenic is poisonous.'

Apron, in engineering, a covering built to protect a surface from the action of flowing water or from heavy shocks.

Apsaras, a race of female beings in Hindu tradition, who bear a strong resemblance to the swan-maidens and seal-women of European folklore.

Apse, in ecclesiastical architecture, the easternmost portion of a church; the recess at the end of the chancel. See Basilica.

Apsheron (Per. 'sweet water') a peninsula at the extremity of the Caucasus range. (See Baku).

Apsides, two points in the orbit of a planet or satellite where the curvature is circular, the moving body there crossing the major axis at right angles.

Apteryx, or **Kiwi**, a ratite bird peculiar to New Zealand, is without obvious wings. The feathers are hair-like in appearance, and the beak is long and curved, with the nostrils nearly at its extremity. Kiwis breed slowly, and will not rear young in captivity. Though now carefully protected, the extermination of the species is imminent.

Apthorp, William Foster (1848-1913), Am. music critic, published *Hector Berlioz* (1879), *Musicians and Music-Lovers* (1894), *By the Way* (1898), *The Opera, Past and Present* (1901).

Apuan Alps, in Italy. The upper layers are composed of some of the finest white marble in the world, which was known to the Romans, and was rediscovered by Michelangelo. See also Carrar and Massa.

Apuleius, Lucius, Roman rhetorician, b. *c.* 130 A.D. in Madaura, N. Africa; educated at Carthage and Athens. On the death of his father, who left him a large fortune, he travelled extensively, visiting Italy and Asia. The knowledge he thereby acquired of priestly irregularities forms the groundwork of many of the stories in his *Golden Ass*. Other ancient writers, mostly philosophical, and of less interest are still extant. *The Golden Ass* is now printed in popular priced editions. See also J. G. Frazer's *Golden Bough*.

Apulia (Ital. *Puglia*), a territorial div. (compartimento) of S. Italy; stretches along the Adriatic, from the river Fortore to the extreme s.e. corner of the peninsula, and embraces the provinces of Brindisi, Ionio, Foggia, Bari, and Lecce; p. 2,886,570; area, 7,442 sq. m. Wine is generally produced; other products are fruits and salt, besides a little cotton, flax, tobacco, and silk. Marble is quarried on Monte Gargano. The chief ports on the Gulf of Taranto are Taranto and Gallipoli. See Gregorovius's *Apulische Landschaften* (4th ed. 1897). See also Italy; and for history, Naples.

Apure, river in Venezuela. See **Orinoco**.

Apurimac. (1.) River, S. America, rises about 15° s. in the Peruvian Andes, and is a head stream of the Amazon. (2.) Department, Peru, S. America. Area, 8,187 sq. m.; p. 280,213. Its cap. is Abancay.

Aqua fortis. See Nitrogen.

Aquamarine, a name given to the transparent bluish-green or sea-green varieties of beryl. It is found in many places, but comes chiefly from Brazil and the Urals. See G. F. Kunz, *Gems and Precious Stones of North America*, and O. C. Farrington, *Gems and Gem Minerals*.

Aqua regia (Lat. 'royal water,' because it dissolves gold), a mixture of nitric acid with from two to four times as much hydrochloric acid, which sets free chlorine; to this its solvent action is due.

Aquarium, tank or vessel, or a collection of these, containing aquatic plants and animals, living as nearly as possible under natural conditions. The basis of the modern aquarium is the mutual dependence of animals and plants, plants absorbing the carbon dioxide generated by animals, and liberating the oxygen necessary for their respiration. Plants, also, are able to utilize the waste materials of animals. Almost all recent aquaria, especially those for public exhibition where a considerable depth and bulk of water is to be maintained, have mechanical arrangements for aerating or renewing the water. A glass aquarium should always contain a few water-snails (*Limnae, Planorbis, Physa*), since these will eat the minute vegetation

THE ARCHER, A SPORTSMAN AMONG FISHES

Although there may be worms in abundance on the river bottom, the archer prefers to shoot down flies and other small creatures from the bank by means of a series of well-aimed "bullets" of water, which it ejects in rapid succession.

(*Confervæ*) which tends to grow everywhere, and so keep the glass clean and clear.

Further information regarding the planning and care of the small home aquarium, with its many varieties of Tropical fish, may be obtained from any store dealing in these supplies.

Extensive experimental marine aquaria are attached to the biological stations of Naples and elsewhere in Europe, and at Wood's Hole, Cold Spring Harbor, and elsewhere in the United States. In the old Fort Clinton (Castle Garden) on the Battery in New York, which was torn down in 1942, was for a half a century one of the largest and finest aquariums in the world. See Taylor's *Aquarium* (1881); Smith's *The Aquarium* (1900).

In vertebrates, the line which separates the typically aquatic and typically terrestrial forms passes through amphibians, which may, as in the frog, be water animals in youth and land animals in adult life. Nevertheless, the crocodiles, turtles, and water snakes among reptiles, many birds, the sirenians, cetaceans, and seals among mammals, illustrate the fact that members of typically terrestrial groups may return to a purely aquatic life.

A very common structure in those aquatic animals which are capable of rising and sinking in the water is some form of hydrostatic organ, or internal reservoir of gas. Though aquatic life is most abundant in warm waters, and near shore, it exists in all climates and at all depths; yet there are few forms which

Roman Aqueduct, the Pont du Gard, Nimes.

Aquarius, a southern zodiacal constellation, and the eleventh sign of the zodiac.

Aquatic Animals. It has become almost an axiom of modern science that life originated in the water, and numbers of animals, especially the simpler forms, still inhabit that medium. This is true of the vast majority of the Protozoa, sponges, Cœlenterata and echinoderms. It is the rule for unsegmented worms, except where these are parasitic; and, among annelids, the earthworms and land-leeches are obviously forms which have later acquired a terrestrial habit. Crustacea are almost all aquatic. Among molluscs, only the gasteropod class includes land forms.

are able to range widely, especially in a vertical direction.

Aquatic Plants, or Hydrophytes, are wholly or partially submerged, but do not include marsh plants. Seaweeds and freshwater algæ are aquatic. The better-known examples of aquatic flowering plants are the water buttercups (*Ranunculus*), and the pondweeds (*Potamogeton*). The majority of water plants are fixed in the soil, but some, like Duckweed (*Lemna*) and Water Soldier (*Stratiotes*), float, or at least are free from the soil. Most aquatic plants expose their flowers above the surface, and thus are subject to the same means of pollination as land

Aquatint

plants. Most aquatic plants are perennial. See the separate articles on the various plants mentioned.

Aquatint, an etching process on copper by which prints are produced imitating the broad effects of India ink and sepia drawings. In this process, areas, not lines, are bitten in by dilute acid on a copper plate, covered with black resin, on which the design has already been traced. See ENGRAVING; ETCHING.

Aqua Tofana, a mysterious poisonous liquid, applied to criminal purposes by a Sicilian woman named Tofana, about the end of the seventeenth century.

Aqua Vitæ (Latin, 'water of life'), ardent spirits; especially, in commerce, the spirits of the first distillation, or unrectified. French *eau de vie* (brandy) has the same meaning, as well as the words *whiskey* and *usquebaugh;* the former a Scotch, the latter an Irish form.

Aqueducts, artificial channels for carrying water. Aqueducts are now carried at will up and down or through mountains, thus saving long detours or costly piers and arches around or across valleys, and at the same time conserving the head or pressure for generating hydro-electric power as the water drops from a higher to a lower elevation. The term aqueducts is usually restricted to relatively large and long conduits leading from a source of supply to a city.

The Romans made little use of pipes under pressure; they raised the channel on arches to keep it at the proper gradient. Where the height was great, they built two or three tiers of arches one above another; and to make the channel impervious to water, the masonry was coated with stucco. Before the end of the first century A.D., Rome was supplied by nine aqueducts, with a total length of over 270 m., of which about 35 m. was raised above ground on arches. The ancient Greek world possessed famous aqueducts at Athens (*c.* 560 B.C.), at Samos (*c.* 625), and at Syracuse (still in use).

United States.—The earliest and for half a century the most important aqueduct in the United States was the Croton Aqueduct (completed 1842). This was surpassed by the new Croton Aqueduct in 1890, and that by the Catskill Aqueduct, completed in 1915. By far the largest American aqueduct was completed by the city of Los Angeles in 1914. Aqueducts have been built by other American cities but most American cities make use of

228

pipe lines or supply mains, rather than aqueducts.

The *Croton Aqueduct* is 38.1 m. long, of stone masonry with a brick lining, horseshoe shaped, 8.64 ft. high, 7.42 ft. wide, with a cross-sectional area of 53.34 sq. ft., and a total fall from Croton River to the Central Park Reservoir of 43.7 ft. The Harlem River is crossed by means of pipes on a masonry bridge, and the Manhattan Valley by inverted cast-iron siphons two m. long.

The *Wachusett Aqueduct,* which supplies the Boston Metropolitan District with water from the Nashua River, has a rated capacity of 300,000,000 gallons and a length of 12 m. including two m. of canal at its lower end.

The *Los Angeles Aqueduct* is longer, has a greater total fall, more diverse elements, and was built under greater difficulties of climate and location than any other of the notable aqueducts of the world. The aqueduct which is about 235 m. long, extends for miles across the Mojave Desert, and at other points up and down and through mountains Notable foreign aqueducts of modern times are those of Glasgow, Manchester, Liverpool and Vienna; also one in Southeastern Italy

See WATER; WATER CONDUITS. Consult Turneaure and Russell's *Public Water Supplies;* White's *The Catskill Water Supply of New York City* (1913).

Aqueous Humor. See **Eye.**

Aqueous Rocks, the name given to those rocks that have been laid down beneath water. See ROCKS.

Aquila, an ancient constellation placed s.e. of Lyra, and traversed by the Milky Way. Nova Aquilæ, photographically discovered by Mrs. Fleming in April, 1899, was then of seventh magnitude.

Aquila, Caspar (1488-1560), the Latin name of a German theologian, ADLER, who aided Luther in translating the Old Testament.

Aquila, Ponticus, a native of Sinope in Pontus, who flourished about 130 A.D. H made a translation of the Old Testamen into Greek.

Aquila degli Abruzzi, province, Italy in the territorial division of Abruzzi an Molise. Cereals, flax, hemp, and fruits are th chief productions. Area, 2,485 sq. m.; p 423,000.

Aquila degli Abruzzi, episcopal see an summer resort, Italy, chief town of the prov ince of the same name. The Cathedral, firs built in the thirteenth century, injured b

Aquila

earthquakes, has been restored. Lace making gives employment to many of the women; p. 24,000.

Aquilegia. See **Columbine**.

Aquileia, or **Aglar**, village, Austria, in Görz and Gradisca, at the head of the Adriatic. It was founded in 182 B.C., was strongly fortified by Marcus Aurelius, and in the 4th century A.D. was the 4th city in point of size and population in all Italy. Aquileia still possesses an eleventh-century cathedral, and has a museum full of valuable Roman anitiquities; p. 2,651.

Aquin, town, Haiti, West Indies. Dyewoods are exported; p. 3,500.

Aquinas, Thomas, 'the Angelic Doctor,' was the son of the Count of Aquino, near which town, situated between Rome and Naples, he was born about 1226. Having received the elements of his education in the monastery of Monte Cassino, he proceeded to the University of Naples, and in his seventeenth year joined the Dominicans. He afterward studied under the celebrated Albertus Magnus at Cologne. Called to Italy by Pope Urban IV. in 1261, he lectured with signal success on behalf of the Church and his order; in 1272 he was made a professor in Naples. He continued his labors in church statesmanship, public lecturing, and writing until his death on March 7, 1274. His remains were deposited at Toulouse. He was canonized in 1323, and made a doctor of the church in 1567.

Aquinas' greatest work is the *Summa Theologiæ*, which exercised an immense influence in his own and later times, and which even today forms the main doctrinal standard of Catholicism. It is designed on a magnificent scale, and its great purpose is to exhibit theology as the synthesis and embodiment of all human knowledge, whether of faith or of reason; in a manner it seeks to realize the famous tenet of Scotus Erigena— namely, the identity of philosophy and theology. The *Summa* is in three great divisions, treating respectively of God, Man, and the God-Man, the last having been left incomplete at his death. Aquinas marks the zenith of scholasticism. His great opponent was Duns Scotus, the Franciscan doctor, who, making the will (*voluntas*) as his principle as Aquinas had taken *intellectus*, the understanding), really transferred theology to the sphere of practice, and so, separating again the provinces of reason and faith, inaugurated the decline of scholasticism, and prepared the way for modern philosophy and the Reformation. Consult Vaughan's *Life*.

Aquisgranum, the ancient name of Aix la Chapelle.

Aquitania, a district of Gaul, lying between the Garonne and the Pyrenees. Its inhabitants were one of the three races which originally inhabited Gaul. The district was conquered (57 B.C.) by Cæsar's lieutenants; and again, after a revolt, in the reign of Augustus.

Aquitanus Sinus. See **Biscay, Bay of**.

Ara, or **Arara**, a cockatoo of Northern Australia and the Malayan Islands.

Ara, an ancient constellation situated to the s. of Scorpio, and possibly embodying a reminiscence of the mound altar of the Tower of Babel.

Arabesque (French), the style of decoration, either sculptured or painted, which the Spanish Moors introduced into Europe. The species of enrichment to which this term is now applied was extensively employed both by the Greeks and Romans. The Egyptians also employed it in their monumental decorations. The arabesque of the Moors confined itself to the foliage, etc., of plants and trees, elaborately intertwined. The arabesques with which Raphael adorned the galleries of the Vatican are at once the most famous and the most beautiful which the modern world has produced.

Arabia, which includes the kingdom of Saudi Arabia, Yemen, Kuwait, Muscat and Oman, is a massive quadrangular peninsula of Asia in the s.w. of the continent, lying between the Persian Gulf and the Gulf of Oman on the e., and the Red Sea on the w., with no natural frontier on the n., the conventional boundary being roughly the parallel of 30° N. Length, n. to s., 1,500 m.; average breadth, 800 m.; area, 1,200,000 sq. m., or about one-third that of Europe. The Red Sea coast, which is extremely deficient in harbors, is fringed with shoals and coral reefs. The s. coast presents a convex shore to the Indian Ocean, and has a number of good harbors, such as Aden, Dafar, and Keshin. The Persian Gulf contains numerous islands, the chief being Bahrein, which is the centre of the Gulf pearl fisheries, valued at about $1,500,000 annually. British influence is predominant in the Gulf.

The coasts of Arabia are among the hottest regions of the world. In several parts of Arabia hardly a refreshing shower falls in the course of the year, and vegetation is almost unknown; in other sultry districts, the date palm is almost the only proof of vegetable life. In general, about two-thirds of the total area is fertile, and one-third is desert and uninhabitable. The modern divisions are the *Sinai Peninsula,* between the Gulfs of Suez and Akabah; *Hejaz* ('the barrier'), fronting the Red Sea, and succeeded by the fertile, well-watered, and well-cultivated country of *Yemen; Tehama,* the low-lying sandy strip, covered with coral *débris,* from 20° N. to 15° N.; *Hadramaut* and *Mahra,* fronting the Gulf of Aden and the Indian Ocean respectively; the mountainous kingdom of *Oman,* the extreme s.w. end of the peninsula; *Hasa,* fronting the Persian Gulf; and *Nejd,* the oasis-studded middle portion of the interior. Knowledge of the interior of Arabia is still imperfect in details.

Products and Industry.—The terraced districts of Arabia are favorable to culture, and produce wheat, barley, millet, palms, tobacco, indigo, cotton, sugar, tamarinds, coffee, senna, and many aromatic and spice plants. Arabia is destitute of forests, but has vast stretches of desert grass fragrant with aromatic herbs, and furnishing admirable pasturage for a splendid breed of horses. Coffee is one of the most important exports. Arabia has few manufactures, but carries on a transit trade in foreign fabrics.

People.—The people are mainly Arabs (Bedouins on the borders of the deserts) and followers of Mohammed (see MOHAMMEDANISM). Estimates of the population of Arabia vary widely, but the best available figures place the total at about 10,000,000. Education is mostly confined to that within th

Moorish Arabesque Ornament, Alhambra.

Arabian Desert Scene.

household. The government is patriarchal, and the chief men of the various tribes have the title of Emir, Sheik, or, in a religious sense, Imam.

History.—Arabian history is divided by Islam into two epochs. Of the pre-Islamic period only a few facts stand out with any distinctness; one is, that the Romans tried in vain to subdue the peninsula. Arab history proper is commonly dated from the breakdown of the great dyke at Mareb, in Yemen, which forced many tribes to seek new habitations in the n. Through Islam, Arabia entered upon the second or political period of its history. Mohammed founded a theocratic state, as chief of which he united in himself the highest secular and ecclesiastical powers.

In the year 1517 a considerable portion of Arabia passed, together with Egypt, under the domination of the Ottoman Sultan Selim. From that time forward until the break-up of the Ottoman Empire four hundred years later, Turkey claimed suzerainty over the greater part of the Arabian peninsula. In the latter half of the eighteenth century, Sheik Mohammed Ibn Saud rose to power with his followers, called the Wahhabis. In 1804 they gained control of both Mecca and Medina in the w. Later Mohammed was defeated in battle, but Abdul Aziz Ibn Saud began to build up the political dominion his forefathers had won and lost. In December, 1915, Great Britain recognized him as independent ruler of Nejd and El Hasa.

Another rival remained in the Hejaz in the person of the Sherif Hussein, who had allied himself with the British during World War I in the hope of establishing under his own moral leadership a great federation of Arab states. Hussein had succeeded in having himself proclaimed 'King of the Arabs' and had won representation for the Hejaz at the Paris Peace Conference. Injustice and corruption flourished in the country and Ibn Saud, as soon as his British subsidy ceased in 1924, was able, with the approval of certain other Moslem countries, to attack Hussein and drive him and then his son Ali out of the Hejaz. By December 25, 1925, Ibn Saud was master of the whole of the Hejaz as well as of Nejd and El Hasa. Not long afterward he extended his influence still further by establishing a protectorate over Asir. Great Britain and Italy agreed, 1938, to respect Arabia's independence. Ibn Saud's wealth increased with discovery of great petroleum deposits in Arabia. These were under concession to the Standard Oil Company of California. Consult Philby's *Arabia of the Wahhabis* (1928); Byng's *The World of the Arabs* (1944).

Arabian Language and Literature. Arabic forms a branch of the Semitic languages, and belongs to its southern group, which also includes Ethiopic. Through the Koran, Arabic was spread over large tracts of Asia, Africa, several islands of the Mediterranean Sea, and Spain. It approaches primitive Semitic speech more nearly than any other member of the family. The ramifications of Arabic grammar are much more numerous than those of any kindred tongue. It is particularly suitable for metric style, and Arabic prosody alone forms a vast chapter in the history of the language. The language has preserved roots lost in the other Semitic dialects. Many obscure words in the Old Testament receive light from Arabic. Persian and Turkish teem with Arabic words.

The pre-Islamic period of Arabic literature consists of poems which lived in the mouths of the people. Native scholars wrote on the lives of the poets, and arranged their works in groups according to their pre-eminence. One of these is the seven famous *Muallakat* ('the suspended ones'). The first prose composition was the Koran, which marks the most important epoch in Arabic literature. (See KORAN.) The composing of the Koran gave an impetus to the compilation of the traditional lore that was needful to establish the minutiæ of Mohammedanism, to fix, or rather embellish, incidents in the life of the prophet, and to collect his real and alleged sayings. This is called the Sunna, and it forms an enormous chapter in Arab literature. The Sunna was followed by writings on the history of the Koran, its reading and exegesis, and biographies of the prophet. There is hardly any branch of human thought to which the Arabs did not devote their attention. The tales of the *Arabian Nights* belong to the world's literature; the *Assemblées* of Hariri have been translated into various European languages. Modern literary advancement has thus far only touched the surface of Arabia and is confined almost entirely to the emancipated few. Consult Green's *Practical Arabic Grammar;* Huart's *History of Arabic Literature* with bibliography; Clouston's *Arabian Poetry for English Readers.*

Arabian Nights Entertainments (Ar. *Alf Laylah wa Laylah,* 'A Thousand Nights and a Night') a collection of tales believed to be in form and substance the Arabic translation of a Persian book, *Hazár Afsánah,* or

'Thousand Tales.' Many translations, generally more or less expurgated, have been published.

Arabian Sea, a body of water forming the northwestern part of the Indian Ocean, stretching from India to Arabia. Its northwestern extension known as the Gulf of Oman, between Persia and Arabia, leads through the Strait of Ormuz into the Persian Gulf. Its southwestern extension, known as the Gulf of Aden, has connection through the Strait of Babel-Mandeb with the Red Sea. See INDIAN OCEAN.

Arab League, a political bloc, including Egypt, Iraq, Lebanon, Syria, Saudi Arabia, Transjordan and Yemen; also Arab factions in Palestine. The League controls an important location with respect to traffic routes.

Arachnida, a class of arthropods, including spiders, harvest-men, scorpions, and mites, and differing from insects in having four pairs of legs instead of three, and in the absence of antennæ, or feelers. The following are the orders usually recognized:—(1) Scorpionida, the true scorpions; (2) Pseudoscorpionida, book scorpions; (3) Pedipalpida, whip scorpions; (4) Phalangida, harvestmen; (5) Solpugida, wind scorpions; (6) Araneida, or spiders; (7) Acarina, or mites and ticks.

Arad, district, Roumania, in the western part; area about 2,500 sq. m. Productions include cereals, wine, tobacco, and iron.

Arad, town, Roumania, capital of the district of Orad, on the right bank of the Maros. It is an important commercial centre and has a large export trade in grain and wine. Until after World War I it was a Hungarian city; p. 77,255.

Araf, (Ar. *Al-Araf*), as stated in the Koran, the Mohammedan purgatory, a raised wall of separation between heaven and hell.

Arafat, or **Jebel-errahm** ('Hill of Mercy'), a granite hill (about 250 ft. high) 15 m. s.e. of Mecca.

Arafura, or **Alfura Sea,** the division of the Pacific lying between the n. of Australia and the western half of New Guinea.

Arago, Dominique (1786-1853), French astronomer and physicist, born near Perpignan. He was appointed professor of analytical geometry in the Ecole Polytechnique. Arago filled that chair for twenty years, and did much to popularize scientific discovery, especially in optics, astronomy, and magnetism. In 1830 he was appointed director of the observatory in Paris. Among his best-known works are his *Autobiog.* (trans. Powell, 1858); *Lectures, etc.* (trans. Smyth and Grant, 1855); *Astronomie Populaire* (1834-5; Eng. ed. 1855-8).

Aragon, an ancient kingdom and former province of Spain, with an area of 17,976 sq. m. and a p. of 912,711; bounded on the N. by the Pyrenees. Cap. Zaragoza. It is now divided into the three provinces of Huesca in the N., Zaragoza in the middle, and Teruel in the s. The soil is sterile, though intersected by the Ebro, but is rich in minerals of almost every kind. From 1282 to 1730 it also embraced Sicily, and from 1416 to 1713 Sardinia. The CANAL OF ARAGON was first projected by the Emperor Charles V. (1528), but was not seriously taken in hand until the accession of Charles III. (1760). See SPAIN.

Aragona, tn., prov. Girgenti, Sicily. Has important sulphur mines; p. 14,126.

Aragonite, an orthorhombic variety of carbonate of lime, first found in Aragon. It crystallizes in six-sided prisms, or in long, narrow, pointed forms, and has the same composition as calcite, though differing from it in specific gravity, crystalline form, and physical properties. (See DIMORPHISM.) Satin spar is a fibrous variety of aragonite.

Araguaya, or **Rio Grande,** a riv. of Brazil, rises in the Serra Cayapo, and joins the Tocantins near São Francisco. It flows N.E., and has a length of 1,300 m., one-half of which is navigable.

Arakan, or **Aracan,** the n.w. division of Lower Burma, ceded to Great Britain (1826); cap. Akyab. Area, 18,540 sq. m.; p. 762,102.

Aral, Sea of (*Aralskoye More*), the second largest sheet of inland water in Asia, fills the lowest part of the W. Turkestan depression. It lies 160 ft. above sea-level, and 245 ft. above the level of the Caspian; measures 280 m. from N. to S., and 140 m. to 190 m. in breadth, and has an area of 26,000 sq. m. The average depth is less than 100 ft.; the deepest part, 220 ft., is towards the N.W. Its water is only slightly saline, and every winter it freezes for several m. all around its shores. Its fish, of which it yields a rich harvest, are fresh-water species.

Aralac, a casein (milk by-product) fiber manufactured by Aralac, Inc., a National Dairy subsidiary. Mixed with other fabrics, rayon, cotton, wool, it creates new textiles.

Aralia, a genus of the *Araliaceæ*, or ginseng family, natives of the temperate and tropical regions. The greenhouse plant, commonly called *A. Sieboldii*, now known as

Fatsia japonica, was introduced from Japan in 1858. Several American species have aromatic rootstocks, as the wild sarsaparilla, and wild spikenard.

Aram, an old Semitic geographical term which included Syria and Mesopotamia, but excluded Palestine. It gave name to a division of the Semitic family of speech, Aramean or Aramaic, the dialects of which formed the group of North Semitic, as distinguished from Middle Semitic (*i.e.* Hebrew and Phœnician) and from South Semitic (*i.e.* Arabic and Ethiopic). Aramaic was divided into two main branches—Chaldee and Syriac. Aramaic was the vernacular of Palestine in the time of Christ, and it is Aramaic that is meant when the New Testament speaks of Hebrew.' **Chaldee (Aramaic) is the language** of the Targums and Talmuds of Jerusalem and Babylon. Syriac, a literary language, embraced the Peshito version of the Bible, and was extensively used from the 4th to the 13th century, though it is now superseded by Arabic. See Nöldeke's *Die Semitischen Sprachen* (1887).

Aram, Eugene (1704-59), an English felon; born at Ramsgill, Yorkshire. He was convicted of a charge of murder of Daniel Clark, his friend, and hanged. The interest attaching to Aram's crime is mainly due to Bulwer Lytton's novel and Hood's poem on the subject of the murder. See Scatcherd's *Memoirs of Eugene Aram* (1838); also the *Annual Register* (1759).

Aran, or **Arran Isles,** a group of small islands at the entrance to Galway Bay, about 4 m. off the w. coast of Ireland. The chief islands are named Inishmore, Inishmaan, and Inisheer. The isles are rich in archæological remains, and their old shrines attract many visitors to 'Aran of the Saints.' The chief industry is fishing.

Aranda, Pedro Pablo Abarc y Bolea, Count of (1718-99), Spanish statesman, born at Saragossa of a noble family. He was sent as ambassador to Paris (1773), and took an active part in the conclusion of the treaty of Paris (1783). Recalled in 1787, he was in 1792 for a short time prime minister, until supplanted by Godoy.

Aranjuez (anc. *Ara Jovis*), tn., prov. Madrid, Spain, on l. bk. of Tagus. It was formerly the spring residence of the Spanish court, and has a beautiful castle built by Philip II., containing many art treasures; p. 12,670.

Aransas Pass, a strait, the entrance to Aransas Bay, an arm of the Gulf of Mexico, on the Texan coast. Here, in Nov., 1864, a battle of the Civil War was fought, in which the Federal troops captured the Confederate fortifications at the Pass.

Arany, János (1817-82), Hungarian poet, born in Nagy-Szalonta, Bihar, won in 1845 a prize from the Kisfaludy Society of Budapest with a humorous epic, *Az Elevszett Alkotmány* (The Lost Constitution.) His epic poems, *Toldi* (1847) and *Murány Ostroma* (The Siege of Murány) (1847), made him the favorite poet of the Hungarian nation. Arany is, after Petöfi, the most popular and important modern poet of Hungary.

Arapahoes, a tribe of North American Indians of Algonquian descent, closely associated with the Cheyenne. The annual sun dance is their chief ceremony; symbolism plays an important part in their customs. Their total number is something over 2,000.

Arapaima, a genus of tropical fishes, including some of the largest known fresh-water forms, remarkable for the mosaic work of strong bony scales with which the body is covered. They are found in the rivers of South America, where specimens 15 ft. in length and 400 pounds in weight have been taken.

Ararat, (Armenian Airarat), the ancient name for the district through which the Aras (q.v.) flows. The association of the region with the landing place of the ark after the Flood, naturally enough led to its being appropriated to the highest peak. The twin mountain of Ararat lies at the point where three empires met—Russia, Turkey, and Persia. It forms an elliptical mass, 25 m. in length from s.e. to n.w., by half that in breadth, rising on the n. and e. out of the alluvial plain of the Aras. The mass stands quite isolated on all sides except the n.w., where a column 7,000 ft. high connects it with a long ridge of volcanic mountains extending westward. Consult Bryce's *Transcaucasia and Ararat.*

Araroba. See **Andira; Chrysarobin.**

Aras (ancient Araxes), large river in Armenia; rises in Erzerum vilayet. For the greater part of its course of 600 m. it forms the boundary between Russia (Cis-Caucasia) and Persia. It flows into the Caspian Sea at Kizil Agach Bay.

Aratus of Sicyon (271-213 B.C.), Greek general and statesman. In 251 B.C. he expelled the tyrant Nicocles, and united (251) Sicyon to the Achæan League (see ACHÆI), and in 245 B.C. was chosen general of the League, an office which he held for many years. The relations between Antigonus' successor, Philip, and Aratus became strained and Philip procured the death of Aratus by poison in 213 B.C. Aratus left thirty books of memoirs (now lost), which were drawn upon by Polybius and Plutarch.

Aratus of Soli, Cilicia, a Greek poet and astronomer, flourished about 270 B.C., only two of whose works are extant, the *Phænomena* and the *Diosemeia*. The former treats of astronomy, and the latter of the weather.

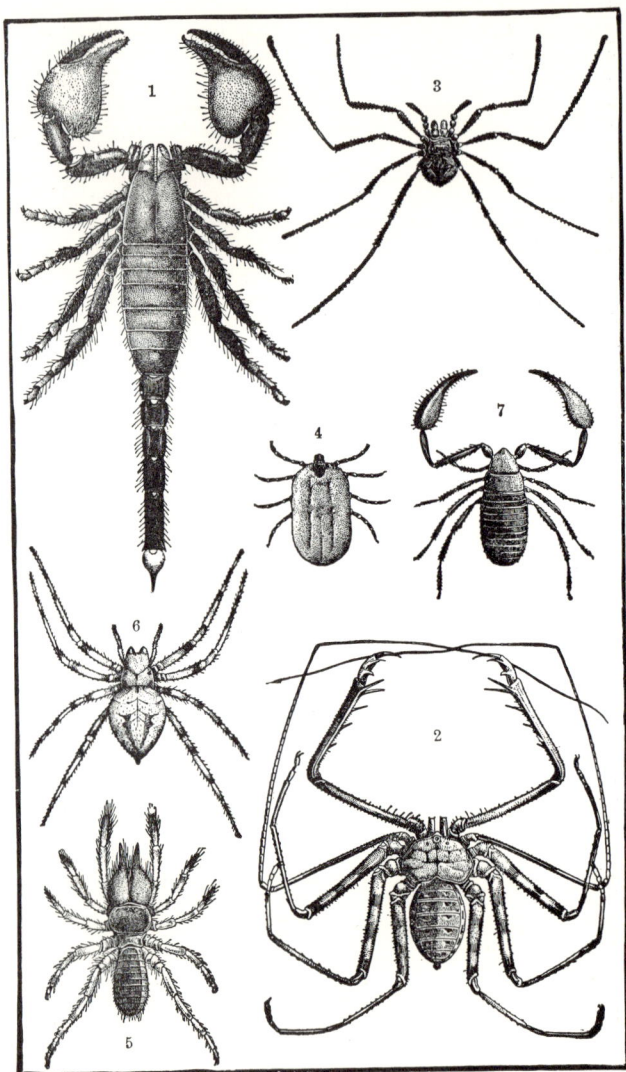

Arachnida.

1. SCORPIONIDA—*Scorpio indicus*, ½ nat. size. 2. PEDIPALPI—*Titanodamon Johnstonii*, ½ nat. size. 3. PHALANGIDA—*Phalangium copticum*. 4. ACARIDA—*Rhypicephalus annulatus*. 5. SOLPUGIDA—*Rhax brevipes*, ½ nat. size. 6. ARANEIDA—*Araneus tarnensis*, nat. size. 7. PSEUDOSCORPIONIDA—*Chelifer sesamoides*. (No. 4, somewhat enlarged; 3 and 7 greatly enlarged.)

Araucania, the country of the Araucos or Araucanian Indians, whose territory comprised that part of Chile which lies between the Bio-Bio and Valdivia Rivers, and bordered n. on the Peruvian empire. The present Chilean province of Arauco, lying between the Andes and the Pacific Ocean, bounded on the n. by Concepción and on the s. by Valdivia, was formed in 1875, and has an area of 2,189 sq. m. and a population of 60,233. Its capital is Lebu, 55 m. s. of Concepción. The Araucanians are an undersized but vigorous race. Their chief industry is the breeding of cattle and vicunas. All are polygamists, and their religion is based on the principle of good and evil (*A po, Pillan*). Araucan, a language of high polysynthetic type, has been reduced to written form, and in it are embodied a large number of myths and national legends.

Araucaria, a genus of evergreen conifers including a number of species of lofty trees native to South America and Australia. They are of a singularly geometrical h a b i t of growth. *Araucaria excelsa,* the Norfolk Island Pine, is the species most commonly seen in the United States, where it is popular as a house plant. *A. imbricata,* the hardiest species, popularly known as the Monkey Puzzle or Chile Pine, is a native of the Chilean Andes. The seed is pleasant to the taste, and is an important article of food to the Indians.

Arauco. See **Araucania.**

Araujo Porto Alegre, Manoel de (1806-79), Brazilian poet and architect, was born in Rio Pardo, in the state of São Pedro, Brazil. He was the founder of the national theatre. His principal poetical works are *Colombo* and *Brasilianas* (1863).

Arawaks, South American aborigines who formerly ranged over a great part of Northern Brazil, the Guianas, and Venezuela, and appear to have formed the chief element in the West Indies and Bahamas. They are still numerous on the mainland. All are rude, uncultured tribes.

Araxes. See **Aras.**

Arbaces, the Mede, who, according to the historian Ctesias, overthrew the Assyrian empire in the 7th century B.C. by defeating Sardanapalus (q.v.), and founded the Median empire. Another of the name was a general of Artaxerxes Memnon in his war with his brother Cyrus (401 B.C.).

Arbalest. See **Crossbow.**

Arbela, now ERBIL or ARBIL, a small town of Assyria, e. of Mosul, famous as having given name to the battle in which Alexander the Great (q.v.) finally defeated Darius (q.v.), 331 B.C. The battle was really fought near Gaugamela, 40 m. n.w.

Arbitrage, a business transaction of a kind common on the stock exchange of New York and of London, wherein the trader buys in a cheaper and sells in a dearer market.

Arbitration is the adjudication by one or more private persons, called arbitrators, appointed to decide a matter or matters in controversy. It may be voluntary, when the parties freely consent to submit the question at issue to arbitration, or compulsory, when they are compelled to do so by statute. At common law all submissions are voluntary, though the court may suggest a reference to arbitrators. Arbitrations are largely resorted to by business men, the object being to have the matter decided by a practical man, and to avoid the comparatively slow and costly procedure of courts of law. See ARBITRATION, INDUSTRIAL; ARBITRATION, INTERNATIONAL.

Arbitration, Industrial. In the settlement of controversies arising between employers and employees, the questions at issue are frequently referred to one or more persons, known as arbitrators, who have been appointed to consider the facts and render a decision or award. This method of settlement is termed Industrial Arbitration. In many countries, statutory provision is made for the formation of permanent official or semi-official boards, before which, either by mutual consent of both parties or upon application of a single party, industrial disputes may be arbitrated. The earliest attempts to avoid industrial conflicts by reference of controversies to industrial courts were those made in European countries. In England, voluntary arbitration through private boards has been encouraged by legislation since early in the 19th century; and in 1896 provision was made for the registration of such boards by the British Board of Trade, and definite rules and regulations governing their procedure were formulated. Compulsory arbitration laws have been enacted in Australasia, the first and most noteworthy of which was that passed in 1894 in New Zealand, and amended in certain respects in 1925.

In 1934, the principle of voluntary arbitration was still operative in Great Britain, Canada, the United States, and South Africa. The awards of the arbitrators are not mandatory and are viewed as 'gentlemen's agreements.' In Australia and New Zealand the state systems of conciliation and arbitration are fully developed and their awards are mandatory. In Germany, since the advent of

Hitler, arbitration has become both compulsory and the function of state agencies.

The Canadian Industrial Disputes Investigation Act, passed by the Dominion Parliament in 1907, applies to all disputes involving ten or more persons employed in mining, or in connection with public-service utilities. The restrictive provisions of the Act make it 'unlawful for any employer to declare or cause a lockout, or for any employee to go on strike on account of any dispute prior to or during a reference of such dispute to a board of conciliation and investigation'. The Canadian Trades and Labor Congress since 1912 has demanded the repeal of the Canadian Act, declaring that 'the right to strike is the one thing that distinguishes the free workman from the chattel slave.'

In the United States, boards of arbitration were established in New York State and Massachusetts in 1886, and at least thirty-six other States have since made statutory provisions for the arbitration of industrial disputes either by special boards or commissions created for this purpose, or by making this one of functions of boards, commissions, or officials having other functions.

Federal statutes providing for the creation of boards or commissions which should endeavor to bring about the settlement of controversies that might arise between railroad employees and employers were enacted in 1888, 1898, 1913, 1920 and 1926. The Newlands Act (passed in 1913) created the United States Board of Mediation and Conciliation. From the organization of the Board in July 1913, up to June 30, 1916, its services were requested in 56 controversies between railroad managers and their employees. In September, 1916, Congress enacted the Adamson law, which provided that eight hours should be the standard measure of a day's work for the purpose of reckoning the compensation of employees engaged in the operation of trains.

The Government took over control of the railroads in December, 1917, and the operations were later transferred to the U. S. Railway Board, created by the Transportation Act of 1920, returning the railroads to private control. The Railroad Labor Board, created by the Act, was to be the appeal body to hear disputes concerning wages, salaries, or disputes not settled by conference between employees and carriers. In 1922, the management of a number of the larger railroads broke away from the Association of Railway Executives and concluded a strike settlement plan, known as the 'Baltimore agreement.'

On May 20, 1926, Congress enacted the Railroad Labor Act, creating the U. S. Board of Mediation which superseded the Railway Labor Board.

The passage of the *National Industrial Recovery Act,* popularly known as N. R. A., in June, 1933, by granting the President the right to require the establishment by private industries of fair competition codes, regulation of production and price, the establishment of maximum hours of work and minimum wage scales, endowed him with dictatorial powers. The legislation was declared unconstitutional by the Supreme Court, 1935.

The National Labor Relations Act was passed in 1935. The board administering the act was criticized by employers and by the A. F. of L. for giving unfair consideration to the C. I. O. In March 1941, in an effort to lay the epidemic of strikes flourishing under the National Labor Relations Act and alarmingly impeding production in national defense industrial operations, Pres. Roosevelt set up the National Defense Mediation Board, of eleven members. See EIGHT-HOUR DAY; INJUNCTION; STRIKES AND LOCKOUTS; TRADE UNIONS.

Consult *Report of the U. S. Board of Mediation and Conciliation* (Senate Document 493, 1916); *American Labor Legislation Review;* and *Special Studies,* of the American Association for Labor Legislation, New York; *Reports of the United States Board of Mediation; Soviet Union Review;* J. R. Commons and J. B. Andrews, *Principles of Labor Legislation* (1927); F. T. Carlton, *Labor Problems* (1933); C. A. Beard and Mary Beard, *Rise of American Civilization* (1927); E. C. Kirkland, *History of American Economic Life* (1932); Publications of the *International Labor Organization,* League of Nations; *International Labour Review;* B. S. Kirsh and H. R. Shapiro, *The National Industrial Recovery Act* (1933).

Arbitration, International. By international arbitration is meant the determination of controversies by international tribunals judicial in their constitution and powers. It differs essentially from mediation, in that the latter is an advisory process, while arbitration is a judicial process—mediation recommends, arbitration decides. Arbitration is unquestionably one of the oldest and most widely used legal devices for the settlement of international disputes. It was among the Greeks that it reached its greatest florescence. Indeed, the efforts to rule their affairs by law led to the development of a rudimentary international organization — the Amphictyonic Council (q.v.), important as a step in the growth of The League of Nations. During the rise and the preëminence of the Roman state the practice of arbitration fell into decay. It is not until well into the mediæval period that records are again found of international arbitration. Throughout Europe, for the greater part of the so-called feudal period, the active principle of the procedural law was that no man could be tried except by his equals or by a superior. One of the important early arbitrations was a dispute submitted to Henry VI. of England by the Kings of Castile and Aragon (1180).

As a general rule, where the dispute was between petty feudal lords, a noble of equal estate and prominence was chosen as arbitrator. The Emperor, the King of France, and particularly the Pope functioned as arbitrators in the more important cases. Indeed, the church was a most potent factor in the development of international conciliation. During the Renaissance the practice of arbitration may be said to have reached the high point in its development.

After the discovery of America and during the rise of the modern national states, the use of arbitration gradually declined. During the 16th, 17th, and 18th centuries the general and incessant condition of warfare brought about the almost complete disappearance of international arbitration. The Jay Treaty (q.v.), of 1794, between the United States and Great Britain, marks an epoch in the history of arbitration.

The most important of the three arbitrations under the Jay Treaty was that which dealt with the claims of the United States for captures made by Great Britain in the war with France, and with the claims by Great Britain on account of the failure of the United States to enforce its neutrality. The American claimants recovered over eleven million dollars for illegal captures. The British claimants recovered $103,428.14.

Practically all of the great disputes between the United States and Great Britain since the war of 1812 have been settled by arbitration. The Treaty of Ghent (1814) which ended the War of 1812, provided for three arbitrations. The acrimonious disputes with Great Britain arising out of the Civil War severely strained the relations of the two countries, and but for the adoption of arbitration as a mode of settlement, serious consequences might have ensued. The Treaty of Washington (1871) provided for four arbitrations. (See ALABAMA, THE.)

Two other important arbitrations of controversies with Great Britain have been held, the Fur Seal Arbitration, 1899, and the Fisheries question, 1910.

With Spain arbitration was employed under the treaty of 1795 down to the Spanish-American War. Between the United States and France, also, various important questions have been arbitrated. Arbitrations have also been held by the United States with Colombia, Costa Rica, Denmark, Ecuador, Germany, Haiti, Nicaragua, Norway, Paraguay, Peru, Portugal, Salvador, Santo Domingo, Siam, and Venezuela.

On April 18, 1890, a plan of arbitration was adopted. While this plan was never approved by the governments represented, it nevertheless marks the commencement of a great and sustained agitation for universal arbitration. The culmination of the popular agitation for arbitration was at the conference which met at the Hague in 1899. The notable achievement of the conference was the Convention for the Pacific Settlement of International Disputes. (See HAGUE PEACE CONFERENCE).

The Convention of 1899 was renewed in 1907 at the Second Peace Conference. At this conference an attempt to make recourse to arbitration obligatory failed. The United States signed and ratified both conventions. The first case decided by the Permanent Court of International Arbitration was the Pious Fund case between the United States and Mexico (Oct. 14, 1902). The Permanent Court of International Arbitration has also rendered awards in the following cases: the Preferential Claims case (Feb. 22, 1904) between Germany, Italy, Great Britain, and Venezuela; the Norwegian-Swedish Maritime Boundary case (Oct. 23, 1909); the Russian Indemnities case (Nov. 11, 1912) between Russia and Turkey and many others. At the Second International Conference of American States, which met at Mexico City in 1901, a second plan was devised and a protocol was signed by all of the delegations except those of Chili and Ecuador looking to adhesion to the Hague Convention. The United States did not sign this treaty but it was signatory to a 3d treaty which regulated the arbitration of pecuniary claims. When the Third International Conference met at Rio de Janeiro (1906) the five years for which the treaty had been concluded had nearly run. A new treaty with some amendments was concluded, therefore. At the Fourth International Conference at Buenos Ayres in 1910 the treaty was renewed with certain amendments.

Compulsory arbitration as a means of furthering peace was agitated in the United States for a considerable period after the First International American Conference. In 1903, a treaty was concluded between France and Great Britain that sought to make arbitration obligatory. Shortly after the conclusion of the Anglo-French convention the United States signed treaties with various powers in the precise terms of the former. Seven of these treaties were submitted to the Senate in January 1905.

The result of these treaties was to produce a radical change in the policy of the United States. Previous to this time the ordinary claims conventions had been made in the form of executive agreements not requiring senatorial consent. Indeed, twenty-seven of the international arbitrations in which the United States had participated up to 1908 had been entered into under executive agreements as against nineteen by formal treaty.

In 1911, two notable agreements were concluded by the United States with France and Great Britain, respectively, commonly known as the Taft-Knox treaties. According to these agreements, all future differences between the contracting parties which were not adjustable by diplomacy, were to be submitted to arbitration. In each case there was to be a special agreement which, in the case of the United States, was to be submitted to the Senate. When the treaties came before the Senate they were so radically amended that they were subsequently abandoned.

In 1913, a paper subsequently published under the title of *President Wilson's Peace Proposal* was handed by Wm. Jennings Bryan, Secretary of State, to the members of the Diplomatic Corps at Washington. The proposal, also known as the 'Bryan Peace Plan,' was that all disputes which diplomacy should fail to adjust should be submitted to an international commission for an investigation and report, and treaties based on the Bryan Plan were concluded with many foreign states.

The outbreak of war in 1914 brought about the temporary suspension of the program of judicial settlement of international disputes. The Treaty of Peace with Germany signed at Versailles (1919), however, made provision for the resumption of arbitration. By article thirteen of the Covenant of the League of Nations the members of the League have agreed that whenever a dispute shall arise between them which they recognize to be suitable for arbitration and which diplomacy cannot settle, they will submit the matter to arbitration.

The 14th article of the Covenant empowers the Council of the League to formulate and submit to the members of the League, plans for the establishment of a permanent court of international justice, to be competent to hear and determine any dispute of an international character which the parties may submit to it. The United States became a member of the Permanent Court of International Arbitration.

The outbreak of the European War in Sept. 1939 ended the League of Nations as an arbitration body and it became ineffective.

In the Charter of the United Nations, signed by the United States in 1945, provision was made for an International Court of Justice. This Court is composed of fifteen members who are elected jointly by the Security Council and the General Assembly. The term is nine years, but in the first election, held on Feb. 6, 1946, five judges were elected for a three year term, five for a six year term, and five for a nine year term; in later elections the normal term will be followed.

Article 92—The International Court of Justice shall be the principal judicial organ of the United Nations. It shall function in accordance with the annexed statute which is based upon the statute of the Permanent Court of International Justice and forms an integral part of the present chapter.

Article 93-1. All members of the United Nations are ipso facto parties to the statute of the International Court of Justice.

This Court was empowered to settle disputes which involved international treaties, laws or obligations. See LEAGUE OF NATIONS; HAGUE CONFERENCES; WORLD COURT. Consult, for history of arbitration, J. B. Moore's *History and Digest of International Arbitrations;* Goebel's *Equality of States* (1923). For modern practice consult J. B. Scott's *The Hague Peace Conferences;* Ralston's *International Arbitral Law and Procedure;* A. P. Higgins' *The Hague Peace Conference;* Moore's *Digest of International Law* and *International Law and Some Current Illusions.*

Arblay, Madame d'. See **Burney, Frances.**

Arboga, town, Sweden, province of Vestmanland, situated on the Arboga River. It is one of the oldest places in Sweden: p. 5,250.

Arbogast (d. 394), a Frank by origin, who distinguished himself as a Roman general under the Emperors Gratian (367-383) and Valentinian II. (388-392). Defeated by Theodocius Arbogast committed suicide.

Arbois de Jubainville, Marie Henri d' (1827-1910), distinguished French philologist and historian, was born in Nancy. He was the author of many important books, as *La famille celtique* (1905); *L'enlevement du taureau divin et des vaches de Cooley* (1907).

Arbor Day, a day set apart in the United States, Canada, and other countries for the planting of trees, especially by children, and for the encouragement of general interest in forestry. The date varies.

Arboriculture. See **Forestry; Gardening.**

Arbor Vitæ (*Thuja*), an evergreen genus of coniferous trees and shrubs allied to the cypress (q.v.). The common Arbor Vitæ (*T. occidentalis*), a native of North America. It is a tree 20 to 50 ft. high; the young leafy twigs have a balsamic smell; and both they and the wood were formerly in high repute as a medicine. The Chinese Arbor Vitæ (*T. Biota orientalis*), a native of China and Japan, is a common ornament of pleasure grounds in Europe. The balsamic smell is very agreeable.

Arbroath, formerly **Aberbrothwick** and **Aberbrothock** ('mouth of the Brothock'), seaport and manufacturing town, Forfarshire, Scotland. Arbroath is the 'Fairport' of Scott's *Antiquary*. The famous Bell Rock is 12 m. s.e.; p. 20,648.

Arbués, Pedro de (1441-85), Spanish inquisitor; appointed (1484) by Torquemada (q.v.). His excessive zeal in the persecution of the heretics led to his assassination in 1485.

Arbuthnot, John (1667-1735), Scottish author and physician to Queen Anne, a close friend of Swift. Consult the *Life and Works*, by G. A. Aitken.

Arbutus, a genus of small trees and shrubs belonging to the order Ericaceæ.

Trailing Arbutus (also known as Mayflower) (*Epigœa repens*) is famous for its early blooming and fragrant, exquisite, pink and white flowers.

Arc (Latin *arcus*, 'a bow'), is any part of a curved line. See CURVE; ASYMPTOTES.

Arc, Electric. See **Electric Lamps; Electro-Metallurgy.**

Arc, Jeanne d'. See **Joan of Arc.**

Arcade, a term in architecture generally used for—(1) a series of apertures or recesses with arched ceilings; (2) a single-arched aperture or enclosure, equivalent to a vault; (3) the space covered by a continued arch or vault supported on piers or columns. The term is also applied, but improperly, to a glass-covered street or lane, with a row of shops or stalls on each side.

Arcadia, (1) mountainous and beautiful country in the centre of the Peloponnesus, Greece. The Arcadians claimed to be the most ancient people in Greece. They were chiefly occupied in pastoral pursuits. Their love of music is responsible for the Arcadia of poetry and romance. Modern Arcadia forms a department of Greece; p. 167,000. (2) Arcadia, Nova Scotia, p. 500.

Arcadius (377-408), first emperor of the East alone, was born in Spain, and was the son of the Emperor Theodosius, after whose death, in 395 A.D., the Roman empire was divided into e. and w. Arcadius lived in Oriental state and splendor, and his dominion extended from the Adriatic Sea to the River Tigris, and from Scythia to Ethiopia

Arcanum, the Great. See **Alchemy.**

Arce, Francisco (1822-78), Mexican settler in California, before the era of the Forty-Niners. He was attacked on June 6, 1846, by some Americans. The Arce Incident was one of several that preceded California's annexation as one of the States of the Union.

Arcesilaus, (316-241 B.C.), Greek philosopher, founder of the Middle Academy.

Arch, a structure of brickwork or masonry, or of iron or steel ribs, whereby a load is supported over an open space, as in doorways, windows, roofs, bridges, and tunnels. The word is not applied to a straight horizontal support. It is to the Romans that the nations of the modern world are indebted for the use of the arch. The Romans most probably derived their acquaintance with it from the Etruscans, who, as well as the Pelasgians of Greece, made their arches pointed. The introduction of the arch by the Romans gradually effected a complete revolution in the architectural forms which they had borrowed from the Greeks. In the Romanesque and Gothic styles the arches sprang freely from the caps of the shafts. The introduction of steel girders has, for many purposes, eliminated the arch.

A typical arch is supported by two piers, the distance between which is the span of the arch. At the apex is reached the keystone, which is the centre of the arch. The diagram shows the most notable forms of arch, indicating the style of architecture with which each is associated. The engineering questions involved are discussed under BRIDGES. See also ABUTMENT; ARCHITECTURE; VAULT.

The Triumphal Arch was originally a monument erected by the Romans in honor of an individual, or to commemorate a great victory. Notable examples are the Arch of Constantine in Rome. The Arc de Triomphe de l'Etoile in Paris and the Washington Arch in New York are later examples of this idea.

Archæan System. A geological term applied to those rocks which are older than the earliest fossiliferous strata. Owing to their resistant nature they usually form elevated plateaus, or even mountainous masses. They are in many places repositories of valuable ores, as in Scandinavia, N. America, and Brazil, where they yield iron, silver, gold, copper, nickel, and often precious stones. See Sir Archibald Geikie's *Text-book of Geology;* Dana's *Geology;* Lapworth's *Intermediate Geol.* (1899); Van Hise, *Correlation Papers —Archean and Algonkian.*

Archæological Institute of America, an association organized in 1879 in Boston with numerous branches in different cities. Its object is the encouragement of research in the antiquities of all lands.

Archæology, the science that deals with the material remains of antiquity. In 1832 Thomsen, a native of Denmark, delimited for the first time the broadest classifications of general antiquity into the Ages of Stone, Bronze, and Iron. The Stone Age was soon divided into Paleolithic and Neolithic, Bronze and Iron into Early, Middle, and late periods.

In many cases definite names of archæological periods have attached themselves to places of origin. It is only the specialist who pretends to keep a detailed list of the names of periods and a chart of cross sections that shows derivative identities or similarities. The word 'pre-history' in all its connotations must be discarded. Nothing is prehistoric which tells truly its own story.

The science of archæology is one with meticulous methods. There are the necessary preliminary studies of ancient and modern writers, of local traditions, of actual roads and probable sites. Then comes the assembling of an archæological outfit, personnel, maps, surveying and photographic implements, materials for the drawing, copying and recording of finds and for preservation, packing and making of objects. There is a technique of excavating and cleaning objects; of determining the dates of pottery by fabric, by style, by shape, etc. and last there is interpretation (called *Hermeneutics*) and publication of the objects discovered. Although isolated finds had often been made as far back as 1506, when the famous Laöcoon group was discovered in Rome, Heinrich Schliemann's discovery of ancient Troy, in 1868), a discovery which was flouted by historians and philologists alike, was seemingly a rock on which the scholarly world was about to split. Schliemann's discovery caused archæology to concentrate on scientific methods in order to substantiate his finds. The many scientific archæologists at

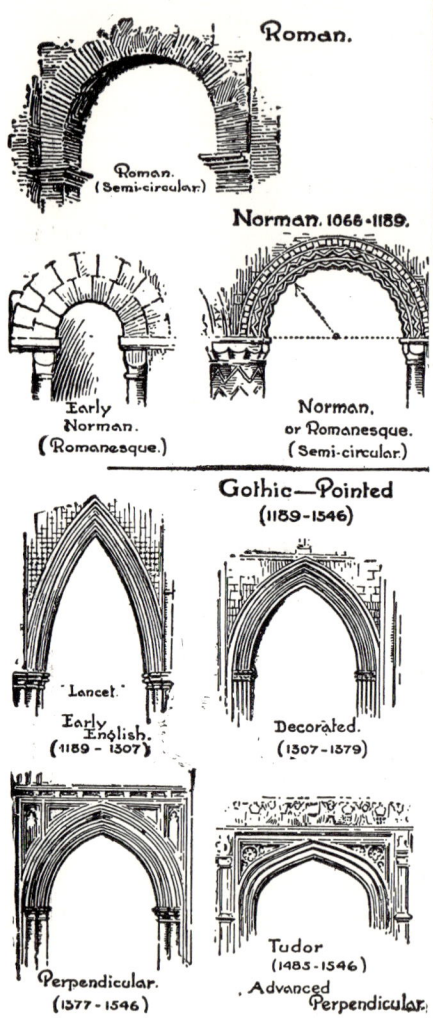

Typical Forms of Arch.

once combined, and as a result Archæology appeared almost overnight as a major scientific subject. An excavation, as now conducted under the auspices of a government grant by experts from a museum or an academic institution, is a marvel in its scientific efficiency.

History has perhaps gained most from the results of archæological research. When the Englishman, Arthur Evans, began in 1900 to work at the site of Cnossus in the island of Crete, the world had no expectation that his discoveries would bring into light a civilization—to which Evans gave the name Minoan—not even dreamed of. Evidence in papyrus MSS. found in Egypt, the many traces of Hittite occupation in Syria and Palestine made it evident that here again, as in Crete, there had come to light the remains of another great civilization.

Within the last decade, two more ancient civilizations have come into the light, also due to the work of archæology: the relics of the early Sumerians and all other recoveries of ancient cultures in upper India. At Harappa and Mohenjo-daro Sir John Marshall uncovered two cities in which are sufficient objects to date this early Indian civilization back to the 4th millennium B.C.

At first the earliest archæological discoveries of importance came at intervals of a century. It was exactly a hundred years after the Laöcoon group of statuary was discovered in Rome that in 1606, also in Rome was found a wall painting to which, from the ownership of the property, was given the title 'The Aldobrandini Marriage.' Excavation began at Pompeii in 1748. Some years later, Herculaneum was the most interesting spot in the archæological world, due to the discovery there in 1753 of more than one hundred ancient marbles and bronzes.

Egypt.—In August, 1799 a stone was found near the Rosetta mouth of the Nile. On it were three inscriptions, one in Greek, one in Egyptian hieroglyphic, and a third in demotic, a sort of shorthand and more common variation of hieroglyphic, both of which latter were undecipherable. It was not until 1822 that the Egyptian inscriptions were read. But for that discovery it may be believed that the history of that famous land would be still classed among the undecipherable past. The excavation of the Serapeum at Memphis was the work of a Frenchman, Mariette. His progress was so notable that he was made an assistant in the Louvre—for which, in 1850, he went out to Egypt to purchase Coptic manuscripts. Mariette excavated in Egypt, during his thirty years there, at thirty-seven different places. His greatest success, after that of the discovery of the Serapeum, was the uncovering of the Ptolemaic temple of Edfu.

Tell el-Amarna is famous in Egyptian annals. First, it was for a time the capital of Egypt during the ascendency of Akhenaten, known to religious history as the 'heretic king,' and to religious philosophy as 'the world's first individual.' Secondly, it is the site which gave its name to the Tell el-Amarna Tablets. These were tablets of clay, inscribed in cuneiform writing, which, accidentally found in 1887, were dated about 1400 B.C. and contained much of the diplomatic correspondence between Egypt and Babylonia. In 1890 the discovery of the Gurob papyrus, and one leaf of the *Antiope* of Euripides, made a great stir in literature. In 1895 the Englishmen Grenfell, Hunt, and Hogarth began to hunt for Egyptian papyri. Their greatest find was on January 13, 1906. A basket of broken rolls of papyrus was found to contain parts of the *Pœans* of the Green Pindar, some of the tragedy of the *Hypsipyle* of Euripides, some portions of the works of Phædrus, and also of a history of Greece. British, French, and Americans now put expeditions into the Egyptian field, all supplied with large funds.

The Pyramids in popular estimation have always stood for Egypt. Many successful attempts were made to find their concealed inner chambers, but when found they proved to be empty, the contents having been rifled in contemporary antiquity.

Egypt has more than 70 pyramids. The excavators in Egypt finally found all but one of the tombs of the Pharaohs, but all had been entered, for the most part in ancient times, and most of the valuables had been stolen. The undiscovered Pharaoh was Tutankhamen.

Theodore M. Davis, the American, held on to his concession for many years, during which time he hunted for the unfound king. In 1906, Mr. Davis discovered a tomb. In it, and near by, he found a number of small articles which had inscribed on them the names of Tutankhamen and his consort. Davis thought he had found the tomb of the lost Pharaoh, and soon thereafter gave up his concession. It was taken over by Lord Carnarvon, associated with Howard Carter. In 1922 Carter and Carnarvon found the four-chambered tomb of **Tutankhamen and the** chambers were full of funerary articles of artistic value, worth many times a king's ransom.

The discovery near the pyramid of Cheops, by Reisner of Harvard University, of the tomb of Hetepheres, the mother of Cheops, is of prime importance. It is an intact tomb of the early period, and afforded for the first time an opportunity to examine the burial of a noble personage, not a Pharaoh.

Mesopotamia.—The materials for building in Mesopotamia were mainly sun-dried or kiln-dried clay in brick form, which have therefore succumbed more readily than the stones and granites of Egypt. The deeper archæological excavations go, the more remote in time are the objects found. The richness in gold and gems found at Ur of the Chaldees quite matches in value, though not in amount, the objects from the tomb of Tutankhamen, and they far outmatch them in artistic and historical value, because they are 2,000 years older.

The pyramid and the mastaba tomb are the outstanding funeral constructions of Egypt. In Mesopotamia, these are matched by the ziggurat and the underground vaulted burial chamber. The ziggurat, of which there are hundreds, is a 'Tower of Babel.' The loft building of today, in its backset stories, is a replica of the ziggurat. The first archæological work in Mesopotamia of scientific consequence began in Babylonia and Assyria, 1811, by Rich, but the first exploit that caused universal excitement was the discovery and copying of the inscription on the Rock of Behistun by H. Rawlinson. As the Rosetta Stone was

Arc de Triomphe de l'Etoile, Paris.

the key to Egyptian hieroglyphics, so the Behistun Rock was the key to cuneiform writing. The entire inscription was translated in 1856 by Edwin Norris.

It is evident from the finds of Sir John Marshall that Indian civilization goes back to 3000 B.C. and beyond. Americans are just entering the field of Indian archæology. The Roerich Museum of New York began work in the year 1930 in the Kulu valley of the Western Himalayas.

Crete and the Ægean Sea.—Both tradition and geographical location seemed to point to the island of Crete as the most probable origin of a civilization in the islands and on the coasts of the Ægean sea. Arthur Evans, the British archæologist, began in 1900 to work at Cnossus, four m. s. of the n. coast seaport Candia. Cnossus was recognized as going back to a time contemporaneous with that of the powers of Egypt and Mesopotamia. The wall paintings portrayed the very people whose pictured presentments had previously

Tomb of Tutankhamen.

Entrance to the Tomb of Tutankhamen.
Howard Carter and his assistants bringing out the richly gilded Hathor-headed Venus, the Goddess of Love.

been found in Egyptian excavations. Soon it was possible to make cross measurements which, even apart from the pottery chronology, settled the comparative dates of culture in Crete and Egypt.

Palestine and Syria.—The discovery of Petra in 1812 by Burckhardt turned the attention of archæologists to the lands that lay between ancient Mesopotamia and Egypt. With the establishment of the Palestine Exploration Fund (British) work was possible on an increased scale. In 1868 the stela of Mesa, known as the Moabite stone, gave to Palestine a discovery in the field of epigraphy somewhat parallel to those of the Rosetta Stone and the Behistun inscription.

The Near East.—Archæology has shown that the Near East was thickly settled from at least 3000 B.C. With 1906 began the most important of the excavations in Asia Minor, which have resulted in restoring the Hittite Empire to its proper place of importance.

Greece.—More sites in Greek lands have been excavated than in any other one country of the ancient world. The British were brought to a high pitch of excitement when they learned that Lord Elgin, their ambassador to the Sublime Porte, was in 1801-03 collecting Parthenon marbles in Athens, and in 1816 the British Museum bought the Parthenon sculptures. The Archæological Institute of America, founded in 1879, started in Athens its first archæological school.

Rome.—The gold mine of Italy consists of the archæological strata of ancient Rome. As might have been expected, the first layer of buried Rome was Christian. De Rossi in 1848 discovered the catacomb of St. Calixtus just outside the city, a find which was the first of many which have been so numerous and so important that Early Christian Archæology is almost a science in its own right.

Tradition in all the lands surrounding the Mediterranean in written records of settlers says that before them there were earlier peoples. We know now that peoples called the Mediterranean race were living on the shores and islands of that sea as far back as 40,000 B.C. Pompeii, Herculaneum, and several other towns were buried by showers of volcanic ash and scoriæ, and overrun to some extent with volcanic mud; all of which hardened considerably when it cooled. Nearly all the inhabitants had time to escape, and later returned to dig out what valuable articles they could. At Herculaneum the scoria was too deep to dig through, and for that reason it is here that excavation brings to light important things. Some of these are now at the Naples Museum.

Continental Europe and Great Britain.—Until late years archæology dealt with remains of Roman civilization in those European countries, and northern Africa as well, which had been Roman provinces. Now earlier remains are known. In Great Britain, in Sardinia, in Brittany, there are menhirs, cromlechs, stone circles, roads, and human remains that are pre-Roman by centuries.

The Americas.—Ethnology set the question before itself as to the racial progenitors of the early peoples in the Americas; archæology settled it. There was some probability inherent in the Mongoloid craniology of the American Indian. Many definite facts were proved when the archæological discoveries in both North and South America traced the objects left by the immigrants from Asia into Alaska down the w. coast of the United States. 'Aboriginal' Peruvians, Maya, Toltec, Aztec, Mixtec, Indians, and the Mound Builders all alike are the descendants of those Asian immigrants.

The most ancient Mayan city, Uaxactum, was discovered in 1916. In 1921 the temple of Quetzalcoatl at Teotihuacan was excavated, and in 1922 Cummings worked at the prehistoric pyramid at Cuicuilco in Mexico. Of late airplanes have helped to discover more. In 1926 the Mason-Spinden expedition explored the ruins of eastern Yucatan. Fine work along these lines is being done at present by the Carnegie Institution.

Archaeological Research from the Air.—Toward the end of World War I there came an important development in archæological research. In Iraq, British and German air pilots discovered markings indicative of archæological remains entirely invisible from the earth. Where earth has been turned in the past, there are slight differences in the color of the soil. This difference in color is carried out in the vegetation, and even trees growing on the site of an ancient ditch or road differ somewhat in color from the neighboring trees. From the air such differences in the color of soil or vegetation or foliage can be readily mapped out and photographed.

Several important archæological discoveries have been made by the use of aeroplanes and aerial photography. This method has also been used to help in mapping archaeological sites already partly excavated, saving considerable work and time. The method is expected to bring to light historic sights in regions difficult to traverse on foot.

Aerial photography has also been used in archæological research of the sea. The sites of cities submerged in the sea and of ancient shipwrecks may be found in this way.

In 1935 an early Christian manuscript which antedates any previously known Christian writings was discovered. It is estimated that this manuscript was written about 150 A.D.

In 1936 a true keystone arch was discovered in a Mayan tomb, the first arch of this type known in Mayan architecture.

In 1940 the tomb of King Psusennes (c. 1000 B.C.) was discovered at Tanis, Lower Egypt. This tomb was intact and contained much rich treasure of archaeological value.

Most Important Archæological Finds.—Rosetta Stone, 1799; discovery of Petra, 1812; discovery of Aphrodite of Melos, 1820; inscription on rock of Behistun 1835; necropolis at Villanova in Italy, 1853; prehistoric caves in France, 1853; Victory of Samothrace, 1863; Moabite stone, 1868; Mycenae, 1876; Hermes of Praxiteles, 1877; Altamira cave paintings, 1879; archives at Tell el-Amarna, 1887; House of Vettii, Pompeii, 1894; Boscoreale silver treasure, 1895; pre-Roman cemetery in Forum, 1902; Egyptian papyri of Greek literature, 1906; Venus of Cyrene, 1913; Treasure of Lahun, 1914; Uaxactum, 1916; oldest Sumerian temple near Ur, 1918; gold statues of Crœsus, 1922; Tomb of Tutankhamen, 1922; Mohenjo-daro and Harappa in India, 1923; Forum of Augustus, 1924; Galilee Skull, 1925; Greco-Celtic bronze flagons near Metz, 1928; Olynthus in Macedonia, 1928; Greek vases in Etruscan cemetery at Valle Treba, 1928.

In 1951 excavators in the Biblical land of Jericho unearthed what is believed to have been King Herod's palace, according to Dr. Jas. B. Pritchard of the Amer. School of Oriental Research. In same year Dr. Carleton S. Coon of the Univ. of Pennsylvania reported evidence that true men lived in Iran about 75,000 yrs. ago. The finding of skeletons of these ancient men (dug up in Hotu Cave nr. Behshahr) may change accepted theories of human evolution, since it indicates the existence of a modern form of man at the same time or earlier than such sub-human species as the Neanderthal or Peking man.

Bibliography.—Consult Marshall's *Discovery in Greek Lands* (1920); Macalister's *Textbook of European Archæology* (vol. 1, 1921); G. G. Maccurdy's *Human Origins* (1924); G. A. Barton's *Archæology and the Bible* (1925); R. A. S. Macalister's *A Century of Excavation in Palestine* (1925); H. B. Walter's *The Art of the Greeks* (1925); W. J. Anderson and R. F. Spiers' *The Architecture of Ancient Rome* (1927); J. R. Moir's *The Antiquity of Man in East Anglia* (1927); D. Randall-MacIver's *The Early Iron Age in Italy* (1927); H. R. Hall's *The Civilization of Greece in the Bronze Age* (1928); G. M. A. Richter's *The Sculpture and Sculptors of the Greeks* (1929); R. C. Thompson and R. W. Hutchinson's *A Century of Exploration at Nineveh* (1929); E. E. Herzfeld's *Archæological History of Iran* (1935).

Archæopteryx, or **Lizard-tailed Bird,** an extinct bird.

Archangel, or **Archangelsk,** most northerly government in European Russia. Area 326,063 sq. m.

Archangel, city, capital of the government of Archangel and chief Arctic port of Russia. Archangel is the chief commercial city for Northern Russia and Siberia; during the year 1915 the growth of Archangel as a trade centre was phenomenal. On Aug. 4, 1918, Allied forces, including an American contingent, were landed at Archangel, defending the port and guarding supplies against seizure; p. 71,000.

Archangel (Gr. 'chief angel'), one of the higher ranks of the angels. See ANGEL.

Archangel, the (plant) deadnettle. See LAMIUM.

Archangelica. See **Angelica.**

Archbishop (Gr. *arch-*, and *episcopos*, 'overseer'), a metropolitan bishop who superintends the conduct of the other bishops in his province, and also exercises episcopal authority in his own diocese. See EPISCOPACY; ARCHES, COURT OF; also Hook's *Archbishops of Canterbury* (12 vols. 1860-76); Raine's *Archbishops of York* (1879); Lightfoot's *Dissertations on the Apostolic Age,* pp. 19, 150, 190 (1892).

Archdeacon, an ecclesiastical dignitary, acting as the bishop's assistant in things temporal, as the archpriest in things spiritual, being in reality the 'bishop's eye' and 'right hand.'

Archduke. Archduchess, titles borne by the members of the imperial house of Austria.

Archegoniata include the moss, fern, and gymnosperm groups of plants.

Archelaus. (1.) A Greek philosopher (c. 450 B.C.). By observation he inferred for the first time the sphericity of the earth. (2.) King of Macedonia (d. 399 B.C.). (3.) Served as general under Mithridates in Greece, where

(86 B.C.) he was twice defeated. (4.) Son of the preceding, became king of Egypt by marrying Berenice, daughter of Ptolemy Auletes, in 56 B.C. (5.) Son of Herod the Great, was bequeathed (4 B.C.) the kingdom of Judæa.

Archer, William (1856-1924), English critic. His works besides his translations (1890-2) of Ibsen's plays, and editions of Leigh Hunt's and Hazlitt's dramatic essays, include *English Dramatists of Today* (1882), *Henry Irving* (1883), *America Today* (1900), *Poets of the Younger Generation* (1901). His dramatic criticisms in *The World* from 1893-7 were republished in book form in annual volumes, under the title of *The Theatrical World*.

Archer Fish, a name for several E. Indian and Polynesian fishes (particularly *Toxotes jaculator*).

Archery, the art, practice, or skill of shooting with a bow and arrows. See Oman's *Art of War in the Middle Ages* (1898); Ascham's *Toxophilus, or the Schole of Shootinge* (1545; or Arber's edition, 1868); Markham's *Art of Archerie* (1634); Ford's *Theory and Practice of Archery* (new ed. 1887); and *Archery* in the Badminton Library (1894)—an excellent bibliography is given at the end of this book.

Arches, Court of. The court of the Archbishop of Canterbury. See *Phillimore's Ecclesiastical Law*.

Archidamus, the name of five kings of Sparta.

Archil, or **Orchil,** a fugitive coloring matter and analogous to litmus.

Archilochus of Paros, Greek poet, lived probably in the earlier half of the 7th century B.C.

Archimage. (1.) The personification of Falsehood in Spenser's *Faërie Queene*. (2.) The personification of Indolence in Thomson's *Castle of Indolence* (1748).

Archimandrite, an Eastern abbot or superior of a monastery.

Archimedean Screw, an apparatus invented by the Greek mathematician Archimedes, for the purpose of raising water from a lower to a higher level.

Archimedes, a genus of fossil shells belonging to the family Fenestellidæ.

Archimedes (c. 287-212 B.C.), the most famous mathematician of antiquity, intermediate in time between Euclid and Apollonius, was a native of Syracuse. Besides making many important discoveries in mechanics and mathematics, he invented numerous mechanical contrivances. See Heath's *Works of Archimedes* (1897).

Archipelago, the term applied to any group of islands considered collectively.

Architects, American Institute of, an association organized in 1857, with offices in Washington, D. C.

Architecture is the art of building according to certain well-defined principles of proportion and symmetry, so that an edifice, when completed, shall not only suit the pur-

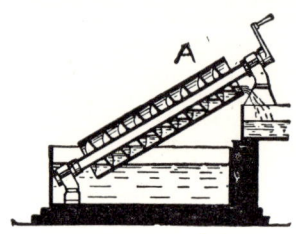

Archimedean Screw (section).

pose for which it was erected, in accommodation and usefulness, but at the same time form a harmonious whole, externally and internally.

PREHISTORIC STRUCTURES. — These include the following:—

Monolith.—Single upright stones. An example is the Carnac stone in Brittany, 63 ft. high, 14 ft. in diameter, and 260 tons in weight.

Cromlech.—Table-stone supported on others that are vertical.

Stone Circles.—The best example is Stonehenge, near Salisbury. The circumference (over 300 ft.) of the circle consisted of numerous uprights, each 18 ft. high, with architrave stones on the top. There are also inside circles of stones, and possibly it was entirely roofed over.

Cyclopean Architecture.—The name given by the Greeks to the prehistoric forms of masonry supposed to have been erected by the Cyclops or giants. The average blocks of stone were 9 ft. long and 4 ft. thick.

Ancient American.—The buildings of Yucatan, discovered in the forests of Mexico, show that that country was at one time peopled by a race of high intelligence.

BABYLONIAN and ASSYRIAN ARCHITECTURE were developed in the valleys of the Tigris and Euphrates, the former from 3800 B.C. till 500 B.C. The designs employed show what seem prototypes of Grecian architecture.

EGYPTIAN ARCHITECTURE.—Among the oldest monuments are the pyramids at Gizeh, n. of Memphis (Cheops, Chephren, and Mycerinus), formed of solid masses of masonry, the sides being stepped from four to five ft. on each course. The great pyramid of Cheops is called after the king of that name. The Great Sphinx at Gizeh is another monument to the genius and ambition of the Egyptians. The temples were of two types, the one excavated out of the solid rock, and the other built in the ordinary manner. Of the former, Abu-Simbel in Nubia (1400 B.C.) is the finest example.

By Ewing Galloway, N. Y.
Famous Flowery Pagoda, Canton, China

CHINESE AND JAPANESE ARCHITECTURE.— The Chinese style of architecture is supposed to be based on the principle of the tent. The roof is the feature of the Chinese style, and has wide projecting eaves turned upwards on the outside. Chinese pagodas are octagonal towers. Japanese architecture resembles the Chinese, except that the decorative details are more refined and delicate. Wood is the chief material used, and the prevalence of earthquakes prevents even the building of towers.

INDIAN ARCHITECTURE.—See special article.

GRECIAN ARCHITECTURE.—The Greeks may be justly called the most perfect masters of the art. Their architecture, which was entirely of the columnar order, exhibits a massiveness and quiet repose. The three distinct orders of Grecian architecture, Doric, Ionic, and Corinthian, are given under CLASSIC ORDERS. The principal ruins in Athens are the Theseum (*c.* 470-50 B.C.) and the Parthenon, finished in 438 B.C. Both belong to the Doric order, which was the favorite order in Greece. The Athenian buildings were built of white marble, and it is supposed that, both externally and internally, they were painted in many bright colors, in conjunction with a considerable amount of gilding. In Athens the three principal Ionic ruins are the temples of Ilissus, Minerva Polias, and Erechtheum; while, of the Corinthian order, the Tower of the Winds and the Choragic Monument are the finest examples. There is, besides, an additional order, called the Caryatic order, in which the statues of women were used instead of columns.

ROMAN ARCHITECTURE.—The Romans almost entirely borrowed their ideas from the Greeks. Until the conquest of Greece by the Romans in 145 B.C., the buildings of the latter were of the rudest description. The warlike Romans had no time to pursue the arts, but left those peaceful occupations in the hands of Grecian workmen. The orders of Roman architecture (Corinthian, Doric, Ionic, and Composite) are given under CLASSIC ORDERS below. Although the Greeks favored the Doric, the Romans preferred the Corinthian. Circular Temples were purely Roman. Among the finest specimens stands the Panthenon at Rome, begun 27 B.C., but rebuilt under Hadrian (117-38 A.D.).

Forums.—All large cities contained several of these buildings. They consisted of a large rectangular court surrounded by a colonnade, through which entrances led to temples, law courts, theatres, etc.

Triumphal Arches.—In Rome we find those built in honor of Titus, Severus, and Constantine. In earlier times they represented a single arch, but latterly consisted of a large central arch flanked by two smaller ones.

Villas.—The private dwellings of the Romans, although built externally of plain brick, surpass those of any other nation in internal magnificence.

Amphitheatres.—These are also of Roman design, ruins existing in most countries conquered by the Romans. The most important is the Coliseum, Rome, built by Vespasian and Titus.

Baths.—It is said that there were at one time as many as 850 baths in the city of Rome, the largest being those of Diocletian, Titus, and Caracalla. At each end, and at the sides, were temples, while the main building contained a large vestibule, with four halls (on each side) for cold, tepid, warm.

and steam baths. In the centre was an immense quadrangle for taking exercise, and, beyond, a hall with 1,600 seats for bathers, while at each end were libraries. In addition there were music, lecture, and dressing rooms, besides gymnasia and swimming baths.

Basilicas.—These were the halls of justice, usually attached to the forum. In later times the walls were raised and roofed in, the part above the colonnade being used as a gallery—one end semicircular in shape—where the judges sat. In many respects these buildings have become models for modern Christian churches.

CLASSIC ORDERS.—In distinguishing between Greek and Roman orders, in addition to the curves of the mouldings being different, there is the variation in the proportion of the diameter of the columns, not only to their height and to the distance they are apart, but also to the depth of the entablature. This is again divided by varying proportions into architrave, frieze, and cornice. For details, consult bibliography.

Grecian Doric Order.—Generally used in Greek temples, and consisting of three parts—stylobate, column, and entablature. At the base the stylobate is from two-thirds to one diameter of the column in height, and is divided into equal courses or steps. Resting on the top step is the column, 4 to 6 diameters in height, and diminishing in a slightly-curved line to the necking or hypotrachelium, where it is between two-thirds and four-fifths diameter at base. It is generally divided into 20 flutes.

ORDERS OF ARCHITECTURE.

Left to Right—1, Greek Doric; 2, Roman Doric; 3, Greek Ionic; 4, Roman Ionic; 5, Greek Corinthian; 6, Roman Corinthian.

Grecian Ionic Order.—This was doubtless borrowed from Assyrian designs. The column, which diminishes to five-sixths at the hypotrachelium, is divided into 24 elliptical flutes and alternating fillets. The capital, three-quarters of a diameter in height is like a paper roll lying on the top of a column, with the rolls or volutes hanging downwards on each side.

Grecian Corinthian Order.—Of this order there are only two remaining specimens in Greece, all others at present standing having been built after the Roman invasion. The Choragic Monument at Athens—circular, and standing on a square pediment—is the best example. This column is 10 diameters in height. The base is two-fifths and the capital 1⅓ diameters in height, composed of a cylindrical core with eight leaves clustered round it, while above are four acanthus leaves cyma recta in contour, surmounted by a moulded abacus curved inwards on each face.

Grecian Caryatic Order.—In this order the statues of women were substituted instead of columns.

Roman Doric Order.—This is a rude imitation of the Grecian design, and seldom used.

Roman Ionic Order.—This design is in many respects similar to the Grecian.

Roman Corinthian.—This was the favorite order adopted by the Romans. The column consists of base, shaft, and capital, 10 diameters in height—the base similar to Ionic, the only difference being that it stands on a square plinth. The capital is 1⅛ diameters in height, consisting of two rows, one above the other, of eight acanthus leaves, surmounted by helices and foliage, and the abacus, with inward curved moulded faces.

Second Corinthian Order.—This order, afterward known in Italian Renaissance as the Composite order, is similar in most respects to the Corinthian. The columns, however, were not quite so high, and have a deeper capital, which in appearance is a combination of Corinthian with 4 Ionic volutes projecting at each corner directly under the abacus.

Early Christian.—This style is an adaptation of the architecture of the declining Roman empire, to the needs of Christian worship. The result in the western world was the Christian basilica; the development of which into the Romanesque and Gothic church forms the history of architecture during the middle ages. Early Christian architecture began soon after the spread of Christianity; it lingered at Rome until the advent of the Renaissance in the 15th century.

BYZANTINE is the Christian architecture of the Eastern empire, as distinguished from the Early Christian in the Western. Its principal characteristic was the development of domical structures. Although the Romans had built domes upon circular walls, and early Christian architects went a step further by converting the lower wall into a colonnade, it was reserved for the Byzantines to construct the largest domes. Another striking characteristic of the Byzantine style, which originated in the love of color peculiar to the Orient, was the glittering mosaic decorations of the interiors. Byzantine influence extended to Italy, dominating Venice, and even extended to Southern France. The most magnificent example in Italy is San Marco at Venice.

ROMANESQUE.—This term is applied to the style of architecture which succeeded early Christian in the western world. Its beginnings date from about 800 A.D.; it lingered in some countries as late as the 13th century. Romanesque architecture differed from the early Christian in that its ground plan was always a Latin cross; in the use of piers in place of columns, and of groined and ribbed vaulting in place of the ancient flat ceilings.

Germany. — The origin of Romanesque architecture was due to the general revival of culture under Charles the Great (*c.* 800), and the seat of its earliest development was the valleys of the Rhine and the Moselle. The normal type of the Romanesque church which displaced the others was the vaulted basilica of the Rhinelands. Examples are the cathedrals of Speyer and Mayence, and the cathedrals of Treves and Worms. The Romanesque lingered longest in Germany.

Norman.—Corresponding to the political division of France during the middle ages and the *langue d'oc* and *langue d'oil* as boundaries of its culture, there were two distinct types of architecture: the flat ceiled basilica of the north, which is best termed the Norman, and the vaulted churches of the south. The chief characteristics of the Norman architecture is the strict insistence upon the Latin cross as the ground form, the use of square instead of round choirs and the extremely long and narrow nave. The Normans imported their own architects from the continent to Great Britain, and soon developed great building activity. The English churches are longer and narrower than the Norman, especially as regards the choir.

Italy.—Owing to the prevalence of antique structures, the development in Italy was slower. The so-called Lombard style in northern Italy, bears much resemblance to those of northern Europe. The earliest example is that of Sant' Ambrogio in Milan. The Tuscan Romanesque is more closely related to the antique. The chief example, the model for Central Italy, is the Cathedral of Pisa (1063-1118), with its Baptistery and celebrated Leaning Tower. The Florentine Romanesque bore even greater resemblance to the antique. In southern Italy and Sicily a peculiar variety of Romanesque originated, with strange admixture of Byzantine, Saracen and Norman elements. The chief characteristic is the splendor of its mosaic decoration. The finest examples are in Sicily, among which the Cathedral of Monreale is pre-ëminent.

GOTHIC.—This term was applied by the Italians to the architecture preceding the Renaissance, in derision of its supposed barbaric character; wrongly so, since it was not German, but originated in France. Its forms were a development of the Romanesque, resulting from the concentration of strains incidental to the universal use of ribbed vaulting. The weight of the vaults was concentrated upon great piers assisted by balanced thrusts in the shape of flying buttresses. The result was a complete dissolution of the masses of the heavy walls, the place of which was occupied by beautiful windows rich in tracery. The pointed arch, which by its downward thrust admits of more lofty vaults, was generally introduced.

France.— Gothic architecture originated in the Ile de France as the result of a combination of Northern and Southern influences. In the latter part of the 12th century arose a series of fine cathedrals, whose massiveness shows the transition from the Romanesque: finest of all, Notre Dame at Paris. The most perfect development was attained in the 13th century in such cathedrals as Chartres. In these buildings the place of the walls is taken by magnificent stained glasses. In the late or florid Gothic period (1375-1525) profuse decoration and cleverness of technical execution replaced dignity of design, finally degenerating into the unrestrained extravagances of the Flamboyant style.

England.— Although Gothic architecture was introduced from France into England, it soon experienced in that country a peculiarly national development. It retained the long and narrow naves of the Norman period and the straight determination of the choir which is usually adorned with a beautiful window. The first example (1174) of Early English Gothic style in England was the choir of Canterbury. The later Decorative or Geometric style is characterized by decorative richness and a lighter construction, among the finest examples being the York Cathedrals. The Perpendicular corresponds with the late Gothic and extends well into the 16th century, when it is called the Tudor style. The college buildings of the English universities are largely built in this style. In general, the most successful features of English exteriors were the lofty and massive central towers.

Spain.—The Gothic style was transplanted into Spain from France during the 13th century. The largest of the Spanish cathedrals, which are themselves more extensive than other European churches, is that of Seville, begun in 1401. The later Gothic in Spain is characterized by overloaded decoration, attributed to Moorish tendencies.

Germany.—Gothic architecture was introduced into Germany at a later period than elsewhere, owing to the tenacity with which the Germans clung to the Romanesque. The most important development took place in the Rhinelands.

Italy.—Among the principal examples are the Cathedral of Milan begun in 1386, a compromise of Italian and Northern methods; and the cathedrals of Siena and Orvieto, begun in 1245 and 1290 respectively, the most beautiful and consistent examples of the Tuscan Gothic. For the development of private dwellings and castles during the Romanesque and Gothic period see article on CASTLE.

RENAISSANCE.—Its principal divisions are the Early or Free Renaissance (1420-1500), the High or Classical (1500-1575), and the Declining Renaissance or Baroque (1575-1780).

Italy.—The Renaissance began in Florence and its early works were by Florentine architects. The founder of the style was Brunellesci who, after long studies at Rome, produced in his cupola of the Cathedral of Florence (1420-64) the first monument of the new style. In Venice, whither the Renaissance was introduced latest of all, it developed into the most richly decorative of the Italian styles. The High Renaissance had much more of the Roman spirit. The decoration, which was much less rich, was subordinated to constructive principles, with the result of a grandiose and severe style, abounding in plain surfaces and colossal details. The study of Vitruvius and of the Roman ruins was accepted as a part of the training of every architect. The pioneer of the style was Bramante of Urbino, whose chief activity was at Rome. His principal successor was Michelangelo, who in his cupola of St. Peter's created a model for the churches of the following period. The tendency was increasingly classical, and about 1450 a period of formal classicism began with Vignola and Palladio. The Baroque or Declining Renaissance was a reaction against

MODERN SKYSCRAPERS, NEW YORK CITY.
Left—A Building in Rockefeller Center. Right—Empire State Building.

classical severity; it emphasized the picturesque rather than the monumental, and was characterized by exaggerated forms and constructions and a general disregard for architectural propriety.

France.—The introduction of the Renaissance into France was greatly promoted by the close political relations with Italy in the latter 15th and early 16th centuries. Its chief result during the 16th century was the transformation of the mediæval castle into a superb modern residence. In the course of the century it became increasingly classic, and in such works as Pierre Lescot's court of the Louvre (1546) the mediæval elements are practically eliminated. It found its chief expression in the magnificent series of châteaux along the Loire. The 16th century saw the development of what may be called the classic period of French architecture, during the reign of Louis XIV., resulting in the Palace of Versailles, the Invalides, and especially in the colonnade of the Louvre.

Germany.—Owing to the religious wars and other conditions inimical to art, the Renaissance did not enter Germany until the early part of the 16th century. The most important monuments are the castles and town halls; such as the castle of Heidelberg. During the later 17th century the Baroque was introduced from Italy.

England.—The Renaissance was introduced into England during the reign of Elizabeth (1558-1603), for which reason the admixture of the Renaissance and Gothic elements of that period is called the Elizabethan style. Under James I classic forms came into more general use, but it was reserved for Inigo Jones, the chief English architect of the early 17th century, to introduce a purer, classic style. His style was further developed by his greatest successor in the later 17th century, Sir Christopher Wren.

MODERN ARCHITECTURE.—What may be called the predecessor of modern architecture was introduced by the so-called Classic Revival, as, for example, all the great constructions of Napoleon, like the Arc de Triomphe and the Madeleine in Paris.

The Gothic Revival.—The reaction against the imitation of classic forms took the form of Victorian Gothic between 1850 and 1870. The corresponding movement in France, which began about 1845 under Viollet-le-Duc, took the form of an accurate and tasteful restoration of mediæval monuments.

United States.—In the period following the first settlement there was little architecture of any special significance. The so-called Colonial style (1753-75) was based upon contemporary English practice, with such modifications of detail as the general employment of wood required.

The Early Republican period was characterized by a series of works of a more monumental character, to meet the requirements of the new state and national life; such as the Capitol at Washington (1793-1830) by Thornton, Hallet, and Latrobe; The White House by Hoban, (1792), the State House at Boston (1795) by Bulfinch, the New York City Hall (1803-12) by McComb and Mangin, and the University of Virginia (1817) by Thomas Jefferson.

The absorption of the people by political activity and industrial progress during the War Period (1850-76) resulted in a decline of taste. Influenced by the Gothic, domestic architecture inclined toward the grotesque. At the end of this period, however, notable achievements in church architecture began, and a general artistic improvement followed. A number of causes contributed to the artistic awakening, among which was the increasing practice of studying abroad. Two pupils of the Ecole des Beaux Arts, R. M. Hunt and H. H. Richardson, exercised a great influence. A school proclaiming the preeminence of Gothic began at this time and is influential to this day, especially in Church and University architecture. Among its achievements may be noted: St. Patrick's Cathedral in New York, by Renwick; St. Thomas's in the same city by Cram, Goodhue and Ferguson; the Princeton University Chapel and the Harkness buildings at Yale; also the Cathedral of St. John the Divine in New York and the Washington Cathedral. But in 1893 the World's Fair in Chicago, whose buildings were designed by the most eminent architects of the time, opened the eyes of the public to the possibilities of monumental effect obtainable through the use of classical architecture. Charles Follen McKim and Stanford White were instrumental in the development of an Italian Renaissance cult. This school also produced a large number of unusually fine buildings throughout the Eastern States, many of them in New York. Among these might be noted St. Bartholomew's Church, the porch by McKim, Mead and White. Stanford White was a leader in this school. With these two influences at work blendings of the styles produced the beginning of a new architecture. Its most notable form was in commercial buildings.

A great innovation in the construction of commercial buildings was caused by the increased use of the elevator and the resulting introduction of the steel cage system of construction, which admits of an indefinite number of stories. The exterior thus became a mere shell. The first quarter of the 19th century produced buildings of structure with simple masses, set back as they rise, in obedience to the requirements of the municipal zoning laws. Later commercial buildings much in advance of those of the beginning of the 19th century, are the Woolworth, showing the Gothic influence predominating, and the more recent Chrysler and Empire State Buildings which show the triumph of a newly evolved style.

The name of Louis Sullivan is especially connected with these efforts to attain a modern style. Frank Lloyd Wright's work influenced design in Europe. American architecture has marched to the front with such rapid strides that the interest of foreign architects in American architecture is evidenced by the annual visits of architects from other countries coming to study American design as well as novel methods of construction. The World's Fair at Chicago in 1933-4 brought about a new interest in uses of new materials and modern forms; these are extended to domestic as well as public buildings. Some authorities assert that architecture suffered a relapse about 1930 and has not yet recovered, but it is safe to say that this field of art has been passing through a period of development and has now reached a stage representative of the time. Thus we may say that architecture has since developed a style of its own—the modern.

Modern style architecture is a result not only of architectural genius, but of a number of direct and indirect causes. Never before has it had such a wealth of materials from which to draw—new types of glass, reinforced concrete, steels and alloys. This, plus influence in design caused by the modern lines in transportation facilities, and the inculcation of practical ideas into the finished structure, all are underlying causes resulting in the modern style.

Architectural structures of today rely upon simplicity of line, yet ingeniously develop that simplicity to a point where it is suggestive of grandeur. The streamline influence has produced 'rounded corners'; realization of the tremendous importance of light has brought about the construction of public buildings whose exteriors are almost entirely of glass; and the increased need for economy of area has resulted in the utmost utilization of space.

So simple in line are some of the modern architectural structures that they cause consternation and opposition on the part of the uninitiated. Such was the case when the railroad station in Florence, Italy, was completed (1936), and it was only after it had been subject to severe criticism that it was finally accepted and officially approved.

In the United States the combination of simplicity and grandeur, plus the almost inexhaustible wealth of materials and methods now available, are adequately shown in the recently completed New York State Roosevelt Memorial, dedicated January 19, 1936, in honor of the late Theodore Roosevelt. John Russell Pope was the architect. The features and design combine illustrations of the widely varied fields of activity indulged in by Roosevelt, and produce a beautifully harmonized whole in which the ancient and modern styles are almost inextricably interwoven.

The prominent features of the Roosevelt Memorial include a façade designed after the Roman triumphal arches, a huge entrance arch 60 feet in height, flanked by gigantic granite columns, and a Memorial Hall 67 feet wide and 120 feet long. The floor of the hall is of marble mosaic, the walls, with the exception of the lower part, are of mellowed limestone, while beneath this they are composed of St. Florient cream-marble. Enclosing the terrace a parapet wall is surmounted with inscriptions signifying Roosevelt's varied activities. A further contribution to the beauty of the hall is a series of murals executed by William A. Mackay which cover a space of 5,230 square feet. The building is managed by the trustees of the American Museum of Natural History.

In 1941 there was destruction by the Germans of much that was valuable beyond price in architecture, masterpieces that can never be restored, while the skill of architects was being extensively devoted to designs for buildings to house defense industries and their workers.

Consult Hamlin's *Text Book of the History of Architecture;* Rosengarten's *Handbook of Architectural Styles;* Fletcher's *History of Architecture on the Comparative Method;* Bibliotheque de l'enseignement des Beaux Arts; Gwilt's *Encyclopaedia of Architecture;* Sturgis's *Dictionary of Architecture;* and *American Architecture of Today* by G. H. Edgell. The two standard works on architectural composition are *Essentials of Composition* by John V. Van Pelt (2d ed., 1914), and Curtis' *Architectural Composition*.

Architrave, the lowest of the three principal members of an entablature. The architrave of a door or window is any moulded or otherwise ornamented band surrounding the opening.

Archives. See **Records**.

Archivolt, the ornamental band of mouldings around an arch.

Archon, originally the lowest, and eventually the highest, magistrate of the city of Athens. Under Solon's constitution the popular courts and the development of the jury system greatly lessened the power of the archons.

Archpriest, a church dignitary whose office was formerly given in each diocese to the priest senior by ordination. He was the helper of the bishop in his spiritual functions, as the archdeacon was in his temporal functions.

Archytas of Tarentum (c. 400 B.C.), Greek general and mathematician, and a friend of Plato, was the first to apply geometry to mechanics. He is known only by references in ancient writers.

Arctic Exploration. The Arctic Sea was first entered by Ohthere or Othere, a Norwegian, who sailed to the north coast of Russia, and made a report of his voyage to King Alfred. About 1001 the west coast of Greenland was colonized by the Icelander, Erik the Red, but no further progress was made in Arctic discovery until 1553, when Sir Hugh Willoughby sighted Novaya Zemlya; in 1596, discovered Spitzbergen, rounded the northern extremity of Novaya Zemlya, and wintered on the east coast. In 1607 Henry Hudson sailed up the east coast of Greenland to Cape Hold with Hope, and crossing over to Spitzbergen, named Hakluyt Headland. In another voyage, in 1610, he discovered Hudson Strait. Captain Carlsen (1863) was the first to sail around Spitzbergen.

As early as 1576 Frobisher made a voyage to the southern extremity of Greenland and the opposite American coast, and in 1585 the strait forming the entrance to the Arctic regions west of Greenland was discovered by John Davis. In 1616 Baffin and Bylot passed through Davis Strait, and sailed up the North Water to Smith Sound. Commander John Ross was sent out in 1818 with the *Isabella* and *Alexander*. He confirmed the accuracy of Baffin's observations. Sir John Franklin in search of a North-West Passage set sail on May 20, 1845, and ascertained the existence of a sea passage from the Atlantic to the channels south of Victoria and Wollaston Lands, leading to Bering Strait. During the last decade of the 19th and the first of the 20th century a large number of explorers visited the Arctic regions. Starting in 1892, Commander R. E. Peary spent several seasons in Greenland and on the neighboring coast. In the summer of 1905 he again sailed northward in the specially built *Roosevelt*, and on April 21, 1906, reached what was then 'farthest north,' 87° 6', 174 nautical m. from the pole. Nansen entered the ice with the *Fram* near the New Siberia Islands in 1893, drifted during two winters toward the pole, and with Johansen marched over the ice to lat. 86° 4' N., while the *Fram* reached lat. 85° 57' to the north of Spitzbergen. In 1905 an expedition under the Duke of Orleans surveyed the east coast of Greenland from Cape Bismarck to lat. 78° 16' N. Roald Amundsen, a Norwegian, started in 1903 to relocate the magnetic pole; this he accomplished in the summer of 1905, and brought his vessel to Alaska in 1905—the first vessel to make the North-West Passage. Mylius Erichsen, leader of a Danish Greenland expedition, after completing the mapping of the unknown coast of Northeastern Greenland, lost his life on the n.e. coast in 1908. On Sept. 6, 1909, the memorable announcement was made to the world by Commander Peary, who had just reached Indian Harbor, that five months previously (on April 6) he had 'nailed the Stars and Stripes to the Pole.' The Peary expedition had left the United States in the summer of 1908. From Etah, the northernmost settlement in Greenland, it proceeded to Cape Sheridan, where quarters were erected, and the long winter night partly spent in transporting stores to Cape Columbia, on the northern shore of Grant Land. From this point, on Feb. 28, 1909, the northward journey to the pole was resumed. Strong winds and bad ice proved heavy handicaps to the party until the 88th parallel was reached. Here Captain Bartlett turned southward, and the expedition was reduced to Peary himself, Henson and four Eskimos, with supplies for forty days. On April 1 the final dash began. Good ice was found and the temperature rose to —15°. Thirty-two miles were made in twelve hours—an observation recorded the latitude as 89° 57'—and then the long-coveted goal was won! Flags were hoisted and the Pole was claimed for the United States (April 6, 1909).

The discovery of the North Pole marked an epoch in Arctic exploration. Since that remarkable achievement numerous important expeditions have been undertaken, and our knowledge of the regions within the Arctic Circle has been greatly extended. The outstanding names of this period are those of Stefansson, and his associate Anderson; Donald MacMillan, **who accompanied Peary** in 1908-09; Vilkitski of Russia; Knud Rasmussen and Koch of Denmark and Roald Amundsen, who had previously distinguished himself in the Antarctic. Not only has much progress been made in mapping the Polar regions, but a vast amount of scientific data has been gathered.

ploration of Crocker Land, which has been sighted by Peary in 1906, northwest of Cape Thomas Hubbard. With his associate, Green, MacMillan succeeded in reaching lat. 82° 30' n. and long. 102° w., only to find that the supposed land was non-existent. The most important recent achievement of Russian explorers was that of Vilkitski, who in 1915 made the first northeast passage ever accomplished from east to west. In *Greenland* Rasmussen disproved the existence of Peary Channel (1912-13), which was formerly believed to form the northern boundary, and made extensive explorations (1916-18) along the Hazen Coast discovered in 1882 by the Greely expedition. In 1918 Roald Amundsen

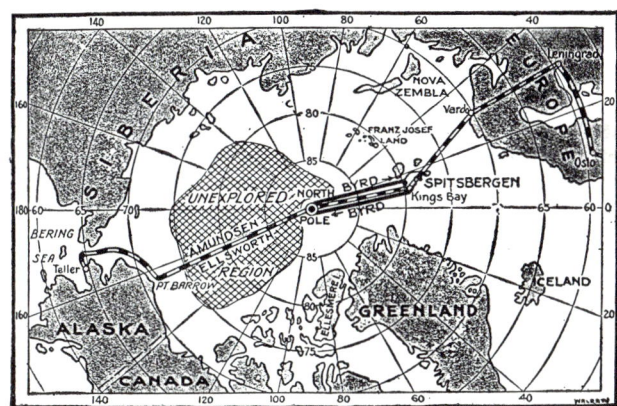

The 1926 Polar Flights
(Reproduced by permission from Current History Magazine)

Vilhjalmur Stefansson made his first expedition to the American Arctic in 1906-07, for the purpose of anthropological study of the Eskimos of the Mackenzie Delta, under the joint auspices of Harvard University and the University of Toronto. A second expedition, undertaken under the direction of the American Museum of Natural History and the Canadian Geological Survey, covered a period of about four years (1908-12). In 1913 a third expedition was organized under the direction of the Canadian government. The purpose of the expedition was chiefly scientific, and a notable group of scientists was brought together to make extensive studies in anthropology, biology, geography, geology, mineralogy, oceanography, and terrestrial magnetism.

In 1913 an expedition under Donald MacMillan left the United States for Ellesmere Island, whence it was to undertake the ex-

sailed from Christiania (now Oslo) on the *Maud,* planning to drift across the top of the world from Alaska to Asia with the Arctic ice. He accomplished the Northeast Passage in 1918-20. The *Amundsen-Ellsworth Polar Flight Expedition,* financed by Lincoln Ellsworth, an American, and under the leadership of Roald Amundsen, took off from Kings Bay, Spitzbergen, May 21, 1925, in the first attempt by airplane to reach the North Pole, 600 nautical m. distant. The flight was sponsored by the Aero Club of Norway and flew under the Norwegian flag. After leaving Amsterdam Island, off the n.e. coast of Spitzbergen, the planes were in the air exactly eight hours, and with their average speed of 75 m. per hour should have reached the Pole but for the head-wind and consequent drift. At the end of that period it was deemed necessary to descend for an observation, afterwards continuing on to the Pole. The planes had become separated in landing, and it was five days before the two parties were able to reunite. During this interval the ever-shifting ice had closed in upon the two planes and it was considered advisable to concentrate all effort on extricating the N. 25 from its icy grip. After 25 days of heroic effort a 'take-off' was effected, and then after five previous attempts had failed. After a flight of eight hours and thirty-five minutes, the N. 25 reached North Cape, Northeastland, Spitzbergen. The scientific results of the expedition included soundings and an air survey covering 64,000 sq. m. of previously unknown region.

The Amundsen-Ellsworth-Nobile Transpolar Flight of 1926 was a continuation of the 1925 Arctic exploration plans of Captain Roald Amundsen and Lincoln Ellsworth and was officially sponsored by the Aero Club of Norway. A semi-rigid airship, built by Italy as the *N-1* and rechristened the *Norge*, was used instead of aeroplanes. At the time of its purchase from the Italian government, Col. Umberto Nobile, designer and builder of the *N-1*, became identified with the expedition as ship commander. The line of flight from Rome was over France, England, Norway, Sweden, and Russia, to Kings Bay, Spitzbergen, a distance of about 5,000 m.; there the *Norge* arrived May 7. At 8:55 A.M. (G.M.T.), on May 11, the start over the Polar Sea was made. The polar pack showed no signs of life north of 83½°. Up to this latitude polar bear and white whale were observed. After leaving the Pole the érst sign of life—a lone polar bear track—was seen at lat. 86°. On reaching the North Pole (600 nautical m. from Spitzbergen) at 1:30 A. M., May 12, the airship was slowed down, and from an altitude of 300 ft., the Norwegian, American, and Italian flags were dropped in the order named. A safe landing was effected at Teller, Alaska, a few minutes before 8 A.M., May 14, after a flight of 71 hours. The mean average temperature during the flight was —10° C. The expedition proved that between the North Pole and Alaska lies only a deep Polar Sea; compiled valuable meteorological and wireless data; bisected the 1,000,000 sq. m. of unknown region by a trail of approximately 100 m. in width, crowning with success the plans and ambitions of the leaders, who had met with such a severe reverse the preceding year.

The month of May 1926 was a notable one in the history of Arctic exploration, for not only was the Pole reached by the *Norge* in its transpolar flight, but three days earlier (May 9, 1926) Lieut.-Com. Richard E. Byrd of the U. S. Navy and his pilot, Floyd Bennett, passed over the Pole in the airplane *Josephine Ford*. The expedition was privately financed in the U. S. The fliers took off from Kings Bay, Spitzbergen, at 12:37 A.M. (Greenwich time) May 9; and reached the Pole at 9:03. They did not land, and taking observations returned to Spitzbergen, which they reached at 4:34 P.M., about fifteen hours after departure, having flown a distance of 1,500 m. On May 29, 1951 Pan American Airways Capt. Chas. F. Blair soloed across the N. Pole. In a single-engine plane (P-51) he flew 3,300 mi. from Bardufoss, Norway to Fairbanks, Alaska in 10 hrs. 29 mins.; reached New York 3,450 mi. away in 9 hrs. 31 mins. Consult Parry's *Journals;* Sir John Franklin's *Thirty Years in the Arctic Regions;* Amundsen's *The North-West Passage;* Peary's *Nearest the Pole* and *The North Pole;* P. L. Simmond's *The Arctic Regions and Polar Discoveries during the Nineteenth Century; The North-West and North-East Passages, 1576-1611,* edited by P. F. Alexander (1915); MacMillan's *Four Years in the White North* (1918); Rasmussen's *Greenland by the Polar Sea* (1921); Stefansson's *The Northward Course of Empire* (1922).

Russia has been the most persistent of all nations in exploring the Arctic within recent years. Russia proposes to maintain a sea path from the White Sea to the Bering Strait.

It has also attempted to make practical its air route between Russia and the United States, via the North Pole. To this end Russia in 1935 sent out 67 expeditions, many of them aerial, to survey the Arctic.

Several additional naval and aerial bases were established along the northern coast of Russia and Siberia in 1936. In 1937, an aerial base was set up on the ice field at the North Pole, which drifted some 1200 miles southward before being abandoned in 1938.

The Arctic zone forms a well-defined geographical region, characterized by many peculiar animals and plants. In certain parts—as in the interior of Greenland—this region is singularly barren and devoid of life; but elsewhere, as in the tundras of Asia, there is, during the brief but hot summer, an exceedingly luxuriant growth of plant life, with a corresponding abundance of insects, birds, and herbivorous and carnivorous mammals. Among the land plants the mosses and lichens deserve special mention, on account of their abundance and importance as food for the reindeer, musk ox, and lemming. In addition, there are many flowering plants. Within the Arctic region proper, trees do not occur, the Arctic species of willow and birch being low-growing plants. The plant life of the sea would not appear to be of great direct importance. Indirectly, the algæ, both large and small, are of great importance, as they furnish ultimately the food upon which the marine organisms depend. Of sea forms, the molluscs are of interest. The Crustacea also deserve notice. Crabs are few, but shrimps, schizopods, and amphipods are abundant; in the case of the ill-fated Greely expedition they formed the only food obtainable by the survivors. In certain parts of the Arctic region fish are extraordinarily plentiful, and reach large size. Of terrestrial animals, the birds in certain regions are very abundant during the summer months. The valuable eider duck, cormorants, mergansers, oyster catchers, puffins, guillemots, terns, auks, razor-bills, and many others literally darken the air in the vicinity of their breeding haunts. In the tundras such land birds as the ptarmigan, the golden plover, and the phalarope abound. The mammals themselves show many striking peculiarities. As the conditions throughout the region are quite uniform, a dominant species is likely to be widely distributed. This is true of the reindeer and the elk; the musk ox, now confined to the northern parts of the western hemisphere, is an apparent exception. Of even greater importance are the aquatic or semi-aquatic mammals, such as the true fur seal. Consult, in addition to the works cited under ARCTIC EXPLORATION, Stefansson's *The Friendly Arctic* (1921) and Mason's *The Arctic Forests* (1924).

Arctic Ocean, one of the great water divisions of the globe, is for the most part enclosed between the northern coasts of Europe, Asia, and North America. Apparently there is no land in the higher latitudes, and the North Pole is a vast sea of comparatively smooth ice. The greatest depth yet sounded in the Arctic is 2,100 fathoms, in 81° N. and 130° E.; or 2,650 fathoms, if we accept the sounding of the *Sofia* made in 1868. The area of the Arctic Ocean is estimated at 5,908,000 sq. m., and it is computed to receive the drainage of 8,614,000 sq. m. In the Polar basin the temperature of the surface water is generally at 29.2°—about the freezing point of salt water. Normally, the ice-pack seldom exceeds from 7 to 13 ft. in thickness. Animal life is fairly abundant in the Arctic regions, though in the highest latitudes no form of life is reported either by Peary or Nansen. The sun remains permanently above the horizon about 160 days and for a corresponding period remains permanently below it—this is, of course, in high latitudes.

Arctinus, of MILETUS (fl. *c.* 750 B.C.), one of the 'cycle' poets, who completed the cycle of epic stories begun by Homer. Only fragments of his poems survive, but he is said to have written two epics—the *Æthiopis*, continuing the story of the *Iliad*, and the *Sack of Troy*. His fragments are collected in Kinkel's *Epicorum Græcorum Fragmenta* (1878) and in Monro's Oxford Text of *Homer* (1896).

Arcturus, Boötis, one of the brightest stars in the northern hemisphere, its magnitude being 0.24. The spectrum of the star is of the KO type, and its rays have a reddish tinge. Arcturus was one of four stars which Halley in 1718 observed had unmistakably shifted their positions since Ptolemy's epoch.

Arcus Senilis, a gray curved band partially or wholly occupying the rim of the cornea of the eye, occurring generally in the aged

Ardebil, Ardabil, or **Ardabeel,** town, Iran, a trading centre on the route to Astara on the Caspian Sea. The shrine of Sheikh Sufi is annually visited by numerous pilgrims; p. 10,000 to 15,000.

Arden, Forest of, a former forest (patches of woodland rather than continuous forest) in Warwickshire, north of the Avon (see Shakespeare's *As You Like It*).

Ardennes, wooded mountain system, Southeast Belgium, between the Meuse and Moselle. Consult Macquoid, *In the Ardennes*.

Ardennes, department, North France, with only the northwestern portion in the Ardennes system. Capital, Mézières; but its neighbor, Charleville, is twice as populous. Area, 2,028 sq. m.; p. 297,448.

Arditi, Luigi (1822-1903), musical composer and conductor, was born in Crescentino, Piedmont. From 1858, he was conductor at Her Majesty's Theatre, London, England. He is known by his brilliant vocal compositions—*e. g., Il Bacio* and *L'Ardita*, and by his opera *La Spia*. Consult his book *My Reminiscences*, 1896.

Are (Latin *area*) in the French metric system is the unit of superficial measurement, being 100 sq. metres, equivalent to 119.6 sq. yds.

Areca. See **Betel-Nut Palm.**

Arenaceous Rocks, a class of sedimentary rocks composed essentially of quartz particles, formed by the disintegration of other silicious rocks. Among the important varieties, depending on the size and state of aggregation of the constituent particles, are sand, gravel, shingle, sandstone, quartzite and conglomerate. See SANDSTONE.

Arenaria, or Sandwort, a large genus of rocks and alpine plants, belonging to the pink family, of wide distribution. They are low, mainly tufted herbs, either annual or perennial; and they have small, sessile leaves and white flowers, generally in terminal heads or cymes.

Arensky, Anton Stephanovitch (1861-1906), Russian musical composer, wrote three operas, besides symphonies, etc. His trio (Op. 32) and quintet (Op. 51) for pianoforte and strings are well known. He revived some interesting ancient forms.

Areopagus, 'Hill of Ares' (Mars), a hill in Athens, w. of the Acropolis; on its northern slope stood the temple of Ares. It gave its name to the council of the Areopagus, which met there.

Arequipa, coast department, Southern Peru, with an area of 21,947 sq. m. It has many active volcanoes; p. 250,000.

Arequipa, city, capital of Arequipa department, Peru, the second largest city in the republic, on the Chile River. The town, which was founded by Francisco Pizarro in 1540, has suffered severely from earthquakes. The city is famed for its beauty and has been the scene of many important events in the history of Peru. It is the centre of commercial activities of southern Peru and has numerous mills, machine shops and factories; p. 70,000.

Ares, the Greek god of war, whom the Romans identified with their god Mars, is represented as the son of Zeus and Hera. Sophocles calls him 'the god unhonored among the gods divine.' His worship originally belonged to Thrace; this 'barbarous origin' lowered the estimate of him in Greece.

Aretæus (c. 100 A.D.), a Greek physician who is ranked next after Hippocrates as a diagnostician. He left two important medical

From Wide World Photos.
The "Norge" preparing to land at Kings Bay, Spitzbergen.

Arms and Armor of the Middle Ages.—You will notice in looking at this picture of arms and armor how strange and fantastic and grotesque much of it is, how many heavy trappings and how many meaningless ornaments there are. If you will contrast this page with the pages that show the arms and armor of Greece or Rome, you will see the difference, not only between good and bad taste, but between efficiency and inefficiency. You will see in this picture a suit of complete armor. These were very heavy and a very great burden to the men who had to wear them; and in the case of cavalry, to the horses as well. The first figure on the left of the top row shows a Swiss soldier in the French service, 1515-47; the two middle figures are French knights of the 12th century. On the bottom row you will see first a knight-banneret of the late 13th and early 14th centuries, and then two foot-soldiers, who are on either side of a man-at-arms in full armor.

works written in elegant and concise Ionic Greek.

Arethusa, a genus of Orchidaceæ, represented in America by *A. bulbosa*. The flower is borne at the top of a scape about a foot high, and is nearly two inches long itself. It is magenta-pink in hue, with a drooping, mottled lip, bearded and crested with white hairs in three ridges.

Arethusa, one of the Nereids, and nymph of the famous fountain of the same name in the island of Ortygia, near Syracuse. See ALPHEUS.

Aretino, Pietro (1492-1556), Italian poet and satirist, was born in Arezzo, whence he was banished on account of his lampoon against indulgences. Pietro enjoyed extraordinary popularity for the wit of his verses and plays. Consult *Lives* by Sinigaglia, Schultheiss, and Bertani.

Arezzo, province of Italy, forming the southeast division of Tuscany, stretching across the main chains of the Central Apennines. Area, 1,273 sq. m.; p. 305,573.

Arezzo (ancient *Arretium*), city, capital of above and episcopal see. It was one of the twelve confederate cities of the ancient Etruscans, and possesses several very interesting buildings of the 13th to the 15th century; p. 58,206.

Argali, an Asiatic mountain sheep (*Ovis vignei*), ranging from Western Tibet to Kamchatka, on the highest ranges and plateaus. The rams carry great coiled horns, often measuring 15 in. around the base and over 40 in. along the curve. The term Argali is sometimes extended to include the whole group of mountain sheep with coiled horns.

Argall, Sir Samuel (*c.* 1580-1626), an English adventurer and naval officer, deputy-governor of Virginia (1617-19). In 1609 he discovered a short route to Virginia; and in April, 1612, by gaining possession of Pocahontas, the daughter of the Indian chief Powhatan, as a hostage, secured the return of English captives held by Powhatan.

Argan, *Argania sideroxylon*, a small, spiny evergreen tree, apparently indigenous to parts of Morocco, bearing an ovate drupe containing a white, milky juice.

Argand Burner, for use in oil lamps, invented by Argand of Geneva about 1782.

Argel, or **Arghel** (Syrian), a name given in Syria and the Levant to *Solenostemma argel*, a plant whose leaves are used in Egypt for the adulteration of senna leaves, from which they are distinguishable by their leathery texture, downy surface, and the symmetry of their sides.

Argemone, a genus of plants belonging to the Papaveraceæ, of which there are about ten species. Among the best known is 'prickly poppy,' found in the Southern United States, and in Mexico, said to possess emetic, narcotic, and cathartic properties.

Argensola, Bartolomeo Leonardo (1562-1631), Spanish poet and historian, was born in Barbastro, in Aragon. With his elder brother Lupercio he was the leader of the so-called Aragonese school of Spanish literature. The two brothers were styled 'the Horaces of Spain.'

Argent, in heraldry is the metal silver, usually represented by white.

Argentera, Punta Dell', the highest summit (10,794 ft.) of the Maritime Alps, s.w. of Cuneo, in Piedmont.

Argenteuil, town, France. Its priory, now in ruins, was turned into a nunnery, of which the famous Heloïse became abbess; p. 32,173.

Argentière, Col d', an easy Alpine pass (6,545 ft.) leading from Barcelonnette, in the French valley of the Ubaye to the Italian valley of the Stura, and so to Cuneo.

Argentina. See **Argentine Republic.**

Argentine, a species of smelt frequenting the southern coast waters of Europe.

Argentine Republic, or **Argentina,** a most progressive South American state, and the second in size. Area, 1,079,965 sq. m. The northern part of the Republic slopes very gradually from the coast n.w. to the Bolivian basin. The southern extremity of the Republic, Patagonia, is a plateau of Tertiary sandstone, interrupted here and there by old eruptive rocks and Archæan schists, which slopes westward to the watershed. Along the watershed—a succession of elevations, 6,000 to 7,000 ft. high—lies a series of lakes. From the great lake Nahuelhuapi the Andes consist of a single chain. Farther north a succession of sierras lies to the e. of the main chain, including the prolongation of the Cordillera Real of Bolivia, with summits rising to 19,000 feet. Near the southern extremity of this region are found the loftiest peaks of the main Cordillera—Aconcagua (in which the American continent culminates at a height of 23,080 ft.). Of the rivers of Patagonia, the Negro is the most important for navigation. The Republic has an Atlantic seaboard of 1,565 m. The mean temperature in the central part of the Republic is not much higher than that of Southern Europe, and the extremes are not excessive.

The fauna is rapidly vanishing. The puma and jaguar are still found in the less populated districts of the Chaco and Patagonia. Birds are more numerous than mammals. They include the condor of the Andes and other birds of prey. There are thirty or more varieties of costly woods now being worked commercially. The *quebracho,* a tanning hardwood, furnishes an important industry.

The nation's principal mineral product is petroleum.

The country is well suited for agriculture. Wheat, maize, and linseed are grown and good cotton is raised in the northern provinces. There are sugar, wine and fruit industries. The area of the Argentine is about 699,278,300 acres, of which about 500,000,000 acres are suitable for agriculture and stock raising. Since the 16th century the cattle industry has flourished on the grassy plains of Santa Fé and Buenos Aires, and stock raising, with its allied meat industry, is important. In Buenos Aires is the largest refrigerating plant in the world. More than half the hides imported into the United States come from here. Aviation has shown rapid advance and there are many regular air routes. The chief industrial establishments are sugar factories, wine depots, flour mills, breweries, and meat-freezing depots. Meat refrigeration is the leading industry, with flour milling second. The chief exports are hides and skins, wool, meat, and other animal products, wheat, corn, linseed and quebracho. The Republic ranks first in the export of linseed and frozen meat, second in wheat and corn. According to an official estimate in 1944 the total population was 13,909,950. Of the country's population, about 25 per cent. are foreign. On December 31, 1939 (official est.), Buenos Aires, the capital city, had a population of 2,364,263. No state religion exists and, although the state supports Roman Catholicism, there is perfect freedom of conscience, and toleration of all other creeds. An admirable system of free, secular, and compulsory education has been introduced for children from 6 to 14 years of age. For higher education there are the universities of Buenos Aires, Córdoba, La Plata, Tucumán, and the University of the Littoral. Service in the army, or national militia, is compulsory for all citizens from 20 to 45 years of age. The army is divided into three grades—the active army or first line, the National Guard, and the Territorial Guard. In 1912 the Argentine navy was augmented by two powerful battleships of the *Dreadnought* type—the *Moreno* and the *Ri-*

vadavia. The government is a federal republic, with Buenos Aires as the capital. The Federal Assembly, or National Congress, is composed of two chambers—a Senate of 30 members, and a House of Deputies of 158 members. The deputies are elected for four years; one-half of the House retiring every two years. Every three years one-third of the Senate is renewed. The president and vice-president are elected for terms of six years. The provincial governors are elected by the people of each province. The capital forms a Federal District similar to the District of Columbia of the United States. Juan Diaz de Solis, a Spaniard, sailed up the estuary of the Rio de la Plata in 1516 and asserted his master's sovereignty over the surrounding country, but no settlement was firmly established until 1580. The settlements continued under the administration of the viceroy of Peru until 1778. In 1810 the general South American revolt against Spain began; and in 1816 was founded the republic of the United Provinces of the Rio de la Plata. A new constitution was declared in 1853. Hipolito Irogoyen became president in 1916 and was re-elected in 1928. The retiring president, Dr. Alvear, attacked the Monroe Doctrine in his last address to Congress. In Sept., 1930, a revolution turned Irigoyen out of office to be replaced by General José Francisco Uriburu, who served a year. On Nov. 8, 1931, Gen. Agustin P. Justo was elected president. Dr. Roberto M. Ortiz became president, Feb. 20, 1938. In 1936, Carlos Saavedra-Lamas, an Argentinian, won the Nobel prize for peace activities.

President Justo, on Dec. 1, 1936, called the Inter-American Conference for the Maintenance of Peace, at Buenos Aires. It was composed of representatives of the twenty-one nations of the two Americas, and included Franklin D. Roosevelt, President of the United States, who recommended that the nations of the New World should unite to help the Old World avert war. Dr. Roberto M. Ortiz, President 1937-42, tried to suppress pro-Nazi conspiracies, but during World War II Argentina alone among Latin American countries, refused to align herself with the Allies. In 1943 the military put Pedro P. Ramírez in as President, but he was ousted in 1944 and Gen. Edelmiro Farrell assumed the position. In 1945 the Allies, over protest of Russia, invited Argentina to the San Francisco conference. In 1946 Juan Perón was elected President. The U. S. State Dept. accused him of Nazi sympathy.

Argentite, or Silver Glance, a gray sulphide of silver and one of the chief sources of the metal.

Argile Plastique (French 'plastic clay'), a series of beds of clay found in the Tertiary basin of Paris, belonging to the Lower Eocene and used for the manufacture of pottery.

Argillaceous Rocks, a class of sedimentary rocks in which clay is an important constituent.

Argo, the largest of Ptolemy's fifteen southern constellations, lies east of Canis Major and Columba.

Argol, known in commerce as CRUDE TARTAR, is an impure bitartrate of potash or cream of tartar, occurring as a hard crystalline deposit in the vats in which wine is fermented, and in bottles of wine, where it is termed 'crust.'

Argolis. See **Argos.**

Argon (Gr. 'inactive'), A 39.9, a gas existing in the atmosphere in the proportion of about .8 per cent., the presence of which was first suspected by Cavendish in 1785, but attracted no further notice till 1895, when Lord Rayleigh and Sir William Ramsay announced its discovery, calling it argon on account of its chemical inactivity. Argon is nearly one and a half times heavier than air; it cannot be made to combine with any other element. The best-known method of obtaining argon on a large scale is from liquid oxygen. Consult Ramsay's *Gases of the Atmosphere* and *Position of Argon and Helium among the Elements.*

Argonaut, or Paper Sailor, a cuttle belonging to the order Octopoda and the genus *Argonauta.* One species (*A. argo*) lives in the Mediterranean, and is called the paper nautilus, though not related to the true nautilus.

Argonautæ, or Argonauts, according to Greek legend, a band of sailors who journeyed to Colchis to secure the golden fleece. The story of the Argonauts contains a number of incidents common not only to European but to savage folklore. For the later story, see JASON, MEDEA, and PELIAS. Consult Euripides' *Medea;* Apollonius Rhodius' *Argonautica;* Kingsley's *Heroes;* Keightley's *Mythology;* Tatlock's *Greek and Roman Mythology* (1916).

Argonauts of '49. See **Forty-Niners.**

Argonne, a wooded region and rocky plateau, departments of Meuse and Ardennes, France, extending from Grand Pré on the north to Thiaucourt on the south. The Argonne figured prominently in the Great War (1914-18) of Europe.

Briefly the Meuse-Argonne offensive is divided into three phases. The first phase started Sept. 25, when the American army quietly took the places of the French, who thinly held the line of the sector. By Oct. 4 the First American Army had advanced over 7 m. through the Hindenburg and Völker lines, but failed to clear the whole of the Argonne Forest.

The second phase of the offensive was opened with a renewed attack all along the line on Oct. 4. This phase is marked by the most violent attacks and counter-attacks. It was found necessary to constitute a second American army, and on Oct. 9 the command of the First Army was turned over to Lieut.-Gen. Hunter Liggett. The command of the Second Army, whose divisions occupied a sector in the Woëvre, was given to Lieut.-Gen. Robert L. Bullard. On Oct. 10 the Germans were cleared out of the Argonne Forest, St. Juvin was taken after a desperate assault a few days later, and Grand Pré, an important German stronghold, was taken three different times—the last time on Oct. 26. A notable incident of this phase was the advance and rescue of the so-called 'Lost Battalion.' On the night of Sept. 27, a battalion of the 308th Infantry, commanded by Major Whittlesey, participated in an attack on a German position deep in the forest, 3 m. n.e. of Binarville. By a single file advance they gained their objective; but at dawn found Germans safely entrenched in front, behind, and on both sides of their position. Thus surrounded, a target for German artillery and machine guns, and without food during the last thirty-six hours, this battalion held out against the enemy for three days. Late on Monday, Sept. 30, it was rescued in an attack of the 307th Infantry led by Lieut. Col. Eugene Houghton.

The last phase of the offensive began Nov. 1 with a desperate assault of Liggett's First Army against the Freya line. The German resistance gave way before the repeated attacks of the First Corps and they began to fall back so rapidly that their retreat bordered on a rout, which compelled the American infantry to follow in motor trucks in order to retain an offensive contact. On Nov 7, the Meuse was crossed and both corps smashed into the German lines with success. In six days the First Army had rushed through to Sedan clearing all on the west bank of the Meuse.

Argos, Argolis, Argia, or **Argolice,** district and town of ancient Greece. Argolis, with Corinth, now forms one of the sixteen nomarchies of modern Greece. Area, 1,442 sq. m.; p. 158,000. The town Argos, with its citadel Larissa, lies on a plain west of the Inachus River; p. 10,000.

Argostoli, seaport, Ionian Islands, capital of Cephalonia, famous for its *Sea Mills;* p. 14,000.

Argot. See **Slang.**

Arguelles, Augustin (1778-1844), Spanish statesman and orator. His oratorical powers won for him the name of the Spanish Cicero.

Argument, in rhetoric or logic, is a reason offered for or against a proposition, opinion, etc.; a debate or disputation.

Argument, in legal procedure, is the address to the jury in which the counsel sets forth the points in his client's case which determine its outcome.

Argun, river, Siberia, called in its upper course the Kerulen, joins the Shilka to form the Amur. It rises in the Great Kinghan Mountains, and forms the frontier between Siberia and China. Length 1,100 m.

Argus, in Greek mythology, a giant with a hundred eyes, only two of which were closed at one time.

Argus Pheasant (*Phasianus argus*), a genus of gallinaceous birds, native to the Indo-Malayan region. The plumage of the male is magnificent.

Argyll, Earls and Dukes of. Archibald Campbell, Fifth Earl (1530-73), was a great-great-grandson of Colin, Lord Campbell, created First Earl of Argyll in 1457. He was involved in the murder of Darnley; and intrigued to deliver Mary from prison. ARCHIBALD (1598-1661) afterward EIGHTH EARL was created marquis in 1641. At the restoration he was called to account by Charles II, for submission to Cromwell's usurpation, and was executed at the Cross of Edinburgh in 1661.

ARCHIBALD, NINTH EARL (d. 1685). For resisting the Test Act of 1681 he was found guilty of treason and finally taken prisoner and beheaded at Edinburgh.

The restoration by William of Orange of ARCHIBALD, TENTH EARL and afterward duke (d. 1703), to his estates, was one of the causes of the rising in the Highlands under Dundee in 1689. His eldest son, JOHN, SECOND DUKE (1678-1743), was created a peer of England for his services in supporting the Union, and served under Marlborough. George Douglas, eighth duke (1823-1900), second son of the seventh duke, was a distinguished orator and politician, and an able writer. His eldest son, John Douglas Sutherland, ninth duke (1845-1914), married, in 1871, Princess Louise, daughter of Queen Victoria.

Argyllshire, a maritime co. in the w. of Scotland. It has an area of 3,165 sq. m., and is very mountainous. The chief town is Inverary; p. 76,862. See Lord A. Campbell's *Records of Argyll* (1885).

Argyria, a bluish gray permanent pigmentation of the skin, caused by the internal use of compounds of silver.

Aria (It.), a rhythmical air, song, or tune. The term is commonly applied to a song for a single voice with instrumental or vocal accompaniment, and introduced into such works as oratorios, operas, and cantatas.

Ariadne, daughter of Minos, king of Crete, the lover and helper of Theseus. Her name is attached to the 43d asteroid.

Arian Controversy. See **Arius.**

Arica, a roadstead and town in the province of Tacna, Chile, connected by a railway (39 m. long) with Tacna; p. 13,140.

Ariège. Dep. S. France, on frontier of Spain and Andorra. Area, 1,893 sq. m. Cap. Foix; p. 172,851.

Ariel, the name of two individuals in the English Old Testament. See Cheyne's *Isaiah.* For Shakespeare's Ariel, see *The Tempest.*

Aries, a zodiacal constellation which originally marked the first sign of the zodiac, entered by the sun at the vernal equinox.

Arikara, or **Arikaree** (horns) a part of the Caddoan linguistic family and members of the Pawnee confederacy. See Coues, *New Light on the Early History of the Greater Northwest* (1897).

Ariosti, Attillio (c. 1660-1740), Italian musician and composer. He composed fifteen operas, of which the most popular was *Coriolano.*

Ariosto, Ludovico (1474-1533), Italian poet, was born at Reggio in Emilia. The *Orlando Furioso,* upon which Ariosto's immortality rests, is one of the great poems of the world, and one of the very first epics in the sphere of chivalry and romance. See *Life* by G. Campori (3rd ed. 1896) and G. S. Nicholson's *Life and Genius of Ariosto* (1914).

Ariovistus, German chief, requested by the Sequani to help them against the Ædui by whom they were hard pressed.

Aristæus, a Greek deity, according to tradition the son of Apollo and the nymph

Cyrene. He was worshipped as the protector of vine and olive plantations, hunters, and herdsmen.

Aristagoras of Miletus (d. 497 B.C.), brother-in-law of Histiæus the despot, who left him governor of the town while he was at the Persian court.

Aristarchus of Samos (*fl.c.* 280-264 B.C.), ancient Greek astronomer, whose one surviving work treats of the distances of the sun and moon from the earth. He appears to have believed the sun to be at rest and the earth in motion.

Aristarchus of Samothrace (*c.* 150 B.C.), ancient Greek grammarian and critic, was educated at Alexandria. It was by his labors that the text of Homer, as we possess it, with the division of both *Iliad* and *Odyssey* into 24 books, was constituted. See Lehr's *De Aristarchi Studiis Homericis* (3rd ed. 1882).

Aristides (fl. 360-330 B.C.), Greek military painter, whose work, *The Capture of a City*, was taken by Alexander the Great to Macedon.

Aristides of Athens (*c.* 530-468 B.C.), son of Lysimachus, surnamed 'the Just,' was a leading Athenian statesman at the time of the Persian wars and afterward. See Plutarch's *Life of Aristides*.

Aristides, Publius Ælius, surnamed THEODORUS (129-189?), Greek rhetorician, was born at Adriani in Mysia. See Baumgart's *Aristeides* (1874).

Aristippus of Cyrene (*c.* 430-360 B.C.), founder of the Cyrenaic school of philosophy, was a pupil of Socrates, lived at the court of Dionysius, the tyrant of Sicily, but returned to Cyrene in his old age. See also Zeller's *Socrates and Socratic Schools* (Eng. trans. by Reichel, 1877), and Ueberweg's *History of Philosophy* (Eng. trans., 1877).

Aristobulus (*c.* 150 B.C.), founder of the Jewish-Alexandrian philosophy. See Schürer's *History of the Jewish People in the Time of Christ* (1886-90).

Aristobulus I. (d. 105 B.C.), high priest of the Jews, a son of the Maccabean prince, John Hyrcanos. In 107 B.C. he was the first after the Babylonian captivity to assume the title of king in Judæa.

Aristocracy (Gr. 'rule by the best') is a government controlled by the nobility or privileged class. See GOVERNMENT.

Aristodemus, hero of the first Messenian War with Sparta (743-724 B.C.), belongs to legend rather than history.

Aristol, an odorless, amorphous powder, of a light-brown color, used instead of iodoform in dressing wounds. It is prepared from iodine and thymol.

Aristolochia, a genus of plants found in temperate and tropical countries, except Australia.

Aristomenes, the chief figure on the Messenian side in their second war with Sparta (685-668 B.C.).

Aristophanes (*c.* 444-380 B.C.), the greatest comic poet of Athens and of Greece. Of his greater works, the *Acharnians* appeared in 425, the *Knights* in 424, the *Clouds* (probably) in 423, and a revised edition in 422: the *Birds* in 414, the *Frogs* in 405, and the *Women in Parliament* in 392. His last play seems to have been acted in 387 B.C. Aristophanes was by far the greatest poet of the old Attic comedy, which was distinguished by its bold and outspoken criticism and caricature of public men by name. As a comic genius he was on a level with Shakespeare and Molière. Editions: text alone, Blaydes (1886); with notes, the editions of separate plays by Kock (German) and Merry (1887-1901). Mitchell has translated the *Acharnians, Knights, Clouds,* and *Wasps* (1822); Frere the same without the *Wasps,* but including the *Frogs* and *Peace* (1871); B. B. Rogers various plays (1867-1902).

Aristophanes of Byzantium (*c.* 264 B.C.), Greek scholar and critic, pupil of Zenodotus and Eratosthenes, and master of Aristarchus, was chief librarian of the Great Library at Alexandria. He introduced the use of accents in Greek.

Aristotle is rightly called by Dante 'the master of them that know'; for he first marked out the path all science was to follow, and first took all knowledge to be his province, although he had little appreciation of mathematical ways of thinking. Aristotle is called 'the Stagirite,' from Stageira (or Stagiros), in Chalcidice, where he was born in 384 B.C. The profession of medicine was hereditary in his family. At the age of seventeen he came to Athens, now 'the school of Greece,' in search of that wider culture of which Isocrates was then the great professor; but it was in the Academy, the school of Plato, alone that he could find intellectual satisfaction.

Aristotle was about 37 when Plato died (347 B.C.). He is said to have been disappointed at not being chosen head of the Academy. Aristotle left Athens in company with Xenocrates, who succeeded Speusippus later on, and the two found a patron in Hermeias, prince of Atarneus in Mysia, whose niece, Pythias, Aristotle married. Before long, however, he was invited, by Philip of Macedon to direct the education of his son Alexander. On the accession of Alexander, Aristotle returned to Athens in 335 B.C. Isocrates was now dead, and Speusippus had been succeeded by Xenocrates, so the way was clear for him to found a school of his own on the model of the Academy. Like Plato, Aristotle set up his school in a 'gymnasium' outside the town. This was the Lyceum, once a favorite haunt of Socrates; and the school itself came to be known as the Peripatos, from a covered walk in which the lectures were given.

The death of Alexander revived the activity of the nationalist and democratic party at Athens, and Aristotle was threatened, like Socrates two generations earlier, with a prosecution for 'impiety.' He fled to Chalcis in Eubœa, and died the next year (322 B.C.). Aristotle's most original creation was the science afterward called Logic, as contained in the collection of treatises to which the name *Organon* ('instrument') was given at a later date.

Aristotle had a love of facts for their own sake, but he always saw them in the light of universal principles. His immediate followers lost themselves in detail, and became antiquarians and collectors of scientific curiosities. The revived Aristotelianism of the middle ages was weak on the other side. The leading principles were grasped clearly enough, but the content was unscientific. The true heirs of Aristotle's spirit are the scientific men of our day.

The chief English works are Grote's *Aristotle* (2 vols. 1872)—deals with the life of Aristotle—the *Organon, De Anima,* and *Metaphysics;* G. H. Lewes's *Aristotle: a Chapter from the History of Science* (1864)—deals chiefly with the physics and biology. For the *Ethics* and *Politics,* see the essays in Sir Alexander Grant's edition of the *Nicomachean Ethics* (4th ed., 1884), 2 vols., and the introduction to Newman's edition of the *Politics* (4 vols. 1887-1901). For the *Poetics,* Butcher's *Aristotle's Theory of Poetry and Fine Art* (3rd ed. 1903); and for the *Rhetoric,* the edition by Cope and Sandys (3 vols. 1877).

Aristoxenus (*c.* 350 B.C.), Greek philosopher, born at Tarentum; was a pupil of Aristotle. He wrote principally on music.

Arithmetic is that branch of the science of mathematics which treats of the properties of numbers and of the operations which can be performed with them. The Roman system was in general use throughout Europe until the end of the 16th century, and is still occasionally seen in dates, numbering of chapters in books, on clock dials, etc. The symbols now in use were introduced some time before 1,200 A.D., from the Arabs, who derived them from the Hindus, to whom also is to be ascribed the introduction of the symbol o, the greatest step ever taken in the history of arithmetical science, and one which completely escaped the Greeks and Romans. By the use of the ten symbols it has been possible to develop the decimal system of numeration by grouping numbers into tens and giving names to the groups (tens, hundreds, thousands, etc.). Of this decimal system, which doubtless arose from the fact that man had ten fingers, traces are found in the early inscriptions of Babylonia and Egypt. Following the introduction of the Arabic system, about 1200 A.D., the science of Arithmetic advanced rapidly. The elementary operations of arithmetic are *addition, subtraction, multiplication* and *division* See ALGEBRA; MATHEMATICS; NUMBERS. Consult Brooks' *Philosophy of Arithmetic;* Smith's *Teaching of Elementary Mathematics* and *Rara Mathematica* (1908); Boole's *Lectures on the Logic of Arithmetic* (1903); Hogben's *Mathematics for the Million* (1937); Miller's *Popular Mathematics* (1942).

Arithmetical Series. See **Series.**

Ari Thorgilsson, (1067-1148), surnamed 'the Learned,' or 'the Wise,' Icelandic historian and genealogist.

Arius, (256-336), an Alexandrian theologian, born in Libya. After having been advanced to the priesthood, he and his followers were deposed and excommunicated by a council of Egyptian bishops at Alexandria (321) for maintaining that Jesus Christ is not of the same essence as God. To settle the resulting controversy, the Emperor Constantine called the Council of Nicæa (325), which adopted the Nicene Creed suggested by Athanasius, affirming the consubstantiality of the Father and Son. Arius and two other bishops refused to sign the creed, and were exiled.

ARIANISM maintained that there is a difference in essence between God and Jesus Christ, which makes the latter secondary. The Western victory in 381 determined both the orthodox doctrine and the orthodox form for its expression. See ATHANASIUS. Consult

Newman's *Arians of the Fourth Century;* Harnack's *History of Dogma;* Bright's *Age of the Fathers* (1903).

Arizona, a State on the s. w. border of the United States. It is bounded on the north by Utah, on the east by New Mexico, on the south by Mexico, and on the west by California and Nevada. The Colorado River forms nearly the whole of the western boundary. The total area is 113,956 sq. m., of which 113,810 are land. The northern part of Arizona consists chiefly of tableland, while the southern part is traversed by numerous mountain ranges. The entire State, however, is mountainous, more than two-thirds of the total area having an altitude of 3,000 ft. or over. The Sierra Nevada and Rocky Mountains, meet in the north-central part, form the southern rim of the Great Basin. The Gila River, the Salt River, its main tributary, and their branches rise in the eastern mountains, and flow across Arizona to join the Colorado about 125 m. above the Gulf of California.

Arizona has a wide diversity of climate. The mean annual temperature varies from 40° in the north to 69° in the south. The rainfall also varies greatly. The greatest obstacle to agriculture is lack of water, and irrigation is being increasingly practised. The Archæan era is represented by widely distributed areas of gneiss and slates, and the Palæozoic by the Tonto sandstone and extensive carboniferous formations. Copper, in which industry Arizona ranks first since 1910, is the most important mineral, but silver, gold and lead are also mined. Arizona ranks first as a producer of natural salt cake and of asbestos.

Cottonwood, sycamore, ash, willow, walnut, ironwood, mesquite, and cherry grow in the lowlands; oak, juniper, piñon, cedar, yellow pine, fir, and spruce on the plateaus and mountain sides. Most of the wooded land is in forest reserves. Agriculture is largely dependent upon irrigation, and remarkable results have been achieved since the completion of the Salt River project (q.v.) in 1917. The project includes Roosevelt Dam (q.v.). The Yuma project (q.v.), which includes Laguna Dam, and the San Carlos project (built under the Indian Service), which includes Coolidge Dam, are also important. The foremost agricultural product of the State in value is cotton. The fruit industry is growing in importance and the raising of cattle, sheep and horses is also an important industry of the state.

By far the largest industry in the State is the smelting and refining of copper. According to the Federal Census of 1940 the population of Arizona is 499,261. The State University of Arizona is situated at Tucson where there is also a State Agricultural School. The present Constitution of Arizona was adopted in 1910. It may be amended by a two-thirds vote of each house, or on the initiative of 15 per cent. of the voters, later ratified by a majority vote of the people. The usual suffrage requirements are exacted. Direct primaries are provided for. Under the Reapportionment Act, Arizona has one Representative in the National Congress. Phoenix is the capital. Arizona was once the home of a highly civilized race some time before it was visited by Spanish explorers. Fray Marcos de Niza was the first white man known to have entered Arizona (1539). Jesuits established missions in the early part of the 17th century, and in the 18th century Tucson and Tubac were founded. Arizona originally formed a part of Mexico, and was ceded to the United States along with New Mexico on Feb. 2, 1848. The Enabling Act of 1910 prepared the way for independent statehood; and after some delay Arizona became a State (Feb. 14, 1912). Consult Sloans' *History of Arizona* (4 vols., 1930); Nelson's *Alluring Arizona* (1927); *The Arizona Historical Review,* published since April, 1928, by the State Historian at Phoenix.

Arizona, University of, a non-sectarian, co-educational institution at Tucson, opened in 1891 under the Morrill Act of 1862, is the only institution of college grade in the State.

Ark of Noah, a huge vessel of gopher wood (possibly cypress), built by the Patriarch for the purpose of preserving the race of man and of the land animals during the flood. It was 120 years in building, measured 300 cubits in length, 50 in breadth, and 30 in height; it had three stories. See DELUGE.

Ark of the Covenant, also called 'Ark of Yahweh of Hosts,' 'Ark of God,' and 'Ark of the Testimony,' was a chest of shittim (acacia) wood overlaid with gold, containing the stone tablets on which were inscribed the Ten Commandments.

Arkansas, (popularly known as the 'Bear State'), one of the South Central States of the United States. It is bounded on the north by Missouri; on the south by Louisiana; on the west by Oklahoma and Texas; and on the east by Tennessee and Mississippi, from which it is separated by the Mississippi River. Its area is 53,335 sq. m., of which 810 m.

are water surface. The northern and central western sections are broken by mountains and foothills. From the northeast corner to the southwest corner runs a belt of rolling country. In the southeast section and along the eastern border the land is low and level, and subject to inundation from the overflowing of the Mississippi and tributaries. The State has some 3,000 m. of waterway. The climate is generally healthful throughout the State, the variation in mean annual temperature in different sections being only about 6° F. The lowlands are fertile, and the alluvial bottoms are remarkably rich. The southern portion of the State is of Tertiary formation, the northern of Palæozoic. They comprise sandstones, limestones, and other building stones.

The mineral industry of Arkansas has increased greatly, due to the discovery of petroleum in the western and southern parts. The four principal products are petroleum, natural gas, natural gasoline, and coal. In 1938, one hundred eighty-eight new oil wells in four different fields, were brought in. In the production of bauxite the State ranks first; second in manganiferous and manganese ore output; fourth in zinc. The only diamond mine in America is in Arkansas. Black building marble is also produced. The value of all mineral products of the State, 1940, was $32,974,389. Arkansas has a forest area of over a million acres, and there are two large national forests in the State in which is located most of the state's timber.

The fishing grounds of the State are mainly the Mississippi River and its tributaries. Arkansas is preëminently an agricultural State. In the northern division the principal products are the cereals and temperate-zone growths; in the southern, cotton, sorghum cane, and other typical Southern crops predominate. Fruits and nuts are also of importance. The poultry industry in Arkansas has developed greatly of recent years, many growers specialize on supplying broilers to the markets. Bee keeping is important. Arkansas contains large deposits of bituminous and semi-anthracite coal, accessible for industrial purposes, while its extensive timber areas provide abundant material for the lumber and timber industry. The State is one of the largest producers of building materials, supplying much of the country's output of hardwood flooring, brick and tile, stone, marble and roofing materials.

The railroad facilities are good except in the mountainous regions of the north-central and west-central sections. The State's navigable rivers have been important factors in its industrial development. According to the Federal Census for 1940, the population of Arkansas is 1,949,387. Of this total, the urban population is 431,910 and the rural 1,517,477. Education in Arkansas is under the general supervision of the Department of Public Instruction. All children between the ages of seven and fifteen are required to attend school for three-fourths of the school session. Aid is provided for the teaching of vocational agriculture and home economics. Separate schools are maintained for white and for colored children. Institutions for higher learning include the University of Arkansas, at Fayetteville.

The present Constitution of Arkansas dates from 1874. A majority vote in both houses, and by the electors, is necessary for an amendment. Provision has been made for the initiative and referendum. Universal suffrage prevails, with residence requirement and payment of a poll tax. Under the Reapportionment Act, Arkansas has seven Representatives in the National Congress. Little Rock is the State capital. The State takes its name from the Arkansas Indians. The first white man to enter it was De Soto in 1541. The first white settlement was by some of Tonti's men in 1686. Until the Louisiana Purchase, Arkansas was a French possession; from 1805 to 1812 it formed part of Louisiana Territory, and until 1819 of Missouri Territory. It was then organized as Arkansas Territory; and in 1836 it became a State.

In 1828 the first steamboat in Arkansas navigated the Arkansas River. Its first railway, the Memphis and Little Rock, was begun in 1854, but was not finished until some years after the Civil War. Although admitted as a slave State, paired with Michigan, there were many Unionists in Arkansas at the outbreak of the Civil War; but an ordinance of secession was finally adopted. The State was readmitted into the Union in 1868. The discovery of oil in 1920 raised the position of Arkansas economically. The attractions of its playgrounds draw increasing numbers of tourists seeking pleasure and health to Diamond Cave in Newton co. and to Hot Springs in middle Arkansas or to the Ozarks. Arkansas has had an era of progress which terrific floods in 1927 and drought in 1930 did not seriously retard. Since 1876 the State has been Democratic. Consult Moorehead's *Archæology of the Arkansas River Bed* (1931);

Moore's *School History of Arkansas* (1924); Thomas's *Arkansas in War and Reconstruction 1861-1874* (1926).

Arkansas River, next to the Missouri the largest affluent of the Mississippi, rises in the high mountains in Central Colorado. Its drainage area is 177,500 sq. mi.; total length, 1,500 m.; navigable for 650 m. It varies in width from 150 ft. near the mountains to about a mile in the sandy regions.

Arkansas, University of, a co-educational institution, at Fayetteville, Ark.

Arkwright, Sir Richard (1732-92), English cotton-spinning inventor, was born in Preston, Lancashire. In 1768 he set up in Preston his first spinning frame. His patent was obtained in 1769, when he set up near Hockley his first mill, driven by horses. Arkwright's invention met with intense opposition, one of his factories being destroyed by the mob. He amassed a large fortune, however, and was knighted in 1786. See COTTON.

Arlberg, Alpine pass in Austria (5,912 ft.) leading from Feldkirch, in Vorarlberg (near the Rhine Valley), to the Inn Valley, near Landeck, Tyrol.

Arles, (ancient *Arelate*), town, France, department of Bouches-du-Rhone on the

George Arliss

Grand Rhone River; 53 m. n.w. of Marseilles. The ancient town was known as 'Gallic Rome,' and was a favorite residence of Constantine; p. 16,400.

Arlington, district, Arlington county, Virginia, opposite Washington, D. C., the home at one time of Gen. Robert E. Lee, and the site of a beautiful national cemetery. Here are the graves of over 18,000 soldiers, mostly of the Civil War period, and also America's Unknown Soldier, buried Nov. 11, 1921. The Lee mansion, of colonial architecture, is still preserved; p. 57,040.

Arliss, George (1868-1946), English actor, born in London. He first played at the Elephant and Castle Theatre, in 1887 and made his first American tour with Mrs. Patrick Campbell in 1901. Among the plays which brought him fame were *Disraeli, Hamilton,* and *The Man Who Played God.* He wrote an autobiography, *Up The Years From Bloomsbury* (1927). His popularity in moving pictures is now firmly established.

He made his first picture in England, *The Iron Duke,* in 1935. Other pictures in which he has starred are *The House of Rothschild, The Last Gentleman, Mr. Hobo* and *Cardinal Richelieu.*

Arm. The upper extremity of the human body may be divided into three parts: the

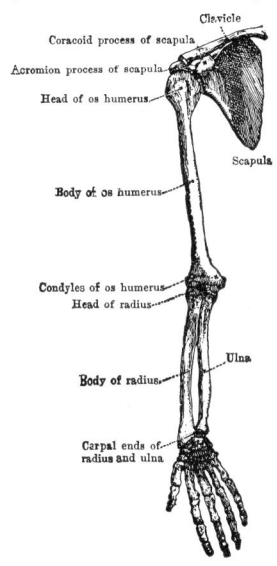

Bones of the Arm.

shoulder, the hand, and the arm, consisting of the upper arm and forearm. The bones are: in the shoulder, the clavicle (collar bone) and the scapula (shoulder blade); in the upper arm the humerus; in the forearm, the radius and ulna; in the hand, the carpal and metacarpal bones and the phalanges. The smooth, round 'head' of the humerus articulates with the glenoid cavity of the scapula, forming the shoulder joint—a ball-and-socket joint. At the lower end of the humerus are two articular surfaces for the bones of the forearm—the outer rounded for the head of the radius, the inner a curved rim for the ulna. These form the elbow joint—a hinge joint. At their lower extremities the radius and ulna articulate with the carpus to form the wrist joint—also a hinge joint.

The arm receives its blood supply from the brachial artery and its branches, and the veins finally unite in the axillary vein. The nerves pass down by the side of the brachial artery, then are distributed as musculo-spiral, ulnar and median.

Armada, in Spanish 'an armed force,' more particularly the great fleet sent against England by Spain in 1588 by Philip II., who had resolved to strike a decisive blow at Protestantism by conquering England. Of its 128 sail, 2 were abandoned to the English, 3 were wrecked on the French coast and 2 on the coast of Flanders, 2 were sunk in action off Gravelines, 19 were known to have been wrecked off Scotland and Ireland, and 35 others never returned to Spain. Thus 63 in all were lost. The effect upon the prestige of the Elizabethan navy was immense. Consult Duro's *La Armada Invencible;* Clowes' *The Royal Navy;* Hales' *Great Armada.*

Armadillo, a name applied to certain tropical American animals belonging to the mammalian order Edentata, characterized especially by the possession of a peculiar armor, consisting of shields on head, neck, shoulders, and rump, and of movable cross bands of plates across the back. The creature is nocturnal in habit and feeds on insects and worms, roots, fruit, and sometimes carrion. The flesh is palatable.

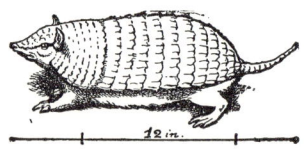

The Six-banded Armadillo
(Dasipus Sexcinctus.)

Armageddon, the battlefield of the Apocalypse, on which the final struggle between good and evil is to be fought. The name is probably derived from Megiddo (q.v.), an important canaanite fortress in Issachar.

Armagh, a co. of Northern Ireland. Oats, potatoes, turnips, wheat and flax are grown. Linen weaving, cotton spinning, and clay working are the chief industries; p. 110,070.

Armagh, cathedral town, Ireland, capital of county Armagh and seat of the Primate of all Ireland. There are marble quarries a short distance from Armagh, and the town is celebrated for its production of brown linens and holland for window shades. Armagh was the Irish metropolis from 495 to the 9th century; p. 6,500.

Armagnac, former name of a district of Southern France, a part of Gascony, now largely included in the department of Gers. It is especially known for its brandy—*eau d'Armagnac.*

Armature. See **Dynamo.**

Armed, a term used in heraldry.

Armed Neutrality, a condition under which a nation that is not belligerent puts itself in a state of defense against the possible aggression of other belligerent nations that threaten its frontiers. See INTERNATIONAL LAW.

Armenia, Socialist Soviet Republic created in 1918, is now one of the sixteen constituent republics of the Union of Soviet Socialist Republics; area 11,580 sq. m. The capital is Erivan. The mineral resources include deposits of copper, silver, lead, and iron, and hot mineral springs. The soil is generally fertile. There are rich vineyards and orchards, fields of cotton, tobacco, rice, hemp, and flax.

The Armenians are Caucasians, rather above middle stature, of dark complexion, with black straight hair, rather large noses, and wide foreheads. Of quick adaptive intelligence and an enterprising commercial spirit, they are especially well suited to trade, and have long constituted an important element in the economic strength of the Turkish Empire. Converted to Christianity in the 4th century, the Armenians have clung to their faith in the midst of a hostile people and in the face of the bitterest persecution. See ARMENIAN CHURCH.

Armenia, like Asia Minor in general, has never really had a history of its own, its fortunes always having been closely linked with those of the greater empires of Media, Persia, Rome, Byzantium, and Turkey. Early in the World War the Russians proclaimed the liberation of Armenia from the Turkish yoke, but the advent to power of the Bolsheviks in November, 1917, altered the whole future trend of Armenian history. A short-lived federal Transcaucasian Republic was formed, but in May, 1918. Armenia, Azerbaijan, and Georgia separated and became independent states. The Allies favored the creation of a big Armenia on both sides of the Russo-Turkish frontier. The Armenians sent representatives to the Peace Conference, their claims were treated with favor and they signed the Treaty of Sèvres in August, 1920. After Denikin's army collapsed, Azerbaijan went Bolshevik, and the Turks launched an attack against Erivan. Armenia collapsed, her very existence was only saved by a pro-Bolshevik government in December, 1920. This event was regulated by a treaty between Angora and the Bolsheviks, which reduced the Armenian territory from 60,000 square kilometers to less than half that size. In 1922 a federation of the three soviet republics of Transcaucasia—Armenia, Georgia and Azerbaijan—was formed; later split up into three separate republics. P. of Armenia S.S.R. is 1,253,985. See CAUCASUS.

Consult Lynch's *Armenia: Travels and Studies;* Gregor's *History of Armenia;* Williams' *Armenia Past and Present;* Arshag Mahdesian's *Armenia, Her Culture and Aspirations;* Hampsotsonmian's *Soviet Armenia.*

Armenia: Language and Literature. The Armenian language belongs to the Indo-Germanic family of languages. It was frequently assigned in the past to the Iranian branch, but it is now recognized as forming a more or less independent branch of its own, more closely akin to the European than to the Asiatic representatives. Syntactically it bears a close resemblance to classical Greek.

The ancient language still survives in the church and literature, but in popular usage has been replaced by several dialects, the chief being the Western (Constantinople) and the Eastern (Tartary, Persia, India): the latter adheres more closely to the ancient language. Armenian literature begins with Mesrop (439 A.D.), who introduced an alphabet of thirty-six characters, to which two more were added in the 12th century. Armenian literature is largely theological, and contains many translations from the Greek and Syriac, chiefly made in the fifth century. Its folk-lore has always been rich in epic and legendary poems of very ancient date; but the introduction of Christianity in particular, if it did not lead to their suppression, at all events afforded no encouragement to their preservation in writing.

In the eighteenth century Armenian literature received a noteworthy stimulus by the erection of printing presses at Amsterdam, Moscow, Smyrna, Vienna, and more especially by the foundation of the Armenian Mekhitarist monks at San Lazarro, Venice. For fuller surveys of Armenian bibliography, consult the related works by Neumann, Somal, Langlois, Patcanian, and Dulaurier.

Armenian Atrocities. The first wholesale massacre of Armenian Christians may be said to have had its beginnings as early as 1885, when revolutionary propaganda on the Nihilist plan commenced to gain adherents among the Armenian population of Turkey. This was easily suppressed, but reappeared in 1893. The Powers pressed the Sultan for action and, after numerous delays and counter-proposals, a complicated program of reform was accepted by the Porte (1895). Meanwhile disturbances continued, and massacre after massacre took place. Entire villages, especially in the provinces of Erzerum and Trebizond, were desolated, and plague and famine attacked those whom the sword had spared. In April, 1909, a terrible massacre broke out in the district of Adana, and, altogether 30,000 Armenian Christians were slaughtered, 6,500 in Adana city alone. In December, 1909, twenty-six Moslems were executed for complicity in the April massacres. Having entered World War I as an ally of Germany, in November, 1914, the Turkish Government proceeded to carry out a systematic massacre and deportation of Armenians that exceeded in cruelty and extent even the massacre of 1909.

In 1918 the Turks captured Alexandropol (now Leninakan) and looted it. Wherever they advanced there were fresh massacres of Armenians and fresh horrors. The sufferings and starvation of the Armenians were indescribable, and the country was overrun by several hundred thousand refugees. The Treaty of Sèvres between Turkey and the Allies, which was signed in August, 1920, recognized Armenia as a free and independent state, but in the following month the Turks again advanced on Alexandropol and massacred almost all the inhabitants. In the autumn of 1922 many thousands of Armenians were driven out of Asia Minor by the Turks. Stripped of everything the fugitives arrived in Greece, Bulgaria and Syria; while great numbers fled again to Russian Armenia.

Consult *The Treatment of Armenians in the Ottoman Empire, 1915-16* (Great Britain Foreign Office, Miscellaneous No. 31).

Armenian Church, the oldest of all national churches, owes its foundation traditionally to St. Bartholomew. The conversion of the Armenians as a nation, however, was due to the labors of St. Gregory the Illuminator, who baptized King Tridates in 301, was consecrated as head of the Church in 302, and for a quarter of a century thereafter devoted himself to its organization. With the invention of an Armenian alphabet early in the fifth century, the Bible was translated into Armenian and a liturgy in the native tongue was prepared.

The Armenian church proper differs from the Church of Rome (see ROMAN CATHOLIC CHURCH) in its belief in the one nature of Christ, and its doctrine that the Spirit proceeds from the Father alone; in its denial of the supremacy of the Bishop of Rome (the Pope); in its rejection of the doctrine of purgatory and of indulgences; and in its lack of any word equivalent to transubstantiation. See ARMENIA; ARMENIAN ATROCITIES. Consult Tozer's *The Church and the Eastern Empire.*

Armes Parlantes, or **Rebus,** in heraldry the term applied to such armorial devices as pun on the bearer's name or attributes, as a bolt through a tun, for Bolton.

Armida, in Tasso's *Jerusalem Delivered,* an enchantress, who by means of a magical girdle attempted to seduce the crusaders from their vows to deliver Jerusalem from the Saracens.

Armillary Sphere, an instrument formed by a combination of several rings, showing the relative positions of the imaginary circles of the celestial concave to which astronomers refer the situations of the sun, moon, and planets. The instrument, by whose aid astronomical problems could be solved, has been superseded by the celestial globe.

Arminianism, a theological system founded by Jacobus Arminius and developed after his death by his followers Johan Wtenbogaert and Simon Episcopius, as a protest against the rigor of orthodox Calvinism. Its principal tenets were formulated in a *Remonstrance* drawn up in 1610 for presentation to the States of Holland. This declares that election is based upon divine foreknowledge, denying the Calvinistic doctrine of absolute predestination; that the atonement is universal, that is, that Christ died for all and not merely for the elect, though only believers receive the benefits of His death; that divine grace is not irresistible but may be rejected; that **there is no Scriptural basis for holding that the** regenerate may never fall away from grace. The Remonstrance met with a strong *Counter-Remonstrance* put forth by the Calvinists, and after several fruitless discussions, the States of Holland, in January 1614, issued an edict of full toleration for both parties. Consult Schaff's *Creeds of Christendom.*

Arminius (18 B.C.-19 A.D.), a famous chief of the German Cherusci, served in the German auxiliary troops with the Roman army.

When Varus, the Roman governor, aroused the German tribes by his exactions, Arminius secretly raised the country against him, cut off his outlying forces, and annihilated his main army in the Teutoburger Wald. Consult Tacitus's *Annals;* Merrivale's *Romans under the Empire.*

Arminius, Jacobus (1560-1609), whose proper name was HARMENSEN, founder of Arminianism, was born in Oudewater, Southern Holland. In 1588 joined the ministry of the Reformed Church at Amsterdam and became a leading theologian and preacher. His views involved him in much controversy, but he successfully defended his position in the ecclesiastical courts, and in 1603 was appointed professor of theology in the University of Leyden, the great training school for the Dutch clergy. Prostrated by persecution, he died at Leyden. See ARMINIANISM. Consult Arminius' *Works,* translated into English by James Nichols; Brandt's *Life of Arminius.*

Armistice, a general suspension of military operations in time of war either by the whole or a large part of the forces engaged. It is within the power of commanders in the field to bring about such a suspension of operations by agreement, but it is more often the result of agreement by the governments of the nations at war as a preliminary to negotiations for a peace or from some high political or religious motive. A brief cessation of hostilities between combatants in the field for the purpose of burying the dead or other cause due to local conditions does not rise to the dignity of an armistice, and is known as a 'suspension of arms.'

The armistice of November 11, 1918 marked German defeat in World War I, and the armistice of June 22, 1940 marked French defeat in World War II. See EUROPE, GREAT WAR OF.

Armor, strictly speaking garments of defence, but, as generally applied, including also weapons. Axe-heads of many different kinds of stone are very characteristic implements of the earliest period. With the use of bronze the variety of weapons increased, in the form of axes, daggers, swords, and shields. The earliest form of bronze dagger is a thin, knifelike blade, broad at the hilt, and fastened to the handle by large rivets of bronze. The leaf-shaped sword, found all over Europe, was cast with the handle-plate in one piece, and was without a guard. Scandinavian bronze swords are longer than British. A narrow rapier-shaped variety occurs frequently in Ireland. Spear-heads of bronze are chiefly leaf-shaped, though barbed examples have been found. The shields of the Bronze Age were circular, with concentric ridges and rows of studs, and the handle was fixed beneath the boss. In Central Europe the Early Iron Age produced swords of iron made of a reed tipped with bronze. Their swordsmen carried straight, double-edged weapons of bronze. The armor of the Etruscans was, in the main, similar to that of the Greeks.

About the first century B.C. the Romans used two varieties of sword—the short,

Specimens of the Armor and Weapons in Use Before the Invention of Gunpowder

formed in exact imitation of the leaf-shaped sword of the previous age.

The Heroic Age in Greece is characterized by a bronze sword; and its defensive armor consisted of helmet, cuirass, greaves, and shield, all of bronze. In the earliest Egyptian period the archers were provided with arrows double-edged *gladius*, and the long, single-edged *spatha*. But of all the weapons carried by the Romans the most characteristic was the *pilum*, a wooden shaft fitted with a stout iron head resembling the modern pike.

Nearer the period prior to the Norman Conquest, most weapons were of iron. A

Norman knight was clad in hose of mail, steel knee caps, a byrnie, gambeson, and helmet, and bore two swords, dagger, spear, and shield. Archery was encouraged in England by statute. The crossbow, at first prohibited by papal decree, came into use toward the close of the twelfth century. With the thirteenth century archers and cross-bowmen increased. With the advent of gunpowder in the fourteenth century, the use of body armor naturally decreased, chain-mail hauberks being discontinued. Leather and whalebone were much used in addition to metals in the manufacture of elbow guards, gauntlets, knee pieces, and sollerets (armed shoes).

Modern arms are classed as firearms, and those wielded at close quarters with a cut or thrust. The modern rifle and revolver used by the leading Powers differ only in points of detail. Of ancient and mediæval weapons in use before the introduction of gunpowder —such as the sword, pike, mace, javelin, axe, etc.—there only remain the various types of bayonet, sword, and lance.

See articles on weapons, especially FIREARMS; RIFLE; REVOLVER; BAYONET; SWORD. Consult Brett's *Ancient Arms and Armor;* Bartlett's *Some Weapons of War;* Ashdown's *Arms and Armor.*

Armored Car, a motor-car so built as to be provided with protective armor and equipped with weapons of offence and defence, as machine guns. While armored cars are chiefly employed in military operations, their use for the transportation of large sums of money and for self-protection by criminals has increased during the past few years.

In military tactics the armored car first came into important use during the World War, especially during the later years and in non-European regions, such as Egypt, Palestine, Persia, and Mesopotamia. They were found to be especially effective for unexpected raids on distant points. A specialized form was the Tank, an armored car on so-called 'caterpillar tracks' instead of wheels, described under that article. Technically armored car units are a part of the Tank Corps of the Army and are organized into companies, each one consisting of four sections with four cars each. Their use to co-operate with cavalry has led to their designation as 'mechanized cavalry.' See also CAVALRY.

Armorial Bearings, the generic term for insignia treated of in heraldry; strictly, those *borne* on the shield. See HERALDRY.

Armorica, a division of pre-Roman Gaul, identified with Brittany, and inhabited by the Armorici. During the Roman occupation it comprised the whole of the country n. of the Loire. After the German invasion the *Tractus Armoricanus* became a sort of federal republic, until annexed to the French crown by Clovis about 500 A.D. See BRITTANY.

Armor, Naval. See **Armor Plate.**

Armor Plate. The first use of iron to protect the sides of ships against hostile shot was made by the French in the siege of Gibraltar, in 1782. The vessels were floating batteries, and were armored with heavy iron bars. They caught fire and burned. The first suggestion to apply armor to a sea-going vessel seems to have been made in 1812 by Col. John Stevens (q.v.). In 1841 his son Robert L. Stevens presented to the United States Navy Department plans for an ironclad steamer of high speed in which all of the machinery, including the propellers, was to be below the water line. The Stevens ship was never completed because Congress refused the necessary money to carry on the work. In 1824 General Paixhans brought out his celebrated shell gun (explosive shells had hitherto been used only in mortars). In 1845 M. Dupuy de Lôme submitted plans for an iron-hulled, armor-plated frigate. He believed that by substituting iron for wood he could save 19 per cent. of the displacement, and this would be sufficient for an armor belt 8 ft. wide and 6.5 inches thick. In 1846, plans of armored floating batteries for coast defence were prepared by the French navy department, but were laid aside. Soon after the outbreak of the Crimean War these plans were taken up and reconsidered.

In September, 1854, Ericsson submitted to the French emperor plans of a cupola or turret vessel which was the forerunner of the monitor. These plans were rejected. On Oct. 17, 1855, three of the French armored batteries took part in an attack upon the Russian forts at Kinburn. The armor of the batteries was not pierced, and their structures were uninjured. This brilliant success decided the question of armor; and France and other countries began almost immediately to build sea-going armor-plated vessels. The first of this character was the French armor-plated frigate, the *Gloire,* which had the hull and machinery of a screw battleship of the old type. The first British armor-clads, the *Warrior* and *Black Prince,* were designed in 1858, laid down in 1859, and completed in 1861-62.

The earlier steel plates were unsatisfactory, not through lack of resistance to perforation, but because they cracked so badly and fell off the backing. In England, and to some extent in France, and Italy, the cracking of steel armor was still regarded with apprehension; and one of the methods whereby it was sought to preserve the impenetrability of steel armor, as well as the resistance to cracking of the wrought iron, was to weld a steel face to a wrought-iron back. The result was called 'compound' armor, and its development both in France and England, held it for the next dozen years on a par with steel. The first really successful compound plates appeared in 1877. Its superiority was not universally conceded until, in September, 1890, the U. S. naval authorities purchased a compound plate of Cammell & Co. and two plates from Schneider, one of steel and one of nickel steel. The defeat of the compound plate by both steel plates was so decisive and convincing that it at once stopped the making of compound armor. After two or three years of experiment the first large plate was tried on Feb. 14, 1891. The plate did all that theory had predicted for a plate which was hard on its face, tough throughout, and soft on the back. Only the best class of projectiles made any impression on it. In the Harvey process the plate is placed in a furnace with the surface to be hardened uppermost; this surface is covered with carbonaceous material, then a layer of sand, and then fire brick. (See HARVEYIZED STEEL).

The next improvement was made by the Carnegie Company in 1895, which found that reforging of plates after carbonizing considerably improved their quality. Of several European armor makers who endeavored to improve the Harvey process, the most successful was Krupp. For cementation he uses gas, which is very rich in carbon, and the plate contains some chromium as well as carbon and nickel. Recent plates of various makers are said to contain other substances, and to give higher resistance to penetration than the Krupp armor of five years ago; and some recent trials confirm these claims.

See BATTLESHIP; GUNS; PROJECTILES; FORTIFICATION.

Consult Very's *Development of Armor for Naval Use; Proceedings* U. S. Naval Institute; Brown's *Armor and Its Attack by Artillery; Annual* of the U. S. Office of Naval Intelligence; Brassey's *Naval Annual*.

Armour, Jonathan Ogden (1863-1927), American merchant, born in Milwaukee, Wis. He became associated with his father, Philip D. Armour (q.v.), in the great Chicago packing house of Armour & Co., and on the death of the latter succeeded him as president. He wrote *The Packers and the People*.

Armour, Philip Danforth (1832-1901), American merchant and philanthropist, was born in Stockbridge, N. Y. He was noted for his philanthropic enterprises. The Armour Institute of Technology and the Armour Mission of Chicago were founded and endowed by him.

Armour Institute of Technology, a technical school founded in 1892 at Chicago, Ill., by Philip D. Armour, to give to young students a knowledge of applied science.

Armpit. See AXILLA.

Arms. See **Armor; Firearms; Bayonet; Revolver; Rifle; Sword; Shooting.**

Arms, Coat of, the bearings on an individual shield, originally embroidered on the sur*coat;* hence the name. See HERALDRY.

Armstrong, John (1758-1843), American soldier and diplomat, was born in Carlisle, Pa. From 1804 to 1806 he was U. S. Minister to France, and from 1806 to 1810 U. S. Minister to Spain. He became Secretary of War in 1813. He published *Notices of the War of 1812,* and Memoirs of Montgomery and Wayne in Sparks' *American Biographies.*

Armstrong, Samuel Chapman (1839-93), American educator and soldier, was born in the Hawaiian Islands, where his father was a missionary. In 1868 he founded and became principal of the Hampton Normal and Agricultural Institute. He did much to improve the methods in use for educating the negro and Indian races in the United States.

Armstrong, William George, first Baron Armstrong (1810-1900), was the son of a Newcastle merchant. In 1845 he invented the hydraulic crane, and soon afterward the hydraulic accumulator, besides making many other applications of hydraulic power. He was the founder of the immense Elswick Engine Works and Elswick Shipyards at Newcastle-on-Tyne. He wrote *Electric Movement in Air and Water.*

Army. An army, in its broadest sense, signifies a body of armed and trained men organized for warfare. Armies may be grouped into three classes—National Armies, Regular or Permanent or Standing Armies, and Field Armies. A *national army* is the total available force of men trained, or partially trained, in the use of arms which a nation can call upon in time of war. A *regular army* is that portion of the national army actually serving with the colors. *Field armies* are those portions of the national or regular army which are engaged in a campaign.

Technically, the organization of an army is of two kinds, tactical and administrative. The former enables the leader of an army to transmit his orders to three or four subordinate commanders, who pass them on to three or four others under them, until through a regular chain of responsibility, the original impulse is communicated to the private soldier (see STRATEGY AND TACTICS). The administrative organization, in a similar manner, divides the army into groups of gradually decreasing size, so that the men may be efficiently paid, fed, clothed, and armed.

The military forces of the earliest times were little better than armed multitudes, possessed of a certain amount of rough organization, but unable to travel great distances, or carry out any very serious operations. The earliest regular military organization is attributed to Rameses II., known to history also as Sesostris, who ascended the throne of Egypt about 1300 B.C.

Little progress was made in military art until the *Persian empire* arose, about a thousand years later. Its soldiers introduced the mass formation, with cavalry in intervals of squares; but the most important feature of the Persian organization was the establishment of what was practically a standing army, divided as garrisons throughout the conquered provinces, and under the control of military governors distinct from the satraps.

In *Greece*, it was not a standing army, but a national militia, subjected to an almost continuous training in the field, that gained Marathon, Platæa, and Mycale. The most important element in the army was infantry, which was divided into two main branches, the *hoplitai* and *psiloi*. The former were heavy troops, and the *psiloi* were lightly armed troops, who carried out the skirmishing duties of the army, harassed the enemy, and hung round the flanks and rear of the phalanx with the cavalry in time of battle. Their cavalry did not come into existence until after the Persian War. The Thebans introduced the column formation, which, being deeper and narrower than the phalanx, was intended to pierce the enemy's line at some one point, and throw them into confusion. Philip, the father of Alexander the Great, established in *Macedonia* the world's second standing army. He brought into use the Macedonian pike, a formidable weapon 24 ft. in length.

The *Roman* armies which ruled the world from about the third century B.C. to the eighth century A.D. were probably the finest, comparatively, that have ever existed, rather because of their perfect discipline and organization than because of individual prowess, which had previously been the main features of hostile armies. They were at first formed entirely of militia. The *legion*, which was the chief unit of Roman armies, was composed, on service, of about 3,000 infantry and a squadron of cavalry, and was lighter and more extended in formation than the Greek phalanx. The infantry of the legion was divided into four classes—*hastati*, young men lightly armed, forming the first line; *principes*, heavily armed men of great strength, forming the second line; *triarii*, the oldest men, heavily armed and armored, in the third line; and *velites*, or light troops, corresponding to the Greek *psiloi*.

With the decline of the Roman power all that remained of scientific warfare was lost for a time. The northern invaders made little use of tactics, but relied chiefly on their personal bravery and on the impetuosity and weight of their attack in column. About the ninth century the feudal system (see FEUDALISM), a form of which prevailed in Egypt about 1900 B.C., and which had been slowly developing for some time past, finally established itself as the basis of European army organization. The Crusades first showed the advantage of co-operation, although the different armies participating were practically independent of each other. The chief branch of the feudal armies was cavalry. The events which led to the downfall of the feudal system were as follows: (1) The success of the English archers against the French at Crécy in 1346, at Poitiers in 1356, and at Agincourt in 1415, England having practically abandoned the feudal system under Edward III. (2) The victories of the Swiss infantry, which was armed with sword and halberd, wore no armor, and fought in wedge-shaped masses, at Morgarten (1315), Sempach (1386), Granson (1476), Morat (1476), and Nancy (1477). (3) The introduction of standing armies, chiefly infantry, and at first largely composed of foreign mercenaries, but later assuming more of a national character.

The Turkish Janissary force, the earliest standing army in Europe, was fully organized in 1362; but the formation of standing armies among Western powers, dates from the establishment of *compagnies d'ordonnance* by Charles VII. of France in 1445. The feudal militia of the Middle Ages was followed by a system of voluntary enlistment in time of peace; if necessary, the standing army was increased by compulsory levies in time of war. Armies were raised by contract, the king paying a fixed annual sum for this purpose to certain of his nobles. Between the beginning of the sixteenth and the end of the eighteenth centuries the proportion of musketeers gradually increased. During the Thirty Years' War (1618-48), Gustavus Adolphus and Wallenstein adopted opposite modes of dealing with masses of infantry: the former spread them out to a great width; the latter adopted a narrower front. In Louis XIV's reign, the prolonged wars introduced the larger grouping into brigades and divisions. Frederick the Great, in the next century, reduced the depth of his infantry formation to three ranks, and introduced a most rigid and exact system of tactics and drills.

The French Revolution effected almost as great changes in the military as in the political organization of Europe. As early as 1793 France had almost exhausted her supply of voluntary recruits, and compulsory requisition was introduced. In 1799 systematic conscription was made the sole law. (See CONSCRIPTION).

From this period also dates the introduction of the short service and reserve system. In nearly all nations some form of a reserve was now built up, intended to augment the standing army, or first fighting line, from a peace to a war strength, and consisting of two classes. A typical example was the army of the German Empire. (See GERMANY).

The principles of organization were also modified in the large armies which took the field in the beginning of the century. In 1792 *mixed divisions,* composed of all arms, had been introduced, and in 1804 Napoleon organized, under his marshals, *corps d'armée,* each in itself a complete army. The Prussian model was generally accepted as the best type of army corps, and in that country originated the territorial system generally adopted by all European powers.

Before the outbreak of the World War in 1914, the immense armies maintained by European countries had come to be a terrific drain upon their respective nations. Of the regular army of Great Britain, only about one-half was serving on the home stations of England, Scotland, and Ireland; while an army officered by Europeans was maintained in India alone. Russia, France, Germany, and Italy also kept large armies constantly with the colors.

See ARMY OF THE UNITED STATES; ARMY IN THE FIELD; MILITIA; ARTILLERY; CAVALRY; INFANTRY; STRATEGY AND TACTICS; FORTIFICATION; AERONAUTICS; BATTLES, FAMOUS; MILITARY AGE; MILITARY EDUCATION; MILITARISM; SANITATION, MILITARY; also the section *Army* in the articles on the principal nations. For a detailed account of the war, see EUROPE, GREAT WAR OF.

Consult Jerram's *Armies of the World;* *Armies of To-Day* (various writers); Köppers' *Armies of Europe* (Eng. trans.); Oman's *History of the Art of War: Middle Ages; Staffs of Various Armies* (issued by the Military Information Division, U. S. War Department).

Army Aeronautics. See **Aeronautics.**

Army and Navy Legion of Valor, U. S. A. See **Medal of Honor, Congressional.**

Army Aviation. See **Aeronautics.**

Army Chaplains. See **Chaplains.**

Army Corps. The corps is the largest peace time formation in the armies of Continental nations. This organization, first adopted by Napoleon in 1803, has been retained in all large armies. In Prussia the territory of the kingdom was divided into army corps districts. The German army corps before the outbreak of the Great War may be taken as a type. Its component parts were the general staff, 2 infantry divisions (to which cavalry and artillery were attached), 1 battalion of rifles, 1 telegraph section, 1 corps bridge train, 1 division machine guns, 1 company pioneers, 6 supply columns, 7 supply parks, 12 ammunition columns, 2 field bakery columns, 12 field hospitals, 2 horse depots. In Great Britain the army corps had never existed prior to the Great War as a permanent fighting unit, the largest formation being the division (see DIVISION).

In the United States the army corps does not exist in time of peace, the highest administrative units being the regiment in the infantry, cavalry, and field artillery, and the district in the coast defence. During the war with Spain the men mustered into the service were organized into army corps. See ARMY IN THE FIELD.

Army Departments. See **Army of the United States.**

Army Education. See **Military Education.**

Army Enlistment. In the United States there is no compulsory military service, except in time of war or defensive emergency and enlistments are voluntary. Army recruiting is conducted by an officer properly detailed and authorized, for each post, regiment, or detachment, and by special officers detailed by the War Department for that purpose. There are general recruiting stations in the leading cities. Any male citizen of the United States or person who has legally declared his intention to become a citizen, if above the age of eighteen and under the age of thirty-five years, able-bodied, and free from disease, of good character and temperate habits, may be accepted for enlistment. If the applicant is a minor, he must have the written consent of his parent or guardian.

the entire force composing the army has been trained and organized for war, and kept by the nation on a paid basis, always ready for war. National armies are those in which the entire available force are the trained men of the nation or those fit to bear arms. A regular or standing army may be part of a national army. A field army, more generally known as a field force, is an army prepared to take the field. Thus, the regular army of the United States, when raised to a war footing, becomes a field force or field army.

The term field army (or armies) has had various meanings, especially in the United States. At times it has meant a group of divisions and at others a group of army corps. The organization of military force changes constantly to meet changing conditions, especially in the case of those engaged in active

Number of U. S. Troops Engaged in Wars of the United States

War	Date	Regulars	Militia and Volunteers	Total[1]	Casualties
Revolution	1775-1783	130,711	164,080	294,791	No record
Northwest Indians	1790-1795	....	....	8,983	1,332
France	1798-1800	....	....	[2]4,593	....
Tripoli	1801-1805	....	....	[2]3,330	....
Creek Indians	1813-1814	600	13,181	13,781	....
Great Britain	1812-1815	85,000	471,622	556,622	5,877
Seminole Indians	1817-1818	1,000	6,911	7,911	82
Black Hawk Indians	1831-1832	1,339	5,126	6,465	65
Cherokee Indians	1836-1837	....	9,494	9,494	....
Creek Indians	1836-1837	935	12,483	13,418	....
Florida Indians	1835-1843	11,169	29,953	41,122	940
Mexico	1846-1848	30,954	73,776	104,730	17,373
Apache, Navajo, and Utah Indians	1849-1855	1,500	1,061	2,561	....
Seminole Indians	1856-1858	....	3,687	3,687	....
Civil War[3]	1861-1865	....	....	2,772,408	359,528
Spain	1898	....	....	[4]274,717	1,688
Philippines	1898-1902	....	....	60,000	7,052
China	1900	5,000	....	5,000	209
World War I	1914-1918	....	....	4,355,000	364,800
World War II	1941-1945	....	....	12,336,901	1,135,054

[1] *Including all branches of the service.* [2] *Naval forces engaged.* [3] *The number of troops on the Confederate side was about 750,000.* [4] *Troops actually engaged, about 60,000.* [5] *Includes 2,890,164 drafted men; does not include Marines serving with the Army.* [6] *Active hostilities ceased 1918.*

Under the existing regulations the original term of enlistment may be for either one or three years. Subsequent re-enlistments must be for three years.

Army in the Field. Regular or permanent or standing armies are those in which campaign in time of war. In time of peace the United States has heretofore had no organization larger than the division. Since conscription became effective and enlargement of the army began in 1940 corps have been formed.

In the United States, when war has been declared the standing army is at once filled up by voluntary enlistment or draft, or both, to its war strength. By recent law the President has the right not only to mobilize the militia, but can even order it outside the boundaries of the country (see CONSCRIPTION and MOBILIZATION).

The commander-in-chief for the army in the field having been appointed, he takes complete charge of operations. The movement across the seas of any large body of troops, with their attendant equipment and stores, necessitates a disembarkation on a seashore, and a preliminary collection and organization of *matériel*. A maritime basis is, therefore, a necessity. The objective of the army may be the opposing force of the enemy, or his capital, or some main source of his supplies. Whatever it is, the army must make a pathway to get to it. This pathway to the objective is called the *line of operations*, and includes not only the country through which the army moves, but all the territory contiguous to it. The *front of operations* includes all territory occupied toward the enemy, and all adjacent territory that must be observed to render it secure against hostile advance. A *zone of operations* is the belt of territory controlled by the moving columns of the army.

As an army moves forward, a *line of communications* becomes necessary, along which the *personnel* and *matériel* necessary to maintain the army in fighting condition are forwarded, and by means of which sick, wounded, prisoners, etc., are removed from the theatre of actual hostilities. The line consists of a chain of military stations connected by a route traversed by rail, road, or river transport, or a combination of all three. As the army advances, the length of the line of communications increases, and it is necessary to organize it into sections.

The usual method by which an army is supplied is an adaptation of the magazine and requisition systems. Arms, ammunition, accoutrements, clothing, harness, tools, and stores in general are forwarded to troops from the nearest magazines; but ordinary transport, and as much as possible of the daily food for men and horses, are drawn from the theatre of war. Food has to be issued daily, as a rule, and the unexpended portion of a ration is carried on the person. (See RATIONS.)

A *general transport* of a semi-military character is worked from the base of operations to the advanced depot in rear of an army, or to the magazines nearest to the troops to be supplied. (See TRANSPORTATION, MILITARY.)

Next to the problem of providing ammunition and supplies, that of a proper medical and sanitary service is most important. (See SANITATION, MILITARY; HOSPITALS, MILITARY.)

In addition to the collection and distribution of supplies, the staff of the line of communications has to utilize and often create postal and telegraph services. The advantage of keeping up communication by wireless, telegraph, heliograph, flying machines, and other means along the route between its various magazines and depots is obvious, and the post of director of telegraph in a campaign is an important one. (See SIGNALLING, MILITARY.)

See ARMY; ARMY OF THE UNITED STATES; STRATEGY AND TACTICS; CAVALRY; INFANTRY; ARTILLERY; AERONAUTICS; FIELD EQUIPMENT; RECONNAISSANCE; RAILWAYS, *Military Railways;* EUROPE, GREAT WAR OF.

Army of the United States. On June 14, 1775, the Continental Congress, recognizing the necessity for a force that would be subject to its orders, authorized the raising of ten companies of riflemen to serve for a period of one year. The following day it took into its pay all of the troops then around Boston, created the office of Commander-in-Chief of all of the forces, raised or to be raised in the defence of American liberty, and appointed George Washington to the office. In 1776 Congress laid the foundation of the present War Department by appointing a Board of War and Ordnance.

For the next hundred years the history of the Regular Army is one of a succession of small increases to meet emergencies, with corresponding decreases after the emergencies had passed. By the act of June 3, 1916, known as the National Defence Act, an effort was made to provide more adequately for national defence. This act provided for the establishing of the Army of the United States, composed of the Regular Army, the Volunteer Army, the Officers' Reserve Corps, the Enlisted Reserve Corps, the National Guard while in the service of the United States, and such other land forces as were then or might thereafter be authorized by law.

Realizing the necessity for a larger force than could be raised through volunteers, Congress, by an act of May 18, 1917, provided for raising a new army through conscription. To distinguish this new force from the Regular Army and the National Guard, it was at first known as the National Army, but in 1918 it was merged with the Regular Army and the National Guard into the Army of the United States. Under the provisions of the act of May 18 (1917) all able-bodied citizens between the ages of twenty-one and thirty years, inclusive, were made liable to military service. Following the armistice (q.v.) and the demobilization of the war army, reorganization of the military forces of the United States was effected through an amendment of the National Defence Act of 1916, passed and approved as the Act of June 4, 1920.

Under the provisions of the Constitution, the President of the United States is the commander-in-chief of the land and naval forces of the United States. In the past he has invariably exercised this office through the Secretaries of War and Navy and through military and naval commanders in the field and at sea. Following World War I, Congress created the office of General of the Armies, and Gen. John J. Pershing was appointed to that rank, which was to continue during the period of his life. With forebodings of war in Europe, 1939 found the U. S. strengthening all branches of the army. In 1940 the first peacetime conscription was voted by Congress. By 1943 U. S. forces were scattered over most of the earth. In time of war the President names the general officers in command.

The Secretary of War is charged with carrying out the policy of the President in military matters and with the general administration of the War Department. (See WAR, U. S. DEPARTMENT OF.)

The Chief of Staff presides over the War Department General Staff and, under the direction of the President and of the Secretary of War, causes to be made by the War Department General Staff the necessary plans for recruiting, organizing, etc. The Staff of the army consists of those corps and departments charged with the administration and maintenance. Primarily, the Staff is divided into the General Staff Corps and the various Technical, Supply, and Administrative Corps and Departments.

The General Staff Corps consists of the War Department General Staff, and the General Staff with Troops.

The War Department General Staff is charged with the preparation of plans for the national defence.

The General Staff with Troops assists Corps Area, Department, and Division Commanders in supervising and co-ordinating the administration, training, supply, and operations of the troops. (See GENERAL STAFF.)

The Adjutant General's Department keeps all records of the army, carries on its correspondence, publishes orders and official books and manuals and manages the recruiting service. (See ADJUTANT GENERAL.)

The Inspector General's Department has general supervision over all that pertains to the efficiency of the army, and with the enforcement of all orders and regulations.

The Judge Advocate General's Department passes upon all legal questions and transacts all other legal business arising in the War Department. (See JUDGE ADVOCATE GENERAL'S DEPARTMENT.)

The Quartermaster Corps, established in 1912 by the consolidation of the old Quartermaster, Subsistence, and Pay Departments, and reorganized in 1920 by the addition of the war-time Construction and Transportation Services and the subtraction of the Finance Department, is charged with the procurement, storage, and issue of all supplies for the army. In a word, it shelters, feeds, clothes, and transports the army. (See QUARTERMASTER CORPS.)

The Medical Department is charged with the care of the sick and wounded and their transportation from the battlefield to hospitals. It consists of the Surgeon General, the Medical Corps, the Dental Corps, the Veterinary Corps, the Medical Administrative Corps, the Army Nurse Corps. (See MEDICAL DEPARTMENT, U. S. ARMY.)

The Corps of Engineers has both line and staff functions. (See ENGINEERING, MILITARY.)

The Ordnance Department supplies the army with all types of arms and ammunition, as well as certain other kinds of equipment. (See ORDNANCE DEPARTMENT.)

The Signal Corps also has both line and staff functions. (See SIGNAL CORPS.)

The Army Air Forces began as a subdivision of the Signal Corps but, during World War I, became a provisional separate service. In World War II they are commanded by a lieutenant general under whom there is a General Air Staff and an Operations Staff. (See AERONAUTICS.)

The Finance Department, under the authority of the Secretary of War, is charged with the disbursement of all funds for the War Department, including the pay of the army and the mileage for officers and the accounting therefor.

The Chemical Warfare Service came into existence as a provisional organization during the World War and was established by Congress in the act of June 4, 1920. It is charged with the investigation, development, manufacture, or procurement, and supply to the army of all smoke and incendiary materials. (See CHEMISTRY: *Chemical Warfare*).

The Bureau of Insular Affairs has general supervision over the affairs of the insular possessions of the United States, particularly the Philippines and Porto Rico.

The Militia Bureau of the War Department has supervision over the organizing, equipping, training, and administering of the National Guard of the United States.

The line of the Regular Army includes the combatant—or fighting branches, such as Infantry, Cavalry, Field Artillery, Coast Artillery, Air Service, Signal Corps, and the Corps of Engineers. The Coast Artillery is occupied chiefly with the fixed defences along the seacoast.

Under the act of June 3, 1916, the National Guard became an important element in the national defence. The act provided that the National Guard should be organized, uniformed, and equipped similarly to the Regular Army. For a full account of the history and present status of the National Guard, see MILITIA.

In 1940, with the German menace causing more uneasiness, Congress passed the Selective Training and Service Act and authorized the President to call the National Guard to active duty. By early 1945 over 8,000,000 men had been called to the colors, and numerous modifications, leading to better co-

U. S. Army Photo

The Marston strip. Douglas A-20A attack bombers landing on one of the portable runways developed by the Army Air Forces.

operation among army, navy, and air forces, had been made in army organization.

Army Register, U. S., an annual publication issued by War Department, which contains a record of the officers on the active or retired list of the U. S. Army, with the department, arm of the service, regiment, corps, and company, and other personal and military data; a list of all persons who have received the Congressional medal of honor, and of those to whom certificates of merit have been granted. It also contains a list of casualties during the year. Similar publications are regularly issued by many other countries.

Army Schools. See **Military Education**.
Army War College. See **Military Education**.

Army Worm, the caterpillar of a dark-colored, night-flying, destructive moth (*Leucania unipuncta*), allied to the cutworms, which sometimes does much damage in the United States to grass, and occasionally to Indian corn. The name is also applied to the larva of the Grass Worm (*Laphynga frugiperda*), and in Europe to the grub of a small black fly (*Sciara militaris*).

Arnason, Jon (1819-88), Icelandic author and writer of folk-tales, was born at Hof, and died at Reykjavik. He is known for his admirable collection of popular Icelandic tales, which won him the title of the 'Grimm of Iceland,' entitled *Popular Legends and Tales of Iceland*.

Arnauld, Antoine (1612-94), French theologian, called 'the Great Arnault,' was born in Paris, and was educated at Sorbonne. He was expelled from the society of the Sorbonne for his support of the Jansenists (see JANSENISM). He gave assistance to Pascal (q.v.) with his *Lettres Ecrites à un Provincial de ses Amis,* and to Lancelot with his *Grammaire*. His great work, the *Logique de Port-Royal,* was written in conjunction with Nicole. Consult Larrière's *Vie;* Sainte-Beuve's *Port-Royal;* Varin's *Vérité sur les Arnaulds*.

Arnaut of Mareuil (in the diocese of Périgueux), Provençal troubadour (fl. c. 1150-1200). About thirty of his poems have come down to us.

Arnaut, Daniel, twelfth-century troubadour, born at Ribérac (Dordogne), France. He was the inventor of the *sestina,* which was imitated by Dante.

Arndt, Ernst Moritz (1769-1860), German poet and patriot, born in the island of Rügen. The son of a serf, he was instrumental in the abolition (1806) of serfdom by his work, *Geschichte der Leibeigenschaft in Pommern* (1803). He wrote patriotic poems and songs. He is familiarly called 'Father Arndt' by the German people. He was a German chauvinist, detesting everything French.

Arne, Thomas Augustine (1710-78), English musical composer, was born in London. He was the first to introduce—in his *Judith* (1773)—female voices into oratorio choruses. Besides oratorios and operas, he composed a large number of glees, catches, and canons; but he is best known by his musical settings of such songs as *Rule Britannia* (the finale of *The Masque of Alfred,* 1740), *Where the Bee Sucks, Under the Greenwood Tree,* and other Shakespearean songs.

Arnhem (ancient *Arenacum*), city, capital of province Gelderland, Netherlands; p. 77,389. Near this beautiful city occurred in World War II (1944) the classic stand of the 'Red Devils,' 1st British Airborne Division, 8,000 of whom were cornered by Nazis, and only 2,000 of whom escaped.

Arnhem Land, most northerly part of the North Territory of South Australia, between the Gulf of Carpentaria and Anson Bay.

Arnica, the dried acrid and aromatic rootlets and rhizome of the Mountain Arnica (*A. montana*) of Middle and Southern Europe. The official preparation is a poisonous tincture which, diluted with water, serves as a remedy for bruises. Internally it has a stimulating effect on the alimentary canal, but is seldom prescribed. Its efficacy seems due to the alcohol in the tincture. Applied too freely to the skin, it may produce erysipelas.

Arnim, Countess von (Mary Antoinette Beauchamp) (1866-1910), English authoress, was born in Sydney, Australia. Her first published book, *Elizabeth and Her German Garden,* published anonymously in 1898, won immediate success in both England and America, and was followed by a number of other successful novels.

Arnim, Bettina (Elisabeth) von (1788-1859), a sister of Clemens Brentano, and wife of Ludwig Achim von Arnim, was born in Frankfort-on-the-Main. The great event of her early life was her enthusiastic attachment to Goethe, whom she first saw in 1807, he being then nearly sixty. The correspondence, published under the title of *Goethes Griefwechsel mit einem Kinde* in 1835, and translated by Bettina into English (*Correspondence of Goethe with a Child*), is mainly fanciful.

Arno (ancient *Arnus*), a river in Italy. The Arno is subject to destructive inundations.

Arnold of Brescia (c. 1100-55), Italian monk, studied under Abélard at Paris. For an attack on the worldliness of the higher clergy he was cited by the bishop of Brescia before the second Lateran Council (1139) as a heretic, and banished. He took refuge with Abélard, but his preaching brought upon him the hostility of St. Bernard, who denounced him. In 1155, being expelled by the senate of Rome at the instigation of Pope Adrian IV., he fled to Campania, but was brought to Rome and crucified. His body was burned and the ashes cast into the Tiber. Consult *Lives* by Giesebrecht, Bonghi, and Hausrath (1892).

Arnold, Benedict (1741-1801), an American soldier, whose services are thrown into the background by his treason to his country, was born in Norwich, Conn. At the outbreak of the American Revolution he raised a militia company for service against the British. As colonel he assisted in the capture of Ticonderoga and Crown Point. He commanded the disastrous 'Kennebec Expedition,' and took a conspicuous part, under Gen. Gates, in the first and second battles of Saratoga. He was afterward in command in Philadelphia, after the evacuation of that city by the British; there he aroused enmities, was accused of disloyalty, was tried by court-martial on charges which apparently had little basis, and was found guilty of two minor offences, for which Washington, directed by the court, mildly reprimanded him. Filled with a sense of wrong and longing for revenge, he entered into treasonable negotiations with the British, and, obtaining from Washington the command of the important fortification of West Point, offered to betray it into the hands of Gen. Henry Clinton, the British commander, then in New York. The loss of West Point would have been an almost irreparable one to the Americans, but the plot was discovered through the capture of Major John André, who had been sent by Clinton to confer with Arnold. Arnold, informed of the capture by a guileless subordinate, escaped to New York, and as brigadier-general in the British army led a pillaging expedition into Virginia and commanded the British force which burned New London, Conn. In Dec., 1781, he went to England, where he lived during most of the time until his death, being everywhere treated with contempt, and being in his last years afflicted with melancholia. The best biography is by I. N. Arnold; see also that by Sparks, Codman, *Arnold's Expedition to Quebec*, J. H. Smith's *Arnold's March from Cambridge to Quebec*, and Abbott's *The Crisis of the Revolution*.

Arnold, Sir Edwin (1832-1904), English poet, born at Gravesend. For a poem on *The Feast of Belshazzar* he gained the Newdigate prize. His works include Poems; *Hero and Leander; The Indian Song of Songs; Light of Asia*, an epic on the life and work of Buddha, which has gone through numerous editions.

Arnold, Henry Harley (1886-1950), U. S. general, was born at Gladwyne, Pa., and grad. from West Point, 1907. Won Mackay Trophy, 1912, 1935. Was Chief of Army Air Corps, 1938; Comdg. Gen. Army Air Forces, 1942; Gen., 1943; Gen. of the Army, 1944; Gen. of the Air Force, 1949.

Arnold, Matthew (1822-88), English poet, critic, and educator, was the eldest son of Thomas Arnold, headmaster of Rugby. He was born at Laleham, Middlesex. On three occasions he drew up valuable reports of continental systems of education. Two of them have been reprinted as *The Popular Education of France* and *Schools and Universities on the Continent*. He died suddenly at Liverpool.

Two early volumes—*The Strayed Reveller* and *Empedocles upon Etna*—were anonymously issued under the initial 'A.' The best of their contents were reprinted in the *Poems* of 1853, on the title-page of which the author's name appeared, and to which he added such masterpieces as *Sohrab and Rustum* (a narrative poem in the Homeric vein) and *The Scholar Gipsy*. Hardly less remarkable than the *Poems* of 1853 was the preface—dwelling on the importance of structure and unity in poetry—that accompanied them. Although the monody on his friend Arthur Hugh Clough, printed as *Thyrsis* in the 1867 volume, is one of his finest single pieces, and he continued to write poetry at intervals until the end of his life, that his strongest work was done. The Oxford lectures, *On Translating Homer* and *On the Study of Celtic Literature* are models of sympathetic, lucid, and graceful discussion of literary problems. Literary criticism, like poetry, Arnold never wholly dropped. Arnold had the gift of crystallizing his views in memorable phrases. Stimulating as his critical works are, it is probably by his poems that Arnold will live in English literature.

Biography: Fitch's *Thomas and Matthew Arnold*, estimating his educational influence; Robertson's *Modern Humanists*, his social influence; and for his literary achievements, Gate's *Three Studies in Literature*.

Arnold, Thomas (1795-1842), historian, divine, and greatest of English schoolmasters, was born at East Cowes, Isle of Wight. He had an acute insight into character, and influenced his pupils by stimulus, moral and intellectual, without subjecting them to needless rules. While at Laleham he had written articles on Roman history for the *Encyclopedia Metropolitana*, and at Rugby, he undertook an edition of *Thucydides*. He died suddenly on June 12, 1842.

There is an excellent biography of Arnold by Dean Stanley in *Arnold's Life and Corre-*

spondence. Consult also Sir. J. Fitch's *Thomas and Matthew Arnold: Their Influence on English Education;* M. Arnold's *Rugby Chapel* and T. Hughes' *Tom Brown's School Days.*

Arnold, Thomas (1823-1900), second son of Dr. Thomas Arnold of Rugby, and younger brother of Matthew Arnold, was born at Laleham, Middlesex. Becoming a convert to Roman Catholicism and an associate of Cardinal Newman, he was appointed professor of English literature in the Catholic University, Dublin. Mrs. Humphry Ward, the novelist, was his eldest daughter. Besides his well-known *Manual of English Literature, History and Criticism,* he was the author of *Chaucer to Wordsworth.* He published also an autobiographical volume, *Passages in a Wandering Life.*

Arnold, William Rosenzweig (1872-1929), American scholar, was born in Beirut, Syria. In 1896 became curator of the Department of Antiquities, Metropolitan Museum of Art. His publications include *Ancient Babylonian Temple Records, The Rhythms of the Ancient Hebrews, The Passover Papyrus from Elephantine.*

Arnoldi, Wilhelm (1798-1864), bishop of Treves, was born at Baden, near Treves. In 1844 he drew vast crowds of pilgrims to Treves by the exhibition of the 'holy-coat,' held to be the seamless coat worn by Christ at His crucifixion and said to have been given to Treves by St. Helena. Revolt against the exhibition led to the formation, under the leadership of Johannes Ronge, of German Catholicism (see GERMAN CATHOLICS).

Arnot, William (1806-75), a popular Scottish preacher and author. He published *Illustrations of the Book of Proverbs,* and *The Parables of Our Lord.*

Arnott, Neil (1788-1874), Scottish physician, was born at Arbroath, Scotland. In 1832 he invented the water-bed; and in 1835 published a treatise on *Warming and Ventilating* in which he described the 'Arnott Stove' and 'Arnott Ventilator.' He was a munificent benefactor to higher education.

Arnsberg, town, Prussia, in the province of Westphalia. It was formerly a centre of the famous Westphalian courts of justice (Vehmgerichte) and was long the capital of Westphalia; p. 11,181.

Arnstadt, town, capital of Thuringia. Features of interest are the Liebfrauen-Kirche, one of the chief ecclesiastical buildings of Thuringia, with fine sculptures, and the 16th century Rathaus. In the vicinity are saline springs and baths; p. 22,000.

Arolla, a group of chalets near the foot of the glacier of the same name (the local term for the *Pinus cembra*). Arolla is one of the most frequented of all Swiss summer resorts.

Arolsen, town, capital of the republic of Waldeck, Germany. The castle contains antiquities from Herculaneum and Pompeii, a good library, and a fine collection of Spanish arms; p. 2,222.

Aromatics, a class of medicines which owe their properties to the essential oils, to benzoic and cinnamic acids, to volatile productions of distillation, or to odorous glandular secretions. Among the plant families which yield the most important aromatics are the Labiatæ, Umbelliferæ, Lauraceæ, Myrtaceæ, Aurantiaceæ, Coniferæ, Scitamineæ, and Orchideæ. Aromatics may be arranged in the following subclasses: (1) Those in which the active principle is an essential oil, as the oil of thyme. (2) Those containing camphor, or an allied body. (3) Bitter aromatics, in which there is a mixture of a bitter principle and an essential oil, as chamomile. (4) Those of which musk is the type, as civet and ambergris; and certain plants with a musk-like odor, as *Malva moschata, Mimulus moschatus,* and *Hibiscus abelmoschus.* (5) Those containing a fragrant resin, as benzoin, which possess stimulant properties. (6) Lastly, those which are artificially produced by destructive distillation, as tar, creosote, benzol, etc.

As a general rule, these substances act as diffusible stimulants of more or less power, and as antispasmodics, while those in which a bitter principle is present, act as vermifuges and tonics.

Aromatic Series, a term applied to a large group of organic chemical compounds, many of which occur in balsams, essential oils, and other substances having an aromatic odor. It was originally limited to the compounds of the benzene group, but it has now been extended so as to include other series homologous with them, and ranging round the group of hydrocarbons.

Aromatic Spirits of Ammonia. See **Sal Volatile.**

Aromatic Vinegar is generally prepared by adding the oils of cloves, lavender, rosemary, bergamot, neroli, and cinnamon to the strongest acetic acid. It is a pleasant and powerful perfume; is very volatile, and when snuffed up by the nostrils, is a powerful excitant, being serviceable in fainting, languor, headache, and nervous debility. The liquid must be cautiously dealt with, as it is very corrosive.

Aronia, a European species of the Cratægus.

Aroostook, river, rising in Piscataquis co., Maine. It possesses a historical interest from its connection with the Northeast Boundary Dispute.

Aroostook Disturbances. See **Northeast Boundary Dispute.**

Aros, African tribe inhabiting the Cross River region north of Old Calabar. A British punitive expedition suppressed their turbulent and slave hunting proclivities in 1901-2.

Arouet, family name of Voltaire.

Arpad (d. 907), the national hero of Hungary, under whom the Magyars first gained a footing in that country, about 884.

Arpeggio, in musical score a chord of which the constituent notes are sounded consecutively from below upwards, instead of simultaneously.

Arpent, an old French land-measure corresponding to the English acre.

Arpino, a town in Italy in the province of Caserta. It is the birthplace of Vipsanius Agrippa (63 B.C.), Caius Marius (157 B.C.), and the painter Giuseppe Cesari (c. 1568); p. 2,647.

Arqua Petrarca, a village in Italy, in the province of Padua, is situated among the Euganean Hills. It was the home of Petrarch (1370-74) and his house and tomb are still shown; p. 1,500.

Arquebus, (more properly HARQUEBUS), an early form of hand firearm used in the 15th and 16th centuries. Soldiers armed with the weapon were designated *arquebusiers.*

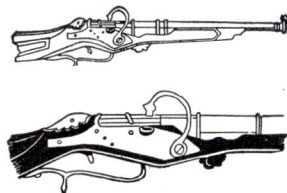

Arquebus, with enlarged View of Lock

Arracacha, a plant of the genus *Umbelliferæ,* with tuberous roots, native to the tablelands of Northern South America. *Arracacha zanthoriza* is much cultivated in the Andes, where its tubers are boiled and used for food as well as for flavoring purposes, the flavor being similar to that of the carrot or parsnip. A starch, similar to arrowroot, is obtained by washing and rasping the root. *A. dugessi* is found in Central America.

Arrack, or **Rack,** an Oriental name applied to various distilled liquors, in particular to that obtained from the fermented juice (toddy) of the cocoanut, date, and other palms. It is sometimes made also from fermented rice and from a combination of rice and molasses. Arrack is made in Batavia, Java, Ceylon, Siam, and Goa, that of Ceylon and Goa being made from palm juice alone. Only small quantities are exported, but large amounts are consumed in India and the East.

Arragon. See **Aragon.**

Arrah, town, India, in the province of Bihar and Orissa, in Shahabad district. During the Mutiny of 1857 it was gallantly held for eighty days by fifty Sikhs and a dozen Englishmen against a force of 10,000 mutineers; p. 48,922.

Arraignment, in criminal procedure the act of summoning a prisoner to the bar to hear the charge contained in the indictment or information filed against him and to plead thereto.

Arran, the largest island in the Firth of Clyde, Scotland, forming part of the county of Bute; p. 8,294.

Arran Islands, Ireland. See ARAN.

Arrangement, in music the transcription or adaptation of compositions to suit other instruments (or voices) than those for which they were composed. A common kind of arrangement is that of adapting orchestral compositions for the piano.

Arras (*Nemetacum*), town, France, capital of the department of Pas-de-Calais. Robespierre was born here; p. 30,000. During the World War (see EUROPE, WORLD WAR I), Arras was occupied by the Germans Aug. 30, 1914, but was shortly afterward evacuated. For subsequent action in the vicinity, see ARRAS, BATTLES OF.

Arras, Battles of, a series of battles in World War I. The first battle of Arras occurred in October 1914. The Allied battle line in the n., which was completed Oct. 19, 1914, stretched a distance of 80 m. or more from Albert to the sea. A successful breach here would have been a decisive step in the German drive for the Channel ports.

Behind Arras ran the line to Amiens by the Ancre valley, and the Doullens line provided three ways for the coming of reserves. The junction of the lines is at Achicourt, and it was obligatory on Maud'huy to hold this point. The chief German attack was on Oct. 24. All day there was desperate fighting. There is little doubt that, but for Maud'huy's stubborn stand, the gates of the north would have been unlocked. All attempts to break the French line failed and by Oct. 26 Maud'huy had begun to retaliate. The fierce French counter-attack pushed the Germans out of their advance trenches, and restored to the French some of the little villages. Bit by bit the circle was widened, till Arras was beyond the reach of the German howitzers; and now Von Buelow's best corps were departing for Ypres (see YPRES, BATTLES OF).

Second Battle.—At the end of the first week of April, 1917, the German armies were secure in defence, if deprived of a first-rate chance of an offensive. The army group under the Crown Prince of Bavaria had been strengthened in men and in material. To meet the Allied artillery, the Germans had increased the range of their field guns by some 2,000 yards; while air work had also vastly improved. They comforted themselves with the reflection that the Allies, wearied with the hectic business of pursuit, were not yet in a position to launch any great attack; and that ere they were ready, the German defences would have become impregnable. The whole defensive belt was from two to five m. deep; but the German command was not content with it. They had designed an independent line running from Drocourt to the Siegfried Line. This, the Drocourt-Quéant line, was not yet completed in April. It was intended as a protection for Douai and St. Quentin, the loss of which would have made the whole Siegfried system untenable.

The city of Arras, though situated less than a mile inside the British lines, had for two years been a place of comparative peace. At the beginning of April, 1917, however, it was a mark which the German guns could scarcely miss. To minimize this danger, the Allied generals had recourse to a bold plan. They resolved to assemble their armies underground. Arras had huge ancient sewers like those of Paris, where three divisions could be assembled in perfect security. The Germans shelled the town intermittently, but there was no real bombardment, and before Arras could be methodically assailed, the enemy had been pushed many miles eastward.

The British front of attack was slightly over twelve m. long. Against Vimy Ridge lay Byng's Canadian Corps. In its constituents the army of assault was largely Scottish.

About April 4 the British guns woke. There was a steady fire upon the great fortress of Vimy Ridge. Easter Sunday, April 8, a lull seemed to fall and the ear-splitting din died away into sporadic bombardments. The attack itself began next day, when, at 5:30 A.M. (zero hour), the British guns broke into such a fire as had never been known on any battlefield. The first stage of the battle lasted three days. Thus far the battle was a remarkable success. Air-craft, artillery, infantry, and tanks had worked in perfect combination. On April 12, the British positions were improved, the second stage of the battle opened; the Germans retired to their third line. The British attack on an eight-mile front on both banks of the Scarpe on April 23, resulted in gains of Gavrelle, Roeux, Guémappe, and Fountainlez-Croisilles at great cost of men to both sides. The attacks on April 28 and 29, also resulted in British gains, both n. and s. of the Scarpe.

Here ended the Battle of Arras as originally planned. That plan, in its ultimate objective, had involved the destruction of the northern pivot of the Siegfried Line, and the consequent reduction of the whole position. But the failure of the French at the southern pivot made this impossible in the immediate future. Haig had, therefore, henceforth to work with a double aim. He had to continue his efforts in the Arras area, partly to ease the pressure on the new French position on the Aisne, partly in order that when the time came for the breaking off of the battle in this sector, he should be able to leave his front in a favorable position for future operations. Likewise, he had to prepare for that great assault upon the German right wing in Flanders, which had long been decided upon as the main British enterprise of that summer.

The Battle of Arras was a limited victory —that is to say, it attained completely its immediate objectives; but, owing to events outside the control of the British Command, it did not produce the strategical result upon the Western front as a whole which was its ultimate design. The vital fact was that the German plan had been defeated. During the last days of the Second Battle of the Somme, the Germans made a desperate but unsuccessful drive for Arras.

The Second Battle of the Marne (see MARNE, BATTLES OF) restored the initiative to the Allies. The Germans had blundered in a trying hour, and had thus given Foch the chance for a *coup* which restored to him the initiative. He was not yet ready for the grand climax, the decisive blow. It was his business to wear down the Germans continuously and methodically by attacks on limited fronts.

Up to August 26, 1918, the Allied Armies had attacked the Germans across and s. of the Somme and on the Aisne, but on that day Haig struck again. At 3 A.M. Sir Arthur Currie, with his Canadians, attacked on a 5-mile front, winning as much in a day as had been won in six weeks in the same area during the Second Battle of Arras in 1917. This was a grave matter for Ludendorff, for he saw both his line and his reserves shrinking with a perilous speed. On August 30, Horne moved along the Arras-Cambrai road, and found the German resistance stiffening. The next day violent counter-assaults against the new British front, between the Scarpe and the Somme, were repelled with ease. Ludendorff's intermediate position had gone, and he was once more a wanderer struggling to find a resting-place short of the main Siegfried Line. The ceaseless pressure of the Allies delayed his going and unless he found some intermediate defence, he might never reach that line.

On Sept. 2, the right wing of Horne's First Army, Currie's Canadian Corps, and Fergusson's Seventeenth Corps of the Third Army, attacked. The attack went clean through all the lines of one of the strongest positions in the West. The feat was one of the greatest in the campaign, and it made Ludendorff's plans for an intermediate stand impossible. He had no time for counter-attacks, but hurried his troops in the south behind the Canal du Nord, and put his trust in the line of water and marsh in the Sensée Valley e. of Etaing which protected Douai. By evening of Sept. 4, the British troops were on the Canal bank.

For a week following, the Allied armies were occupied only in pressing the German retreat. They struck no great blow, for their immediate task was to secure the kind of front upon which to launch a final battle for which Foch had been preparing since July. The whole front which Ludendorff had vainly hoped to establish for the winter in impenetrable defences, was a thing of angles and patches, and parts of it as fluid as wax under a flame. Ludendorff finally set to work strengthening every natural defence. He also prepared positions well to his rear, and evacuated the civilian population of Douai, Cambrai, and St. Quentin.

Between March and May, 1917, the British had forced the Germans back to the Siegfried zone, taking in the process 21,000 prisoners and 257 guns. In 1918, starting from a front many miles further west, they had performed the same feat in one month, and had 70,000 prisoners and 700 guns to their credit.

Arrebo, Anders Christensen (1587-1637), Danish poet, was born in Ærö. He was styled 'the father of Danish poetry.' He published *Hexaëmeron* (1641-61). Consult *Life* by Rördam.

Arrest. The act of taking a person into custody by authority of law. Arrest is the ordinary process of apprehending a person accused of crime. It may be on warrant or without warrant. Any justice may issue a warrant for the arrest of any person for any offence upon a sworn information being laid before him.

Arrest of Judgment. A permanent stay of judgment on a verdict rendered in a court of law by reason of a fatal error in the proceedings or a fatal and incurable variance between the allegations and the proof or between the proof and the verdict.

Arretium, Italy. See AREZZO.

Arrhenius, Svante (1859-1927), Swedish chemist, was born near Upsala. He was professor of physics at Stockholm, and received the Davy medal in 1902, and the Faraday medal in 1914. His publications include *Electrochemistry,* (1901); *Worlds in the Making* (1908); *Life of the Universe* (1909); *The Destinies of the Stars* (1918); *Chemistry and Modern Life* (1919).

Arrianus or **Arrian** (*c.* 90-170 A.D.), Greek historian, pupil and friend of Epictetus, was born in Nicomedia, in Bithynia. In 147 he became Archon Eponymos in Athens. He is best known for his *Anabasis of Alexander the Great.* Arrianus' style is clear and simple; as a critical historian he deserves great credit for having made use of authoritative matter now lost.

Arrondissement, the principal civil division of the department in France, governed by a sub-prefect and council.

Arrow, a wooden shaft tipped with stone, metal, or bone, and notched and feathered at the butt, discharged by hand from a bow. It is one of the most ancient objects made by man. Prehistoric flint arrow-heads display numerous forms, range in length from half an inch to three inches. In America flint triangular arrow-heads, notched at the base so that they could be bound to the shaft with sinew thread, were in general use among the Indians. See also ARCHERY.

Arrowgrass, two small, erect, grass-like plants of the genus Triglochin.

Arrowhead, any member of the genus Sagittaria.

Arrowrock Dam, the chief engineering feature of the Boise Project, Idaho. It is 349 ft. high, 1,100 ft. long, and contains 585,200 yards of concrete. The dam was completed in 1915 at a cost of nearly $4,500,000. See BOISE PROJECT.

Arrowroot, an edible starch obtained from the root stock of various plants. The true arrowroot comes from the rhizomes of *Maranta arundinacea,* a West Indian plant of the order *Marantaceæ.* Brazilian arrowroot is obtained from the *Cassava* (q.v.).

Arrowsmith, John (1790-1873), British cartographer, one of the founders of the Royal Geographical Society (1830), and publisher of a long and important series of maps from 1858 on.

Arrow Worms, small, transparent creatures often found in enormous numbers at the surface of the sea. The common genera are Sagitta and Spadella.

Arsaces, the founder of the Parthian empire. He raised a revolt among the Parthians against Antiochus II. of Syria, and was the first king of Parthia, about 250 B.C., reigning two years. His name was borne by all his successors, of whom the last was Arsaces XXXI. (Artabanus IV.), whose power was overthrown by the Persians in 226 A.D. A branch of the dynasty ruled over Armenia from 147 B.C. to 430 A.D.

Arsenal, a government establishment for the manufacture, repair, storage, and issue of arms, ammunition and munitions of war for the land forces. As early as 1776 the U. S. Government undertook the manufacture of gunpowder, and the next year Washington selected Springfield, Mass., as the site of the first arsenal. Harper's Ferry, the next arsenal, was built in 1795, and others were erected at various times, until, in 1900, the United States had seventeen establishments of the kind, several of which have since been abandoned. See ORDNANCE DEPARTMENT.

Arsenic (As, 75.96), a semi-metallic element widely distributed in nature. It rarely occurs native, but usually combined with sulphur, iron, and other elements, as in realgar, As_2S_2, arsenical iron, and particularly as mispickel or arsenical pyrites, $FeSAs$. Arsenic is a steel-gray, brittle, crystalline solid that sublimes when heated, being deposited partly in crystals and partly as a black, amorphous solid. It tarnishes in air, and is rapidly oxidized if heated with it. It is chiefly used to harden and improve the sphericity of shot, for bronzing, and in pyrotechny. Arsenic forms two oxides, As_2O_3 and As_2O_5, both of which are acid anhydrides.

The largest use of arsenic at the present time is in various insecticides, as the arsenates of calcium and lead and Paris green. As an insecticide in agriculture where arsenic is used as a spray, there is supposed to be some danger from absorption of the pigment. The ease of application, however, keeps it in use. (See INSECTICIDES). Medicinally the salts of arsenic are used as tonics and alteratives. (See also SALVARSAN).

Arsenical Poisoning. Acute arsenic poisoning due to an overdose of the drug.

Arsenius, surnamed THE SAINT (c. 354-450), an Egyptian monk. He is honored in the Greek Church on May 8, and in the Latin on July 19.

Arsenius, surnamed ANTORIANUS, was appointed (1255) patriarch of Constantinople by Theodorus Laskaris II., and also guardian of his son, John IV.

Arsinoë, a Greek legend, a daughter of Phegeus and wife of Alcmæon.

Arsinoë, in Egyptian history, the name of several women famous among the Ptolemies. Among them were (1) the mother of Ptolemy I.; (2) the daughter of Ptolemy I.; (3) the daughter of Lysimachus and Nicæa, first wife of Ptolemy II.; (4) a daughter of Ptolemy XI., who was recognized as queen by the Alexandrians but later taken to Rome as a prisoner.

Arsis and **Thesis** (Gr. 'elevation' and 'depression'). In prosody, *arsis* signifies the strong or primary accent in a word, *thesis* the weak or secondary accent. In music, they denote respectively the strong and the weak beat in a bar.

Arson. The act of unlawfully and maliciously setting fire to a house, barn, or other building of another.

Arsphenamin, or **Arsphenamine,** another name for Salvarsan.

Ars Poetica, a poetic epistle by the Roman poet Horace (1st century B.C.), in which he tried to set forth the laws of poetic composition. Subsequent works, written with a similar view, include Vida's *Ars Poetica* (1527); Sir Philip Sidney's *Apology for Poetry* (1595); Pope's *Essay on Criticism* (1711).

Art has been defined as 'the manifestation of emotion obtaining external interpretation, now by expressive arrangements of line, form, or color, now by a series of gestures, sounds or words governed by particular rhythmical cadence' (Véron). In virtue of the organs through which the arts severally appeal to the mind, they are usually grouped as (1) 'arts of the eye,' including architecture, sculpture, and painting; (2) 'arts of the ear' —literature and music. The drama and the music drama, may be described as 'composite.' Excluding the minor arts, the function of which is to give pleasure by adorning articles of use, all the arts have a common origin in the desire to reproduce the feeling awakened in the artist by the contemplation of life and nature. Popular usage usually limits the term 'art' to architecture, sculpture, and painting, and such handicrafts as goldsmith's work, enamelling, pottery, and wood-carving, related to them by skill of workmanship and display of taste. In this sense art may be said to be the materialized expression of man's delight in beauty. It is not until something has been added to adorn an article already adapted for its purpose that art can be said to begin. The decorative element appeals to the senses alone, and it is the essential, if not the sole, characteristic of the applied arts. On the other hand, the expressive arts—architecture, sculpture, and painting—appeal vividly to the senses, and through the senses to the intellect and the imagination.

Architecture has been called the 'mother of the arts.' As soon as men commenced to erect huts and temples, the art of architecture, thus originated, provided a great and suggestive field for the exercise of the arts of sculpture and painting. Religion had much to do with shaping the course of the arts—in Egypt and in Greece originating temple and tomb architecture, sculpture, and painting, and even supplying decorative motives for the lesser arts; in France and England, during the Middle Ages, producing the Gothic cathedral and objects of ecclesiastical art in metal and enamel, ivory and textiles. The most important works were inspired by the religious instinct, desire for beauty expressed itself in domestic and warlike furnishings also. With the Renaissance and the Reformation other elements, including desire for beauty for its own sake, came into play.

All works of art are more or less colored by the individuality of the artist. Even among the Greeks, whose sculpture has as a general ideal the perfect beauty of the human form, the masters are distinguished from one another by individual treatment of common motives, and Phidias and Praxiteles have given their names to epochs of sculpture. During the earlier Renaissance the individuality of the artist displays itself in the conception of his subject—be it a Crucifixion, a Holy Family, or a saintly legend. It is, however, in the painting of the matured schools of the 16th and 17th centuries that personality, combined with a great but flexible technical tradition, first fully asserts itself. And it is towards greater individual freedom that art has since tended to move.

Convention exercises a great influence in the arts. Indeed, to practise an art at all, it is necessary to conform to its conventions. Thus, in painting, the artist must express his impression of the visible world, or his dreams and imaginings, in color and form (or in black and white, as in etching) upon a flat surface, in terms conformable to the laws and habit of vision, at the same time giving due consideration to the decorative or merely pleasing aspect of the result. In sculpture, again, in which real form is imitated in its three dimensions, or suggested as in relief, the nature of the imitation is controlled and determined by the material characteristics of the medium—stone or marble, bronze or silver—which, in its turn, should be so used as to bring out its inherent beauty as that is affected by mass and the play of light upon the modelled surfaces. Finally, architecture is largely conditioned by the use to which a building is to be put, by the structural possibilities of the building materials available, and by the necessity of providing against the prevailing weather.

Tradition also influences artistic form. It serves to preserve sound technical methods, and transmits from one generation to another the experience gained in experiment with new subjects or new processes. Sometimes, however, under the form of academicism, it sets up an arbitrary ideal of subject and style, founded upon past achievements, and tends to stereotype and conventionalize art. Thus, tradition may become the enemy of self-expression and of experiment.

Today, in every capital in Europe, there is a strong body of 'seceding' artists. Of the many books treating of the origin and theory of the arts, the following are selected: Ruskin's *Art Culture;* Loveridge's *Appreciation of Art;* Henri's *The Art Spirit* (1923); Mullen's *An Approach to Art* (1923); Neuhaus' *The Appreciation of Art* (1924); Ruckstuhl's *Great Works of Art and What Makes Them Great* (1925); Cortissoz' *Personalities in Art* (1925); Cheney's *Story of Modern Art*

(1941); Wright's *Modern Painting: Its Tendency and Meaning.* See also names of artists and of schools of painting.

Arta, city, Greece, capital of the province of Arta. It has a large trade in wine and tobacco; p. 9,626.

Artaxata, city, ancient capital of Armenia, on the Aras; 68 m. from Erivan. It was here that Hannibal took refuge. The Romans destroyed this city (A.D. 58), and after rebuilding, it was sacked by the Persians (A.D. 370). Later the patriarch Joseph presided over its council. Its ruins are now known as Ardashir.

Artaxerxes, a name borne by four ancient Persian kings. ARTAXERXES I., surnamed LONGIMANUS, was a son of Xerxes, who reigned from 464 to 425 B.C., and is mentioned in the Book of Nehemiah. ARTAXERXES II., surnamed MNEMON, reigned from 405 to 358 B.C. The chief events of his reign were the defeat of Cyrus and his 10,000 Greeks at Cunaxa (401 B.C.); the war with Archelaus, king of Sparta (401-394); the conclusion of the peace of Antalcidas (387). ARTAXERXES III., surnamed OCHUS, reigned from 358 to 338 B.C. ARTAXERXES IV. reigned from 226 to 240 A.D., and waged war with Alexander Severus, the Roman Emperor.

Artel, the Russian coöperative organization of artisans or skilled workmen.

Artemidorus, (*c.* 100 B.C.), Greek geographer, a native of Ephesus, who made voyages in the Mediterranean and Red Seas, to Iberia and Gaul, and as far as the Southern Ocean. His work, called *Periplus,* is not extant, but some fragments have been collected in Hudson's *Geographi Græci Minores* (1826), vol. i.

Artemidorus, surnamed DALDIANUS, from Daldis, a town in Lydia, his mother's birthplace, was a native of Ephesus. He lived in Rome from about 140-180 A.D., and wrote a work on dreams, which is extant.

Artemis, called DIANA by the Romans, one of the chief divinities of the Greeks, and twin sister of Apollo, was the daughter of Zeus (Jupiter) and Leto (Latona). She was born in the island of Delos, and was worshipped under a variety of aspects. The general conception of Artemis in Greek literature, beginning with Homer, is that of the virgin huntress, in close association with her brother Apollo. See also DIANA.

Artemisia, daughter of Lygdamis and queen of Halicarnassus, the birthplace of Herodotus, who tells her story. Another Artemisia was the wife and successor of the Carian prince Mausolus, who reigned from 352-350 B.C. She is famous as the builder of the mausoleum at Halicarnassus to her husband's memory.

Artemisia. See **Wormwood.**

Artemus Ward. See **Browne, Charles Farrar.**

Artery, any of the numerous blood-vessels which convey blood from the heart to the various parts of the body. The arterial system is similar in its distribution to a many-branching tree, of which the aorta, arising from the left ventricle of the heart, is the trunk. The main arteries usually follow comparatively straight courses and are fairly well protected from pressure and other dangers.

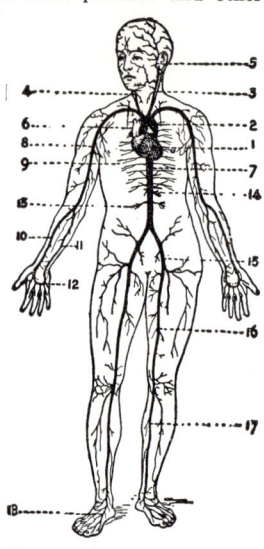

Diagram showing the Principal Arteries

1. Heart. 2. Arch of aorta. 3. Left carotid. 4. Right carotid. 5. Temporal [6. Vena cava]. 7. Thoracic aorta. 8. Brachial. 9. Intercostal. 10. Radial. 11. Ulnar. 12. Palmar arch. 13 Renal. 14. Cœlic axis and mesenteric. 15. Iliac. 16. Femoral. 17. Tibial. 18. Dorsalis pedis.

The branches, through an elaborate system of subdivision, extend to every part of the body except the hair, nails, epidermis, cartilages, and cornea, ending in minute vessels called arterioles, which in turn, open into the capillaries (q.v.). Those arteries which do not anastomose with other arteries either directly or through their branches are known as 'end arteries' or 'terminal arteries.'

The arteries are capable of extension and distention—a property of great service in the maintenance of normal blood pressure and velocity. The loss of this elasticity, occurring during degeneration of the arteries from disease or senile changes, is a precursor of softening and final rupture, an accident which usually causes death when occurring in the brain. The arteries may be the seat of *thrombus* formation or of *embolism*.

Arteriosclerosis, popularly known as hardening of the arteries, is one of the almost inevitable accompaniments of advancing age; it may be due also to toxic or infectious causes, and may occur in association with high blood-pressure. An *aneurism* is a dilatation of the arterial walls forming a sac filled with blood.

Artesian Wells, deep borings into the earth to obtain water. In the United States the term has come to be applied to all wells in which the water rises above the strata in which it is found. The conditions necessary for such a rise are a pervious stratum between the two impervious strata, the pervious stratum being exposed to moisture at some point higher than that at which the well is located. They are largely used for city water supply and in the arid regions for irrigation. The sections of the United States where artesian wells have been most largely developed and used for irrigation are the James River Valley in South Dakota, Southern Texas, Pecos Valley in New Mexico and Texas, and Southern California. See ARTESIAN; Senate Executive Document No. 41, 52d Congress, First Session; *Artesian Wells as a Means of Water Supply*, by Walter Gibbons Cox.

Artevelde, Jacob van (1285-1345), Flemish patriot, was a wealthy brewer of Ghent, who assisted the people in their struggle against Louis, Count of Flanders. His son PHILIP (c. 1340-82) was placed at the head of the citizens of Ghent in 1381, and after defeating the Count of Flanders he became regent. See Hutton, *James and Philip van Artevelde* (1882).

Arthritis. See **Joints**.

Arthrophycus, a genus of fossil sea plants.

Arthropoda (jointed feet), the name of a series of invertebrate land and water animals, including such diverse forms as crustaceans, insects, and arachnids. Arthropods have bilaterally symmetrical, segmented bodies, some of the segments bearing jointed appendages; the body is covered by a tough cuticle made of chitin; the heart lies above the food canal, and the nervous system below it, except for the dorsal brain; there is no distinct body cavity between the food canal and the body wall. The chief classes of Arthopoda are as follows: Crustacea, including crabs, lobsters, and their allies; Protacheata; Myriapoda: the millipedes and centipedes; Insecta: the insects; Arachnoidea: spiders, scorpions, and mites; Palæostraca: the living king crab and the extinct trilobites.

Arthur, a famous British chieftain who distinguished himself in the wars with the Saxons during the latter part of the 5th and commencement of the 6th centuries. We may accept as historical the fact that Arthur fought a series of successful engagements with the invaders, ending in the crushing defeat inflicted upon the Saxons at Mount Badon; probably he was betrayed by his wife, and met his death in conflict with a near kinsman.

About 1135 Geoffrey of Monmouth wrote his *Historia Regum Britanniæ*. Here the historic Arthur, *dux bellorum,* becomes Arthur the king of Britain and world-conqueror. Geoffrey's work was translated into French verse, about 1155, by Robert Wace, who himself found a translator in the Anglo-Saxon monk Layamon, each of them adding, from his own knowledge of popular tradition, to the picture drawn by Geoffrey. It is more especially on the version of Wace that the popular conception of Arthur is founded. Here he is the son of Uther Pendragon; king of Britain; conqueror of Scandinavia, Gaul, and Rome; the founder of the Round Table, and the centre of a brilliant circle of heroes. Victim of the joint treachery of his wife and his nephew Modred, he is wounded in battle with the latter, and retires to Avalon to be healed of his wounds. For popular knowledge of the Arthurian legends, see Sir Thomas Malory's *Morte D'Arthur* and Tennyson's *Idylls of the King*.

Arthur, Duke of Connaught. See **Connaught**.

Arthur, Prince of Brittany (1187-1203), grandson of Henry II. On the death of his uncle, Richard I., Arthur's claim as son of Geoffrey, elder brother of John, king of England, was upheld by several French provinces, and, at first, by Philip Augustus of France. John captured Arthur in 1202, and imprisoned him at Falaise and at Rouen, where he disappeared in 1203, murdered, it is said, by the hands of his uncle. See Shakespeare's *King John* and Norgate's *John Lackland* (1902).

Arthur, Prince (1486-1502), eldest son of Henry VII. of England.

Arthur, Chester Alan (1830-86), the twenty-first President of the U. S., born at

Fairfield, Vt., Oct. 5, 1830. He was admitted to the bar in N. Y. City in 1854. Strongly opposed to slavery, he took part, as one of the counsel, for the slaves concerned, in the famous *Lemmon Slave Case*. He joined the was the collector of customs for the port of N. Y., by Pres. Grant's appointment, from 1871 until 1878. Arthur was nominated for the vice-presidency, on the ticket with Garfield in 1880. Succeeding Garfield, after the

Arthropoda.

INSECTA—1. Butterfly. PROTOTRACHEATA—2. Peripatus. PALÆOSTRACA—3. King or Horseshoe Crab; 4. Eurypterus (fossil); 5. Trilobine (fossil). MYRIAPODA—6. Centipede. ARACHNOIDEA—7. Scorpion. CRUSTACEA—8. Masked Crab. (King Crab one-twelfth natural size; all others two-thirds nature.)

Republican Party soon after its organization, and during the first two years of the Civil War rendered valuable service as quartermaster-general of the N. Y. state troops. He latter's assassination, he became President (1881-5). His administration was marked by the passage of an Act Restricting Chinese Immigration (1882), of the Pendleton Civil

Service Act (1883), and of a Contract Labor Act (1885), and by the exposure of the 'star-route' postal frauds. Arthur was defeated for a renomination in 1884.

Arthur, Timothy Shay (1809-85), American novelist and story-writer, was born at Newburgh, N. Y. Of his twenty-odd books, perhaps the most popular was his *Ten Nights in a Bar-room* (1860).

Arthur's Seat, hill (822 ft.), Holyrood Park, Edinburgh, figures in Scott's *Heart of Midlothian*.

Artichoke, two different plants of the order Compositæ—the globe artichoke, or *Cynara scolymus*, and the Jerusalem artichoke, or *Helianthus tuberosus*. The plant, introduced into Europe from North America in 1616, is indigenous to the upper Mississippi and parts of Canada. It was one of the few plants cultivated by the American Indians.

Article, in grammar, one of a class of limiting words. In English there are two articles—*the*, definite article, and *a* or *an*, indefinite article. See PARTS OF SPEECH.

Articles of Association, in law, a written agreement setting forth the rights, powers, and duties of the persons concerned in a joint enterprise. In the United States, articles of association, when duly executed and filed, have the effect of a charter of incorporation, and this is the usual method for incorporating companies. See CHARTER; CORPORATION.

Articles of Confederation, The, fundamental law of the United States from 1781 to 1789, were adopted by Congress on Nov. 15, 1777, but did not go into effect until ratified by the various States. All the States gave their adhesion by May, 1779, except Maryland, which for important reasons did not sign until March 1, 1781. (See UNITED STATES, *History*.)

The Articles provided for a loose confederation of the various States, in which the central government had little real power. The latter could not levy taxes nor effectually control foreign commerce; it could not coerce any individual State into obedience to its acts, even in cases in which it nominally had jurisdiction; and it could not enforce its authority by arresting and punishing individual offenders. Administrative, legislative, and judicial affairs of the Confederation were to be vested in a general Congress, a single chamber with little real power, in which each State was to have one vote, and was to be represented by not less than two nor more than seven members, none of whom was to serve more than three years in any term of six years. In general, the central government was to have charge of foreign relations, with the exclusive power of declaring and waging war; was to settle disputes between the States through the agency of a commission or court appointed jointly by Congress and the contestants; and was to have the right of regulating the coinage, Indian affairs, and the postal service. None of the more important powers of Congress could be exercised without a prior affirmative vote of at least nine of the thirteen States.

After the Revolution the defects of the system of government provided by the Articles of Confederation became more and more apparent, and in 1789 the Articles were superseded by the present Constitution (see CONSTITUTION OF THE UNITED STATES). The text of the Articles of Confederation may be found in Macdonald's *Select Documents of United States History*. Consult McLaughlin's *The Confederation and the Constitution* ('American Nation Series').

Articles of Faith, a summarized statement of religious belief. Important articles of faith are the Apostles' Creed, the Nicene Creed, the Athanasian Creed (see CREEDS), the Thirty-nine Articles (q.v.) of the Church of England, the Augsburg Confession, the Westminster Confession, and the Articles of the Methodist Episcopal Church.

Articles of War, ordinances for the government of troops, seamen, and camp followers, providing for the punishment as crimes of acts or omissions which in civil life would be regarded as mere breaches of contract—e.g., desertion or disobedience of orders. The Articles of War in the United States number 121, and are prescribed by Chapter II of the Act of Congress approved June 4, 1920 (41 Stat. L., 759).

Articles, Thirty-nine. See **Thirty-nine Articles.**

Articulata (Lat. *articulus*, 'a joint'), the term formerly used to include animals, such as crustaceans and insects, which bear jointed appendages. See ARTHROPODA.

Articulation. See **Joints.**

Artificer, (Latin *artifex*), a soldier who is a blacksmith, mechanic, carpenter, harness-maker, wheelwright, machinist, etc.

Artificial Limb, a mechanical contrivance taking the place of an absent limb in use and appearance. In the Museum of the London College of Surgeons there is an artificial leg made of bronze, wood, and iron, which was discovered in 1885 in a tomb at Capua along with other relics dating from 300 B.C. Recent years, particularly since the Great War, have seen great advances in the adaption of these mechanical contrivances to varied requirements. The first desideratum in an artificial limb is lightness. In other respects, however, important differences exist between what is desirable in an artificial arm and in an artificial leg. In the former, *mobility*, to the extreme limit compatible with control over its movements, is sought; in the latter, *stability* is of prime importance.

Artificial Respiration. See **Resuscitation.**

Artificial Silk. See **Silk.**

Artigas, the most northerly department of Uruguay; p. 30,000. Capital, San Eugenio.

Artillery, in the general sense, includes not only the guns, but also the mounts, equipment, personnel, and transport of that branch of the military service which is charged with the service of the guns in action.

All artillery is grouped in two general classes viz., field artillery and coast artillery. Field artillery is that which accompanies the armies in the field, and coast artillery, or garrison artillery, as it is sometimes called, is that designed for the defence of the coasts against naval attack.

During ancient times, the large number of fortified walled cities encountered in military operations made necessary the introduction of engines of war of greater power than those that could be transported and operated by the individual soldier. These heavy engines of war, the precursors of artillery as we now understand the term, were the *ballista, catapult* (qq.v.), and similar engines for hurling heavy darts and stones. These weapons were heavy and cumbersome, difficult to transport, slow in operation, and consequently were used only in the deliberate and prolonged attack of fortified places.

Cannon were introduced into Europe very shortly after the discovery, by Schwartz, in 1320, of a method of granulating powder, and it is said that Edward III., in his campaign against the Scots in 1327, used what were called 'Crakeys of War,' but no accurate description of these weapons has been found. Froissart states that at the siege of Quesnoy (1340) the French were repulsed, 'their horses being frightened by weapons which made a great noise and shot pieces of iron'; and the English apparently used cannon at the Battle of Crécy (1346). These first cannon were of small calibre, low power, and of little efficiency. From the middle of the 14th century the use of cannon rapidly increased. Artillery soon came into general use for the defence of fortified cities and on ships of war.

In the Thirty Years' War great improvements were made in artillery through the genius of Gustavus Adolphus, who not only improved the material but gave to the arm greater importance and value by changing the method of its employment.

In 1765 Gribeauval, sometimes called the father of modern field artillery, began the reorganization of the French artillery. He provided separate material for field, siege, garrison, and coast service; and made interchangeable all parts of the same type of gun or carriage. The guns were made shorter and lighter and were provided with stronger but lighter carriages. The powder charge was reduced in weight to one-third that of the projectile. Artillery played a prominent part in Napoleon's operations and he, like Frederick the Great, increased the proportion of artillery to the other arms as the quality of his infantry declined.

Between 1814 and the Crimean War the artillery of all nations was improved. During the Civil War in the United States, half of the Federal artillery was equipped with 3-inch rifled guns and half with 12-pounder Napoleons, introduced by Napoleon III. in 1852. The extreme ranges of these two guns were about 2800 yards and 1520 yards.

In the Austro-Prussian War each army had a large force of artillery. In the Franco-German War the Prussians abolished their reserve artillery and assigned the artillery as divisional and corps artillery. Four field batteries were assigned to each infantry division, and four field and three horse batteries to each corps. The guns were steel breech loaders and assigned in the proportion of 3.7 guns per 1000 rifles.

Following the introduction of the breech-loading steel cannon, few changes were made in artillery until the latter part of the 19th century. A factor retarding the rate of fire of field guns was the dense smoke from the powder following each discharge, which prevented the gunners from seeing the target and delayed relaying the piece. This difficulty was eliminated by the introduction of smokeless powder in 1895. At the time of the World War the other principal powers followed the lead of France in adopting a long-recoil type gun for their artillery. In this type of gun the shock of discharge is absorbed by the recoil mechanism and, aside from an occasional slight correction in the laying of the gun, it is not necessary to relay after each shot for the same target and the rate of fire is greatly increased.

Along with the introduction of the long-recoil type, came improved telescopic sights, range finders, observation telescopes, and other fire-control instruments. The improvements in observation instruments enabled artillery commanders to obtain the maximum advantage at the longer ranges, and the improved sights permitted concealment of the guns from view of the enemy, behind an intervening mask, from which position they could fire upon designated targets with the same degree of accuracy as though the targets were visible to the gunners. Great improvement was also made in ammunition and fuses. Fixed ammunition, in which the powder charge and projectile are assembled as a unit, was adopted for the use of field artillery. This improvement permitted the entire round to be inserted in the breech of the gun at one time, obviated ramming the projectile, and thus increased the rapidity of fire. In the early days of artillery one round every half hour was considered as a very satisfactory rate of fire. Today field guns of the '75' type may be fired at the rate of 20 to 25 rounds per minute. Although the '75' is effective as an antitank weapon, it is too light for general artillery work and is being replaced by the 105 mm. howitzer. During World War II, however, the standard medium field piece was the 155 mm. howitzer. The 16-inch coast defense rifle fired a shell weighing over a ton. Antiaircraft guns were of various types, ranging from 37-mm. guns firing 120 rounds per minute to large 105-mm. guns, sometimes mounted on heavy tank destroyers.

Great advance was also made in the tactical employment of the arm. Concealment of the guns from observation by the enemy became an absolute necessity for field artillery, due to the great rapidity and accuracy of its fire and the advent of the airplane.

As a result of experiments made during World War I, it was found that a considerable increase in range could be obtained by a change in the form of the projectile, which reduced the resistance offered by the air. During this war the Central Powers first made use of guns and howitzers with their mobile forces of a weight and calibre previously considered prohibitive with field forces. These weapons were used with terrible effect in the early stages of the war in overcoming the resistance of fortified places in Belgium and France. Never before had artillery played such a prominent part in a war nor had it ever been used to such an extent. Forests and even the hills were in certain localities obliterated by the fire of artillery. At the beginning of the war and even much later it was the practice to precede every attack of any consequence by artillery preparation, varying in duration from a few hours to several days. During the latter stages of the war the period of artillery preparation was shortened and in some cases omitted entirely in order that the enemy might be taken by surprise.

Railway artillery, for shelling distant bases and routes of communication, was employed to a considerable extent in the war. Among the largest of the railway guns was a 14-inch naval gun mounted on a special car, having an extreme range of 44,000 yards and firing a projectile weighing 1,400 pounds. The gun with which the Germans shelled Paris was at first 8.4 inches in calibre, but was later re-bored to 9.6 when it became worn. Its range was approximately 70 miles. It did little material damage to Paris, but its moral effect was considerable. Railway artillery in World War II was handled by the Coast Artillery. The large 8-inch railroad guns stood far behind the lines and shelled large targets of importance, as enemy ammunition dumps and battery positions.

But the leading defensive weapon of the infantry in World War II was the heavy machine gun, a weapon that fired more than 250 shots per minute and required a squad of seven men to serve it. An adaptation of this 30-caliber gun was the light machine gun, which could be more easily hidden or carried from place to place. The U. S. Superfortress of 1944 (Boeing's B-29) carried ten or twelve 50-caliber machine guns and a 20-mm. cannon.

See AMMUNITION; COAST ARTILLERY; FIELD ARTILLERY; GUNNERY; GUNS (*Field guns and Siege, Railway, and Seacoast Guns*); ARMY OF THE UNITED STATES.

Bibliography.—Consult Berkheimer's *Historical Sketch of the U. S. Artillery;* Owen's *Modern Artillery;* Birnie's *Gunmaking in the United States;* Wagner's *Organization and Tactics* (1905); Spaulding's *Notes on Field Artillery* (1914).

Artillery Company, Ancient and Honorable. In 1637 there was formed in Massachusetts Bay Colony 'the Military Company of Boston,' which 20 years later became the 'Artillery Company.' The company was armed with brass three-pounders, and was

Artillery very active during the Revolutionary War. Its functions are now mainly social, although it still preserves its military organization.

Artillery Company, Honorable, an ancient military organization in Great Britain, formed in the days of the Tudors in 1537. The organization rendered excellent service in the South African War.

Artillery Corps. See **Army of the United States.**

Artillery Practice. See **Target Practice.**

Artillery Schools. See **Military Education.**

Artiodactyla. The great mammalian order Ungulata is usually divided into two suborders, the *Perissodactyla*, the 'odd-toed' or 'solid-hoofed' forms, including the horse, tapir, and rhinoceros, and the *Atiodactyla*, the 'even-toed' or 'cloven-footed' ungulates, such as the sheep, cow, and pig. The Artiodactyla may again be divided into two groups—the *Non-Ruminantia* and the *Ruminantia*.

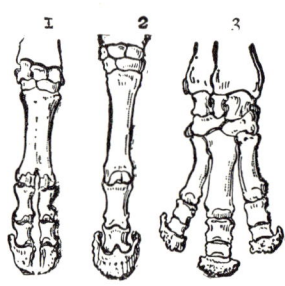

Comparison of Even-toed Ungulate with Odd-toed.
1. Pig (artiodactyl); 2. Horse; and 3. Rhinoceros (perissodactyl).

Artists, Society of American. See **National Academy of Design.**

Artocarpaceæ, an order of plants confined to the tropics, containing a milky juice. The best-known species are the Upas Tree of Java, the Bread Fruit Tree of the Pacific Islands, the Cow Tree of South America.

Artois, former province of France, now forming the greater part of the department Pas-de-Calais. Artois belonged (863) to Flanders; was French from 1180 to the middle of the 13th century; became then a Burgundian and afterward (1493) an Austrian possession, finally reverting to the French (1659-1713).

Arts. The term 'Arts,' or 'Liberal Arts,' as technically applied to certain studies, came into use during the Middle Ages; and on the establishment of universities, the term 'Faculty of Arts' denoted those who devoted themselves to science and philosophy, as distinguished from the faculty of theology, and afterward of medicine and law. See DEGREE; UNIVERSITY.

Arts, American Federation of, an association of organizations and individuals, formed at a convention held in Washington in May, 1909. The Federation publishes a monthly illustrated magazine, *Art and Progress*, and also the *American Art Annual*. The Federation maintains at Washington a general bureau of information.

Art Schools. See **Schools of Art.**

Art Students' League of New York, a well-known school of art, founded in 1875, and located in the American Fine Arts Building, New York City.

Aru, Aroe, or **Arru Islands,** small Dutch archipelago, East Indies, 80 m. s. of Papua. Coralline in formation and well wooded, the group produces trepang, sago, cocoanuts, rice, maize, mother of pearl, edible swallows' nests, betel nuts, sugar, and tobacco. The birds and fauna are of great interest. Chief town, Dobo. Area of group, 3,305 sq. m.; p. 18,176.

Arum, a genus of plants belonging to the natural order Araceæ or Aroideæ. This order is chiefly tropical, and comprises herbaceous plants, some of which are stemless; shrubby plants, some of which are arborescent; and plants which climb by aerial roots, clinging to the trees of tropical forests. The Arrow Arum (*Peltandra*) is an American plant. The Calla or Calla Lily (*Calla palustris*) is the Bog Arum or Water Arum.

Arundel, Earls of, a British peerage which has descended through several noble families from Roger de Montgomery, a follower of the Conqueror.

Arundel, Thomas (1353-1414), Archbishop of Canterbury, chancellor five times under Richard II. and Henry IV. He was banished for complicity in the conspiracy against Richard II. (1397); and returned with Henry IV., on whose head he placed the crown, in 1399.

Arundel Marbles, the collection of ancient sculptures preserved in the Ashmolean Museum at Oxford. They include the celebrated 'Parian Chronicle,' a slab recording the outlines of Greek history from 1582 to 263 B.C.

Aruwimi River, a right-bank tributary of the Congo River, explored for 100 m. by

Stanley in 1883, and by it Stanley advanced to the relief of Emin Pasha in 1887.

Arvad, a famous Phœnecian town on a small island north of Gebal, called Arados in Greek (now Er-Rûâd); also known as Amrit and Marathos.

Arval Brethren (*Fratres Arvales*), a kind of priestly college in ancient Rome who in the end of May conducted the *ambarvalia,* or progressions round the ploughed land, chanting as they went hymns of invocation to Dea Dia, probably Ceres, or to the Lares of the fields, praying that they might grant them a rich harvest. Consult Frazer's *Golden Bough.*

Arverni, a Gallic tribe in Aquitania. In early days they were the most powerful people in Gaul, and under Vercingetorix offered a stubborn resistance to Cæsar (52 B.C.), but were subdued in 121 A.D. by the Romans.

Arya, Aryan, Aryanism. Arya is a Sanskrit word, the general connotation of which is nobility, historical and personal, 'belonging to good family' (*cf.* Latin *gentilis*), in opposition to *anarya,* 'unworthy,' 'vile,' In the Rig-Veda, from the language of which classical Sanskrit was derived and formed, it was used as the national designation of the invading tribes from the northwest. But the more ordinary use of the term Aryan is for the whole family, which is also known as Indo-Germanic and Indo-European. This use of it was introduced chiefly by Max Müller and Pictet.

The problem of the Aryan race and its origin has long been a vexed question with scholars, because of the evidence of two fundamental races in Europe. According to one view, the classical civilization of Europe is of Mediterranean origin, but Aryanized in speech. The advocacy of the opposite theory is termed Aryanism—that Europe owes its culture and civilization to the Aryan, a tall, blond dolichocephalic race represented by the modern Germans, Scandinavians, and English. Consult Schrader's *Prehistoric Antiquities of the Aryan Peoples* (trans. by Jevons); Sergi's *Mediterranean Races* (with a bibliography); Morris' *The Aryan Race: its Origin and its Achievements;* Humphrey's *Mankind: Racial Values and Racial Prospects* (1917); Dutt's *The Aryanization of India* (1925); Childe's *The Aryans: a Study of Indo-European Origins* (1926).

As, the Roman *libra,* or pound. Eventually the name came to denote a coin, the *as,* which weighed half an ounce.

As, in northern mythology.

Asa, king of Judah (*c.* 918-877 B.C.), son and successor of Abijah. He showed great energy in purging his kingdom of idolatry.

Roman As (reduced)

Asafœtida, (Lat. 'fetid gum'), a gum resin from the living root of various species of *Ferula,* found chiefly in Tibet, Afghanistan, Persia, and the Punjab. It is one of the aromatics.

Asakusa, popular Buddhist temple to the 'thousand-armed Kwan-non,' the goddess of mercy, in a suburb of Tokyo, Japan.

Asaky, or **Asachi, George** (1788-1869), Roumanian author, one of the leaders in the regeneration of his country. He established the first Roumanian theatre (1817), set up the first press for printing books in the Roumanian language, and founded, and edited for 30 years, the first Roumanian paper (*Albina*).

Asama-yama, active volcano (doleritic lava), in the province of Shinshu, Japan, 80 m. n.w. of Tokyo. It is the largest and most treacherous volcano in Japan. In 1908, 1911, and 1912 serious eruptions occurred and in 1783 a violent one, lasting 88 days, spread terror and destruction for miles.

Asaph, chief musician in the time of David and Solomon.

Asaphus, a genus of trilobites.

Asarum, a genus of plants of the order Aristolochiaceæ. They are low-growing perennial herbs with purplish brown flowers, found in shady woods. An American species, *A. canadense,* is the snake-root or wild ginger.

Asbestos (*Gr.* eternal, indestructible), a term used in mineralogy to designate three minerals, whose fibrous, crystalline structure and the special property of being more or less acid and fire proof mark them from all others.

The use of asbestos can be traced back to the Romans, who named it amianthus, considering it a vegetable substance. It was probably the amphibole asbestos found in the Ural and Alps mountains, whose brittle fibres they wove together with threads of linen, to make burial cloth, in which to wrap their dead, in order to retain the ashes when the body burnt on the funeral pyre. Plutarch records the use of asbestos in the wicks of the Vestal Virgins' lamps, and Marco Polo in the 13th century noted the use of amianthus in Siberia. All knowledge of asbestos, however, was buried with the past, for it was not until 1868 when it was rediscovered in the Aostro Valley, in the Italian Alps, that it became known to the modern world. Even then it was not until 1878 when chrysotile asbestos was discovered in large quantities that any real progress was made in the industry. Since then its exploitation and development has been rapid and today asbestos, in one form or another, is indispensable in the electrical and engineering worlds, and plays an important part in our domestic life.

Commercially the asbestiform minerals are divided into three groups: Chrysotile, or serpentine asbestos, known as cross fibre; Amphibole asbestos or slip fibre including crocidolite, tremolite, and actinolite; Anthophyllite, or mass fibre. Anthophyllite is quarried extensively in the United States, principally in the Gall Mountains in Georgia. Chrysotile, 80 per cent. of which comes from Canada, where it is quarried in open pits, is used in the making of yarns and fabrics, packing, brake linings, and insulating material. Recent successful experiments with long-fibred amphibole found extensively in the somewhat inaccessible Grand Canyon of Arizona, greatly reduce the United States' present dependence on foreign sources of supply.

Asbjörnsen, Peter Christian (1812-85), Norwegian author and writer of folktales, was born in Christiania. Asbjörnsen is the Norwegian story-teller, *par excellence,* though he wrote in Danish.

Asbury, Francis (1745-1816), first American bishop of the Methodist Episcopal Church, and joint founder with Thomas Coke of Methodism in the United States, was born in Handsworth, Staffordshire, England. He early came under the influence of the Wesleys, and at twenty-two was one of John Wesley's chosen lieutenants. He went to Philadelphia in 1771. The great development of Methodism in the United States was largely due to his untiring efforts.

Asbury Park, city, New Jersey, in Monmouth co., on the Atlantic coast. It was long a favorite place for religious and educational meetings; p. 14,617.

Ascalon or **Ashkelon,** one of the five chief Philistine cities, now in ruins. It is situated on the Mediterranean, about 40 m. s.w. of Jerusalem. One of the oldest cities in the world. It passed into the hands of the Philistines in the 12th century B.C., later was conquered by Alexander. The city was taken by the Crusaders in 1153, recaptured by Saladin in 1187 and finally destroyed in 1270.

Ascanius, the son of Æneas and Creusa, who as a boy escaped with his father after the fall of Troy.

Ascaris, a genus of round worms or nematodes, including some intestinal parasites.

Ascendant. See **Astrology.**

Ascension Island, in the S. Atlantic Ocean; a Br. possession since 1815. Area 34 sq. m. Since it is a valuable midway station from America to Africa, Russia, and the East, the U. S. built an airport there 1942.

Ascension Day, or **Holy Thursday,** commemorates, in most of the Christian churches, the ascension of Christ into heaven, held to have taken place 40 days after the resurrection, and thus placed in the calendar 40 days after Easter.

Ascension, Right. See **Right Ascension.**

Asceticism, means the continual mortification of bodily desires, even of such as are lawful in themselves, in order to attain purity of soul and more perfect union with God. The principle of asceticism is common in varying degrees to most religions, as in Brahminism and Buddhism. After the Christian era, the Roman Stoics, and later still the Neo-Pythagoreans and Neo-Platonists, pursued ascetic modes of life. Early in the 2nd century A.D. a special class of men and women arose, known as ascetics. From them came monasticism, which is the legitimate outcome of the ascetic life. The ascetic principle is still maintained in the Roman and Eastern Churches.

Asch, Sholem (1880-) novelist, dramatist of Jewish extraction, was born in Poland; later came to America. Many of his works have been translated into English. Among his important plays may be noted *God of Vengeance, Kiddush ha-Shem,* and *Sabbatai Zevi.* With the publication of his trilogy *Three Cities* in English, his importance as a novelist became firmly established. Translations include *Salvation* (1935); *Mottke the Thief* (1936); *In the Beginning* (1936); *The Nazarene* (1939); *The Apostle* (1943); *East River* (1946); *Moses* (1951).

Ascham, Roger (1515-68), English writer and scholar, one of the earliest masters of English prose, was born in Kirby Wiske, near Northallerton.

Ascidians (Ascidiacea), an order of tunicates or sea-squirts, including all the familiar members of that class.

Ascites, an accumulation of fluid in the peritoneal cavity.

Asclepiadaceæ, an order of plants closely related to Apocynaceæ, or Dogbanes. **Many are characterized by a milky juice** (*latex*).

Asclepiades, a Greek poet of Samos (fl. 280 B.C.).

Asclepiades, Greek physician, a native of Bithynia who lived in the 1st century B.C. The salient features of his treatment were such as are approved by most modern physicians—*viz.* a generous diet, the use of alteratives, open-air exercise, bathing, etc.

Asclepiadic, a metre supposed to be so-called because of its connection with the poet Asclepiades.

Ascoli Piceno, city, Italy, capital of Ascoli Piceno province. The ancient cathedral is alleged to have been built by Constantine the Great, on the site of a former temple of Hercules; p. 18,500.

Ascomycetes, a class of fungi which develop their spores in membranous sacs called asci. See FUNGI.

Asconius Pedianus (2 B.C.-83 A.D.), Roman grammarian, famed especially for his commentary on the speeches of Cicero.

Ascot or **Ascot Heath,** a famous race course, nearly 2 m. long, in Berkshire, England. The races, instituted in 1711, are held annually in June.

Asellio, Gasparo (1581-1626), a celebrated Italian surgeon, native of Cremona. An early advocate of vivisection, and an accomplished anatomist, his greatest claim to distinction is his discovery (1623) of the lacteals.

Asepsis, the neutral condition in which there are neither the germs of putrefaction nor any active antiseptic agents: water boiled for half an hour in a covered vessel is *aseptic,* containing no living germs of putrefaction, but is not *antiseptic* until an antiseptic has been added to it.

Asexual. See **Sex; Parthenogenesis; Reproduction.**

Asgard, home of the Aesir, in Scandinavian mythology.

Ash (*Fraxinus*), a genus of trees belonging to the family Oleaceæ, and including 30 species, half of which are found in all except the coldest sections of the New World. The wood is white, tough, and elastic, and is valuable in cabinet work. The most important American species is the White Ash (*F. Americana*). Other common species are the Black Ash (*F. nigra*). the Red Ash (*F. Pennsylvania*), and the Oregon Ash (*F. Oregona*), also a valuable shade tree found on the Pacific coast.

Ashanti, or **Ashantee,** a district of the Gold Coast, lying inland behind the Prah River, until 1896 a native kingdom of West Africa, dating from the beginning of the 18th century. Gold is the principal mineral product, the output in a single year amounting to 85,019 oz., valued at £361,360. The chief town is Kumasi, with 44,627 inhabitants.

Ashburton, Alexander Baring, Baron (1774-1848), was the head of the British banking firm of Baring Brothers. As special commissioner to Washington, 1842, he concluded the Ashburton Treaty.

Ashburton Treaty, or **Webster-Ashburton Treaty,** an important treaty between the United States and Great Britain, negotiated at Washington, D. C., in 1842, by Daniel Webster, then Secretary of State, on behalf of the United States, and Alexander Baring, Lord Ashburton, on behalf of Great Britain. By this treaty the boundary between Maine and Canada was agreed upon. The treaty was particularly important in that it settled a long-standing dispute concerning the northeast boundary of the United States. (See NORTHEAST BOUNDARY CONTROVERSY.) The text of the treaty is to be found in Macdonald's *Select Documents of United States History, 1776-1861.*

Ashby-de-la-Zouch, town, England, in Leicestershire. Features of interest are the ruins of the Castle, built about 1474 and famous as the scene of several events in Scott's *Ivanhoe.*

Ashby-Sterry, Joseph (1860-1917), English artist, journalist, and critic, was born in London. He became widely known in England as the writer of the 'Bystander' papers in the London *Graphic.*

Ashdod, a great city of the Philistines called Azotus in the Apocrypha and New Testament.

Ashdown Park, in Berkshire, England. Near here was fought the sanguinary battle in which Ethelred and Alfred defeated the Danes (871). See Scott's *Kenilworth.*

Ashe, John (1720-81), American Revolutionary soldier, was born in Grovely, N. C. He was presiding officer (1762-5) in the Colonial Assembly. In 1775 he aided in the capture of Fort Johnson, and equipped a regiment to defend the first Provincial Congress of North Carolina. Asheville, N. C., was named in his honor.

Asher, Jacob's eighth son, whose mother was Zilpah, the handmaid of Leah.

Asherah, a Hebrew word (pl. *asherim; asheroth*), the sacred pole of the Phœnicians and Babylonians, the symbol of fertility.

Ashes, the mineral residue obtained by the combustion of animal and vegetable substances, and consisting of the fixed salts contained in these substances. Ashes are economically useful as fertilizer.

Asheville, city, North Carolina, county seat of Buncombe co., at the junction of the French Broad and Swannanoa Rivers. It is picturesquely situated at an elevation of 2,350 ft. above sea-level, and is one of the best known health resorts in the United States; p. 51,310.

Ashhurst, John (1839-1900), American surgeon; professor of clinical surgery in the University of Pennsylvania, and later president of the Philadelphia College of Physicians. He wrote *Injuries of the Spine* (1867) and *Principles and Practice of Surgery* (1871).

Ashio, town, Japan, on Hondo Island, 12 m. s.w. of Nikko. It is the site of a famous copper mine covering an area of over 2,000 acres and producing annually over 30,000,000 pounds of copper ingots; p. 47,000.

Ashmun, Jehudi (1794-1828), American missionary, prominent for his efforts in developing the negro republic of Liberia, was born in Champlain, N. Y. Becoming interested in colonization, he was appointed agent of the American Colonization Society, and in 1822 conducted a party of negroes to Liberia, where he remained for six years, displaying great valor and remarkable executive ability.

Ashokan Reservoir. See **Catskill Aqueduct.**

Ashraf, town, Iran, was the residence of Shab Abbas the Great in the 16th century, and remains of its earlier glory are still evident.

Ashtabula, city, Ohio, Ashtabula co. Its excellent harbor is one of the largest ore-receiving ports of the world, as well as a great coal-shipping port; p. 21,405.

Ashwanipi Hamilton, or **Grand River,** Labrador, flows from Ashwanipi Lake into Esquimaux Bay or Hamilton Inlet, after a course of several hundred miles. The Grand Falls of Labrador are 316 ft. high.

Ash Wednesday (Ger. *Aschermittwoch;* Fr. *Le jour des cendres*), the first day of Lent in the Western Church, said to derive its name from the custom of sprinkling ashes on the heads of penitents.

Asia, the largest of the continents so extensive that when the sun at the equinoxes is rising on its western extremity, Cape Baba, in Asia Minor (26° E.), it is nearly setting on its farthest eastern shores, Cape Dezhneff (170° w.), 6,000 m. away. For some weeks every year continual night reigns at the northernmost point, Cape Chelyuskin ($77\frac{1}{2}°$ N.); while day and night are always nearly equal at the most southerly point, Cape Romania ($1\frac{1}{3}°$ N.), 5,400 m. distant, and within 90 m. of the equator. The Mediterranean and Black Seas form natural physical western limits to the continent; as does the Red Sea, lying between Asia and Africa, which are connected by the isthmus of Suez, 72 m. wide. The modern Suez Canal may here be taken as the boundary. The Ural River and Mountains are the common conventional boundaries with Europe n. of the Caspian. The Manych depression and the crest of the Caucasus are both used as the limits of Asia between the Black and Caspian Seas. The former is the better. The low northern coast borders the Arctic Ocean into which the Taimyr peninsula projects, and out of which the New Siberian Islands rise. Bering Strait, 50 m. wide, separates Asia from America; and the St. Lawrence and Aleutian Islands are reckoned with the latter, the Komandorski Islands with the former. The east coast borders the Pacific. Three great peninsulas, which have some analogies with those of Southern Europe, project southwards.

Within these limits the continent has an area of over 16,000,000 sq. m.—roughly, one-third of the land of the globe. The coast-line bounding it is some 44,000 m. The continent may be divided into four great natural regions: The Great Lowlands, in the N.; the Great Central Mountain System; the Eastern Margin of Fringing Basins and Volcanic Islands; the South and Southwest Tablelands of the Deccan and Arabia.

The Pamir plateau and the Tibetan plateau contain some of the world's highest mountain ranges. On the south are the Himalayas, with Mount Everest, 29,000 ft. and Kanchan-Janga, 28,156 ft. The Himalayas are pierced by the gorges of the Indus, Sutlej, Ganges, Gogra, Gandak, and Brahmaputra.

Three great rivers and a number of smaller ones rise in the plateaus of Asia, and break across the escarpments to the sea—the Amur, the Hwang-ho, and the Yang-tse-kiang. The fringing islands are mainly volcanic, and form part of the 'girdle of fire' which encircles the Pacific and rises above the greatest depths of the ocean. The southern chains of the Central Mountain system N. of the tropic form the climatic divide between the N. and S. of Asia, between the regions of cold and those of warm winters, between the regions of light summer rains and the monsoon lands, which, except in North Arabia, receive heavy summer rains.

Asia may be divided into ten climatic regions:—(1.) The region fringing the Arctic Circle, belonging to the cold, dry northern or Arctic climatic region, where the average temperature of the warmest month is not over 50° F. (2.) The Siberian continental region, N. of 50° with a July temperature of 50° to 70° F., and a January temperature under 0° F. (3.) The Siberian coastal plain, with a similar summer and a slightly higher winter temperature, and a heavier rainfall. (4.) The Turanian region, with a July temperature between 75° and 90° F., a January temperature between 10° and 40° F. (5.) The Mediterranean region, with cool winters and warm summers, and rain during the winter half-year. (6.) The mountain region, from inner Asia Minor to the Khingan, and from the Altai to the crest of the Himalayas; dry everywhere with very cold winters, especially on the lofty plateaus, and warm summers, especially in the depressions. Both annual and daily ranges of temperature are very great. (7.) The east monsoon region, including China and Japan, with a uniform July temperature of over 70° in Japan and over 80° F. in China, but with a January temperature that varies from 60° F. in the S. to below freezing-point in the N. (8.) The south monsoon region, including India and Farther India, where the temperature is never lower than 60° F. (9.) The Indian desert region, which differs from the rest of India in having hardly any rain. (10.) The southwestern desert region, including Arabia with warm winters and very hot summers, and scarcely any rain, and that falling in winter.

Hydrography.—The rivers flowing to the Arctic Ocean are ice-bound in winter, and, as their upper waters thaw before the lower, great floods occur in the middle and lower basins every spring. The rivers rising in Tibet are fullest in summer, when the snow melts and the rainfall is abundant, causing heavy floods. The flood waters of the Yangtse flow into the Tung-ting and Po-yang lakes, and those of the Mekong into the Tonle-sap, which act as regulators, and prevent disastrous floods. Most of the lakes have no outlet, and are salt and brackish.

The mineral wealth of Asia is very great. The older mountains, like the Altai, the Khingan, and the Chinese mountains, are rich in many kinds of minerals. The gold-mining in the regions N. and S. of the Amur may one day rival that of the American mountains in similar latitudes on the other side of the Pacific. The precious stones of Ceylon, Burma, and the Yablonoi are famous. The coal and iron of China are among the richest known, and have scarcely yet been touched. Petroleum is abundant in Sumatra, Burma, and the Caucasus.

The vegetation areas correspond to the climatic ones. The tundras are found N. of the Arctic Circle, and in patches as far S. as 60° N. See TUNDRA. The cold temperate forests of larch, spruce, fir, and birch lie between 50° and 60° N. The thin-stemmed trees are covered with lichens and dark-green mosses, and the forest is strewn with wreckage of storm and fire. The vine, fig, orange, citron, and pomegranate are among the fruits; the cedar, Aleppo pine, cork, and evergreen oak among the timber trees. The western steppes and deserts cover most of the plateaus of Iran, Arabia, and the heart of Asia Minor. Pistachio and junipers are characteristic bushes of the less arid parts, and date-palms are the trees of the oases. Salt steppes cover much of Iran and sand-dunes Arabia, whose southern heights are a savanna region yielding important cultivated plants. Wherever water is found, vegetation flourishes. The high mountain and plateau regions of Tibet, the Pamirs, and the great mountain chains are treeless.

In Japan two regions can be distinguished —the northern, with dense temperate forests of deciduous trees, thick undergrowth, and innumerable lianas, due to the heat and moisture of the vegetation period; and the southern, where evergreen trees abound, such as camphor, camellia, magnolia, and other laurels, oaks, etc. Similar vegetation is characteristic of Korea. The savannas of Southern and Eastern Asia are found in the higher and drier regions, and produce the alang-alang grass, between 3 and 5 ft. high. The wet jungles of heavy monsoon rains are characteristic of the lower flood plains of the S. and S.E. peninsulas and islands.

Animals.—The E. to W. trend of the mountains separates Asia into two great faunal realms, the palæarctic and the oriental, with a transition region in the e. The n. tundras and forests are the home of many fur-bearing animals. The seal, walrus, and other aquatic mammals are found in Arctic waters. The polar bear, reindeer, dog, arctic fox, wolf, ermine, lemming, arctic vole, musk ox, deer, and brown bear are among the characteristic mammals. Some tigers and Kamchatkan sheep are still found in the e. of this region. Ptarmigan, snow owl, and guillemot are among the birds. In the steppe lands s. of the forests a different fauna exists. The horse, ass, and camel are among the animals of this region and the argali, a large, handsome sheep, lives in the mountains. The jerboa, marmots, some deer and gazelles, and a few tigers are found. The lofty plateau of Tibet, with its severe climate and scanty vegetation, deserves to be reckoned as a special region. The yak, wild ass (kulan), Hodgson's argali, and some rodents are peculiar to it. The Sino-Japanese region is a transition one for animals as well as for plants. Monkeys are found, and tigers exist on the mainland. Many deer, some of which exchange white-spotted coats for brown winter ones, are found. The sea-otter occurs round the coast. The giant salamander is peculiar to Japan.

Races.—Asia is the home of the Mongolians. They are divided by Keane into the Northern Mongols, found throughout the lowlands, in parts of Iran, and Asia Minor; the Southern Mongols, in China, Tibet, Indo-China, Formosa, and some parts of Malaysia; and the Oceanic Mongols in Malaysia, the Philippines, Formosa, and the Nicobar Islands. In w. Asia the white man predominates, mainly the central or alpine type. In the s.e. are numerous oceanic negroes, mainly Negritos. The Northern Mongols are related by their languages. They include such different races as the Japanese in the e., the Magyars and the Finns in Europe, the semi-nomadic Mongols and the Khirgiz and Turkomans of the steppes, the agricultural Turks of the Asia Minor and the Balkan (European) peninsulas in the w., and the Manchus and Koreans in the e., while the Northern tribes are nomadic fishers and hunters, with herds of reindeer. The Southern Mongols are darker than the Northern ones. They include such different peoples as the Tibetans, Gurkhas, Burmese, the different tribes of the mountains between Tibet and Burma, the Lao and other tribes of n. Siam, the Annamese, the Cochin-Chinese, and the Chinese themselves. Oceanic Mongols may be divided into Proto-Malays and Historic Malays. In the Asia Minor and Iranian plateaus, as well as in the plains of Hindustan, numerous peoples are found corresponding to the southern or Mediterranean-European type, some Kurds, most Persians, Afghans, Dards, Kafirs, and Hindus. In the extreme s.w. the white type is represented by the Arabs. The population of Asia is over 1,000,000,000.

Political Divisions.—Since World War I many changes have occurred in the political status of parts of Asia. In the w. the Turkish Empire has been succeeded by a smaller Turkish Republic, Syria and Lebanon becoming French mandates while Great Britain held the mandates for Palestine and Transjordania. In 1932 Great Britain gave up the mandate for Iraq and in 1946, for Transjordan. Arabia is divided into Saudi Arabia, Yemen, Kuwait, Muscat and Oman. Asiatic Russia is composed of a number of federated republics. Tsingtao, in the Shantung Peninsula, which had been captured by the Japanese from the Germans in 1914, was restored to China in 1922 but held by the Japanese 1938-1945. India, Ceylon, Cyprus, Aden, islands in the Indian Ocean, are under British control. France possesses Indo-China, but it is seeking its independence. Portugal owns three settlements in India, Macao in China and the eastern half of the island of Timor. The Philippines were administered by the United States, and the remaining islands of s.e. Asia belonged to the Dutch before the Japanese invasion in World War II. Great Britain has relinquished the lease of Wei-hai-wei.

Exploration.—Little was known of e. Asia prior to the 13th century when Marco Polo brought back to Europe accounts of his journey across the continent. See POLO, MARCO. Much detailed work of exploration was accomplished in the 19th century, in particular the discoveries of Col. Younghusband, Sven Hedin and Sir Aurel Stein. More recently the work of Roy Chapman Andrews, in Chinese Turkestan, under the auspices of the American Museum of Natural History, has brought to light valuable information regarding prehistoric man. The Ruba-el-Khali, the great southern desert of Arabia, was crossed for the first time by a European, in 1931, when Bertram Thomas made the journey from Salalah on the Arabian Sea to Dohah in the Persian Gulf.

Communications.—In most parts of Asia communications are being developed at a rapid rate by road, rail and air. From West Europe through trains cross the continent to Vladivostok, and railroads are being extended in many directions. In India 41,724 m. of railroad are in operation, and a line now links Singapore with Bangkok and also with w. Siam. Automobiles now cover the continent, and scheduled services from the Mediterranean cross the roadless desert to Bagdad. Air transport links England with India and Holland with the East Indies.

Religions.—The great religions of mankind had their beginnings in Asia. The teachings of Confucius are followed by 350 million people, while 230 millions are Hindus and 138 millions Mohammedan. The Buddhists number 150 millions, the Christians 21 millions, Animists 45 millions and Shintoists 25 millions.

Bibliography.—E. Reclus, *Nouvelle Géographic Universelle;* Stanford's *Asia;* E. Suess' *Face of the Earth;* Buxton's *Peoples of Asia* (1925); Dixon's *Racial History of Man* (1923); Haddon's *Wanderings of Peoples* (1911); Dennery's *Asia's Teeming Millions* (1931); Sven Hedin, *Southern Tibet* (10 vols. 1917-1922); John Gunther's *Inside Asia* (war edition, 1942); Pearl Buck's *American Unity and Asia* (1942); Nathanial Peffer's *Basis for Peace in the Far East* (1942). See also the various Asiatic countries, ARABIA, AFGHANISTAN, CHINA, INDIA, IRAN, MONGOLIA, PALESTINE, etc.

Asia, Western, a general term including all that part of Asia which lies westward of a line drawn from the Caspian Sea to the Persian Gulf, including Turkey, Syria, Arabia, and the British protectorate of Aden. With the exception of Southern Arabia, Western Asia may be said to belong to the temperate zone, but geographical differences produce within this zone a great variety of climate. The races of men represented within the region are similarly various, though the prevailing type is the Semitic. The primitive seat of the Semitic race was probably Northern Arabia. Babylonian civilization was a continuation of Semitic and Sumerian elements. Already, in 3800 B.C., Babylonian armies made their way to the shores of the Mediterranean, bringing with them the culture of Babylonia, which included its script and language, religion and laws. Two thousand years later the cuneiform characters and language of the Babylonians had become the medium of literary and diplomatic intercourse throughout Western Asia, and the Egyptian Pharaohs carried on their foreign correspondence in the Babylonian language and script. Before the 10th century B.C. the cuneiform syllabary had been superseded in the west by the so-called Phœnician alphabet, and a new electic form of culture, which may be termed Phœnician, took the place of the older Babylonian. Meanwhile a religion had arisen in Palestine which was destined to have a profound effect upon the civilized world, and which found its literary instrument in the Phœnician alphabet. The Jewish exile brought it under the immediate influence of Babylonian culture, and so united the two streams of literary thought which were flowing from Palestine and Babylonia.

The empire of Asia now passed into the hands of the Indo-European Persians, whose official religion was Zoroastrianism, and who were therefore inclined to look with favor on the adherents of a monotheistic form of faith. The Greek conquest of Asia, however, brought with it once more a revival of polytheism, this time in an artistic form; but the triumph of polytheism was short-lived. Judaism made way for Christianity, which from Western Asia, spread throughout the world. Henceforth the supremacy of Christianity in the civilized East was disputed only by Mohammedanism. With the rise and decline of Mohammedanism, the influence of Western Asia upon the history of the world came to an end. It gave to us our religion, our alphabet, and the elements of our civilization; it was the earliest home of the arts and sciences, of organized government and legal codes.

Asia Minor, or **Anatolia,** the name applied since the 5th century B.C. to that part of Asia which extends as a peninsula between the Black Sea on the n. and the Mediterranean Sea on the s. to the Ægean Sea on the w. It now constitutes the Turkish Republic. The climate of Asia Minor is greatly diversified. Forests of oak, fir, beech, ash, and plane still clothe the slopes along the Black Sea coast, but have almost disappeared from the mountain lands, which were once densely wooded. Wild animals include the wolf, the bear, the hyæna, the lynx, and the wild boar. Camels and asses are used for beasts of burden, horses for riding, and the buffalo for farm work. The Angora goat is bred for its characteristic silky hair. Bees are kept in great numbers. The mineral wealth of Asia Minor is abundant, but the deposits have not been largely worked. Agriculture occupies most of the people, although it is in a backward state. Manufacturing is confined to the production of silks, the weaving of rugs and carpets, shawls, and mohair cloth, and to the making of wine. Fishing is carried on in the Ægean Sea. The chief ports are Trebizond, Samsun, Sinope, Smyrna, Adalia, and Mersina. The roads are in a wretched condition, and internal trade is thus greatly hindered. See BAGDAD RAILWAY.

The population numbers 13,660,275, and consists of the most various races. The dominant race is the Osmanli Turks, who number about 1,200,000, and are spread over the whole country. The Greeks and Armenians are the most progressive elements in the population.

Asia Minor has long been a battle ground for warring nations. At the close of World War I a peculiar situation arose as the result of the growth of a nationalist movement which culminated in the calling of a Grand National Assembly at Angora in April, 1920. Kemal Pasha was elected the first President of a Turkish Republic in 1923, the Caliphate was abolished, and the capital transferred to Angora. The Treaty of Lausanne was accepted by Turkey and the European Powers concerned, in 1923, the capitulations being annulled. Consult Ramsay's *Historical Geography of Asia Minor;* Childs' *Across Asia Minor on Foot* (1917); Hawley's *Asia Minor* (1918).

Asiatic Association, American, a society organized in 1898 to foster the trade and commercial interests of United States citizens in China, Japan, the Philippines, and elsewhere in the East.

Asiatic Societies, organizations for the study of Oriental religions, languages, history, and antiquities. The oldest Asiatic Society, the Dutch Colonial, was established in Java in 1779, and the Asiatic Society of Bengal in 1784. In 1843 the American Oriental Society was founded at Boston. Tokyo and Peking have similar organizations.

Askew, or **Ascough, Anne** (1521-46), English Protestant martyr, accused of heresy, was tortured; but, refusing to recant, was burned. Consult Bale's two Tracts *On the Examination of Anne Askew* (1546 and 1547).

Askhabad, or **Askabad,** town, capital of

Turkoman Soviet Socialist Republic, U.S.S.R.; p. 53,690.

Askja, (Ice., 'basket'), the largest volcano in Iceland.

Asmodeus, probably a corruption of Æshma Dæva, an evil genius in the ancient Persian religion. He is the supernatural cicerone in Le Sage's *Le Diable Boiteaux.*

Asmoneans, or **Hasmoneans,** the Greek denomination of the first members of the Jewish dynasty of the Maccabees.

Asoca (*Jonesia asoca*), a tree of the order Leguminosæ, common throughout India, where it is associated with poetry and mythology.

Asoka, emperor of India from B.C. 272-232, notable as a great monarch and as a zealous propagandist of Buddhism.

Asolo, a walled town in the province of

Treviso, Italy, 18 m. n.w. of Treviso. It was a favorite resort of Robert Browning, and possibly the source of inspiration for parts of *Pippa Passes* and *Sordello*.

Asp (*Vipera aspis*), a poisonous snake about 2 ft. in length, common in the wooded elevated regions of Southern Europe generally.

Asparagine, amido-succinamic acid occurs in asparagus, peas, and many other plants. It can be prepared synthetically, and forms transparent crystals, soluble in water.

Asparagus, Common (*Asparagus officinalis*), a genus of the order Liliaceæ, indigenous to Europe, Asia and South Africa. In spring its perennial underground stems (rhizomes) produce a large number of fleshy, aerial stems bearing small scale-leaves, which are eaten, and are often blanched.

Asparagus-Beetle. A chrysomelid beetle (*Crioceris asparagi*), the most important of the insects that attack asparagus. See *Bulletin No.* 10, of the U. S. Department of Agriculture.

Asparagus Stone, certain yellowish-green varieties of apatite.

Aspasia. (1.) Of Miletus, the most famous of Greek courtesans. She came to Athens, and Pericles lived with her until his death. Aspasia shared to the full the highest culture of the day; popular gossip gave her the credit of much of Pericles's statesmanship. See Landor's *Pericles and Aspasia* (1836). (2) The younger, a Phocæan, the favorite mistress of Cyrus the younger.

Aspect in astronomy refers to the relative positions of two planets as seen from the earth.

Aspen (*Populus sp.*), certain trees belonging to the willow family. Even in calm weather the leaves tremble in upward currents of air which are not strong enough to stir those of other trees. There is an old tradition in Scotland that the leaves are never at rest because the cross was made of aspen wood.

Asperges, in the Roman Catholic Church, is an antiphone taken from the *Miserere*.

Aspergillus, a genus of hyphomycetous fungi. See MOULD.

Asphaltum. A natural mineral pitch belonging to the bitumens, and therefore allied to natural gas and petroleum. Physically it ranges from liquid form to the dense brittle variety. The solid varieties have a black or brown color, a splintery fracture, and burn with a smoky flame. Though deposits of nearly pure asphaltum occur, more often the mineral is admixed with earthy matter, or else is distributed through the pores and cavities of rocks such as limestone and sandstone. Asphaltum is quite widely distributed in nature. One of the most remarkable deposits occurs at Pitch Lake, island of Trinidad, where it fills a basin to a depth of nearly 100 ft. The material is solid enough to support a horse and wagon, but has a slow motion which closes up the cavities made by excavation. In the United States most of the asphaltum is obtained from bituminous sandstone and limestone. The principal use of asphaltum is in the construction of pavements. Besides its use as paving material asphaltum finds application in the manufacture of paints, varnishes, and cement, as an insulating or water-proofing material and for roofing purposes. See articles in the volumes of *The Mineral Resources,* U. S. Geological Survey, Washington.

Asphodel, a plant of the order Liliaceæ. The asphodel, being sacred to Proserpine, was in the days of the Romans used in funeral ceremonies.

Asphodel, Bog (*Narthecium ossifragum*), also called 'Lancashire asphodel,' is a small plant of the order Liliaceæ, whose blossom gives an orange tint to many peat bogs in Europe during July and August. The specific name, meaning 'bone-breaking,' is derived from the unfounded belief that when sheep eat leaves their bones become fragile.

Asphyxia is commonly used to denote the condition following upon total deprivation of oxygen for respiration, from whatever cause. Drowning, strangling, irrespirable gases, and mechanical obstruction of any kind to the entrance of oxygen to the lungs, are common examples. Recovery is possible while the heart beats, and may even be hoped for a little later still, in some cases, if the heart's work be made easier by bleeding.

Asphyxiants are substances which cause death by the production of asphyxia. Examples of these are carbonic acid gas, coal gas, marsh gas, and acetylene.

Aspidistra, a Chinese genus of the order Liliaceæ, now much cultivated. Three species are grown, but *A. lurida* is the one commonly seen in rooms. The plant is popularly known as 'parlor palm.'

Aspidium. See **Male Fern.**

Aspinwall, William H. (1807-75), a New York merchant and shipowner who obtained a concession in 1850 to construct a railway across the isthmus of Panama. It was completed in February, 1855, and the eastern terminus, now called Colon, was named after him. He was also one of the organizers of the Pacific Mail Steamship Co.

Aspirate (Lat. *ad*, 'to;' *spirare* 'to breathe'), in phonetics, is the strong breathing of a letter, approximating the guttural sound. The habit of 'dropping the *h*' when (according to modern usage) it ought to be retained is prevalent in the English lower class, and this is accompanied by the contrary habit of prefixing an *h* where it is not wanted. In the English of the cultivated class of to-day there is a tendency to restore the aspirate in some words and to drop it in others. See *The Aspirate*, by G. Hill (1902).

Aspirator, an apparatus used to draw air or gases through pipes or other apparatus connected with it. The name is also given to a surgical instrument for removing fluids from body cavities, as in pleurisy, ascites, abscesses, retention of urine, etc.

Aspirin, the trade name for acetyl salicylic acid.

Aspromonte, a wood mountainous district, in the extreme south of Italy. Here Garibaldi was defeated and taken prisoner (1862).

Asquith, Rt. Hon. Herbert Henry (1852-1928), English statesman; Premier of England from 1908 to 1916, when he resigned. At the General Election in 1918, Mr. Asquith was defeated in East Fife, which he had represented since 1886. He continued active in politics for a number of years. His *Memories and Reflections* was published shortly after his death. Politicians and publicists of all shades of opinion expressed regret at the disappearance from the parliamentary arena of a statesman who, during a long career, preserved the amenities of public life and maintained at a high level the best traditions of British statesmanship.

Ass, a name given to a group of species of the genus *Equus*, including the domestic ass (*E. asinus*), or donkey, and the wild asses of Africa and Asia. The ass differs from the horse in its long ears, the absence of long hairs at the base of the tail and of 'chestnuts' on the hind legs. When treated with kindness, it is often scarcely inferior to the horse in usefulness, and is far less expensive to keep, being less liable to disease and less particular as to diet.

Assai Palm, (*Euterpe*), a tree of tropical America, much cultivated for its pulpy fruit, *assai*, from which is prepared a thick creamy beverage.

Assam, province of British India, lies at the northeastern corner of the peninsula of India. The climate is generally hot, enervating and malarious, while the Assam hills have the heaviest rainfall in the world, normally 450 inches. Earthquakes are of frequent occurrence. The soil is fertile and yields an abundance of tea, rice, and mustard-seed. Over 700 varieties of orchids are found, and palms, bamboos, and teak trees flourish. Fish abound in the rivers and furnish a large portion of the native food. Mineral products include coal, petroleum, iron, gold, manganese, limestone, and mica. The bulk of the people are Ahoms, an offshoot of the Shans of Northern Burma. The government is in the hands of a Chief Commissioner, with headquarters at Shillong. In 1842 Matak and Sadiya were incorporated in British territory. In 1905 Assam and Eastern Bengal were united to form a new province, and in 1912 Assam became once more a separate province; p. 7,606,200.

Consult E. A. Gait's *History of Assam;* L. W. Shakespear's *History of Upper Assam, Upper Burma, and the Northeastern Frontier* (1914).

Assandune. See **Ashdown Park.**

Assassination, a term sometimes applied to any murder, but usually restricted to the killing of some prominent person from fanatical or political or religious motives.

Assassins, a fanatical sect which flourished in Persia and Syria from the 11th to the 13th century. It was founded by Hassan-ibn-Sabbah, who seized, in 1090, the fortress of Alamut in Persia, where he established his society, consisting of a supreme ruler, the 'Old Man of the Mountain' of European historians, besides three grand priors, priors, associates, and the assassins proper, who, when selected for the commission of a murder, were first intoxicated with hashish (hemp), the origin of the name assassin, from hashishin (hemp-eaters). This society soon made its power felt, and the reign of its rulers was marked by a long series of assassinations of famous men. See F. Walpole, *The Ansayrii, or Assassins* (1851); Guyard, *Fragments relatifs à la Doctrine des Ismaéliens* (1874).

Assault. An offer of personal violence to another. Thus, to threaten to strike a person within striking distance, or to shake one's fist in his face, or to present a gun at him when within range, to pull a rosette off his coat, or to incite a dog to attack him, or to attempt to kiss a woman, or to do any act accompanied by circumstances which denote both intention and ability at the time to molest or do violence to the person, is an assault. If a blow is struck or violence actually used, it is a battery; but the word assault is frequently used in the sense of a battery. Verbal abuse does not amount to an assault. A person actually struck is justified in striking back in self-defense, but not in revenge. His retaliation must, therefore, not be greater than is necessary to put an end to the assault.

Assaying. The term 'assaying' in its widest sense, comprises that section of analytical chemistry which has for its object the estimation of the value of ores and metallic products. In general, two classes of methods are followed: one, the 'dry' or 'fire' assay, and the other the 'wet' or more strictly scientific methods of gravimetric and volumetric analysis, the latter including colorimetric determinations. The chemical reactions in the dry assay are accomplished by the aid of high temperatures obtained in a furnace, while in the wet assay these reactions take place in cold, or only slightly heated solutions. In its limited sense the term assaying is restricted to the determination of the precious metals in coins, jewelry, silver and goldplate and other commercial alloys. The standard assays to determine the purity of these alloys are made at the Goldsmith's Hall, Great Britain, and at the various government mints and assay offices in the United States and other countries.

It is impossible to present in a limited space a detailed description of the methods of chemical analysis. The reactions vary in each class of work and frequently the manipulations differ according to the individual practice of the assayer or chemist. The first step in assaying an ore or furnace product is to select, by hand or machine, a proper representative sample. Various methods of sampling ore are used, the simplest, called 'quartering,' consists in taking every tenth shovelful of ore as it is discharged from the ore cars until about 10 tons have been obtained. This is shoveled into a conical heap, which is then flattened out into a circular cake and divided diametrically into quarters. Two opposite quarters are taken for a second conical heap, which is likewise flattened and quartered, and the operation repeated until the sample has been reduced to a few pounds. This small quantity is then ground until it will pass through a very fine sieve, and constitutes the final sample for assay. Solid metallic products are drilled or punched, the drillings or punchings forming the sample. Molten products are sampled by ladling out a small portion of the fluid material.

There are, in the United States, assay offices at New York, New Orleans, Carson City, Boise, Helena, Seattle, and Salt Lake City. These offices serve the public by making assays of ores and bullion.

See Berringer's *Textbook of Assaying* (1902); Rickett's *Notes on Assaying* (1893); Lodge, *Notes on Assaying* (1905).

Assegai, the Zulu spear, of which there are two varieties—the long javelin, or throwing-spear; and the shorter 'stabbing' assegai, for use at close quarters.

Assembly. See **General Assembly**.

Assembly, National. See **France**—*History*.

Assembly, Unlawful. An assembly of three or more persons with intent to commit a crime, or with intent to carry out in common any purpose, lawful or unlawful, which is likely to lead to a breach of the peace. See RIOT.

Assessment. See **Taxation; Rating**.

Assessors. Persons associated with a court for the purposes of consultation and advice. The term assessor is also employed in the United States to describe officers charged with the duty of appraising or assessing property for purposes of taxation.

Assets. Property of a decedent or an insolvent debtor which is available for distribution among creditors. See BANKRUPTCY.

Asiento (Span. 'treaty'), a contract made between Spain and other powers by which the monopoly of importing slaves into Spanish America was conferred upon the latter.

Assignation. See **Assignment**.

Assignats. During the period immediately preceding the French Revolution, the National Assembly declared the church lands to be national property, and offered them for sale to the various municipalities throughout the country; accepting, in lieu of cash payment, paper notes or bonds of equivalent value, consequently styled assignats. Assignats were in circulation in France from 1790 to 1796.

Assignment. In the most general sense a transfer of any species of property, real or personal, by any mode of conveyance. Thus interpreted the term is nearly identical in meaning with conveyance or alienation. See INSOLVENCY. The Scotch equivalent for assignment is ASSIGNATION.

Assimilation, the process by which organisms take up and transform foreign substances into their own tissues, as in digestion and respiration.

Assiniboines ('stone boilers'), a division of the Sioux Indians. At present they are found on several small reservations in Canada and the United States. See Coues *New Light on the Early History of the Greater Northwest* (1897).

Assisi (the ancient *Asisium*) tn. and episc. see, prov. Perugia, Italy, the birthplace (1182) of St. Francis Bernardone, founder of the Franciscian order (1209); p. 17,240.

Assisi, St. Francis of. See **Francis.**

Assistance, Writ of. A chancery process in England and the United States directing the sheriff or other proper officer to enforce an order or decree awarding to the petitioner the possession of lands.

Association of Ideas, the manner in which, or principle according to which, ideas or images succeed each other in the mind when their succession is not interrupted from without, or determined by logical thinking. For a general view of the place of association in mental life, see PSYCHOLOGY. For more special criticism of the psychological doctrine of association, see James, *Principles of Psychology* (1893); and articles in *Mind*, July, 1893, and Oct., 1894, by Ward. For the philosophical doctrine of associationism, see HUME and MILL.

Assonance, a kind of imperfect rhyme

The Nile Reservoir and Dam, Assuan.

Assize of Clarendon (1166), Henry II.'s first measure of judicial reform, remarkable by its institution, in criminal trials, of the germ of the jury system—the justices and local sheriffs trying accused persons by grand juries of the county.

Assizes. The sittings of a circuit court, of a court which moves about from place to place to try causes.

Associated Press, largest of the American news gathering agencies, with a membership in 1935 of 1,300 newspapers in the United States, South America, Europe and China. Its correspondents are stationed throughout the United States and in the major capitals of the world. In 1934 the Associated Press news service was supplemented by a picture service, and a wire-photo service. It was sued as a monopoly in 1942 by the U. S. Govt.

consisting of the recurrence of the same vowel sounds. It differs from rhyme proper in paying no regard to the accompanying consonants. See RHYME. *Pain* and *care, waver* and *fairest,* are examples of perfect assonants. Its most striking development is to be found in Celtic poetry, which compensates for its almost total absence of perfect rhyme by the establishment of a highly artificial and intricate system of assonantal harmonies. Assonance is only suitable to languages in which the vowel sounds predominate over the consonants. Hence, while rejected in English, it is tolerated in Scottish poetry.

Assuan, or **Aswan,** a town of Upper Egypt, at the first cataract of the Nile; p. about 12,000. Here is a *barrage* or dam, the largest work of the kind in the world, built by the Egyptian government after the design of Mr. W. Willcocks, at a cost of $24,000,000. The dam, which is 2,187 yards long, is designed to form a reservoir regulating the flow of the Nile. It is built of solid masonry, weighing a million tons, with a sloping buttress throughout its length, and having 180 under-sluices, which when opened will allow free passage to the early floods—the later annual inundation being, of course, conserved. The dam was completed on July 31, 1902. See *The Nile Reservoir Dam at Assuân*, by W. Willcocks (1901).

Assumption, capital of Paraguay. See **Asunción.**

Assumption of the Virgin (Aug. 15), a day observed by the Oriental and Roman Catholic Churches, but ignored by Protestants. Her bodily resurrection was a Roman Catholic doctrine until proclaimed a dogma by Pope Pius XII on Nov. 1, 1950.

Assur, Asur, or **Asshur,** the ancient national god of Assyria.

Assurance, Legal. A technical term of English law for a conveyance of land. The term is not in common use in the U. S.

Assyria. (the Hebrew, Asshur) is the ancient name for the tract of country with Mesopotamia on the west, Babylonia on the south, and Armenia on the north. The country was exceedingly fertile, with excellent clay for brickmaking and pottery and also good building stone, in the possession of which it had the advantage over Babylonia. The ancient capital, Assur, now called Kalaat Shergat, about 60 m. below Mosul, was the residence of the early kings and viceroys; but the place was seemingly abandoned as the capital about 1300 B.C., and Nineveh substituted. Nineveh is now represented by the mounds of Kuyunjik and Nebi Yunus, opposite Mosul.

Assyrian Sculpture.—Copper Relief from Tell-el-Ubaid, pre-flood or Sumerian Period.

The date when the colonists from Babylonia established themselves in Assyria is doubtful, but it is generally regarded as having taken place about 2500 B.C., when the amalgamation of the Semitic and the non-Semitic elements of the population had already been accomplished. On entering Assyria, the migrants brought with them the civilization, the manners, the customs, the religion, and the literature of the Babylonians, with whom they originated, and it is largely owing to them that that literature has been preserved.

Aster Novæ Anglicæ.

The history of Assyria falls into three periods: 2300 to 1650 B.C. when the country was dependent upon Babylonia (q.v.); 1745-745 B.C. when the country became increasingly aggressive and a rival of Babylonia; 745-606 B.C. when the country reached the height of its power only to fall under a combination of the forces of the Medes and Babylonians at Nineveh 607-606 B.C.

Thus ended the great Assyrian empire. Of the same race with the Babylonians, whom they closely resembled, the Assyrians added to their love of art, letters, and capacity to rule a great power of organization and warlike energy. Like the Babylonians, they were excellent agriculturists and equally good builders. Boastful as they were bold, they were fond of long inscriptions and the frequent writing of reports to the King.

One of the most remarkable characteristics of the Assyrians was that aptitude which brought about their success in war. In all probability this was due to their superior mobility and also to the perfection of their defences and their engines of attack. In the sieges which they carried on, they constructed enormous towers on wheels, which were pushed up specially-constructed causeways, approaching so close to the walls that battering-rams worked from within the towers could be brought into play. To this must be added their skilfully-made chain-mail and scale armor, which, with their enormous wicker shields, enabled their soldiers to fight to the greatest advantage. Indeed, it is not impossible that they were the masters and teachers of the ancient world in the art of war.

The religion of the Assyrians was practically the same as that of the Babylonians, the chief difference being that they gave their national god, Assur, the highest place in the pantheon. To all intents and purposes he replaced the god Merodach, who was also worshipped by the Assyrians, and with whom he seems to have been identified. See Maspero's (ed. by Sayce) *The Dawn of Civilization* (1896), and *The Struggle of the Nations* (1897); Roger's *Babylon and Assyria* (1901); Omstead's *History of Assyria* (1923). Compare also BABYLONIA and CUNEIFORM.

Astaire, Fred (1899-   ), American actor and dancer born in Omaha, Neb. Educated in public schools, at the age of twelve he appeared on the vaudeville stage. Being under age he was forced to abandon his career until 1916 when with his sister Adele he toured the U. S. and Canada in a vaudeville act. He was called to the N. Y. stage to take leading roles in a number of musical comedies and appeared in well over a dozen between 1918 and 1928. In 1923 and 1926 he went to England to play in musical comedies on the London stage. It was not until 1933 that he heeded the call of Hollywood. With his first picture, *Dancing Lady*, he scored an instantaneous and overwhelming success. Ginger Rogers and Rita Hayworth have been his dancing partners. Some of his greatest successes were *Roberta, Top Hat, Follow the Fleet,* and *Swingtime.* He retired in 1946. He later opened a dancing school.

Astarte, the Syrian Venus, is identical with 'Ashtaroth the abomination of the Zidonians' and with the Ishtar of Assyria, besides having affinities with other classic deities.

Astatic Needle. See **Galvanometer.**

Astatki is the residue from the distillation of Russian petroleum.

Aster, a genus of Compositæ, which is chiefly American, and comprises at least 250 species, and many varieties. They are mostly perennial herbs, of branching habit, with flowers, both tubular and radiate, generally corymbose or paniculate. They are often very showy with a wide range of white, pink, blue, and purple shades. The asters, or starworts, are a hardy crowd, often flourishing in sandy, dry soil. When cultivated as they often are, in Europe, under the name of 'Michaelmas daisies,' they increase in height and brilliancy, and the various species bloom through the fall months, in succession, quite up to frost.

Aster, China, (*Callistephus hortensis*), a species of Compositæ, native of China and Japan.

Asteroids, small planets circulating between Mars and Jupiter. They seem to replace a single large planet, conjecturally located, before they were found, in the wide interval occupied by them, and collectively represent a term in the series of planetary distances designated as 'Bode's Law.' The first asteroid (see CERES) was discovered on Jan. 1, 1801; and on Jan. 1, 1903, the known members of the family numbered about 540. These bodies differ greatly in size. The largest has a diameter of nearly 500, the smallest of probably less than 20 m. and there may be multitudes beyond the range of perception, constructed on the modest scale of shooting stars. None can possess appreciable atmospheres; yet their markedly diverse albedoes suggest unexpected varieties in physical constitution. Their joint mass is almost certainly much smaller than that of the moon, but cannot be estimated with any approach to precision. The zone tenanted by the asteroids is fully 200 millions of miles in width. See authorities cited under ASTRONOMY.

Asterophyllites (for which the synonym Calamocladies is used by some botanists) is supposed to be the foliage of certain fossil Equisetaceæ, such as calamites, which flourished principally in the Carboniferous epoch.

Asthenopia, weakness of the organs of sight. It is accompanied by pain, headache, and impaired vision.

Asthma, a respiratory disease spasmodic and recurrent in character, marked by great temporary difficulty of breathing. The majority of cases occur in the early years of life and heredity is believed by some to play a rôle. Premonitory symptoms—varying with the individual, but constant in recurrent attacks—may be observed — malaise, cough, coryza, etc. The attack itself is characterized by a feeling of intense suffocation and marked dyspnea. The patient fights for breath, with slow, loud, convulsive respiratory efforts, in which every muscle of the body seems to be strained.

The paroxysms are frequently nocturnal in character, and the duration varies from a few minutes to several hours. The frequency of recurrence is also extremely variable. The nature of the attack is such as to make the diagnosis comparatively simple. The important thing, however, is to determine the exciting cause.

Asti, town and episcopal see, Italy; p. 42,000.

Astigmatism, a defect of vision in which the rays of light proceeding from a point do not reach the retina as a point, but as an area or spot. It means that one set of rays passing through a certain axis of the cornea and lens is not focused on their axial area of the retina. One set of rays is focused ahead (myopia) or behind (hypermetropia). The wearing of corrective glasses is essential.

Astilbe, a perennial herb of the saxifrage family. It has beautiful dark green foliage and small white, pink, or purplish flowers, growing in dense spikes.

Astle, Thomas (1735-1803), English bibliophile, author of the *Origin and Progress of Writing* (1784; new ed. 1876), a work of importance, for its explanations of mediæval handwriting. The valuable MSS. of his collection are now in the British Museum.

Astor, John Jacob (1763-1848), American merchant, founder of the American Fur Company, was born in Waldorf, near Heidelberg, Germany. He went to the United States in 1783. He prospered exceedingly, and at his death left a legacy of $350,000 to found a public library in New York City (see NEW YORK PUBLIC LIBRARY).

Astor, John Jacob (1864-1912), great-grandson of John Jacob Astor (q.v.). invented several useful mechanical appliances, and published *A Journey in Other Worlds: A Romance of the Future* (1894). He was drowned in the *Titanic* disaster.

Astor, Nancy Witcher Langhorne, Viscountess (1879-   ), the first woman member of the British House of Commons, was born in Virginia. She was elected in 1919, becoming the first woman to obtain a seat in the House of Commons. She has been re-elected at every General Election since then and enjoys great popularity and has real influence. She is the author of *My Two Countries* (1923).

Astor, (William) Vincent (1891-   ), American financier born in New York City. He is the present head of the American branch of the family. His various offices include those of trustee or director in railroad companies, Chase National Bank, Metropolitan Opera Company, New York Public Library, and Western Union Telegraph Company. He holds membership in more than 30 clubs. The magazine *Today* was at one time published by him.

Astor, William Waldorf (1848-1919), writer and diplomat, great-grandson of John Jacob Astor was born in New York City. He was naturalized as a British subject in 1899, and in 1916 was created Viscount of Hever Castle.

Astorga, town, Spain. Notable features are the 17th century town hall, the Cathedral dating from the 15th century, the bishop's palace and Priests' Seminary; p. 6,312.

Astoria, city, Oregon. Founded by J. J. Astor in 1811, it was in its early history noted for fur trade; p. 10,389.

Astor Library. See **New York Public Library.**

Astor Place Riot, a serious disturbance which took place in New York City on the evening of May 10, 1849, at the Astor Place Opera House. The English actor William C. Macready (q.v.) was billed to play *Macbeth,* but partisans of the American actor Edwin Forrest (q.v.), made a violent attack on the opera house.

Astrabad, or **Asterbad,** town, Iran. It

Astræa, is a dilapidated but picturesque town surrounded by a mud wall flanked with round towers; p. about 9,000.

Astræa, in Greek mythology the goddess of justice, daughter of Zeus and Themis, or of Aristæus and Eos (Aurora). The name Astræa was often applied to Queen Elizabeth.

Astragal, a small moulding usually applied to the bars in windows which carry the glass.

Astragalus, one of the bones forming the ankle-joint. See ANKLE; FOOT.

to designate the higher and invisible part of man's physical nature. See THEOSOPHY.

Astringents, drugs which contract tissues chiefly by coagulating albumin. When applied in the form of lotions or ointments, they reduce the congestion of mucous membranes, and thus assist in the healing of wounds and ulcers; when taken internally, they are useful in cases of hæmorrhage or diarrhœa.

Astrocaryum, a genus of palms native to tropical America. Thirty or more species are known, many of which bear edible fruit,

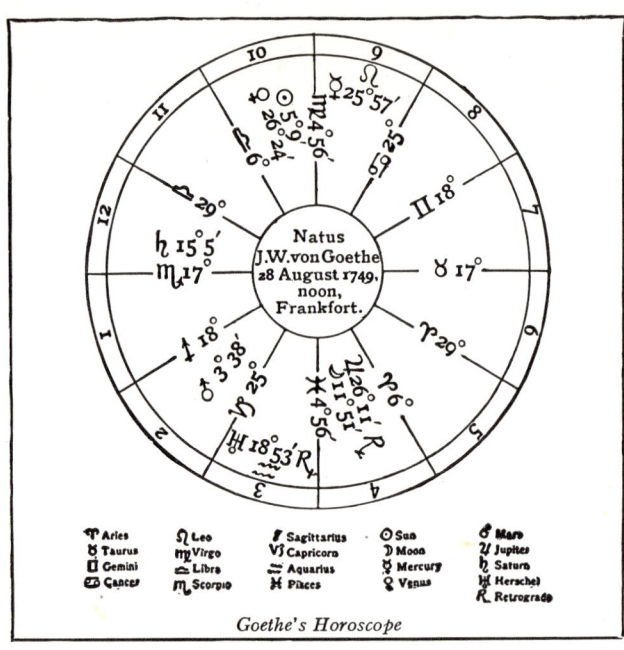

Goethe's Horoscope

Astragalus, a large genus (about 1,000 species) of plants, of the order Papilionaceæ, found in almost every country except Australia, and commonly known as Milk Vetches or Rattle Weeds. Two American species, *A. crassicarpus* and *A. Mexicanus*, the ground plums, have edible, fleshy fruits, *A. mollissimus*, is the poisonous Purple Loco, Woolly Loco Weed or Crazy Weed (see LOCO WEED.)

Astrakhan, city, Russia, capital of Astrakhan government, is built on an island in the Volga delta; p. 239,681.

Astrakhan Fur, also known as **Karakul**, a black or gray fur prepared from the pelts of Bokhara lambs.

Astral Body, a term used by Theosophists

with a melon-like flavor. From the leaves of the Tucum palm, the natives obtain a fine, strong fibre of which they make cordage for bowstrings and fishing nets.

Astrolabe, an arrangement of rings representing the equator, prime meridian, ecliptic, etc., which was used by astronomers in the middle ages. An instrument used by mariners in the age of the great discoveries for ascertaining the altitude of the sun was also called an astrolabe.

Astrology, a pseudo-science whereby celestial phenomena are interpreted for the direction of mundane affairs. Astrology and astronomy were long regarded as a single science, but eventually a distinction was made and astrology was restricted to the sphere of foretelling the future. It is one of the oldest sciences known to man. Careful and extensive research has ascertained that after reigning supreme in Babylon it spread to Syria and Egypt, Phœnicia and Persia, China and India. About the beginning of the Christian era it flourished in Greece and Rome; in the latter city especially, astrologers, or 'soothsayers' as they were called, occupied a prominent position in society and were consulted on many important questions. The Arabs of the desert were firm believers in astrology, and the teachings of Mohammed in regard to predestination accord well with astrological predictions. In the 16th and 17th centuries the astronomical discoveries of Copernicus, Galileo and Kepler tended to discredit the science of astrology and since that time its influence has greatly declined.

Astrology proceeds from the assumption that a study of the stars may serve as a guide to life. The astrologer's judgment is based on the configuration of the heavens at a given moment.

The astrologer's first care is to draw a figure of the heavens, visible and invisible, divided into twelve houses, and to mark on it the zodiacal signs and the planets at their proper places. This is called 'casting the horoscope,' or the 'nativity' if it refers to the birth of a child. He next observes which sign is rising and takes the planet whose mansion it is for the 'lord of the ascendant,' or the querent's significator. Then, if a significator is wanted for person inquired about, he looks to the sign in the proper house. Thus, the lord of the seventh would stand for the querent's wife, the lord of the fourth for his father, etc. When all the evidence has been carefully weighed, judgment may be given.

Consult Cumont's *Astrology and Religion among the Greeks and Romans;* Leo's *Practical Astrology;* Heindel's *Simplified Scientific Astrology;* Thompson's *Astrology* (1930).

Astronomical Society, American, a society organized in 1898 for the advancement of astronomy, astrophysics, and related branches of physics.

Astronomy, the science of the celestial bodies, first took definite shape in Babylonia, where, in the third millennium B.C., the sphere began to be measured, the zodiac was delimited and divided, and many of the constellations were named. It developed into a coherent science only through the formative influence of Greek genius. The Greeks received a considerable amount of astronomical knowledge and observational material from the Babylonians and Egyptians, but few general principles had been deduced.

The theory of homocentric spheres invented by Eudoxus of Cnidus (406-350 B.C.) and elaborated by Aristotle, represented a memorable effort to grapple with the problem of celestial movements; but the line of great astronomers started with Hipparchus (about 140 B.C.), whose adoption of the epicycles and eccentrics of Apollonius decided the plan of the great edifice raised by Claudius Ptolemæus three hundred years later. Even Copernicus did not attempt its subversion. He changed the point of view, but not the principle of interpretation. Ptolemy's *Almagest,* though undermined, stood erect until brought to the ground by the impact of Kepler's discoveries.

The Copernican system, interpreting the daily motion of the sun, planets, and stars from east to west as an apparent motion produced by the rotation of the earth about an axis, and substituting the sun for the earth as the centre of planetary motion, was much simpler than the Ptolemaic and represented equally well the motions of the planets. It soon became evident, however, that a really stringent and decisive test between the two theories could not be applied until observations of greater accuracy and in greater abundance were available. This was realized and, to the best of his ability, supplied by Tycho Brahe (1546-1601). Through the plain sights—for the telescope had not yet been invented—placed far apart on his great mural quadrant, he was able greatly to increase the accuracy of aiming at the heavenly bodies and thus measuring their positions. He was fortunate, also, in securing Kepler as his assistant.

Wren, Hooke, and Halley all divined the law of gravitation but failed to apply it as the mainspring of the planetary machine. Newton came to the rescue; and his continental successors, Euler, D'Alembert, Lagrange, and Laplace, using the flexible methods of analysis, needed a full century to complete in its details the colossal work he had reared on a massive base. Laplace's *Mécanique Céleste* (1799-1805) was the complement to Newton's *Principia* (1687), and presented astronomy under the aspect of a solved mechanical problem.

Meanwhile, descriptive or telescopic astronomy, initiated by Galileo (1564-1642), was assuming predominant importance through the labors of William Herschel (1738-1822). Attention had until then been concentrated on the solar system—stars and nebulæ being regarded incidentally. Herschel originated their systematic study, prescribing determinations of their positions and movements. For the latter purpose the transit circle is essential. It consists of a telescope movable in the plane of the meridian, attached with a large graduated circle to a rigid hori-

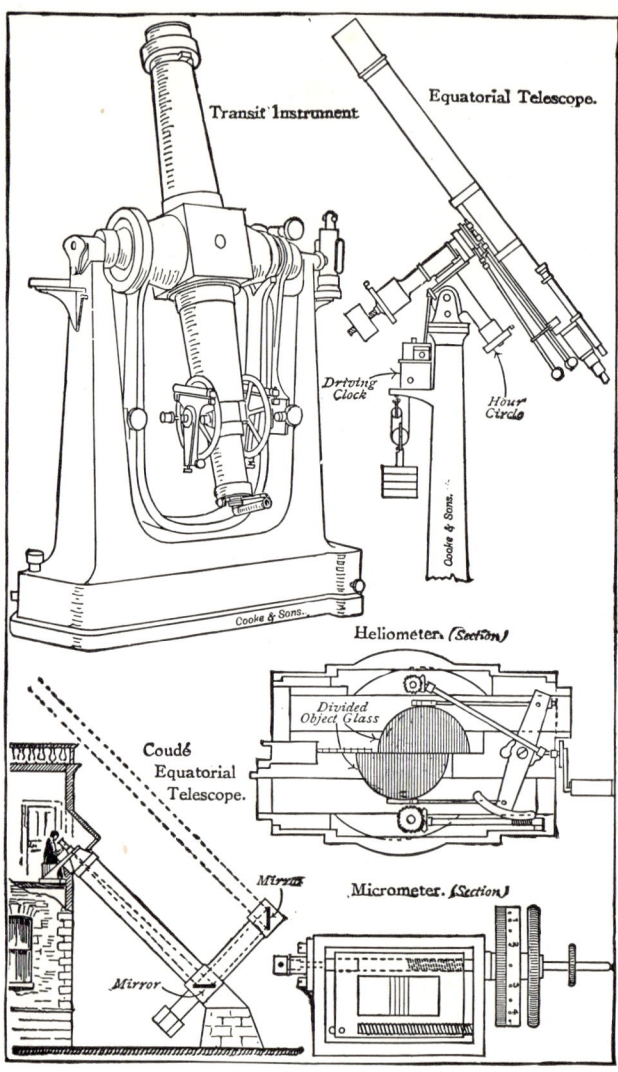

Astronomical Instruments

some of the leading methods of modern astronomy.

Astrometry.—A typical 20th-century observatory combines astrophysics and astrometry. Investigations into the nature of the heavenly bodies proceed side by side with zontal axis. The culmination of a star is fixed by noting the successive instants of its transits across a set of vertical spiderlines, an electric chronograph serving as the recorder, while the corresponding declination is read off on the perpendicular circle. Fifty or 60 such complete observations constitute a good night's work, and the material accumulated serves, when reduced and corrected, for the construction of star catalogues, and for the improvement of solar, lunar, and planetary tables. The observation of star transits determines the correct local time and the error of the clock. Comparison, by means of telegraph, transportation of chronometers, or radio, with the local time of another place, gives the difference of longitude. Radio broadcasting of time signals has made it possible for many observatories to discontinue their own time service.

The relative situations of adjacent objects in the sky can be accurately ascertained by means of an equatorial and micrometer. A telescope is said to be equatorially mounted when it follows, actuated by clockwork, the diurnal revolution of the heavens. One of a pair of crossed axes, directed towards the pole, carries the 'hour circle'; the other, at right angles to it, supports the telescope and 'declination circle.' Any object with known co-ordinates can then, by setting the circles, be readily brought into the field of view; to keep it there, it is necessary only to start a driving-clock, by which uniform rotation, once in twenty-four hours, is imparted to the polar axis. In the 'Coudé' form of equatorial, adopted at Paris, a revolving plane mirror reflects the objects to be observed into the polar axis of the telescope, which itself remains stationary.

A profound change has been brought about in the scope, no less than in the methods, of astrometry by the adoption of the camera as an instrument of precision. Plans were made at the Paris Astronomical Congress in 1887 to photograph the entire sky on plates each covering four square degrees, eighteen observatories co-operating in the work. The vision of E. C. Pickering in inaugurating, toward the close of the last century, a programme of systematically and repeatedly photographing the entire sky on small scale plates has produced an enormous storehouse of astronomical information.

The characteristic astrophysical instrument is the spectroscope or rather the spectrograph; for the spectra of the heavenly bodies are now ordinarily recorded photographically. (See SPECTRUM.) By means of spectroscopic investigations, the heavenly bodies have been assimilated chemically, as they were physically by the discovery of gravitation, to our common earth. Many of the properties of stars are related to their spectra. Much interest has been shown in recent years in the order of evolution of the stars. That they are gradually changing from one type to another we cannot doubt. They radiate vast quantities of heat and light into space. But this change is exceedingly slow. The geologic records convince us that the amount of heat received by the earth from the sun has not materially changed in hundreds of millions of years.

The rigidity of the earth is being studied through the rhythmic oscillation of the axis of rotation, first detected by Chandler in a variation of latitude of places on the earth; the tides produced in the crust of the earth by the moon and sun; the waves which originate in an earthquake and record themselves on seismographs at great distances (see EARTHQUAKES).

The sun itself presents a crowd of pending problems. Its peculiar mode of rotation; the nature of sunspots, the motion of material in and about them and the attendant magnetic peculiarities; the pressures prevailing at different levels; the sources of maintenance of the sun's heat; the constitution of the photospheric cloud-shell, its relations to the faculæ which rise from it, and to the surmounting vaporous strata; the nature of prominences; the alternations of coronal types; the affinities of the zodiacal light—all these problems are being vigorously attacked. The entirely new field opened up in the investigation of the structure of an atom, and the conditions under which it emits or absorbs light of certain wave-lengths, is leading, at an astounding rate, to an understanding, through their spectra, of conditions prevailing in the heavenly bodies. The theory of relativity requiring, for its substantiation, the observational proof of a slight change in direction of light from a star passing close by the sun, and of a small shift in the lines of the solar spectrum, has given fresh impetus to the observation of solar eclipses and to the careful study of the individual factors which determine the position of a spectral line. Both these proofs have been recently furnished. The third proof required by Einstein, an advance of the perihelion of Mercury, has existed for many years as an outstanding problem.

The origin of meteors, and the part played by them in the scheme of things, are still largely enigmatical. The mystery of non-gaseous nebulæ—mostly spiral in form—is rapidly giving way before the measurement of their velocities, of the motion of material spirally outward along the arms, of the distribution of their intrinsic luminosity, of their location with respect to the galaxy, and mathematical researches concerning possible modes of development into their present form.

The announcement of the sudden apparition of a new star is followed, immediately, by a spirited campaign to record its life history, as shown in change of brightness and of the character of its spectrum. New theories of the cause of 'novæ' are constantly advanced. A great band of amateur astronomers adds, without interruption, to the mass of information concerning long-period variables, collecting the material which will solve the problem of intrinsic variation of a star's brightness. The general outline of the evolutionary history of the stars cannot long remain in doubt before the combined efforts of astronomers, physicists and chemists, and mathematicians.

To meet the need of being able to express the enormous distances of many of the stars and clusters in figures of convenient size, a new unit of measurement has been quite generally adopted. This unit is the distance at which a star's parallax (see PARALLAX) would be one second of arc. It is known as the *parsec*, and is the equivalent of 3.26 'light-years' or of 206,000 times the earth's distance from the sun. The further need has arisen of a means of distinguishing the intrinsic brightness of a star from the apparent brightness, which latter depends on the distance of the star.

Astronomical enterprises tend more and more to assume an international character. England commands both hemispheres through the activity of the sister establishments at Greenwich and the Cape. The organization centered at Harvard University has been extended from pole to pole by the foundation of a post at Arequipa.

An expedition was sent to South America a few years ago under the auspices of the Carnegie Institution to observe, with the meridian circle, a large number of the brighter southern stars. Large telescopes are being sent to South Africa by the universities of Yale and Michigan, the one to be used in the measurement of parallaxes of southern stars, the other in the measurement of southern double stars. The International Astronomical Union has been formed and, through its committees, is co-ordinating the efforts of astronomers, issuing reports of progress and suggesting needs for further research in all the various phases of astronomical activity.

Great strides have been made in popularizing astronomy in recent years with the construction of planetariums in Chicago, Philadelphia, Los Angeles, and New York.

Evidence of the existence of cosmic dust in space was reported by astronomers at the Yerkes Observatory in 1935. Early in that year a star with alternating periods of brightness and faintness was discovered. Studies of the planets show that several have atmospheres composed to a large extent of marsh gas. A total eclipse of the moon, observed from a balloon at a height of four miles on January 8, 1936, provided much new material for study. The smallest astral body ever discovered by astronomers, a planetoid only $1/3$ of a mile in diameter, came into view for a short time early in the same year. Investigations of meteor showers concluded recently led to the belief that eight billion meteors reach the atmosphere of the earth every year. Two new satellites of Jupiter (the 10th and 11th), were discovered by Professor Nicholson of the Mount Wilson Observatory in 1938. Both are exceedingly faint. See: ASTEROIDS; Cluster; Comet; Constellation; Double Stars; Earth; Eclipse; Equinox; Falling Stars; Fixed Stars; Geodynamics; Leo; Leonid Meteors; Moon; Multiple Stars; Nebula; Observatory; Orbit; Orion; Perihelion; Planet; Pleiades; Satellites; Saturn; Siderostat; Solar System; Libra; Magnetism; Mars; Mercury; Meridian, Celestial; Meteors; Milky Way; Spectroheliograph; Spectrum; Stars; Sun; Telescope; Variable Stars; Venus.

Consult: W. J. Leytun, *Pageant of the Stars* (1929. *National Geographic Magazine*, Nov. 1932, et al.; *The Splendour of the Heavens* (1923), an authoritative popular work, fully illustrated, written by members of the Royal Astronomical Society; Nordmann's *The Kingdom of the Heavens* (1923); Gregory's *Vault of Heaven* (2d ed., rewritten, 1923). *Books for Amateur Telescopists:* Webb's *Celestial Objects for Common Telescopes* (6th ed. in 2 vols. 1917); Kelvin McKready's *A Beginner's Star-Book*.

Children and beginners should read Miss Giberne's *Sun, Moon, and Stars* and *Radiant Suns;* Olcott's *The Book of the Stars for Young People*.

See: Asteroids, Cluster, Comet, Constellation, Double Stars, Earth, Eclipse, Equinox, Falling Stars, Fixed Stars, Geodynamics, Leo,

Leonid Meteors, Libra, Magnetism, Mars, Mercury, Meridian, Celestial, Meteors, Milky Way, Moon, Multiple Stars, Nebula, Observatory, Orbit, Orion, Perihelion, Planet, Pleiades, Satellites, Saturn, Siderostat, Solar System, Spectroheliograph, Spectrum, Stars, Sun, Telescope, Variable Stars, Venus.

Astrophel (Gr. 'star-lover'), the name under which Sir Philip Sidney addressed his sonnets to Stella ('Star') or Penelope Devereux.

Astrophysics. See ASTRONOMY.

Astruc, Jean (1684-1766), born March 19, 1684, at Sauve, in Languedoc, French biblical critic, author, and physician. He is known chiefly for his publication in 1753 of a penetrating criticism of the Pentateuch, in which he traced two main sources to the book of Genesis. The work was published anonymously, under the title *Conjectures sur les mémoires originaux dont il paraît que Moyse s'est servi pour composer le livre de la Genèse*. Later he acknowledged authorship. He died in Paris in 1766.

Astura, an ancient town of Italy, in the province of Rome. Here Cicero had a villa, where after the death of his daughter, he spent many unhappy days.

Asturias, former principality, Northern Spain, now forming the province of Oviedo (q.v.). See SPAIN.

Astyages, son of Cyaxares, was the last king of Media, reigning from 585 to 550 B.C. See CYRUS.

Astyanax, in Greek legend the son of Hector and Andromache.

Asunción, city, capital of Paraguay. It is built opposite a wide stretch of the Paraguay River, and is connected with Buenos Aires and Montevideo by regular steamers. The city has many modern improvements and its buildings include a National theatre and a national library with many rare books. In its earlier history it was the scene of oppression and bloodshed and the city still bears many marks of former terrible fighting; p. 104,820.

Asylums for the Insane, institutions for the care and treatment of those of unsound mind. The first asylum of which historical mention is made is one said to have been erected in the latter part of the 5th century, by the monks of Jerusalem. Spain seems to have taken the lead among European countries in providing for this class, but the treatment adopted there, as elsewhere, was brutal and cruel, with the result that many who were not originally beyond hope of recovery became permanently deranged. In the United States the first hospital treatment of the insane was undertaken in Philadelphia, in 1750, when a small hospital in which the patients were to be treated as 'sick persons' was established.

In all civilized countries today, insane persons are regarded as ill persons. The old asylums, with jail-like architecture within and without, have been supplanted by comfortable buildings, in which classification is possible. Restraint has largely been abandoned; the physiological problems of faulty nutrition have been studied; and if the cases cannot be cured, at least as much is made of the life of the patient as is possible in view of his mental and moral limitations. Separate provision is generally made for the criminal insane.

Asymptotes (Gr. 'not coinciding'), are lines which continually approach a curve, but which, though they and their curve were infinitely continued, would never meet.

Asyndeton (Gr. 'not bound together'), a figure of speech consisting in the omission of the usual connectives, as, *Veni, vidi, vici*.

Atabrine, trade name for a recently developed substitute for quinine.

Atacamite, the native hydrous oxychloride of copper, a not uncommon mineral in veins of copper ores, and usually a decomposition product.

Atahualpa (d. 1533), a son of Huayna Capac, the great Inca emperor of Peru. Consult Prescott's *Conquest of Peru*.

Atalanta, a heroine of Greek mythology, concerning whom tradition has two legends. The Arcadian Atalanta is said to have been the daughter of Iasus and Clymene. Her father, disappointed because of her sex, exposed her on the Parthenian (virgin) hill; she was suckled by a she-bear, and grew to maidenhood famous for her prowess in the chase. The Boeotian Atalanta was a daughter of Schoeneus. It seems certain that in both cases, Atalanta is only another form of Artemis. For the story of Atalanta consult Ovid's *Metamorphoses* (bk.x.).

Ataulf (d. 415?), king of the Visigoths, was assassinated at Barcelona.

Atavism, the inheritance from a more or less remote ancestor of any bodily or mental quality which has failed to show itself in intervening generations. See HEREDITY.

Ate, an ancient Greek divinity, daughter of Eris (Strife) according to Hesiod, and of Zeus according to Homer.

Atef Crown, a symbolic headdress worn by Egyptian deities.

Atellanæ Fabulæ, so called from Atella, a town of Campania, are a kind of unpolished popular drama which was performed in Roman theatres.

A tempo, or **A tempo prima,** in musical score, denotes a return to the original time after any acceleration or retardation.

Athabasca, formerly a district of the Dominion of Canada, now included in the provinces of Alberta and Saskatchewan.

Athabasca Lake, a large lake lying partly in Alberta and partly in Saskatchewan, Canada.

Athabasca River, or **La Biche,** 'Red Deer or Elk River,' Canada, rises in Alberta, e. of Mt. Hooker.

Athaliah, Old Testament character, married Jehoram, king of Judah. She usurped the throne, which she occupied for six years (841-836 B.C.). Handel and Mendelssohn have treated the subject musically, and Racine's drama *Athalie* is founded on the story.

Athamas, in classical mythology, son of Æolus and Enarete, married the goddess Nephele, but secretly loved Ino.

Athanaric (d. 381), king of the Visigoths, waged war against the Emperor Valens, but was defeated (369).

Athanasian Creed, one of the three so-called ecumenical creeds of Catholic Christendom. See CREEDS.

Athanasius, (c. 293-373), Bishop of Alexandria, father of Greek orthodoxy, and most eminent theologian of the 4th century. He was a deacon at the time of the outbreak of the Arian controversy. In 325 he was with Bishop Alexander at the Council of Nicæa, at which 318 bishops were assembled to deal with questions which had arisen over the teaching of Arius. While there he displayed something of those unusual powers of mind and determination which afterward established him as champion of the orthodox faith. When he returned to Alexandria he was elected bishop by acclamation. In defiance of the imperial command, he refused to admit Arius to communion. He was repeatedly banished returning again and again until in 367, he remained undisturbed till his death in **373**. The theological dispute was by this time virtually ended and the final verdict in favor of Nicene orthodoxy came at the council of Constantinople in 381. The writings of Athanasius include *Defense of the Nicene Creed* (351); *Apology to Constantius* (357); *History of the Arians for Monks* (358); *Letter to the Africans* (369); and many other letters and sermons.

Consult Robertson's *The Life and Theology of Athanasius,* in *Nicene and Post-Nicene Fathers;* Farrar's *Lives of the Fathers* (vol. 1); Taylor's *Athanasian Creed in the Twentieth Century.*

Athapascans, or **Athabascans (Tinné),** a linguistic family of North American Indians, notably the Navahos and Apaches (qq.v.). They can scarcely be said to have a distinctive culture. Consult Hodge's *Handbook of American Indians.*

Atheism, in its narrowest sense, a disbelief in or denial of the existence of God, in contradistinction to Agnosticism (q.v.), which merely disclaims knowledge of Him. The word has often been loosely employed as a term of opprobrium to designate any one taking a stand against current theological doctrine.

Athelstan (895-940), king of the English, was a son of Edward the Elder and grandson of Alfred the Great.

Athena, or **Athene,** also **Pallas Athene,** or **Pallas,** one of the greatest of the Greek divinities, was the daughter of Zeus (Jupiter) and Metis (Counsel). The legend is that she sprang, full-armed, from the head of Zeus, because, having beer warned that any child born of Metis would overthrow its father, he had enticed Metis to transform herself into a fly and had then swallowed her. This parentage indicates the character of the goddess —a combination of might and wisdom. Athena is represented in ancient art with a somewhat masculine figure, and a serious countenance. She is always clothed, or draped and generally wears the helmet, the ægis, and a shield with the Gorgon's head. Athena is also known under the title Hippia, and as Nike. The Romans identified the Etruscan goddess Minerva with Athena.

Athenæum, the temple of Pallas, at Athens, where poets and philosophers met to read their works.

Athenæum, The, an English weekly journal of literature, music, science, and the fine arts, merged on Feb. 19, 1921, with *The Nation.*

Athenæum Club, a London club, instituted in 1824 for the association of persons of scientific, literary, and artistic attainments, liberal patrons of learning, and those attaining distinction in public service.

Athenæus, (*c.* 230 A.D.), a native of Naucratis, in Egypt, a man of great learning, known today only by his *Deipnosophistæ*, or *Banquet of the Learned*.

Athenagoras, an Athenian philosopher and Christian apologist.

Athens, city, capital of Greece. The city and its surroundings occupy a group of low hills, in the centre of the plain, chief of which is the Acropolis, the site of ancient Athens, some 300 ft. above the town. Below, to the west, is the rocky hill of the Areopagus, while still farther west are the Hill of the Muses,

Greek antiquities. The central authority for all antiquarian research in Greece is the Greek Archæological Society. This body carries on excavations, publishes annual reports and monographs, and undertakes the preservation of ancient monuments. Commercial and manufacturing interests are few; p. 292,991.

Ancient Athens was undoubtedly situated on the Acropolis and probably extended below it to the south and west. Excavations have disclosed remains of a massive wall surrounding the Acropolis and also portions of a wall enclosing the town below. This lower

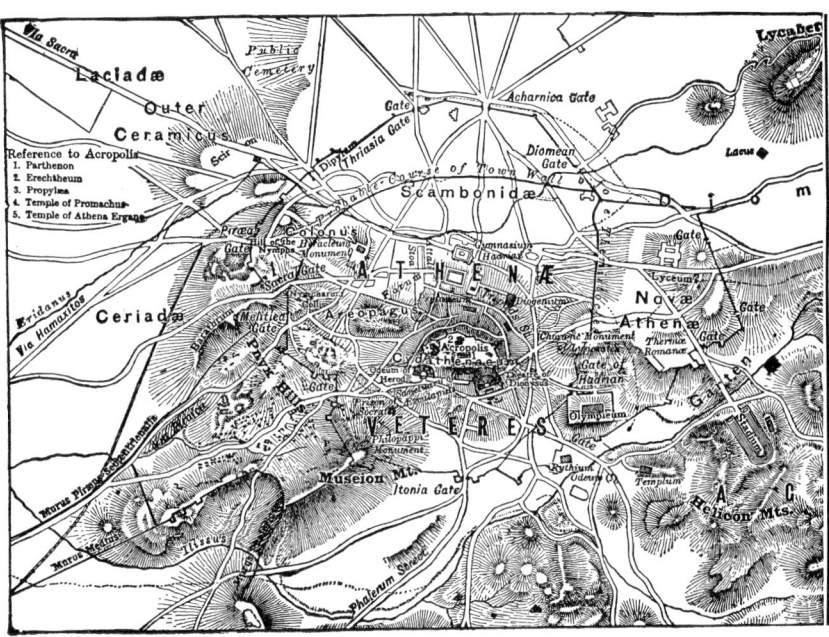

Plan of Ancient Athens.

the Pnyx, and the Hill of the Nymphs. Northeast of the Acropolis rises the abrupt slope of Mount Lycabettus.

Modern Athens—Known as the Neapolis, is an attractive city with fine buildings, good shops, and paved streets. Important buildings in modern Athens are the Parliament building; Academy of Science; University; Library; Polytechnic Institute; National Archæological Museum, containing a fine collection of antiquities; the Royal Palace, erected in 1834, with its beautiful gardens; the Zappeion, an exhibition building for Greek industries and manufactures. Of interest, also, are the schools of archæology, established by different countries for the study of

wall was pierced by nine gates, the most remarkable of which was the Dipylon, which formed the principal entrance to the city. Just without it was a great cemetery, in which many important excavations have been made. The dominating feature of ancient Athens was the Acropolis, the earliest seat of the Athenian kings, later devoted solely to the gods. The ancient temple and shrines were destroyed by the Persians in 480-79 B.C., but under Themistocles, Cimon, and Pericles, the Acropolis was reconstructed, and the ruins now standing are among the most magnificent in the world. Surmounting the Acropolis are ruins of the Parthenon (q.v.), the chief glory of ancient Athens. North of the Parthenon is the Erechtheum (q.v.), which was devoted to the worship of Erectheus and of Athena Polias, and before the east facade are the remains of a small round temple to Roma and Augustus. Fronting the northeastern corner is a relic of the great sacrificial altar of Athena. At the base of the Acropolis are the ruins of the Odeum of Herodes Atticus, an ancient theatre, which later served as a sort of outwork of defense for the Acropolis. Here, also, are the theater of Dionysus once the centre of Greek dramatic art, partly excavated in the solid rock of the hills; the Asklepeion, a temple and altar erected to Asklepios (Æsculapius); and the Stoa Eumenia, a colonnade leading from the Odeum to the theatre of Dionysus.

Southeast of the Acropolis was the Arch of Hadrian, an isolated gateway adorned by columns, leading to the temple of the Olympian Zeus. Near the Olympieum was the Stadium, the scene of the Panathenaic games. This imposing structure, originally erected in the 4th century B.C., has been recently restored, and here in 1896 and 1906 the Olympic Games (q.v.) were held. Below the Acropolis, to the west, is the rocky plateau known as the Areopagus or Hill of Mars. Here the ancient court of Athenian citizens held its sittings. On the slope of the Areopagus was a large inclosure containing wine vats and temples; in the valley between the Areopagus and the Pnyx was an ancient street which led from the Acropolis to the ancient Agora, or market place, where extensive excavations have been agreed upon by the Greek government and the American School of Classical Studies in Athens. North of the Acropolis and west of the market place stands the Theseum (or Hephæsteum), the best preserved ruin in Greece. It is an imposing temple of Pentelic marble in Doric style.

The site of Athens was probably occupied in the far distant past by the Pelasgians, who were expelled by immigrant Ionians, though the Athenians always proudly considered themselves autochthonous, or sprung from the soil. They regarded Cecrops as the founder of the town, but Theseus is generally held to have established the city in the year 1259 B.C. It was ruled by kings until the death of Kodros, when kings were replaced by archons, about 1058-752 B.C., at first elected for life, but later for ten, and eventually for but one year. In the 7th century the supremacy of the nobles, Eupatridæ, became greatly weakened, and in 594 the revision of the constitution by Solon (q.v.) gave a share of power to wealth apart from birth, opened the highest offices to all free citizens, and established choice of judges by lot. For further details of Solon's reforms and for the subsequent history of Athens up to the Peloponnesian War, see GREECE.

Athens, Greece.—Entrance to the Stadium with the Acropolis in the right background and the Hill of Philopappos on the left.

The Peloponnesian War (432-404), though it ended in terms humiliating to Athens and deprived her of much of her political power, did not greatly affect her cultural supremacy, which remained unchallenged for centuries. The Gothic raid of 258 A.D. and consequent refortification, the spoliation of the temples by Constantine (330), and the invasion of Alaric (396) are landmarks of decline, and the suppression of the schools of law and philosophy by Justinian (529) completed the transformation. Under the Frankish dukes Athens regained prosperity and culture, but since it lay off the pilgrim routes, was little known in the west. Under Turkish rule the Greek Church was at first reinstated, but the Parthenon and other buildings were soon converted to Moslem uses. The best preserved Turkish building is the 18th century mosque adjoining the governor's palace. The introduction of artillery and the Venetian raid of 1466 brought fresh fortifications and more destruction. The Propylæa was blown up in 1636, and the Parthenon in 1687. The Nike Temple (reconstructed in 1836) was demolished in 1686, and thenceforward destruction was rapid. At the Greek revolt of 1822 Athens was at once seized by the insurgents, but was captured by the Turks in 1827. In 1833 the Turkish troops evacuated the citadel, in 1835 Athens became the capital of Greece. It was occupied by the Germans, 1941; liberated by the British, 1944. Consult Stuart and Revett's *Antiquities of Athens* (revised ed., 4 vols.); Gardener's *Ancient Athens*; Butler's *The Story of Athens;* Tucker's *Life in Ancient Athens.*

Athens, city, Georgia. It is the seat of the University of Georgia; the State College of Agriculture, a State normal school for girls, and the Lucy Cobb Boarding School. Of special interest is the 'tree that owns itself,' a tree to which Col. William H. Jackson made a deed of several sq. ft. of land; p. 20,650.

Atheroma, a soft, yellow, cheesy material replacing normal tissues in the walls of arteries, weakening them.

Atherton, Gertrude Franklin (*née* Horn) (1857-1947), American novelist, born in San Francisco. Her works include: *The Conqueror* (1902); *Tower of Ivory* (1910); *Julia France and Her Times* (1912); *Perch of the Devil* (1914); *California—an Intimate History* (1914); *Black Oxen* (1923); *The Sophisticates* (1931); *The Adventures of a Novelist* (1932); *The House of Lee,* 1940.

Atherton Resolutions. See **Gag Rules.**

Athletics, a term used in a broad sense to cover all games or sports depending in whole or in part upon feats of physical strength or skill. It is frequently applied to field sports as distinguished from indoor gymnastics.

Athletic sports were practised in various forms by the ancient Egyptians, and the ancient Greeks. In Great Britain they have been cultivated since Celtic times, different varieties of sports being in favor at different periods. The Amateur Athletic Union, which now controls amateur athletes throughout the country, was organized in 1888.

In 1894 delegates in Paris instituted the first modern Olympic games, international in scope and to be held quadrennially beginning 1896.

There are six national organizations regulating amateur athletics in the United States: Amateur Athletic Union of the United States; American Olympic Association; Intercollegiate Association of Amateur Athletes of America; National Amateur Athletic Federation; National Collegiate Athletic Association; and National Federation of State High School Athletic Associations. Groups or individuals engaged in amateur athletics in any form are affiliated in some way with one or more of these six organizations. The best known is the A.A.U. which conducts annual national championships in all amateur sports, 20 or more in number, and governs these sports as to amateur status, licenses for entry in competition, records, and international relations. The emphasis upon record-breaking in all forms of athletics is unfortunate, if the good of the many, or even of the individual is to be considered.

Football is by far the most popular of college and school athletics. Its prominence in shaping athletics policies is due partly to the financial profit accruing from the football season. Fabulous gate receipts have caused schools and colleges to initiate huge programs in other sports—including extensive building projects, and, in some cases, even the laying out of golf courses. The football coach has come to be an extremely important person, often better known than the presidents of the schools they serve. The school has resorted to newspaper publicity in athletics as a means of advertising the institution. The various phases of commercialism in school athletics is presented in *American College Athletics* (1929), Carnegie Foundation for Improvement of Teaching, Bulletin No. 23. See **Football.** Consult Carnegie Foundation for the Advancement of Teaching Bulletin 24, *The Literature of American School and Col-*

lege Athletics, by Ryan (1929); Leonard's *Guide to the History of Physical Education.*

Athletics, Latest Records. The 1948 Olympic Games were held in Wembley, England, July 29-Aug. 14. The first 10 official team point scores by nations were: United States, 662; Sweden, 353; France, 230½; Hungary, 201½; Italy, 183; Great Britain, 170; Finland, 158; Switzerland, 151½; Denmark, 143; The Netherlands, 119. In the track and field events (men) the following records were made: 800-meter run, 1 m. 49.2 s., by Mal Whitfield, U. S.; 5,000-meter run, 14 m. 17.6 s., by Gaston Reiff, Belgium; 10,000-meter run, 29 m. 59.6 s., by Emil Zatopek, Czechoslovakia; 10,000-meter walk, 45 m. 13.2 s., by J. F. Mikaelsson, Sweden; 110-meter hurdles, 13.9 s., by William Porter, U. S.; 400-meter hurdles, 51.1 s., by Roy Cochran, U. S.; discus, 52.78 m. (173 ft. 2 in.), by Adolfo Consolini, Italy; 16-lb. shot, 17.12 m. (56 ft. 2 in.), by Wilbur Thompson, U. S.; pentathlon, 16 pts., by W. O. G. Grut, Sweden. In the track and field events (women), the following records were made: 200-meter run, 24.4 s., by F. Blankers-Koen, Holland; 80-meter hurdles, 11.2 s., by F. Blankers-Koen, Holland; high jump, 1.68 m. (5 ft. 6⅛ in.), by Alice Coachman, U. S.; broad jump, 18 ft. 8¼ in., by V. O. Gyarmati, Hungary; javelin, 45.57 m. (149 ft. 6 in.), by H. Baume, Austria. In the swimming events (men), the following records were made: 100-meter free style, 57.3 s., by Wally Ris, U. S.; 400-meter free style, 4 m. 41 s., by William Smith, U. S.; 200-meter breast stroke, 2 m. 39.3 s., by Joseph Verdeur, U. S. In the swimming events (women), the following records were made: 400-meter free style, 5 m. 17.8 s., by Ann Curtis, U. S.; 100-meter back stroke, 1 m. 14.4 s., by Karen M. Harup, Denmark; 200-meter breast stroke, 2 m. 57.2 s., by Nel Van Vliet, Holland.

The next Olympic Games are scheduled for Helsinki, Finland, in 1952, and for Melbourne, Australia, in 1956. See also OLYMPIC GAMES.

Athor, Aythor, Hether, or **Hathor,** an Egyptian goddess, daughter of Ra, in whom the Greeks recognized their Aphrodite. The cow was her symbol.

Athos, a mountain 6670 ft. high on the Acte peninsula, Chalcidice, Macedonia, Greece. It has been occupied since the 9th century A.D. by monastic communities of the Greek Rule of St. Basil and is called the "Holy Mountain." As Mount Athos, it was declared an autonomous republic in 1927. Area, 111 sq. m.; p. 4,858.

Athrepsia, the wasting of infants due to malnutrition. Treatment consists in correcting faults in the diet. See also DIET AND DIETETICS.

Athyroidism, deficiency of the secretion of the thyroid gland.

Atitlan, Lake, department of Solola, Guatemala, 4,700 ft. above the sea, 64 m. in circumference, of great depth, and with no visible outlet.

Atjeh, Atchin, or **Achin,** residency of the Netherlands Indies, in Northern Sumatra, with an area of about 21,380 sq. m.; p. 1,003,062.

The inhabitants are engaged in agriculture, silk manufacture, fishing, and the fashioning of weapons. In 1873, the Dutch sent an expedition against Atjeh, and, after a campaign of about forty years, costly in both lives and money, Atjeh was placed under the authority of a military commandant.

Atka, or **Atcha,** an island of the Andreanov group in the chain of Aleutian Islands (q.v.), in long. 195° w. It contains a good harbor. Area, about 500 sq.m.; p. 89.

Atka Fish, or **Atka Mackerel,** a species of fish belonging to the rock-trout family (Hexagrammidæ), extremely numerous in the kelp beds around the Aleutian Islands, in the North Pacific.

Atkins, Tommy, originally a supposititious name used in enlistment forms issued by the British War Office, whence it came to be applied generally to the British regular soldier.

Atlanta, city, capital of Georgia, county seat of Fulton co., is situated 7 m. s.e. of the Chattahoochee River, at an altitude of 1,050 ft. In the Civil War it was a base of supplies for the Confederate armies and was captured by General Sherman Sept. 7, 1864. It is the commercial centre of the Southeastern States; p. 326,962.

Atlantic, Battle of the, 1941-43; the Axis powers' effort to destroy Allied supply lanes in the Atlantic. By 1943 United Nations had gained supremacy in the Atlantic.

Atlantic Cable. The idea of uniting Europe and America by telegraphic communication first assumed definite form in 1845, when Messrs. John and Jacob Brett registered a company entitled 'General Oceanic Company.' After a period of eleven years, these gentlemen joined a syndicate, of which Cyrus Field (q.v.) was the leading spirit, for the establishment of telegraphic communication between Ireland and Newfoundland. Trinity Bay, Newfoundland, was the American terminus for the cable and Valentia Bay, Ireland, was the British, and construction was begun in 1857. On Aug. 17, 1858, the first message was cabled across the Atlantic. Consult Bright's *Submarine Telegraphs*.

Atlantic Charter, The.

THE JOINT DECLARATION
(Issued by the White House, August 14, 1941.)

The President of the United States of America and the Prime Minister, Mr. Churchill, representing His Majesty's Government in the United Kingdom, being met together, deem it right to make known certain common principles in the national policies of their respective countries on which they base their hopes for a better future for the world.

First: Their countries seek no aggrandizement, territorial or other;

Second: They desire to see no territorial changes that do not accord with the freely expressed wishes of the peoples concerned;

Third: They respect the right of all peoples to choose the form of government under which they will live; and they wish to see sovereign rights and self-government restored to those who have been deprived of them;

Fourth: They will endeavor, with due respect for their existing obligations, to further the enjoyment by all states, great or small, victor or vanquished, of access, on equal terms, to the trade and to the raw materials of the world which are needed for their economic prosperity;

Fifth: They desire to bring about the fullest collaboration between all nations in the economic field, with the object of securing for all improved labor standards, economic adjustment and social security;

Sixth: After the final destruction of the Nazi tyranny, they hope to see established a peace which will afford to all nations the means of dwelling in safety within their own boundaries, and which will afford assurance that all the men in all the lands may live in freedom from fear and want;

Seventh: Such a peace should enable all men to traverse the high seas and oceans without hindrance;

Eighth: They believe that all of the nations of the world, for realistic as well as spiritual reasons, must come to the abandonment of the use of force. Since no future peace can be maintained if land, sea or air armaments continue to be employed by nations which threaten, or may threaten, aggression outside of their frontiers, they believe, pending the establishment of a wider and permanent system of general security, that the disarmament of such nations is essential. They will likewise aid and encourage all other practicable measures which will lighten for peace-loving peoples the crushing burden of armaments.

FRANKLIN D. ROOSEVELT
WINSTON S. CHURCHILL

Atlantic City, city and popular Atlantic coast resort, Atlantic co., New Jersey, 60 m. s.e. of Philadelphia, is one of the most attractive winter and summer resorts in the United States; p. 64,094.

Atlantic Fisheries Arbitration, The, before the Permanent Court at The Hague in 1910, was instituted for the purpose of settling the rights of U. S. fishermen to fish in the waters of n.e. Canada. The issues involved grew largely out of the true interpretation of Article 1. of the Treaty of 1818.

Atlantic Ocean, a large body of water stretching from the Arctic Ocean in the n. to the Antarctic Ocean in the s., and lying between the shores of Europe and Africa on the e. and those of North and South America on the west. The Atlantic is about 9,000 m. long from n. to s., and its breadth varies from 4,500 m., between Florida and the Saharan coast, to 1,600 m. between Brazil and the African coast. Its area is estimated at from 23,000,000 to 30,000,000 sq. m. Directly or indirectly it receives about one-half the entire rainfall of the globe. The floor of the Atlantic is a gently undulating plain (average depth, 2,200 fathoms), with a narrow ridge, at less than 1,700 fathoms, along the centre, roughly parallel to the Europeo-African coasts, the volcanic peaks of the Azores representing its greatest elevation. The deepest sounding thus far, is that of the Nares deep (70 m. n. from Porto Rico), 4,561 fathoms, or nearly 5¼ m. There are relatively few oceanic islands, but numerous continental islands, such as the British Isles, Newfoundland, the West Indies, the Falklands, and others.

The surface temperature over the greater part of the North Atlantic average 40° F., increasing to 50° F. near the shores of Europe. For the characteristics of the deposits on the Atlantic floor, see OCEANS; for the currents, see OCEAN CURRENTS and GULF STREAM; and for the winds, TRADE WINDS.

Since the 16th century the Atlantic has been the chief commercial highway of the world. Consult works cited under OCEAN; Hull's *Monograph on the Sub-Oceanic Physiography of the North Atlantic Ocean* (1912).

Atlantis, according to ancient tradition a great island w. of the Strait of Gibraltar, opposite Mt. Atlas, the inhabitants of which were very prosperous and powerful. As a result of recent palæontological research, geologists have concluded that in the Tertiary epoch such an island really existed. Consult Archer-Hind's and Th. H. Martin's editions of the *Timæus of Plato;* Steiner's *Submerged Continents of Atlantis and Lemuria*. Compare ISLES OF THE BLEST.

Atlantosaurus, or **Titanosaurus,** a member of the order Dinosauria, the largest land animal which is known to have at any time inhabited the globe. Consult Marsh's *Dinosaurs of North America*.

Atlas, one of the Titans in Greek legend,

Atlas   322   **Atom**

son of Iapetus and Clymene; said to have been the leader of the Titans in the war against the gods, and to have been condemned, as a punishment, to the task of bearing the heavens on his shoulders.

Atlas (pl. Atlantes), in architecture, a term applied to statues of men, analogous to caryatides (q.v.), set in the place of columns to bear the entablature, etc.

Atlas, a collection of maps, first used in this sense by Mercator, evidently from the common decorative use of Atlas bearing the heavens as a symbol of earth.

Atlas, in anatomy, the highest vertebra of the spinal column, which supports the skull. See SPINAL COLUMN.

Atlas Mountains, an extensive system of folded mountains in North Africa, stretching from the shores of the Atlantic Ocean, to which it has given its name, through Morocco, Algeria, and Tunis, in a general s.w. to n.e. direction, to the shores of the Gulf of Tunis. See ALGERIA; MOROCCO.

Atlas Powder, an explosive of the dynamite class, consisting mainly of nitroglycerine absorbed in wood fibre, with additions of sodium nitrate and magnesium carbonate.

Atlin, Lake, Canada, with an area of 343 sq.m., of which 331 are in British Columbia and 12 in the Yukon Territory.

Atmolysis is the method of separating gases of different densities by means of porous tubes or other septa. By diffusion the gases pass through the porous septum at rates inversely proportional to the square roots of their densities. See FILTER.

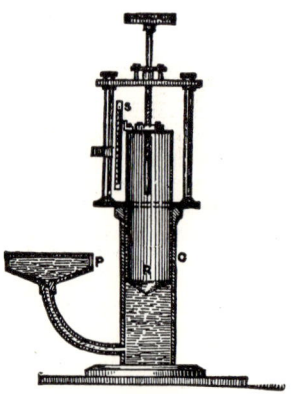

Von Lamont's Atmometer

Atmometer, an instrument for the determination of the amount of water passing into the air by evaporation.

Atmosphere (Greek, 'sphere of vapor'), a gaseous envelope surrounding a body in space. The atmospheres of the several planets differ greatly in quality. Those of Jupiter, Saturn, Uranus, and Neptune appear to be dense and cloud-laden; that of Mars, although much less dense than terrestrial air, almost certainly includes a considerable ingredient of water-vapor. Mercury is believed to be still more thinly covered; and refractive phenomena on Venus indicate her possession of an atmosphere fully comparable with our own. The atmosphere of the earth may extend in a highly rarified state to a height of 200 m., and meteors give rise to conspicuous light at elevations up to 120 m. Above 45 m., however, the effects of refraction cease to be perceptible. With each ascent of $3\frac{1}{2}$ m. the density of the air is halved. For each 300 ft. of ascent the temperature falls about 1° F. (See GASES AND VAPORS).

Atmospheric air is a mechanical mixture of 79.04 volumes of nitrogen with 20.93 of oxygen and 1 of argon; a small percentage (0.03) of carbon dioxide is also present, besides traces of free hydrogen and helium (probably supplied by mineral springs), of neon, krypton, and xenon. The ceaseless convection currents due to the sun's heat keep the atmosphere mixed, and of uniform composition. It also contains a variable but all-important proportion of water-vapor. It is through the thermal opacity of this part of its atmosphere that the earth is rendered habitable, the heat received from the sun being, through its intervention, stored, distributed, and hindered from departing uselessly back into space. Water-vapor, too, is the mainspring of atmospheric circulation and the amount suspended over a given area largely determines the type of prevalent weather. (See METEOROLOGY).

The total weight of the atmosphere, as computed by Sir John Herschel, amounts to $11\frac{2}{3}$ trillion tons, or $\frac{1}{1,200,000}$ that of the solid globe itself. See CLIMATE; TEMPERATURE.

Atoll. See **Coral.**

Atom—from the Greek, meaning indivisible—the name applied to the ultimate portions of matter which are supposed to be the smallest quantities which can enter into chemical combination. The notion of a granular structure of matter is a very old one and seems to have been first suggested by the Greek, Democritus, 400 B.C., who explained all matter as being made up of minute granules, alike in their sizes and qualities.

The modern investigation of the atom begins with the work of Dalton, the English chemist, about the end of the 18th century. According to Dalton, certain substances are found in nature which are called elements, or elementary substances—as gold, iodine, bismuth, aluminum, oxygen—which cannot be broken up into other substances. The smallest amounts of these substances which can enter into chemical combination are the atoms. Chemical combinations are brought about by the attractions between the atoms. In such combinations a definitely fixed amount of any one element always combines with a fixed amount of some other substance.

The so-called 'atomic weight' of any substance is figured as the relative weight of an atom of the substance when compared to some element as a standard, as for instance in a table of atomic weights reckoned with hydrogen as standard. (See ATOMIC THEORY). In what is said above concerning the atomic weights of substances, it is assumed that the atoms are all just alike. But it has been found that there are variations in atomic weight among especially the heavier elements but having the same chemical properties. The elements with these variations are known as isotopes. (See ISOTOPES). The atomic weight of such an element is, therefore, approximately the average weight of all the several isotopes.

From the time of Democritus efforts were made to determine the real nature of the atom, its real 'structure.' During the last century, it was recognized that the simple, solid atom assumed by Democritus and his immediate successors could not be acceptable.

With the discovery of radio-activity by the Curies, there came an epochal change in the theory of the nature of the atom. Observation showed that radium and other radioactive substances constantly emitted streams of particles, which were found to be electric charges. It also showed that radium was constantly at a higher temperature than the surrounding medium. Later experiments indicated that uranium gave off successive emissions, or radiations, and at the end turned into lead, with helium, a gas, as one of the by-products of this radioactive transformation, this transmutation of the elements (see RADIO-ACTIVITY). The dream of the alchemist was come true, one metal was transmuted into another, but the noble into the base. From that day to the present, there have followed in rapid succession a series of theories about the structure of this small particle of matter, each with elements of truth, but each discarded or changed to fit newly discovered observations. Certainly the atom can no longer be regarded as simple, but must be thought of as complex, as having a structure, and therefore, as being divisible. It cannot now be looked upon as the smallest portion of matter that can exist, for the nucleus, which contains practically all the mass of the atom, must be considered as such.

There have been two ways of picturing atomic structure: Bohr and Rutherford see electrons as moving around a nucleus in a prescribed orbit; A. H. Compton believes electrons are distributed so as to be found in certain places at certain times. Prof. Millikan has calculated that 1 hydrogen atom is equivalent to 1,845 electrons. Little is known of the structure of the nucleus; Rutherford and Chadwick have partially broken apart nuclei of some lighter elements by using high speed alpha particles; Aston has, with the spectrograph, fairly accurately measured and studied the nuclei of some elements. The neutron (unchanged particle) has been isolated, and physicists have been searching for an X-particle pre-named neutrino (little neutron). In 1937 Dr. Carl David Anderson at the Calif. Inst. of Technology declared flatly for its existence, and Dr. Street of Harvard in 1000 photographs of cosmic ray activity appears to have accumulated sufficient data to prove Anderson's contention. Dr. Otto Hahn, in Berlin, 1939, bombarding a bit of uranium, accidently exploded an atom, releasing two million volts of low-amperage electricity; he obtained ekarhenium, a heavy element, which he was seeking, and also, as a surprise, atoms of barium and krypton.

Since 1905, when Einstein developed the equivalence of mass and energy, matter has been considered as highly concentrated energy, which can be transformed into energy and back into matter.

Consult Tolansky, Samuel, *Introduction to Atomic Physics* (3rd ed., 1949); Gaynor, Frank, ed., *Pocket Encyclopedia of Atomic Energy* (1950); Humphreys, R. F., and Beringer, R., *First Principles of Atomic Physics* (1950).

Atomic Bomb, a bomb capable of a large scale atomic explosion whose energy depends on smashing the atom; secretly developed at a cost of over $2,000,000,000 by European and American scientists working in U. S. 1941-1945. It was first used in combat on Aug. 6, 1945, when one was dropped from the B-29 Superfortress, *Enola Gay*, piloted by Col. Paul Tibbets, on the Jap army base city of Hiroshima (pop. 344,000) on the island of Shikoku, destroying 4.1 sq. mi., 60% of the city; 82,000 persons were dead or missing. The second and only other atomic bomb used was dropped on Nagasaki, Kyushu, Japan, on Aug. 9, 1945. An improved model, it destroyed 30% of its target city. The existence of, and past work on the bomb was disclosed to the world by Pres. Truman sixteen hours after the first was used. In 1940 Prof. Nier of U. of Minn. isolated a minute quantity of a rare form of uranium, U-235, and this was put under the cyclotron, or atom smasher, at Columbia U. A Jewish refugee from Ger., Dr. Lise Meitner, discovered that U-235 is present in small quantities in uranium. In 1941 scientists perfected a process for manufacturing the atomic explosive from U-235, and it was discovered in 1942 that Ger. scientists were also working on an atomic bomb. Three huge plants were built: at Oak Ridge, Tenn., at Pasco, Wash., at Los Alamos, N. M. Many famed scientists headed by Dr. Vannevar Bush, head of the Office of Scientific Research and Development, worked on the project which was known to all but a select few as the 'Manhattan Project.' Functioning of the atomic bomb is based on atomic chain reaction, initiated by division of an atom of U-235 set off by bombardment of this atom by neutrons obtained from a mixture of radium and beryllium. Split nucleus of U-235 atom formed barium and krypton atoms which disseminated gamma and beta radiation and finally spread neutrons. These neutrons, slowed by graphite, ignited other uranium nuclei and in a fraction of a second penetrated a mass of uranium, containing trillions of atoms, resulting in a tremendous explosion. One bomb had more power than 20,000 tons of **TNT**, and could cause the same destruction as 2,000 B-29's loaded with fragmentation bombs. Details of the size, weight, methods of manufacture and other secrets relating to the atomic bomb were not disclosed. Political and military leaders of the U. S., Gr. Br. and Can., the three nations possessing the secrets of the bomb, hesitated to use it until the Japanese government ignored their surrender demand, in the form of the Potsdam Declaration, in July 1945. Its use undoubtedly shortened the war and is believed by many to have caused Russ. to declare war on Jap. on Aug. 8, 1945, rather than wait until Aug. 15, a date purportedly agreed on by Roosevelt, Stalin and Churchill at the Yalta Conference in Feb. 1945. See **Atom; Atomic Energy.**

Atomic Energy, power released continually and spontaneously by certain elements, the heavy metals. This process, known as radioactivity, was discovered by Henri Becquerel in 1896. Albert Einstein propounded the theory that energy is equal to mass multiplied by the square of the velocity of light (186,000 miles per second), expressed by formula as $E=mc^2$. In 1934 Jean-Frederic and Irene Joliot-Curie made aluminum, boron and magnesium artificially radioactive. Artificial radioactivity is the essence of the functioning of the atomic bomb. Leading scientists have predicted that the harnessing of atomic energy will revolutionize civilization. In a report issued by the U. S. War Department in August, 1945, prepared by Prof. H. D. Smyth, chairman of the physics department at Princeton University, he wrote, "Should a scheme be devised for converting to energy even as much as a few per cent of the matter of some common material, civilization would have a means to commit suicide at will." Niels Bohr, a Danish scientist whose research in Denmark and at Princeton University had aided greatly in the creation of the new atomic age wrote, "Against the new destructive powers no defense may be possible, and the issues center on worldwide cooperation to prevent any use of the new source of energy which does not serve mankind as a whole."

Atomic Energy Commission, U. S. An independent civilian administrative agency of the Federal Government established by the Atomic Energy Act (McMahon Bill) of 1946 and charged with the formulation and operation of the national atomic energy program.

On January 1, 1947, the Commission took over from the Army's Manhattan District the research, development and production facilities, on which $2,000,000,000 had been spent during World War II in connection with the atomic bomb project. Subsequent appropriations for the atomic energy program through fiscal year 1951 total about $2,500,000,000.

The major AEC facilities are:

1. Hanford Works, Richland, Washington, plutonium production.

2. K-25 Plant, Oak Ridge, Tennessee, uranium 235 production.

3. Los Alamos Scientific Laboratory, New Mexico, weapons research and development.

4. Argonne National Laboratory, DuPage County, Illinois, reactor development.

5. Oak Ridge National Laboratory, Tennessee, chemical engineering.
6. Brookhaven National Laboratory, Long Island, physical science and biology.
7. Savannah River Plant, Aiken, South Carolina, production of materials, for either weapons or fuel.
8. Radiation Laboratory, Berkeley, California, physical and biological research using high energy accelerators.
9. Reactor Test Station, Arco, Idaho.
10. Weapons Proving Ground, Eniwetok.

The production of fissionable materials (U-235 and plutonium) for weapons and potential fuel for power is the central activity of the atomic energy program. This involves procurement of uranium ores and preparation of feed materials for the two main production lines. Uranium hexafluoride is the feed material for the gaseous diffusion plant at Oak Ridge in which fissionable uranium 235 is separated from the heavier, non-fissionable uranium 238. The gas is pumped through barriers, each containing billions of small, molecule sized holes. The lighter molecules, containing U-235, pass through the barrier more rapidly than the heavier U-238 molecules resulting in a slight degree of enrichment. By repeating the process hundreds of times almost any desired degree of enrichment may be obtained.

Plutonium is produced in enormous nuclear reactors at Hanford, Washington. A Hanford reactor consists essentially of a huge cube built of graphite bricks of exceptional purity, containing a lattice of holes into which natural uranium metal slugs are placed. Natural uranium contains one atom of U-235 to 140 atoms of U-238. Neutrons released in the fission of U-235 are captured by U-238, which through a process of radioactive decay becomes plutonium. The plutonium is finally separated from the unused uranium and an accumulation of fission products by complicated chemical processes.

Weapons research and development is centered at Los Alamos, and production of weapons is administered by the Sandia Laboratory near Albuquerque, New Mexico. The first post-war tests of new atomic weapons were conducted at Bikini Island in the South Pacific, while subsequent tests have been held at the proving ground at Eniwetok Atoll in the Marshall Islands.

It is expected that utilization of atomic energy for ship and aircraft propulsion and stationary power plants will come about as a result of the Commission's reactor development program. Reactor research is conducted at the Argonne National Laboratory, Chicago, and the Knolls Atomic Power Laboratory, Schenectady. Three experimental reactors are located at a reactor test station near Arco, Idaho. These include: an Experimental Breeder Reactor, to test the possibility of producing more fissionable material than is burned, a Materials Testing Reactor, having a very high neutron flux to pre-test materials believed suitable for reactor construction, and a Ship Thermal Reactor, a land-based prototype reactor to propel submarines. Many other types of reactors are in various stages of design. In addition to the plutonium production reactors at Hanford, research reactors are in operation at Argonne, Oak Ridge, Brookhaven, and Los Alamos. The first privately owned and operated reactor will be built at North Carolina State College.

In connection with its primary programs the Commission conducts a widespread research program in physical, biological and medical sciences. Research work is done both in the national laboratories and by contract with universities, clinics, and industrial laboratories throughout the country. Special training and fellowship programs have also been established.

World-wide distribution of radioactive and stable isotopes for research was started in 1946. During the first four years more than 15,000 shipments of these valuable research tools had been made.

In January 1950, President Truman directed the Commission to continue work on new weapon developments including the so-called hydrogen or H-bomb, which will utilize a fusion process involving the light elements instead of the fission or splitting process used in the A-bomb. In connection with this program a new 250,000-acre Savannah River Plant in South Carolina is being built.

The Commission consists of five members appointed by the President with consent of the Senate for five-year terms. The General Manager is appointed by the Commission.

Atomic Heat. Dulong and Petit of Paris were the first to show (1819) that an approximate relation exists between the specific heat and the atomic weight of elements—*viz.*, that the specific heat is inversely proportional to the atomic weight; the higher the specific heat, the lower the atomic weight. Expressed in another way, the same quantity of heat is required to raise an atom of mercury, an atom of iron, an atom of sulphur, and an atom of lithium, or an atom of any solid element, through 1° C.

Atomicity, or **Valency,** denotes the number of atoms of hydrogen which an element will unite with or displace: it is practically the atomic weight divided by the equivalent. All those elements which combine with hydrogen, atom for atom, are termed *monads*, the valency being 1. Others are dyads, triads, etc.

Atomic Theory. The atomic theory is the foundation on which modern chemical science is built. John Dalton, in the first decade of the 19th century, revived the idea of atoms, which was first taught by the ancient Greek philosopher Democritus, 400 B.C.

While the structure of the atom is still a matter of discussion, atomic weights (See ATOM) as related to one another are known. The atom of hydrogen, being the lightest, was formerly taken as the standard, but oxygen as 16 is now eccepted. Hydrogen thus has an atomic weight of 1.0080, and uranium is 238.07. When a chemical change takes place, it is due to the union or separation of atoms, and it necessarily follows from the indivisibility of the atoms that this union or separation must occur in definite or fixed proportions by weight—*i.e.* the weights of the atoms themselves. For example, if the atoms of nitrogen and oxygen weigh respectively 14 and 16 times as heavy as a hydrogen atom, then, according to the theory, they can only unite 1 to 1, 2 to 1, 3 to 1, 3 to 2, etc.; and the proportion of nitrogen to oxygen in the compound formed will be that of 14 parts by weight of nitrogen to 16 of oxygen, 14 x 2 to 16, 14 x 3 to 16, 14 to 16 x 2, and so on. And this we know by experiment to be the case.

Though Dalton was unable to understand and explain all his facts, he laid down the following laws of definite (or constant) and multiple proportions:—(1) The same compound always contains the same elements, combined in the same proportion by weight; or, in every chemical compound, however produced, the proportion by weight of the elements is always the same. (2) When two elements unite with each other in more than one proportion by weight, the quantity of one of these being constant, the weights of the others vary in simple ratio. Further advances were made by the investigations of Gay-Lussac and Avogadro.

It is impossible to describe here how atomic weights are determined, or all that the atomic theory leads to, but one result is that we can employ symbols, formulæ, and equations. A *symbol* of an element indicates (1) its name, (2) one atom of the element, (3) the weight of the element compared with hydrogen or its atomic weight. A *formula* indicates (1) the name of the substance, (2) the number of atoms in the molecule, (3) the composition of the molecule (*i.e.* the elements which by combination produce it), and (4) the weight of the molecule (molecular weight) compared with the atom of hydrogen. *Equations* describe or express chemical change. They indicate graphically the nature of the combinations or decompositions which take place, the relative weights of the substances involved, and, in the case of gases, their volumes.

A table of the atomic weights of the chemical elements, compiled by the International Committee of Atomic Weights, will be found in the article on ELEMENTS. Certain important relations which atomic weights bear to one another, pointed out by Mendeleyeff, are indicated in the article PERIODIC LAW. See also ATOM; ATOMIC BOMB; ATOMIC ENERGY; ATOMIC HEAT; CHEMISTRY. Consult bibliography at end of ATOM article.

Atom Smashers. Machines used in atomic research to disintegrate the nucleus of the atom. They are generally of three types: (1) an early type was to use natural radioactive elements; but their power was limited to the natural energy obtained; (2) an electrostatic machine whereby power is built up on a large metal ball; and (3) the cyclotron. (See also CYCLOTRON).

Atonement, the name given in (English) Christian theology to the work of Jesus Christ as the Saviour of sinners. The word occurs but once in the King James version of the New Testament, and not at all in the Revised Version, in which the more accurate rendering of the Greek—'reconciliation'—is employed. The term is common, however, in the sacrificial language of the Old Testament law, in the sense of propitiation or expiation, and it is in this latter sense that it has been applied to the work of Christ, which is looked upon as an expiatory offering, 'propitiating an offended deity and reconciling him with man.' Some authorities regard atonement (removal of guilt) as one important element in primitive conceptions of sacrifice; while others point out that the sin offering or atoning sacrifice, as such, is admittedly a late development. Men offered sacrifices before they realized the need of propitiating the divine anger and afterward employed the rite for a new exigency.

Many modern writers deny any form of satisfaction or expiation but explain the doctrine of atonement as a sort of moral influence exerted upon man; some writers teaching that Christ suffered with us through sympathy so as to give Him the power of quickening and moulding men by love and example; others that His death and suffering were designed to illustrate the beauty of self-sacrifice; and still others, notably M'Leod Campbell, that Christ so identified Himself with us as sinners that He offered to God a perfect confession and adequate repentance for our sins and thus met all the demands of the law.

Atonement, Day of, a Jewish fast day, on which the high priest, clad in robes of white, entered the holy of holies with the sacrificial blood which he offered as an expiation for the sins of himself and his people. It is the tenth day of the seventh month (Tishri), and is known in the Talmud as 'the great day.' It is looked upon generally as the most sacred day of the Jewish year.

Atony, a medical term, indicating a want of tone; weakness; debility.

Atossa, queen of Persia, was daughter of Cyrus the Great, and wife successively of her brother Cambyses, Smerdis the usurper, and Darius Hystaspis, to whom she bore Xerxes and three other sons.

Atrak, or **Atrek,** river of Persia, rising in Khorassan. It flows n.w. and then w. and enters the Caspian Sea at Hassan Kuli Bay. Its total length is about 350 m.

Atrato, river in Colombia, South America, rising on the west flank of the Western Cordillera and flowing n. to the Gulf of Darien. It is about 400 m. long, drains a basin of 11,400 sq.m., and is navigable for 250 m.

Atrebates, an ancient Celtic people of Gallia Belgica, having as their capital *Nemetacum* or *Nemetocenna* (now Arras). A branch was also settled in England, in what is now Berkshire, their chief town being *Calleva* or *Calleva Atrebatum* (i.e. Silchester).

Atreus, in Greek legend, the son of Pelops and Hippodamia, and grandson of Tantalus. The misfortunes of the house of Atreus supply the theme for many Greek tragedies, notably the *Agamemnon, the Choephoræ* and *Eumenides* of Æschylus, the Electra of Sophocles, and the *Electra* and *Orestes* of Euripides.

Atri, a town in Italy. It has a fine Gothic cathedral. See Bulfinch's *Age of Fable;* p. 12,735.

Atriplex, a genus of the Chenopodiaceæ, the species of which are commonly called Oraches, or Salt Bushes or Salt Sages. They are either annual or perennial herbs and low shrubs, and are often silvery or scurfy. It is the perennial salt bushes which are important, *A. nuttallii,* or Nuttall's Salt Bush, is the most useful, and is the one usually referred to as 'Salt Sage.' Many of these plants are very valuable forage plants in arid regions; and both young shoots, foliage, and fruit are highly nutritive, besides affording salt, in their tissues, to live stock.

Atrium, the principal apartment of a Roman house; in the earliest times, no doubt, the only chamber. It had a hole in the roof, called the *compluvium,* which collected the rain and conducted it to a cistern in the floor. In later times other rooms were built on to the atrium, but, with Roman conservatism, it retained its original character as the chief room of the house. In early Christian churches the trium was an open court in front of the basilica, a place of abode for penitents, sometimes also as an asylum for criminals. See Preston and Dodge's *Private Life of the Romans* (1893).

Atrophy, a general or local wasting of the body. In children, general atrophy is most commonly due to unsuitable food (see ATHREPSIA), to catarrh of the digestive organs, to tubercle, or to worms in the alimentary canal. In adults it is generally the result of grave organic disease. Local atrophies of muscle and nerve may be caused by disuse, as in paralyzed limbs; more rarely by overwork. It is sometimes congenital, the normal growth of a part being arrested.

Atropine, or **tropine,** an alkaloid which occurs along with hyoscyamine in all parts of the *Atropa belladonna* (deadly night shade), and in the seeds of *Datura stramonium.* It is a powerful poison, but used medicinally it is valuable to dilate the pupil of the eye, quicken the heart's action, and relieve cardiac distress, and as an external application for the relief of pain. See BELLADONNA.

Atropos, the eldest of the three Fates. Her functions were to render the decisions immutable, according to Plato, and to sever the thread of life (spun by her sisters) with the scissors with which she is pictured, her features darkly veiled.

Atrypa, a genus of fossil brachiopods of the family Atrypidæ, found abundantly in the silurian and Devonian. See BRACHIOPODA.

At sight, a commercial term used upon bills of exchange, equivalent to 'on demand.'

Attacca (Ital.), in music a term signifying

that a succeeding movement is to be begun without stopping for any intermediate pause.

Attaché, Military. To the embassy or legation representative of a nation at the seat of government of a foreign power there is usually appointed a military or naval attaché. The duties of these officers are to make themselves thoroughly acquainted with every change that takes place in military or naval matters, and to report from time to time on the mobilization, armament, and equipment of the power to whom they are accredited. In time of war the privilege of being attached to the headquarters staff of an army is usually conceded to representatives of friendly nations.

Attachment. A process for placing a person or personal property in legal custody. *Attachment of persons* is commonly employed in this country to compel the attendance of a delinquent juror or witness or a person guilty of contempt of court. See ARREST; EXECUTION. *Attachment of Goods* is not generally available to a creditor except as a special proceeding based upon proof that the debtor is concealing the goods to avoid legal process or is about to remove them from the jurisdiction for the same purpose. It is a purely statutory proceeding and is strictly regulated by law. *Attachment of Debts* is a creditor's process whereby a judgment creditor, in satisfaction of his judgment, secures the payment to himself of a sum of money due from a third person to the judgment debtor. See GARNISHMENT.

Attainder. The extinction of all civil rights as a consequence of a judgment of treason or felony. Attainders was a necessary result of such a judgment at common law. In the United States a man may be attainted for treason, but the condemnation does not involve corruption of blood. The Constitution of the United States and those of the several states limiting the attainder to a forfeiture of estate only for the life of the person attainted. (U. S. Const., Art. III., Sec. 3).

Attalus, the name of three kings of Pergamus. (1) Surnamed SOTER, reigned from 241 to 197 B.C. He was distinguished for his great wealth and his patronage of literature. (2.) A. PHILADELPHUS, reigned from 159 to 138 B.C., second son of (1), and like him an ally of the Romans; he overthrew Pr·'sias of Bithynia. (3). A. PHILOMETOR succeeded (2), who was his uncle; he reigned from 138 to

The Atrium of a House in Pompeii (restored).

133 B.C., and by his will left his kingdom to the Romans; it formed their original province of Asia.

Attar, or **Athar, Ferid ud-Din** (1119-1230), Persian poet of the mystic school, and author of the *Mantik ut-Tair,* or *Conversations of the Birds,* a series of thirty moral tales, describing, in terms of Sufic thought, the progress of the human soul to Nirvana.

Attar, or **Otto, of Roses,** a perfume which consists of the volatile or essential oil distilled from certain varieties of rose. The manufacture is carried on in India, Persia, and Bulgaria.

Attention, the process in which, or activity by which, an object is brought from the *margin* to the *focus* of consciousness, and thus acquires additional clearness and distinctness. It has been a matter of controversy within recent years whether attention is to be conceived as a complex process explicable in more ultimate terms, or as a unique activity incapable of further analysis. See James' *Principles of Psychology* (1890), vol. i. ch. xi.; Ribot, *Psychology of the Attention* (trans.).

Atterbom, Peter Daniel Amadeus (1790-1855), the most distinguished poet of the romantic school in Sweden. In 1828 he was appointed professor of philosophy, and in 1835 professor of æsthetics and literary history, at Upsala University.

Attestation, the verification by a witness of the due execution of a legal document. An attestation is usually effected by the addition of the signature of the witness to the instrument attested.

Attica, a division of ancient Greece, with the Ægean Sea to the e. and s.w., and Bœotia to the n. It was divided into several independent states, but before the dawn of history they were united into one polity (by Theseus, according to the legends); Athens was the capital city. Area 2,472 sq.m.; p. 623,399. See GREECE.

Atticism, a term used to denote a well-turned phrase, was, among the Athenians applied to those grammarians (Atticists) who endeavored to retain the pristine purity of the Attic dialect. *Attic wit* and *Attic salt* signify a poignant and delicate wit characteristic of the Athenians.

Atticus (*c.* 400 A.D.), patriarch of Constantinople and successor of Chrysostom. He wrote a treatise, entitled *De Fide et Virginitate,* opposing Nestorian views.

Atticus, Titus Pomponius (*c.* 109-32 B.C.), a Roman knight, whose full name was Quintus Cæcilius Pomponianus Atticus. The last name was given him because of his residence in Athens (86-65 B.C.) and his attainments in Greek literature and culture. In philosophy he was an Epicurean.

Atticus Herodes, Tiberius Claudius (104-180 A.D.), celebrated Greek rhetorician of the 2d century. He possessed great wealth, even after presenting five minæ—nearly $100—to every Athenian citizen in fulfilment of his father's will. He taught rhetoric both in Athens and Rome, having for pupils the Emperors Marcus Aurelius and Lucius Verus.

Attila, or **Etzel,** king of the Huns, succeeded to the kingship in A.D. 434. In the reign of Attila (434-453) the supremacy of the Huns is said to have extended from the Caspian Sea to the Rhine, due largely to the resistless energy and masterfulness of their great leader. In 441 Attila laid waste Thrace and Illyria, withdrawing his forces only after exacting a heavy fine. In 451 Attila gave battle to the allies on the Catalaunian Fields (451). The Huns were defeated; but in the following year Attila laid waste Northern Italy, and even threatened Rome. He died in 453 on the night of his marriage with the Burgundian princess, Hilda or Ildiko.

Attleboro, city, Massachusetts, Bristol co., has manufactures of silverware, cotton, and jewelry; p. 22,071.

Attlee, Clement Richard (1883-   ), Prime Minister of Great Britain 1945-   , was born in London, studied at Oxford, and later engaged in social work in East London. 1913-22, lecturer, London School of Economics; Major in World War I and retired when wounded; Mayor of Borough of Stepney 1919-22; Member of Parliament from Limehouse 1922-45. In 1924 Under Sec'y of State for War; 1931 Postmaster General and Deputy Leader of the Opposition; 1940-42 Lord Privy Seal; 1942-43 Sec'y of State for the Dominions; 1944-45 Deputy Prime Minister and represented Great Britain at San Francisco and Berlin Conferences. July 1945, as leader of the Labor Party, won 390 seats in Parliament, was elected Prime Minister.

Attorney, in the most general sense, any person appointed by another to act in his behalf. An *attorney in fact* is an agent with specific authority to bind his principal, the authority being usually conferred by a writing known as a 'power of attorney' or 'letters of attorney.' In a specific sense, an attorney, or *attorney at law,* is one who represents another, known as his client, in legal proceedings. The term attorney has never been applied in England to the superior order of lawyers known as advocates and barristers. In the United States, however, all classes of lawyers have been described as attorneys, and that is still the name by which they are commonly known. For a description of the functions of the attorney and his place in the administration of justice see BAR; LAWYER. See also DISBAR.

Attorney General, in the United States and Great Britain, the principal law officer of the government. He is the public prosecutor and standing counsel for the government in all its legal proceedings, as well as the legal adviser of the various governmental departments. In the United States the Attorney General, who was made a member of the first cabinet of President Washington (1789), is fourth in rank of the great appointive officers of the government, and the head of the Department of Justice. He is the legal adviser of the President and of Congress. Each of the States has a similar officer. See JUSTICE, U. S. DEPARTMENT OF.

Attornment, the formal recognition by a tenant of another person than his lessor as landlord. The necessity for an attornment was done away with by statute in 1705 (4 Anne, c. 16), but it may still be employed so as to affect the rights of parties in certain cases. See LANDLORD AND TENANT.

Attraction, the tendency of bodies to approach each other and unite; the force which brings bodies together and resists their separation. Attractions are divisible into two classes: (1) those which act at sensible and measurable distances, as gravitation, magnetic and electrical attraction; and (2) those which extend only to extremely small and insensible distances, as capillary, molecular, and chemical attraction. (See CAPILLARITY; AFFINITY; CHEMICAL; MAGNETISM; ELECTRICITY.)

Attribute, a term employed in logic to denote the opposite of substance. See also SUBSTANCE.

Attu, the most westerly of the group of Aleutian Islands, in the Northern Pacific. Occupied by the Japanese, June, 1942, it was retaken by American airmen, May, 1943.

Atwill, Lionel (1885-1946), actor, born at Croyden, England. He made his first appearance on the stage in *The Walls of Jericho*, at the Garrick Theater in London in 1905 and toured in plays of Shakespeare, Shaw, etc. In 1915 he came to New York with Mrs. Langtry and has since appeared in *The Dolls'* *House; Caesar and Cleopatra; Napoleon* and *The Silent Witness*, etc. Since 1932 he has appeared in motion pictures including *Dr. X, Song of Songs* and *Nana*.

Atwood's Machine, a machine invented by George Atwood to demonstrate the laws of uniformly accelerated motion, and to illustrate the relations of time, space, and motion in the case of a body falling under the action of gravitation.

Atys, or **Attis,** a beautiful Phrygian shepherd beloved by the goddess Cybele, who made him her priest, then changed him into a fir-tree. The story is related by Ovid and by Catullus. The versions vary widely.

Aubanel, Théodore (1829-86), poet and dramatist of the Provençal language, and one of the leaders of the development of Provençal poetry, was born in Avignon, where he carried on the business of publishing.

Aube, river, France, a tributary of the Seine.

Aube, department, Central France, consisting for the most part of the parallel valleys of the Seine and its tributary the Aube, with an area of 2,326 sq. m. The capital is Troyes; p. 238,253.

Auber, Daniel François Esprit (1782-1871), French operatic composer, was born in Caen. In 1842 he was appointed director of the Conservatory in Paris; and in 1857 Napoleon III, made him Maître de Chapelle. He wrote over forty operas, among which are *Fra Diavolo* (1830), and *Le Rêve d'Amour* (1869).

Aubergine, another name for the Eggplant.

Aubervilliers, town, France, department of the Seine, forming a suburb of Paris to the northwest; p. 47,881.

Aubrietia, or **Purple Rock Cress,** a genus of small plants belonging to the order Cruciferæ. About 3 inches high, producing masses of violet, lilac, and purple flowers adapted for borders, and rock gardens.

Aubry de Montdidier, courtier of Charles v. of France. The popular drama, *Le Chien d'Aubry,* is founded on the story of his assassination known also as *The Dog of Montargis.*

Auburn, city, New York, county seat of Cayuga co., situated at the foot of Owasco Lake. Among the public institutions are the Auburn Theological Seminary and a State prison, which is widely known for the reformatory character of its discipline; p. 35,758.

Auburn-Lissoy, village in co. Westmeath, Ireland, 8 m. n.e. of Athione. It is famous as the scene of Oliver Goldsmith's *Deserted Village*.

Auburn Theological Seminary, a divinity school under Presbyterian control at Auburn, N. Y., founded in 1818, associated with which is a School for Religious Education.

Aubusson, town, France, department of Creuse, is picturesquely situated on the Creuse. It is noted for its carpet and tapestry factories, one of them established by Colbert in 1665. This industry is said to have been introduced by the Saracens, who are supposed to have founded the town after their defeat at Tours (732 A.D.); p. about 6,000.

Aubusson, Pierre d' (1423-1503), 'the shield of the Church,' was grand master of the Knights of St. John of Jerusalem, and by his successful defence of Rhodes (May-July, 1480) against an army of 100,000 Turks, checked their victorious course after the fall of Constantinople (1453).

A.U.C. (Lat. *anno urbis conditæ*, 'in the year from the founding of the city'). In Rome a particular year was usually described by the names of the consuls for that year; but later Roman writers reckoned from the year of the founding of Rome—according to Varro, B.C. 753.

Aucassin et Nicolette, a romantic French love story of the 13th century, written in alternate prose and assonant verse of seven syllables.

Auchenia, or **Lama,** the genus to which belong the llama, alpaca, guanaco, and vicuña. They are entirely confined to South America and are not known outside this continent.

Auckland, provincial district, North Island, New Zealand; area 25,364 sq. m. It is hilly, well timbered, and well watered, and has an extensive seaboard, with many good harbors; p. 369,618.

Auckland, the largest and most important city of New Zealand, in North Island, is situated on an isthmus at the head of Waitemata Harbor, an inlet of Hauraki Gulf. The harbor, one of the best in New Zealand, has ample accommodation for shipping. The city was founded in 1840 and until 1865 was the seat of colonial government; p. 209,800.

Auckland Islands, a group of uninhabited, mountainous, volcanic islands about 180 m. s. of New Zealand, to which they belong; total area, about 350 sq. m. The islands were discovered in 1806 by Bristow and annexed by Great Britain in 1886.

Auction, a method of selling property by which the vendor agrees to sell to the highest bidder. Auction sales and the business of conducting them are carefully regulated by statute, both in England and the United States.

Auction Bridge. See **Bridge.**

Aucuba Japonica, an Asiatic shrub of the order Cornaceæ.

Aude, maritime department in Southern France, lying along the Mediterranean coast; area 2,448 sq. m. Carcassonne is the capital; p. 287,052.

Aude, river, France, rising in the department of Pyrénées-Orientales, crossing the department of Aude, and entering the Mediterranean after a course of 139 m.

Audhumla, in Scandinavian mythology, the cow whose milk nourished the giant Ymir, the first created being, and his race.

Audiometer, an instrument, invented by Professor D. E. Hughes in 1879, to accurately measure the sense of hearing. It consists of an adaptation of the telephone.

Audiphone, a device for improving the hearing of persons partially deaf. It consists of a thin fan-shaped sheet of ebonite or other suitable material, which is pressed against the upper front teeth, and capable of being varied in convexity. Sound vibrations are conveyed through the bones of the head.

Auditor, a person employed to examine and report upon the financial condition of a private business or undertaking, or of a corporation, or of a public office or department, municipal, state, or federal. He is often a permanent official of industrial corporations. There are six auditors of the treasury department at Washington.

Auditory Nerve, the eighth cranial nerve, consists of two roots (auditory, vestibular) with different functions and distinct peripheral and central connections, and should be regarded as two distinct nerves. The auditory nerve is concerned solely with hearing, passes from the cochlea, and for that reason is known as the cochlear nerve. It leaves the trunk of the eighth nerve and enters the pons by the posterior, lateral or cochlear root. See also BRAIN; EAR.

Audley, Sir James (?1316-69), British knight, a 'first founder' of the Order of the Garter (1344), famous as a brave companion of the Black Prince.

Audran, Edmond (1842-1901), French

musical composer, was born in Lyons. His operas include *Olivette, La mascotte, La Cigale* and *La poupée*.

Audran, a family of French artists who flourished in the latter half of the 17th and the early part of the 18th centuries. The best known are: GÉRARD (*c.* 1640-1703), JEAN (1667-1756), CLAUDE II. (1644-84), CLAUDE III. (1658-1734).

Audsley, George Ashdown (1838-1925), architect and writer, was born in Elgin, Scotland. He went to the United States in 1892 and settled in New York City where he practised as an architect. His writings include a *Handbook of Christian Symbolism* (1865), *The Art of Chromolithography,* and a number of beautiful volumes on Japanese art.

Leopold Auer, Violinist.

Audubon, John James (1780-1851), American ornithologist, was born in Mandeville, near New Orleans, La. His father early recognized his son's talent as a draughtsman, and sent him to study under the artist David, in Paris. On his return (1798) young Audubon went to the Mill Grove farm, near Philadelphia, Pa., where he had unlimited facilities for collecting natural history specimens, making his drawings. He there met Miss Lucy Bakewell, whom he was to marry (1808). In 1826 went to England to arrange for the publication of the great volume of *The Birds of America* (1830-9). This work was characterized by Cuvier as 'the most magnificent monument that art has yet raised to ornithology.' Consult *Life* by Buchanan from materials supplied by his widow; Coues' *Audubon and his Journals;* Herrick's *Audubon, the Naturalist* (1917).

Audubon's Peak, one of the Rocky Mountains, situated in Colorado. Height, 13,173 ft.

Auenbrugger von Auenbrugg, Leopold (1722-1809), Austrian physician. He introduced the method of diagnosing chest and abdominal diseases by percussion.

Auer, Aloys (1813-69), Austrian printer, was born in Wels, Upper Austria. He made many typographical inventions and also published the Lord's Prayer in over six hundred languages.

Auer, Leopold (1845-1930), Hungarian violinist, was born at Veszprim, and studied music at Vienna and later with Joachim at Hanover. He emigrated from Russia to Scandinavia and in 1918 made New York his residence. His best known pupils are Elman, Zimbalist, Heifetz and Seidel.

Auerbach, Berthold, (1812-82), German author, was born of Jewish parentage in Nordstetten. He is chiefly known as the founder of the contemporary German 'tendency novel'. Many of his works have been translated into English; the best known being *Village Tales* (1846); *Edelweiss* (1861); *Der Forstmeister* (1879); *Brigitta* (1880).

Augean Stables. See **Hercules.**

Augershell, an elongated, closely coiled, carnivorous gastropod mollusc, of the family Terebridæ, inhabiting the tropical seas and the Southern Pacific. Over 200 varieties are known.

Augite, a common variety of pyroxene, rich in iron and aluminum, and specially important as a rock-forming mineral.

Augmentation, in music, is the reproduction or imitation of a theme or subject by doubling the time value of the notes in which it was first introduced.

Augmentation, Honorable, in heraldry an addition to a coat-of-arms granted by the sovereign for distinguished service.

Augsburg, city, Bavaria, situated at the confluence of the Wertach and the Lech; about 40 m. n.w. of Munich. Some of the gates of the mediæval fortifications are still extant. Augsburg was founded by the Romans about 15 B.C.; p. 168,000.

Augsburg Confession, the chief statement of faith of the Lutheran church. Melanchthon, aided by suggestions from Luther and others, drew up the Confession of Faith which at the request of Charles v. of Germany was presented to the Diet on June 25, 1530.

Augsburg Interim. See **Interim.**

Augur and **Auspex,** names given to the Roman diviners, meaning primarily 'diviners by birds'. The Roman augurs formed a priestly collegium and in ancient times no public transaction took place without consulting them. See DIVINATION.

August. See **Year.**

Augusta, name of several ancient cities built by or called after Augustus and other Roman emperors.

Augusta, or **Agosta,** a fortified seaport in the province of Syracuse, Sicily, is situated on a small island close to the southeastern coast. The town was founded in 1232; p. 16,000.

Augusta, city, Georgia, county seat of Richmond co., at the head of navigation on the Savannah River, 175 m. s.e. of Atlanta. The cotton trade is one of the largest in the South. Augusta was captured by the British in 1779 and in 1780, and recaptured by Gen. Henry Lee in 1781; p. 65,919.

Augusta, Maine, the State capital, population (1940) 19,360. On the Kennebec River, 62 m. n.w. of Portland. Industries: cotton mills, pulp and lumber mills, printing and publishing concerns, boot, shoe and shirt factories.

Augustales. (1.) Games in honor of Augustus held at Rome and in other parts of the empire. After B.C. 11 the senate decreed their celebration annually on the birthday of Augustus. (2.) Two classes of priests, one at Rome (*sodales augustales*) and the other in the municipia, instituted by Tiberius to attend the worship of Augustus and the Julia gens.

Augustana College and Theological Seminary. A Lutheran institution at Rock Island, Ill., established in 1860 at Chicago.

Augustan Age, a term applied to the period of the Roman emperor Augustus (31 B.C. to 14 A.D.). The great names of the Augustan age were Ovid, Horace, Livy, Virgil, and Catullus.

Augusta Victoria (1858-1921), German Empress and Queen of Prussia, daughter of Frederick, Duke of Schleswig-Holstein. In 1881 she married Prince William of Prussia, who became William II.

Augustine (Aurelius Augustinus), the greatest of the Latin fathers of the Christian church, was born on Nov. 13, 354 A.D., at Tagaste, a small Numidian country town. He taught in Carthage, Rome, and Milan, where in 386 he became a Christian. He returned to Africa and in 395 was created bishop of Hippo. No theologian has produced a larger and deeper impress on the mind of Christendom than the bishop of Hippo. This he has achieved not only by his writings, but by the exhibition of Christian fervor and devotion which is given in the story of his inner life. As a philosopher and a moralist he anticipated many of the problems of modern times. But Augustinianism — the doctrines with which the name of Augustine is universally identified—was developed by its author in controversy with Pelagius, a British monk, and others who more or less entirely supported his views. The point of conflict was the relation between truth and individuals—the conditions and process of salvation.

Augustine's writings are voluminous, but the two best-known compositions are undoubtedly the *De Civitate Dei,* or 'City of God' (413-426) and the *Confessions* (397). An English edition, including most of the important works, except the *Retractiones* (428), was published at Edinburgh (T. and T. Clark) in 1872-80. See also *Nicene and Post-Nicene Fathers* (ed. by Schaff, 1886-8, 8 vols.). For an unfavorable estimate, see Allen's *Continuity of Christian Thought* (1894).

Augustine, or **Austin, St.,** first Archbishop of Canterbury, originally a monk of the Benedictine convent at Rome, was sent by Pope Gregory to convert Britain to Christianity. Accompanied by 40 monks, Augustine landed on the Isle of Thanet (596). Through the intercession of Bertha, wife of Ethelbert, king of Kent, he was permitted to preach, and succeeded in making the king himself a convert to his cause. He was consecrated Archbishop of Canterbury. He died c. 607, and was buried at Canterbury. See A. J. Mason's *The Mission of St. Augustine to England* (1897). The chief source is Bede's *Eccles. Hist.* (ed. Gidley, 1870).

Augustinians, fraternities in the Roman Catholic Church who follow the rules referred to St. Augustine; but the origin of the order is in dispute. The principal congregations are the Canons Regular, the Hermits, the Special Congregations (of which Luther was a member), and the Barefooted Augustinians. See Speakman's *Rule of St. Augustine* (1902); and Dugdale's *Monasticon,* VI. 37.

Augustulus, Romulus, the last Roman emperor of the West, (476).

Augustus (63 B.C.-14 A.D.), the first and greatest—unless Julius Cæsar is reckoned—

Augustus of the emperors of Rome, was the son of C. Octavius, by Atia, daughter of Julia, the sister of Julius Cæsar, who adopted him. His name before adoption was C. Octavius; afterward it was Gaius Julius Cæsar Octavianus, the title Augustus ('the revered') being added by the senate and people in 27 B.C. Augustus was studying at Apollonia, in 44 B.C., when the news of the murder of Cæsar reached him. Proceeding to Rome, at first he professed adherence to the republican party, and fought against Antony at Mutina. Antony fled across the Alps, and both the consuls fell in the battle. Augustus, on his return to Rome, compelled the senate to support his election to the consulship. He then proceeded against Antony, but was reconciled to him by Lepidus; and the three formed the second triumvirate, which was to last for five years. In 42 B.C. Augustus and Antony defeated Brutus and Cassius at Philippi, thus destroying the hopes of the republican party. Returning to Italy (B.C. 41), Augustus had to wage war with L. Antonius, brother, and Fulvia, wife, of the triumvir. The capture of Perusia decided the contest favorably for him. Antony now threatened him, but, thanks to Fulvia's death a reconciliation was affected between them at Brundusium. Antony then took the east, Augustus the west of the empire, and Lepidus Africa. In 36 B.C. Augustus put down the power of Sextus Pompeius, son of Pompey the Great, who had for years held Sicily with a powerful fleet, and deposed Lepidus, whom he allowed to live at Rome as *pontifex maximus* ('chief priest'). Meanwhile Antony's repudiation of Octavia, his wife, Augustus's sister, led to the decisive struggle for supreme power, which was ended by Augustus's victory at Actium (Sept. 31). Next year he went to Egypt, and the death of Antony and Cleopatra left him undisputed master of the Roman world. In 29 B.C. he returned to Rome, and held a triple triumph.

Though Augustus was really an absolute monarch, he appeared to preserve the republican constitution. His reform of provincial government was his best title to fame and literature was much encouraged by his patronage. Ancient authorities: Cicero's *Letters and Philippics;* Tacitus's *Annals,* bk. i.; Plutarch's *Antonius; Dion Cassius,* bks. XLV.-LVI.; Baring-Gould's *Tragedy of the Cæsars,* and Shuckburgh's *Life of Augustus.*

Augustus, elector of Saxony (1526-86), born at Freiburg, was brought up at Prague a Calvinist, in intimate friendship with Maximilian, afterward emperor of Germany. He was mainly instrumental in negotiating the peace of Augsburg (1555).

Augustus II., Frederick, The Strong, elector of Saxony and king of Poland (1670-1733), second son of John George III. of Saxony, was born at Dresden, and succeeded his brother, John George IV., as elector in 1694. Joining Peter the Great and Denmark he fought against Charles XII. of Sweden.

Augustus III., Frederick, elector of Saxony (1696-1763), son of the preceding, was born at Dresden. Succeeding his father (1733), he was chosen king of Poland (1734) by a party of the Diet, prevailing over Stanislaus. He was embroiled in the three Silesian wars.

Auks, or **Alcidæ,** a family of marine birds with heavy bodies, large heads, and compact plumage. The wings are always short, and the great auk, or gare-fowl, now extinct, was flightless. See Newton, *Dictionary of Birds* (1896). See GAREFOWL.

Aula Regia, or **Regis,** a court instituted by William the Conqueror, formed of the great officers of state, and afterward regulated by Magna Charta.

'Auld Lichts.' See **Presbyterianism.**

Aulic Council. The Emperor Maximilian, in 1501, set up in Vienna the Aulic Council. Though at first it dealt only with Austrian business, the Aulic Council gradually encroached upon the Imperial Chamber and usurped many of its functions. With the dissolution of the empire in 1806, the term Aulic Council was applied to the emperor of Austria's council of state.

Aulis, seapt. in Bœotia, Greece, on the Euripus. It was the scene of the detention of the Greek fleet, Trojan War, and of a part of the famous story of Iphigenia, the subject of two plays by Euripides.

Aumale, Count and Duke of. The former title was granted by William the Conqueror to Eudes, son of Henri Etienne, count of Troyes and Meaux, in the 11th century. The male line of this family terminated with the third generation, when the title passed by marriage to the family of Castille. Confiscated by Philippe Auguste (1194), it was granted in succession to various other houses and finally, in 1679, it passed by marriage to the house of Orleans, the fourth son of Louis Philippe bearing the title.

Aumale. (1.) Charles de Lorraine, Duc d'Aumale (1554-1631), the last of the old dukes, was a prominent member of the Holy League, instituted by the Duke of

Guise (1576). (2.) **Henri Eugéne Philippe Louis d'Orleans, Duc d'** (1822-97), fourth son of Louis Philippe, was born in Paris. He devoted himself to literature, mainly military and historical, his chief works being *Les institutions militaires de la France* (1867) and the *Histoire des Princes de Condé* (1869). See E. Daudet's *Le Duc d'Aumale* (1898).

Aune, an old European cloth measure corresponding to the English ell, varying between 27 and 54 in. It survives in Switzerland, where the aune is 47¼ in.

Aungerville, Richard (1281-1345), called also Richard de Bury, from his birthplace, Bury St. Edmunds; tutor to the Prince of Wales, afterward Edward III.; became bishop of Durham (1333), lord high chancellor (1334), and treasurer (1337). *Philobiblon* is his chief work (1473); ed. by E. C. Thomas, 1902.

Aura, any strange sensation which gives warning of the approach of an epileptic or a hysterical fit. It often resembles a breath of cold air moving up the body to the head; whence the name.

Aural Diseases. See **Ear.**

Auray, tn., dep. Morbihan, France. '*Le Pardon d'Auray*' gathers yearly thousands of Bretons round the Chapel of St. Anne; p. 6,485.

Aurelianus, emperor of Rome from 270 to 275 A.D., was born of humble parents, probably at Sirmium, in Pannonia, c. 212. Elected by the army to succeed Claudius II., he defeated the Goths and Vandals, who had crossed the Danube, and repelled a German invasion of Italy. In the east he overcame (271) Zenobia, queen of Palmyra, and brought her captive to Rome. Next he recovered Gaul, Spain, and Britain from the usurper Tetricus.

Aurelian Wall, the wall which the Emperor Aurelian built round Rome in 271 A.D., though it was completed by Probus in 280. See J. H. Middleton's *Remains of Ancient Rome* (1892); Burn's *Rome and the Campagna* (1870).

Aurelian Way (*Aurelia Via*), one of the principal ancient military roads of Italy, which, starting from Rome near the Janiculan gate, ran northwards along the west coast, (Civita Vecchia), to Antipolis (Antibes) in Gallia. The part north of Pisa was constructed by Augustus.

Aurelius, Marcus (121-180 A.D.), Roman emperor, whose birth-name was M. Annius Verus, was born at Rome. In 138 he was adopted by his uncle, the Emperor Antoninus, taking on himself the new name of Marcus Aurelius Antoninus. He succeeded to the throne in the year 161. The influence of the emperor's philosophy became apparent in the broader and more beneficent interpretation of Roman law. In 166 the frontiers of Italy were menaced by northern barbarians. Aurelius first took the field in person in 167, and the uncongenial business of war occupied him almost continuously until the year 175. In Dec. 176, the emperor returned to Rome, where he was accorded a triumph. But he left again for the field in Aug. 178. The campaign was successful; but Aurelius died, either at Vienna or Sirmium, March 17, 180. The emperor's twelve books, or rather short chapters, form one of the famous books of the world. They are the jottings of his lonely reflections in the moments snatched from rest or action during his campaigns—*Among the Quadi, At Carnutum,* etc. The *Thoughts* unite high nobility with complete sincerity and tenderness. M. Aurelius wrote in Greek —the accepted philosophical speech of his age—but hardly with perfect ease. The first translation of Aurelius' own book into English was that of Meric Casaubon, issued in 1634 (recent edition, 1900, by W. H. D. Rousse); but the two standard modern translations are Long's (2nd ed. 1880) and G. H. Rendall's (1898). Walter Pater introduced M. Aurelius into his romance of *Marius the Epicurean.* Consult also Matthew Arnold's *Essays in Criticism.*

Aureole, a radiance or luminous cloud surrounding the body of Christ, the Virgin Mary, or the saints, in sacred art, emblematic of the influence of the Holy Spirit.

Aurès Mountains, (the *Mons Aurasius* of Procope), a range in Southern Algeria, province of Constantine, about 75 m. in length, overhanging the Sahara, and enclosing fertile valleys and plains.

Aureus, (Lat. *aurum,* 'gold'), the first and standard Roman gold coin, issued tentatively about B.C. 217, and afterward permanently by Julius Cæsar and the Roman emperors, until Constantine substituted for it the *solidus.* Its average weight was 121 grains. Its value was about $5.00.

Auricle. See **Heart** and **Ear.**

Auricula. See **Primrose.**

Auriga (Lat. 'the Charioteer'), an ancient constellation, situated between Perseus and Taurus, of which Capella is the principal star. There is little doubt of its Euphratean origin.

Aurignacian, an important culture stage

Aurillac

(the first division) of the upper Palæolithic period, probably began 25,000 or 30,000 years ago. The people were artistically more developed than their predecessors, and were probably the first to decorate the walls and roofs of their caves with outlines.

Aurillac, town, France, capital of the department of Cantal. The church of St. Géraud, begun in the 15th century and completed about 1890, and an old castle now used as a normal school are the most notable buildings; p. 18,036.

Aurochs, a modern name for the European bison (see BISON).

Aurora (Gr. *Eos*), goddess of the dawn, daughter of Hyperion and Thia. Every morning she rose from her couch to announce the coming of the sun, in a chariot drawn by swift horses.

Aurora Borealis, or **Northern Lights,** a luminous meteorological phenomenon seen in the northern sky, taking the form of streamers, arches, or patches, which vary in shade considerably, being sometimes smoky black or steel gray, and at others brilliant yellow, green, violet, or fiery red. As usually seen, the aurora commences with the formation of an arch with its apex to the magnetic meridian. Underneath the arch the sky is apparently darker than the rest of the heavens, this gloomy portion being known as 'the dark segment'; stars are visible through this part of the sky as well as through the aurora itself. Slender streamers of well-defined bright light extend up from the arch usually to a distance of from 20 to 30 degrees, towards the magnetic zenith. The arch is sometimes evenly illuminated, but is at times convoluted like a folded curtain. Sometimes the sky is entirely covered with brilliant coruscations shooting up from the horizon, converging in a quivering blaze of feathery flame high in the sky, nearly in the direction shown by the south end of a magnetic dipping-needle. This is known as the corona.

Auroral displays are most frequent and brilliant in relatively high latitudes. In the torrid zone it is rarely observed, not more than six auroras in a century being seen as far south as lat. 20°. The generally received theory is that the aurora is due to the ascent of positive electricity from the intertropical water surfaces, which flows towards the poles, wafted by the higher aerial currents. In the region of the poles it descends towards the earth, and comes in contact, in a highly rarefied atmosphere, with the terrestrial negative electricity, which results in luminous discharges of great brilliancy. The Aurora Australis, which is the name applied to auroral displays seen in the southern hemisphere, differs in no striking feature from the Northern Lights. See text-books of meteorology, and *The Polar Aurora* by M. Angot (Inter. Scientific Series, 1896).

Aurungabad, walled town in the state of Haidarabad (Deccan), India, 67 m. n.e. of Ahmednagar and 180 m. from Bombay. It contains the ruins of a palace built by Aurungzebe, and the mausoleum of a favorite daughter. There are caves, partly Buddhist, a m. w. of the town. Embroidery, silverware, silk, and cotton are produced; p. 35,000.

Aurungzebe, Mohammed Muhi ed-Din Aurungzeb Alamgir (1618-1707), Mogul emperor, ascended the throne of Delhi in 1658, when he put to death his two brothers, Dara and Murad Baksh, drove his third brother, Shuja, into exile, and imprisoned his father, the Emperor Shah Jehan, for the rest of his life. Consult S. L. Poole's *Aurangzib* and Sarkan's *History of Aurangzib* (1913).

Ausable Chasm, village, New York, Clinton co., at a point where the stream falls 70 ft. and flows through a narrow, deep chasm between vertical rocks of Potsdam sandstone, from 90 to 175 ft. in height. It is a famed rock formation and a resort for tourists.

Ausable Lakes, two small bodies of water, called Lower and Upper Ausable Lake, situated in the Adirondack Reserve, New York, about 2,000 ft. above sea-level.

Ausable River, river of New York, rising in the Adirondacks, in Essex co., in two small streams which unite at Ausable Forks. It follows a northeasterly course and discharges into Lake Champlain. See AUSABLE CHASM.

Auscultation, in medical practice listening to the sounds (especially respiratory and cardiac) of the body, with a view to diagnosis. It was introduced regularly into practice by Laënnec.

Ausgleich, the compromise between Austria and Hungary, effected in 1867, which governed the relations between the two halves of the monarchy prior to its dissolution in 1918. See AUSTRIA-HUNGARY.

Ausonius, called Decimus Magnus (309-c 394), Latin poet and man of letters. Of his works, *Mosella* is the most famous.

Austin, Alfred (1835-1913), English poet laureate, 1896-1913, was educated at Stonyhurst and Oscott College. His *Autobiography* appeared in 1911.

Austen, Jane (1775-1817), English novelist, was born in Steventon, Hampshire, of which parish her father was rector. Her first four novels which were published anonymously were *Sense and Sensibility* and *Pride and Prejudice, Mansfield Park,* and *Emma.* The first two were written before she was twenty-two years old. *Persuasion* was published posthumously, with *Northanger Abbey,* in 1818, with a memoir prefixed, and the author's name for the first time on a title-page. These six stories, with a shorter tale in letters, called *Lady Susan,* and the fragment already referred to, constitute Jane Austen's entire contribution to English literature. She died on July 24, 1817, and was buried in Winchester Cathedral.

Jane Austen's novels are the earliest and the best example of the so-called domestic novel in English. Consult Hill's *Jane Austen;* Mitton's *Jane Austen;* Chapman's *English Literature in Account with Religion;* Austen-Leigh's *Jane Austen: Her Life and Letters; A Family Record* (1913); Firkin's *Jane Austen* (1920).

Auster, called *Notus* by the Greeks, the south or southwest wind, which was usually wet, but at certain seasons dry and unhealthful; the modern Italian sirocco.

Austerlitz, Battle of, a famous battle of the Napoleonic Wars, fought in the country west of the town of Austerlitz (a small town in Moravia, Austria, on the Littawa), on Dec. 2, 1805, in which the French army under Napoleon I. routed the combined forces of the Austrians and Russians. As a result of the battle, Austria was forced to sign the Treaty of Pressburg (Dec. 26, 1805).

Austin, city, capital of Texas. It is the educational centre of the State, being the seat of the University of Texas and other colleges and schools. Austin is a trade centre for farm products and live-stock, and is noted for its brick and white lime manufactures; p. 87,930.

Austin, Alfred (1835-1913), English poet, was born in Headingley, near Leeds. He was graduated from London University in 1853, and was called to the bar. In 1896 he was appointed poet-laureate, in succcession to Tennyson. A collected edition of his *Poems* appeared in 6 vols. (1892). Among his prose works are *In Veronica's Garden* (1895); *Spring and Autumn in Ireland* (1900); *Autobiography* (1911).

Austin, John (1790-1859), founder of the modern English school of analytical jurisprudence, and friend of Jeremy Bentham and John Stuart Mill, was born in Creeting Mill, Suffolk. He was called to the bar, but met with slight success and retired from practice in 1825. The real work of his life was the summary of his lectures on jurisprudence, the first part of which was published in 1832 and re-edited by his widow in 1861. His great merit consists in his having been the first English writer to attach precise and intelligible meanings to the terms which denote the leading conceptions underlying all systems of jurisprudence. Consult Mill's *Autobiography;* Brown's *Austinian Theory of Law.*

Austin, Stephen Fuller (1793-1836), American pioneer, one of the founders of Texas, was born in Wythe co., Va., the son of Moses Austin (1767-1821), who just before his death obtained from the Mexican government a tract of land in Texas, on which he planned to establish a settlement of Americans. Stephen Fuller carried out his father's plan early in 1822, founding the city now known as Austin (q.v.).

Australasia, ('Southern Asia'), a popular term, sometimes used to comprehend the Malay Archipelago, the Philippines, Australia, and all the islands of the Pacific; at other times confined to the British possessions of Australia, Tasmania, and New Zealand, to which New Guinea and Fiji are sometimes added. As a geographical term it is best applied to the greater Australian region, which includes the islands of Australia, Tasmania, New Guinea, the Bismarck, Solomon, and New Hebrides archipelagoes, New Caledonia, and New Zealand (qq. v.). See MELANESIA.

Australia is the name applied, at the suggestion of Captain Matthew Flinders, to the island continent which lies between latitude 10° 39' and 39° 11½' s., and longitude 113° 5' and 153° 16' E. It includes the island of Tasmania. The Territory of Papua in New Guinea is adjacent to Australia and is administered by the Commonwealth.

The Commonwealth of Australia comprises the states of New South Wales, Queensland, South Australia, Victoria, Western Australia, and Tasmania; the Territory of Northern Australia, and the newly-created Federal Territory of Canberra. The Commonwealth also administers the Territory of New Guinea (late German New Guinea) under mandate from the League of Nations. The area of the island of Australia is 2,948,366 sq. m.; of the Commonwealth, 2,974,581 sq. m., exclusive of Papua (90,540 sq. m.). From Steep Point, in the west, to Cape Byron, in the east, is a distance of about 2,400 m., and from Cape York in the north, to Wilson promontory, in the south, nearly 2,000 m. Australia is bounded on the n. by the Timor and Arafura Seas and Torres Strait, on the w. by the Indian Ocean, on the s. by the Southern Ocean, and on the e. by the Pacific. The coast line, exclusive of minor indentations, is 12,210 m. in length.

The general physical appearance of Australia has been roughly compared to an inverted saucer. There is a rich, low-lying coastal belt of fertile soil, averaging 40 m. in width, separated from the vast plains of the interior by the mountain ranges of the e. and w. In the e. is the Great Dividing Range, stretching the length of the continent in a line parallel to the coast. In the n. a rugged table land of moderate elevation rises sharply from the low coast lands and extends well into South Australia. The western half of Australia is also a table land, with a mean elevation of between 1,000 and 1,500 ft. Along the southern coast no mountains occur as far e. as Spencer Gulf, the principal physical feature being the sandstone cliffs bordering the Great Australian Bight. Although Central Australia is in general not mountainous, there are a few isolated mountain groups. The chief river of Australia is the Murray (q.v.), in the s.e., which, with its great tributary, the Darling, drains an area of 414,253 sq. m.

Area and Population of Australia

	Area square miles	Population 1950, est.
New South Wales.	309,432	3,175,935
Queensland........	670,500	1,160,300
South Australia...	380,070	697,873
Tasmania.........	26,215	284,245
Victoria..........	87,884	2,164,331
Western Australia..	975,920	544,815
Northern Territory	523,620	13,850
Federal District...	940	19,530
Total........	2,974,581	8,050,892

The Tropic of Capricorn crosses Australia midway between n. and s., and the temperature is never very low except in the mountains of the s. Indeed, Australia is less subject to extremes of climate than almost any other similar area in the world; and with the exception of some of the low-lying coast lands, even the tropical zone is healthful. The mean annual temperature varies from 85° F. in the n. to 54° F. in the s. The s.e. trade winds prevail at most seasons over the greater part of the continent. Unequal distribution of rainfall, varying from 150 in. in certain districts in Eastern Queensland to 5 in. in the Lake Eyre district is characteristic of Australia. In Tasmania the rain falls at all seasons, but is most plentiful in the winter. The most fertile districts are on the coast, where there are abundant rainfall and rich alluvial deposits; but there are also great expanses in the interior, which with an annual rainfall of only 12 or 15 in. are extremely productive. With water conservation and irrigation, many of the more arid districts may be made suitable for agricultural purposes.

Australia seems to be built up chiefly from Palæozoic and Cenozoic or Tertiary formations, while Mesozoic or Secondary deposits have also been laid open in various quarters. Tertiary deposits, mostly Pliocene it is supposed, occupy an immense area of Australia, comprehending the desert sandstone, the coral limestone, and a large part of the conglomerates and clays of the gold diggings. The most striking feature of the plant life of the Australian continent is the eucalyptus or gum tree. There is a rich tropical vegetation on the eastern and northeastern coasts. The Australian fauna is remarkable for its primitive mammals, and for the absence of all higher forms except rodents and bats, and the dingo or wild dog, possibly introduced by man. The Tasmanian devil (confined to that island), the pouched kangaroos, opossums, wombats, and bandicoots are among the distinctive mammals, all marsupials. The duck-billed platypus (*Ornithorhyncus*) and the echidna, or spiny ant-eater, belong to the other class of Australian mammals, the monotremes. Birds are numerous, and lizards and snakes abound. The forest area of Australia is estimated at 69,000,000 acres, or 3.6 per cent. of the entire area. The principal timber regions are in the eastern and southern portions of the country, including Tasmania, and in the southwest. Among hardwood timbers, the ironbarks, species of eucalyptus, are highly valued for building purposes because of their great strength and durability. Many varieties of food fish are caught on the coast, and in the lakes and streams. Pearl oysters are found in the waters along the northern and western coasts, and the pearl industry is of importance.

Although the presence of valuable mineral deposits in Australia has long been known, a large portion of the continent has not yet been adequately prospected, and the mineral-bearing areas have been only superficially worked. There are vast coal beds and extensive deposits of iron ore, as well as a great variety of other minerals, including gems and building stones. Gold, silver, copper, and tin are produced in large quantities. The most important gem mined is opal; diamonds, sapphires, emeralds, garnets, topazes, and other precious and semi-precious stones are also found.

Australia is preëminently a pastoral country; agriculture ranks second among the country's sources of wealth, and is of growing importance. The soil in many sections is of great fertility, the climate especially favorable, and danger from frosts unknown. While drought constitutes a source of danger, the soil has unusual powers of recuperation even after prolonged periods of dryness. Wheat is the principal crop of the Commonwealth, over half of the entire cultivated area being devoted to it. With flour it constitutes an important item of export. Hay is second in value only to wheat.

By far the most important Australian industry is the raising of horses, cattle, sheep, pigs, goats, and other live stock, and the list of pastoral exports includes live animals, meats, hides, wool, and tallow. The mildness of the climate, making housing for the cattle unnecessary at any time of the year, and the excellence of the Australian grasses are great advantages to the dairy farmer. The sheep is not a native of Australia, but sheep breeding was begun at the end of the 18th century, and has been characterized by a continuous and remarkable growth, due largely to the fine grazing facilities of the country, especially the grassy Downs in the east. In addition to wool and meat, sheepskins, both with and without wool, form an important item of export. Cattle raising is carried on in all the states, both for slaughtering and dairying purposes. Dairying has also grown greatly in importance during recent years. Condensed and concentrated milk are made, and poultry and bee farming carried on, in conjunction with other agricultural industries. The country is well adapted to horse breeding, and Australian horses compare favorably with those of other lands.

Owing to the lack of navigable rivers to furnish communication between the coast and the interior, Australia is especially dependent on its railways for transportation. In the eastern, southeastern, and southern parts railway lines connect the chief ports with each other and with the surrounding industrial districts. Some of the eastern lines run inland more than 600 m., and one main line runs from Adelaide northward for nearly 700 m. Western Australia also has a connected system of lines between its ports and the agricultural, mining, and pastoral districts. There are a number of disconnected lines in Northern Queensland, Northern Territory, and Tasmania. On June 30, 1947, there was open a total length of government and private railways of 27,827 m., of which 648 m. were under private ownership. The mileage was distributed as follows: New South Wales, 6,128; Victoria, 4,748; Queensland, 6,566; South Australia, 2,547; Western Australia, 4,348; Tasmania, 641; Federal Capital Territory, 5; Northern Territory, 316. The staff comprised about 110,500 persons. The Trans-Australian Railway was completed in 1917. By 1950, the total railway mileage had increased to 28,000.

Nearly one-fourth of the value of Australian production is contributed by the manufacturing industries. The richness of the country's resources, and the policy of the Commonwealth Government to encourage local industries by means of protective duties and the payment of bounties and bonuses, promise much for the future development of manufacturing. Measured by the value added to the raw material, the most important group of industries is that of metal working and machinery, which includes the manufacture of agricultural implements, cutlery, railway carriages, brass and copper works, iron works and foundries, smelting, tin smithing, and wire working. Wool is by far the largest item of export. Other leading exports are wheat, butter, sheepskins, frozen beef, lamb, and mutton. About half of the Commonwealth's exports go to the United Kingdom and British possessions; France comes next with about 12 per cent., and the United States third. Australia derives about one-fourth of its imports from the United States. The principal items are automobiles and automobile parts, chemicals, machinery, and petroleum. Australia is the United States' largest foreign market for automobiles, and about a fourth of her total imports come from the United States, most of the rest coming from Great Britain.

The population of Australia in 1950 was estimated at 8,000,000. The aboriginal population is estimated at 60,000. The average density is about 2.3 persons to the sq. m., and the only districts which may be considered well populated are those on the coast. The great proportion of the population are either Australian or British born. There is no established state religion, but by far the larger proportion of the people belong to the Church of England.

Education is in the hands of the separate states, and in the primary grades is free and compulsory throughout Australia. There are universities at Sydney, Melbourne, Brisbane, Adelaide, Hobart, and Perth. Military education is offered at the Royal Military College, Duntroon.

Sydney, capital of New South Wales, is a first-class naval station, and has been the headquarters of the British fleet in Australia.

According to the Federal Constitution, the Commonwealth of Australia is governed by a Governor-General appointed by the British Crown, and assisted by a Cabinet responsible to the Australian Parliament. The Parliament consists of a Senate of 36 members (six elected by each of the six original states for six years, half retiring every three years), and a House of Representatives, numbering 75 members and elected every three years. The number of the Representatives sent from each state is proportional to its population (excluding aborigines), but may not number less than five in the case of any of the original states. Each state has a state governor, who represents the sovereign for the state, and a parliament which exercises all rights not delegated to the Federal Parliament. There is a High Court, consisting of a chief justice and five justices appointed by the Governor-General in Council, exercising original as well as appellate jurisdiction.

Ethnographers differ as to the origin of the native Australian race (aborigines), many holding that the numerous tribes scattered over Australia were not originally of common descent. Sir G. Grey, however, believed that, notwithstanding apparent differences between tribes, their common origin and fundamental unity must be admitted. A fundamental connection with the negro stock, whether Oceanic or African, is shown in the dark color, the shape of the skull (highly dolichocephalic, or long-headed), and several other physical characteristics. The aboriginal population is estimated at 60,000. The state parliaments have made humane and adequate provision for the protection of these peoples.

The precise date of the discovery of Australia is doubtful. It has been asserted that Magellan's followers sighted Western Australia in 1522, and that a Spanish ship passed Torres Strait in 1545. In a French chart of 1542 it figures as 'Java la Grande.' It is next distinctly referred to in a book by Cornelius Wytfliet (Louvain, 1598), in which it is con-

Sydney, Australia.

Australia

jectured to measure one-fifth of the world. The first definite knowledge of the country was brought to Europe by the *Duyfken*, a Dutch ship, which explored the north coast in 1606. In the same year Torres, a Spaniard, passed through the strait which bears his name. In 1616 exploration of the west coast was carried on by Dirk Hartog. The Dutch vessel *Arnhem* in 1618 explored the coast of Arnhem Land, and in 1627 the *Guldene Zeepard*, also Dutch, sighted a large part of the south coast from Cape Leeuwin eastward. Another Dutchman, Tasman, discovered Tasmania, which he called Van Diemen's Land, in 1642, and William Dampier, an Englishman, visited the continent in 1688 and 1699. A century later (1770) Captain Cook came upon this island continent, in the course of his circumnavigation of the globe, exploring the whole eastern coast from Gipps Land on the s.e. (now Victoria) to Cape York. The exploration of the whole coast of Australia was completed by the *Beagle* (in which Charles Darwin sailed), 1837-43. The first British settlement having been made in 1788 at Port Jackson (where Sydney now stands), inland exploration followed. One of the greatest and most successful of all Australian explorations was the crossing of the continent, from south to north, from Adelaide to a point west of Chambers Bay, in 1862, by J. M. M'Douall Stuart. The first civilized settlement in Australia was made at Botany Bay in 1788 by 1,030 persons, mostly convicts. In 1825 Moreton Bay (now Queensland) was settled as a part of New South Wales, attaining in December, 1859, the position of a separate colony. The settlement of Western Australia (the Swan River Settlement, as it was then called) dates from 1829. It continued to be a penal settlement from 1851 to 1868. Port Phillip (now Victoria), then a part of New South Wales, was first colonized in 1835, and on July 1, 1851, was constituted an independent colony. The colonization of South Australia by British emigrants dates from 1836. All the colonies were granted responsible government between 1850 and 1860, except West Australia, which, on account of its sparse population, was not granted self-government until 1893. The definite movement for Federation began in 1885, and a constitution was drawn up by a special convention and accepted by the various colonies in 1899. In 1900 the constitution was submitted to the British Parliament, and on Jan. 1, 1901, the six colonies were proclaimed a British colonial federation, under the title of 'The Commonwealth of Australia.' Australia's part in World War I was a notable one. More than 362,000 volunteers, equipped and trained, were sent to the front.

To encourage immigration into Australia, the Australian Government reached an agreement with the British Government in April, 1925, under which it was proposed to lend money, up to $170,000,000 at low rates of interest to the governments of Australian states, to make suitable areas of land available for settlement and to aid their development by the construction of public works. Australia declared war on Ger., Sept. 1939. Early in the war with Japan, Australia was threatened and great concern was felt for her safety. In March 1942 Gen. MacArthur arrived and took supreme command of the Allied Forces in the South-West Pacific. With the Allied attack on Guadalcanal the danger began to lessen. In Nov. 1943 the Duke of Gloucester was appointed to succeed Lord Gowrie as Governor-General; he went to Australia in Jan. 1945. In July 1945 Prime Minister John Curtin died; he had headed the Labor Party. In Sept. 1945 Australia ratified the United Nations Charter.

Bibliography.—Bean's *Official History of Australia in the War of 1914-18* (12 vols., 1921-43); Jose's *History of Australasia* (15th ed., 1930); Elkin's *The Australian Aborigines* (1938); Fitzpatrick's *The British Empire in Australia* (1941); Grattan's *Introducing Australia* (1942); Miller's *Australian Literature from Its Beginnings to 1935* (1942); Deakin's *The Federal Story* (1944); Fitzpatrick's *A Short History of the Australian Labour Movement* (2nd ed., 1944); Haskell's *Waltzing Matilda: A Background to Australia* (5th ed., 1945); Smith's *Place, Taste and Tradition: A Study of Australian Art Since 1788* (1945); Denning's *Inside Parliament* (1946); Evatt's *Australia in World Affairs* (1946); Fitzpatrick's *The Australian People, 1788-1945* (1946); Gentilli's *Australian Climates and Resources* (1946); Greenwood's *The Future of Australian Federalism* (1946); Mitchell's *The Pronunciation of English in Australia* (1946); Neville's *Australia's Coloured Minority* (1948).

Australian Alps, a mountain range of Southeastern Australia. The loftiest summits are Mount Townsend (7,347 ft.) and Mount Borong (6,508 ft.).

Australian Ballot, a method of voting in which the ballots, printed by the government and having the names of all the candidates of all parties inscribed thereon, are handed to each voter as he enters the voting booth, that he may designate the candidates he desires to support with his vote, absolute secrecy and freedom of choice being thus secured in the ballot. See BALLOT.

Australian Gum Tree. See **Eucalyptus.**

Australian Literature, while essentially part of English literature, is yet sufficiently distinctive to justify a separate classification. The first Australian poet worthy of the title is Charles Harpur (1812-68), whose *Bushrangers and Other Poems* appeared in 1853; Henry Clarence Kendall (1842-82), in whose work the Australian genius finds its first real expression; Adam Lindsay Gordon, author of *Bush Ballads and Galloping Rhymes,* although a Scotsman, is considered by some the real pioneer poet of Australia. Among other Australian poets are Brunton Stephens, George Gordon M'Crae and many others. Marcus Clarke (1846-81) is probably the best all-round man of letters Australia can claim. He was a critic, short story writer, and novelist. Henry Kingsley (1830-76), brother of the more famous Charles Kingsley, though not an Australian, was the author of two novels which portray most vividly the pastoral epoch of Australian history. Mrs. Campbell Praed has done more than any other novelist to depict the political and social side of Australian life. Other Australian writers of note are Ada Cambridge, Madame Couveur ('Tasma'), Mary Gaunt, Louis Becke, Guy Boothby, 'Steele Rudd,' Ethel Turner, Hume Nisbet, Price Warung, and the historical and philosophic writers, Charles Henry Pearson, William Edward Hearn, and G. W. Rusden.

Consult Turner and Sutherland's *The Development of Australian Literature;* Stevens' *Golden Treasury of Australian Verse;* Nettie Palmer's *Modern Australian Literature;* H. M. Green's *An Outline of Australian Literature.*

Austrasia, or **Kingdom of the East** (as opposed to *Neustria,* which formed the KINGDOM OF THE WEST), a large part of Frankish Gaul, was founded in 511, and governed from the 6th to the 8th century by a succession of Merovingian kings, ultimately being merged, under Charlemagne's successor, into Germany, as Neustria was into France.

Austremoine, or **Stremonius, St.,** apostle and first bishop of Auvergne. He introduced Christianity into Issoire, France, in the 3d century.

Austria, a republic of Europe, constituting, prior to World War I, the western half of the Austro-Hungarian monarchy. See AUSTRIA-HUNGARY. By the terms of the Peace Treaty (1919) this area was greatly reduced. The reconstituted nation, known as the Republic of Austria, consisted of 9 provinces—Vienna, Burgenland, Lower Austria, Upper Austria, Salzburg, Styria, Carinthia, Tyrol, and Vorarlberg. With the exception of

Area and Population of Austria **(1937)**

Provinces	Area (Square Miles)	Population
Vienna........	107	1,874,130
Burgenland.....	1,532	299,447
Lower Austria..	7,452	1,509,076
Upper Austria..	4,626	902,318
Salzburg.......	2,762	245,801
Styria.........	6,323	1,015,106
Carinthia......	3,680	405,129
Tyrol..........	4,882	349,098
Vorarlberg.....	1,005	155,402
Total........	32,369	6,760,233

Switzerland, Austria is the most mountainous country in Europe, the greater part of the surface being covered by the ranges and peaks of the Eastern Alps. Austria is for the most part well watered. The principal river is the Danube which traverses the country for a distance of 234 m. and, with its tributaries, waters over half the country. Vorarlberg is dominated by the Rhine, which forms a boundary line between Switzerland and Austria. There are numerous small mountain lakes. Owing to the wide diversity in altitude, the climate is extremely varied, and the geographic conditions are accompanied by a similar diversity in its flora. The forests, many of which are state property, are extensive, more than a third of the total cultivated area being woodland. The mineral resources of the old Austrian Empire were so extensive as to be practically inexhaustible. The loss of Bohemia, Silesia, and Moravia by the terms of the Peace Treaty deprived Austria of her richest coal lands and of valuable deposits of iron, silver, lead and graphite; while the loss of Galicia meant also the loss of large quantities of petroleum and rock salt. The mineral wealth of the country is, in spite of these losses, considerable.

Although the growth of modern industrial life in Austria has attracted large numbers from the soil, agriculture remains an important industry and has shown steady improvement since World War I.

The manufacturing industries enjoy several

natural advantages, such as good water supply, equable distribution of fuel, abundance of raw materials, cheap labor, and fairly good and economical means of communication. Following World War I Austrian industries suffered severely. The chief industries are the manufacture of agricultural and industrial machinery and automobiles; textiles, cotton, wool, leather, woodwork, furniture, paper, and fancy goods. By virtue of an agreement between Austria and Hungary, made in 1867 and renewed every ten years, the two countries under pre-war conditions formed a single customs territory. Their commercial importance to each other was paramount. During the war, trade could be carried on only with the countries allied to Austria-Hungary and with the neutral countries of Switzerland, the Netherlands, Denmark, Norway, and Sweden; production naturally decreased. In 1937 the foreign trade reached its highest level for several years.

The net proceeds of the customs of Austria and Hungary were devoted to the administration of common affairs, the expenditures in excess of the customs revenue being divided between the two countries. At the break-up of the old empire by the terms of the Peace Treaty, Austrian finances were in a state of chaos. The attempt to meet the problem by the issue of paper currency served only to increase the difficulty. Generous foreign loans gave merely temporary relief. The League of Nations plan for the rehabilitation of Austrian finances was completed and the protocols embodying the details were signed by Great Britain, France, Italy, Czechoslovakia, and Austria, On Oct. 4, 1922. This plan was almost immediately effective. The loan, of about $26,000,000, was raised without delay, and the general economic condition of the country improved markedly.

At the close of 1939 the population of Austria was 7,009,014. Before World War I the empire of Austria-Hungary had a population of about 51,000,000.

The religious creeds then were as numerous as the nationalities represented among its people. Religious liberty was a leading principle, but the Roman and Greek Catholic churches predominated. The educational system is of the German type. Elementary education was free and compulsory.

In addition to the common army of the dual monarchy Austria formerly maintained *Landwehr* forces to the number of about 50,000, military service being compulsory and universal. Naval affairs were administered by the Naval Department of the common War Ministry. (See AUSTRIA-HUNGARY: *Defence*). By the treaty of St. Germain (Sept. 10, 1919), universal compulsory military service was abolished, and the country's military forces were limited to 30,000 men. The only Austrian war vessels were four patrol boats on the Danube. The armed force of the country did not include any military or naval air forces. The manufacture, importation, or exportation of aircraft or aircraft parts was prohibited.

Prior to World War I Austria and Hungary formed a dual monarchy with a common ruler and common Ministries of War, Foreign Affairs, and Finance (see AUSTRIA-HUNGARY). Otherwise, Austria had its own parliament, ministry, and administration. According to the new Austrian constitution, promulgated Nov. 10, 1920, the Austrian republic was a confederation of nine independent states, with its capital at Vienna. A new constitution was adopted Dec. 7, 1929. The legislative power was vested in two chambers—the Assembly (*Nationalrat*), and the First Chamber (*Bundesrat*). The two houses together formed the Federal Assembly, which convened only for the purpose of declaring war and electing the president. Each province had its provincial diet (*landtag*) and a governor chosen by the diet from its membership.

The Austro-Hungarian monarchy originated in a margravate founded by Charlemagne at the end of the 8th century, to the east of Bavaria, as a defense against the Avars. It was afterward called *Oesterreich*, or Austria, being first mentioned in 996. After a period of confusion and some fighting, Ottokar, king of Bohemia, gained possession of the Austrian territories (1252), to which he added by inheritance Carinthia and Carniola in 1269. In 1276 he lost them all through his refusal to recognize as emperor Rudolf of Hapsburg, who gave (1282) Austria, Styria, and Carniola in fief to his sons Albert and Rudolph, and thus founded the future greatness of the house of Hapsburg which rapidly rose to a powerful state. By the acquisition of Netherlands in 1477, of the crown of Bohemia in 1526, and of Hungary in 1527, Austria rose to the rank of a European monarchy. Between 1439 and 1526 Hungary and Bohemia were ruled by other princes, but by prudent policy and clever marriages the Hapsburg power steadily grew. The death of Charles VI., in 1740, threw open to Europe the imperial crown, and the succession to the Austrian possessions. In

1864 Austria joined Prussia in wresting Schleswig-Holstein and Lauenburg from Denmark; but in 1866 the allies fell out and went to war. After the Franco-Prussian War of 1870-1, Bismarck established with Austria and Russia the Alliance of the Three Emperors, to preserve the *status quo* in Europe, and to oppose all revolutionary movements. But owing to the events in the Russo-Turkish War of 1877-8, the friendship of Austria and Russia came to an end. (See TRIPLE ALLIANCES.) The war which finally broke out between Turkey and the Balkan states and in which Austria was thus largely implicated, had as one of its results the fourth tragedy of the Hapsburg family during the reign of Emperor Francis Joseph. The heir apparent, Archduke Francis Ferdinand, and his wife, the Duchess of Hohenberg, were shot to death by a native of Herzegovina on June 28, 1914, at Sarajevo, the capital of Bosnia. The investigation into the assassination of Archduke Francis Ferdinand led to the sending of an ultimatum to Servia on July 23 which practically constituted an indictment of that country, and which demanded a reply within forty-eight hours. On July 26 Austria proclaimed martial law and severed diplomatic relations with Servia, and despite the offer of Servia to submit the case to The Hague, Austria declared war on July 28, and the next day bombarded Belgrade. The history of Austria for the next four years is closely bound up with the history of the World War, during the early part of which the Austrian armies were engaged chiefly in Servia, Galicia, Albania, and Montenegro. In the latter half the main Austrian activity was on the Italian front. For details of campaigns and battles see the article EUROPE, WORLD WAR I.

Austria.—Houses of Parliament, Vienna.

By the terms of the Treaty of St. Germain, signed Sept. 20, 1919, establishing peace, Austria was recognized as a new and independent state under the name of the Republic of Austria, about one-fifth its former size, losing Galicia, Bukowina, Bohemia, Moravia, Silesia, Southern Tyrol, Carniola, Croatia, Slavonia, Bosnia Herzegovina, Dalmatia, the Adriatic Coastlands, and parts of Carinthia and Styria. She was required to recognize the independence of the Czechoslovak Republic and of the Jugoslavs and to accept the frontiers of these states, as well as of Bulgaria, Greece, Hungary, Poland, and Roumania, as determined by the Allies. See EUROPE, GREAT WAR OF.

On Nov. 10, 1920, the new Austrian constitution (see *Government*) came into operation, and on Dec. 9, 1920, Dr. Michael Hainisch was elected first president of the republic. A period of economic chaos ensued, in which the very existence of the republic was threatened. An appeal for help was eventually made to the League of Nations, of which Austria had become a member in October 1920. Dr. Wilhelm Micklas was elected President, 1928, and re-elected October 9, 1931, for six years.

In January, 1934, Austria demanded of Germany that it respect Austrian independence and cease Nazi propaganda across the border. On Feb. 1, Austria received and rejected Germany's reply. On July 26, Chancellor Engelbert Dollfuss, Austrian Anti-Nazi and Anti-Socialist dictator, was killed by Austrian Nazis led by a former army sergeant. Kurt Schuschnigg, Minister of Education, was named chancellor of Austria by Pres. Micklas on July 30. The anti-Dollfuss group who had seized a broadcasting station and announced the success of their Nazi putsch were tried by a court in Vienna and nine were immediately hanged.

Chancellor Schuschnigg consolidated his position as dictator in 1936. He readopted universal military service for all men between 18 and 42 years of age as a preliminary to rebuilding a conscript army in defiance of the St. Germain treaty, which limited the regular army to 30,000. On May 14, he forced out of the cabinet Vice-Chancellor von Starhemberg, head of the Heimwehr. On July 11 he announced a reciprocal agreement with Chancellor Hitler of Germany, with Italy's approval. He accepted the resignation of the two Heimwehr members of his cabinet on October 10, 1936, issued a decree that eliminated the Heimwehr as an organization (consisting of 150,000 men) and absorbed the members as individuals in the national army which was to comprise about twice the number, after which he took back the former Heimwehr ministers, thus obtaining what amounted to absolute power.

Under German military pressure a union of Austria with Germany was effected during March and April, 1938. Vienna was bombed by the Russians in World War II; it was captured by them in April 1945. At the end of the war, in 1945, Austria was restored to her 1937 borders. A republic was approved by the Allied Council and elections were held.

Consult Bryce's *The Holy Roman Empire;* Fisher's *The Mediæval Empire;* Coxe's *House of Austria, 1218-1792;* Austria-Hungary and the Hapsburgs; Drage's *Austria-Hungary;* Lennhoff's *The Last Five Hours of Austria* (1938).

Austria-Hungary, officially the Austro-Hungarian Monarchy (*Oesterreichisch-Ungarische Monarchie*) was, previous to World War I, a dual sovereignty of Europe, embracing the empire of Austria and the kingdom of Hungary. The total population of Austria-Hungary in 1910 was 51,390,223.

The two halves of the monarchy were perfectly independent of each other, possessing each its own constitution, legislature, and executive for most state affairs. The bond of union was a common dynasty, and a close and intimate political alliance. The dual agreement was brought about by the so-called *Ausgleich* (Agreement) of 1867.

Military service was universally compulsory, though all men were not actually called upon to serve with the colors. During World War I Austria-Hungary's mobilized strength was estimated at 6,500,000. The navy was organized chiefly for coast defence, and in accordance with the terms of the armistice at the close of the World War, the fleet was surrendered to Italy, March 2, 1919. The multiplicity of races within the dual monarchy with their rivalries and mutual jealousies long rendered the task of the central government a delicate and difficult one. When World War I came, the conflict of race interests and race ideals made internal dissension inevitable. The subject races broke away and declared their independence, and a few days after the armistice was signed, Nov. 11, 1919, the German-Austrians set up a provisional government and declared Austria to be a republic (see AUSTRIA). Hungary, in the meantime, after a bloodless revolution, in the latter part of October 1918, declared its independence; and the peace treaty recognized the two nations as independent republics. See AUSTRIA; HUNGARY; EUROPE, WORLD WAR I; WORLD WAR II.

Austria, Lower, province, Austria, a crown land of the former Austrian Empire, is divided by the Danube into a northern and a southern half. The southern half is occupied by secondary ranges and foothills of the Eastern Alps. The north is a tableland, tilted east toward the low plain of Marchfeld.

Austria, Upper, province, Austria, a crown land of the former Austrian Empire, is divided into two unequal parts by the Danube.

Auteuil, former village of the department of Seine, France, now incorporated in Paris. See PARIS.

Author and Publisher. See **Copyright; Publishing.**

Auto, in Spain and Portugal, a kind of short religious play, analogous to the miracle and mystery play of the Middle Ages. Such plays were in vogue from the 12th to past the middle of the 18th century; but were forbidden in Spain in 1765, though they are still presented in Portugal.

Autobiography, the record of one's life, written by himself. It may take the conventional narrative form, or it may consist of letters, as those of Pliny in ancient times or of Robert Louis Stevenson in our own day. Again, it may be in the form of a diary, as that of Evelyn, found in an old clothes basket in 1817.

The autobiography of Benvenuto Cellini gives a spirited picture of the Italian Renaissance. Among the many distinguished later works are Benjamin Franklin's *Autobiography*, Theodore Roosevelt's *Autobiography* (1913), Anna Howard Shaw's *Story of a Pioneer* (1915), *The Education of Henry Adams* (1918).

Autochthones, the Greek name for the original inhabitants of a country, not settlers, considered as having sprung from the soil itself. The Latin equivalent term was *aborigines.*

Autoclave, or **Digester,** is an apparatus for heating substances under pressure, invented by Dr. Papin about 1690. It is used in separating gelatine from bones; in slaughter houses, to obtain lard and tallow from carcasses too poor for marketable purposes; and in extracting tannin from nut-galls.

Autocles, an Athenian general and orator of the 4th century B.C.

Autocracy (Gr. 'sole mastery,' 'ruling by one's self'), a term signifying that form of government in which the sovereign unites in himself the legislative and the executive powers of the state, and thus rules uncontrolled. Such a sovereign is called an autocrat.

Auto da Fé. See **Inquisition.**

Autodidactus, The, ('Self-taught man'), an Arabic romance setting forth the growth, into knowledge of nature and God, of a child cast upon a desert island; by Abu-Bekr-ibn-Tofail. Lat. trans., *Philosophus Autodidacticus*, E. Pocock; *The Improvement of Human Reason*, S. Ockley.

Autographs, documents of any kind in the handwriting of their authors. Interest in autographs dates back to antiquity. The Greeks and Romans had notable collections, as did also the Chinese. The British Museum contains several of these albums, with signatures of celebrities of the reigns of Elizabeth and James I., in whose time they were especially popular. The New York Public Library contains the most valuable known collection of American autographs, and also the best set of signers of the Declaration of Independence.

Autogravure, a photo-etching process patented by J. R. Sawyer in London, 1884. If an ordinary autotype carbon print is placed on silvered copper instead of on paper, the slight relief that the picture possesses is enough to admit of an electrotype being taken from it (see AUTOTYPE).

Autogiro. See **Aeronautics.**

Auto-intoxication, self-intoxication, or poisoning by uneliminated toxins generated within the body. While it may include a number of varieties of internal poisoning, it is applied usually to toxæmias which arise from the intestinal tract owing to faulty digestion and elimination, and the putrefaction of the retained waste products by intestinal bacteria.

The symptoms include loss of appetite, headache, and abdominal distress, becoming more and more marked as the case proceeds, accompanied by nervous and vasomotor disturbances. The treatment consists largely in dietetic measures, and the taking of proper exercise.

Autolycus, an ancient Greek hero, the son of Hermes, and father of Anticleia, the mother of Odysseus. He was famous for his craft and cunning.

Autolycus of Pitane (*c.* 300 B.C.), Greek astronomer, wrote two works on the sun and stars.

Automatic Action, a term applied in physiology to instinctive or involuntary movements. Sleep-walking may be given as an example of automatic action.

Automatism, the doctrine according to which all the actions of living beings, including the voluntary actions of man, are completely explained in purely physiological terms. Consult Huxley's essay on 'The Hypothesis that Animals are Automata'.

Automaton (Gr. 'self-moving'), a machine contrived to imitate the motions and actions of some living creature. In ancient history many automata are reported as having been invented by Archytas, Hero, and others. The most famous modern invention was Vaucanson's flute-player. All automata were surpassed by the specimens invented by Mr. Maskelyne, and exhibited at the London Egyptian Hall, 'Psycho' (1875), a figure seated on a glass cylinder, which played cards against all comers, and worked arithmetical questions of great difficulty. See ROBOT.

Automobile. See **Motor Cars.**

Autonomy, in political economy, is a polity in which the citizens of any state manage their own government. The term is used specifically of states and territories which combine self-government in local matters with subordination in foreign relations.

Autonomy, in its philosophical sense, a term used by Kant to express the principle that the moral reason, or conscience, cannot recognize as binding any law which is not affirmed by the moral reason itself, but merely imposed from without. A law thus imposed from without is termed by Kant *heteronomous.*

Autoplasty (Gr. 'self-formation'), a surgical operation whereby a diseased or injured part is replaced by tissues taken from the same body. Skin-grafting is another example.

Autopsy. See **Post-mortem Examination.**

Autosuggestion, or **Self-Suggestion,** a suggestion conveyed to the individual without external intervention. Auto-suggestion may be voluntary or involuntary. The subject may, by concentrating his thought upon a certain line of action, induce that action, or he may, unconsciously act upon suggestions started in his consciousness by others.

Autotype, a photographic process by which permanent prints are produced in a carbon pigment. A sheet of paper coated with a film of bichromatized gelatin, in which lampblack or other permanent pigment has been held in solution or suspension, is exposed to the action of light, in a printing-frame, beneath an ordinary photographic negative.

Autrefois Acquit—Autrefois Convict. Technical pleas in bar of a second prosecution for one and the same offence. It is an ancient principle of the common law that a person accused of crime shall not, after one conviction or acquittal, be a second time subjected to the hazard of a trial for the identical offence for which he was previously tried. If so indicted he may plead verbally or in writing *autrefois acquit* or *autrefois convict*—i.e. that he has already been acquitted or convicted on the same charge, either at home or abroad, by a court of competent jurisdiction.

Autumn is that season of the year which begins astronomically in the northern hemisphere when the sun enters the zodiacal sign Libra—*viz.* about Sept. 23. Autumn ends and winter begins on or about Dec. 21, when the sun has reached its lowest position south of the equator.

Autun (anc. *Augustodunum*), district capital and episcopal see, department Saône-et-Loire, France. Originally the seat of a Druidical school, it was under the Romans famous for its school of rhetoric. Industries, especially textiles, tanning, paper-making, and brewing, are important; p. 14,150.

Auxerre (Rom. *Autissiodorum*), town, capital of department Yonne, France. There are manufactures of cloth, and a trade in wines (Burgundy), coal, wool and chemicals; p. 21,980.

Avalanche, a mass of snow or ice which slides or rolls from the mountain slopes into the valleys, often causing great damage to villages and forests. Avalanches occur particularly in spring and early summer when the snow and underlying soil are loosened by melting. Drifts or powder avalanches which frequently take place in winter consist of light snow set in motion by the wind. In the upper courses of glaciers, masses of ice may become detached from the main body and fall down the slopes.

Avalon, 'the island-valley of Avilion' of Tennyson's *Morte d'Arthur,* is the paradise of the departed heroes of Celtic tradition. Its 'magic apples' suggest a connection between Avalon and the garden of the Hesperides. The Celtic legends of the journey to the soul-kingdom formed one of the sources of Dante's poem. For one of the most perfect of them see Whitley Stoke's trans. of *Fis Adamnain.*

Avampace, surnamed **Ibn-Say eg** or **Ibn-Badia** (d. 1138), Arab philosopher, physician, astronomer, and poet, was born in Saragossa. His great philosophical work, *The Conduct of the Individual,* is known to us only through its mention by Averrhoës, and notes upon it by Moses of Narbonne.

Avars. (1.) A people of Uralo-Altaic race. In 558 A.D. they offered their services to the Byzantine emperor Justinian, who commissioned them to subjugate the Bulgarians, who had invaded Mœsia (now Bulgaria). Having performed this task, they settled in Pannonia (the present Hungary) and in 566 helped the Longobardi to break the power of the Gepidæ, or Goths. After the death (630) of their chief, Bajan, their downfall was rapid. Nevertheless, during the 8th century they made frequent incursions into Germany and Italy, until Charlemagne took the field against them, and completely destroyed their power in 796.

Avatar (Sanskrit 'descent'), applied to the 'descent' (incarnation) of the principal deities in Hindu mythology; especially applied to Brahma, Siva, and the ten incarnations of Vishnu.

Avatcha, or **Avacha,** bay, town, and active volcano with double peak (8,500 and 10,000 ft.) southeast of Kamchatka, on the shore of the bay Petropavlovsk.

Avebury, or **Abury,** Wiltshire, England, an ancient artificial mound and 'Druidical circle' or 'heathen temple,' now almost obliterated. It resembled Stonehenge, which lies 17 m. s. of it.

Avellaneda, industrial and commercial city, Argentine Republic, separated from Buenos Aires by the Riachuelo River. It is practically a part of the capital; p. 193,431.

Avellino, town, episcopal see, Italy, capital of province of the same name, has for centuries been famous for its hazel-nuts. Orchards, vineyards, farms and gardens provide the chief industries, but there are also some manufactures. Close to it is the famed monastery of Monte Vergine, with a wonder-working image of the Virgin, and the tomb of Catherine of Valois; p. 29,611.

Ave Maria, or **Angelica Salutatio,** a prayer used in the Roman Catholic Church, addressed to the Virgin Mary. The addition, 'Holy Mary, Mother of God, pray for us sinners, now and in the hour of our death,' dates from the 15th century, but was first authorized for daily use in the breviary by Pius v. in 1568.

Avens, plants of the genus Geum, or their allies.

Aventine Hill (*Aventinus Mons*), one of the seven hills of ancient Rome. Ancus Martius colonized it with the inhabitants of the conquered Latin towns. Servius Tullius brought it within the fortified part of the city, and built upon it the celebrated temple of Diana. After 455 B.C. it was the special plebian quarter of Rome. At the present time it is almost deserted, being covered with gardens, vineyards, and a few old churches.

Aventinus, Johannes (1477-1534), whose proper name was TURMAIR, known as the 'Bavarian Herodotus,' a German historian, studied under Celtes at Ingolstadt, in 1495.

In 1517 he was appointed historiographer of Bavaria. His *Annales Boiorum* and its German edition appeared after his death. His *Chronica* is the first important work on German history based on a critical examination of the sources. See his *Life* by Döllinger, and by Wegele.

Average, in law. General average is the term applied to the rule by which losses or sacrifices arising on a voyage are recouped by an average contribution from all parties who benefit by such loss or sacrifice. For this purpose the adventure is considered as consisting of three parts—ship, freight, and cargo. In order that there may be a general average contribution, the following conditions are necessary: (1) The loss must be an intentional one. (2) It must be for the benefit of all parties. (3) It must be incurred under pressure of immediate and unusual necessity. (4) It must not arise from the negligence of the parties.

Averescu, Alexandre (1859-1938), Roumanian soldier and politician. He served with distinction in the World War. After the Roumanian defeat Averescu was appointed premier to conduct the peace negotiations with the Central Powers, but he resigned rather than accede to the harsh terms of the German conquerors. He was premier again in 1920-21 and 1926-27.

Avernus, Lake, Italy, now called **Lago d'Averno,** where the ancients placed the entrance to the infernal regions. (*Cf.* '*Facilis descensus Averno*,' Virgil's *Æneid*, VI.), Agrippa, at the command of Augustus, connected the lake with the sea, and built a naval port, which existed down to 1538, when the volcanic uprising of Mount Nuovo destroyed it.

Averrhoës or **Averroës,** whose name was ABUL-IBN-ROSHD (1126-98), Arab philosopher, was born at Cordova in Spain. He regarded Aristotle as the incarnation of all human wisdom, he was for ages famous as the great commentator of his master, and at Padua his school flourished until nearly the middle of the 17th century. Roger Bacon and John Baconthorpe were the most conspicuous of the English Averrhoists. Averrhoës drew the clearest distinctions between human science (knowledge) and religion, and discriminated sharply between this last and the logic-chopping subtleties of theology. The best Latin edition of his commentaries was issued at Venice in 1552 and later years. See J. Müller's *Philosophie und Theologie;* Renan's *Averroës et l'Avérroisme;* Mehren's

Etudes sur la Philosophie d'Averrhoës; Christ *Psychology of the Active Intellect of Averrhoës* (1926).

Avianus, Flavius, a Latin fabulist of the 4th century, author of 42 fables in imitation of Phædrus and Babrius, still extant, set forth in elegiac verse. See *The Fables of Avianus.*

Aviary, a large cage or enclosure for keeping birds. Such structures are permissible only in summer in most of the United States, and hence are uncommon except in zoölogical gardens. See CAGE BIRDS.

Aviation. See **Aeronautics; Airplane.**

Avicebron, or **Salomon ibn-Gabirol** (1020-70), Jewish poet and philosopher, born in Spain. He is the author of the philosophical work *Fons Vitæ,* or *Fons Sapientiæ,* written in Arabic, which had a great influence on the scholastic writers of the middle ages. He composed numerous poems and hymns, several of which now form part of the synagogue prayer-book. See Kaufmann's *Studien über S. Ibn Gabirol;* Geiger's *S. Gabirol und seine Gedichte;* Munk's *Mélanges de Philosophie Juive et Arabe.*

Avicenna, or **Ibn-Sina** (980-1037), Arabian philosopher and physician, born near Bokhara; died at Hamadan, in Persia. His principal work is the *Canon of Medicine,* written in Arabic, early translated into Latin, and for centuries (to the middle of the 17th century in some) a leading text-book in European universities. His philosophical doctrine is mainly Aristotelian, adapted in many parts to the religious faith of the Koran. See Munk's *Mélanges de Philosophie Juive et Arabe* (1857); and Carra de Vaux's *Avicenne* (1900).

Avicennia, or **White Mangrove,** a genus of Verbenaceæ, evergreen trees and shrubs indigenous to the tidal estuaries and salt marshes of most tropical countries. The astringent bark of the *A. tomentosa* is much used in Rio Janeiro for tanning.

Avienus, Rufus Festus, a Latin poet who wrote on geographical and astronomical subjects in the 4th century. See Wernsdorf's *Poetæ Latini Minores.*

Avignon (Latin *Avenio*), town, capital of department Vaucluse, Provence, France. The

The Palace of the Popes, Avignon.

citadel-like palace of the Popes, built 1336-70, with six towers and walls 18 ft. thick, is the chief object of interest. The metropolitan church, Notre Dame des Doms (12th century), perched on a rock (280 ft.), between which and the river is the well-known Promenade des Rocher des Doms, and a multitude of other ecclesiastical structures, are interesting (*la ville sonnante* of Rabelais). A continuous belt of walls (1349-68) encircles the city. Villeneuve, on the r. bk. of the river, is connected with Avignon by the famous bridge built in 1108, and partly destroyed in 1669. Petrarch first saw Laura in Avignon, and she was buried in the church of the Cordeliers, now destroyed. Silk spinning is the principal industry and the town is the chief warehousing place in s.e. France for grain and wines; p. 59,172.

Avila (Ancient *Abela*), city, Spain, capital of province of the same name. The ancient city is falling into picturesque decay, though its Moorish walls and towers stand almost intact. Avila was the birthplace of Santa Teresa; p. 13,704.

Aviz, Order of St. Benedict, a Portuguese military and religious order founded in 1162 to oppose the Moors. In 1211-23 King Alfonso removed the order to the fortress of Aviz, whence the name. It is now since (1879) simply a miltary order. See Lawrence-Archer's *Orders of Chivalry.*

Avoca, or **Ovoca,** short riv., in Co. Wicklow, Ireland, famed for its silvan scenery for Thomas Moore's well-known lines, (*Irish Melodies,* 1779).

Avocado Pear. See **Alligator Pear.**

Avocets, widely-distributed birds belonging to the genus Recurvirostra, allied to the plovers and sandpipers, and characterized by the long up-curved beak.

Avogadro, Count Amadeo (1776-1856), a professor of physics who discovered 'Avogadro's law'—that equal volumes of different gases, at the same temperature and pressure, contain the same number of molecules.

Avoirdupois. See **Weights and Measures.**

Avon, Upper or Warwickshire river, rising near Naseby, Northamptonshire and flowing through Warwickshire and Worcestershire to join the Severn on the left bank at Tewkesbury, passing Stratford, hence Shakespeare's designation 'Swan of Avon.'

Avondale, par., 10 m. s.w. of Hamilton, West Lanarkshire, Scotland, with the battlefield of Drumclog (1679), immortalized in Scott's *Old Mortality.*

Avulsion. The rapid wearing away or separation of land through the action of the sea or of a natural watercourse. The process is in legal effect opposed to accretion, whereby the shore line is altered by imperceptible degrees. See ACCRETION.

Awaji, largest island in the Inland Sea of Japan. Its scenery is very beautiful and the island is much visited by tourists.

Award. The judicial finding of a referee or arbitrator. The term is sometimes employed to describe a judgment or decree of a court assessing the damages due a litigant, but it is more commonly used in connection with extra-judicial proceedings, as the assessment of damages on the condemnation of land for public use, the determination of questions in dispute by arbitrators, and the like. See ARBITRATION.

Awn, a bristle-like growth, called also *beard,* which arises from the backs or apices of the outer flowering glumes of many species of grasses and cereals; a prolongation of the midrib.

Ax, or **Ax-les-Thermes,** town, department Ariège, France, famous for its warm sulphur springs; p. 1,503.

Axe (spelt *ax* in the Bible), an instrument used for hewing and chopping wood; formerly also a weapon of war. (See BATTLE-AXE.) It was in the earlier ages made of flint or bronze, but is now made of iron with a cutting edge of steel.

Axel Heiberg Glacier, between New Zealand and the South Pole, flows from the Queen Maud Range of the Antarctic Continent on to the Ross Ice Barrier on the Atlantic Ocean.

Axestone, a hard variety of mineral, jade or nephrite, of a greenish color; so called from its use by the Maoris and the South Sea islanders for axe-heads. See JADEITE and NEPHRITE.

Axil, the upper angle between a leaf and the stem from which the leaf arises. The old term was *ala.*

Axilla (Lat. 'armpit'), is, strictly speaking, the armpit, or any other part of the body which forms a similar angle; but for practical purposes axilla is applied to the armpit only.

Axinite, a comparatively rare mineral composed of silica, boron, aluminium, and calcium. It occurs in clove-brown, triclinic crystals with acute edges.

Axinomancy, an ancient Greek ordeal for the discovery of crime. See DIVINATION.

Axiom, a proposition or premise which, being self-evident, requires no proof, and is taken for granted. As a technical term the word 'axiom' is now restricted to the self-evident premises of geometry, the corresponding term in philosophy being intuition.

Axis, in general, an imaginary line about which any solid body rotates, or about which any geometrical figure or organic structure is symmetrical. In human osteology the name is applied to the second cervical vertebra.

Axis Deer, a deer of southern Asia, profusely spotted with white.

Axis Powers, the alliance of Germany, Italy and Japan which originated in the Italo-German pact of Oct. 25, 1936, and opposed the United Nations in World War II.

Axminster, a town in Devonshire, England, noted, before 1835, for its carpets.

Axolotl (*Amblystoma,* or *Siredon pisci-*

formis), a Mexican and North American amphibian, which resembles a newt in shape, and has a powerful tail and three pairs of simple external gills. This amphibian is eaten by the Mexican Indians.

Axum, Axoum, or **Aksum,** ruined town, Tigré, Abyssinia, formerly the capital of a powerful Ethiopian kingdom. (See ETHIOPIA.) Axum has been Christian since the 4th century. There are numerous remains of Greek architecture; p. 5,000.

Ayacucho, town, Peru, capital of dep. of same name. In 1539 Pizarro founded the town of San Juan de la Victoria on the site of the Indian Huamanga (Falcon Rock); and after the victory of General Sucre over the Spaniards (1824) the independence of Peru was secured, and the name of the town was changed to Ayacucho; p. 20,000.

Ayala, Pedro Lopez de (1332-1407), Spanish poet and historian. His great work is the *Crónicas de los Reyes de Castilla*.

Aydin, a province, in Turkey, produces most of the olive oil yield in that country. It is rich in mines. Iron, manganese, emery, lignite, mercury and arsenic are found here; area, 2,926 sq. m.; p. 261,078.

Aye-aye (*Chiromys madagascariensis*), a remarkable lemur, nocturnal in its habits, and confined to Madagascar, where it inhabits the dense forests. A notable peculiarity is the rodent-like structure of the front teeth. The hands are also very remarkable, the middle finger being exceedingly long and very slender; it is said to be used in picking out wood-boring insect larvæ. The aye-aye is about as large as a cat, and has large naked ears.

Ayeshah, wife of Mohammed. She died at Medina (677). See MOHAMMED.

Aylesworth, Merlin Hall (1886-), American executive, born in Cedar Rapids, Ia. A public utilities executive (1914-26), he was president, National Broadcasting Co. (1926-36).

Aymaras, a numerous and formerly powerful South American people whose territory lay chiefly on the Bolivian plateau round Lake Titicaca. Their civilization was antecedent to that of the Incas, but was in some respects more highly developed, judging from the stupendous monuments of Tiahuanaco.

Aymon, or **Haimon,** of Dordogne, the father of four sons—Renaud, Guiscard, Alard, and Richard—whose adventures form one of the most popular romances of the Middle Ages.

Ayr, town, Scotland, capital of Ayrshire. The leading industries are manufactures of carpets, lace, woolen and leather goods, boots, shoes, and chemicals. Nearby is the cottage where Robert Burns was born; p. 38,000.

Ayrshire, maritime co. in the southwestern part of Scotland. It is rich in minerals, coal, limestone and iron, and there are valuable fisheries; p. 299,254.

Ayuthia, town, Siam, built principally on piles. Remains of the castle and many temples attest to its former glory. It was taken by the Burmese in 1767 after a two years' siege; p. about 50,000.

Azalea, a genus of ornamental shrubs of the order Ericaceæ. The hardy azaleas are all deciduous, and are native to North America and South Europe. The commonest ones in the northern United States are the wild honeysuckle, or pinxter flowers, and the

Wild Azalea or Honeysuckle.

white azalea, or swamp honeysuckle. A southern species (*A. lutea*), the flame azalea, has orange-red, or red blossoms, which make the shrub a favorite for cultivation. The beautiful Asiatic azaleas (*A. indica*) are usually grown in greenhouses. See also RHODODENDRON.

Azan, ('announcement'), the Moslem call to prayer, chanted or recited five times daily by the muezzin, with his face towards Mecca.

Azerbaijan, or **Aderbaijan,** a fertile and

Azerbaijan   **Aztecs**

mountainous province in Iran. Wheat, maize, cotton, hemp, and tobacco are grown in considerable quantities and there is much mineral wealth; p. estimated at over 2,000,000.

Azerbaijan, a Transcaucasian Soviet Republic consisting chiefly of the two former Russian provinces of Baku and Yelisavetpol. Baku, the capital, is the centre of a great

point of the horizon through the west from 0° to 360°.

Azores, (Portuguese *Açores* or 'Hawk Islands'), a group of islands in the Atlantic Ocean w. of Portugal, of which they form a constituent part. Agriculture, dairying and needlework are the chief occupations. Horta is a seaplane base on Pan American Airways' route from N. Y. to Lisbon and is one of the

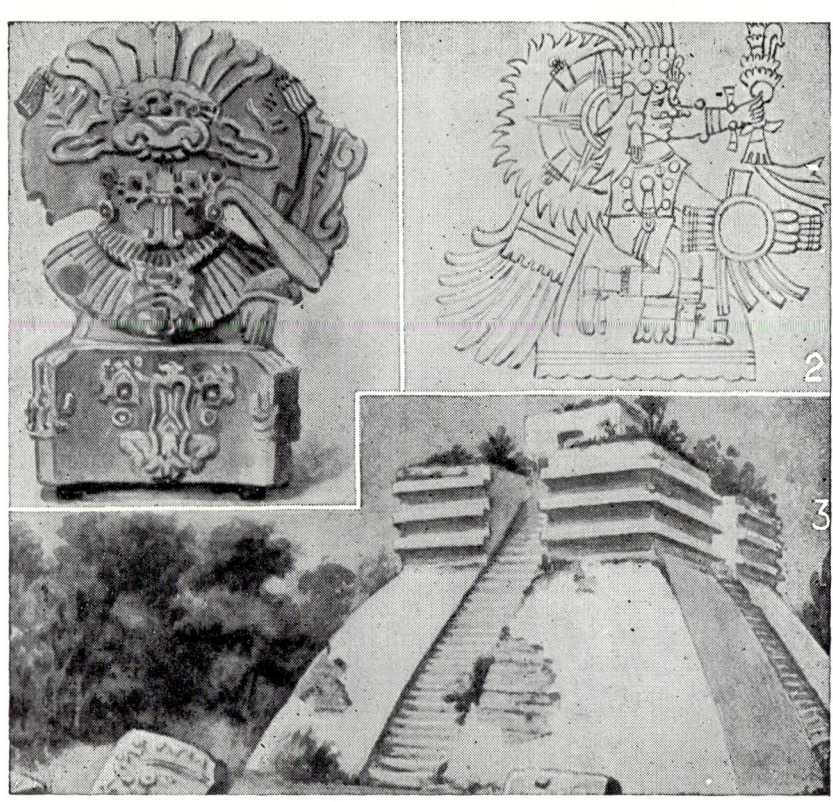

Aztec Remains.
1. Terra-cotta fanciful bust covering square box or hollow pedestal, probably to contain jewels or incense; found near Zachila. 2. Aztec representation of Tonatish, the substance of the sun. 3. Pyramid near Tehuantepec.

petroleum industry. Other industries include cotton, fisheries, cattle breeding, sericulture, and cereals; p. 2,096,973, of whom nearly 75 per cent. are Mohammedans.

Azimuth, the angular distance of a celestial object from the northern or southern point of the horizon, or the angle comprised between the meridian and a vertical plane passing through the object. In the northern hemisphere it is usually reckoned from the south

world's principal **cable stations;** a. 922 sq. m., p. 246,000.

Aztecs, one of the chief cultured peoples of the New World; so called from Aztlan, the fabulous land of the 'Seven Caves' in the north, whence they migrated southwards, and founded a powerful empire in the valley of Mexico, some three or four hundred years before the discovery of America. Their polytheistic religion was largely their own, and was characterized by the worship of the sun and human sacrifices. Their astronomy was mainly astrological, or used for astrological purposes—the determining of good and evil days, divination, the taking of horoscopes, and the like. See Peñafiel's *Monuments of Ancient Mexican Art;* Payne's *History of the New World;* Bancroft's *Native Races of the Pacific States;* also works cited under MEXICO.

Azurite, or blue copper ore, known as chessylite, from its abundance in beautiful crystals at Chessy, near Lyons. It is a basic carbonate of copper, and like malachite, is found chiefly where copper ores have been exposed to water containing carbonic acid. It was formerly much used by painters, but is liable to change to malachite and become green: this is believed to be the origin of the green skies in some old paintings. As an ore of copper, azurite is chiefly important in the copper mining region of southeastern Arizona.

B

B. This letter represents a sound which differs very slightly in different languages. Before utterance the stream of breath is stopped by the lips, hence the modern classification of B as a stop consonant; it is the voiced labial stop. Like other stop consonants, it tends to change into the corresponding spirant, *v*. In this way the letter may come to represent the sound *v*. In English *b* has shown a tendency to become silent before *t* and after *m* ('debt,' 'lamb').

B, in music, is the seventh degree or 'leading note' of the natural scale of C. In French and Italian it is called *si*; in German, H (*Ha*), with B for our B♭. The key of B natural has five sharps; that of B♭ has two flats.

Baal, a word found in all Semitic languages meaning 'owner, proprietor.' When used of a god the article is often prefixed and a word is added expressing the place or thing possessed, or indicating a characteristic. The theory which makes Baal the proper name of a god typifying the sun is not consistent with this multiplicity of local baals (Heb. pl. *baalim*) and lacks corroborative evidence. The baalim were rather local deities each of whom gave fertility to his district and thus became an object of worship. The Israelites found the cult everywhere when they entered Canaan and naturally adopted it. See Sayce, *Hibbert Lectures*; Baethgen, *Beitrage zur semitischen Religions-geschichte*; Robertson Smith, *Religion of the Semites*.

Baalbek (Gr. *Heliopolis*, 'city of the sun': Scrip *Baalath*), ancient city of Syria, chiefly remarkable for the magnificence of its ruins, which occupy a site analogous to that of the Acropolis of Athens. The early history of Baalbek is lost in the mists of antiquity; but as it stood on the route between Tyre and Palmyra, it early became a great entrepôt of Oriental commerce. During the Crusades the city was frequently the centre of warlike operations. It is now a poverty-stricken little village, with about a hundred mean houses. See Wood's *The Ruins of Balbec*; Lortet's *La Syrie d'aujourd'hui*; Frauberger's *Die Akropolis von Baalbek*.

Baba (Slav. 'old woman'), the name of a fantastic being who plays a great rôle in the folk-lore of the Slavonic peoples, especially the Russian, where she is called Iaga-Baba. See Ralston's *Russian Folk-tales*.

Babbage, Charles (1791-1871), a scientific mechanician, who, with Herschel and Peacock, gave the first impulse to an English mathematical revival. He is famous for his unfinished calculating machines, and wrote a good little book called *Economy of Machines and Manufactures*, also *Tables of Logarithms*.

Babbitt, Irving (1865-1933), American literary critic and philosopher, born Dayton, Ohio. Almost contemporaneously with the rise of the postbellum iconoclastic American school of thought represented by H. L. Mencken and Sinclair Lewis, Professor Babbitt began to turn his attention to promulgating a philosophy of life stressing the value of ideals over ideas and the necessity of standards over unbridled self-expression. As a humanist, he emphasized the importance of the individual, while with the progenitors of the humanistic school believing that man is by no means entirely good. Among his books are *The New Laokoon*; *The Masters of Modern French Criticism*; *Rousseau and Romanticism*; *Democracy and Leadership; On Being Creative*.

Babel, Tower of. Modern scholarship is disposed to identify the 'Tower of Babel' with the *zikkurat* of the temple E-sagilla, the extensive ruins of which are now known as Amran in Babylon itself. See Sayce's *Fresh Light from the Ancient Monuments*, and his edition of G. Smith's *Chaldæan Account of Genesis*.

Bab-el-Mandeb, strait uniting the Red Sea with the Indian Ocean. The island of Perim divides it into two unequal channels. The cape of the same name is on the Arabian side of the strait.

Baber (the Tiger), **Zehir ed-Din Mohammed** (1483-1530), first Mogul emperor in India, and founder of the Mogul dynasty, which lasted to the beginning of the 19th century, was a descendant of Timur-Beg (Tamerlane), and succeeded his father, Sheikh Mirza, at the age of twelve on the throne of Andijan in Ferghana. Baber was also a poet, writing in both Turkish and Persian; but the most important of his literary works is his *Autobiography* or *Memoirs*, which he wrote in Turkish, at the end of his life. See Lane Poole's *Baber*.

Babi and Babiism. The term Babiism denotes the tenets of a school of religious reformers who arose in Persia in the middle of the 19th century. The founder was a young sayid, Mirza Ali, son of Mohammed, who was born at Shiraz in 1819, and who, while resident near Bagdad, in 1844, began to preach a faith which differed in many respects from the orthodox Sufiism of Persia. Regarding himself as the latest prophet of God, he took the title of *Bab al-Din*, whence he became known as 'the Bab' and his disciples as 'Babis.' Later he styled himself the *Nuqta*, believing that in him all previous dispensations centered. Mohammed, Christ, and Moses he revered as prophets, but as *his* forerunners. The doctrine which he preached was largely a healthy protest against the ideas of the Persian hierarchy. See E. G. Browne, *A Traveller's Narrative, written to illustrate the Episode of the Bab*, *The New History of the Bab*, Khayru'llah, Mac-Nutt, *Beha'u'llah*. See BAHA, BAHAISM.

Babington, Anthony (1561-86), English Roman Catholic conspirator, served as page to Queen Mary of Scotland, to whom he was devoted. He led the conspiracy to kill Elizabeth, confided the plot to Mary, who wrote her approval in the letter which brought her, Babington, and the other conspirators to the scaffold. See W. D. Cooper's *Notices of Anthony Babington*, *State Trials*, Turnbull's *Letters of Mary Stuart*, and Froude and Lingard's *Hists. of England*.

Babington, William (1756-1833), English physician and mineralogist; was the founder of the British Geological Society, and author of *A Systematic Arrangement of Minerals Reduced to the Form of Tables*, and *A New System of Mineralogy*.

Baboon, a name which should strictly be applied only to African monkeys of the genus Cynocephalus. These monkeys are distinguished by the fact that the fore and hind limbs are nearly equal, and that the animals are thus adapted for quadrupedal progression on the ground, rather than for arboreal life like other monkeys. The baboon which was sacred to the ancient Egyptians is supposed to have been the hamadryad. For examples, see MANDRILL, CHACMA, DRILL.

Babrius, a Greek poet, probably before the time of Augustus. His work, called *Fables*, in ten books, was a version of *Æsop's Fables* and seems to have been the base of all the various Aesopean fables which have come down to us. In 1842 a Greek named Minas discovered 123 fresh *Æsop's Fables*, under the name of Babrius, in a MS. at Mount Athos; and others were discovered in MSS. in the Vatican library by Knöll in 1877; and yet others on wax tablets at Palmyra by Von Assendelft in 1891. See Bentley's *Dissertation on the Fables of Æsop*, Tyrwhitt's *Dissertatio de Babri*, and Conington's *Miscellaneous Writings*.

Babson, Roger Ward (1875-   ), statistician, was born in Gloucester, Mass. He was the founder and now is the president and chairman of the board of Babson's Statistical Organization, at Wellesley Hills, Mass., with branch offices in 26 American cities; also founder of Babson's Institute.

Babu, a native of India who possesses a superficial education in English; though, strictly speaking, the term is equivalent to 'Mr.' For an admirable travesty of 'Babu English,' see Anstey's *Baboo Jabberjee, B.A.*

Babul Tree, of India (*Acacia arabica*), yields a transparent gum which is used medicinally and also as food. The wood is used for railway sleepers, and the bark yields a brown tanning dye.

Babuyanes, fertile island group, largely volcanic, of the Philippines. Products: tobacco, rice, maize, and tropical fruits; p. about 9,500.

Baby. See **Infant.**

Babylonia. This name is derived from the native *Bab-ili* (rarely *Bab-ilani*), 'gate of God' (or 'of the gods'), the name of the city which, after the accession of the royal house known as the first dynasty of Babylon, became the capital of the country. The history of the name Bab-ili is unknown, but it is not improbably due to a folk etymology, as is suggested by the fact that Nebuchadnezzar the Great often gives the name as Babilam (a form ending with *a*, and provided with the 'mimmation'), a way of writing it which bears a likeness to a city name read as Babalam, mentioned in an inscription of King Gaddas. Both form and meaning, however, are of sufficient antiquity, as is shown by the fact that it was at an early date translated into the primitive language of the country under the form of Ka-dingira, with the same meaning.

Besides the city of Babylon which was the capital of the country in later days, Babylonia contained a number of other cities of the most remote antiquity, equaling, or perhaps exceeding, in that respect, Babylon itself.

Numerous inscriptions found in the ruins of the cities testify to the success of the ancient Babylonians as agriculturists. The plain is still covered with a network of old canals, some of them of considerable extent, which anciently not only irrigated but also drained the land, keeping the inundation within due limits, and rendering healthier and more cultivable what is at present in too many cases a marsh. The digging of a new canal was considered, 2000 B.C., as being of sufficient importance to date by.

until a comparatively late date; and that when it does come to the front, its kings gradually reduce all the other petty states to subjection, and the latter are not heard of afterward except as integral parts of the Babylonian empire. Yet the city of Babylon must have had a past as glorious as any of the others. Its history practically begins with the royal house called the dynasty of Babylon, consisting of eleven kings, who reigned, in all, about 290 years, beginning about 2200 B.C.

The names of many kings occur, but very

Temple of Jupiter, Baalbek.

As is indicated by the tablets and the sculptures, at least two races anciently inhabited the country, each speaking its own language, and living side by side, until, in the course of centuries, they became one people.

The beginnings of Babylonian history are lost in obscurity, but were certainly of considerable antiquity. According to the American explorers, the rubbish accumulations of the ancient city Nippuru (Niffer) go back no less than 10,000 years—that is to say, as far as 8000 B.C.

Exceedingly interesting is the history of the northern kingdom of Akkad. As far as can at present be ascertained, it was the state in which Semitic influence predominated, and seems, therefore, to have given to Babylonia its first dynasty of Semitic kings.

It is noteworthy that though Sargon of Agade came into contact with Babylon, that city does not appear as a place of importance

little history, until the time of the Kassite dynasty, the first ruler of which was named Gandas or Gaddas (*c.* 1800 B.C.). This ruler calls himself 'king of the four regions, king of Sumer and Akkad, king of Babalam.' Seven reigns later we have the name of the celebrated king Agu or Agu-kak-rime.

Another notable ruler was Nebuchadnezzar I., son of Ninib-nadin-sumi, who warred in Elam and the east generally, and in Syria (Amurru). In 747 B.C. Nabonassar came to the throne, but all that is stated of his reign is that a revolt occurred in Babylon and Borsippa, but was quelled. As to his reign having commenced a historical era, there is no trace of that in the inscriptions. Perhaps the true explanation is that systematic astronomical observations were recorded in his time.

Much has still to be discovered ere we know all about the remarkable ruler, Nabo-na'id, to whom students of Babylonian history owe so much. The son of a princely family of Babylon, he was to all appearance learned, well read, and an antiquarian. The accounts of his researches in the foundations of the ancient temples for records of his predecessors are of the highest value. He seems to have given over the direction of the military affairs of the kingdom into the hands of his son Belshazzar. During his reign the renown of Cyrus began to be spread abroad, and the Babylonian chronicle records that this conqueror attacked a petty ruler in the neighborhood of Arbela. In the year 539 B.C. he began the subjugation of Babylonia and Gobryas, his general, entered the capital on the 16th of Tammuz of the following year. At this time, to all appearance, Belshazzar was at the head of affairs, and practically king, and he seems to have been killed on the night of the 11th of Marcheswan, 539 B.C., in an attack made by Gobryas. The next year the king of Anzan, as Cyrus is called, found himself completely master of Babylonia, and assumed the reins of government. Babylonia had thereafter no separate existence. From time to time she tried to revolt, but always without success. The inhabitants saw with grief their ancient glories disappearing; and the foundation of Seleucia on the Tigris by Seleucus Nicator (312-280 B.C.) completed the ruin of the city. The Semitic Babylonian language, however, continued to be spoken and used in contracts almost, if not quite, until the Christian era, and the worship of their deities is said to have been carried on until the 4th century of the Christian era.

Though it is uncertain whether the ancient Babylonians were more civilized than their Egyptian contemporaries there is but little doubt that they were the pioneers of civilization in the whole of Western Asia before Greece and Rome came to the front. Four thousand years B.C. their system of writing had already been developed, and applied also to the Semitic Babylonian tongue. Fourteen hundred years B.C., as the Tell-el-Amarna tablets testify, its use extended over the whole of Western Asia as far as the Mediterranean and Egypt. (See CUNEIFORM.) Though not a war-like people, the Babylonians possessed more than once what might have been described at the time as a world-wide empire. They were energetic, intelligent, polished in their way and fond of letters. From 4000 B.C. onwards excellent sculptures and engravings on hard stone exist to testify to their skill and artistic instincts. Representations of musical instruments imply also that the art of harmony was not altogether unknown to them. To this must be added agriculture, mensuration, and mathematics, such as they were; and their legal enactments, codified apparently by Hammurabi, are, in their way, noteworthy productions. In the matter of literature we owe to them no less than three accounts of the creation, two accounts of the Flood, one of them put into the mouth of the Babylonian Noah. It is difficult to judge which was the more predominant characteristic of the Babylonians, their trading instinct or their reverence for their gods, for both are equally marked. They had intercourse by means of trade with Elam on the east, Syria on the west, and many other places on the north and south whose names are not recorded. Slavery was common, and contracts concerning the buying, selling, and hiring of slaves are frequently met with. The Babylonians seem at all times, but especially at the earlier period, to have been very prone to litigation, and the large number of tablets of this class which exist show that though the men had generally only one wife, a second was at times taken, often to wait upon the first. Whether a man had children or not, he would, if it seemed good to him, adopt sons or daughters, to whom he was then under legal obligation to give part of his property.

In common with all Semites, the Babylonians were exceedingly religious, and were consequently greatly in the power of their priests, through whom tithes and offerings to their numerous gods were made. Their earliest chief divinity was apparently the god Ea, lord of the deep, possessor of unsearchable wisdom, and creator of all things. When, however, Babylon became the chief city of the united states of Babylonia, Merodach, the god of that city, assumed the first place. He was a reflection of the sun, or the light of day, and was worshipped as he who constantly sought to do good to mankind. His chief title was Bel, 'the lord.' Other divinities were Samas, the sun-god; Sin, the moon-god; Nebo, the prophet or teacher; Nergal (Ura), the god of death and the grave; and many others. It is noteworthy that the names of most of the deities of Babylonia are not Semitic, but in the language of the early Sumero-Akkadian inhabitants of the country. See Hommel's *Geschichte Babyloniens und Assyriens;* Geo. Smith's and A. H. Sayce's *Hist. of Babylonia;* Maspero's *The Dawn of Civilization; History of Art in Chaldea and Assyria;* Loftus's *Travels and Researches in Chaldæa and Susiana;* and Radau's *Early Babylonian Hist.*

Babylonish Captivity. See **Israel, History of.**

Baca, The Valley of, through which the pilgrims march towards Zion.

Baccarat. The origin of the game of baccarat, or baccara—called more familiarly bac—is not known. It became the French gambling game *par excellence* during the latter portion of the reign of Louis Philippe, and still retains its pre-eminence in France.

Baccarat, town in Meurthe-et-Moselle department, France. It possesses one of the most celebrated artistic glass factories in Europe, founded in 1765; p. 7,014.

Bacchæ, also called Mænads and Thyiades, the female attendants of Bacchus. The name was also applied to the priestesses in the Dionysian festivals.

Bacchantes, male and female devotees of Bacchus in his festival processions.

Bacchus. See **Dionysus.**

Bacchylides (*c.* 510-450 B.C.) of Ceos, one of the great lyric poets of Greece, was a nephew of Simonides. Until 1896 only fragments of his poetry were extant, but in that year the British Museum obtained from Egypt a papyrus which contained twenty of his poems, of which six are practically perfect. Bacchylides's poetry is distinguished by elegance and smoothness; he does not possess the depth and magnificence of Pindar, nor his difficulty of thought and language. Editions: Kenyon, the *edition princeps;* Blass, trans. by Poste.

Bach, Johann Christian (1735-82), the youngest son of Sebastian. In 1754 he became organist at Milan, whence he removed to London in 1759, and was appointed conductor to the queen. He wrote many compositions for the piano; several operettas, of which *Orione* had a great success, and another, *La Clemenza di Scipione,* was played as late as 1805.

Bach, Johann Sebastian (b. Eisenach, Mar. 21, 1685; d. Leipzig, July 28, 1750), musical composer. Johann Ambrosius (1645-95), the father of Sebastian, gave his son lessons on the violin. Sebastian, a violinist in the orchestra of Prince Johann Ernst at Weimar, held successively the posts of organist in Arnstadt in Muhlhausen at the court chapel of Weimar and of capellmeister to Prince Leopold at Köthen (1717). In 1723 he was appointed cantor at the school of St. Thomas, Leipzig. Bach's development of all forms of composition marks an epoch in the history of music. His orchestral works, chamber music, and sonatas hold a unique position. Bach was perhaps the greatest organist of his generation. His introduction of a new system of fingering exerted an enormous influence upon the modern art of piano playing. Bach, who tuned his own claviers, invented our present system of equal temperament. The most complete edition of his works is that issued at Leipzig by the Bach Society between 1850 and 1900, in 59 folio volumes. Consult Spitta's exhaustive work (Eng. trans. by Bell and Fuller-Maitland), *Lives* by Miss Kay Shuttleworth, R. Lane Poole, C. F. A. Williams, Rutland Boughton, Sir Hubert Parry and Schweitzer.

Bach, Karl Philipp Emanuel (1714-88), third son of J. S. Bach (q.v.). Among his many compositions is the oratorio *The Israelites in the Wilderness.* He wrote also *Versuch uber die Wahre Art, das Klavier zu Spielen.*

Bach, Wilhelm Friedemann (1710-84), eldest and most talented son of J. S. Bach. (q.v.). Organist Dresden (1733); Halle (1746-64).

Bache, Alexander Dallas (1806-67), American physicist, grandson of Benjamin Franklin. In 1836-42, president of the trustees of Girard College; from 1843 to 1867 superintendent of U. S. Coast Survey. He made valuable investigations in physics and chemistry. He published *Observations at the Magnetic and Meteorological Observatory at Girard College* (3 vols., 1840-7).

Bacheller, Irving Addison (1859-1950), American author. His books include *The Master of Silence* (1890); *Eben Holden* (1900); *Silas Strong* (1906); *The Light in the Clearing* (1917); *The Winds of God* (1941).

Bachelor, Latin form, *baccalarius,* signified a cowherd; then it came to mean novices in monasteries, and persons passing through the probationary stages of knighthood (q.v.). Subsequently the *Bachelor's Degree* came to be conferred as the lowest academical degree in universities. The term at present signifies an unmarried man.

Bachelors' Buttons, the popular name for cornflower.

Bacillus, properly, rod-shaped Bacteria; inaccurately, bacterium.

Back Bay, section of Boston, Mass.

Backbone. See **Spinal Column.**

Backgammon, a game played upon a board with dice, and disks similar to those used in checkers. Backgammon is played by two persons, each with two dice, and fifteen disks called 'pieces' or 'men,' distinguished by their colors, red and black or—less commonly nowadays—black and white. Often a backgammon board is drawn on the reverse side of a chess board. It has a raised border, and a

Backgammon

dividing ridge in the center. Unlike chess or checkers, but like parcheesi, the men are played around the board, not across. Object of the game: to get one's own men into one's own inner table, where they can be 'played off.' Black moves from his outer table into white's outer table, then into white's inner table, and finally into his own inner table. White of course moves in the same way from his outer table, etc.

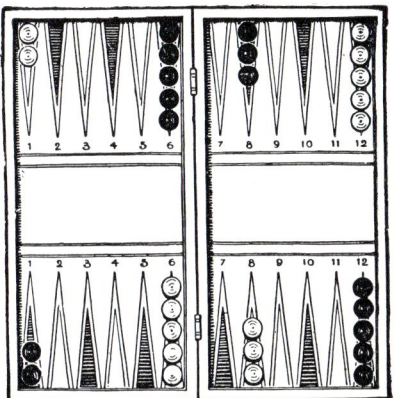

BLACK
Black's Home, or Inner Table.   Black's Outer Table.

White's Home, or Inner Table.   White's Outer Table.
WHITE
The Game of Backgammon.

The moves are decided by throwing dice; one man is moved a number of points equal to the numbers on both dice thrown or two men are moved, one for the number of points indicated on the one dice, and the other for the number of points indicated by the other dice.

If the point at which any move ends is occupied by 2 or more hostile men, that move is blocked, and some other move must be made, if possible. A point occupied by only one man is called a 'blot,' and if an enemy's man reaches such a point the man on the blot is 'hit' or captured.

When all a player's men have reached his inner table he begins to *play* or *bear* them off the board. Pieces now count according to the point they are on: throw a 5 and a 2 and you may remove one man from point 5 and one from 2. The player who throws off his men first wins. If the enemy has not borne any of his men he wins a 'double' game or 'gammon.' If the adversary has a man remaining in either of the winner's tables, it counts as a 'triple' game or 'backgammon.'

To play backgammon well requires some knowledge of the law of chances. See Nicholas, *Modern Backgammon* (1928).

Backlash, the shock which occurs in cog wheels or other such gearing when reversed suddenly; also the lost motion in screw threads and gearing caused by wear or imperfect fitting.

Bacon, the back and sides of a pig, cured. See PORK.

Bacon, Francis (1561-1626), Baron Verulam and Viscount St. Albans, English lawyer, statesman, man of science and letters, was born in London. He was a younger son of Sir Nicholas Bacon by the daughter of Sir Anthony Cooke, tutor to Edward VI. At the age of twelve Bacon entered Trinity College, Cambridge, where he remained for three years, returning to London in 1576 to take up the study of law at Gray's Inn. The following year he went to France in the suite of Sir Amyas Paulet.

Through the favor of Lord Burleigh, his uncle, Bacon was employed by Elizabeth in queen's counsel business. He was specially utilized by the Earl of Essex (q.v.). Besides this, he was in active and zealous Parliamentary service, studied science, meditated on a great work to revolutionize philosophy by turning its material from speculative metaphysics to experimental science; and wrote somewhat, including some of his famous *Essays.*

Essex fell into treasonous ways, and drew away from Bacon, who had been over-frank in his warnings. Bacon was given a leading part in the prosecution which sent Essex to the block, and in preparing the government's justification. But he was not proficient in the arts of rising. He remained poor and out of office, and gained his positions late and hard by sheer abilities, though in 1603 he was knighted. But he gratified James by Parliamentary help, and at last, became Lord Chancellor and baron and in 1620 viscount.

As Chancellor, Bacon was a great and sound judge, and almost none of his decisions were reversed. While his rise had been cruelly slow, his fall was swift and irrevocable. He had not reformed a bad old custom, then tolerated, of taking or letting his underlings take presents from suitors for speedier hearings; but he owned his wrong. Deprived of his office in 1620 and ruinously fined, he wrote: 'It was the justest censure that was in Parliament these two hundred years.' The fine was remitted, and he was pensioned, and in 1624 recalled to the House of Lords; but his public career was ended.

The world was the gainer thereby. He had written on law, and other subjects; in 1605 issued the *Advancement of Learning;* by 1617 wrote the *New Atlantis;* and in 1620, the immortal *Novum Organum.* Thenceforth, however, his whole energies went to writing. In 1623 appeared his magnum opus, *De Augmentis Scientiarum,* a Latin version of the *Advancement,* much enlarged and recast; in December, 1624, the *Apophthegms,* a collection of short stories and jokes, still capital reading; in 1625 his *Translations of Some of the Psalms,* which show that he wished to prove himself a poet but proved amply that he was not one. *Sylva Sylvarum* and *The New Atlantis* appeared posthumously together. Lord Bacon's mighty fame as head of English science and philosophy is deserved: it is the triple one of prophet, vast vital influence, and literary architect. More than any other, he pointed out science's and intellect's line of march, though his tools were impotent to level the road; and his best prose is a leading glory of English literature.

Bacon, Henry (1866-1924), American architect associated with the architectural firm of McKim, Mead & White; and Brite & Bacon. He is the designer of the Lincoln Memorial (Washington, D. C.).

Bacon, Nathaniel (1648-76), American colonist. See BACON'S REBELLION.

Bacon, Robert (1860-1919), American public official, from 1909 to 1912 American Ambassador to France.

Bacon, Roger (*c.* 1214-94), English philosopher and scientist, made discoveries and inventions feared as the work of magic. In 1266 Pope Clement IV. desired to see his works, and Bacon accordingly drew up his *Opus Majus, Opus Minor,* and *Opus Tertium;* of their reception nothing is known. Bacon later issued his *Compendium Studii Philosophiæ,* attacking church and clergy. In 1278 the general of the Franciscan order, forbade the reading of Bacon's books.

Although a believer in astrology and the philosopher's stone, Bacon was far in advance of his time as a scientist and philosopher. Consult Bacon's *Opera Inedita* (edited by Brewer); *Lives* by E. Charles, in French, and by Schneider and Held, in German; J. H. Bridges' *The Life and Work of Roger Bacon* (1914).

Bacon Beetle (*Dermestes lardarius*), a hairy beetle. See DERMESTES.

Bacon-Shakespeare Controversy, the generic popular term for the many theories of non-Shakespearean authorship of Shakespeare's works: *i.e.,* that those works were written either singly by Francis Bacon (q.v.), or by a person unknown, or by a group; Shakespeare, in any case, being a mere ignorant actor who fathered them. Scouted generally as a crazy conceit, its amazing growth and tenacity had two deep roots: (1) a feeling that the known Shakespeare did not explain the works; and (2) as furnishing an easy and exhaustless field of scholarship. A number of persons have worked out cipher schemes by which the author reveals himself. The most ambitious of these is the Great Cryptogram of Ignatius Donnelly (q.v.), making the entire set of *printed* works one vast cipher interlaced from title page to colophon.

Bacon's Rebellion, in American colonial history, an uprising in Virginia in 1675-6, under the leadership of Nathaniel Bacon. The navigation laws of 1651, 1660 at once bled the colonists and destroyed their chief purchasing medium, tobacco. This being also currency for taxes, the poorer planters for years leagued to refuse payment. In addition, the Restoration governor, Sir William Berkeley (q.v.) was growing rich on the Indian fur trade; and when, in 1675, the savages massacred hundreds, and reduced a large district to wilderness, he refused to form a defence, or let the citizens do so. At last a border county defied him, raised 300 men, and for leader chose Nathaniel Bacon, a young English planter of Berkeley's own council. The entire colony revolted and occupied Jamestown; Berkeley had to replace his Assembly with one heavily against him, including Bacon. The new Assembly restored universal suffrage, and voted a regiment for Indian service. The aristocracy, which was really aimed at, clove to Berkeley; but Bacon's force drove out Berkeley, and burned Jamestown. When Bacon died of malaria the rebellion collapsed; and Berkeley hanged the leaders wholesale. Consult John Fiske's *Old Virginia;* Edward Eggleston's 'Nathaniel Bacon' (*Century Magazine,* vol. xl., 1890).

Bacteria and **Bacteriology.** The *Bacteria* are microscopic plants. Among the smallest of living things, they are also among the most abundant, swarming in soil and dirty water, and in all substances in which organic decomposition is going on. Their multiplication is so rapid and their physiological activity so great that they set up far-reaching chemical changes in the surrounding media. The results they produce are sometimes useful and sometimes prejudicial; many are the inciting causes of some of the most serious diseases.

The bacteria were first clearly described by Anton von Leeuwenhoek (q.v.), in 1683. During the next century and a half these minute objects, looking like dots, dashes, and spirals, which could be seen moving about in decomposing fluids, remained only curiosities for the naturalist. They were studied by O. F. Muller in 1786, and by C. G. Ehrenberg (q.v.) in 1838; but the recognition of their practical importance dates from the investigations of *Louis Pasteur* (q.v.). On the basis of Pasteur's early work *Joseph Lister* (q.v.), the English surgeon, founded our modern practice of antiseptic and aseptic surgery; while the German

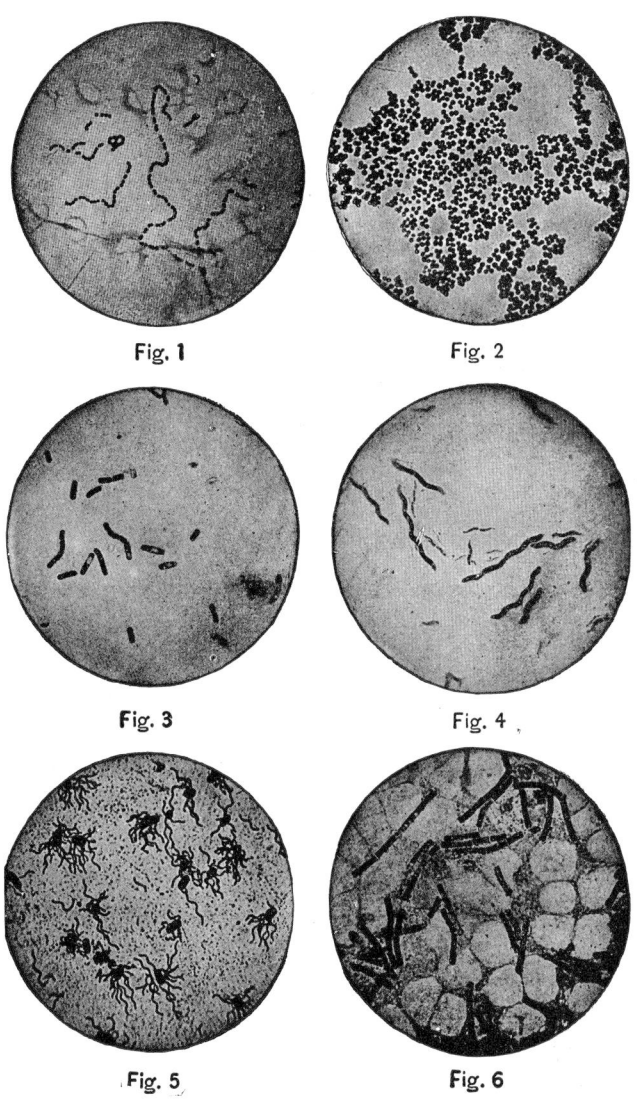

Photo-Micrographs of Bacteria.
Fig. 1. Streptococcus from pus. Fig. 2. Large micrococci from air. Fig. 3. Spore-bearing bacilli (malignant œdema). Fig. 4. Large spirilla. Fig. 5. Typhoid bacilli (showing flagella). Fig. 6. Anthrax bacilli. (From Atlas der Bakterienkunde, Fraenkel and Pfeiffer.)

physician, *Robert Koch* (q.v.), in 1882 devised the method of cultivating bacteria on solid culture media, and in 1884 discovered the bacillus of tuberculosis. The Bacteria constitute the simplest group of the *Fungi* (q.v.). The technical name of the group is *Schizomycetes* (Fission Fungi); and its members are distinguished from the higher fungi by the direct splitting of one cell into two (fission fungi). The term *microbe* (little living thing) includes not only the bacteria, but certain of the higher fungi (yeasts and moulds). (See MOULDS; YEASTS; PROTOZOA.)

The bacteria range in *size* from a sphere less than one micron in diameter to a large spiral form about 40 microns in length. Some 400,000,000 bacteria of average size could be packed into a grain of granulated sugar. The *shape* is either spherical (*coccus*), rod-like (*bacillus*), or ranges from slightly curved to spiral (*spirillum*). When the bacteria split the cells sometimes do not separate but remain attached forming pairs of spherical cells (*diplococci*), chains of spherical cells (*streptococci*), masses of spherical cells (*staphylococci*), regular packets of spherical cells (*sarcinæ*), chains of bacilli, or long convoluted spirals.

The bacterial cell, as a rule, shows no *internal structure* except the ordinary granular network characteristic of protoplasm. In certain forms, however, special areas give a differential stain with aniline dyes (*metachromatic granules*). In some species a jelly-like mass, or *zooglæa*, is formed. Mother of vinegar illustrates this phenomenon. Some bacteria in *motile* stage swim in an appropriate liquid medium. This locomotion is effected by means of long lashes or *flagella*, which may grow out singly or in groups from one or both poles of the cell, or may extend in various directions from its surface. (See FLAGELLUM.) The spores of bacteria are highly resistant to heat and poisons and other harmful physical and chemical conditions. The spores of certain species, for example, may survive boiling for many hours.

At one extreme are *prototrophic* organisms, capable of securing their life energy by the oxidation of such simple substances as methane, carbon monoxide, nitrites, and ammonia. Many of these forms are hampered in their development by small amounts of the organic matter which is so essential to the life of other types. At the other end of the scale are *paratrophic* bacteria, which have become so closely adapted to life in the fluids of the animal body that they cannot grow under natural conditions anywhere outside of it. Between these two extremes are the great mass of *metatrophic* forms, which thrive upon non-living organic matter of various sorts.

Many of the activities of the bacterial cell are effected by means of soluble ferments or *enzymes*, substances which stimulate definite chemical changes. In the life of certain bacteria, particularly those which are parasitic on man and the higher animals, specific complex substances are formed which are highly poisonous, and are known as *toxins* (q.v.).

Light is inimical to bacterial development. *Moisture* is essential to the growth and multiplication of bacteria. The reaction of bacteria to *oxygen* varies widely in different groups. *Temperature* is one of the most important of all factors in controlling bacterial growth and development. There is a *minimum temperature*, below which growth will not occur, which varies from 0° c. for some of the phosphorescent bacteria to 42° c. for forms that develop in fermenting manure heaps. Below this minimum (even down to the temperature of liquid hydrogen, about —250° c.) the bacteria are not killed off promptly, but gradually die off as a result of internal chemical changes, just as they do when dried. Above the minimum, an increase of temperature causes a regular and progressive increase in bacterial growth and activity until an *optimum temperature* is reached, which varies for different species from 20° c. to 70° c. Shortly above the optimum is a *maximum temperature*, above which growth ceases, and a still higher temperature destroys bacterial life entirely.

Many *chemical substances* exert a powerfully poisonous action upon bacteria. In dilute solution such substances merely check growth (*antisepsis*). In stronger concentration they destroy bacterial life (*disinfection* or *sterilization*).

The more important characteristics of the bacteria can be studied only by cultivating the bacteria in various media, by observing the physical and chemical effects that they produce. More recent physiological studies have not yet been systematized into a thoroughly satisfactory basis of classification.

Most modern processes of sewage disposal depend on the activity of one or both of these groups of bacteria to change the decomposable organic matter, which would otherwise putrefy and create a nuisance, into a harmless mineral form; while the fertility of the soil is constantly being enriched by the action of the nitrifying bacteria upon the products of organic decomposition. (See SEWAGE AND SEWAGE DISPOSAL.)

There is an even more important service

rendered to the agriculturist by groups of bacteria which possess the remarkable power of absorbing the free nitrogen of the atmosphere and storing it in organic form. When the products of bacterial activity happen to be of value it is frequently of advantage to grow the organisms in question in pure culture. Certain cheeses are made by using pure cultures of particular bacteria and moulds which impart their peculiar flavors to the products.

Medicine has made great advances in utilizing acids, alcohols, and ketones formed by bacteria from waste sugar. Lactic acid from milk is used as a cathartic. Rancid butter acid is excellent for burns and various skin infections. Vinegar acid, obtained from alcohol, is the base of aspirin and several anesthetics, and is used in the treatment of dysentery. Prolonged bleeding is checked by citrus acid obtained from sugar. From wood alcohol is obtained a dental antiseptic; from green apples an antidote to hysteria; from fusel oil a disinfectant; glycerin is changed to nitroglycerin, valuable as a gargle and lotion, as well as an explosive.

When, on the other hand, bacteria decompose our foods or other materials that we do not want destroyed, they become our enemies, and must be diligently combated. The bacteria with which we are unfortunately most familiar are those which have become adapted to a parasitic existence, so that they grow on the surfaces or in fluids of the body and produce disease. Among *human diseases* more and more are being definitely traced to specific bacterial causes; the causative organisms of many have not yet been isolated.

Bacteriology is therefore of supreme importance in the control of communicable diseases. The use of vaccines and sera, which produce an artificial immunity against specific diseases, is an important aid in the prevention and cure of disease, based upon the results of bacteriological and clinical experimentation. Consult G. C. Frankland's *Bacteria in Daily Life;* G. Newman's *Bacteriology and the Public Health;* E. F. Smith's *Bacteria in Relation to Plant Diseases* (Carnegie Institution of Washington); C. E. Marshall's *Microbiology;* A. C. Abbott's *Principles of Bacteriology;* W. H. Park and A. W. Williams' *Pathogenic Microorganisms* (1914); E. O. Jordan's *Text Book of General Bacteriology;* Buchanan's *Agricultural and Industrial Bacteriology* (1921); Cunningham's *Practical Bacteriology* (1924); Thorne's *Microscopic World* (1940); Turner's *Microbes that Cripple* (1944); Rahn's *Microbes of Merit* (1945).

Bacterioids, Bacteroids, involution forms of bacteria which produce the tubercles on the roots of leguminous plants. They form and accumulate free nitrogen, enriching the soil. See FERTILIZERS.

Bactria, or **Bactriana,** ancient territory in Central Asia. In 327 B.C. Alexander the Great married Roxana daughter of the Bactrian chieftain. The inhabitants of ancient Bactria were closely related to the Persians (see ARYA), and from this region probably sprang Zoroastrianism (see ZOROASTER). Consult Rawlinson's *Bactria, the History of a Forgotten Empire.*

Badajoz, the largest province of Spain; p. 645,658.

Badajoz, city, Spain, capital of Badajoz province; principal industries: pottery, hats, soap, linens, woolens and leather.

Badajoz was the *Pax Augusta* of the Romans; p. 37,967.

Baden, a constituent part of Germany. There are universities at Heidelberg and Freiberg-im-Breisgau. The capital is Karlsruhe; p. 2,208,503.

Baden, or **Baden-Baden,** town and famous health resort, Germany, in the state of Baden. Baden is said to have been founded by Hadrian in the second century A.D. From 1808 to 1872 it was popular for its public gaming tables, then the most renowned in Europe; p. 25,444.

Baden, or **Baden bei Wien** ('Baden near Vienna'), city, Lower Austria. It is much frequented for its warm mineral springs; p. 14,083.

Baden-Powell, 1st Baron (1857-1941), British General, was a commander in the Boer War; he organized the Boy Scouts.

Badges
1. The Red Hand of Ulster. 2. Tudor Rose.
3. Fleur-de-Lys.

Badge, any device used as an emblem, a token, or a decoration. The term badge is also applied to the distinctive decoration of an order of knighthood, and to society emblems. See COCKADE; FRATERNITIES, COLLEGE; HERALDRY.

Badger, a genus of carnivores of the Mustelidæ or weasel family including the European Badger, the American Badger, the Sand Badger of India, and the Ratel and Honey Badger of Africa and India.

The *American badger, or taxus* (*Taxidea americana*), is a distinct, more carnivorous

Badger

form, differing in dentition and in its broad, massive head. Its prevailing color is hoary gray in winter, and yellowish brown in summer. The hair grows very long, and is woolly in winter. The American badger is possessed of extraordinary burrowing powers, and preys on small animals.

Consult Blakeborough and Pease's *The Life and Habits of the Badger* (1914).

Badger Dog. See **Dachshund.**

Badger State, a popular name for Wisconsin (q.v.).

Badghis, or **Badghiz,** a region in Northwestern Afghanistan.

Bad Lands, a term designating certain rough and barren tracts in the western part of the United States, developed by the action of occasional rains upon arid plateaus of soft, incoherent rock.

Badminton, a game resembling lawn tennis, but differing from it in one essential point —the use of a shuttlecock instead of a ball. It was named for Badminton, a village in Gloucestershire, England.

Badoglio, Pietro (1871-), Italian general in World War I. After the fall of Mussolini (July, 1943) he became head of the new Italian government, resigning April, 1944.

Badrinath, peak in Garhwal district, India. It is 23,210 ft. above the sea and on one of its slopes is a shrine of Vishnu.

Bæda. See **Bede.**

Baedeker, Karl (1801-59), German author and publisher. He issued an admirable series of handbooks in German, French, and English.

Bætica, old name of Southern Spain, called after the river Bætis (now the Guadalquivir), which traversed it. It fell into the possession of the Vandals, whence is derived the name of Andalusia.

Baeyer, Johann Friedrich Wilhelm Adolph von (1835-1917), German chemist. In 1905 he received the Nobel Prize for chemistry.

Baffin, William (1584-1622), British navigator. He joined Captain Robert Bylot in 1615 to search for the Northwest Passage by Davis Strait. Unsuccessful in this, he discovered and charted Baffin Bay. Consult Markham's *Voyages of William Baffin.*

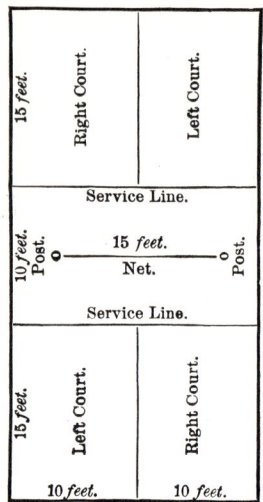
Diagram of Badminton Court

Baffin Bay, or, more correctly, **Baffin Sea,** lies between Greenland and Baffin Land, with the Arctic Circle for its southern limit and 77° 30′ n. lat. for its northern. Long. 51° to 80° w. William Baffin (q.v.) discovered and explored it in 1616.

Baffin Land, an island of British North America, lying between lat. 62° and 72° n., with Lancaster Sound on the north, Baffin Bay and Davis Strait on the east, the Gulf of Boothia and Fox Channel on the south.

Bagasse, a by-product of sugar-cane, being the sugar-cane stalk after the juice has been pressed out for sugar making. A high grade pulp, suitable for book paper, can be produced.

Bagatelle, a game played on an oblong table. At the semicircular upper end of the table are nine holes or cups, numbered from 1 to 9, into which it is the object of the player to drive by means of a cue the nine balls—eight white and one red—that enter into the game. The playing of all the balls by a player is a round, and any agreed-upon number of rounds may be played for the game.

Bagdad, or **Baghdad,** vilayet of Iraq (Mesopotamia), in the basin of the Lower Euphrates and Tigris Rivers. The capital is Bagdad.

Bagdad, or Baghdad, city, capital of Iraq (Mesopotamia), and of the vilayet of Bagdad, is situated on both banks of the Tigris River, 500 miles from its mouth in the Persian Gulf. The Eastern section of the city covers an area of about 600 acres, and was formerly enclosed by a semi-circular wall of brick, now mostly

Baghdad.
Street Scene in the Capital City of Iraq.

in ruins. The ancient moat is represented by a deep ditch, and the fortified gates of the city, with one exception, have been destroyed or sealed up. Here are located the Governor's Palace, the European consulates, the principal bazaars, and the more important commercial houses. The Western section is about one-fourth the size of the Eastern, and constitutes the principal Persian quarters. Pontoon bridges across the Tigris join the two sections.

Feature of interest in the city is the traditional tomb of Zobeida, favorite wife of Haroun al-Raschid. The climate is dry and invigorating.

While the trade of Bagdad is still considerable, the city has declined in commercial importance since the opening of the Suez Canal (q.v.). Exports are wool, grain, gum, galls, skins and hides, opium, carpets, and dates. The population is 400,000, largely Mohammedan.

History.—In 1848 Rawlinson discovered bricks at Bagdad bearing the name of Nebuchadnezzar (604-561 B.C.); but the historical city dates from 764 A.D., when it was founded by Al-Mansur (q.v.). It was capital of the Abbaside califate; was enlarged and improved in the 9th century by Haroun al-Raschid, immortalized in the *Arabian Nights;* and under the latter's son, Al-mamun, became the seat of Arabian learning, literature, and romance. After many vicissitudes it came into the hands of the Turks in 1638. Bagdad formed an important objective in the campaign of the allied armies against Asiatic Turkey during World War I.

Bagdad Railway. The railway from Constantinople across the Anatolian Peninsula and down the Mesopotamian Valley to Bagdad. The Bagdad Railway—which, because of its connection with the Austrian railways and because of the predominant position of German capitalists in its ownership and control, came to be popularly called the Berlin-to-Bagdad line—was intended to open up the potential wealth of the Ottoman Empire, particularly in oil and minerals; to bring the trade of the Near and Middle East in more direct and more rapid touch with Europe; and to strengthen the political and military position of Turkey in the Near East. Because of the great strategic importance of the railway, it early came into prominence as a source of Russo-German and Anglo-German imperialistic rivalries.

As the construction of the Bagdad Railway progressed, German economic penetration of the Ottoman Empire became more potent, and the Bagdad Railway became the symbol of German prestige. From a railway it became a state of mind and one of the stakes of pre-war diplomacy. In October, 1903, at the instigation of the French Government, the Paris Bourse excluded all Bagdad Railway securities from the privileges of the exchange. In spite of the Government's attitude, however, French financiers retained their interests in the Bagdad Railway Company. British objections to the Bagdad Railway were not so much directed at the project itself as at the rising economic and political prestige of Germany.

On the eve of World War I international animosities arising out of the Bagdad controversy had been almost completely adjusted. In 1910 Russia and Germany had completed the so-called Potsdam Agreement, by which Russian objections to the Bagdad line were withdrawn in return for German recognition of Russia's sphere of interest in Persia. During February and March 1914, German and British capitalists carried on a series of successful negotiations for the adjustment of overlapping and competitive claims. These agreements, settled amicably practically every outstanding question between England and Germany in the Near East.

Bahia (Salvador de Bahia). Mountain Street.

Unsuccessful attempts were made by the Allied Governments following the First World War to divide among themselves the Bagdad Railway and other German economic rights in Turkey. Mustapha Kemal Pasha and the Turkish Nationalists, whose resurgent power led to the striking diplomatic victory of Lausanne, upset all pre-arranged plans. Turkey herself gained undisputed control of the Anatolian sections of the Bagdad line, while the British, by purchasing German interests, appear to have acquired ownership of the Mesopotamian sections. The length of the main line is about 1,900 miles and there are some 2,400 miles of branch lines.

Consult E. M. Earle's *Turkey, the Great Powers, and the Bagdad Railway* (1923).

Bagehot, Walter (1826-77), English economist, journalist, and critic. His most important works on economic and political subjects are *Physics and Politics* (1869); *Lombard Street* (1873), a fresh and lucid description of the money market; and *The English Constitution* (1867), a keen analysis of the English system of government, widely used as a textbook.

Baggage is the personal property which a traveller may properly carry with him to minister to the comfort and convenience of his journey.

Baggara, Arab tribes living chiefly in Southern Kordofan, in the Anglo-Egyptian Sudan. They are hunters and herdsmen and own large herds of humped cattle, horses, and sheep. They are a warlike people and in the Mahdi's revolt against the Egyptians (1882) constituted his greatest strength.

Bagot, Sir Charles (1781-1843), British diplomatist and administrator. While he was minister to the United States the treaty known as the Rush-Bagot Convention was negotiated (1817), by an exchange of notes with Richard Rush, then acting Secretary of State. The agreement, which is still in force, placed a limit on the number, size, and equipment of war vessels which each nation should maintain on the Great Lakes. In 1841, Lord Bagot succeeded Lord Sydenham as governor-general of the Canadas.

Bagpipe, a musical reed wind instrument believed to have been in existence before the Christian era. It was common in Germany and England as early as the 15th century, and is referred to by Chaucer, Spenser, and Shakespeare; and is still used in Italy, in Southern France, and in Great Britain (Ireland, Scotland, and Northumberland). The Highland bagpipe, which is now the most familiar, consists of an airtight leathern bag, a wind-tube for blowing, three wooden pipes called drones, and the chanter, a pipe with notes, which produces the melody, the compass consisting of nine notes only.

Bagshot Beds, an important group of rocks found in the Eocene of the Thames basin, where they rest upon the London clay, and in the Isle of Wight. They are shallow marine and fresh-water deposits, consisting of sands, layers of flint pebbles, and occasional thin seams of pipe-clay.

Bagster, Samuel (1772-1851), English publisher of Bibles, chiefly polyglot, and New Testaments in Syriac and Hebrew. He also issued the famous *English Hexapla* (1827). The firm still exists, under the title of Samuel Bagster and Sons, London.

Baguet, or **Baguette** (architectural), a small, round, convex moulding. Also, a modern rectangular cut in jewelry.

Bagworm, Basketworm, or **Dropworm** (*Thyridopteryx ephemerœformis*), a caterpillar moth belonging to the family Psychidae, common throughout the United States, particularly in the south.

Baha, Abdul, or **Abbas Effendi** (1844-1921), leader of the Bahai movement, was born in Shiraz, Persia, the eldest son of the prophet Baha-Ullah, upon whose death (1892) he became the leader of the Bahais. He was proscribed by the authorities and spent a great part of his life in exile or prison, but was released in 1907 and thereafter lived in Haifa. In 1921 he visited the United States. He was a man of learning and character and his home was a sort of Mecca for Bahais throughout the world. His writings include many letters, known as the *Tablets of Abdul Baha*, which were written to individuals and assemblies, and translations of his teachings, talks, and prayers.

Bahadur, Shah (Abu-l-Mozaffar Siradsch ed-din Mohammed) (1767-1862), the last of the Grand Moguls of the House of Tamerlane, and leader of a Mohammedan revolt against the British (1857). After the British capture of Delhi, he was taken prisoner. He was well known as a poet, some of his verses having been published under the title *Safar* (Victory).

Bahaism, a development of Babism which acknowledges Houssein Ali (1817-1892) as the Baha Ullah, whose coming was prophesied by the Bab. The basic principles of the Bahai religion are the oneness of mankind, the independent investigation of truth, the accord of religion with science and reason, the unity of all religions, the equality of the sexes, universal peace, universal education, an international auxiliary language, and an international tribunal. Some years before his death Baha Ullah declared his son Abbas Effendi (Abdul Bdha, the 'Servant of God') to be his successor; Abdul, who died in 1921, named his grandson Shoghi Effendi as head of the executive work of the cause.

The Bahai movement has spread throughout Persia and other Eastern countries, Europe, Canada, and the United States, and numbers over 1,000,000 adherents. A Bahai temple, standing for unity between all races, creeds, and classes, has been erected in Chicago. Consult Phelps' *Life and Teaching of Abbas Effendi;* Holley's *Bahai, The Spirit of the Age* (1921).

Bahamas, the most northerly group of the West Indies, extending 780 m. between Florida and the east end of Santo Domingo. They comprise 29 inhabited islands and a large number of islets and reefs called keys, with an area of 4,404 sq. m. They are generally long and narrow, covered with low, rounded hills of wind-blown shell and coral sand. The climate is agreeable and healthful, and the islands are popular as a winter resort. Nassau, on New Providence, is the capital, and the only town of importance; p. 70,332.

The Bahamas were discovered by Christopher Columbus in 1492, and in 1718 were taken by the British. During the American Civil War, Nassau was the headquarters of the blockade runners and became exceedingly prosperous. The Duke of Windsor was governor of the islands, 1940-1945.

Bahawalpur, native state of India, under the political control of the Punjab government. It is largely desert, only about one-fifth being cultivated. The capital is Bahawalpur. The rulers, Abbasi Daudputras, claim descent from the Abbasid khalifs of Egypt; p. 781,191.

Bahawalpur, city, capital of the native state of Bahawalpur. It is an important trade center; p. 18,494.

Bahia, mountainous state of Brazil; p. 3,334,465.

Bahia, or **São Salvador da Bahia,** city, Brazil, capital of the state of Bahia. The city consists of two parts, an upper and a lower, connected by means of hydraulic elevators. Center of the tobacco, sugar, and cocoa trade, and exports, also, rubber, piassava, and tropical fruits. It was founded in 1510 and from 1549 to 1763 was the capital of the country; p. 363,700.

Bahia Blanca, city, Argentina, on the Naposta river, 3 m. from its outlet into a deep, well-sheltered bay of the same name. It is the natural shipping port for La Pampa and Neuquén, from which great quantities of wheat and wool are exported. Bahia Blanca is a modern city and ranks close to Buenos Aires in commercial importance; p. 72,002.

Bahr, Arabic term connoting river or lake—Bahr-el Abiad (White River).

Bahraich, chief town Bahraich district, India. The shrine of Masaud is visited by Mohammedans and Hindus; p. 30,000.

Bahrein Islands, a group of islands under

Bahr-el-Ghazal

British protection, in the Persian Gulf; p. 110,000, chiefly Mohammedans.

Bahr-el-Ghazal, a river rising in the Sudan and flowing into the White Nile. It is the main source of the floating vegetation of the Nile.

Bahr-el-Ghazal, an arm of Lake Chad, Africa, appearing periodically on the eastern side.

Baiæ, ancient town in Campania, Italy. It was a favorite watering-place of the Romans.

Bailey, Gamaliel (1807-59), American anti-slavery journalist. In 1847 he became editor at Washington, D. C., of the *National Era,* in which Mrs. Stowe's *Uncle Tom's Cabin* first appeared (1852).

Bailey, Liberty Hyde (1858), American agriculturist and author. He was professor of horticulture and landscape gardening at Michigan Agricultural College (1883-8), and professor of horticulture (1888-1903) and director of the College of Agriculture (1903-13), Cornell University. He has given special study to the subjects of botany and horticulture and to rural problems, was chairman of the Roosevelt Commission on Country Life in 1908, and has written numerous works on agriculture, rural affairs, nature, and kindred subjects. Among them are: *Evolution of Our Native Fruits; Beginners' Botany; Principles of Fruit Growing; Principles of Vegetable Gardening; The Holy Earth; Universal Service; Wind and Weather* (verse).

He has edited also: *Cyclopedia of American Horticulture* (4 vols.); *Cyclopedia of Agricul-*

Photo from Publishers Photo Service.
The Bahamas—A Street in Nassau.

Baikal, the third largest lake in Asia, and the deepest fresh water lake in the world, is situated in Southern Siberia in the government of Irkutsk. It is 400 m. long, from 18 to 56 m. wide, and covers an area of 13,185 sq. m. The trans-Siberian railway passes around the southern end.

Bail, the process of surrendering a person in legal custody to a competent person who undertakes to become responsible for the production of the former in court when wanted. The character and amount of security sufficient to procure the release of a prisoner is sometimes fixed by statute, but is more often left to the discretion of the court.

ture (4 vols.); *Standard Cyclopedia of Horticulture* (6 vols.).

Bailey, Solon Irving (1854-1931), Amer. astronomer, was born in Lisbon, N. H. He was graduated from Boston University (1881; A.M., 1884), and from Harvard (A.M., 1888), founded a branch of the Harvard observatory in the southern hemisphere, at Arequipa, in Peru, 1889, and in 1893 established on the summit of Misti (19,000 ft.) the highest scientific station in the world. In 1908 and 1909 he carried on special astronomical investigations in South Africa.

Bailiff, in Great Britain an official exercising a delegated authority. A private bailiff is an agent in the care of property, real or personal. In the United States bailiffs are usually called deputy-sheriffs. See SHERIFF.

Bailiwick, the district over which the jurisdiction of a bailiff or sheriff extends.

Bailment. The deposit of personal property with a person not the owner so as to confer on the depositary a definite right to the possession thereof. Among the more common forms of bailment are the pawn or pledge, the common-law lien, the custody of goods by a common carrier, an innkeeper or a warehouseman, the hiring and the loaning of chattels, and the like.

Baily, Francis (1774-1844), English astronomer, practised as a stock broker in London from 1799 to 1825. On his retirement from business he devoted himself to astronomy; discovered Baily's Beads; founded the London Astronomical Society (1820); revised the star catalogues of Flamsteed, Lalande, Lacaille, and others; reformed the *Nautical Almanac;* and repeated, in his own house, the 'Cavendish' experiments to determine the earth's density. He wrote a biography of Flamsteed (1835). Consult Herschel's *Memoirs of Francis Baily.*

Baily's Beads, a phenomenon in eclipses of the sun, first fully described by Francis Baily (q.v.). Just before the beginning and after the end of the obscuration by the moon of the sun's disc, the unobscured portion of the sun seems usually to become suddenly discontinuous, and looks like a belt of bright points, varying in size and separated by dark spaces. The resulting appearance has been compared to a string of beads.

Bain, Alexander (1818-1903), Scottish philosopher. His chief works are: *The Senses and the Intellect* (1855), and *The Emotions and the Will* (1859). He based his analyses upon physiological states and processes, and largely determined the direction and methods of modern British psychology. He knew J. S. Mill well, and supplied him with many illustrative examples drawn from the experimental sciences. Consult his *Autobiography* (1904).

Bainbergs, plate armor for the protection of the legs, worn over chain mail in the 13th century.

Bairam, or **Beiram,** the Persian and Turkish name for a Mohammedan festival analogous to Easter. It commences immediately after the fast of Ramadan or Ramazan, which corresponds in its abstinence to Lent.

Baird, David, Jr. (1883-   ), United States Senator from New Jersey, by appointment (1929-1931), a Republican leader of Southern New Jersey.

Baird, John L. (1890-1946), British radio engineer, one of the first to demonstrate (1926) practicability of television.

Baird, Spencer Fullerton (1823-87), American naturalist. His special work was the development of the National Museum, which made its beginning under his direction in 1850; in 1878 he became secretary. In 1874 he was appointed the first U. S. Commissioner of Fish and Fisheries, and in that capacity organized the science of fish culture in the United States. Next to Louis Agassiz, natural history in America is perhaps most indebted to Baird. A bibliography of his writings up to 1882 contains 1,063 titles. Consult *Life* by his son; W. H. Dall's *Spencer Fullerton Baird* (1915).

Bairnsfather, Bruce (1889-   ), British cartoonist, playwright and lecturer best known for his war play, *The Better 'Ole.*

Bait Fishing ranks next to fly fishing as a sportsmanlike branch of angling. *Spinning* is usually accomplished with an artificial bait.

Baize (Old French *baies*), a coarse woolen cloth with a long nap on one side, used mainly for coverings, curtains, and linings, but in some countries for clothing also.

Baja, market town of Hungary, on the Danube, 90 m. s. of Budapest. It has a large trade in grain and wine; and is also noted for its annual swine fair; p. 19,133.

Bajazet I., or **Bayazid** (1347-1403), sultan of the Turks, succeeded his father, Murad I., in 1389, and began his reign by murdering his younger brother Yakub. In three years he conquered Bulgaria, with parts of Servia, Macedonia, and Thessaly; and his swift subjugation of Asia Minor gave him the name of Ilderim, or 'Lightning.' Bajazet tried to destroy the Greek empire, but Timur completely defeated him (1402). Bajazet was captured, and travelled in a litter with Timur's camp; which gave rise to the story that he was imprisoned in a cage.

Bajazet II., or **Bayazid** (1447-1512), son of the Sultan Mohammed II., the conqueror of Constantinople, ascended the Ottoman throne after his father's death in 1481. He was a patron of learning and the builder of many fine mosques and bridges.

Bakelite (oxybenzyl-methylene-glycolanhydride), a substance produced from the chemical union of phenol and formaldehyde. It is amber-like, characterized by electrical insulating properties, great strength, insolubility in all known solvents, and resistance to most chemicals.

In one of its preliminary conditions bakelite is a liquid which solidifies by the application of heat, enabling impregnation of coils for dynamos or motors, and the hardening of wood and other porous bodies. Compounded with asbestos, wood pulp, and similar fillers, it furnishes strong and accurately moulded articles. Bakelite is the invention of Dr. Leo H. Baekeland.

Baker, Sir Benjamin (1840-1907), English civil engineer, designed the ship that brought the obelisk Cleopatra's Needle from Egypt to London. He also invented the pneumatic shield for tunneling under rivers.

Baker, Frank Collins (1867-1942), American zoologist. He published: *A Naturalist in Mexico* (1895); *Mollusca of the Chicago Area* (1898-1902); *Shells of Land and Water* (1903); *The Lymnœidæ of North and Middle America* (1911); *Relation of Mollusks to Fish in Oneida Lake* (1916); *Life of the Pleistocene* (1920).

Baker, George Fisher (1840-1931), American financier, industrialist and railroad magnate. During the Civil War, before he was 25, Baker was invited to Washington and consulted on financial affairs by President Lincoln's Cabinet officers. About 1875 Baker began buying up railroads that were in low water and building them up to heights of prosperity. When the public first became aware of the tremendous financial power wielded by Baker, he admitted that the money power of the country lay in his and Morgan's hands. Of his vast wealth he devoted many millions to philanthropy, to educational institutions and museums.

Baker, George Pierce (1866-1935), American educator. Professor of English Harvard (1905), later at Yale. At Harvard as director of the '47 Workshop' he carried on active instruction in dramatic writing. Director of the various Elizabethan works. He published *Principles of Argumentation, The Development of Shakespeare as a Dramatist* (1907), and *Dramatic Technique* (1919).

Baker, Moses Nelson (1864-   ), American editor and writer. A recognized authority on municipal government, engineering, and sanitation. He edited the *Manual of American Water Works* and the *Municipal Year Book*, and wrote several works on sanitary and municipal engineering.

Baker, Newton Diehl (1871-1937), Secretary of War in the cabinet of Woodrow Wilson. He discharged the huge task of creating the draft army, sending the American Expeditionary force abroad and demobilizing the troops at the end of the war. He is generally credited with the selection of General John J. Pershing as commander-in-chief of the American forces. He was City Solicitor of Cleveland, O., and from 1911 to 1915 was Mayor of that city. President Coolidge appointed him to the World Court in 1928, and in 1931 he was selected by President Hoover as a member of the Wickersham Commission to investigate enforcement of the prohibition laws.

Baker, Ray Stannard (1870-1946), American author, known also by the pseudonym 'David Grayson.' During 1918 he was sent by the U. S. Department of State as special commissioner to Great Britain, France and Italy, and in 1919 he was director of the Press Bureau of the American Commission to Negotiate Peace, at Paris. His published works include *The Boys' Book of Inventions* (1899); *What Wilson Did at Paris* (1919); *The New Industrial Unrest* (1920); *Woodrow Wilson and World Settlement* (3 vols. 1922). Under his pseudonym appeared: *Adventures in Contentment* (1907); *Great Possessions* (1917). In 1927 he published the first two volumes of an authorized biography of President Wilson, in 1931, volumes III and IV.

Baker, Sir Samuel White (1821-93), English explorer, who, after exploring the Blue Nile and tracing the course of the White Nile, in 1864 reached the great fresh-water lake which he named Albert Nyanza.

Baker, Mount, volcano, Whatcom county, Northwest Washington. It is in eruption from time to time, and was active in 1843 and 1880. Altitude, 10,827 ft.

Bakersfield, city, California, county seat of Kern co. Industries include oil refineries, machine shops and foundries, planing and flour mills, and packing houses; p. 29,252.

Baker University, a coeducational institution of learning at Baldwin, Kans., founded in 1858 by the Methodist Episcopal Church.

Bakhchi-Sarai, Tartar town, Crimea, Russia. It contains the ancient palace (1519) of the Tartar khans; p. 9,500.

Bakhtegan, or **Niris,** a salt lake in the Persian province of Farsistan.

Baking. See **Cookery.**

Baking Powder, a compound used in cooking in the place of yeast, consisting of an acid and an alkali. Bicarbonate of soda is the alkali generally used, and cornstarch is the usual filler, but the acid constituent varies, often being tartaric acid. When the powder is moistened, carbonic acid gas is generated and puffs up the doughy mass. See BREAD.

Bakony Wald, a broad, hilly region of Hungary. Large herds of swine are annually driven hither. The swineherds were formerly the robbers celebrated in the ballads of the Hungarian people.

Bakshish, or **Backshish** (Persian 'a gift'), a word used throughout the East for a gratuity or 'tip' for services rendered; though it is demanded, often, with threats.

Bakst, Léon Nikolajewitsch (1868-1924), Russian decorator and designer. He earned distinction for his elaborate stage settings, especially in connection with the productions of the Imperial Russian ballet.

Baku, Russian government of the Eastern Caucasus. Its greatest importance arises from its oil wells, mostly located in the vicinity of the city of Baku. Area, 15,060; p. 1,050,000. See CAUCASUS.

Baku, city, seaport, and administrative center of the government of Baku, Russia, is situated on the Apsheron peninsula, and has a fine natural harbor on the Caspian Sea. The soil around Baku is saturated with petroleum, and oil refining constitutes the chief industry of the town; p. 575,200, largely Tartars and Armenians.

The ancient Parsees or fire worshippers made Atesh-Ga an object of pilgrimage, as there natural gas, or naphtha, issued from the ground and ignited spontaneously. The Persians possessed Baku from 1509 to 1723, when the Russians captured it. After twelve years it was restored to Persia, but Russia finally took possession in 1806. In 1901 a disastrous fire visited the city. Consult Marvin's *The Region of Eternal Fire;* Henry's *Baku, an Eventful History* (1906).

Bakunin, Michael (1814-76), Russian revolutionist and anarchist. He took an active part in the revolutionary movements at Prague and Dresden, being arrested in Saxony (1849). He was given up to Russia, sent to Siberia in 1855, but managed to escape in an American ship to Japan. In 1869 he founded the Alliance of the Social Democracy, which soon joined the International Workingmen's Association. As the leader of militant anarchism, Bakunin was in the International the opponent of Karl Marx. In 1872 he was expelled from the International, and retired to Switzerland. He wrote a large number of works, the chief being: *Dieu et l'Etat.*

Balaam, a prophet, seer, or soothsayer, who, according to Scripture, was summoned by Balak, king of Moab, to pronounce a curse upon Israel, and thereby arrest the march of that people toward Canaan. Nearly all the references to Balaam in Scripture, particularly in the New Testament, speak of him with opprobrium, and hold him up as a warning example of those who love the hire of unrighteousness.

Bala Beds. The rocks of the Bala district, North Wales, contain two limestones, separated by some 1,400 ft. of arenaceous and slaty strata. The lower limestone (25 ft.) is called the Bala limestone, and has been followed over a considerable area; the upper, or Hirnant limestone, is local. Bala beds form a group of the Lower Silurian.

Balachong, a condiment used in China for eating with rice. It is made of shrimps or small fish pounded with salt and spices and then dried.

Balaghat, ('above the Ghats'), the elevated table land of Berar, India, which lies between the Eastern and Western Ghats.

Balakireff, Mili Alexeievitch (1837-1910), Russian musical composer. His works include: *King Lear; Tamara* and *Russia,* both symphonies; *Islamey,* an Oriental fantasia for the piano; an interesting collection of Russian popular songs (1866); and many overtures with Russian, Spanish, and Czech (Bohemian) themes. He edited a selection of Tausig's pianoforte pieces in 1908.

Balaklava, or **Balaclava,** port and health resort, southwest coast of Crimea. The harbor, which affords secure anchorage for the largest ships, till 1860 was a naval station. It is chiefly memorable for the charge on the Russian guns by the Light Brigade. Consult Kinglake's *Invasion of the Crimea;* Paget's *The Light Cavalry Brigade in the Crimea.*

Balalaika, a musical instrument very much used in Russia for the accompaniment of popular songs. It is a stringed instrument, with, generally, two strings, and resembles a guitar.

Balance, an instrument for determining the relative weights or masses of bodies. There are many varieties of balance. The ordinary balance consists of a lever of the first kind, called the beam, which is supported on a fulcrum in the middle, and from the extremities of which are hung two scale pans, one for the weights, the other for the object to be weighed.

The following are the requirements of a good balance:—1. The two arms of the beam must be precisely the same length, otherwise unequal weights in the scale-pans will be necessary to produce equilibrium of the lever. 2. The balance should be in equilibrium when the scale-pans are empty. 3. The center of gravity of the beam, when horizontal, should be in the same vertical line with the knife-edge of the fulcrum, and a short distance underneath the latter, in order to insure that the beam, when at rest, shall assume a position of stable equilibrium. 4. The balance should be delicate— i.e. should answer to the least alteration of the weights in the scale-pans. This is effected (a)

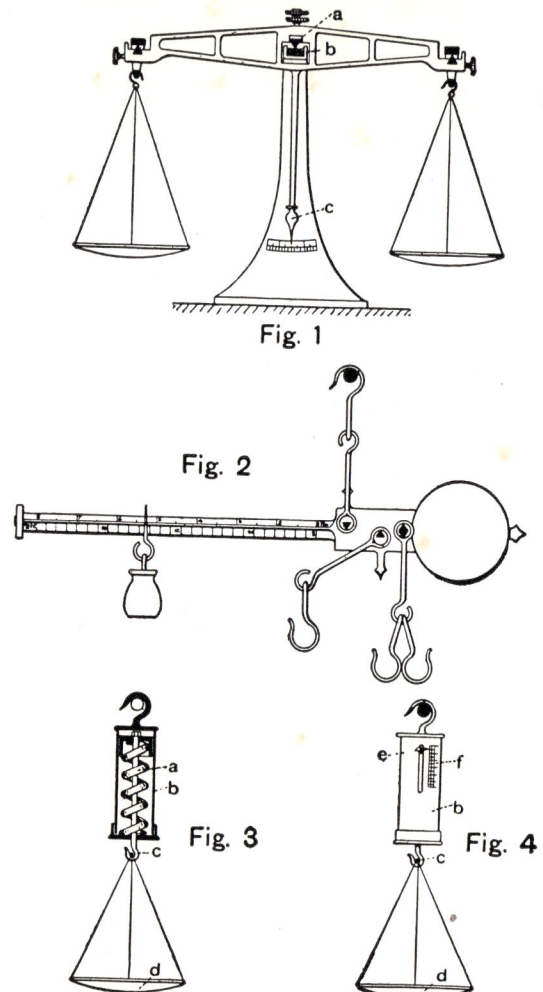

Common Form of Balance.

Fig. 1 Ordinary balance—*a*, knife edge, and *b*, polished plane, of steel or agate; *c*, pointer. Fig. 2. Steelyard. Figs. 3 and 4. Spring balance, interior and front view—*a*, spring; *b*, case; *c*, hook; *d*, scale pan; *e*, index-finger; *f*, scale.

by making the arms of the balance long, while their weight is reduced as far as the necessary rigidity will permit; (b) and by having the center of gravity but little below the knife-edge of the fulcrum; while (c) due attention must be given to diminishing friction by having the knife-edges of the supports as sharp, and the bearings as hard, as possible. See Glazebrook and Shaw's *Practical Physics* (1893).

Balance of Power. A principle of world politics implying an international equilibrium of forces such that no single State or group of States shall dominate the others. The theory is ancient, but was first applied in modern Europe in the 17th century, at which time the European nations combined in a federation based on the balance of power, agreeing that it was the duty of every State to prevent, by force of arms if necessary, any violation of the agreement by any member. The League of Nations (q.v.) was undertaken as an effort to substitute a community of power for the pre-war balance of power system, but in recent years the nations have reverted to alliances based on the balance of power.

Balance of Trade. See **Trade**.

Balance Spring. See **Horology**.

Balancing of Machinery. In most machines the inertia of the moving parts originates forces which tend to cause the frame of the machine to vibrate as a whole. Such a machine is said to be unbalanced, and in the case of high-speed machinery it is often necessary to balance these forces wholly or partially by means of suitably disposed weights. A perfectly balanced machine, if hung up and set in motion, would not vibrate as a whole. Machines, such as dynamos, turbines, and centrifugal pumps, whose moving parts consist of rotating masses symmetrically situated about the axis of rotation, are naturally in balance, and only require adjusting for errors due to slight lack of symmetry in the different parts; but in machines such as the steam-engine, having unbalanced reciprocating masses, it is impossible to obtain perfect balance as regards all the forces, and in practice a compromise has to be arrived at.

Balanoglossus, a small (1-6″) worm found in sand and mud in various seas, of much zoölogical importance from the fact that it is found to possess distinct gill-slits, like those of the lower vertebrates, and, more doubtfully, some other vertebrate characters. See Parker Hawell's *Text-book of Zoology* (1898).

Balanophoraceæ, an order of fungus-like leafless plants in the sub-class Apetalae, found in the equatorial zone.

Balasor, dist. at the n.e. angle of the Orissa div., Bengal, India; produces rice, and salt is manufactured by a crude process. The chief town, Balasor, was one of the earliest English settlements in E. India (1642); p. 21,000.

Balas Ruby, or **Precious Spinel,** a precious stone, consisting of alumina and magnesia, which occurs in small crystals with eight triangular faces (octahedra), and is a little softer than the true ruby. Burma, Afghanistan and Ceylon are the principal sources of supply.

Balata, a substance resembling gutta-percha, of a dirty reddish-brown color, with a rather greasy feel, and obtained as an exudation from a tree in Venezuela and Guiana.

Balaton, Lake, or **Plattensee,** the largest lake in Hungary, 47 m. long and 7 m. to 9 m. broad.

Balbo, Italo (1896-1940), Italian aviator who in 1933 commanded a squadron of twenty-four planes in a flight from Rome to Chicago. In 1931 he led twelve planes across the South Atlantic from Rome to Brazil. Premier Mussolini detached him from the cabinet as Minister of Air in 1933 and appointed him Governor of the Italian colony of Libya in Africa.

Balboa, Vasco Nuñez de (1475-1517), Spanish explorer, born at Xeres de los Caballeros. He accompanied Rodrigo Bastidas to America in 1500. In 1513 he crossed the isthmus to verify the reported existence of a great ocean on the other side of the mountains, and saw, first of Europeans, the eastern waters of Pacific Ocean. He entered the waters of the Pacific (which he called the South Sea) and took formal possession of it and of all shores washed by it for the kings of Castile, the name, Gulf of San Miguel, which he gave to the arm of the ocean that he discovered, being still retained. He was executed at Acla for treason.

Balboa, a town, Panama Canal Zone. It is the port for Panama City from which it is 3 m. distant.

Balbriggan ('town of Brecan'), seaport and market town, Ireland, county Dublin. 'Balbriggan hose,' of fine unbleached cotton, take their name from the town; p. 2,500.

Balchen, Bernt (1899-   ), Norwegian aviator who accompanied Commander Richard E. Byrd in his North Pole expedition in 1927, piloted Byrd over the South Pole in 1929 and accompanied Byrd's transatlantic flight as co-pilot in 1927. In 1934 he made a second expedition to Antarctica with Lincoln Ellsworth.

Baldachin, a canopy of silk cloth borne over the head of a dignitary, especially in the East, sometimes also over the eucharist when carried processionally. The term has been extended to the canopy of metal or stone, sometimes called *ciborium,* supported by pillars or suspended over the high altar, in the Eastern and Roman Churches, from which is suspended a vessel containing the host.

Balder, or **Baldr,** the central figure of one of the most significant of the Scandinavian myths, and the personification of purity and innocence, was the son of Odin and Frigg, the brother of Thor, and the husband of Nanna. Consult Bulfinch, *Age of Fable.*

Baldpate, an American gunner's name for the widgeon. Some other white-headed birds, as a variety of domestic pigeon, are also called baldpate or bald-head.

Baldric, a belt worn from either shoulder, and crossing the body diagonally; used as an ornament, or to sustain a sword, dagger, or horn.

Baldung, Hans (*c.* 1476-1545), called also **Grun** or **Grien,** German painter and engraver. Of his paintings the chief are his *Coronation of the Virgin* and others which form the altar-piece of Freiburg Cathedral.

Baldwin, the name of nine counts of Flanders of whom the most important are Baldwin I. (d. 879), surnamed *Bras de fer* ('Iron Arm'); Baldwin v. (d. 1067), *Le Debonnaire,* who assisted William of Normandy in his conquest of England; and Baldwin IX., who as Baldwin I. was the first Latin emperor of Constantinople.

Baldwin, the name of a number of Latin kings of Jerusalem.

Baldwin, James Mark (1861-1934), American psychologist. He was professor of psychology at Princeton (1893-1903); professor of philosophy and psychology at Johns Hopkins (1903-9). He founded the *Psychological Review* (1894). His publications include *Handbook of Psychology* (2 vols. 1889-91); *Mental Development* (2 vols. 1895-7); *Story of the Mind* (1898); *Development and Evolution* (1902); *History of Psychology* (2 vols. 1913); *Genetic Theory of Reality* (1915).

Baldwin, Stanley (1867-1947), British statesman. He became Chancellor of the Exchequer in 1922 and in May 1923 he succeeded the late Andrew Bonar Law as prime minister. His party suffered defeat in the election of early 1924, when for the first time in British history a Labor Ministry came into power, under J. R. MacDonald. Baldwin again became prime minister late in the same year and was succeeded by MacDonald in 1929. Baldwin returned as prime minister in 1935 and continued as such until his voluntary retirement in 1937 following the abdication of Edward VIII and the coronation of George VI. He was succeeded by Neville Chamberlain. Upon his retirement he was made an Earl.

Bale, Basel, city, Switzerland, capital of Basel-Land, is situated on both banks of the Rhine, here crossed by four bridges. In Great Bale, on the left bank, are a picturesque 14th century minster, a museum with a fine picture gallery rich in works of Hans Holbein the Younger, a 16th century town hall, the University, the Church of St. Paul, and a large zoological garden. Little Bale, on the right bank, contains ribbon factories, paper, silk, and thread mills, and dye works; p. 150,750.

Bale, Council of (1431-49), the last of the three reforming church councils held in the fifteenth century, met in Bale, or Basel. In 1449 the Council was dissolved, and the schism was ended by the general acceptance of Pope Nicholas v.

Balearic Islands, ('Slingers' Islands'), a group of islands belonging to Spain, lying in the Mediterranean, about 125 m. off the eastern Spanish coast. The group consists of Majorca, Minorca, Iviza, Formentera, and several smaller islands, with a total area of 1,936 sq. m. The islands are for the most part rocky, with precipitous coasts, but with a number of excellent harbors. The climate is delightful; the soil is generally fertile; and vines, olives, almonds, and many varieties of fruit are raised. Palma is the capital. The p. was estimated in 1935 at 376,735, mostly Spanish. Recently Majorca has been much favored as a winter resort. See MAJORCA; MINORCA.

Consult Bidwell's *The Balearic Islands;* Markham's *The Story of Majorca and Minorca.*

Balfe, Michael William (1808-70), British composer, was born in Dublin, and in his 9th year made his debut as a violinist. Of his numerous operettas and other compositions, the most successful have been *The Bohemian Girl* (1843); *The Rose of Castile* (1857).

Balfour, Arthur James, first Earl of (1848-1930), English statesman, son of James M. Balfour of Whittinghame, Haddingtonshire, Scotland. When Sir Michael Hicks-Beach, Chief Secretary for Ireland, retired, because of ill-health, in 1887, Mr. Balfour succeeded to the office, applying himself to the task of 'restoring the reign of law and order,' as he expressed it, with a vigor and resolution that provoked the bitter hostility and resentment of Mr. Parnell and his followers. In 1891-2 Mr. Balfour was first lord of the treasury; in Lord Salisbury's 3d administration (1895-1902) he resumed the leadership of the House of Commons: and he was continued in this office when, in October, 1900, the general election was fought on the question of the South African War. On July 12, 1902, on the retirement of Lord Salisbury, Mr. Balfour became prime minister and Lord Privy Seal, with the office of First Lord of the Treasury, serving until his resignation in 1905.

Mr. Balfour re-entered Parliament in 1906 as representative of the City of London, assuming the leadership of the Unionist Party, which he retained until 1912, when he was succeeded by Bonar Law. He was made Secretary of State for Foreign Affairs in December, 1916, and in that capacity headed the British War Mission to the United States in the spring of 1917. He was the author of *Criticism and Beauty* (1909); *Theism and Humanism* (1915) and other philosophic writings.

Balfour, Francis Maitland (1851-82), Scottish embryologist, brother of Arthur James Balfour, was born in Edinburgh. His fame rests on his work, *Comparative Embryology*, (1878-83).

Balfour, Sir James (d. *c.* 1583), of Pittendreich, Scottish lawyer and politician. He became one of the most shameless political intriguers of his time, frequently betraying both Queen Mary's party and that of her opponents. In 1561 he was appointed lord president of the Court of Session.

Bali, or **Little Java**, island of the Dutch East Indies, belonging to the Lesser Sunda group, lies immediately e. of Java. It is about 75 m. long by 50 m. broad, and has a total area of 2,100 sq. m. Agriculture is the chief employment, rice, indigo, cotton, fruits, maize, and edible roots being raised. Dutch rule was established in 1849; p. 946,387. It was invaded by the Japanese in 1942.

Balin and **Balan**, in Arthurian legend, two brothers, knights, who came to Arthur's court. They met abroad, and, not recognizing one another, fought, and slew each other.

Baliol, The Family of, an Anglo-Norman family that played a prominent part in Scottish history. GUIDO DE BALIOL, crossed from Normandy with William I.—JOHN DE BALIOL (d. 1269) was regent of Scotland, and founded Baliol College (see OXFORD).—JOHN DE BALIOL (1249-1315), king of Scotland, was 3d son of John de Baliol. He died at Castle Galliard, Normandy (1315).—His son, EDWARD DE BALIOL (d. 1363), king of Scotland, who was the last of his race, surrendered the kingdom to Edward III. (1356) in return for a pension of £2,000.

Baliuag, market town, province Bulacan, Luzon, Philippine Islands, on a branch of the Rio Grande de la Pampanga. It was the first place in the Philippines to receive municipal government at the hands of the Americans after their occupation; p. 21,000.

Balkan Mountains, Great and **Little,** a calcareous chain on the east side of the Caspian Sea, south of Aji Daria Bay, between 39° and 40° n. lat. The highest point, toward the southeastern extremity of the range, is about 5,310 ft.

Balkan Peninsula, or **Illyrian Peninsula,** the most easterly of the three great Mediterranean peninsulas of Southern Europe. It stretches southward from the Danube River and its tributary, the Save, as a broad quadrilateral of nearly 200,000 sq. m., having the Black Sea on the east, the Sea of Marmora and the Aegean Sea on the southeast and south respectively, and the Ionian Sea and the Adriatic on the west. It includes Albania, Greece, Jugo-Slavia, Bulgaria, Roumania and European Turkey.

The term Balkan Mountains (ancient *Haemus; cf.* Cape Emine) is loosely applied to the whole mountain region of the north, but specifically to the range which sweeps round from the Iron Gates of the Danube. Important factors in the political, social, and economic development of the peninsula are the passes, many of which afford mere tracks for baggage animals. The two highest passes over this range are the Rabanica (6,285 ft.) and the Rosalita (6,160 ft.). The chains show the peculiar features of the karst region, the loftiest peak being Mount Dinara (6,010 ft.), a dazzling mass of hippurite limestone. The only river of size entering the Black Sea is the Danube.

The wolf and bear are found in the mountains; the deer and wild pig in the forests; the jackal, buffalo, and Oriental fat-tailed sheep in the southern plains; vast flocks of water fowl along the Danube; and pheasants and partridges everywhere.

The population of the Balkans is extremely heterogeneous and includes Albanians, Greeks, Roumanians, Slavs, Bulgars and Turks. It cannot be classified by racial differences nor religions, still less by political boundaries. The earliest historical inhabitants were the Illyrians, Greeks, and Dacians. The Illyrians are now represented by the Albanians, and the Dacians by the Rumanians. There are also considerable numbers of Jews, Armenians, and Hungarians (Magyars). These races retain their own religions and social customs, and numerous wars have been caused by lack of union and opposing interests.

Balkan War, 1912-13. In February, 1912, the four Christian States of the Balkan Peninsula—Bulgaria, Servia, Greece, and Montenegro—after long endeavor on the part of some of their far-seeing rulers and statesmen, formed an alliance for the promotion of their common interests and the improvement of their standing in the family of nations. Their condition was indeed deplorable, and it was one of the reproaches of the civilized world, but the Powers formed *ententes* to keep matters as they were; and after thirty-four years, Bulgaria and Servia, which in the meantime had been growing more cultivated and humane, realized that only by joint action could the wretched *status quo* be destroyed.

Military preparations went on quietly during the spring and summer of 1912, and an imperative ultimatum for administrative reform, presented to the Porte by Servia and Bulgaria was rejected. The Powers labored in vain to avert a conflict; and on Oct. 8, Montenegro, apparently acting on instructions from Bulgaria, declared war upon Turkey. Turkey would listen to no proposition involving the league's interference in her internal affairs, and on Oct. 17 she declared war on Servia and Bulgaria. Turkey at that time had about 200,000 regular troops in Europe; but at least 150,000 more were available in the Asiatic provinces, and they were moved as rapidly as possible. Nazim Pasha, the War Minister, was generalissimo of the forces.

The Montenegrin Advance.—The Montenegrin army was about 40,000 in strength, commanded by Crown Prince Danilo. It was divided into three parts—the Northern army, headed by General Vukovitch; the Eastern, or Central, by General Lazovitch; and the Western, by General Martinovitch, the War Minister. The last two made Scutari their objective; the Northern army set out across the vilayet of Kossovo to join one of the Servian columns. The chief defence of Scutari, which Martinovitch reached with slight difficulty, was Tarabosch Mountain. Its four forts had been admirably built by German military engineers; but they had overlooked a spur of the mountain, and by Oct. 23 this was in possession of Martinovitch's forces, which had hastily blasted a road to the top with dynamite. The two Montenegrin columns now began the siege of Scutari. Meanwhile Vukovitch was making his way through the vilayet of Kossovo and on Oct. 25 joined the Western Servian column at Sienitza.

The Servian army numbered about 200,000 troops. General Putnik was commander-in-chief, and the force operated in four separate columns. The objective point of the first two armies was Uskub; while Zievkovich, in the west, was to operate with the Northern army of Montenegro. There was fierce close-range fighting, and the Servian artillery made frightful havoc among the Turks, who were completely routed (Oct. 24). Zekki now found himself in danger of envelopment. He evacuated Krupulu, which the Serbs entered on Oct. 29, and retired upon Monastir. The last of the Turkish soldiers fled from Novibazar into Austrian territory, while Servia proceeded methodically to occupy the conquered territory.

The Bulgars in Thrace.—The Bulgarian army numbered about 340,000, under the chief command of General Savoff.

Leaving a garrison of 40,000 under Shukri Pasha to cope with the Bulgarian bombardment of Adrianople, which began Nov. 1, Abdullah fell back upon Lule Burgas, and formed a new line between that place and Viza. Abdullah counted on an energetic assault by Mukhtar with the Third Corps, seconded by the flank attack of an Ottoman division which had just debarked at Midia, on the Black Sea. But the Turkish commander realized that Mukhtar was too hard pressed to render him assistance; his own troops were completely exhausted; and he had to abandon all his positions. This move rendered necessary the retreat of the Third Corps on the following day (Oct. 31), and the whole army fell back in complete disorder.

Movements of the Greeks.—Greece, whose attitude had been uncertain, went to war on Oct. 17 under the command of Crown Prince Constantine. Preparations for investment had been begun on the night of Nov. 1, when a Greek torpedo boat drove a Turkish cruiser from the harbor. The commander at Salonica, Tahsin Pasha, found it impossible to hold out against forces at least three times the strength of his own, coming from all directions. On Nov. 8 he capitulated, and next day the Greeks and Serbs entered the town. Greece was the only member of the league with an adequate navy, and her fleet blockaded Turkish ports and seized a number of islands in the northern Aegean.

After his flight from Uskub, Zekki Pasha and his remaining troops joined Djavid Pasha and the Seventh Corps at Monastir. Djavid was successfully resisting the Greek attack from the south when a Servian army appeared from the north. Monastir, with over 40,000 troops, surrendered on Nov. 17; but the generals managed to escape.

The Bulgars made a rapid flank movement upon the Turks in their headlong flight after Lule Burgas, striking the rear guard a savage blow at Tchorlu (Nov. 6), while the cavalry penetrated as far as Rodosto, on the Sea of Marmora. A new line was formed opposite the Turkish position at Tchataldja, and preparations for attack were made at once. After some preliminary fighting, the main battle began on Nov. 17 and continued until Nov. 19. For the first time the Bulgars found themselves outranged in artillery, for the Turks had heavy siege guns, and a number of others had been brought up from the fleet.

But Turkey had had enough. Albania had declared herself independent in the middle of November, and a provisional government, with Ismail Kemil Bey as president, was set up. A truce was declared, and this led to an armistice on Dec. 3. Meanwhile, the Serbs were completing the occupation of Macedonia; Dibia and Ochrida were taken, with many prisoners and stores.

The Last Phase.—Of all the allies, Servia had up to this time accomplished most in the way of effective conquest. To Bulgaria there remained the tasks of reducing Adrianople and piercing the Tchataldja line.

The first real victory fell to the lot of the Greeks. On March 6, Janina surrendered to the Crown Prince, who twelve days later became King of the Hellenes when his father, King George, was shot and killed by a weak-minded Greek at Salonica (March 18).

On March 24, Djavid Pasha and 15,000 men yielded up their arms to the Serbs on the Skumbra River, while March 26 witnessed the fall of Adrianople. Shukri Pasha capitulated to Ivanoff, after the eastern front of the city had been furiously stormed and most of the batteries captured.

Meanwhile, the Powers had succeeded in determining the frontiers of the new state of Albania, and on March 27 Nicholas was invited to raise the siege of Scutari and withdraw from Albanian territory. The Servian allies did so; but the King of Montenegro replied by a more vigorous attack upon Tarabosch Mountain. A joint naval demonstration of the Powers was made off Antivari (April 4), and the coast blockaded, while Austria prepared to use military pressure. Essad Pasha finally surrendered the city on April 23, but it was not until May 4 that Nicholas, in defiance of his ministers, finally yielded, and in return for financial assistance relinquished the place to the Powers.

Elsewhere the war was over. The offer of mediation by the Powers, so constantly requested by Turkey, was accepted at last by the allies. On April 14 a truce had been declared between the opposing forces at Tchataldja. The ambassadors of the Powers met in London, and on May 16 representatives of the five states assembled to ratify the terms of peace. As in the previous winter, they were disposed to wrangle and accuse each other of intrigue; but the British government served notice that no delay would be tolerated, and on May 30 the Treaty of London was signed.

According to the terms of the treaty, Turkey was to pay no indemnity, but her entire European continental possessions west of a line drawn between Enos, on the Sea of Marmora, and Midia, on the Euxine, together with the island of Crete, were handed over to the allies. The future of Albania and the captured Aegean Islands was left to the Powers. Financial questions were referred to a commission sitting in Paris; other points were regarded as matters for settlement by the interested parties themselves.

Disruption of the League, Second Balkan War.—Even while the delegates in London were concluding terms of peace, the Greeks and Serbs were forming an anti-Bulgar alliance, and frequent conflicts had taken place with the Bulgars in Macedonia; but now, at the end of June, 1913, the fighting blazed into real warfare. King Constantine won a victory at Morfassa, retook Gyevegli, and captured Kukush (July 2), Doiran, Strumnitza (July 10), Drama (July 15), and finally reached Nevrekop, only twenty m. from the South Bulgarian frontier.

Bulgaria's position was most critical, and the Porte was emboldened (July 2) to demand the withdrawal of 60,000 of her troops, which were encamped near Rodosto, because the Turkish army was still mobilized. To this the Sofia government agreed on condition that Turkey remain neutral in the present conflict. But now, in Bulgaria's extreme hour, the opportunity to regain the lamented Adrianople was more than the wisdom of the Turks could neglect, or human nature could resist. On July 12, an Ottoman force under Enver Bey started unopposed across Thrace, and recaptured Lule

Burgas, Bunar Hissar, Viza, and finally Adrianople (July 22). It then entered Bulgaria, burned many villages, and committed other outrages. The Bulgarian premier sent General Paprikoff (July 20) to negotiate with Servia and Greece at Nish. The very day that the armistice was concluded (July 30), there raged a hard battle for possession of the southern gateway into Bulgaria; the Greeks occupied Gumuldjina, and captured Dedeagatch; the Servians continued to bombard Widin until Aug. 3.

The treaty of peace was signed at Bucharest on Aug. 10. It gave to Servia the whole of Macedonia under her occupation, and some territory east of the old vilayet of Kossovo—over 15,000 sq. m. in all. Her area was thus nearly doubled. Greece made the greatest relative advance in political importance. Her share (18,700 sq. m.) consisted of parts of Macedonia, Albania, and even a small portion of Thrace. Bulgaria surrendered 2,000 sq. m. of her northeastern territory to Rumania, and had to be content with only 7,000 sq. m. on the s. and w.—a much smaller area than that allotted by the Treaty of London. Montenegro's reward was a small addition on the south and east, corresponding to the aid rendered Servia in the second war.

Negotiations between Turkey and Bulgaria over Eastern Thrace were then begun, and on Sept. 17 an agreement was reached by which the former regained a considerable area, including Demotika, Adrianople, and Kirk Kilisseh. On Nov. 13, 1913 Greece and Turkey came to an agreement in regard to their unsettled differences. In World War II Germany overran and held the Balkans.

Balkh, district of Afghan Turkestan, the most northerly province of Afghanistan. It corresponds to ancient BACTRIA. The natives are Uzbegs, whose character differs in different districts.

Balkh, former capital and chief town of Balkh district, is a place of great antiquity, famous as the cradle of Zoroastrianism. Between the 7th and 12th centuries it was a center of Buddhism, and seems (from Sven Hedin's and Stein's discoveries) to have extended its influence as far as the now sand-buried cities of East Turkestan. It was sacked by Jenghiz Khan in 1220. The capital was removed to Mazar-i-Sherif, 10 m. to the east, in 1877.

The modern city occupies but a small part of the former area, and is surrounded by a mud wall; p. 15,000, mostly Uzbegs.

Balkhash (Kirghiz *Tengis* or *Tenghiz;* Chinese *Sihai*), a great inland lake near the eastern borders of Russian Central Asia. Lying 900 ft. above sea level, it extends 340 m. southwest; its breadth at the western end is 53 m., at the eastern from 4 to 9 m.; the area is 7,120 sq. m. The water is clear, but intensely salt. See ASIA.

Balkis or **Bilkis**, according to Mohammedan tradition, the name of the Queen of Sheba, who visited Solomon.

Ball. Games with balls were among the favorite gymnastic exercises of the ancients. The Greeks prized such games as a means of giving grace and elasticity to the figure. The balls were of various kinds; they were generally of leather, and filled with air; others were stuffed with feathers or hair (*pila*). In the 16th century ball playing was in great favor in the courts of princes, especially in Italy and France; and it is still practised by the people in Italy and Spain. Lawn tennis is the lineal descendant of the *jeu de paume*, which was so popular an amusement at the French court. The American game of lacrosse originated among the American Indians; and football is so wide-spread that its origin is impossible to trace. See BASEBALL; BASKETBALL; BILLIARDS; CRICKET; CROQUET; FOOTBALL; GOLF; HANDBALL; LACROSSE; LAWN TENNIS; POLO; SOFTBALL.

Ball, Thomas (1819-1911), American sculptor. His best known work is the famous equestrian statue of Washington in the Boston Public Gardens (1860-4). Some of his best known sculptures are *Eve Stepping into Life*, *Emancipation* (at Washington), *Daniel Webster* (Central Park, New York). He wrote *My Threescore Years and Ten* (1891).

Ballad. The word ballad is derived through the medium of French from the Late Latin *ballare*, 'to dance,' and thus meant originally a song sung to the rhythmic movement of a dancing chorus—a dramatic poem sung or acted in the dance, of which a kind of survival is seen in the ring songs of children's games at the present day. The name is sometimes applied to a simple song, usually of a romantic or sentimental nature, in two or more verses, each sung to the same melody. But in literature the name Ballad means more particularly a simple, spirited, narrative poem in short stanzas of two or four lines (without counting the burden or refrain), in which a story is told in straightforward verse, often with great elaborateness and detail in incident, but always with graphic simplicity and force. Coleridge's 'Rime of the Ancient Mariner,' Tennyson's 'Revenge,' Browning's 'Herve Riel,' and Rossetti's 'King's Tragedy' have, however, preserved the best traditions of the ballad. The ballad poetry of modern versifiers is not to be compared with the genuine ballads of old times.

The ballad, like the popular tale (*marchen*), is, as a dance song, an invention of the folk, with savage origins and direct modern survivals. The word 'ballad' has long lost the special sense of a dance song. As early as 1568 the poems in fourteen lines each, said to have been addressed by Mary Queen of Scots to the Earl of Bothwell, were spoken of indifferently as 'sonnets' or 'fond ballads.' The ballad, in short, is a popular form of verse, often adapted—during the last four centuries at least—to the purposes of educated men of letters. The verse, as a rule, runs in this measure:

'The king he writ a letter then,
   A letter which was large and long;
He signed it with his own hand,
   And he promised to do him no wrong.'

In the traditional ballads of England and Scotland we must not look for exact dates; but there is ample evidence that a large part of that poetry existed in much the same form as now, more than three hundred years ago. Many of the themes, of course, are much older, and undoubtedly many of the versified ballads also. It was not till Bishop Percy published his famous *Reliques of Ancient English Poetry*, in 1765, that Englishmen awakened to the fact that their popular poetry was poetry at all. Perhaps no book ever had a greater or more immediate effect. A similar return to the simplicity of truth and nature took place about the same time in France and Germany, and ere long showed its results as plainly in the lyrical work of Andre Chenier, of Goethe, Schiller, and Heine.

Nowhere has there been a richer growth of really popular ballads than in Sicily, where Pitre tells us that as many as seven thousand examples have been gathered. It is interesting to note that many of these ballads have the same tone, the same incidents, the same iteration of words and ideas as the traditional ballads of England and Scotland, of Scandinavia, of Greece, of Germany, of Italy, of France, and of Spain. This discovery widens our interest in the question enormously. The plots and situations of many of our traditionary folk songs are the immemorial inheritance of Celts and Saxons, of Greek and Slavonic peoples—of unknown and prehistoric antiquity. They do not belong to one nation in particular, but are the property at least of all the peoples of the Aryan family. Entirely apart from questions of origin, the popular ballads of the English-speaking peoples will repay the most diligent study on their literary side alone.

The best collection of ballads, in all their varying versions, is Professor Child's great work, *English and Scottish Ballads* (first published in 5 vols. in 1857-9); and a one-volume edition, edited by Mrs. Child Sargent and Professor Kittredge (1904), contains all but five of the 305 ballads. Allingham's is a good anthology. Among notable collections have been: Percy's *Reliques of Ancient English Poetry* (3 vols. 1765; a beautiful and excellent edition by H. B. Wheatley, 3 vols. 1886); Scott's *Minstrelsy of the Scottish Border* (3 vols. 1802-3, with its admirable introduction and notes); and Motherwell's *Minstrelsy, Ancient and Modern* (1827), with an excellent introduction. Indispensable books are Chappell's *Popular Music of the Olden Time* (1855-9; new ed. 1893), and Hales and Furnivall's reprint of the *Percy Folio Manuscript* (3 vols. 1867-8). Consult also F. B. Gummere's *The Popular Ballad* and *The Beginnings of Poetry* (1901); Sir A. T. Quiller Couch's *Oxford Book of Ballads* (1910).

Ballade, a poem divided into one or more triplets, each formed of seven or eight lined stanzas, the last line being a refrain common to each stanza. In the ballade of eight lines there are only three rhymes, thus—A, B, A, B; B, C, B, C. An *envoi* is usually attached. Its four lines repeat the rhymes of the last four lines of the stanza. The foregoing is the strict application of the term—it is now frequently used somewhat more loosely of any poem divided into stanzas of equal length. The ballade should not be confused with the ballad. The two have no connection, apart from their common derivation from the Latin *ballare*, 'to dance.'

Ballarat, or **Ballaarat,** city, Victoria, Australia, next in importance to Melbourne. Owing its rise to the discovery of gold there in June, 1851, it is still the center of a rich goldfield; p. 45,000. Consult Withers' *History of Ballarat*.

Ballast, employed to give a ship sufficient immersion in the water, so as to insure her safe sailing with spread canvas, when her cargo and equipment are too light, may consist of iron, stone, gravel, sand, or water. The term is also used of the broken stone, cinders, or gravelly material laid as a packing between railroad ties. The word ballast is also applied to the sand which is carried in a balloon, and which is thrown out from time to time in order to enable the balloon to ascend to higher altitudes.

Ball Bearings, a device for reducing friction, usually applied to the shaft or axle of a rotating wheel or disc, as in the motor car and bicycle, and consisting of a series of hardened and perfectly true steel balls, one-eighth inch in diameter and upward. Each ball is separate, and rotates with the shaft.

Ball Bearings.
Hub of motor car, showing two outer rows of balls taking the journal bearing load, and two inner taking the end thrust in both directions.

Ballet, a series of solo and concerted dances with mimetic actions, accompanied by music and scenic accessories, telling a story. The ballet, combined with dialogue and vocal music, was introduced as a court entertainment into France from Italy about 1550 by Baltasarini, under the patronage of Catherine de' Medici. As an exclusively dancing establishment the ballet came into being with the foundation in 1669 of the *Académie Royale de Musique et de Danse* in Paris. The ballet, as an independent entertainment, owes its origin to Jean Georges Noverre, who wholly parted it from opera about 1776. The ballet was introduced into England from France about 1734 by two female dancers—De Subligny and Sallé, and flourished especially during the first half of the 19th century, after which time it suffered a serious decline.

The *Russian Ballet,* which has risen to a position of pre-eminence since the decline of the ballet in France, was instituted by the Empress Anne in 1735. Among its leading recent exponents are Anna Pavlowa, Waslaw Nijinsky, Mikail Mordkin, Tamar Karsovina and Lydia Kyasht. Consult Pougin's *Dictionnaire Historique du Theatre;* Flitch's *Modern Dancing and Dancers;* Perugini's *The Art of Ballet;* Karsovina's *Theatre Street;* Haskell's *Balletomania; Nijinsky.*

Ball-flower, an ornament in Gothic architecture of the 13th and 14th centuries, in which the petals of a sculptured flower, three or, rarely, four in number, enclose a ball, instead of pistils or stamens.

Ballin, Hugo (1879-   ), American artist, was born in New York. In Rome and Florence, he devoted much time to mural painting, in which he attained some striking effects through his lavish use of color. His decorations for the capitol building at Madison, Wisconsin, are typically American in spirit and conception. He has produced and mounted many feature motion pictures.

Balliol College, Oxford. See **Oxford.**

Ballista, or **Balista,** an ancient military engine in the nature of a catapult, used in throwing large stones or darts.

Ballistic Pendulum, an apparatus invented (about 1740) by Benjamin Robins to ascertain the velocity of projectiles fired from a gun. It is now superseded by other contrivances, as the electro-ballistic chronograph.

Ballistics. See **Gunnery.**

Ballistite, a smokeless powder resembling cordite, introduced in 1886 by Alfred Nobel.

Balloons. There are two classes of lighter-than-air craft: 1. balloons which are non-steerable and without motive power except as provided by the winds; 2. dirigibles or airships which are powered and can be steered.

1. There are captive balloons which are restrained from free flight by means of a cable, and free balloons whose ascent and descent can be controlled by releasing ballast or gas and whose direction is determined by the winds.

2. Dirigibles may be rigid, non-rigid or semi-rigid.

The free balloon, usually spherical, was the first successful air vehicle. Until recently the gas-carrying bag was made either of cotton or silk and rubberized or varnished to minimize diffusion of the contained lifting gas. A cord netting around the gas bag has attached to it the basket in which passengers, instruments and ballast are carried. Hydrogen, coal gas or helium are most used. A balloon rises because it is lighter than the volume of air it displaces by virtue of the gas-filled bag.

The first man-carrying flight of a balloon (See Aeronautics for early history) in 1783 covered a distance of about five miles. In 1914 a balloon carried three passengers 1,897 miles. Used early in the pursuit of scientific investigations, Charles Green, by 1838, had attained altitudes of 20,352 feet. On November 11, 1935, Captain A. W. Stevens and Captain Orville A. Anderson, riding in an aluminum alloy sphere, ascended by balloon from a spot in South Dakota to an altitude of 72,395 feet, the highest point yet reached by man.

Not only transoceanic but transpolar flights engaged the imaginations of 19th Century balloonists. In 1897, Andree and two companions took off from Spitzbergen in a free balloon attempt to fly over the North Pole. It was not until 1933 that their bodies were found on White Island, not too far away. One of the most dramatic military uses of the balloon came during the Franco-Prussian War when, in 1870-1871, 164 persons and 20,000 pounds of mail were sent out of beleaguered Paris by air. Two of the 65 balloons so used were blown by storm 600 miles to Norway before landing.

With development of the dirigible, with its advantages of power and steerability, interest in ballooning dwindled, except for specialized purposes. In World War I, captive balloons were used extensively for observation, although they proved most vulnerable to gun fire and enemy planes. In World War II their use was even more confined, as aerial barrages over vital areas. Still used in 1951, free balloons are sent skyward carrying instruments to record information about weather conditions, and also cosmic rays at high altitudes. This information is either sent automatically by radio to ground receivers, or is recorded and recovered by parachute when the balloon bursts. Altitudes up to 120,000 feet have been reached by giant balloons made of plastic.

Development of the Dirigible. It was not until the close of the 19th Century, when internal propulsion engines were perfected, that the dirigible's possibilities (See Aeronautics) could be exploited fully, although in 1884 Renard and Krebs had made a circular flight of 5 miles with an electrically powered airship. In 1901, Santos-Dumont won a 100,-000 franc prize for a closed course flight of 7 miles in less than 30 minutes. In 1906 the Lebaudy Brothers built a semi-rigid airship for the French Government, the first dirigible to be constructed on special order from a government which in the following year made a controlled flight of 130 miles.

Great Britain purchased an airship from a French firm in 1910, and on its delivery flight it crossed the Channel during the 242 mile nonstop trip. In the early 1900's the Parseval nonrigid airships in Germany enjoyed some success.

In the United States the story of the dirigible begins in 1904 when Captain Thomas S. Baldwin constructed the "California Arrow." In 1908 Captain Baldwin built a nonrigid airship, capable of making 19 mph, which the Army bought for $10,000. It was 94 feet long, powered by a 20 hp. engine and manufactured by Glenn Curtiss. It attained speeds up to 30 mph.

Walter Wellman, an American explorer and journalist, made unsuccessful efforts to reach the North Pole by air and to fly the Atlantic during the years 1906-1910 in a French-built dirigible. It was at first 185 feet long, but was later enlarged to a length of 228 feet. On the Atlantic crossing attempt, Wellman and his crew were rescued from the twin-motor airship 400 miles off the Coast. Melville Vaniman, a member of the Wellman crew, constructed another dirigible, the *Akron,* with which he proposed to attempt the transatlantic crossing. During a trial flight July 12, 1912, it burst into flame, causing the death of the crew of five.

The British carried forward development of completely nonrigid dirigibles, which became generally known as blimps, and used them widely in World War I. In the United States, too, blimps were developed under Navy sponsorship. In 1950, construction was completed by the Goodyear Aircraft Corporation of the first of the "N" type blimps. The largest nonrigid airship ever built, it has a gas capacity of 875,000 cubic feet and is 324 feet long. Its engines are housed within the control car with power transmitted by shafts and gearing to the outboard propellers. It was designed for use as a member of the Navy's antisubmarine warfare team. During World War II, some 160 blimps, capable of top speed of approximately 75 mph, were manufactured for the Navy. They ranged in size from the "G" class, 187 feet long, with 183,-000 cubic feet gas capacity, to the "M" class, 308 feet long, with 725,000 cubic feet gas capacity. Most of the blimps constructed during this period were of the "K" class, 251 feet long, with 456,000 cubic feet gas capacity. It has been estimated that the blimps served as escorts to 90,000 surface vessels without loss to submarines of a single ship.

Other nonrigid airships deserving of mention would include the semirigid Italian design, the *Roma*. This dirigible had a keel for almost the entire length of 412 feet, and had a gas capacity of 1,200,000 cubic feet. First flight trials in 1920 were successful, after which the *Roma* was sold to the U.S. Army, dismantled, shipped to America and reassembled. Its first American flight was in November, 1921. Later, its six Italian engines were removed and as many Liberty engines were installed. On February 21, 1922, during a flight from Langley Field, Virginia, it became unmanageable, and in a rapid descent, hit an electric power line and exploded, causing the death of 34 of the 45 men aboard. The Italians also built the *Norge* which Amundsen flew over the North Pole May 12, 1926, and the *Italia*, in which Nobile duplicated this feat in 1928, only to crash on May 25th, with the loss of seven of the crew.

The Zeppelin. Credit for practical development of the rigid airship must be given the German, Count von Zeppelin, who, curiously, made his first balloon ascent from St. Paul, Minnesota, in 1863, when he was an observer with the Union forces. In 1889, Count Zeppelin had proposed construction of rigid airships, but government support was not forthcoming, and it was not until 1898 that he organized a stock company and began construction of an airship 419 feet long. Its framework was of aluminum and its gas capacity 338,000 cubic feet. First trial flights in 1900 were successful to the point where additional public support was quickly forthcoming. By 1909 one of his Zeppelins had crossed the Alps during a 235 mile flight, and the following year commercial passenger service was inaugurated over a five-city 300 mile route. By 1914, when World War I began, 34,228 passengers had been carried.

During World War I, 72 Zeppelins were in commission. They were used mostly for scouting and bombing. The first Zeppelin air raid on England was in January, 1915, and a total of 53 such raids were made on Britain. By 1917, defenses had been so perfected that the airship raids were no longer profitable. Had the Germans had helium instead of inflammable hydrogen, the Zeppelins doubtless would have been more effective. As it was, they were credited with killing 556 persons and wounding 1,326, doing considerable bomb damage and having a noticeable effect on morale. Perhaps the outstanding Zeppelin flight of the War was in March, 1917, when the L-59 flew 4,225 miles nonstop in a flight from Bulgaria to Africa with medical supplies and ammunition. Part way on the voyage wireless reports told of surrender of the German colonial troops, otherwise the flight might have been even longer.

British airship construction during World War I was not great, but the R-34, which made its test flights the week of the Armistice, November 11, 1918, was historic in that it was the first to cross the Atlantic in July, 1919. This airship, which had a length of 643 feet and a gas capacity of about 2,000,000 cubic feet, was followed by the larger R-38 (695 feet in length, 2,720,000 cubic feet gas capacity). It was to be bought by the U.S. Navy for $1,500,000. On August 24, 1921, during turning trials, its frame buckled and it broke in half, killing 45 of the 50 men on board. Another airship of this period was the L-72, which the Germans completed 3 days after the Armistice, only to have it turned over to the French and become the Dixmude. After an earlier 4,000 mile flight in December, 1923, it was caught in a violent storm over the Mediterranean and was lost with a crew of 50.

The first rigid airship to use helium was the *Shenandoah*, 680 feet long and with 2,100,000 cubic feet gas capacity. By September, 1925, it had been in the air 740 hours and had flown more than 25,000 hours. On September 2, 1925, it was caught in a violent line storm in Ohio and broke apart. The control car remained attached to the rear section and most of the men were carried safely to earth. Fourteen of the crew were killed. The United States acquired the ZR-3, called the *Los Angeles*, from Germany in 1924. For ten years this airship was used widely, covering most of the United States and participating in naval maneuvers over both the Atlantic and Pacific. The final British effort to build rigid airships resulted in the R-100 and R-101. The R-100, somewhat the larger, had a gas capacity of 5,000,000 cubic feet and was 706 feet long. Both were intended for commercial air travel to Canada and the Far East. In 1930, the R-100 made a round-trip Atlantic crossing. On its maiden voyage, October 4, 1930, the R-101 crashed and exploded near Paris, killing 56 persons. The R-100 was dismantled not long after.

In 1932 and 1933 the *Macon* and *Akron* were constructed. These had 6,500,000 cubic feet gas capacity and were 785 feet long. The *Akron* was lost off the New Jersey coast during a violent storm on April 4, 1933, with the loss of 7 men, including Rear Admiral William N. Moffett, USN. February 12, 1935,

Acme Newspictures

Dirigible Hindenburg crashes at Lakehurst in May 1937. The German zeppelin Hindenburg is seen in this remarkable photo as it crashes to the earth in flames at Lakehurst, New Jersey, following explosion on board just as she was about to be moored to her mast.

the *Macon* also crashed at sea, off the California coast. Only two members of the crew were killed of the crew of 80.

As a result of the Locarno Treaty of 1925, restrictions were relaxed which permitted resumption of airship construction. The first of the post-war German dirigibles was the *Graf Zeppelin I*, with 3,700,000 cubic feet gas capacity, completed in 1928. In the nine years following it made more than 200 flights, covering 775,000 miles. During regularly scheduled flights across the North and South Atlantic it carried 12,500 passengers and more than 110,000 pounds of mail and freight. In 1929, from August 1 to September 4, it flew 31,011 miles, including a round-the-world flight in 21 days, 7 hours and 12 minutes.

Dr. Hugo von Eckener, who had succeeded Count von Zeppelin, felt that the *Graf Zeppelin I* was too small for commercial passenger work. In 1936, the *Hindenburg* was launched. It was 813 feet long and had a gas capacity of 7,000,000 cubic feet. It was quickly put into schedule, both to North and South America from Germany. May 3, 1937, on her first North Atlantic flight of the season, the *Hindenburg* burst into flames as it was being moored at Lakehurst, New Jersey. Miraculously, only 36 of the 97 persons aboard were killed.

Because the *Hindenburg* disaster was clearly due to the fact that the airship used hydrogen, Germany at once requested the United States to provide sufficient helium for th *Graf Zeppelin II,* a sister ship of the *Hindenburg*, which was nearing completion, and for the *Graf Zeppelin I*, which was still serviceable. Harold Ickes, then U.S. Secretary of the Interior, faced considerable public criticism when he refused to authorize export of the helium, on the ground that there was insufficient guarantee that Germany might not use the dirigibles for warlike purposes. Outbreak of World War II, hardly two years later, gave substance to his fears.

Finally, of course, the rapid development of heavier-than-air transport in the '30's made further development of the airship unprofitable. By 1935, regular service had begun across the Pacific, and by '39 similar service was inaugurated across the North Atlantic (See *Airplanes*).

See *Aeronautics;* Lehmann's *Zeppelin,* 1937; Magoun and Hodgin's *History of Aircraft,* 1931; *The Airman's Almanac, 1945;* and *The Aircraft Yearbook,* 1919.

WALTER T. BONNEY, *Information Specialist. National Advisory Committee for Aeronautics.*

Ballot, or secret voting, is a very old institution practised both in Greece and in Rome. In America the employment of the ballot in elections dates from early colonial times. Since the Revolution voting by ballot has been the general practice. In Great Britain voting by ballot was advocated by reformers at least as early as 1817. A modern development is the voting machine, now used in many large cities. This device, so constructed as to mark the voter's ballot when a lever is pulled after adjustment of the machine, minimizes the possibility of alteration of ballots after they have been cast. Voting by ballot in some form has been introduced into nearly every country governed in accordance with constitutional methods.

Ballot, Buys (1818-90), Dutch chemist, physicist, and meteorologist. The 'law' by which he is most widely known defines the relation of the wind to the isobars.

Ballou, Hosea (1771-1852), American clergyman. Of his numerous books may be mentioned *Notes on the Parables* (1804), and *Examination of the Doctrine of Future Retribution* (1834). He was one of the most active founders of Universalism in the United States.

Ballou, Maturin Murray (1820-95), American journalist. In 1872 he was a founder of the Boston *Globe,* and was its editor for many years. Author of several books of travel and various miscellaneous books.

Ballymena, market town, Ulster, Ireland, with a flourishing trade in brown linens (yearly average, $5,000,000) and an old linen market (manufacture introduced 1732); p. 11,376.

Balm of Gilead, or **Mecca Balsam,** an aromatic gum or powder with supposed medicinal qualities, which, if not produced in Gilead, was at least a well-known article of commerce in that region.

Photograph published by the Stereoscopic Company.
Balmoral Castle, the Highland Residence of the British King.

Balme, Col de, famous mountain pass in the Pennine Alps, on the dividing line between France and Switzerland.

Balmoral Castle (Gael, 'the majestic dwelling'), royal residence, Scotland, purchased by Queen Victoria in 1848. In 1853 the present red granite Scotch baronial castle replaced an old one.

Balsa, a raft or surf-boat, made of the extremely light balsa-wood of Peru and Brazil. The name is also employed for a life raft used in the navy and on merchant vessels, consisting of two floats so joined as to form a platform on which people and goods can be sustained.

Balsam. 1. Various species of the order

Balsamineae. The principal genus is known as Impatiens, because the ripe capsule bursts spontaneously or when touched. There are over a hundred species of Impatiens; many have been introduced from the East for greenhouse cultivation. 2. *I. Balsamina*, from India, is a commonly cultivated annual, often called 'lady's slipper.' BALSAM TREE of Jamaica is *Clusia flava* of the order Guttiferae, yielding a gum-resin which is used as pitch in the West Indies.—CANADA BALSAM, obtained from the Canadian balm of Gilead fir, is used in microscopic work for the permanent preservation of sections on glass slides.— BALSAM OF PERU is taken from the trunk of *Myroxylon peruiferum*, after beating, scorching, and removing the bark. Its volatile oil contains cinnamic and benzoic acids, which give its fragrance. It has the general qualities of balsams, and is used chiefly as a disinfectant expectorant in bronchial affections.

BALM-OF-GILEAD is a fragrant liquid resinous substance obtained from *Commiphora opobalsamum* or *Balsamea meccanensis*. In the United States a variety of *Populus balsamifera* is called Balm-of-Gilead Tree.

Balta, town, Odessa Region, Ukraine, U.S.S.R., on a tributary of the Bug River about 112 m. n.w. of Odessa. The center of an agricultural region, it raises grain and cattle. In World War II it was held by the Germans, 1941-44, but retaken by Russia in 1944. P. 21,374.

Balthazar, one of the three wise men (Magi) of the Nativity, and one of the fabulous three kings shown in Cologne Cathedral.

Baltic Port or **Paldiski,** seaport, Estonia, Russia; p. 662.

Baltic Provinces, the name formerly applied to the Russian provinces of Estonia, Livonia, and Courland, or Kurland. They later formed two republics: Estonia and Latvia; reannexed by Russia, 1940.

Baltic Sea, or **East Sea,** an inland sea of Northern Europe, surrounded by Denmark, Germany, Poland, Russia, Finland, and Sweden, and communicating with the Atlantic through the Skagerrak and the Kattegat, which leads to the channels of the Sound (Oresund), the Great Belt, and the Little Belt, between the Danish Islands.

The Baltic is generally shallow (20 to 100 fathoms). The sea is fed by numerous streams, some of them considerable rivers, such as the Vistula, and Oder. In winter the smaller bays and creeks, especially in the northern parts of the sea, invariably freeze, and so suspend navigation; and in severe winters the Gulf of Bothnia becomes frozen from side to side. The tides are barely perceptible east of the Danish islands.

The Kaiser Wilhelm Canal, more commonly called the Kiel Canal, affords a short cut between the Baltic and the North Sea.

Baltimore, largest city of Maryland; p. 941,809. Baltimore is divided into two general parts by a stream called Jones' Falls, which is covered by the Fallsway, the great commercial highway of the city. On the west side is the most important residence section, while on the east is the 'Old Town,' with many of the principal manufacturing industries. There are 79 public squares, triangles and parks. The most celebrated is the beautiful Druid Hill Park. Baltimore is often called 'The Monumental

The First Lord Baltimore.

City,' from its many monuments. The city is noted also for the splendid architecture of its public buildings. Educational institutions are many and prominent, the most notable being Johns Hopkins University, one of the finest universities in the country.

Baltimore is a manufacturing city of the first importance. The leading industries are the manufacture of clothing and of copper, tin, and sheet iron products, slaughtering and meat packing, and the making of fertilizer.

The city stands high in the manufacture of cotton duck, straw hats, men's clothing, and the canning of oysters. There are immense steel works at Sparrow's Point, nine m. from the city, and shipbuilding is a leading industry, which was given an additional impetus when the United States entered the World War.

The location of Baltimore near the head of Chesapeake Bay, midway between the North and South, makes it a commercial center of the first importance. A canal across the State of Delaware connects it with Philadelphia, and an inland waterway system reaches south to New Bern, N. C.

Most of the Baltimore piers are owned by railroads. The port has grown steadily in recent years. With occasional exceptions, passenger business since the World War has been restricted to coastwise travel. The exceptions include passenger and freight service, more or less regular, to Germany, England, Puerto Rico, Bermuda. Baltimore has long been one of the leading grain exporting centers of the United States. Leading articles of export, besides grain and breadstuffs, are tobacco, coal, cotton, naval stores, iron, steel, meats, and canned fruit and oysters.

Baltimore, which was founded in 1729, took its name from Lord Baltimore the founder of the Maryland Colony. It was incorporated as a city in 1796 and early became noted for commerce and shipbuilding. The city was extended by seven different Acts beween 1732 and 1918, and separated from Baltimore co. by the Constitution of 1851. Francis Scott Key composed the words of *The Star Spangled Banner* in Baltimore during the War of 1812.

On Feb. 7, 1904, a great fire started in the business section, burning for thirty hours, with an estimated loss of $125,000,000. The city is the seat of a Roman Catholic archbishop, whose see is the oldest in the United States.

Consult Love's *Baltimore: The Old Town and the Modern City;* Coyle's *The Baltimore Book; Baltimore Municipal Journal;* Mayor's *Quadrennial Message to Baltimore City Council.*

Baltimore, George Calvert, first Baron (?1580-1632), English statesman, entered Parliament in 1609, and ten years later became secretary of state. The failure of the Spanish marriage scheme, however, made him very unpopular, and in 1624 he resigned office, at the same time declaring himself a Catholic. On his retirement he was created (1625) a baron, and was granted large estates in county Longford, Ireland.

He applied for a grant of land in America (1632) which was named 'Maryland,' but he died before the patent was issued and the grant descended to his son Cecil. See MARYLAND. Consult Browne's *George Calvert and Cecilius Calvert;* Wilhelm's *Life of George Calvert* (Md. Histor. Soc. monograph); Kennedy's *Life and Character of George Calvert.*

Baluchistan, name of two states in India bounded on the n. by Afghanistan, on the e. by British India, on the s. by the Arabian Sea, and on the w. by Iran. The province has an area of 134,000 sq. m., and the whole territory (except British Baluchistan) is under native rule. The few fertile spots in the province are peopled by pastoral tribes, chiefly Brahui and the more settled Baluchis, and Kurds from Kurdistan, all of whom are zealous Mohammedans; p. 858,000. Baluchistan, with its scanty population, and products, owes its importance to its position on the British Indian frontier, and its command of the trade routes between Iran, Afghanistan, and India. Quetta (p. 60,272), capital of British Baluchistan, is an important centre of trade on the route through the Bolan Pass to India.

Baluster, a small circular pilaster, of Italian invention, supporting a hand-rail, coping, balcony, or terrace.

Balzac, Honoré de (1799-1850), a celebrated French novelist, was a native of Tours. Educated at Vendôme, and at the Sorbonne, Paris, for some years he lived in a state of penury. Success came when, in his thirtieth year, he published, under his own name, *Les Derniers Chouans* (1829), after which he continued to send out an enormous number of novels, some historical, but mainly illustrative of French contemporary life and manners. These he afterward grouped under the collective title of the *Comédie Humaine,* in which he describes the manifold aspects of human life. Often gross and brutal, Balzac is yet one of the great writers of the world, being the father of the realistic school of fiction. Of his works, which were very numerous, the best known are *Eugénie Grandet* (1833); *Le Pére Goriot* (1835). See also Saintsbury's *French Novelists* (1891), and Balzac's *Life,* written by his sister (1858); Lovenjoul's *Histoire des Œuvres de H. de Balzac* (2d ed. 1886); Théophile Gautier's *H. de Balzac* (1859); Sainte-Beuve's *Causeries du Lundi* (vol. ii.) and *Portraits Contemporains* (vol. ii.); Taine's *Nouveaux Essais de Critique et d'Histoire* (1865); and Faguet's *Etudes Littéraires sur le XIXe Siécle* (1887). See, also, for bibliography Saltus's *Balzac* (1888).

Bamangwato, a native district and people

Bambara in the Bechuanaland Protectorate, ruled over by the chief Khama.

Bambara, or **Bambarra,** people of French W. Africa. The majority are slaves, the upper classes being Mohammedans.

Bambino (Ital. 'The Babe'), a term applied to the wooden figure of the child Jesus.

Bamboo, or **Bambusa,** a genus of grasses with woody aerial stems.

Bamian, former town; Afghanistan. Noteworthy for its five colossal human figures sculptured out of the conglomerate of the valley wall, and described about 630 A.D. by a Chinese Buddhist monk, Hwen Thsang.

Bamra, native state in Sambalpur district, Central Provinces, India; p. 123,378.

Banana, a plant of the order Musaceae. Though some have distinguished many species in cultivation, De Candolle (*Origin of Cultivated Plants*, 1884) shows that there is only one, *Musa sapientum* of Robert Brown; even the plantain, or pisang (*M. paradisiaca* of some botanists), is merely a sub-species or variety of *M. sapientum*. The original home of the banana is doubtful, but most evidence is in favor of the East Indies. It is now cultivated in every tropical and sub-tropical country, where its nutritious fruit, rich in starch, sugar, and nitrogenous matters, forms the principal food of millions. Certain varieties, notably *Musa coccinea, M. superba, M. assamica,* and *M. ensete,* may be grown for decorative purposes without the application of great heat. All the plantain-tree species have handsome foliage, and some yield a fiber.

The variety of banana which is most suitable, as it is most frequently grown, for market purposes, is the large yellow Martinique or Jamaica. These, when intended for export, are gathered green, and allowed to ripen on the voyage and after reaching their destination. In the tropics the banana is among the most important articles of food. The consumption of bananas has increased enormously during the last few years. The fruit comes chiefly from the West Indies.

Banana-quits, small, active, fly-catching birds of the 'honey-creeper' group Certhiola, so-called in the West Indies because they frequent banana orchards, where they are welcome for their pretty ways and melodious notes.

Banbury, a market town in Oxfordshire, England. The celebrated Banbury cake has had a reputation since 1608. Roman remains have been discovered; p. 13,463.

Banco, in finance, equivalent to 'bank value,' or the standard money in which certain European banks, especially the banks of Hamburg, Genoa, Amsterdam, and Venice, formerly kept their accounts.

Banana Plant.

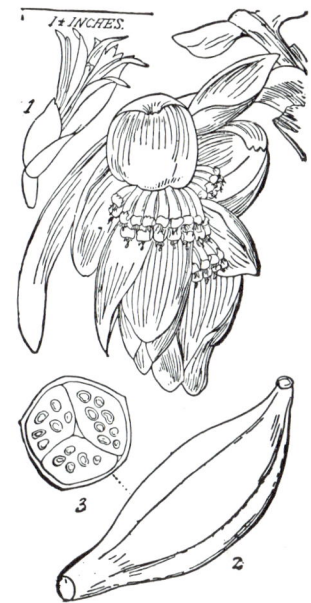

Inflorescence of the Banana.
1, Flower; 2, fruit; 3, section of fruit.

Bancroft, George (1800-91), American historian, statesman, and diplomat, was born in Worcester, Mass. In 1835 he began work on his *History of the United States* (1834-76), and completed the 10th volume in 1876. During the war with Mexico, Bancroft not only accomplished effective service with the navy in Mexican waters and secured California to the Union, but was instrumental in bringing about the Oregon compromise with Great Britain; and during his brief term of office (1845-6) he developed the Naval Observatory at Washington and established the Naval Academy at Annapolis. From 1846 to 1849 he was U. S. minister to Great Britain. Subsequently he prepared and published the *History of the Formation of the Constitution of the United States* (1882). The whole series was revised and reissued under Mr. Bancroft's supervision as *History of the United States from the Discovery of America to the Inauguration of Washington* (1884-5). See West's *George Bancroft*.

Band, in architecture, is any ring or collar encircling a shaft or tower, or, any flat ornament continued horizontally along a wall, such as a frieze.

Band, Military. The earliest record of regimental bands is contained in a French decree of April 19, 1766, assigning a band of music to each regiment, but it was near the close of the century before the institution was thoroughly established. Individual bandmasters first began to attract attention about 1850. The most celebrated in the United States army was Patrick Sarsfield Gilmore. Some of his successors were D. W. Reeves, Victor Herbert and John Philip Sousa. For further details of U. S. army bands, see U. S. Army Regulations.

Banda, capital of district of same name N. W. Provinces (United Provinces of Agra and Oudh), India; p. 631,058.

Banda. (*1.*) A group of islands in the Dutch E. Indies. The chief town and center of trade is Nassau in Banda Neira. Up to 1873 the islands enjoyed a monopoly in the production of nutmegs, which still form the chief export; p. 9,500. (*2.*) BANDA SEA, division of the Pacific lying between the Moluccas.

Bandage and **Bandaging.** The bandage may be used to fix splints or dressings, to prevent or to lessen swelling, to stop haemorrhage, to drive the blood from a limb before operation, to support a limb, or to prevent or lessen movement. It is made of muslin, linen, cheese cloth, or of flannel. When applied to a wound it may be of gauze, medicated with carbolic acid, or some other antiseptic. It may be stiffened with starch, plaster of Paris, or waterglass, when it is intended to replace a splint. An elastic rubber bandage is sometimes used in cases of varicose veins in the leg. Bandaging always proceeds from below upwards, to help the blood onwards, and to lessen the risk of stopping circulation.

The roller bandage is the one chiefly used; but the triangular bandage, made by doubling a handkerchief diagonally, is useful for covering the head and for making a sling. See Leonard's *Bandaging*.

Bandana, an Indian term properly applied to the rich yellow or red silk handkerchief, with diamond spots left white by exceedingly great pressure applied to prevent their receiving the dye. It has now come to mean a kind of calico printing in which white or brightcolored spots are placed upon a Turkey-red or dark ground.

Banderole. (*1.*) A scroll very common on engravings of the 16th-18th centuries, containing a motto, or title, or description of the picture. (*2.*) The piece of bunting attached to a lance or spear, and formerly often decorated with the crest or badge of the bearer.

Bandicoot, a name applied to various small Australian marsupial mammals of the family Peramelidae. The hind feet resemble those of the kangaroo, while the fore feet have two or three of the middle toes of equal length, with strong, sharp claws, and the other toes rudimentary. All are either omnivorous or insecteating.

Bandolier, or **Bandoleer**, a cartridge belt woven of stout canvas, with a separate pocket for each cartridge or clip of five cartridges, intended to be worn over the shoulder. It dates from mediaeval times.

Bandoline, a gummy substance produced from gum tragacanth, quince seeds, Irish moss, or Iceland moss, with perfume added, used by hairdressers to make the hair glossy.

Baneberry, a name given to two members of the genus Actaea, belonging to the order Ranunculaceae. They are hardy, herbaceous plants, about 2 feet high.

Banff, town, province of Alberta, Canada. It is the headquarters for the famous Rocky Mountains Park (2,751 sq. m.), controlled by the Dominion government.

Banffshire, maritime co., in the northeastern part of Scotland, with an area of 630 sq. m.; p. 51,700.

Bangalore, city, India, capital of the native state of Mysore, 150 m. w. of Madras; p. 306,470. When Mysore was restored to its rajah in 1881, Bangalore was reserved as a British cantonment. Important as a railway centre and manufactures silks and carpets.

Bangka, a district in the Netherlands East Indies; area 4,611 sq. m.; p. 205,363.

Bangkok, city, capital of Siam, on the River Menam, 25 m. from its mouth. It covers an area of about 15 sq. m. on both

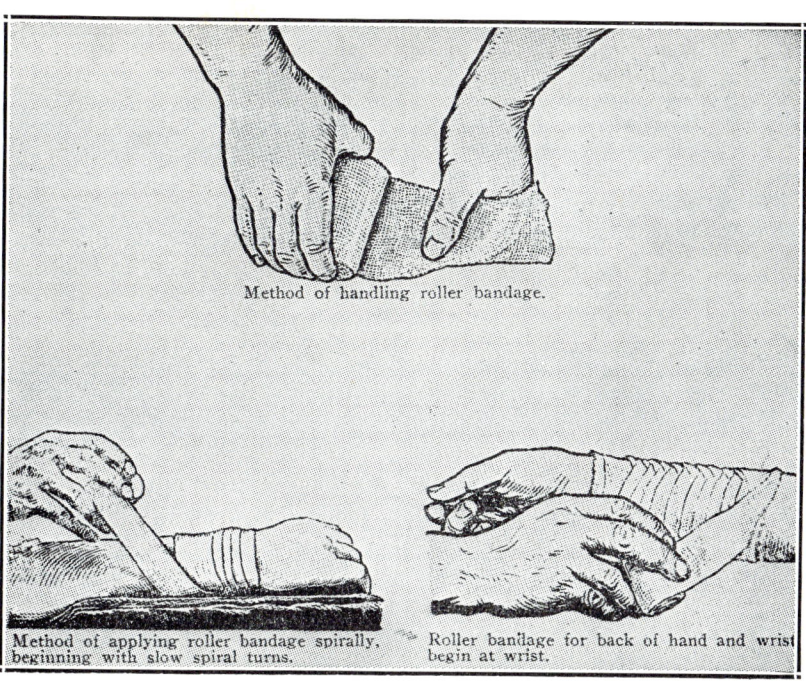

Method of handling roller bandage.

Method of applying roller bandage spirally, beginning with slow spiral turns.

Roller bandage for back of hand and wrist; begin at wrist.

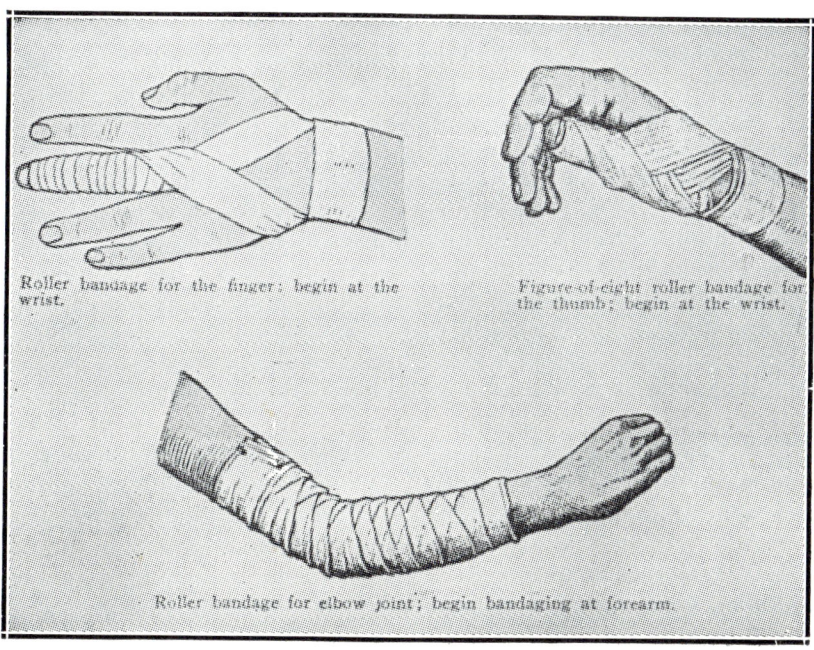

Roller bandage for the finger; begin at the wrist.

Figure-of-eight roller bandage for the thumb; begin at the wrist.

Roller bandage for elbow joint; begin bandaging at forearm.

Bangor   388   **Banking**

sides of the river, the larger and more important part lying on the east bank. Bangkok is the chief port of the kingdom, and trade is largely in the hands of Europeans and Chinese; p. 931,170.

Bangor, city, Maine, county seat of Penobscot co., situated at the head of navigation on the Penobscot River, 60 m. from its mouth. The place was founded by settlers from Massachusetts in 1769 under the name of Sunbury. In 1791 it was incorporated as the town of Bangor, and the city charter was granted in 1834; .. 29,822.

Bangs, John Kendrick (1862-1922), American humorist and editor, was born in Yonkers, N. Y., and was graduated (1883) from Columbia University. He was associate-editor of *Life* (1884-8), a member of Harper & Brother's editorial staff (1888-1900), editor of the *Metropolitan Magazine* (1902-3) and of *Puck* (1904-05). His publications include over forty books, chiefly of a humorous character. Among these are *A House-Boat on the Styx* (1895); *From Pillar to Post* (1916); *The Cheery Way* (1919).

Bangweolo, or **Bemba, Lake,** Africa, in Northern Rhodesia, 3,800 ft. above the level of the sea. It was discovered by Livingstone in 1868.

Banian, a name given to the merchant class in India. The banians belong to the Vaisya caste and are worshippers of Vishnu.

Banian Tree. See **Banyan.**

Banishment, a form of punishment which consists in sending a person out of a country, district, or town, under penalties in the case of his return. Banishment was first inflicted as a punishment in England by a statute of Elizabeth. In modern times banishment for political offences has been practiced by Russia, prior to the revolution, and Turkey. See OUTLAWRY.

Banjermassing, or **Banjermasin,** capital of Dutch Borneo, in the East Indies. Built on piles, it stands near the southern coast, on the Martapura, a few miles from the Barito River; p. 50,000. From the Middle Ages down to 1857 there existed an independent Malay state of the same name, its capital being Martapura.

Banjo, a musical stringed instrument made popular by the American negroes and minstrels. The strings, from five to nine in number, rest upon a bridge, and are stopped with the fingers of the left hand and plucked with those of the right.

Bankers' Association, American, an organization, founded in the United States in 1875. The first convention of the Association, at Saratoga, 1875, was attended by three hundred bankers. Its membership, 1947, was about 15,500.

Bankhead, John Hollis (1842-1920), American legislator, was born in Moscow (now Sulligent), Ala. In 1907 he was appointed a member of the Inland Waterways Commission and was appointed U. S. Senator to fill the unexpired term of J. T. Morgan, deceased (1907), being re-elected in 1913 for two succeeding terms.

Bank Holidays, certain days on which the business of banking is suspended. In the United States generally, Sundays and all public holidays are bank holidays; in some of the States Saturday has also been made a bank holiday, in whole or in part. In England, the bank holidays are Sundays, Good Friday, Easter Monday, Monday in Whitsun week, the first Monday in August, Christmas Day, and Dec. 26.

Banking is a term rather loosely used to describe the operations of almost any institution whose business is concerned chiefly with the handling of money or claims to money. The term bank (French 'banque,' Italian 'banco') is a word of doubtful derivation. Most authorities maintain that it comes from the Italian word for bench which was erected in the market place where it was customary to exchange money. It is known that commercial instruments including promissory notes, bills of exchange, and transfer checks not unlike the modern bank check, were used in Assyria, Phoenicia, and Egypt long before they obtained fuller development in Greece and Rome. It was not until after the ascendency of Athens and Rome, however, that banking came under official regulation. In its earliest forms banking consisted primarily of money changing. Lack of uniform coinage handicapped the financing of foreign trade and money changers arose to overcome this difficulty. The danger of loss and robbery led traders to deposit their money with money changers for safekeeping and transfer. Money changers issued receipts and gave transfer orders which soon became instruments for making international trade payments. These were the forerunners of the modern bills of exchange.

Before the fall of the Roman Empire banking had attained a development which in many respects resembled that of financial institutions of the 18th century. The Bank of Venice, formed in 1157 is generally given as the first bank, but it was, in the first instance, merely a transfer office of a national debt. The origin of modern banking is more properly attributable to the money lenders of Florence, but the principal function of a modern bank—that of keeping depositors' money safe but accessible—was perhaps first undertaken on a large scale by the Bank of Amsterdam, founded in 1609.

In their competition for business, banks have adapted their services to their customers' present and prospective needs until the large modern bank is a veritable department store of financial services. Of these many services three merge into prominence and banks may be classified according to the predominance of one or the other of these. (1) Commercial banking, which has as its main function the gathering together of the short-time funds of the community and making them available for current use in business, supplying in the process a form of credit which serves as our chief medium of exchange, namely, that which is called deposit currency. (2) A second banking function deals with more permanent types of capital and includes all investment institutions such as saving banks, bond houses and investment banks, which allocate that portion of the community's income not utilized for the satisfaction of current wants to corporate and governmental units seeking investment funds. (3) Trust companies which engage in fiduciary operations not strictly of banking nature, but in the course of which it is found expedient to add banking functions so as to care for and better manage the trusts accepted. Today trust companies carry on most complete and inclusive financial operations.

Deposits represent rights to draw on the bank for money. Depositors may get such rights in any of several ways: By deposits of cash or cash items, or time items for collection and credit; by the process of loan and discount; by receiving credit as proceeds from the sale of securities or other property to the bank.

The loan and investment policy of the individual bank must inevitably be based upon the condition of its reserves since borrowers make loans at the bank because they need more funds than they already possess. The bank must be prepared to honor checks drawn against the balances established. If the recipients of these checks are depositors in other banks, reserves will be reduced when remittances are made. By increasing its outstanding loans, therefore, a bank increases its cash obligations or decreases its cash holdings. The relationship involved in the operation may be summarized as follows: the bank lends cash or a claim to cash. If the borrower prefers credit the bank's cash remains intact and loans and deposit liabilities increase *pro tanto*. If the borrower utilizes the proceeds of the loan by cashing checks the bank's liabilities are reduced by a corresponding reduction in cash. If the borrower's balances are left unused, or if transferred to another depositor's account in the same bank, the reserve ratio remains unchanged. In practice the bank borrower does withdraw part of the proceeds of the loan and yet as a rule an unused balance remains on deposit. The net result is that the individual bank can expand its credit more or less in proportion to the 'free' reserves, depending upon the customary bank balances left by borrowers and the conventional reserve found to be safe in meeting current demands for cash.

Bankers perform the important function of remitting money from one place to another, by setting off the amount of the drafts payable in one place against those payable in the other. They also often receive plate and other valuables belonging to their customers for safe custody and they frequently issue letters of credit for the transmission of money, either within the country or abroad. A letter of credit is an authority from the banker who signs it to the banker or other person named in it, and who produces the letter. He alone is entitled to draw the drafts or to receive payment, and a letter of credit is not a negotiable instrument. (See BILL OF EXCHANGE; CHECK; NEGOTIABLE INSTRUMENT.)

In a country with a large number of banking units, if financial chaos is to be avoided, some degree of coöperation and coördination must be obtained through voluntary agreements. Originating locally such coöperation spreads in broader concentric circles through the bank system until district, national and even international bank relationships have been established. The germ or nucleus of a real banking system has begun when certain coöperative institutions and practices have developed to knit independent banks together so that all act in unison to achieve a given aim or to avoid the consequences of a crisis.

In the United States beginning with the clearing house association founded in New York City in 1854, clearing houses have been established in nearly every large city. At first established to facilitate the clearing and collection of checks, these institutions took on new functions, and clearing houses formed to facilitate clearing and collection of checks between banks under panic conditions, resolved themselves into protective units where reserves are pooled and conserved and clearing house loan certificates issued for settlement of bank balances. Since the inauguration of the Federal Reserve clearing system for member and non-member banks the whole country has been knitted together into twelve clearing systems and one large district clearing system.

United States.—In early days such a thing as a banking system hardly existed and a conception of what a bank should be and what it should do was wholly unlike that now prevailing. A century ago deposits were unknown in banking operations; today they constitute the chief source of banking funds. Circulating notes were the banks' main earning instrument; today only one in four banks issues its own notes. Notes were formerly issued on the

A Modern Bank Building, New York City.

basis of doubtful security and losses were large; today there are no losses from note issue. Banking was then a common law right and it was an easy transition for any merchant to become a banker since he performed in some fashion banking functions when he made advances in cash as well as selling goods on credit, and at times even issued his own notes to meet a scarcity demand for currency.

The Colonial Period.—The early conception of banking brought over from the mother country was that of a note issuing institution. In fact the word bank as first used in this country meant the issue of paper money, and the colony of Massachusetts resorted to a number of 'banks' in the 17th and early 18th centuries to pay soldiers for their services. Other colonies followed until the British government undertook to put a stop to the trend of monetary chaos which might result from these issues, by prohibiting the emission of letters of credit except for necessary government expenses. These were called 'anti-bubble' acts. The Revolutionary War brought further experiences with depreciating bills of credit. Worthless continental currency was indeed partly responsible for the beginnings of sound banking in the United States. In 1781 Robert Morris, Superintendent of Finance under the Continental Congress, persuaded that body to charter a bank modelled somewhat after the Bank of England as it existed at that time. The Bank of North America rendered conspicuous service during the last years of the war, supplying funds to the government and aiding in correcting currency disorders. It was rechartered in Pennsylvania in 1787 and still exists today. In 1784 two more banks were established, one in Massachusetts, the other in New York. These three banks were the only ones in existence at the time of the adoption of the Constitution.

1791-1836.—In 1791, at the instance of Alexander Hamilton, Congress established the First Bank of the United States with branches in eight cities, its capital being fixed at $10,-000,000, one-fifth of which was subscribed by the government. Though not positively authorized to issue notes this function was taken for granted. These were at all times convertible into cash, were receivable for all payments to the government, and hence circulated freely and set a high standard for notes of other institutions. The bank was employed as an agent by the government in financial transactions, and deficits in public revenues were frequently met by loans from the bank. From the outset this scheme met with much opposition, particularly from Thomas Jefferson and his political adherents, and at the expiration of the twenty years for which the charter was granted, Congress refused to renew it, and the institution went out of existence. It was a most unfortunate time for the country, on the verge of a war with England, to be deprived of the services of a Federal bank. State banks sprang up on every hand to take its place. Depreciation and suspension of specie payments resulted, with only New England remaining on a sound money basis. These conditions led to a strong agitation for the reestablishment of the Federal bank.

The Second Bank of the United States received a twenty year charter in 1816. It was capitalized at $35,000,000, one-fifth of which was subscribed by the government. This bank was mismanaged at first, and its endeavors to control the issues of State banks rendered it unpopular in many sections of the country. In 1819 there was a change in the administration of the bank, and in the following decade, especially under the competent management of Nicholas Biddle, it became a powerful financial institution and performed valuable services to both government and business. Unfortunately the bank got into politics during the administration of President Jackson. The matter of charter renewal was made the chief issue of 1832. The policies of the bank irritated the President, who arbitrarily removed government deposits and placed them in 'pet' State banks. The Second Bank, thereafter, declined in importance until its charter expired in 1836. The Government's experiences with State bank depositories was most unfortunate, and finally in 1846, the Government refused to place any further dependence on them and established its own 'Independent Treasury' for the custody of public funds.

The State Banks before 1863.—Some 28 State banks were in existence at the beginning of the 19th century. In 1811, when the charter of the First United States Bank expired, the number had increased to 88, and during the period prior to the chartering of the Second United States Bank it is estimated that the number had increased to 246, with an aggregate note circulation of approximately $100,000,000.

During 1811-1816 and 1836-1863 State banks grew up and carried on their operations unhampered by control or competition of Federal banks. The history of pre-Civil War banking is largely the story of successful and unsuccessful experiments in regulating and controlling the issue of bank notes. Wild cat banking was profitable to the issuers who could circulate irredeemable notes, but noteholders suffered great loss and inconvenience in those cases where notes were at a heavy discount in terms of specie, and where high rates of exchange were charged to obtain remittances. The most successful attempts to remedy the situation were: (1) the Suffolk System, developed in Boston in 1818; (2) the Safety Fund System (1829); and (3) Free Banking System (1838), both contributions cf New York experiences; and (4) certain notable experiments such as branch banking in Indiana under the law of 1834, and the well regulated system in Louisiana after 1842.

National Banks.—Prior to the Civil War State bank notes constituted the only form of paper money in the United States. Many of these were worthless because counterfeited or because the issuing bank had failed. The evils of a decentralized, heterogeneous currency condition intensified financial difficulties when the Civil War broke out. One paramount need of the government in 1860 was, therefore, sound and uniform currency, another was the urgent need of public revenue. Taxation proved inadequate and paper money issues (greenbacks) were resorted to, but loans were necessary and government credit needed support.

The Act of 1863 was passed with the double purpose of providing a uniform currency and at the same time creating a market for Government bonds; but not many banks entered under its provisions so a revision was made in 1864, which remedied many of the features to which banks objected.

As the law stands now any number of citizens, not less than five, may organize a National bank, if they possess the necessary capital, by applying to the Comptroller of the Currency for a charter. It is not mandatory upon the Comptroller to grant such applications, and in practice charters are granted only in those cases in which a survey shows that there is a general demand for a bank and that it is well sponsored. The general supervision of the system is committed to a separate bureau established in the Treasury Department under the direction of the Comptroller of the Currency. The Comptroller appoints examiners who 'examine' all National banks. These banks are also required to report at least three times a year. The law provided for double liability of shareholders in case of failure of the bank, and provision is made for building-up surplus for additional protection to the bank's creditors. One chief cause of bank losses and failures has been unsafe and non-liquid loans and advances. Regulations in this matter limit the advances of National banks both with regard to character and amount, so as to insure a reasonably safe diversification and liquidity of assets. National bank notes may be issued to the value of United States bonds deposited with the Secretary of the Treasury. Before 1913 every bank was required to invest a part of its capital in Government bonds whether it took out circulation or not; but this provision was repealed by the Federal Reserve Act. Notes are redeemable at the issuing bank, and at all National banks, and at the Treasury of the United States, where, since the Act of 1874, there has been kept a five per cent. redemption fund contributed by the banks for this purpose. To clear the way for the new National bank notes and in order to abolish the chaotic circulation of State banks a prohibitory tax of ten per cent. was imposed in 1865 on all notes issued by State banks. The immediate result of this provision was a rapid decrease in number and importance of State banks, which were practically wiped out by 1873; the ultimate result, however, spelled a relative decline in the importance of the bank note, and the increased use of deposit currency shifted the competitive advantage of banking to State and private institutions enjoying the advantage of more liberal laws. The National Bank Act was liberalized in 1913 and finally in 1927 the McFadden-Pepper Act considerably broadened National bank powers.

Federal Reserve System.—The defects of the National Banking System were recognized almost from the start, but monetary problems, greenbacks and free silver, overshadowed questions of banking policy. Nothing resulted from the experiences of the crises of 1873 and 1884, but the distressing need of an emergency currency during the panic of 1893 started an agitation which resulted twenty years later in the adoption of the revolutionary changes embodied in the Federal Reserve Act. Progress was slow until the collapse in the panic of 1907. In the following year Congress passed the Aldrich-Vreeland Act, which provided for temporary emergency currency until permanent measures could be devised; and also for a National Monetary Commission, which was to study the whole subject of banking reform and propose suitable legislation. The Commission's official programme of currency reform, the Aldrich Plan, failed of passage in a Democratic Congress, but the ground was prepared for the drafting and adoption of an act, full of compromises, but incorporating the thought of a generation of students who had grappled with the problem of currency and banking reform.

Its purposes may be summarized as follows: (1) To furnish an elastic currency; (2) To centralize and mobilize reserves and to afford means of rediscounting commercial paper; (3) To obtain cheaper and more effective clearance and collection of checks and a more efficient transfer system; (4) To facilitate foreign trade financing; (5) To afford a satisfactory depository and fiscal agent for the government.

Administrative Organization and Structure.—To carry out the purposes of the reform the organization of the Federal Reserve was effected in the following manner: the country was divided into twelve districts (not less than eight nor more than twelve) and a Federal Reserve bank was established in each. These banks were superimposed upon an undisturbed structure of National and State banks, and an attempt was made to obtain institutions of approximately equal strength by adjusting the size of geographical areas to their respective jurisdictions. Despite the tradition against branch banking, these were allowed, and Federal Reserve banks have at the present time 24 branches and two agencies, most of these being located in large districts where access to the Reserve bank is difficult.

In order to give cohesion there was established in Washington a centralized mechanism in the form of a *Federal Reserve Board*, consisting of eight members, the Secretary of the Treasury and the Comptroller of the Currency *ex-officio*, and six others appointed by the President. They rotate in office and have a ten-year term of tenure. They have important coordinating, regulating, and supervisory powers over the Reserve banks, and exert a large measure of control over their policies.

Federal Reserve Banks are incorporated under Federal charter; each bank must have a capital of at least four million dollars subscribed by member banks, one-half of a subscribed capital must be paid up; it is thus a 'bankers' bank' with regard to ownership. This stock carries a cumulative dividend of six per cent. per annum; net profits in excess of this amount go to build up surplus until it is equal to the subscribed capital; thereafter one-tenth goes to surplus while the remaining ninety per cent. is paid to the Government as a franchise tax.

With regard to management each Reserve bank is controlled by a board of nine directors.

The membership of the system is composed of all National banks, which were required to become members or relinquish their Federal charters, and all State banks and trust companies satisfying certain eligibility conditions regarding capitalization and character of their business.

The Functions of Reserve Banks.—The Reserve banks, like ordinary commercial banks, receive deposits, extend credit, furnish a medium of exchange, but unlike ordinary commercial banks their operations are not dominated by considerations of profits but are governed by principles which are peculiar to central bank practice, namely, they must envisage the whole credit and economic situation of the country to develop their policies, to promote the general welfare of society as a whole. Their chief functions are, therefore, to serve member banks and the government, with which they deal directly, and non-member banks and business, with which they come into contact through clearings and collections and open market operations, so as to best promote the general interests of commerce and business. These functions may be enumerated as follows: (1) to hold the ultimate reserves of the banking system; (2) to extend credit to member banks; (3) to issue notes and to furnish currency; (4) to act as fiscal agent for the government; (5) to operate a clearings and collections system; (6) to facilitate foreign trade financing; (7) to control the volume of credit of the banking system.

Reserves.—Under the old banking system reserves were scattered among thousands of individual banks and laws governing reserves were so inflexible that reserves could not be used in times of emergency. The Reserve system made two great changes in these requirements; (a) it concentrated the reserves into twelve great reservoirs intimately connected in order to make them mobile and accessible; (b) it provided a plan of credit expansion based upon these reserves.

Prior to the establishment of the Federal Reserve System four kinds of paper money were in general use, all of which are still in circulation: first, gold certificates covered by gold and susceptible of increase or decrease only as gold in the United States Treasury is increased or decreased; second, silver certificates secured dollar for dollar by silver, the amount of which is limited by law; third, United States notes or greenbacks, still limited by statute to $346,000,000; and fourth, National bank notes, limited by the amount of the United States bonds carrying the circulating privilege. None of these forms of currency fluctuate in any relation to usual or abnormal changes in business demands.

The presence of the Reserve banks relieves the Government Treasury of much of the direct responsibility which it formerly assumed in the money market. The Reserve banks, in constant touch with the money market, and with offices in all parts of the country, are able to perform the fiscal operations required by government business with expedition and effect. Collections, remittances and transfers are made in huge amounts, practically without charge. During the war and after the Reserve banks proved invaluable in aiding the flotation of bonds, and by furnishing machinery for securing credit; expansion made war financing possible.

Credits and Collections.—Because of the absence of any other organization in the United States capable of operating a nation wide clearings and collection system the Federal Reserve was compelled to establish an elaborate mechanism which has united the whole country into a single money market. What the local clearing house did for local settlements the reserve clearing system has done for out of town settlements. All member banks are compelled to remit checks at par, that is, they may not charge one another, or the Federal Reserve bank, for cashing their own checks. Non-member banks are invited to become members of the 'par list,' assuming the obligation of paying their checks without exchange charges, and in return benefiting by the operation of the system. Clearings and collections within the single district involve a simple process of settling transactions by debit and credit entries affecting members' accounts on the books of the Federal Reserve bank.

Recent Trends.—In addition to National banks, State-chartered banks, and Federal Reserve banks, are banks for extending agricultural credits, operating under the jurisdiction of the Farm Credit Administration; also Federal Home Loan Banks, organized under the Federal Housing Loan Act of July 22, 1932, for the purpose of making advances upon the security of home mortgages.

National banks organized after June 16, 1933, are required to have capital of not less than $50,000. Since then they have been permitted to have branches in the States in which they are located. After July 22, 1932 they were permitted to issue circulating notes secured by United States bonds, bearing interest at a rate not exceeding 3 3-8 per cent.

Early in March, 1933, the time of the crisis, all the banks in the country were closed by the Federal government; but they were later opened under official license.

During the past ten years a business revolution has been taking place, and with it, a trend away from the multiplicity of independent banking units. Big business has been accompanied by big banking. This movement has been characteristic in most commercial countries. In Canada ten banks and their branches do all the commercial banking in the country. In England the Big Five with their branches, control about four-fifths of the total banking resources, and the German Big Four approximately seven-tenths. Mergers and consolidations have been the order of the day, especially in the last two years, but even now the five largest banks in the United States represent less than ten per cent. of the total banking resources in the country.

Branch banking is a system of banking in which a large bank increases and extends its operations through a number of smaller banks the latter forming a definite part of the organization. There are numerous advantages of such a system. The size of such a banking organization permits large reserves; facilities for handling huge business projects; and the employment of expert officials. The large reserves and the variety of assets of the big institution tend to safeguard against economic fluctuations, and the incompetence of the small, poorly equipped bank.

On the other hand there is the danger of one or a few large banks buying up all smaller concerns thus establishing a monopoly. In the hands of an efficient government such a centralized banking system might be desirable. Canada furnishes an example of centralized banking; and in England the practice has been carried to greater extremes than in any other country.

Banks for International Settlements. Under the Dawes Plan reparation payments were to go through the Reichsbank, where they were deposited to the account of the Agent General. Disposition of this account was made by the Transfer Committee of Reparations Commission. In 1929 the Young Plan was devised to more satisfactorily solve the problems of debts and reparations, and to free Germany from political control. The Bank for International Settlements or World Bank, was therefore established. This bank became the trustee of the creditor accounts in dealing with the reparations annuities. The Bank was also designed 'to promote the coöperation of central banks, and to provide additional facilities for international financial operations'; in effect to become an international clearing house, thus eliminating the necessity of shipping gold in the settlement of international transactions.

The bank of International Settlement, located at Basle, Switzerland, commenced business in May, 1930, with capital equivalent to one hundred million dollars, one-fourth paid in; shares were offered for public subscription in seven countries.

The control of the bank is vested in the board of directors consisting of fourteen to sixteen members, plus no more than nine additional elected members.

The drastic banking reform act of June 16, 1933, aimed to correct conditions which led to the March crisis, prohibited interlocking directorates between commercial and private banks, prohibited private banks from doing both an investment and deposit business (such as J. P. Morgan & Co. had carried on), limited the borrowing of any executive officer from his own bank, and limited loans to 10 percent of capital and surplus.

This law also created the Federal Deposit Insurance Corp. and provided for maximum deposit insurance of $5,000. No bank was permitted to join the Federal Reserve system unless it subscribed to the corporation's stock. Early in 1925 the FDIC announced that more than 98 percent of all depositors in the 14,208 insured banks of the country were protected by the insurance system which, it was conceded, had done much to restore the public's confidence in the banks.

The Banking Act of 1935 enlarged the authority of the Federal Reserve Board over the nation's credit policies. The continued decrease in bank earnings during the depression became strikingly noticeable in 1939 with marked reductions by banks in rates of interest allowed on deposits. Gold imports by the United States during 1939-40 were far in excess of such imports for any like period in the past. In January 1941 the total value of gold reserves of all the world's countries was about 29 billions of dollars, of which about 75 per cent was in the United States. Rates of interest on deposits continued low through 1952.

Bibliography.—General. Consult W. F. Mitchell's *The Uses of Bank Funds* (1925); G. W. Dowrie's *American Monetary Banking Policies* (1930); C. Hazelwood's *The Bank and Its Directors* (1930); F. C. James' *Money, Credit, and Banking* (1930).

United States (See also references above) Dewey and Chaddock's *State Banking Before the Civil War;* O. M. W. Sprague's *History of Crises Under the National Banking System;* P. M. Warburg's *Federal Reserve System; Its Origin and Growth* (1930).

England.—L. A. Harr's *Branch Banking in England* (1929); H. W. Greengrass' *The Discount Market in London* (1930).

France.—Andre Leisse's *Evolution of Credit and Banks in France from the Founding of the Bank of France to the Present Time* (1909); H. E. Fisk's *French Public Finance* (1910);

E. Dulles' *The French Franc 1914-1928* (1929).

Germany.—K. Bergmann's *History of Reparations* (1927); H. Schacht's *Stabilization of the Mark* (1927).

Canada.—R. M. Breckinridge's *The History of Banking in Canada;* J. F. Johnson's *The Canadian Banking System.*

Banking—Gold Standard. Following the banking crisis of March, 1933, the United States suspended gold payments. A joint resolution of Congress, adopted June 5, 1933, voided payments in gold. It was upheld by the Supreme Court in the celebrated gold clause case (1935) by a 5 to 4 vote.

President Roosevelt, after moving to take into the Treasury all gold held by private citizens and corporations, signed the Gold Reserve Act of January 30, 1934, which sequestered the Reserve Banks' gold. The effect of this was to put the country on what was called an international gold bullion standard. In popular terminology, the United States had "gone off gold."

This same legislation authorized the President to reduce the gold content of the dollar. He did so by proclamation on January 31, 1934. His order reduced the dollar's gold weight from 25.8 grains to 15 5-21 grains, making its value approximately 59 cents when compared with the $1 par fixed by the 1900 valuation act.

The President also announced that the government would pay $35 an ounce for gold mined or delivered to the United States. The old price had been $20.67.

The gold profit to the Treasury from dollar devaluation enabled the President to set up a $2,000,000,000 stabilization fund, which the Secretary of the Treasury immediately proceeded to use so as to keep the dollar at or near 59.06 cents on international exchange.

In departing from an unqualified gold standard basis, the U. S. took the course which England had adopted in 1931. By midyear 1935 only France, Switzerland and the Netherlands were left in Europe's so-called gold bloc, Belgium having been forced off gold earlier in the year.

In 1936, Netherlands suspended convertibility of its notes, Switzerland did likewise and devalued its franc, and France devalued its franc. By 1937 the old gold standard as formerly known had ceased to exist in any of the principal countries of the world. Managed currencies continued to be the method in general use.

Bank Note, a promissory note by an authorized bank of issue payable on demand. See PAPER MONEY.

Bank of North America, the first banking institution of a national character organized in the United States, was incorporated by the Continental Congress in 1781, and $250,000 of its $320,000 capital stock was subscribed by Congress.

Bank Rate, a term used to denote the rate of discount charged in the chief financial centers by the state bank, or the leading bank, as opposed to the rate in the open market.

Bankruptcy, a state of insolvency ascertained and declared in appropriate judicial proceedings. The principle of the state of bankruptcy may be stated as follows: One who is unable to pay his debts in full may be discharged therefrom upon giving up all his property for ratable distribution among his creditors.

Under the present bankruptcy acts in the United States, proceedings may be begun either by the debtor himself (voluntary), or by the creditors (involuntary). In either event, the case is begun by filing a petition.

In *voluntary* bankruptcy the debtor himself petitions that he be adjudicated a bankrupt; in the other case, *involuntary* proceeding, creditors file a petition, asking that their debtor be adjudicated a bankrupt.

In involuntary proceedings, creditors must allege grounds for asking the Court to declare the debtor bankrupt.

The debtor against whom a petition has been filed may oppose it; other creditors also may oppose it. Upon hearing, the debtor is either adjudicated or the petition dismissed.

The bankrupt must file a schedule of all of his assets and liabilities which must be sworn to. He must in the schedule claim any exemptions to which he believes himself entitled under the State Law. The Trustee takes title of all assets of bankrupt, and the latter must make full disclosure of all his acts and conduct.

There are criminal provisions in the law, which apply under certain conditions, and there are provisions applying to farmers, also provisions applying to wage earners. The law provides for certain reorganization phases, in cases of corporations, to come before the Securities and Exchange Commission.

The first national bankruptcy law of 1800 followed closely the contemporary English statutes. From 1878 to 1898 there was no national bankruptcy act.

The most recent laws relating to bankruptcy include the Municipal Debt Adjustment Act, approved August 16, 1937; the Frazier-Lemke Farm Mortgage Act, approved August 29, 1935 (held constitutional by the U. S. Supreme Court March 29, 1937; the Railroad Reorganization Act of March 3, 1933, amended by act known as Section 77, approved August 27, 1935; and the Chandler Bankruptcy Act, approved June 22, 1938, effective as of September 22, 1938.

All proceedings in bankruptcy in the United States come under the Federal law and are administered by Federal Courts. See DEBT; INSOLVENCY.

Banks, in navigation, are shelving elevations in the sea or the bed of a river, rising to or near the surface, composed of sand, mud, or gravel. When tolerably smooth at the top, they constitute shallows, shoals and flats; but when rocky, they become reefs.

Banks, Nathaniel Prentiss (1816-94), American soldier, lawyer and public official, born at Waltham, Mass. He was speaker of the lower State legislative house; chairman of the State constitutional convention, 1853; Member of Congress, becoming Speaker, 1855-7; and governor of Massachusetts, 1858-61. During the Civil War he entered the Federal army and became Major General of volunteers; served in the Shenandoah Valley, where his inferior force was defeated at Cedar Mountain by Stonewall Jackson; later in command at New Orleans; captured Port Hudson; and commanded the unsuccessful Red River expedition. After the war he was again a Member of Congress, and was U. S. marshal for Massachusetts.

Banksia, a genus of the Australian order Proteaceae, named in honor of Sir Joseph Banks. They are abundant in all parts of Australia, forming, indeed, a characteristic feature of its vegetation, and are called honeysuckle trees.

Banksian Cockatoo, an Australian cockatoo. The plumage is black or brown, flecked with red or orange.

Banks Islands, group, South Pacific Ocean.

Banks Land, an island in the Arctic Ocean, part of the Dominion of Canada. It was discovered by Parry in 1819, explored by McClure in 1850, and named by him Baring Island.

Banks Peninsula, on the eastern coast of South Island, New Zealand. It is a high table land with extinct volcanoes; 50 m. long and 25 m. wide.

Bankura, capital of Bankura district, Bengal, India, on the River Dhalkisor. The district has an area of 2,621 sq. m. and a population of 1,200,000, over 90 per cent. of whom are Hindus.

Banner, a term sometimes loosely used to signify any military ensign or standard, but in a more strict sense denoting a square flag charged with the coat of arms of the owner. See FLAG.

Bannock (Gaelic *bannach*, a cake), a cake of home-made bread, common in Scotland and the north of England.

Bannockburn, an historic village of 2,500 inhabitants, 3 m. s.e. of Stirling, on the Bannock Burn, a small affluent of the Forth, Scotland. In the famous Battle of Bannockburn, fought on June 24, 1314, Robert Bruce, gained a signal victory over Edward II., and secured his throne and the independence of Scotland. See SCOTLAND; BRUCE.

Banns (German *bann,* order or edict) is a word signifying the announcement of an intended marriage made in the presence of a congregation assembled for divine worship. The system of publishing banns is found in the earliest ages of the Christian Church, and was promulgated in England by the Council of London in 1200 A.D. See MARRIAGE.

Banshee, a female fairy common to Celtic myth, but more particularly to the folklore of Ireland and Western Scotland. Her mournful wail is looked upon as a herald of death.

Bantam Fowl, a variety of domestic fowl remarkable for its small size. See POULTRY.

Bantayan, pueblo, Philippine Islands, on the southwest coast of Bantayan Island, in the province of Cebu. There is a leper settlement on a small island off the coast; p. 14,812.

Banting, Frederick Grant (1891-1941), Canadian physician, was born in Alliston, Ontario, Canada. He was the discoverer, with C. H. Best, of Insulin (see DIABETES). For this Dr. Banting has been the recipient of several medals and prizes, notable among which is the Nobel prize in Medicine awarded him (jointly with Prof. J. J. R. Macleod), in 1923.

Banting System, a method of treating corpulency by a restricted diet, proposed by Harvey, but first effectively practised by William Banting (1797-1878) of Kensington.

Bantock, Granville (1868-1946), English musician, was born in London. He was editor and proprietor of *The New Quarterly Musical Review* (1893-6), and later, became director of the Birmingham and Midland Institute School of Music and professor of music in Birmingham University. Among his published compositions are *Hebridean Symphony* (1920); *The Song of Songs* (1922); *The Seal-Woman* (opera, 1924).

Bantu, a group of negro tribes occupying Central and South Africa, possessing a common language, with numerous dialectic variations.

Banyan Tree (*Ficus benghalensis*), Indian tree, so called because it is frequently used as a market-place by the Banians or Indian merchants. It is a species of fig tree, bearing large heart-shaped leaves and small red fruit.

Baobab, also called **Monkey Bread** and **Sour Gourd** (*Adansonia digitata*), a tree of the order Malvaceae, found in most parts of tropical Africa, and in the East Indies. It is one of the largest and oldest trees in the world, with a trunk often more than 20 ft. in diameter. The bark is fibrous, and is stripped off for making ropes and clothes.

Baptanodon, a late ichthyosaurian, the only type of the aquatic ichthyopterygian reptiles found in America. It was fish-like in appearance, about 10 ft. long, and had short, broad paddles.

Baptism, a rite of the Christian church, performed either by sprinkling the candidate with water, pouring water upon him (affusion), or immersing him in water. The immediate origin of Christian baptism would appear to be what is called 'the baptism of John.'

The distinctively Christian rite is not only a symbol of a moral change in the recipient, but is further the outward expression of a *new life* to the individual submitting to it, and of his union with Christ, which privileges were conferred by the gift of the Holy Spirit. The converts were to be baptized 'into' the name of the Trinity.

The question of the eligibility of the infants of Christian parents for baptism hardly seems to have arisen in New Testament times, the converts being necessarily of sufficient age to make profession of their faith. The early church seems to have sanctioned the practice, which soon became general. The opponents of infant baptism, however, point out that the practice is nowhere commanded or even countenanced in Scripture.

There is little doubt that the original practice was immersion but it is equally undeniable that sprinkling was sometimes substituted at a very early period.

Can baptism be properly administered by the clergy only? or is it equally valid when performed (in certain cases) by the laity? It has generally been held that baptism by duly qualified ministers is desirable; but in cases of imminent death, when no minister was at hand, the administration of the rite by laymen was deemed perfectly valid.

Baptistery, or **Baptistry,** the name given sometimes to a separate building, sometimes to the portion of the church in which the ceremony of baptism is performed. Originally Christian baptism was performed at the riverside, or at founts where springs of water flowed. The first baptisteries were not, as now, within the church, but without, and connected with it only by a passage or cloister. Afterward they formed a constructional part of the church, toward the west end.

The celebrated baptistery of Florence is an octagonal structure, measuring about 100 ft. in diameter. It stands detached from, but in the immediate vicinity of the west end of the cathedral. The magnificent bronze doors, with their beautiful bas-reliefs, are remarkable features of this famous baptistery. The most celebrated of the three doors was executed by Lorenzo Ghiberti, the earliest being the work of Andrea of Pisa. Next in importance, and of even greater size, is the baptistery of Pisa. It is circular in form, the diameter measuring 116 ft. The largest baptistery ever erected is supposed to have been that of St. Sophia, at Constantinople.

Baptists, a denomination of Christians, so named because of their distinctive views regarding the ordinance of baptism, which they administer by immersion to believers only.

The Baptists hold the inspiration and supreme authority of the Holy Scriptures as a revelation from God; the equal deity of the Son and the Holy Spirit in the unity of the Trinity; the direct relationship of the individual soul to God; faith as a prerequisite for entrance into the Kingdom of God; the supreme headship of Jesus Christ in that kingdom; and the freedom and responsibility of the individual Christian; but they have among them many shades of belief. They maintain the necessity of regeneration and holiness of life as essential to true religion, and that 'without holiness no man shall see the Lord.' They have ever stood for complete liberty of conscience, and for absolute separation of church and state. They acknowledge but two ordinances, Baptism and the Lord's Supper.

Looking upon the church as a completely spiritual institution, they maintain that the membership, and therefore the ordinance of baptism, ought to be confined to believers only—thus excluding the baptism of infants. They hold that the only correct mode of administering the ordinance is by immersion.

The Baptists are divided among themselves regarding communion—one portion receiving conscientious members of other sects at the Lord's table; the other refusing this privilege to any but baptized believers. The former are called 'open' communionists; the latter, 'strict' communionists. Both agree in regarding the Supper as commemorative only, and in no sense sacrificial.

The form of church government of the Baptists is congregational. They maintain that the only officers of a New Testament church are pastors and deacons; that each church is a spiritual democracy, possessed of the power of self-government under its exalted head, Jesus Christ; that discipline is to be exercised in the presence and with the consent of the members of the church.

Famous Italian Baptisteries.
1, Pisa: Interior; 2, Exterior. 3, Asti: S. Pietro. 4, Florence.

The doctrine of congregational independence is held to render unnecessary any general creed or confession; but it is assumed that all ministers and members of Baptist churches accept the principle of liberty of conscience and of the divine authority of Scripture.

Baptist associations and conventions exist, to which most of the congregations belong; but these unions have no legislative or judicial functions, and exercise no control over the individual churches.

According to the *American Baptist Year-Book*, there are 14 Baptist bodies in the United States. There were a total of 14,035,590 Baptists in the U. S. in 1945. The Northern Convention included 7,603 churches with 1,555,000 members; the Southern Convention had 24,840 churches and 5,667,600 members; and the National (colored) Convention had 24,000 churches and 3,796,600 members. Combined totals for the three conventions showed 56,443 churches. The Baptist Missionary Society has 425 missions in India, China, Jamaica, Africa, and Ceylon. In Canada the Baptists controlled 1,260 churches, 883 ordained ministers, 141,384 church members, and church property valued at $5,882,200. In Mexico there were 95 churches, 50 ordained ministers, 6,107 church members and 3,519 Sunday scholars.

The first Baptist church in America was founded in Providence, R. I., in 1638, by Roger Williams (q.v.), who had been banished from the colony of Massachusetts for advocating 'unsettling and dangerous' views. About 1644 a second church was established in Newport; and in 1655 the First Baptist Church of Boston was organized. In 1683 or 1684 Baptist refugees from New England founded the first church in the South, near Charleston, S. C.; and by 1740 there were Baptist churches in all the colonies. From the period of the Great Awakening (1743) the Baptist church in America experienced a rapid growth.

Bibliography.—Consult Evans' *Early English Baptists;* Newman's *History of the Baptist Churches in the United States;* Vedder's *Short History of the Baptists* (rev. ed. 1907); Carlile's *Story of the English Baptists* (1905); Glothlin's *Baptist Confessions of Faith* (1911); Carroll's *The Religious Forces of the United States* (1912); Christian's *A History of the Baptists* (1922); *The American Baptist Year Book* (annual); *The Baptist Handbook* (English annual).

Bar, Aramaic for 'son'; a common constituent of Jewish names—Bar-jesus, Bartimaeus, Bartholomew.

Bar, in heraldry, one of the *honorable ordinaries*. It differs from the fess only in its size (*i.e.*,height), which is but one-fifth of the field, and in the fact that it may be borne in any part of the shield. *Bar sinister,* the popular, but erroneous, term for the 'baton sinister,' the mark of illegitimacy. See HERALDRY.

Bar, in music, an upright line drawn across the stave to regulate the accent and divide the music into equal portions as determined by the time signature. Each portion is termed a *measure,* but is sometimes also called a bar. A *double bar,* consisting of two lines, denotes the end of a complete section or movement, or the introduction of a change of time or key.

Bar (Heraldry)

Bar, in hydrography, is a bank of sand, silt, etc., opposite the mouth of a river, which obstructs or *bars* the entrance of vessels. See SAND BANKS; DELTA; DREDGING.

Bar, in law, has several meanings. Thus, it is the term used to signify an enclosure or fixed place in a court of justice where lawyers may plead. Again, the dock, or enclosed space where persons accused of felonies and other offences stand or sit during their trial, is called the bar; hence the expression, 'prisoner at the bar.' In particular, bar is a collective term for all those members of the legal profession who have the right to appear in court on behalf of suitors. See BAR ASSOCIATIONS; LAWYER; BARRISTER; ADVOCATE.

Barabbas ('son of the father,' 'teacher'), a criminal, whose release was demanded from Pilate in preference to that of Jesus.

Bar Associations, voluntary organizations of lawyers in the United States, formed to maintain the dignity and influence of the legal profession—*i.e.*, maintaining the honor and raising the standards of the bar, and securing the elevation of fit members. Admission to the bar is in the United States vested in the legislatures of the several States or in the courts. The AMERICAN BAR ASSOCIATION, organized in 1878, is composed of the State bar associations, and includes most of the prominent lawyers of the country.

Barataria, (from Spanish *barato,* part of a gamester's winnings given 'for luck' to bystanders), the name of the island assigned in *Don Quixote* to Sancho Panza; also the name of the retreat in the delta of the Mississippi of the notorious Jean Lafitte and the imaginary kingdom in Gilbert and Sullivan's *Gondoliers.*

Barb, the tip of an arrow or a fish hook, with difficulty extracted from a wound.

Barb, a distinct variety of the Arabian

horse, developed among the Moors of Barbary.

Barbados, or **Barbadoes**, the most easterly island of the West Indies. The climate is almost ideal, but hurricanes have caused great loss of life and property. Barbados was first colonized in 1625 by the English, who have held uninterrupted possession; p. 198,023. Consult Schomburgk's *History of Barbados;* Stark's *History and Guide to Barbados and the Caribbee Islands; Barbados Blue Book* (annual). See WEST INDIES.

Barbados Cherry, the fruit of two small trees of the order *Malpighiaceæ*, natives of the West Indies.

Barbara, Saint, a saint of the Roman Catholic Church who suffered martyrdom about 235 A.D. She is the patron saint of artillerists; her feast is on December 4.

Barbarians (Gr. *barbaros*), a term applied among the ancient Greeks to all foreigners. An important period in European history was that of the barbarian invasions (395-527 A.D.). The invasion of Greece by the Visigoths under Alaric (396 A.D.) led to the dismemberment of the western half of the empire, and about the same time barbarian hordes entered Spain. They were a mixed band of Vandals, Suevians, and Alans. The Vandals were two German tribes; the Suevians were Teutons, and the Alans a Caucasian race. They were scarcely settled when, in 412 A.D., the Visigoths swooped down on them. In 429 A.D. the Vandals crossed to Africa. The Emperor Honorius, for the services of the Visigoths in Spain, rewarded them with two large territories in Gaul.

The next of the barbarian invasions was that of the Franks, who took possession of the greater part of Visigothic Gaul. The Huns—Asiatic nomads—are the next to figure as invaders, under Attila. Defeated by the confederated German tribes, the power of the Huns was destroyed. The Alemanni settled in the northern part of Rhaetia, and they had as neighbors the Thuringians.

Italy also suffered from the invasions of barbarians, which continued till the Ostrogothic kingdom was formed (489) under Theodoric, whose rule extended from Dalmatia to the Atlantic. The Eastern empire held on for many centuries afterward, notwithstanding continual invasions of barbarians, such as the Saracens.

Barbarossa. See **Frederick I.**

Barbarossa ('Red-beard'), **Horuk** (*c.* 1473-1518) and **Khair ed-Din**, two celebrated Turkish corsairs of the 16th century. Horuk in 1515 made himself master of Algiers. He was defeated and slain by the Spanish general Gomarez near Oran in 1518. The war was continued by his brother Khair ed-Din. During the next ten years, until his death in 1546, he was the terror of the Mediterranean.

Barbaroux, Charles Jean Marie (1767-94), Girondist orator and revolutionist. He led the Marseilles battalion on Aug. 10, 1792, and was a Girondist deputy to the Convention. He denounced Marat and Robespierre, he was proscribed as a royalist, and was forced to flee from Paris. But he was captured and guillotined at Bordeaux (June 25, 1794).

Barbary Ape, or **Magot** (*Macacus inuus*), a macaque, remarkable in that it is the only tailless macaque, and that it is found on the Rock of Gibraltar, and the opposite shore of Africa, while its allies are confined to Asia.

The Barbary Ape
(The only native European monkey.)

Barbary Pirates. See **Barbary States.**

Barbary States, an extensive region of North Africa, stretching from Egypt to the Atlantic, and from the Mediterranean to beyond the Great Atlas, and comprising the countries of Morocco, Algeria, Tunis, Tripoli and Barka. It was variously known to the ancients as Mauritania, Numidia, and Africa Propria; it reached its zenith under the Carthaginians; but during the 7th century it passed under the sway of the Arabs. Warfare between the Christian powers and the Barbary States was chronic from the beginning of the 15th to the beginning of the 19th century, the Barbary States seizing trading vessels, and even smaller war-vessels. Gradually a practice obtained of paying tribute for immunity to these states. During the War of 1812 with Great Britain the Barbary States, and particularly Algiers, took advantage of the preoccupation of the United States to commit depredations; in 1815 the United States declared war against Algiers. Decatur forced the dey of Algiers to agree in the same year to a treaty of peace relinquishing all tribute money. In spite of the fact that the European powers were unable in the Congress of Vienna (1815) to agree upon concerted action against the Barbary States, the individual powers soon followed the example of the United States, and piracy was finally suppressed. See TRIPOLITANIA, TUNISIA, ALGERIA, CYRENAICA, and MOROCCO.

Barbecue, an American outdoor feast which originated in the Southern States. The main food is meat roasted or broiled on wooden racks laid over trenches made for the purpose.

Barbel, a general name applied to the numerous species of a genus (*Barbus*) of Cyprinoid fishes closely related to the carp.

Barber (Lat. *barba*, 'a beard'), one who shaves and trims the beard and cuts the hair. The trade of barber is one of great antiquity. At one time the barber added to his duties as hair-dresser that of surgeon, especially in simple cases such as blood-letting. The sign of the barber (a pole with spiral bands of red, and a pendent brass basin with a semi-circular opening in its rim) symbolizes the old function of the barber—blood-letting.

Barberini, an Italian family of the 17th century, of Tuscan origin, whose greatness dates from the elevation of Maffeo Barberini (1568-1644) to the papal chair as Urban VIII. in 1623 (see URBAN). The valuable library collected by Francesco Barberini was sold to Pope Leo XIII. in 1902.

Barberry, shrubs of the genus Berberis, natural order Berberidaceæ. They are hardy shrubs, native to both temperate zones, cultivated chiefly for their handsome foliage. *B. vulgaris,* the Common or European Barberry, is a thorny shrub naturalized in North America, which in early summer bears yellow, many-flowered, pendulous racemes. The scarlet fruits afford a brilliant display in autumn.

Barber's Itch, or **Ringworm of the Beard.** See **Ringworm.**

Barbette, a low, fixed armored breastwork surrounding and protecting the turntable on which the heavier naval guns are mounted as well as certain parts of the machinery used to operate these guns.

Barbican, a word introduced during the Crusades to describe an outwork to protect the entrance to a castle or fortified town.

Barbier, Paul Jules (1825-1901), French dramatic writer, celebrated chiefly for his librettos for operas.

Barbison, or **Barbizon,** village, France, near Fontainebleau. Its fame is due to the Barbison School (1840-75), an illustrious group of French artists—Corot, Millet, Diaz, Rousseau, Troyon, Daubigny—who lived and worked there. Characterized by a reaction against false romanticism, the work of Millet and Rousseau especially was the result of a return to nature.

Common Barberry.—Inflorescence, single flower, pistil and stamen, and fruit.

Barbour, John (?1316-95), one of the earliest Scotch poets. His fame rests on his heroic poem *The Bruce,* completed in 1375-6, detailing the fortunes and adventures of Robert Bruce. Consult Irving's *History of Scottish Poetry.*

Barbusse, Henri (1874-1935), French author, was born in Asnieres. He wrote a scathing indictment of war, entitled *Le Feu,* which went through more than two hundred editions and was translated into many languages.

Barcarolle (Ital. *barcaruolo,* 'a boatman'), a name given to songs, which originated with the gondoliers of Venice.

Barcellona, city, Sicily, in the province of Messina; p. 26,172.

Barcelona, province in the northeastern part of Spain, in the center of Catalonia, with an area of 2,968 sq. m. The surface is mountainous. The coast lands are fertile, and agriculture is well developed. The mountains are rich in iron, lead, and salt; p. 1,349,282.

Barcelona, city and seaport, Spain, capital of the province of Barcelona, on the Mediterranean Sea. It is the chief industrial and commercial city of Spain, and the second in size in the kingdom. The harbor is wide and deep. In mediaeval times Barcelona was an important factor in Mediterranean commerce. Here the famous sea-laws, known as the 'Consulate of the Sea,' were in all probability promulgated in 1279. It is in connection with this port, too, that we find the first mention of marine insurance; p. 738,498.

Barcelona was founded by the Phoenicians, raised to the rank of a Roman colony by Augustus, and during the second century became a place of considerable importance. It grew and flourished under the Visigoths. After 874 it was the seat of the Counts of Barcelona and rivalled Genoa and Venice as a trading port, but in the 15th century its prestige began to decline. In more recent times Barcelona has been the center of repeated separatist, and republican movements; suffered much from airplane bombing in civil war 1936-39.

Barcelona, city, Venezuela, capital of the state of Anzoategui, is situated in the northern part, near the coast; p. 10,833.

Barcelona Nuts, a variety of hazel nut or filbert, sometimes grown in the United States, but usually kiln-dried and imported from Barcelona, Spain.

Bard, one of an ancient Celtic order, whose province it was to celebrate in verse, song, and play the deeds of the heroes. The bards were especially active in recasting and adding to the Arthurian cycle. In Ireland bards were divided into three classes—those who sang of war and religion, those who dealt with genealogy and family history, and those who chanted the laws. In modern usage the term bard signifies a poet, as the 'bard' of Avon (Shakespeare), the Ayrshire 'bard' (Burns).

Barebone's Parliament (July 4 to Dec. 12, 1653), an assembly summoned by Cromwell after the 'Rump' had been expelled, so called in derision after one of its prominent members, Praise-God Barbon or Barebone, a leather-seller of Fleet Street. Consult S. R. Gardiner's *History of the Commonwealth and Protectorate*.

Barege, a gauze-like fabric made of silk and worsted, or of cotton and worsted, and used for women's dresses.

Bareges, summer health resort, France, in the department of Hautes-Pyrenees. Its hot sulphur springs are said to be efficacious in the treatment of skin diseases and wounds.

Barents, island in the Spitzbergen group, between Edge Island and West Spitzbergen. It is named after Willem Barents, the Dutch navigator.

Barents, Willem (?-1597), Dutch explorer. In 1594 he sailed from Holland in search of a northeast passage to China and explored the coast of Novaya Zemlya. He made a voyage in 1596, during which he discovered the island of Spitzbergen. He then sailed eastwards to Novaya Zemlya, but encountered such heavy ice that he and his companions were forced to winter in Ice Haven on the east coast, where they suffered extreme hardship. The following summer the survivors started for the mainland but during the voyage Barents and four of his companions died.

Barents Sea, a division of the Arctic Ocean between Spitzbergen and Novaya Zemlya.

Baretti, Giuseppe (1719-89), Italian poet and critic, was born in Turin. To Englishmen he is best known as the author of a *Dictionary of the English and Italian Languages* (1760; new ed. 1873), long a standard work of reference.

Barfleur, (anc. *Barofluctum*), seaside resort, France, in the department of La Manche, on the northern coast. Here Edward the Confessor embarked in 1042 for England, and the *White Ship* left the port in 1120 on its disastrous voyage.

Barge, flat-bottomed boat for carrying freight on rivers and canals, or for loading and unloading ships (lighters).

Bari, or **Bari delle Puglie,** province of Southern Italy, on the Adriatic seacoast, forming a part of the Apulian plain; p. 952,511.

Bari (anc. *Barium*), seaport, Italy, capital of the province of Bari, on the Adriatic. Features of interest are the cathedral of San Sabino, with paintings by Tintoretto and Veronese; the church of San Nicola, and the Apulian Historical Museum; p. 120,807.

Bari, district, Uganda, Africa, in the northwestern part, between the Nile and the Tu.

Bari, a negro tribe living on the White Nile, near Gondokoro.

Barie, a unit of pressure equal to 75 centimeters of mercury, or to 'one atmosphere,' and corresponding to the pressure of one dyne to the square centimeter.

Barilla, the ash, containing about 20 per cent. of sodium carbonate, of certain plants that grow near the sea, principally in Spain.

Baring, the name of one of the most important financial houses in Great Britain. The house of Baring Brothers & Co., of London, was founded in 1770 by Francis and John Baring, sons of John Baring, a German who settled in England early in the 18th century.

Barite, a mineral consisting of sulphate of barium and known also as 'heavy spar' from its high specific gravity (4.5.). One of the commonest of veinstones, it usually accompanies silica and ores of lead.

Baritone, the male voice intermediate between the bass and the tenor. Its compass is from about A on the first space of the bass clef to the F above the stave.

Barium (Ba., 137.4), a metallic element found only in combination, chiefly in heavy spar (sulphate) and witherite (carbonate). The metal, prepared by electrolysis, is soft, like lead, silver-white, and of specific gravity 3.75. Barite, heavy spar, or barium sulphate, is the most common ore of barium and is the starting point of the manufacture of most of its compounds. *Blanc fixe* is precipitated barium sulphate prepared by adding sodium sulphate to barium sulphide solutions. Barium chloride is prepared by adding calcium chloride to the coke-barite mixture in the furnace, or by dissolving witherite (barium carbonate) in hydrochloric acid. Barium nitrate and chlorate are used largely to impart a green color to flames in pyrotechny. The insoluble sulphate is used to some extent in x-ray diagnosis of abdominal conditions, to render human viscera opaque.

Bar-jesus, nicknamed **Elymas,** a Jewish sorcerer who was smitten with blindness for withstanding Paul when he preached before the Roman proconsul, Sergius Paulus, at Paphos.

Bark, a term which is often used indiscriminately but which in non-technical usage generally means all the tissues of a tree or shrub outside the cambium. The outer portion of bark consists of epidermis and green cortex, while the inner portion is pale-colored and

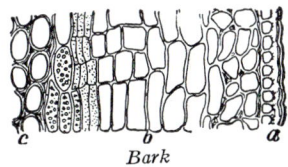

Bark
a. Outside layer or epidermis. b. Fibrous or bast layer. c. Inside or cambium layer.

fibrous, forming the phloem or 'bast' region. In the first or second year of growth a cylinder of cells, usually in the cortex, but sometimes in the epidermis, becomes an outer cambium, known as the 'cork cambium' or 'phellogen.' This shows numerous horizontal channels, composed of loosely attached cells; and through these paths, called lenticels, air and moisture pass out and in during the growing season; in winter, however, the last-formed autumn cells in the innermost layers of the lenticels remain firmly attached, like the ordinary cork cells, and render the passage impervious. In spring these special cells again separate, and allow the lenticels to resume their function. As tree trunks grow old the outer cork cells die and as the girth increases so does the pressure on the bark; the outer cork, therefore, often cracks, but the inner layers having greater elasticity, remain complete.

Barka, or **Barca** (anc. *Cyrenaica*), formerly a Turkish vilayet, North Africa, bounded on the e. by Egypt and on the w. by Tripoli and the Gulf of Sidra, and extending to the Libyan Desert in the s. By the treaty of Ouchy (1912) it was ceded to Italy and now forms a part of Italian Libia; p. 300,000.

Bark Beetles, known also as **Engraver Beetles,** insects belonging to the family Scolytidae, of the order Coleoptera. They are exceedingly destructive, and in spite of their small size do much damage. All attack wood, on which they live, and which may be completely riddled by their burrows.

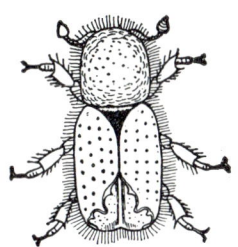

Bark Beetle (*much enlarged*)

Barker, Harley Granville (1877-1946), British author and playwright, was born in London. He began his career as an actor, appearing in many of the plays of George Bernard Shaw. Among his publications are *The Voysey Inheritance* (1907); *The Morris Dance* (1916); *The Secret Life* (1923).

Barker, Robert (1739-1806), Irish portrait and miniature painter. He is said to be the inventor of panoramas, his chief ones being those of Edinburgh (1789) and London (1794), and the battles of Trafalgar and Aboukir.

Barker, Thomas Jones (1815-82), English historical painter. Among his more important pictures are *The Meeting of Wellington and Blucher* (1851); *The Relief of Lucknow* (1860); *A Riderless War-horse at the Battle of Sedan* (1873); *Balaklava—One of the Six Hundred* (1874).

Barker's Mill, the simplest form of hydraulic engine, or prime mover, invented by one Dr. Barker in the late seventeenth century.

Barkla, Charles Glover (1877-1944), British physicist, was born in Lancashire. He was professor of physics (1907-13) in the University of London, and in 1913 became professor of natural philosophy in the University of Edinburgh. In 1917 he received the Nobel Prize in physics. His research work has been mainly connected with electric rays, x-rays and secondary rays.

Barkley, Alben William (1877-   ), American statesman, born in Graves Co., Ky., ed. at Emory Coll. and U. of Va. In U. S. Congress, 1913-27; U. S. Senate, 1927-49; Vice Pres. of the U. S., 1949-   .

Barley (*Hordeum sativum*), one of the oldest cultivated plants known. It is supposed to have originated in Western Asia. It was grown

Barley

1. Four rows. 2. Two rows. 3. Side view of grain. 4. Cross section of grain. 5. Pearl barley.

by the early colonists of the United States and is an important crop in Russia, Germany, Austria, France, and Great Britain.

The barley resembles the wheat plant, but differs from it in the structure of the head, and in its generally lower habit of growth. The head consists of one-flowered sessile spikelets of which three are borne side by side on each joint of the central stem. Barley contains more starch and more crude fiber than wheat. The straw of the two plants is similar in composition. The legal weight per bushel of the grain is usually 48 lbs. Barley has a wide distribution. It thrives best on a friable, calcareous, well-drained loam soil. In the United States and Canada and many parts of Europe the seed is sown in the spring, but along the Mediterranean barley is a fall crop and in some of the Southern States of America it is a winter crop. Barley is used principally for malting, breakfast food preparations, flour, and for feed. The crop is grown for hay, and the straw is used for forage and bedding.

Barlow, Joel (1754-1812), American poet, was a chaplain in the Revolutionary War and performed diplomatic missions for the U. S. He wrote *The Columbiad,* an epic poem of American history.

Barmecides, a rich and influential Persian family who came to power under the Abbasside caliphs of Bagdad. One member acted as tutor and companion to Haroun al-Raschid and after Haroun's accession to the caliphate (786) became his vizier, with unlimited power. The expression *Feast of the Barmecides* comes from one of the tales in the Arabian Nights.

Barnabas, otherwise **Joses** or **Joseph,** a Levite, born in Cyprus, and one of Paul's most distinguished fellow-workers.

Barnabas, Epistle of, an important Christian work found in some early MSS. of the Bible, and actually accepted as genuine by Origen and Clement of Alexandria.

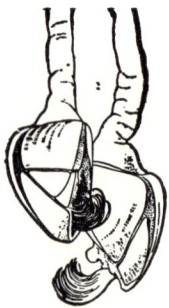

Ship Barnacle.

Barnacle, a name applied generally to the members of the crustacean order Cirripedia. In the United States the name is applied popularly to the non-stalked or sessile sorts (Balanus), which cover rocks, wharf-piles, and the like, between tidemarks with their white acorn-shaped shells.

Barnacle, or **Bernicle Goose,** an Arctic bird, gray and black in color, with white markings and black bill and feet, about 25 inches in length and weighing about five pounds. It migrates southward during winter as far as the Mediterranean and the Central United States.

Barnard, Edward Emerson (1857-1923), American astronomer, was born in Nashville, Tenn. From 1887 to 1895 was astronomer at the Lick Observatory, Cal.; and after that professor of practical astronomy at the University of Chicago and astronomer at the Yerkes Observatory, Williams Bay, Wisconsin. He discovered the 5th satellite of Jupiter (1892) and 16 comets, and is known for his important work in celestial photography.

Barnard, Frederick Augustus Porter (1809-89), American mathematician and educator. From 1837 to 1854 he was professor in the University of Alabama. In 1864 he was elected president of Columbia College, which position he held until 1888, when he resigned because of ill health. During his long connection with Columbia he did much for its advancement and improvement, transforming it into one of the great universities of the country. He bequeathed to it the bulk of his property, and Barnard College is named for him. He was one of the incorporators of the National Academy of Sciences; U. S. commissioner to the Paris Expositions of 1867 and 1878, and editor-in-chief of *Johnson's New Universal Encyclopaedia*.

Barnard, George Grey (1863-1938), American sculptor, was born at Bellefonte, Pa., and studied at the Ecole des Beaux-Arts, Paris, 1884-7. He received gold medals at the Paris exposition of 1900, the Pan-American exposition at Buffalo, 1901, and the St. Louis Exposition, 1904. Among his works are *Brotherly Love; Two Natures; The God Pan* (Central Park, New York); *The Hewer; Adam and Eve;* statues for the State Capitol, Harrisburg, Pennsylvania, and many busts.

Barnard, Henry (1811-1900), American writer on education, was born in Hartford, Conn. He was president of the University of Wisconsin (1857-9) and of St. John's College, Annapolis (1865-6); and first U. S. Commissioner of Education (1867-70). He organized the Bureau of Education, and founded (1855) the *American Journal of Education*, of which he was long editor.

Barnard College, New York City, the undergraduate college for women of Columbia University, founded in 1889, and named for F. A. P. Barnard, president of Columbia, who worked for many years to introduce coeducation into that institution. The buildings of the college occupy a site on Broadway just west of Columbia.

Barnegat Bay, Atlantic coast of Ocean co., New Jersey. Island Beach and Long Beach protect it from the ocean. Between these is Barnegat Inlet, at the mouth of which is a light-house.

Barnes, Alfred Smith (1817-88), American publisher, was born in New Haven, Conn. In 1838 Mr. Barnes established the firm of A. S. Barnes & Co. at Hartford. It removed to Philadelphia, 1840, and to New York, 1845, where it afterward remained, five of Mr. Barnes's sons eventually entering the firm as partners. Mr. Barnes made his home in Brooklyn, N. Y., and was a liberal benefactor of that city's institutions.

Barnes, Julius Howland (1873-), corporation official was born in Little Rock, Ark. He was president of the U. S. Food Administration Grain Corporation Aug. 1917-July 1919; and president of the U. S. Grain Corporation from July 1919-July 1920. He is also president of the International Development Co., and chairman of the board of several companies. He was president of the Chamber of Commerce of the United States 1921-24; and chairman of the board 1929-31.

Barnum, Phineas Taylor (1810-91), American showman, was born at Bethel, Conn., and kept store with more or less success. His first venture in the show business was the exhibition of a colored woman said to be 167 years old. He ran small shows in the South, and established Barnum's Museum in New York, 1841, where he exhibited 'Gen. Tom Thumb' and other freaks of nature. He made a large fortune (1849-51) as manager for Jenny Lind. He settled at Bridgeport, Conn., and lost $1,000,000 by a bankruptcy, but was able to start again. After travelling with Tom Thumb in Europe, he again opened his Museum and established, 1871, his 'greatest show on earth,' which toured the country annually, and even visited Europe. See his *Autobiography* (1854 and 1888); and *Life* by Benton (1902).

Baroda. State, situated in the Gujarat division of Bombay, India; is one of the three large Mahratta feudatories of the British Indian empire, and is ruled by a chief called the Gaekwar. Area, 8,570 sq. m.; p. 1,950,927.

Barometer (Gr. 'a measure of weight'), an instrument for determining the pressure of the atmosphere. An observation by Galileo, who remarked that water would not rise in a pump more than 'eighteen cubits,' led to the discovery, in 1643, of air-pressure by his pupil Torricelli. His classical experiment consisted in filling a tube about three feet long, and closed at one end, with mercury. This he inverted, immersing its lower end into a basin filled half with mercury and half with water. The mercury descended in the tube, remaining stationary at a height of thirty inches, a vacant space of about six inches being thus left at the top of the tube, which is still known as the 'Torricellian vacuum.' On raising the open end of the tube above the level of the mercury, but still under the surface of the water, all the mercury in the tube rushed rapidly out, its place being taken by the water, which completely filled the tube. He thus concluded that the elevation of the column of liquid which will stand in any tube is determined by the specific gravity of the liquid composing the column and by the atmospheric pressure.

In the construction of a barometer much care has to be taken that pure mercury, of sp. gr. 13.594, is employed. This is introduced into a glass tube about 34 in. long, and the mercury is boiled in the tube, so that any air and moisture may be got rid of. The tube, which in first-class instruments is of large bore, stands vertically in a cistern of mercury. The height of the mercurial column in the tube above the level of the cistern is measured by means of a graduated scale; but if great accuracy is required, a cathetometer is employed. The glass tube is fixed in a frame to protect it from damage, and the divisions of the scale, unless the instrument is intended for use on a mountain, vary from 26 to 32 in. In barometers for scientific purposes the scale and the frame are both made of brass, of which metal the expansive coefficient is well known. It is thus possible to make allowances for the alteration by heat in the length of the scale, which has to be taken into account in the re-

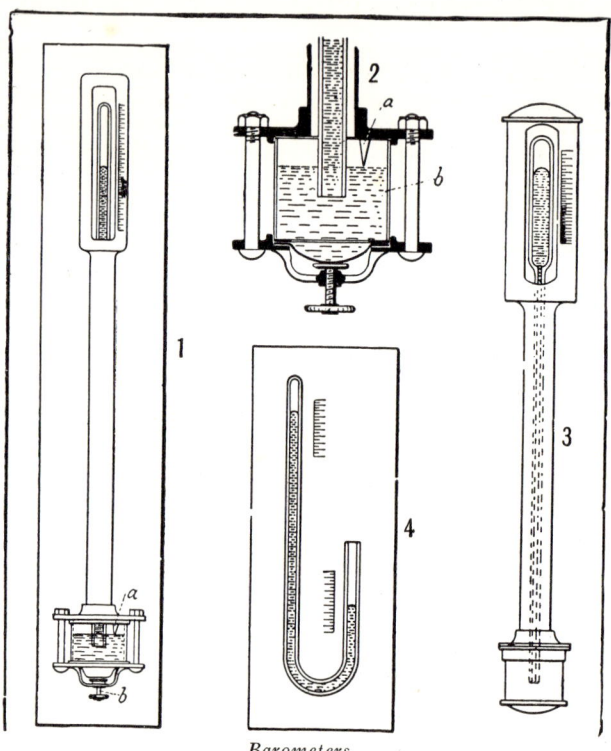

Barometers.

1, Fortin Barometer. 2, Lower part enlarged: a, ivory pin; b, adjusting screw. 3, Kew Barometer. 4. Siphon Barometer.

duction of barometric observations to a fixed temperature.

In the Fortin barometer a modified form of which is used by the U. S. Weather Bureau, the starting-point of the scale is formed by an ivory pin, which is placed in the cistern of mercury. When a reading is to be made, the mercury is raised or lowered by means of a screw until its surface just touches the pin, the lower end of which corresponds with the zero of the scale. The Green pattern, used by the Weather Bureau and American meteorologists, has the advantage of portability as well as affording the desired accuracy. The Kew barometer is admirably suited for observations on shipboard, or in situations where there is much oscillation. The ordinary wheel barometer, or 'weather-glass,' a siphon type, was invented in 1665 by Robert Hooke, secretary to the Royal Society of London.

As mercury expands its bulk for every degree of temperature, it is necessary, in taking observations of scientific accuracy, to apply a correction for temperature. A thermometer is thus usually attached to the barometer in such a way as to give the temperature of the barometer tube itself. Tables have been prepared showing at a glance the corrections to be applied for the varying temperature of the mercurial column, the readings being reduced to 32° F. Those published by the Smithsonian Institution and the U. S. Weather Bureau are available for workers.

Barographs, or self-registering barometers, are employed to give a continuous automatic record of pressure fluctuations on a revolving drum driven by clockwork. In this class of

Barograph, or Self-Registering Barometer.

instrument the record may be either mechanical or photographic, the latter method being the more reliable owing to the elimination of friction. One of the best-known forms of this instrument is the Richard barograph, or recording aneroid. See ANEROID; also works on meteorology and meteorological instruments, such as the treatises by Cleveland Abbe (1887), R. H. Scott (1883), and especially the publications of the U. S. Weather Bureau. Of the latter, *Barometers, and the Measurement of Atmospheric Pressure* (1901), by Prof. C. F. Marvin, will be found very useful.

Baron, a word which has come to mean first a 'king's man' and afterward a 'noble.' The title was unknown in Britain prior to the Norman conquest, and its earliest usage shows that it was applied to all the nobility. By the time of Edward I. only the greater barons could claim to be summoned to the House of Lords. The creation of barons by patent dates from the year 1387. A baron's coronet consists of a gold circlet with six pearls set on it, surrounding a cap of crimson velvet and ermine.

Baronet, originally a title given to the lesser barons, a meaning now obsolete, is a title of hereditary rank, in degree next to that of baron, instituted by James I. in 1611.

Sir James Matthew Barrie.

Baronius, Caesar (1538-1607), controversial historian of the Roman Catholic Church; born in S. Italy. His famous *Annales Ecclesiastici a Christo Nato ad Annum 1198* (12 vols. 1588-1607), were written in reply to the Protestant *Magdeburg Centuries.*

Barons' War, The (1263-7). See **England** —*History* (Henry III.).

Barony, in England strictly the domain of a baron, but also applied to the tenure by which a baron held of his superior; also military or other 'honorable' tenure.

Baroque, a term at first applied to ill-shaped pearls, now denotes fantastic, bizarre, and decadent forms in art and architecture.

Barotse Land, or **Northwestern Rhodesia,** a region in the Upper Zambezi, British C. Africa. It is well watered and populous.

Barque, a three-masted ship, square-rigged on the fore and main masts, and fore-and-aft on the mizzen. A BARQUENTINE differs from a barque in being only square-rigged on the fore mast.

Barr, Amelia Edith (1831-1919), American author, was born (Huddleston) at Ulverston, Lancashire, England. She was married to Robert Barr, the son of a Scottish clergyman, 1850, and came to America with him in 1854. Among her numerous novels are *Jan Vedder's Wife* (1885), *A Bow of Orange Ribbon* (1886), and *Thyra Varrick* (1903).

Barracks, permanent shelters for troops in contradistinction to bivouacs, camps and cantonments, which are temporary shelters. Barracks of some sort have been built in the United States at fully two-thirds of the almost 5,000 forts, batteries, stations, etc., which have been occupied by government troops since the beginning of the Republic. The term barracks is applied to several important military posts in the United States where there are no fortifications. Officers do not live in any part of the barracks in the U. S. service as is the case in some foreign armies, but in separate buildings called Quarters. See ARMY OF THE U. S.

Barranquilla, town, Colombia, Bolivar dep.; stands at the head of navigation of the river Magdalena. It is the most important trade centre in Colombia; p. 150,000.

Barras, Paul Francois Jean Nicolas, Vicomte de (1755-1829), who played a conspicuous part in the French Revolution. As commander of the army besieging Toulon, he shared the responsibility for the cruel measures attending the reduction of that city by the republic. Again in Paris, he arrested Robespierre at the Hôtel de Ville. Nominated general-in-chief, he, or rather Bonaparte, whom he had selected as general of artillery, crushed the insurgents (Oct. 5, 1795). Thereupon appointed one of the five members of the Directory, and next (1797) practical dictator, he set up quite a royal establishment at the Luxembourg, which led to his overthrow (Nov. 9, 1799).

Barré, collective names of numerous South American aborigines who constitute a semi-independent confederacy about the headwaters of the Rio Negro, an affluent of the Amazon, and range thence across the Cassiquiari into the Upper Orinoco basin. They are one of the few progressive nations of South America, and since about 1800 their speech (a stock language radically distinct from all others) has become a sort of *lingua franca* throughout an extensive region above the Orinoco cataracts and in the Brazilian province of Amazonas.

Barré, Isaac (1726-1802), the son of a French refugee in Dublin, was with Wolfe at Quebec. He held office under Bute, Pitt, and Shelburne, and gained the favor of the Americans by a spirited speech against the Stamp Act in 1765. The 'Sons of Liberty' got that name from his use of the phrase in a speech. Barre is one of those to whom the *Letters of Junius* have been ascribed.

Barrel. A barrel of wine or brandy in the U. S. and Great Britain contains 31 1-2 gallons; a barrel of flour, 196 lbs.; a barrel of butter, 224 lbs.; and a barrel of pork or beef, 200 lbs. But the dry barrel is not a legalized measure, and quantities should be specified in pounds or bushels.

Barrel Organ, a portable mechanical organ played by a rotary handle.

Barrere, George (1876-1944), French flutist who became the best known player of the flute in the United States.

Barricades, obstructive works thrown up in haste to arrest an enemy's progress through a street or give cover to the besieged, were used by the city of Saguntum against Hannibal. At the siege of Carthage the Romans took some six days to surmount the barricades opposed to them. Historic barricades of Paris are those of July 27-30, 1830, when Charles X. was dethroned, and of June 23-26, 1848.

Barrie, James Matthew (1860-1937), Scottish novelist, dramatist, born at Kirriemuir, Forfarshire. His first notable book was *Auld Licht Idylls* (1888). This was followed by *A Window in Thrums* (1889) and *My Lady Nicotine* (1890). *The Little Minister* (1891) was his first serious attempt at a long novel. *Margaret Ogilvy* (a biography of his mother) and *Sentimental Tommy* appeared in 1896, the latter being followed by a sequel, *Tommy and Grizel,* in 1900. His first play, *Walker, London* (1892), was produced by Mr. J. J. Toole. It was followed by *Jane Annie* (1893), written in collaboration with Conan Doyle. *The Professor's Love Story* was produced at the Garrick Theatre (London) in 1894, followed at the Haymarket (London) in 1897 by *The Little Minister,* an adaptation of his novel, played very successfully by Miss Maude Adams. *The Wedding Guest* was produced at the Garrick in 1900, and *What Every Woman Knows* at the Duke of York's Theatre in 1908. Other dramatic successes have been *The Admirable Crichton*, played in the United States in 1904, and *Little Mary*. For Christmas, 1904, he produced a children's play, *Peter Pan*, and later, *Alice Sit-by-the-Fire* (1905). See the edition of his *Novels, Tales, and Sketches* in 8 vols. (1897), and Hammerton's *J. M. Barrie and his Books* (1900).

Barrier Reef. See **Great Barrier Reef.**

Barrier Treaty, a treaty concluded in 1709 at the Hague between England and the Netherlands, by which the Netherlands republic obtained the right to occupy certain fortified places in the Spanish Netherlands.

Barrington, E., pen-name of Mrs. L. Adams Beck, English novelist, who wrote also under her own name.

Barrister. An advocate in the higher law courts of England and Ireland. In England he must be called by one of the Inns of Court. Barristers have an exclusive right of audience in the High Court and Court of Appeal, and may have the same right in quarter sessions on an order by the justices.

Barron, James (*c.* 1768-1851), American naval officer, born in Virginia. He became a captain in the U. S. navy in 1799. He commanded the *Chesapeake* when that vessel was fired upon in time of peace, June 22, 1807, by the British ship *Leopard*, and Barron was forced to surrender three of his crew. See CHESAPEAKE.

Barrow is a term applied by antiquaries to the sepulchral mounds which are so numerous in the British Isles, and indeed throughout a great part of the world. Sometimes they are earthen mounds, sometimes heaps of stones or cairns.

Barrow-in-Furness, seaport, and manufacturing center, Lancashire, England. Once a fishing village, Barrow has since 1847 made extraordinary progress owing to the discovery of pure haematite iron ore at Park, in the neighborhood. Furness Abbey forms a picturesque feature towards the n. Shipbuilding forms an important industry. There are huge steel and iron works (Bessemer steel works dating from 1863), engineering shops, foundries, jute factories, paper and pulp works.

Barry, Sir John Wolfe (1836-1918), English engineer. He designed the Blackfriars, Kew, and Tower bridges over the Thames, and built the Barry docks, docks at Hull and Middlesbrough, and numerous railways in England, Scotland, India, and elsewhere.

Barrymore, Ethel (1879-), American actress, daughter of Maurice Barrymore and niece of John Drew. Her debut, in 1896, was followed by leading roles in *Captain Jinks* (1900), *A Doll's House* (1905), *The Second Mrs. Tanqueray* (1925), and other well-known plays. She married Russell Griswold Colt. Her first talking picture was made with her brothers John and Lionel in *Rasputin and the Empress*. She has three children, John, Samuel and Ethel Barrymore Colt.

Barrymore, John (1882-1942), American actor and film star, son of Maurice Barrymore and nephew of John Drew, born in Philadelphia. His theatrical debut, as Max in *Magda*, Chicago, 1903, was followed by seasons in New York, London, and Australia. In 1925 he went to London, organized his own company, played *Hamlet*, and was accorded high acclaim during a long season. He has been as popular in films as on the stage. Consult his *Confessions of an Actor* (1926). Some of his most successful sound films are: *Don Juan, Bill of Divorcement, Reunion in Vienna*, and *Counsellor-At-Law*. In 1936, he married Elaine Barrie

Barrymore, Lionel (1878-), American actor and film star, son of Maurice Barrymore and nephew of John Drew. His debut, 1893, was made in *The Rivals*, in which his grandmother, Mrs. John Drew, was appearing as Mrs. Malaprop. In addition to many starring successes on the stage, he has achieved marked popularity in motion pictures.

Barthelmess, Richard, (1897-), American film star, appeared in *War Brides* in a role offered him by Nazimova. *The Dawn Patrol* a most successful talking picture brought him great popularity. This was followed by *The Finger Points* and *The Last Flight*.

Bartholdi, Frederic Auguste (1834-1904), French sculptor, of Italian ancestry, commissioned by the French government to execute a huge statue of Liberty for presentation to the American government in commemoration of the centenary of its independence. This statue, *Liberty Enlightening the World*, was erected on Bedloe's Island in New York Harbor in 1886 (see LIBERTY, STATUE OF).

Bartholomew, son of Talmai, one of the twelve disciples of Jesus, frequently, though not conclusively, identified with Nathanael.

Bartholomew, Massacre of St., the massacre of the Huguenots which began in Paris on St. Bartholomew's Day, Aug. 24, 1572.

Barthou, Louis (1862-1934), French public official. He became Minister of Public Works in 1894, and between 1896 and 1913 was successively Minister of the Interior, of Public Works, and of Justice. From May to December 1913 he was Premier. During World War I he was Minister of State and subsequently was Minister of Foreign Affairs and of War. He was Minister of Foreign Affairs when slain at the time of the assassination of King Alexander of Yugoslavia at Marseilles, in October, 1934.

Bartlett, John (1829-1905), American author, best known by his *Familiar Quotations* (1854), an admirable and much-used compilation of selections from standard prose and poetry.

Bartlett, John Russell (1805-86), American author, statesman, and bibliographer, whose publications include: *Dictionary of Americanisms* (1850; 4th ed. 1877); and *Bibliotheca Americana* (1865-71).

backgrounds beyond the practice of his contemporaries; he was the inventor of the lay figure. Among the best of his numerous paintings are a *Pieta*, a *Resurrection*, and *Salvator Mundi* in the Pitti Palace, Florence; *Last Judgment*, and *Enthronement of the Virgin*, Uffizi Gallery, Florence; and *The Marriage of St. Catherine*, Louvre, Paris. Consult Scott's *Fra Bartolommeo*.

Barton, Clara (1821-1912), American philanthropist, was born in Oxford, Massachusetts. During the Civil War she devoted herself to the care of sick and wounded soldiers. At the close of the war she inaugurated and carried on a systematic search for missing men, thus gaining a national reputation. She worked with the International Red Cross in the

John, Ethel, and Lionel Barrymore, in the motion picture 'Rasputin.'

Bartlett, Paul Wayland (1865-1925), American sculptor, was born in New Haven, Conn. Among his important works are statues of Columbus and Michelangelo; the *Ghost Dancer;* figures on the pediment on the National House of Representatives, and six allegorical figures for the New York Public Library.

Bartlett, Robert Abram (1875-1946), American explorer, born in Newfoundland. He was awarded the Chas. P. Daly medal by the American Geographical Society. He is the author of *Last Voyage of the Karluk*.

Bartolommeo di Pagholo del Fattorino, Fra, known also as **Baccio della Porta** (c. 1475-1517), one of the greatest of the Florentine artists, was born in Soffignano, a village near Prato, the son of a muleteer. Bartolommeo left a great number of masterpieces characterized by deep religious feeling. His influence upon Italian art was fourfold: he preceded Raphael in a scientific system of composition, based on principles of strict symmetry; he combined harmony of tone with brilliance of color; he elaborated his landscape

Franco-German War, 1870-71, and by her efforts established and became the first official president, 1881-1904, of the American Red Cross. Besides work in the Russian famine, 1892, and following the Armenian massacre, 1896, she performed field duties in the Spanish-American War, 1898, and in the Boer War, 1899-1902, as well as superintending other relief work carried on by the Red Cross. She published reports of her work and *History of the Red Cross in Peace and War* (1898), *Story of the Red Cross* (1904). Consult *Lives* by Epler and by Wm. Barton.

Bartram, John (1699-1777), American botanist, founded the first botanical garden in the United States, 1728, near Philadelphia. See *Memoirs of John Bartram*, by William Bartram.

Baruch, The Apocalypse of, a remarkable work, made known to scholars by the discovery of a Syriac MS. in 1866. Consult R. H. Charles's *Apocalypse of Baruch* (1896).

Baruch, Bernard Mannes (1870-   ), American economist and public official. He was appointed by President Wilson a member

Barus   411   **Baseball**

of the Advisory Commission of the Council of National Defence. In March, 1918, he became chairman of the War Industries Board. He was attached as economic adviser to the American Commission to Negotiate Peace; was a member of the President's Conference for Capital and Labor, 1919, and the President's Agricultural Conference, 1922. His financial career was launched when he became a partner in the Wall Street brokerage firm of A. A. Housman & Co., where his aptitude for market operations brought him a substantial fortune. He retired from the Stock Exchange in 1917, aided in negotiation of the peace treaty which ended World War I, and for a time retired from active operations in the market. He interested himself in politics, contributing generously to the Democratic campaign in 1920, 1924, 1932. In 1942, chairman of a committee to investigate the rubber situation. Appointed, 1946, by Pres. Truman as U. S. representative on Atomic Energy Commission, gave plan for atomic energy control.

Barus, Carl (1856-1935), American physicist, distinguished for his pioneering researches in physical geology and meteorology published in the Bulletins of the U. S. Geological Survey and of the Weather Bureau—over 30 volumes.

Barye, Antoine Louis (1795-1875), one of the greatest of French sculptors, recognition of his talent coming from America through his friend Mr. Walters, whose fine art collection at Baltimore contains many of his best bronzes, such as *The Orleans Group*, *The Hunt of the Wild Ox*. Barye was unexcelled in illustrating groups of animals in vigorous action, the best example being his *Lion Struggling with a Snake* (1832), in the Tuileries.

Barytes, a white mineral, also called heavy-spar, sulphate of barytes, or barium sulphate, $BaSO_4$, is sometimes confused with the mineral witherite, $BaCO_3$. It is a common ingredient, sometimes used as an adulterant, of paints. A finer quality of barytes is used for dressing cloth and leather and for making a smooth coat for 'art' papers.

Basalt. Certain volcanic or eruptive rocks possess a micro- or crypto-crystalline structure, consisting of crystals embedded in an amorphous or glassy ground mass. Mineralogically, rocks of this group consist essentially of some form of feldspar, with hornblende or augite and quartz. Basaltic rocks are usually black, dark brown, or greenish black, and vary from a fine-grained to a coarsely crystalline structure, with a tendency to cleave into hexagonal columns. Basaltic rocks are abundant and widely distributed in those regions which have undergone more recent volcanic disturbances.

Bascule Bridge, a lifting bridge opened by means of a bascule or balanced lever.

Base, in chemistry, is a term applied to any substance which forms hydroxyl ions in solution or which is capable of neutralizing an acid to form salts. See also ACIDS, SOLUTIONS.

Base, in heraldry, is the lower portion of a shield.

Baseball is a game that was invented in the United States. It has earned the title of the 'National Game' which it deserves. It has been claimed that it is an evolution of an English game called Rounders. The only thing in common between Rounders and Baseball is the fact that players in both games circle bases.

The man who devised the field diagram of base ball was Colonel Abner Doubleday then in the United States Army. The first game was played in Cooperstown, New York in 1839. His conception of a diamond, with bases 90 feet apart, was a complete departure from any other game of bat and ball that had been invented in the world. The first code of rules was formed by the Knickerbocker Club of New York City.

The first undertaking toward making baseball a national sport was in 1857. A convention was called in New York City. Twenty-five clubs were represented by delegates. A national organization was perfected at that meeting. It had a membership of sixteen clubs and most of them were located in New York and Brooklyn. They adopted their own rules, improving on the Knickerbocker Code as they did so, and from that date the game of baseball can be recognized as the national sport of the United States.

The Atlantics of Brooklyn were acknowledged national champions in 1864 and held the title until almost to the close of the season in 1867. Their principal competitors were the Athletics of Philadelphia—a club name holding good to this day—and the Mutuals of New York City. In 1869 the Cincinnati team under Harry Wright did not lose a ball game. This was the first loud note of defiance that the West had voiced in baseball. In 1868 professionalism began to manifest itself in baseball. This was largely due to the fact that many cities, in which baseball was played, needed one or two strong players to round out the local team and engaged experts at a small salary to help them. Arthur Pue Gorman, took the first baseball team from Washington over the Allegheny mountains throughout the West. George Wright, one of the greatest baseball players of the United States, was its captain. The team won one game after another until it met, in Chicago, the Rockford, Ill., nine. Albert G. Spalding, eventually to be one of the great figures in baseball, pitched for Rockford. His team won by 29-23 and the seventeen-year-old pitcher was a hero.

In 1868 a Cincinnati team was organized on semi-professional lines and in 1869 every player on the team was paid a salary. This was the first open professional team of record. In 1870 disagreement began to take place between amateur baseball players and the professionals. The upshot was the organization of an amateur association in 1872. It lasted but two years, the fact being proven quickly that amateur baseball, as an organized sport, could not vie with professional baseball on purely showman-like lines.

In 1871 the National Association of Professional Baseball Players became the first prominent factor of its kind in the history of the game and from that time on organized baseball established an existence which is maintained until this day. Its history has been replete with disputes but organized control has lived through it all. The National Association was disbanded in 1875 because there was dishonesty on the part of players and the public would no longer lend its encouragement to the game.

The National League of Professional Baseball Clubs was formed in 1876 and is now at the height of its career. This league is known as the senior major league of organized baseball. Its original membership was made up of the Athletics of Philadelphia, Boston, Chicago, Cincinnati, Hartford, Louisville, the Mutuals of New York City, and St. Louis. In 1934 the circuit of the National League was made up of Boston, New York, Philadelphia, Brooklyn, Pittsburgh, Cincinnati, Chicago and St. Louis.

No by-laws of leagues existed for six years which prevented one club from preying upon another by luring away its best players. This condition of affairs, if longer prolonged, would have wrecked baseball. In 1883 an agreement was adopted between three principal leagues to prevent player piracy. Afterward this became known as the national agreement and in one way or another, has been in effect since. It prevents a player being illegally taken from a club of any league by a club of any other league. Thus it establishes stability for the promoters of ball clubs and ensures to them a certain continuous financial solidity.

The American League is known as the junior major league. It began as the Western League and was brought to the height of its success by Byron Bancroft Johnson, who had been the president of the Western League, and continued in the capacity of chief executive when the Western League became the American League by the simple process of changing its name in 1900. The first circuit of the league was made up of Chicago, Milwaukee, Indianapolis, Detroit, Kansas City, Cleveland, Buffalo, and Minneapolis. The circuit in 1934 was Boston, New York, Philadelphia, Washington, Cleveland, Detroit, Chicago and St. Louis.

The American Association of 1882 was organized as a rival to the National League. It was not a well attempted league and it never played fair with itself. Most of its owners were scheming to obtain membership in the National League. Its slogan was 'baseball for twenty-five cents.' It played Sunday games which, for a long time, were forbidden in National League. It was merged with the National League in 1891 because of its internal weaknesses.

When the National League and the American League became reconciled a new National Agreement was adopted and a new form of government was agreed upon. In most of its essentials the principles of this agreement were like those of previous agreements. The principal authority of baseball was placed in the hands of a National Commission which was composed of the two presidents of the major leagues, they, in turn, to elect a chairman of the commission.

In addition to the major leagues in baseball there is also an organization known as the National Association which embraces all of the minor leagues of the United States.

As a result of alleged dishonesty on the part of players, and other disturbances, organized baseball leagues changed their organization somewhat in 1921 by placing one man, a Commissioner of Baseball, at the head of its government to act as final authority on questions of rules, conduct of players, etc. Judge Kenesaw Mountain Landis received the first appointment and after his advent there was continued confidence in the management of the games. He served until his death, 1944.

The World Series is the most important event of the year. It is played by the club winning the championship of the National League and that which wins the championship of the American League. The games alternate, the first two being played in that city which

Baseball

did not open the series the year before. Three following games are than played in the other city and after that, if necessary, the clubs return to the city in which the series began. The receipts in recent years in a single World Series have amounted to as much as one million dollars. This sum is divided among the Advisory Council: the players of the clubs competing, the owners of the clubs, and each league.

WORLD'S SERIES RESULTS

YEAR	WINNERS	LOSERS
1932	New York, Am.	Chicago, Nat.
1933	New York, Nat.	Washington, Am.
1934	St. Louis, Nat.	Detroit, Am.
1935	Detroit, Am.	Chicago, Nat.
1936	New York, Am.	New York, Nat.
1937	New York, Am.	New York, Nat.
1938	New York, Am.	Chicago, Nat.
1939	New York, Am.	Cincinnati, Nat.
1940	Cincinnati, Nat.	Detroit, Am.
1941	New York, Am.	Brooklyn, Nat.
1942	St. Louis, Nat.	New York, Am.
1943	New York, Am.	St. Louis, Nat.
1944	St. Louis, Nat.	St. Louis, Am.
1945	Detroit, Am.	Chicago, Nat.
1946	St. Louis, Nat.	Boston, Am.
1947	New York, Am.	Brooklyn, Nat.
1948	Cleveland, Am.	Boston, Nat.
1949	New York, Am.	Brooklyn, Nat.
1950	New York, Am.	Phila., Nat.
1951	New York, Am.	New York, Nat.
1952	New York, Am.	Brooklyn, Nat.

In 1942 the St. Louis Cardinals by a late season spurt won the National League Pennant, and became World's Champions by beating the New York Yankees, 4 games to 1. In 1943 the New York Yankees won over St. Louis by 4 games to 1.

Among the many names which have made baseball history are those of A. G. Spalding, known to all through his library of athletic sports, including the Spalding Guides; John McGraw, manager for many years of the New York Giants; Miller Huggins, manager of the New York Yankees; Connie Mack (Cornelius McGillicuddy), manager of the Philadelphia Athletics; Ty Cobb, batting champion and generally rated the greatest all-round player of all time; Christy Mathewson and Walter Johnson, pitchers; Babe Ruth, home-run king; and Rogers Hornsby, Bob Grove, Hughey Jennings, Wilbert Robinson, Ed Walsh, Bill Terry, Tris Speaker, the Dean brothers, Eddie Collins, and many others.

Baseball is played with nine men on each side. These players are also known as a team. They are catcher, pitcher, first baseman, second baseman, short-stop, third baseman, left fielder, center fielder, and right fielder. Each nine, or team, has a captain, if so wished, and in modern days a manager has been added. In professional baseball the authority of the manager usually exceeds that of a captain.

A regulation game is nine innings long for each side. If the side second at bat is ahead in its completed eighth inning it need not play its half of the ninth and wins. If the score is tied at the end of nine innings, play is continued until one side has scored more runs than the other in any equal inning after the ninth. Provision is made for temporarily stopping any game because of rain, snow or panic. One team is always at bat and the other is always in the field.

Positions of the fielders are assigned by the captain. The batter takes his place in the batsman's box at home plate equipped with a round hardwood bat, not exceeding two and three-fourths inches in the thickest part, or more than 32 inches in length. The ball must not be more than 5 1-4 ounces avoirdupois in weight nor less than that. It must not measure less than 9 inches in circumference nor more

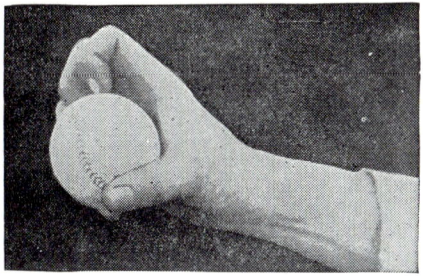

Pitching the 'Knuckle Ball.'

than 9 1-4 inches. The pitcher throws the ball—it is called 'delivers it'—to the batsman. The latter in a specially located rectangular box at home plate is presumed to strike at every fairly delivered ball that passes over any portion of home plate not lower than his knee nor higher than his shoulder. If such a ball is pitched and he does not strike at it the umpire must call it a strike. After three failures either to strike at or to hit such ball the batsman is out, provided the third ball is caught by the catcher before it touches the ground or is thrown to first base and held before the batter reaches there. If four pitches are not at the regulation height over the plate and are called 'balls' the batter takes first base in safety whether he has a strike or not.

Associated Press, Photo.   *Baseball.*
Upper, A Scene at the Polo Grounds, New York City, during a Major League Game.
Lower, A Close Play.

The batsman tries to hit the ball inside of the foul lines in such a manner as to enable him to make the circuit of the bases in the various ways provided for by the rules. After making what is called a base hit, or when he has been given four called balls, or has been hit by the pitcher, or on a missed third strike, the batsman becomes a base runner and he

Baseball

scores one run after he has touched first, second, third and home bases in succession without being put out.

Much of the team play in batting and in base running is assisted by signs and signals which are given by the players and by the manager if he remains on the bench. A manager may play if he elects to do so. Any player may give signals but they are frequently entrusted to the catcher because, from his position, he has a full view of the game. Sometimes the batsman will sacrifice his own

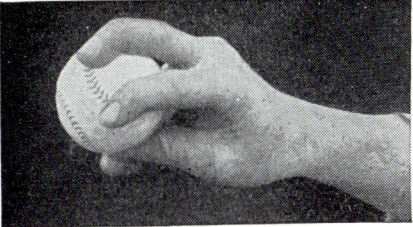

Pitching the 'Screw Ball.'

chances by bunting—which is really tapping the ball—toward an infielder expecting to be put out himself but hoping by a well placed hit to advance the runner. The baseball rules are printed annually in the Spalding Base Ball Guide and the Reach Base Ball Guide.

A simple manner in which to lay out a ball field is first to establish the position of home plate. From this the positions of the other bases are located. It is 90 feet from home base to first base, 90 feet from first to second, 90 feet from second to third and 90 feet from third to home plate. The bases are located on surface lines in the shape of a diamond. That is why the term 'diamond' often is used in connection with baseball. It is 60 feet 6 inches straight away from home plate to the pitcher's plate. It is 127 feet 3 and 3-8 inches from home plate to second base and the same distance from first base across the diamond to third. The size of the pitcher's plate is 24 inches by 6 inches. Canvas bags are used for bases and they must be 15 inches square.

An easy method of laying out the field is this: Obtain a piece of rope or cord, measuring off 60 feet 6 inches and making a knot, then measure 90 feet, making another knot, then 127 feet 3 and 3-8 inches with another knot. Fasten the rope on a peg at what will be home plate. Walk straight out 60 feet 6 inches. This will be the point of location of pitcher's plate. Continue walking to the knot at 127 feet, 3 and 3-8 inches and here will be second base. Walk to the right from home plate 90 feet and this will be first base. Turn left and walk to the point where second base has been located. This will constitute the base line between first and second. Upon arrival at second turn left again and walk 90 feet. When this point has been reached turn left again and from there it will be a straight walk of 90 feet to home plate. A diamond can be laid out in this manner in a very short time as all distances between bases are equal and the pitcher is nearly in the center of the area.

Consult Richter's *History and Records of Baseball* (1914); *Spalding's Official Baseball Guide* (annual).

Basel, Switzerland. See **Bale.**

Basel, Council of. See **Bale, Council of.**

Base Line, or **Base,** in surveying, is a straight line measured on the ground, from the two ends of which angles can be measured. See SURVEYING. In architectural designs, the base line is the lowest horizontal line, marking the bottom of the design; in perspective, it means the trace of the picture plane on the ground plane.

Basket Ball.

Base of Operations, in warfare, is the receiving depot where everything required for prosecuting the campaign is collected and organized before being forwarded to the front, and to which the sick and wounded can be sent back for removal to their homes when opportunities occur. See ARMY IN THE FIELD.

Basic English, an 850-word vocabulary which can be learned in two weeks. It was invented by C. K. Ogden of Cambridge, England, and I. A. Richards, in the early 1920's. Consult I. A. Richards, *Basic English and Its Uses* (1943).

Basil, various herbaceous plants of the order Labiatae. Sweet Basil (*Ocimum basilicum*) is a native of India, the young leaves being used for seasoning dishes.

Basil, St. (329-379), surnamed THE GREAT, a father of the Greek Church, born at Caesarea, of which he became bishop (370). There is an English translation of his work in *Nicene and Post Nicene Fathers*.

Basil, two Byzantine emperors. BASIL I. (867-886); BASIL II. (957-1025), who became emperor in 976.

Basilica (Greek *basilike*, from *basileus*, 'a king'), in ancient times a market place, exchange, and place of meeting generally. It contained an apse, in which the praetor conducted his court of justice. The basilica strongly influenced the form of the earliest churches.

Basilica, name given to a legal code published 887 A.D. for the Byzantine empire.

Basilicon, an ointment composed of yellow wax, resin, and olive oil, with suet and turpentine added for basilicon proper.

Basilisk, name given by the Greeks and Romans to a fabulous serpent-like monster. It has been applied by zoologists to certain harmless American tree lizards.

Basin, in geology, a depression in the rocks at the earth's surface caused by differential movements, by folding, or by erosion. Basins formed by folding occur in mountainous regions (see SYNCLINE). The coal-fields of Pennsylvania afford examples of this type. Erosional basins are produced by the action of water or ice upon the earth's surface. Most river basins have been formed in this manner.

Baskerville, John (1706-75), English printer. He made his own paper and prepared his own ink, and specimens of his work are now of great value.

Basketball, a game invented in 1891 by James Naismith, following a suggestion from Dr. L. H. Gulick that an indoor game might properly fill in the time between the football and the baseball seasons. It was originally played by branches of the Young Men's Christian Association and was subsequently taken up by athletic clubs, schools, and colleges. Certain very definite rules and regulations govern play, and special rules for women, adopted in 1899, and revised later, offer some modification of the men's game. Consult Spalding's *Official Basketball Guide* (annual); Wardlaw and Morrison's *Basket Ball*. Basketball has grown tremendously in popularity in the last few years. It is fast, exciting, and yet without the danger of serious physical injury inherent in football. There are eleven intercollegiate league conferences. In 1938 Dartmouth was the mythical 'National Champion,' heading the Eastern League with 8 victories and 4 defeats.

Basket Fish, the popular name of a group of echinoderms related to the star-fishes, and other species. The name is derived from the animal's habit of folding its branching arms around its body when it is threatened.

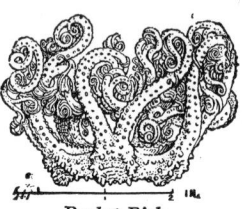

Basket-Fish

Baskets and Basket Making. Baskets are vessels made of osiers, reed, raffia, rush, straw, or hemp, in a great variety of shapes and sizes and put to a corresponding variety of uses. Their manufacture is one of the oldest of all handicrafts. The ancient Israelites used baskets in offering sacrifice, the early Britons were skilled in basketry, the Chinese and Japanese have for centuries produced baskets of great beauty, and the American Indians reached a high degree of proficiency. For ordinary baskets osiers (q.v.)—the cut branches of certain willows—are most commonly used. Consult Okey's *Art of Basket Making*; Gill's *Practical Basketry* (1916); Collier's *Basket Making* (1920).

Basking Shark (*Selache maxima*), the largest shark of the Atlantic, sometimes exceeds thirty feet in length. The liver yields much oil, and the shark is widely hunted on this account.

Basnage, Jacques (1653-1725), French Protestant clergyman, one of the best of the church historians, his books being accepted by Catholics and Protestants alike. He published *Histoire de la Religion des Eglises Reformes* (1690; much enlarged in 1725), and also *Histoire des Juifs depuis Jesus Christ* (1706).

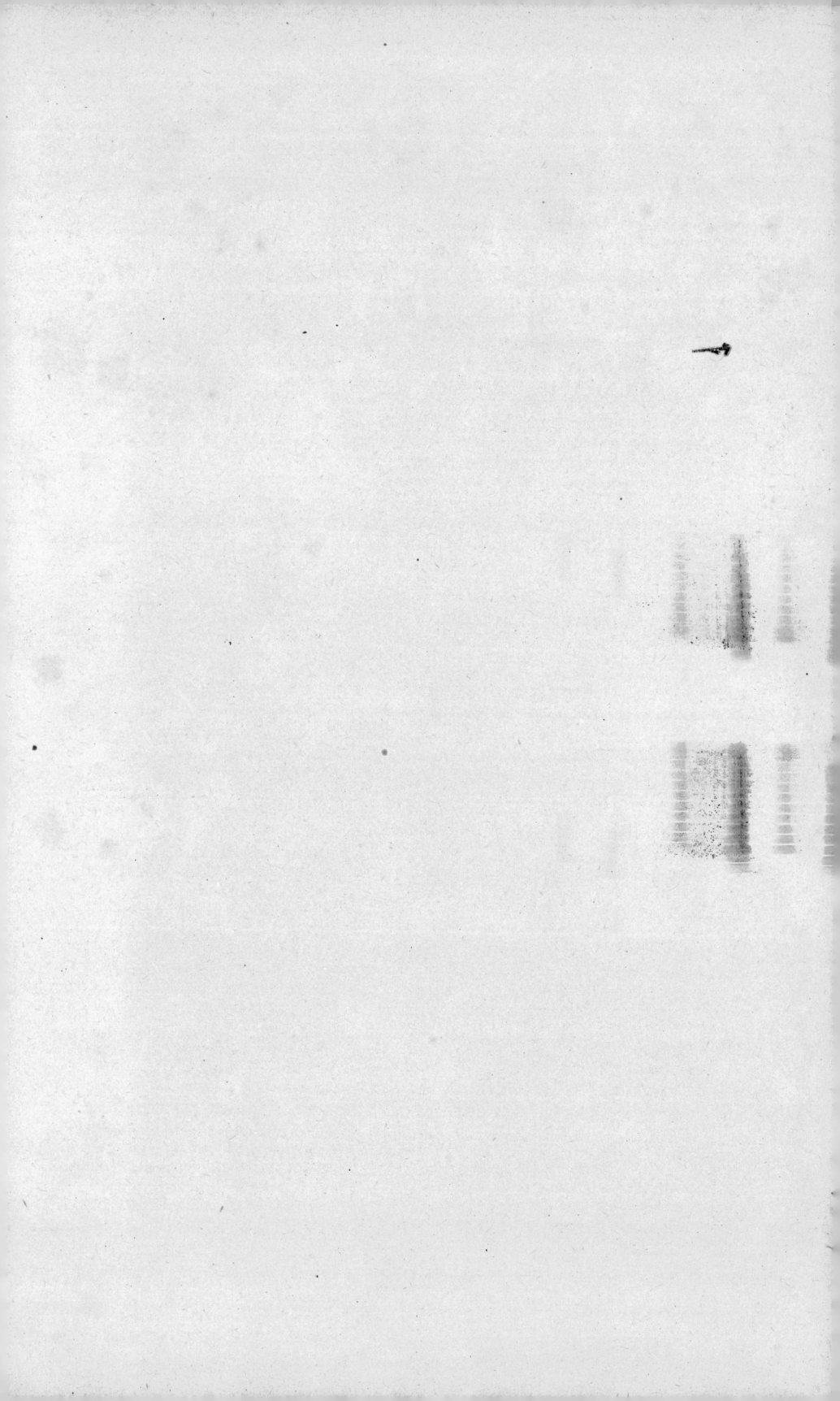